I0729601

NO SIGNAL

FUNK STILLE

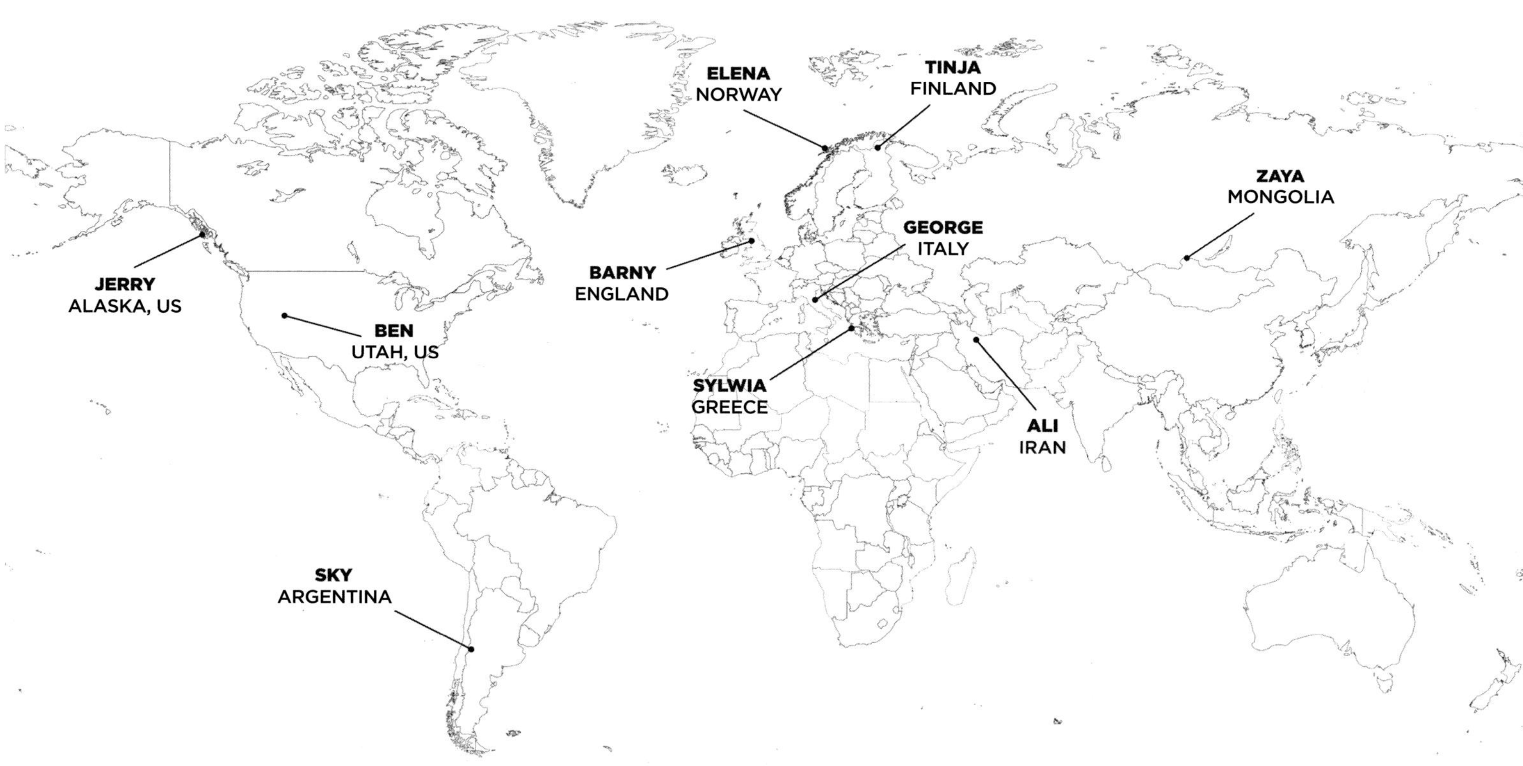

ELENA
NORWAY
TINJA
FINLAND
ZAYA
MONGOLIA
BARNY
ENGLAND
GEORGE
ITALY
JERRY
ALASKA, US
BEN
UTAH, US
SYLWIA
GREECE
ALI
IRAN
SKY
ARGENTINA

BRICE PORTOLANO

NO SIGNAL

FUNK STILLE

LIVING IN THE HEART OF NATURE
TEN PORTRAITS

———

ZEHN LEBENSENTWÜRFE
IM EINKLANG MIT DER NATUR

teNeues

CONTENT | INHALT

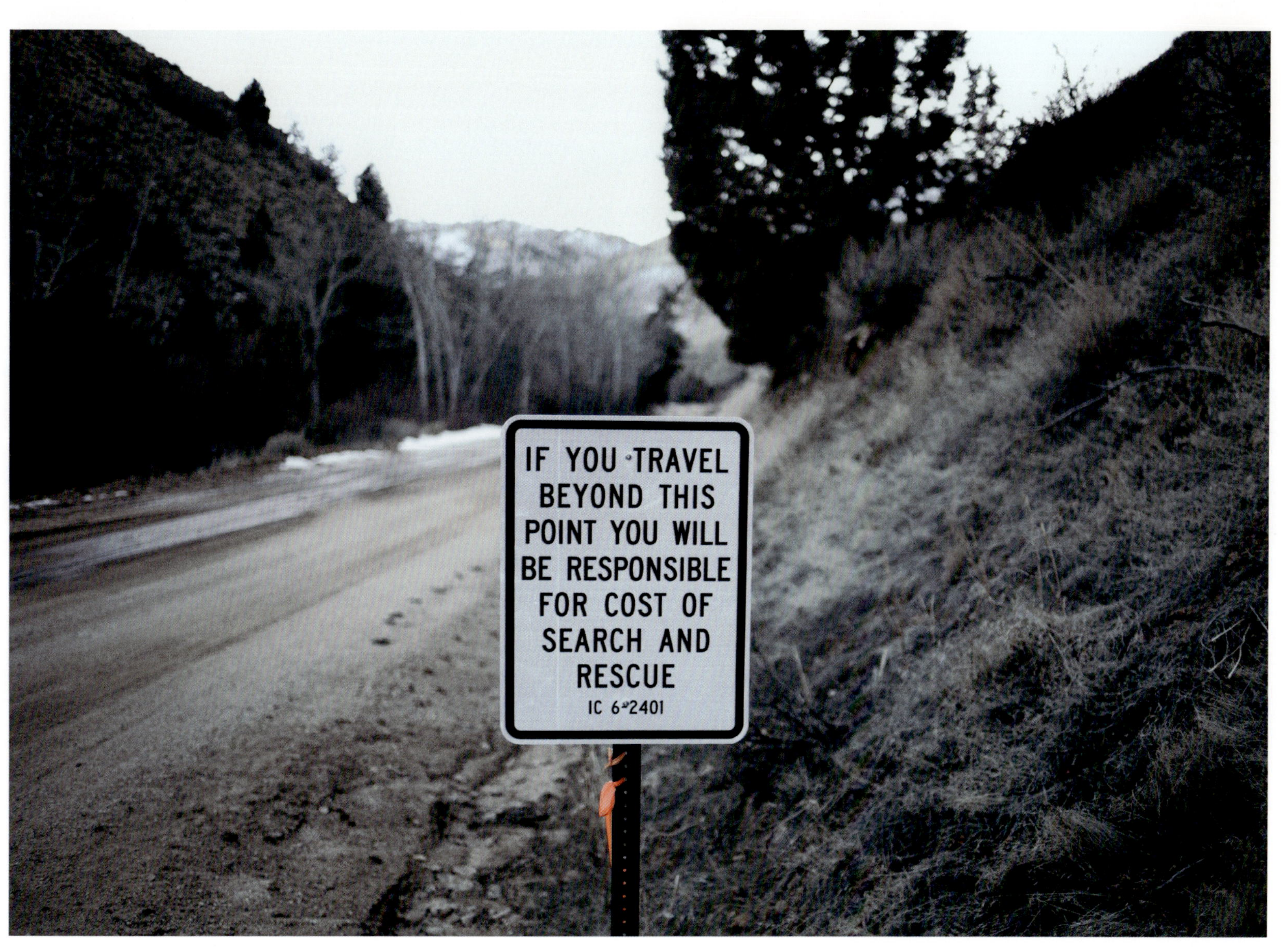

IF YOU TRAVEL
BEYOND THIS
POINT YOU WILL
BE RESPONSIBLE
FOR COST OF
SEARCH AND
RESCUE
IC 6-2401

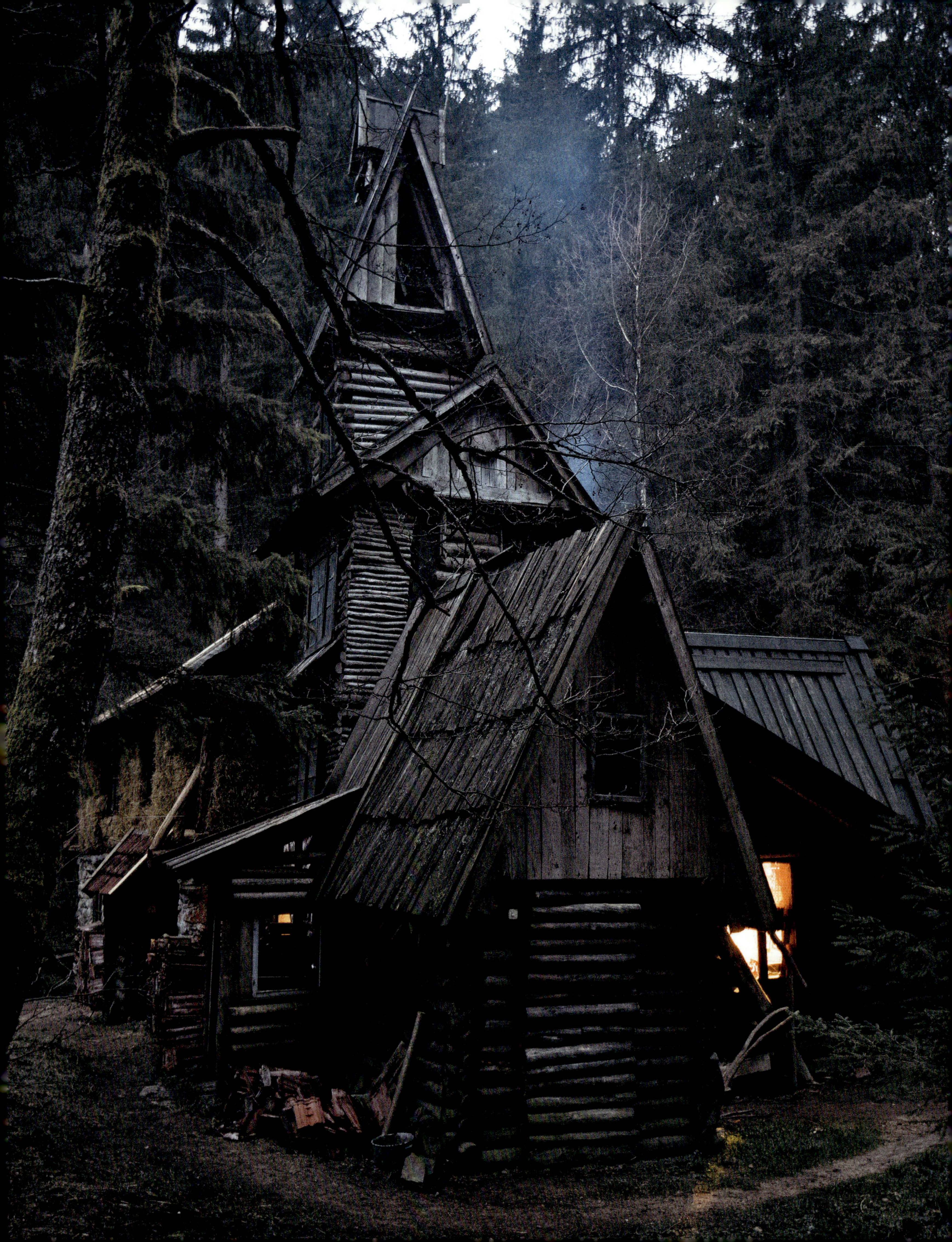

"I went to the woods because I wished to live deliberately, to front only the essential facts of life, and see if I could not learn what it had to teach, and not, when I came to die, discover that I had not lived. I did not wish to live what was not life, living is so dear; nor did I wish to practice resignation, unless it was quite necessary. I wanted to live deep and suck out all the marrow of life, to live so sturdily and Spartan-like as to put to rout all that was not life, to cut a broad swath and shave close, to drive life into a corner, and reduce it to its lowest terms, and, if it proved to be mean, why then to get the whole and genuine meanness of it, and publish its meanness to the world; or if it were sublime, to know it by experience, and be able to give a true account of it in my next excursion."

HENRY DAVID THOREAU
Walden; or, Life in the Woods

„Ich zog in den Wald, weil ich den Wunsch hatte, bewusst zu leben, dem eigentlichen, wirklichen Leben näherzutreten, zu sehen, ob ich nicht lernen konnte, was es zu lehren hatte, damit ich nicht, wenn es zum Sterben ginge, einsehen müsse, dass ich nicht gelebt hatte. Ich wollte nicht das leben, was kein Leben war; das Leben ist so kostbar. Auch wollte ich keine Entsagung üben, außer es wurde unumgänglich notwendig. Ich wollte tief leben, alles Mark des Lebens aussaugen, so hart und spartanisch leben, dass alles, was nicht Leben war, in die Flucht geschlagen wurde. Ich wollte einen breiten Schwaden dicht am Boden mähen, das Leben in die Enge treiben und auf seine einfachste Formel reduzieren; und wenn es sich als niederträchtig erwiese, dann wollte ich seiner ganzen unverfälschten Niedrigkeit auf den Grund kommen und sie der Welt verkünden. War es aber erhaben, so wollte ich dies durch eigene Erfahrung erkennen und imstande sein, bei meinem nächsten Ausflug Rechenschaft darüber abzulegen."

HENRY DAVID THOREAU
Walden oder Leben in den Wäldern

In 1842, the young American writer Henry David Thoreau decided he wanted to escape the trappings of civilisation. He left his home town of Concord in Massachusetts and started a new life a few kilometres away on the banks of Walden Pond. With his own two hands, he built himself a wooden cabin where he lived for two years, two months and two days. There he lived a simple life, free of all indulgences and distractions, and spent his days observing the natural world, reflecting on philosophical questions and conversing with any visitors that passed his way.

Twelve years later he published *Walden; or, Life in the Woods,* his own account of his experiences. The book became a masterwork of American literature and today remains a valuable reference text for modern ecological thinkers, who see in it the foundations of environmental awareness and the idea of returning to nature. The text itself is rich and diverse, overflowing with philosophical thinking and exquisitely detailed descriptions of the small lake that gives the book its name, as well as practical observations from Thoreau's time at the cabin. In it, Thoreau describes his natural surroundings – the rocks, plants, trees, animals and weather conditions – as well as their internal workings and how they change over time.

Throughout the book, you see Thoreau's indifference towards those who consider him eccentric, as well as evidence of his non-conformist views which would later lead him to write *Civil Disobedience*, a work that inspired Gandhi and Martin Luther King among others. Thoreau would also later spend a night in prison for his own act of civil disobedience when he refused to pay his taxes in protest against the war that the American government wanted to wage against Mexico.

In *Walden*, Thoreau advocates the choice of a simple life, at one with nature, where you take no more from Mother Nature than what you really need. He adopts the most rudimentary of lifestyles. He defies the fashion of the day by choosing to dress in simple clothing produced in the local area, and eats what he can forage for himself – fish from the lake, a muskrat that crosses his path or some wild vegetables. Even though he sees fewer people at his cabin away from the town, he considers these relationships to be more meaningful and authentic.

As you read through the book, his reflections reveal how he values his free time over material possessions, even those simplest of items: "I had three pieces of limestone on my desk, but I was terrified to find that they required to be dusted daily, when the furniture of my mind was all undusted still." Among the very limited furniture in his small makeshift cabin were just three chairs: "one for solitude, two for friendship, three for society…".

Thoreau wanted to unpick what life was truly about. He wanted to get to the very essence of what life is, with minimal concessions to societal convention, and so he rejected everything that was superfluous, be it material, intellectual or spiritual. He immersed himself in nature in its purest and rawest form and fostered a simple and timeless relationship with nature, observing with fascination the rhythms of the flora and fauna and noting every minute change in his corner of the natural world. In his quest to find the truth – and escape the pretences for which he held society partly responsible – his solitary retreat, with its long walks and wealth of experiences, freed him to develop a deeper understanding of himself.

A Christian by upbringing, he maintained his connection to the sacred world through religious rituals that were simple, primitive and universal: "Every morning was a cheerful invitation to make my life of equal simplicity, and I may say innocence, with Nature herself… I got up early and bathed in the pond; that was a religious exercise, and one of the best things which I did." And yet on his death he was almost refused a burial in consecrated ground since he had stopped going to church.

Thoreau wanted to awaken his compatriots to what is truly real once all appearances are cast aside. He therefore takes a scientific approach to his work, based on both observation and experimentation. Like a chemist or a mathematician, he seeks to "reduce life to its simplest terms", to extract the very essence of life and to share his findings from his research.

He published *Walden* in 1854 and although the book achieved only modest success, it did get Thoreau noticed among the transcendentalist circle frequented by his mentor Emerson. And even though certain detractors in his own country dubbed the book pagan and backward, it was very well received in France, notably by the *Le Mercure de France* magazine, which drew parallels between the works of Thoreau and the artist Cézanne.

Thoreau like Cézanne depicts the natural world as he experiences it himself and both men seek to represent those essential, timeless and metaphysical qualities of nature that reveal themselves in our human relationship with our natural surroundings. Thoreau himself was considered by some to be a visionary philosopher, but it was not until the 20th century that *Walden* was finally recognised as a seminal literary work.

Almost two centuries later, I discovered *Walden* just after returning home from a long trip away. As I turned the pages of the book, Thoreau's words really resonated with me, reawakening feelings from my childhood in Provence surrounded by an unspoilt natural landscape of towering pine trees and olive groves. It's a world away from the New England that so inspired Thoreau, but I was struck by the relevance of his ideas and by the connection with the natural world that he describes – so much so that I was determined there must be other modern-day Thoreaus out there; people who have chosen to follow a different path that brings them closer to nature.

So I set about the enormous task of finding them. I made contact with lots of people, disturbing a few hermits who were not so keen on visits along the way. I bombarded countless travel guides with my questions, and I devoured piles of adventure novels and travel guides. And finally, armed with my camera, I set off on a series of extended trips around the world. With spring awakening, I donned an oilskin and immersed myself in the day-to-day life of an oyster farmer, who had swapped his former career as an estate agent for life in a small wooden hut floating out at sea in southeast Alaska. In the depths of the Arctic winter, I learnt how to handle a team of sled dogs at -40 °C, and on the other side of the Atlantic, in the Andes in Argentina, I helped a gaucho move her herd to new grazing grounds.

Over the course of five years I met all sorts of people who had rejected the conventional path in life and embraced freedom. As I shared in their day-to-day lives, I always kept my camera in the background, conscious that I wanted to capture them as authentically as possible and become one of them, if only for a short time. I discovered the immense resilience and perseverance it takes to pursue such a bold life choice and became fascinated by the sheer force of these people's personalities.

At the end of each trip, I found it more and more disconcerting to return to my city life in France. I felt compelled, as if by some magnetic force, to take yet another trip to these isolated places, without any running water, electricity, internet or, in most cases, even a phone line. Surrounded by unspoilt nature, I felt a world away from the hustle and bustle of human life and our noisy towns and cities. And I started to like what I saw. Despite all the challenges, the rejections, the lost baggage and the odd frostbite, I remained driven by the need to meet new people and share something of their lives.

I am convinced that every human being needs some connection with nature, no matter how subtle that connection may be. All the people I have met and the discussions I have had during my years of research confirm this. I have seen the great wealth that can be found in a humble and honest relationship with our natural world. We have a visceral need, embedded in our genetic memory, to connect with nature. It is vital to our deep sense of well-being, and also our very survival, as individuals and as a collective. Yet perhaps the human race first had to master nature before it could understand that it too is part of the natural world.

Like Henry David Thoreau, all the people in *No Signal* have heard nature calling and changed their lives as a result. They have not all read *Walden*, and they are not necessarily militant about their cause, but their words echo those of Thoreau in his book. They too are looking for greater meaning and a way of life that nurtures them as individuals as well as the wider natural world. They have embraced a way of life that may seem tough and precarious. But like Thoreau, they know that each of us must find our own path and create a life that's tailored to us – a life which philosopher Edgar Morin described as a constant process of creation, destruction and reorganisation.

"Simplify! Simplify!" Two centuries ago, Thoreau implored us all to open our eyes and free ourselves from the smokescreen that stands between us and reality: the futile tasks that distance us from our true selves, the obligations created to satisfy needs that don't really exist, the superfluous possessions, and the distractions that divert our attention from what really matters. In an age where, for many of us, screens have become our all-important window onto the world, can we really choose simplicity and go in search of the very essence of life that so eludes us? And does that mean giving up our sense of material and emotional security – the comfort that we draw from a life lived within the bounds of conventionality? "Just because I live in a deserted village where nature runs wild and unchecked, that doesn't automatically mean I have to give up my internet connection." That's what Sylwia told me when I visited her small Greek village nestled in the heart of an isolated valley. Like the other people in this book, her daily life is proof that living closer to nature does not necessarily mean rejecting the modern world. But we do need to use the technology available to us more consciously. By changing the way we live in this way, we are not taking a step backwards. On the contrary: we are moving forwards by opening up new perspectives. We are shifting the paradigm and redefining, in the simplest of terms, the quality of life that underpins each of our individual decisions. The people in this book, like Thoreau before them, wish for everyone to make a conscious choice to live their life in a way that allows them to be their true selves. But more than that, they want everyone to enjoy the same precious freedom that has allowed each of them to follow their dreams.

"Life should be nothing but a tribute paid by adults to their childhood dreams."

SYLVAIN TESSON
The Consolations of the Forest: Alone in a Cabin on the Siberian Taiga

Im Jahr 1842 beschließt der junge Schriftsteller Henry David Thoreau, fernab der Zivilisation zu leben, und verlässt seine Heimatstadt Concord im US-Bundesstaat Massachusetts, um sich ein paar Kilometer entfernt am Ufer des Walden-Sees niederzulassen. Er erbaut eigenhändig eine Holzhütte, in der er zwei Jahre, zwei Monate und zwei Tage ein einfaches, ungekünsteltes Leben führt, mit Naturbeobachtungen, philosophischen Betrachtungen und Gesprächen mit Zufallsbesuchern.

Zwölf Jahre später erschien sein Buch *Walden oder Leben in den Wäldern*. Dieser Bericht über seine Erlebnisse sollte zu einem Hauptwerk der US-amerikanischen Literatur werden und ist bis heute ein Standardwerk der modernen Klimabewegung, die darin die Anfänge des Umweltbewusstseins und des Gedankens der Rückkehr zur Natur sieht.

Dieses vielschichtige, lebendige Werk ist reich an philosophischen Gedanken, sorgfältigen Beschreibungen des namensgebenden Sees und Überlegungen zu Thoreaus Erfahrungen. Er schildert die umliegende Natur mit ihren Felsen, Pflanzen, Tieren und Wetterphänomenen, aber auch seine eigenen Gemütszustände und Wandlungsprozesse.

Thoreaus Bericht lässt die Gleichgültigkeit gegenüber denjenigen, die ihn für einen Sonderling hielten, ebenso erahnen wie den Nonkonformismus, der sein späteres Werk *Über die Pflicht zum Ungehorsam gegen den Staat* prägen sollte; es inspirierte unter anderem Gandhi und Martin Luther King. Übrigens verbrachte Thoreau selbst eine Nacht im Gefängnis, weil er in einem Akt zivilen Ungehorsams seine Steuerzahlung verweigert hatte, um gegen den Krieg zu protestieren, den die US-amerikanische Regierung gegen Mexiko führen wollte.

In *Walden* rühmt Thoreau die freiwillige Einfachheit und das Leben im Einklang mit der Natur, der er nur das entnimmt, was er braucht, und plädiert für einen möglichst schlichten Lebensstil. Er ignorierte Moden und trug schlichte, lokal produzierte Kleidung. Seine Nahrung bestand aus dem, was er fand: einem im See geangelten Fisch, einer Bisamratte, die zufällig seinen Weg kreuzte, oder ein wenig wildem Gemüse. Und obwohl er weniger Umgang mit anderen Menschen pflegte, seit er fernab der Stadt lebte, war er der Meinung, dass seine Beziehungen wertvoller und authentischer geworden waren.

Die Reflexionen in seinem Buch zeigen, dass er freie Zeit materiellen Besitztümern vorzog, seien sie auch noch so unschuldig: „Ich hatte drei Kalksteine auf meinem Pult liegen, fand aber zu meinem Entsetzen, dass sie tägliches Abstauben benötigten, während mein geistiger Hausrat noch unabgestaubt dastand." Die Möblierung seiner kleinen Hütte beschränkte sich auf das absolute Minimum, darunter drei Stühle – „einen für die Einsamkeit, zwei für die Freundschaft, drei für das Sozialleben".

Es war das Leben, das echte Leben, mit dem Thoreau sich auseinandersetzte. Um dessen Wesenskern mit möglichst wenig Zugeständnissen an gesellschaftliche Konventionen aufzudecken, tilgte er alles aus seiner Existenz, was materiell, intellektuell oder spirituell überflüssig war. Zur Natur in ihrem Urzustand entwickelte er eine einfache, zeitlose Beziehung, beobachtete fasziniert die Rhythmen der Wildnis und nahm aufmerksam die kleinsten Veränderungen seiner natürlichen Umgebung wahr. Auf der Suche nach Wahrheit, fern jener Scheinwirklichkeit, für die er zum Teil das Gesellschaftsleben verantwortlich machte, bot ihm sein Rückzugsort die Freiheit, seine Selbsterkenntnis durch lange, einsame Wanderungen und mannigfaltige Erlebnisse zu vertiefen.

Dieser von der christlichen Kultur geprägte Mann, dem eine Bestattung in geweihtem Boden beinahe verweigert worden wäre, weil er nicht mehr in die Kirche ging, pflegte seine Beziehung zum Heiligen über universelle religiöse Rituale: „Jeder Morgen war eine frohe Aufforderung, mein Leben so einfach und, ich darf sagen, so unschuldig zu gestalten wie die Natur selbst. [...] Früh stand ich auf und badete im Teich; das war eine religiöse Übung, eine der besten Handlungen, welche ich beging."

Sein Ziel, andere Menschen für die Natur zu sensibilisieren, verfolgte Thoreau mit einem wissenschaftlichen Ansatz, durch Beobachtungen und Experimente: Wie ein Chemiker oder Mathematiker wollte er das Leben „auf seine einfachste Formel reduzieren", ihm das Mark aussaugen und die Ergebnisse seiner Forschungen mit anderen teilen.

So veröffentlichte er 1854 *Walden oder Leben in den Wäldern*, dessen – bescheidener – Erfolg ihm Anerkennung im Kreis der Transzendentalisten verschaffte, zu denen sein Mentor Ralph Waldo Emerson gehörte. Und obwohl einige Kritiker in seiner Heimat *Walden* als heidnisch und rückwärtsgerichtet bezeichneten, wurde das Buch in Frankreich wohlwollend aufgenommen und mit Paul Cézannes Malerei verglichen.

Tatsächlich stellen beide Künstler ihre Umwelt so dar, wie sie sie wahrnehmen, und versuchen ihren zeitlosen, metaphysischen Wesenskern wiederzugeben, der sich in der Beziehung zwischen Natur und Mensch offenbart. Obwohl Thoreau manchen als visionärer Philosoph galt, wurde sein Buch erst im Lauf des 20. Jahrhunderts allmählich zum literarischen Standardwerk.

Fast zwei Jahrhunderte später entdeckte ich *Walden oder Leben in den Wäldern* nach der Rückkehr von einer langen Reise. Bei der Lektüre klangen Thoreaus Worte kraftvoll in mir nach, und ich entdeckte Gefühle in seinem Buch wieder, die ich als Kind in der Provence empfunden hatte, inmitten von wilder Natur, alten Pinien und Olivenbäumen – ganz anders als die Natur Neuenglands, die Thoreau inspirierte. Angesichts der verblüffenden Klarheit seines Denkens und der Beziehung zur Natur, die er beschrieb, wuchs in mir die Überzeugung, dass es auch unter den Männern und Frauen unserer Zeit Persönlichkeiten geben müsse, die sich wie einst Thoreau für einen anderen Weg entschieden haben: den der Annäherung an die Natur.

Ich begann, intensive Recherchen durchzuführen, und nahm Kontakt zu zahlreichen Menschen auf; ich störte Eremiten auf, fragte Ortskundige aus, verschlang Abenteuerromane und Reiseberichte, bis ich schließlich mit meiner Kamera zu einer langen Reise aufbrach. Im Frühjahr streifte ich im Südosten Alaskas mein Ölzeug über und wohnte in einer schwimmenden Holzhütte auf dem Meer, um am Alltag eines ehemaligen Immobilienmaklers teilzunehmen, der Austernzüchter geworden war. Bei -40 °C erlernte ich im tiefsten arktischen Winter, ein Gespann Schlittenhunde zu führen, bevor ich den Atlantik überquerte, um bei den Gauchos in den argentinischen Anden an einem Viehtrieb teilzunehmen.

Im Lauf von fünf Jahren lernte ich außergewöhnliche Persönlichkeiten kennen, freie Geister auf unkonventionellen Wegen. Indem ich ihre Lebensweise teilte, ließ ich meine Kamera mit der Umwelt verschmelzen, um sie besser fotografieren zu können, und gehörte eine Zeitlang zu ihnen. Diese starken Persönlichkeiten faszinieren mich nach wie vor; ihre Schicksale spiegeln Widerstandsfähigkeit und Durchhaltevermögen wider.

Nach jeder dieser Reisen wurde die Rückkehr nach Frankreich, in mein städtisches Leben, befremdlicher. Eine magische Anziehungskraft trieb mich immer wieder dazu, an diese abgeschiedenen Orte zu reisen, ohne Strom oder fließendes Wasser, ohne Internet und meist auch ohne Telefonnetz. Von wilder Natur umgeben, war ich weit entfernt vom geschäftigen Treiben der Menschen und dem Lärm der Städte und begann, daran Geschmack zu finden. Trotz aller Schwierigkeiten, Absagen, verlorener Gepäckstücke und einiger Frostbeulen trieb mich weiterhin der Wunsch an, neue Menschen kennenzulernen und eine Zeitlang ihre Schicksale zu teilen, die symptomatisch für eine sich selbst in Frage stellende Menschheit stehen. Denn ich bin fest davon überzeugt: Jedes menschliche Wesen hat das innere Bedürfnis, eine Verbindung zur Natur aufrechtzuerhalten, wie subtil sie auch sein mag.

Im Lauf der Jahre bestätigten die Begegnungen und Gespräche diese Überzeugung, und ich erkannte, welcher Reichtum in einer demütigen und offenen Beziehung zur Natur steckt. Eine solche Verbindung scheint als instinktives, in unser genetisches Gedächtnis einprogrammiertes Bedürfnis absolut unerlässlich für unser wahres Wohlergehen, aber auch für unser individuelles und kollektives Überleben zu sein. Vielleicht musste der Mensch die Natur erst zähmen, um zu erkennen, dass er ein Teil von ihr ist.

Genau wie der amerikanische Philosoph haben alle Protagonisten in *Funkstille* einen Ruf vernommen, der sie dazu brachte, ihr Leben zu ändern. Und auch wenn sie nicht alle *Walden* gelesen haben, wenn sie nicht alle engagierte Aktivisten sind – in ihren Worten klingt das Echo von Thoreaus Schriften nach: die gleiche Suche nach Sinn, nach einer Lebensweise, die mit unserer inneren und der äußeren Natur im Einklang steht. Sie stehen zu ihrem frei gewählten Alltag, der rau und unsicher scheinen mag. Wie Thoreau wissen sie, dass es uns allen selbst überlassen ist, unseren eigenen Weg zu finden und ein Leben zu finden, das zu uns passt – ein Leben, das der Philosoph Edgar Morin als ständigen Prozess der Schöpfung, Zerstörung und Neuentstehung beschreibt.

„Vereinfache, vereinfache!" Es ist schon beinahe zwei Jahrhunderte her, dass Thoreau mit diesen Worten dazu aufrief, die Augen zu öffnen und uns von allem zu befreien, was uns von der Wirklichkeit abschirmt: nutzlose Beschäftigungen, die uns von uns selbst entfremden, Verpflichtungen, die nur der Erfüllung künstlicher Bedürfnisse dienen, überflüssige Gegenstände und Zerstreuungen, die vom Wesentlichen ablenken. Können wir uns in einer Zeit, in der Bildschirme für viele von uns die unentbehrliche Schnittstelle zur Welt geworden sind, überhaupt noch für das Einfache entscheiden und auf die Suche nach dem Wesentlichen machen? Braucht es dafür einen Bruch, einen Verzicht auf materielle und psychische Sicherheit, auf den Komfort, der zu einem konventionellen Leben gehört?

„Nur weil ich in einem verlassenen Dorf mitten in der Wildnis wohne, muss ich doch nicht aufs Internet verzichten", meint Sylwia, die in einem abgelegenen griechischen Tal lebt.

Ihr Alltag zeigt – wie auch der anderer Menschen aus diesem Buch –, dass ein naturnahes Leben nicht unbedingt bedeuten muss, das moderne Leben abzulehnen; es geht eher um einen bedachten Umgang mit den Technologien, die es uns bietet. Diese neuen Lebensweisen sind nicht rückwärtsgewandt, sondern stellen im Gegenteil einen echten Fortschritt und einen Paradigmenwechsel dar, bei dem auf selbstbewusste Weise die Lebensqualität wieder ins Zentrum individueller Entscheidungen rückt. Und wenn diejenigen, die in diesem Buch vorkommen, wie Thoreau möchten, dass jeder den eigenen Weg bewusst und passend zu seiner Identität wählt, liegt ihnen dabei vor allem eines am Herzen: dass alle Menschen jene kostbare Freiheit genießen können, die es ihnen erlaubt, ihre Träume zu verfolgen.

„Das Leben sollte nichts anderes sein als das:
eine Huldigung des Erwachsenen an die
Träume seiner Kindheit."

SYLVAIN TESSON
In den Wäldern Sibiriens

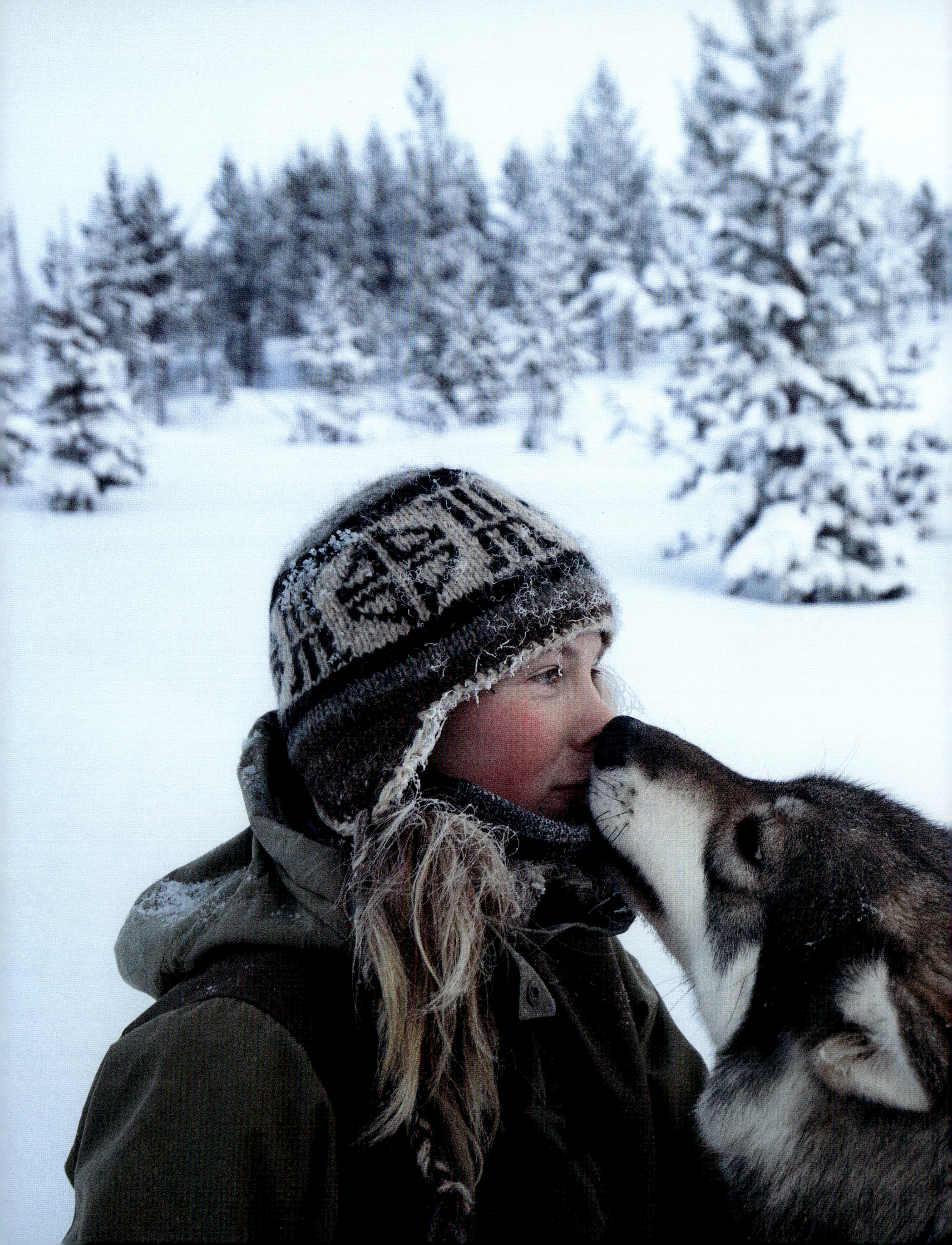

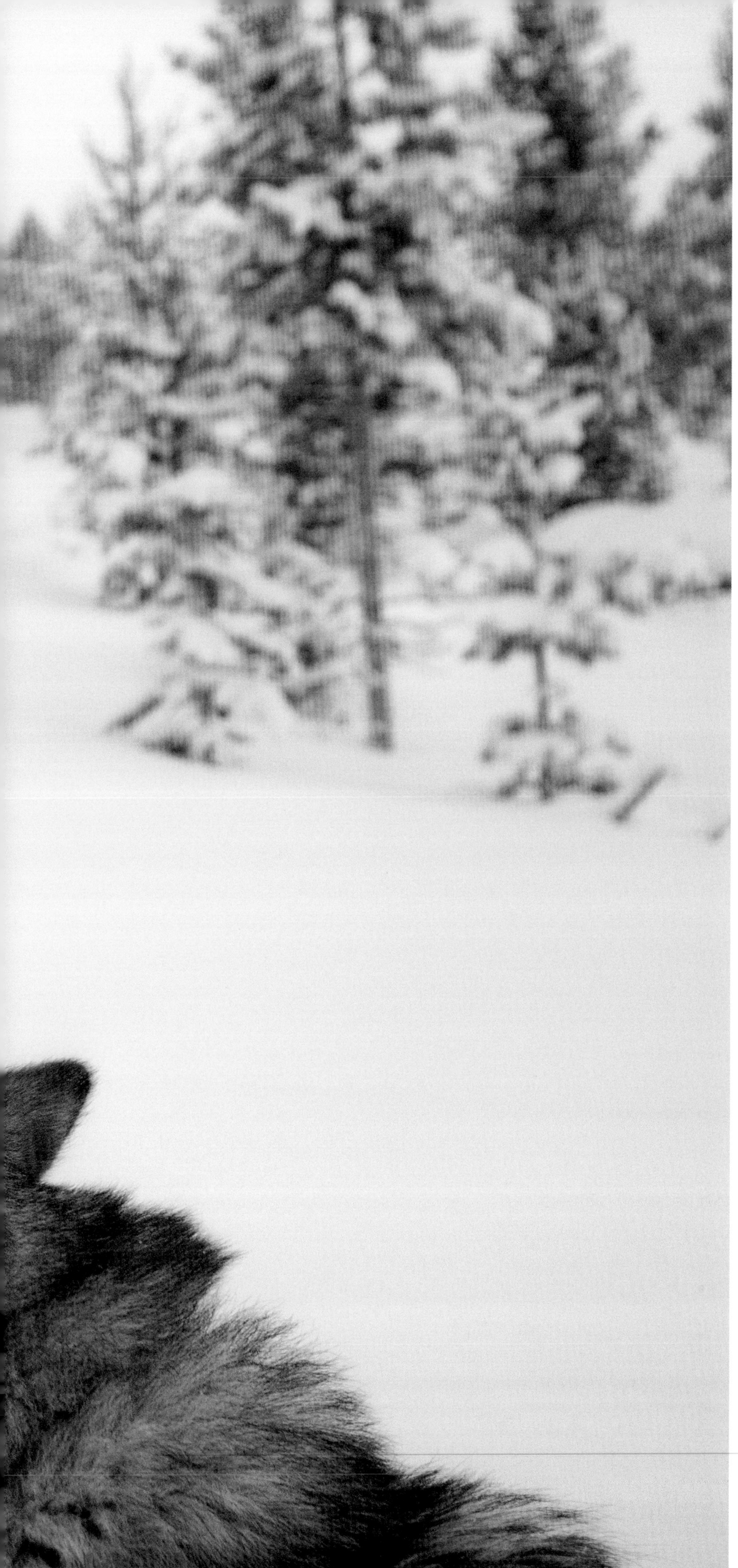

TINJA

"MATERIAL GOODS
DON'T MATTER MUCH TO
ME… NATURE GIVES ME
EVERYTHING I NEED."

„MATERIELLE GÜTER SIND
MIR NICHT WICHTIG, DIE
NATUR GIBT MIR ALLES, WAS
ICH ZUM LEBEN BRAUCHE."

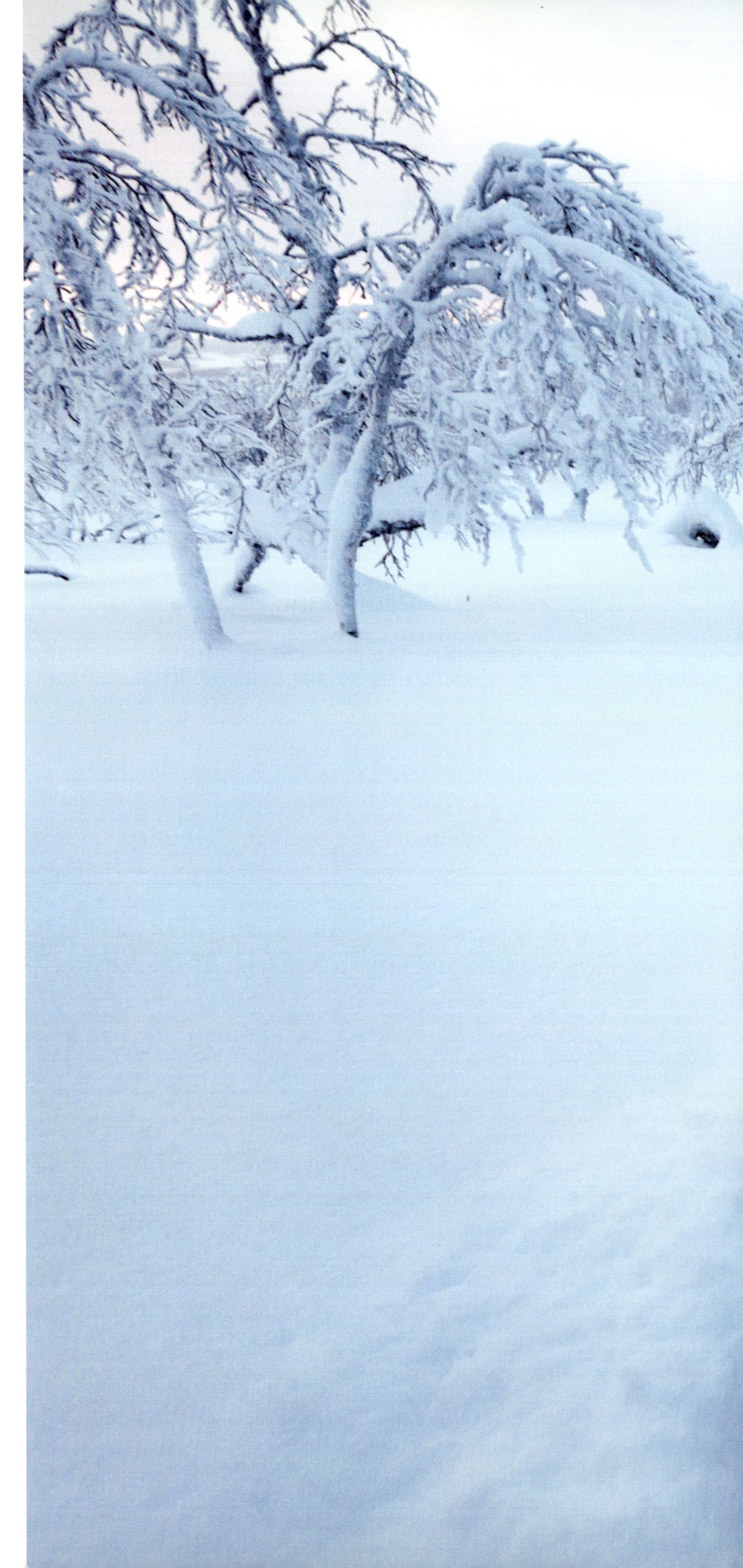

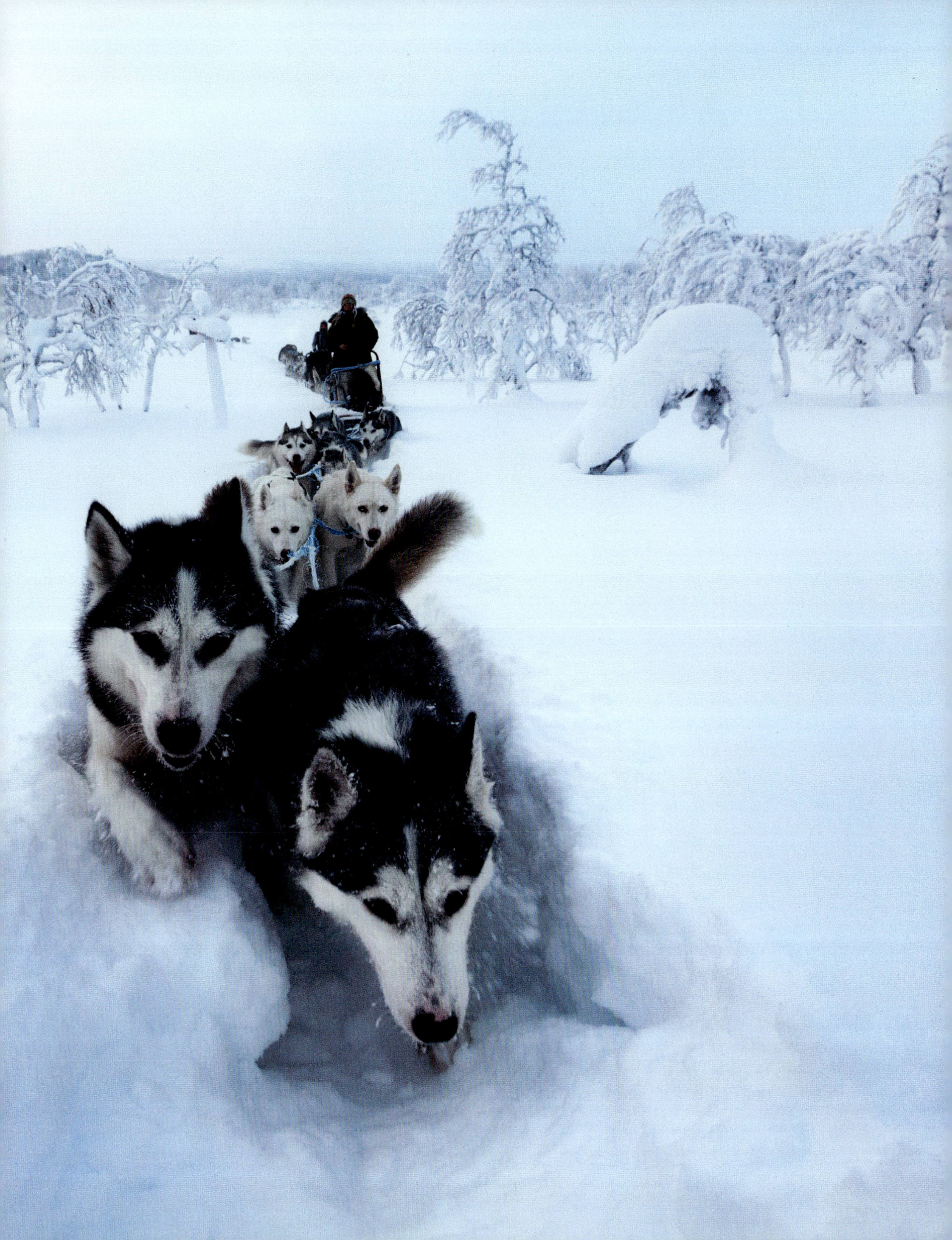

AN ARCTIC DREAM

INARI, FINLAND

Tinja lives in Finnish Lapland in a small wooden house, with no running water or electricity,
350 kilometres away from the nearest big town. After spending six years in the south of the country,
she decided to leave urban life behind and return to Lapland.

Tinja now lives several hundreds of kilometres away from the nearest big town, in a small wooden house without any water or electricity, after falling in love with the magical landscapes of the far north. Only a river separates her cabin from the Muotkatunturi Wilderness Area, a huge uninhabited tundra that now serves as a playground for the young Finn and her sled dogs.

At home, she relaxes in the unique hideaway that is her living room, decorated with photos of huskies alongside medals won for sled races, Scandinavian knives and leather artefacts she works on during the long winter nights. She shares this space with her 15 horses, among them Fjord, Icelandic and mustang breeds, as well as, of course, her 85 huskies – and the mere mention of her noisy, affectionate tenants makes the thirty-year-old's eyes light up. "They're my best friends. It doesn't matter how you're feeling in a given moment, they make everything better."

When she was little, Tinja was often left to her own devices. She would spend all of her time with her childhood dog in the woods, even building a sled for her four-legged companion, inspired by Jack London novels. She was already very drawn to nature, with her animals as friends. She quickly discovered the exhilaration of sledding in the great wide open, with all the speed, peace and quiet and freedom it offered.

"Material goods don't matter much to me," she says. "Nature gives me everything I need. I like being alone with my dogs and my horses. For me, I'm most at peace when I'm in nature."

Her decision to live in the wilderness and return to Inari, where she grew up, was a gradual one, made over the course of several years living in towns or cities doing the same absurd things every day. For the young woman, the thought of refrigerating her food while it is cold outside is foolish, and running water from a tap when you could simply fetch some from the river doesn't make any sense. And so Tinja left town and its absurdities behind after six years of studying biology at the University of Jyväskylä, in the south of Finland – and she hasn't looked back since. In studying biology, her original plan was to find a job that would allow her to combine professional life with her passion for wildlife, but it would ultimately turn out to be too human-centric for Tinja.

Instead, she swapped theory for practical work, paving the way to move closer to – and eventually form a deeply symbiotic relationship with – the Arctic nature that had fascinated her for so long. She makes do with very little to live a frugal and simple life, using only old materials, leather and wood, and has close ties with the local Sámi reindeer herders, whose territory overlaps with the immense tundra landscape of Lapland.

Don't be fooled by her petite frame. Tinja can quickly reduce a tree into a pile of logs and guide a sled through the snow and ice for hours on end in temperatures dipping to -40 °C. To provide for her dogs and be able to stay with them at all times, however, she has also had to reluctantly dip her toes into the world of tourism, and now organises expeditions for visitors to the far north. But little by little, Tinja is managing to reduce her reliance on tourism and can now pick and choose which trips she wants to do, allowing her to keep a good balance and continue to enjoy her peaceful life with the dogs.

Strong and agile yet unpredictable and wild at heart, Tinja is the head of the pack in the icy kingdom – with its biting, piercing cold – that she loves so much. "In winter I'm always full of energy.

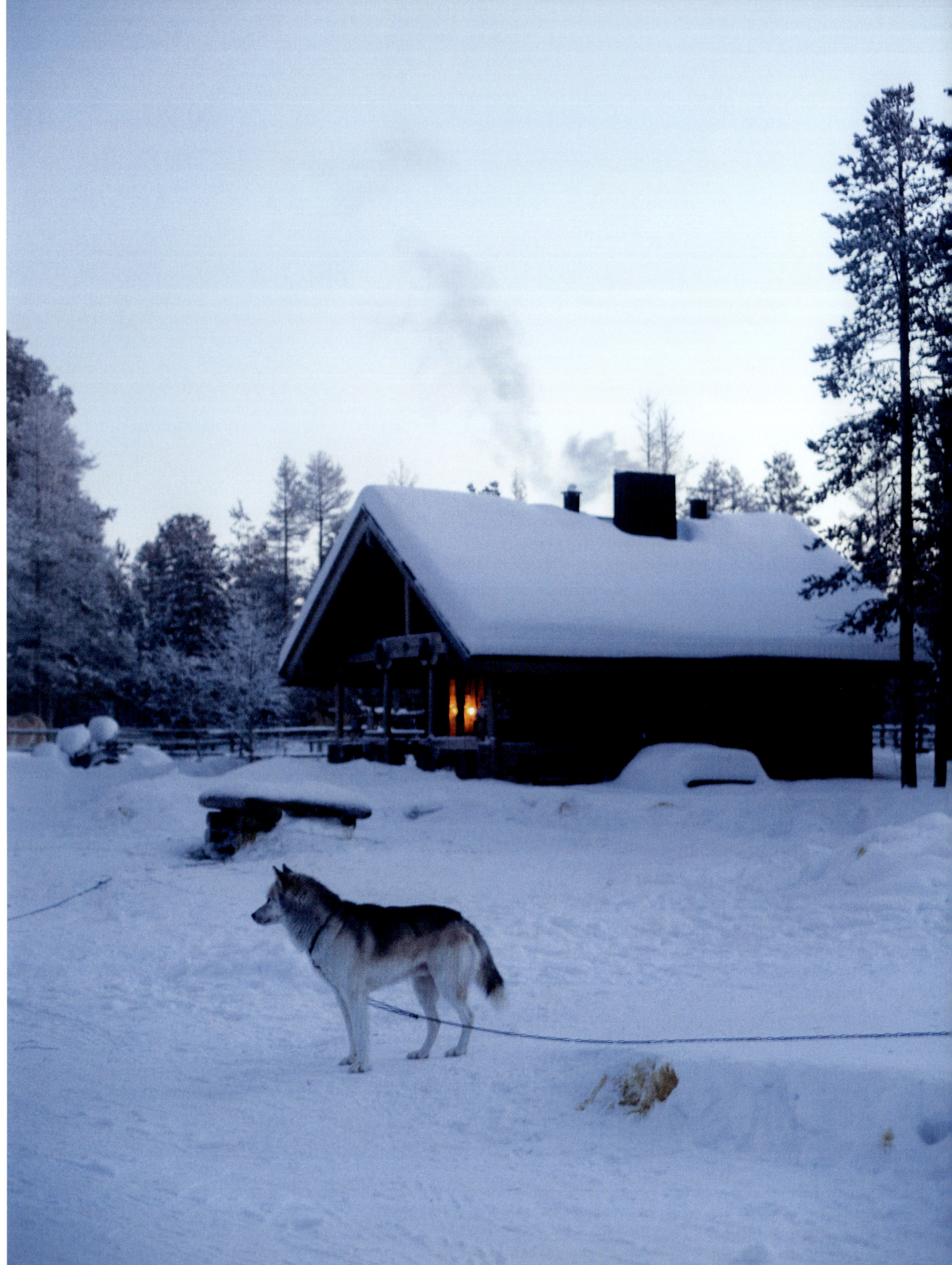

The air is so fresh and invigorating. It's the most beautiful season, the time of year when the Arctic is revealed in all its glory – from the sky and the stars to the northern lights. It's so beautiful that you never grow tired of it."

With these Arctic temperatures comes the need to take certain precautions and always remain vigilant, however. At -20 °C, the moisture on the inside of your nostrils starts to freeze. Once the temperature dips down to -30 °C, the tears freeze on the end of your eyelashes and frost starts to form on the hair. Over the years, the musher, strapped into her felt boots – which offer the best protection from the very low temperatures – has learned to perfect the art of layering clothing to stop frostbite.

During the short winter days, Tinja wakes up early to clean out the paddocks housing her dogs and horses. This allows her to spend time with each of them, as well as keep an eye on their health and identify any – even tiny – problems. Some of her huskies were abandoned by their owners before they came to her, and she tries to give them all of her attention.

Here, there is no running water or electricity. Tinja uses a wood-fired stove to cook and stay warm, and goes down to the river every morning to break the ice and fetch water. She lives by the seasons, which leaves little time to get bored. When she isn't out with her dogs, the musher spends her day doing manual tasks – such as repairing fences or harnesses – or sewing. When evening comes, she feeds the pack with kibbles or reindeer carcasses.

The same herders also hunt wolves, and so it has been a long time since howling has been heard in the forests. But Tinja's dogs have stepped up to the plate and, several times a day, the pack can be heard howling in unison – a sound that can be perceived for miles in all directions.

In winter, she sometimes ends the day with a scorching hot sauna, where she can have a wash and escape from the monotony of the cold. This is also where Tinja washes up and does her laundry. Heat is precious when the outdoor temperatures fluctuate between -30 °C and -40 °C. This is a tough life where every movement is an effort, but Tinja doesn't think of this as a heavy price to pay. She considers human beings as a kind of sickness for the planet – so much so that in another life she would like to be reincarnated as a dog.

Until then, Tinja, who embarked on this journey solo, is no longer alone. She now lives with Alex, who she met several years ago during a sled dog race. "Life is better as a pair," she says, despite her solitary tendencies. "I knew instantly that Alex would make a good companion." After a career as a professional skier, Alex started rearing his own competition dogs. Tinja finds it fun to help him from time to time.

Together, the couple roam the vast stretches of wilderness, setting up camp and making the most of being on the edge of a protected area to explore the far north, venturing a little further with every trip. Here, in the forest, Tinja is part of a whole. She is home.

EIN ARKTISCHER TRAUM

INARI, FINNLAND

Tinja wohnt im finnischen Teil Lapplands in einem kleinen Holzhaus ohne fließendes Wasser oder Strom, 350 Kilometer von der nächsten Großstadt entfernt. Nach sechs Jahren im Süden des Landes beschloss sie, die Stadt zu verlassen und wieder in Lappland zu leben.

Hunderte von Kilometern von der nächsten Großstadt entfernt, in einem Holzhaus ohne Strom und fließendes Wasser, lebt Tinja, eine junge Finnin, die sich in die märchenhaften Landschaften des hohen Nordens verliebt hat. Nur ein Fluss trennt ihre Hütte vom Naturschutzgebiet Muotkatunturi, einer riesigen, wilden, unbewohnten Tundra, die den Spielplatz der jungen Frau und ihrer Schlittenhunde bildet.

An den Wänden ihres höhlenartigen Wohn- und Schlafraums drängen sich Husky-Fotos neben Medaillen von Hundeschlittenrennen, skandinavischen Messern und Lederarbeiten, die in den langen Winternächten entstehen. Sie teilt diesen Ort mit ihren 15 Pferden, darunter Fjordpferde, Islandponys und Mustangs, und natürlich mit ihren 85 Huskys. Schon die Erwähnung dieser lärmenden und liebevollen Mitbewohner lässt die Augen der Dreißigjährigen aufleuchten. „Sie sind meine besten Freunde. Egal, in welchem Seelenzustand man gerade steckt – im Zusammensein mit ihnen verfliegt alles."

Als kleines Mädchen war Tinja viel sich selbst überlassen und verbrachte ihre Zeit in den Wäldern mit ihrem Hund, dem sie – inspiriert von Jack Londons Romanen – ein Zuggeschirr gebastelt hatte. Schon damals war sie der Natur nahe, mit Tieren als einzigen Freunden. So entdeckte sie auf dem Schlitten die herrlichen Momente lautloser Schnelligkeit und Freiheit in den riesigen Weiten.

„Materielle Güter sind mir nicht wichtig", sagt sie. „Die Natur gibt mir alles, was ich zum Leben brauche. Ich bin gern mit meinen Hunden und Pferden allein ... Für mich gibt es keine friedlichere Lebensweise als die in der Natur."

Ihre Entscheidung, in der Wildnis zu leben und nach Inari zurückzukehren, wo sie aufgewachsen ist, reift im Lauf der Jahre, die sie in der Stadt mit ihren täglichen Absurditäten verbringt. Es kommt ihr bizarr vor, Lebensmittel einzufrieren, während draußen Frost herrscht. Wasser aus einem Wasserhahn laufen zu lassen, wenn man es einfach am Fluss holen kann, ergibt ebenso wenig Sinn. Ohne Bedauern verlässt Tinja die Stadt und ihre Ungereimtheiten nach einem sechsjährigen Biologiestudium an der Universität Jyväskylä in Südfinnland. Tinja hatte diesen Weg gewählt, um ihren Beruf mit ihrer Leidenschaft für das wilde Leben zu verbinden; aus ihrer Sicht erwies er sich letztlich als zu sehr auf den Menschen und zu wenig auf die Natur ausgerichtet. Indem sie die Theorie durch praktische Arbeit ersetzte, fand die Dreißigjährige einen Weg, sich der arktischen Natur anzunähern, die sie fasziniert und zu der sie ein zutiefst symbiotisches Verhältnis pflegt. Sie braucht nur wenig für ihr bescheidenes, einfaches Leben, verwendet alte Materialien wie Leder oder Holz und pflegt Beziehungen zu den Sámi-Rentierzüchtern, deren Territorium sich über die riesige Tundra Lapplands erstreckt.

Man sollte sie besser nicht nach ihrer zarten Erscheinung beurteilen: Tinja kann einen Baum in einen Stapel Feuerholz verwandeln oder bei -40 °C einen Schlitten stundenlang durch schnee- und eisbedeckte Landschaften steuern. Um für den Unterhalt der Hunde zu sorgen und immer bei ihnen zu sein, musste sie sich zu einem vorsichtigen Schritt in Richtung Tourismus durchringen; sie organisiert Expeditionen für Besucher des hohen Nordens. Inzwischen konnte sie die Zahl der Teilnehmer reduzieren; sie sucht sie sorgfältig aus, um das Gleichgewicht und die Ruhe ihres Lebens mit den Hunden nicht zu sehr durcheinanderzubringen.

Tinja ist stark und leichtfüßig, unberechenbar und wild – die Rudelführerin in ihrem eisigen Reich, dessen scharfe, durchdringende Kälte sie so liebt. „Im Winter fühle ich mich energiegeladen. Die Luft ist frisch und belebend. Das ist die schönste Jahreszeit; die Arktis zeigt sich in ihrer ganzen Pracht. Der Himmel mit den Sternen, die Nordlichter ... So schön, dass man nie genug davon bekommen kann."

Die arktischen Temperaturen erfordern dennoch bestimmte Vorkehrungen und ständige Wachsamkeit. Bei -20 °C lässt die kalte Luft die Feuchtigkeit in den Nasenlöchern vereisen. Ab -30 °C gefrieren die Tränen am Ende der Wimpern und auf dem Haar bildet sich Raureif. Die Hundeschlittenführerin trägt Filzstiefel, durch die keine Kälte dringt, und hat im Lauf der Jahre perfekt gelernt, wie man sich durch Schichten von Kleidung vor Frostbeulen schützt.

An den kurzen Wintertagen steht Tinja früh auf und macht die Hunde- und Pferdegehege sauber. So kann sie mit jedem Tier ein wenig Zeit verbringen, aber auch ihren Gesundheitszustand überprüfen und kleine Probleme rechtzeitig erkennen. Viele ihrer Huskys hat sie aufgenommen, nachdem sie von ihren Eigentümern im Stich gelassen wurden, und Tinja widmet ihnen bewusst ihre volle Aufmerksamkeit.

Hier gibt es weder fließendes Wasser noch Strom: Ein Holzofen dient zum Kochen und Heizen, und jeden Morgen muss man zum Fluss gehen, das Eis aufhacken und Wasser schöpfen. Ein Leben im Rhythmus der Jahreszeiten, das wenig Zeit für Müßiggang lässt. Zwischen den Ausfahrten mit den Hunden wird der Tag von handwerklicher Arbeit strukturiert – Reparaturen an

Zäunen und Hundegeschirren oder Näharbeiten –, und abends muss die Meute mit Trockenfutter oder Rentierkadavern gefüttert werden, die sie preiswert bei den Sámi-Hirten der Region kauft. Deren Jagden haben dafür gesorgt, dass schon lange keine Wölfe mehr in den Wäldern heulen. Aber Tinjas Hunde übernehmen diese Aufgabe; mehrmals täglich bricht die Meute in einstimmiges Geheul aus. Es klingt kilometerweit ins Land.

Im Winter enden die Tage manchmal mit einer heißen Sauna, die Tinja Gelegenheit zur Körperpflege gibt und die Monotonie der Kälte durchbricht. In diesem Raum spült Tinja auch ihr Geschirr und wäscht ihre Kleidung. Hitze ist kostbar, wenn die Außentemperatur zwischen -30 und -40 °C schwankt. Ein raues Leben, bei dem jede Bewegung Anstrengung erfordert, aber Tinja betrachtet das nicht als Nachteil. Sie sieht die Menschen als eine Art Krankheit des Planeten und würde im nächsten Leben gerne als Hund wiedergeboren werden.

Inzwischen ist Tinja nicht mehr allein. Alex, den sie vor einigen Jahren bei einem Hundeschlittenrennen kennengelernt hat, lebt mittlerweile an ihrer Seite. „Zu zweit ist es besser", gibt sie zu, trotz ihres Hangs zur Einsamkeit. „Und ich wusste sofort, dass Alex ein guter Gefährte sein würde." Nach einer Karriere als Profi-Langläufer züchtet er heute Hunde für Schlittenrennen. Hin und wieder nimmt auch Tinja teil, nur zum Spaß.

Zusammen durchquert das Paar riesige unberührte Weiten, biwakiert dort und nutzt die Lage am Rand eines Naturschutzgebiets, um in die weißen Weiten vorzudringen, jedes Mal ein bisschen tiefer. Hier im Wald fühlt Tinja sich zu Hause und einem großen Ganzen zugehörig.

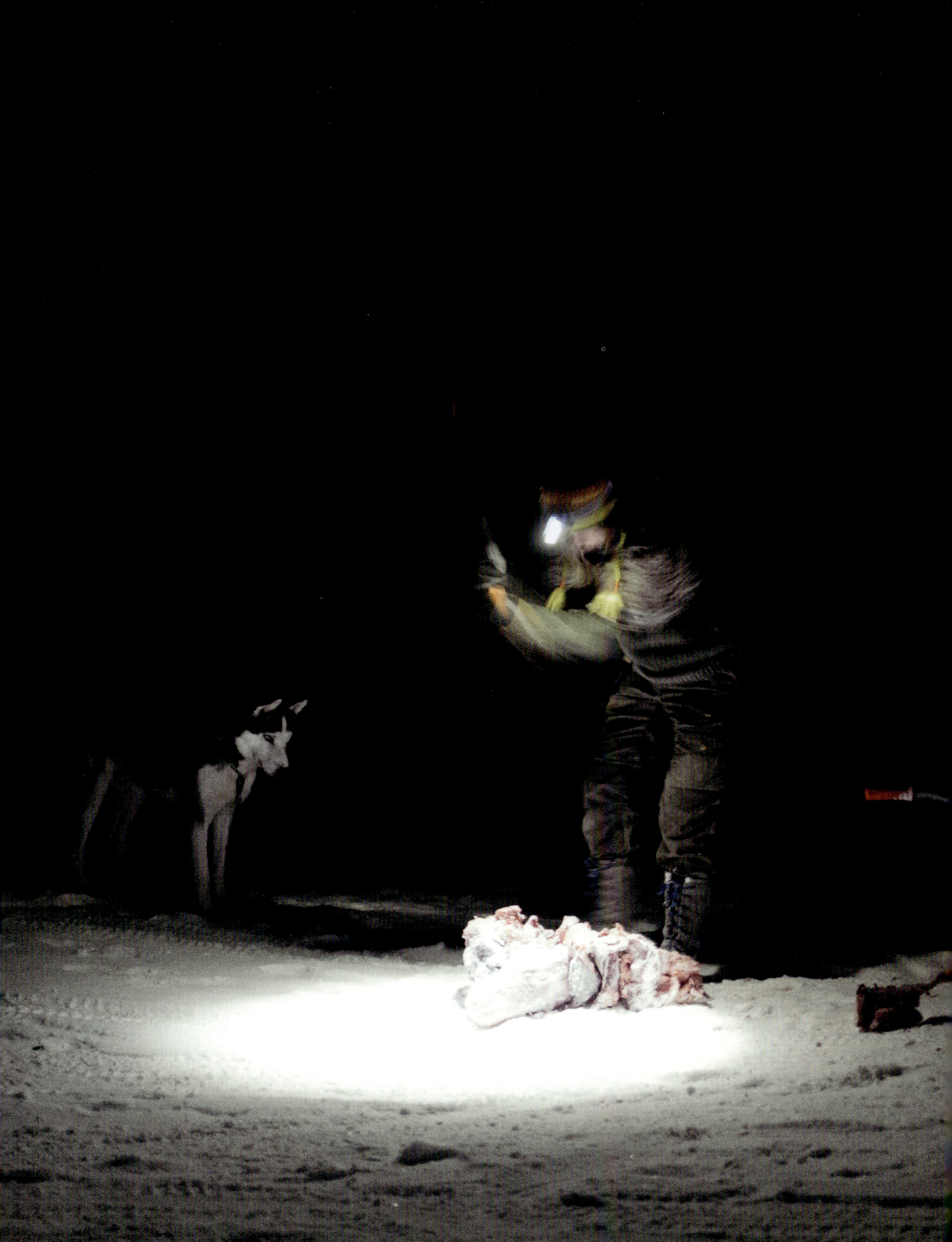

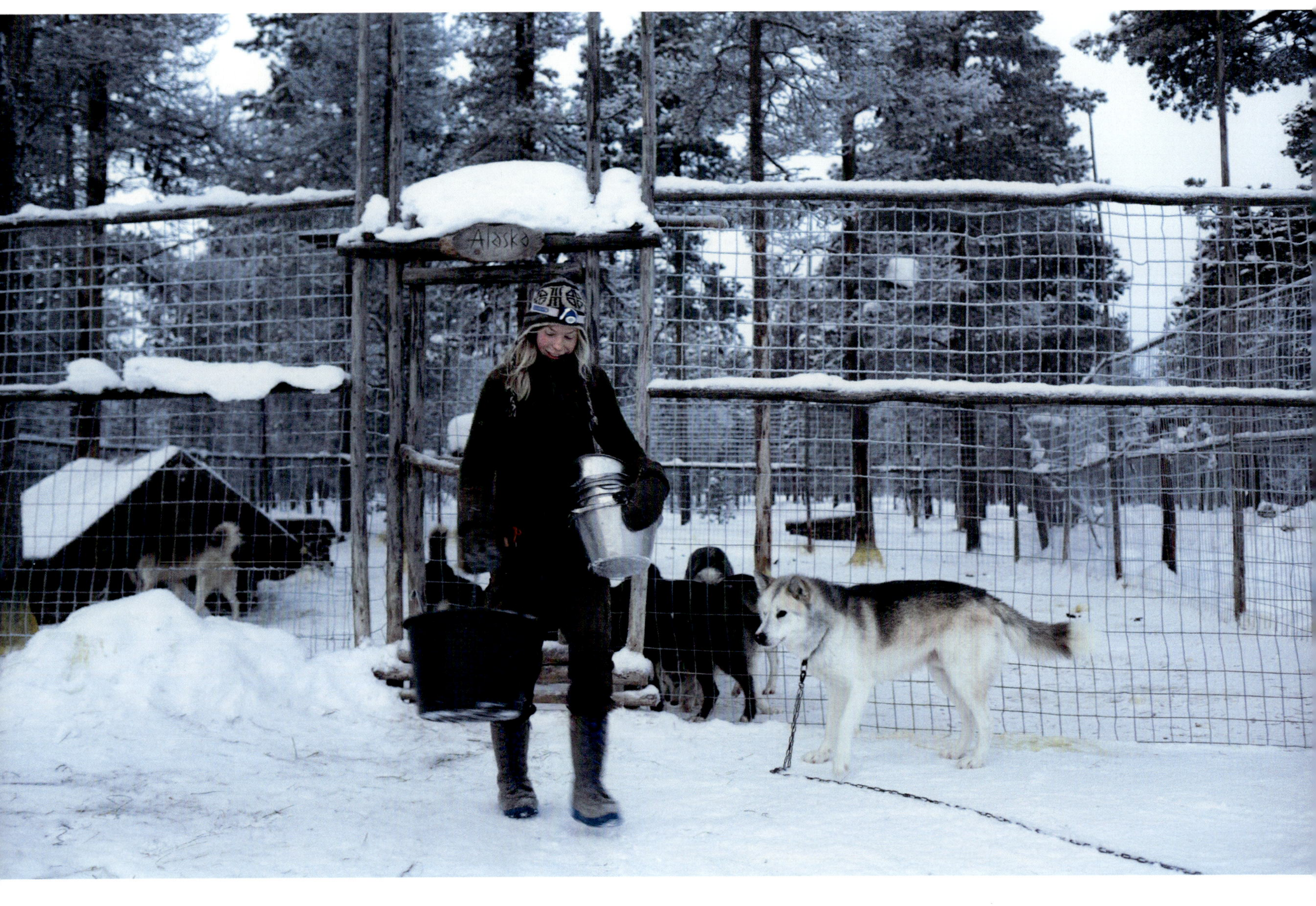

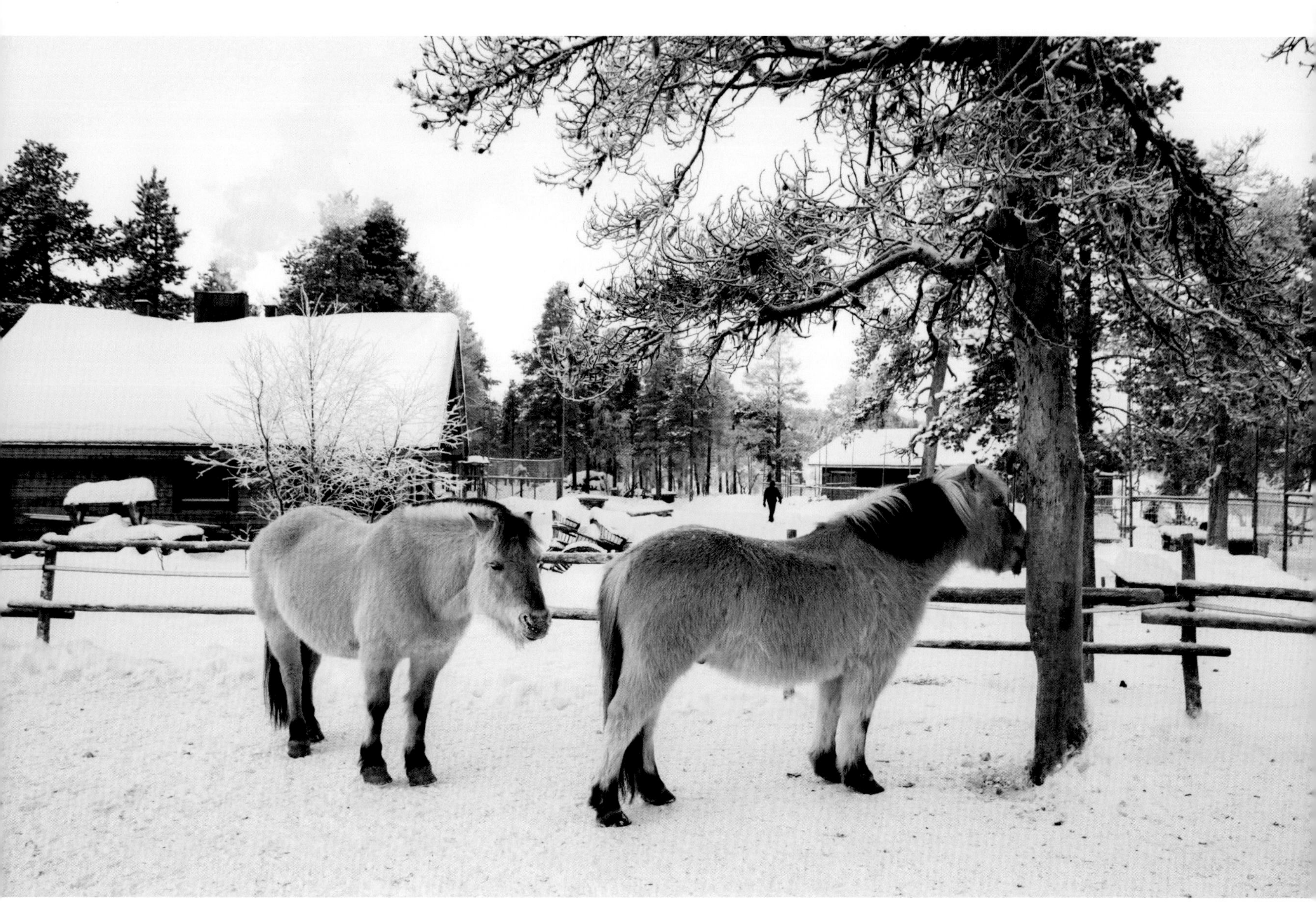

"Simplicity, simplicity, simplicity!
I say, let your affairs be as two or three, and
not a hundred or a thousand; instead of a
million count half a dozen, and keep your
accounts on your thumbnail."

HENRY DAVID THOREAU
Walden; or, Life in the Woods

„Einfachheit, Einfachheit, Einfachheit!
Lass deine Geschäfte zwei oder drei sein,
sage ich dir, und nicht hundert oder tausend;
statt eine Million zu zählen, zähle ein
halbes Dutzend und führe Buch auf
deinem Daumennagel!"

HENRY DAVID THOREAU
Walden oder Leben in den Wäldern

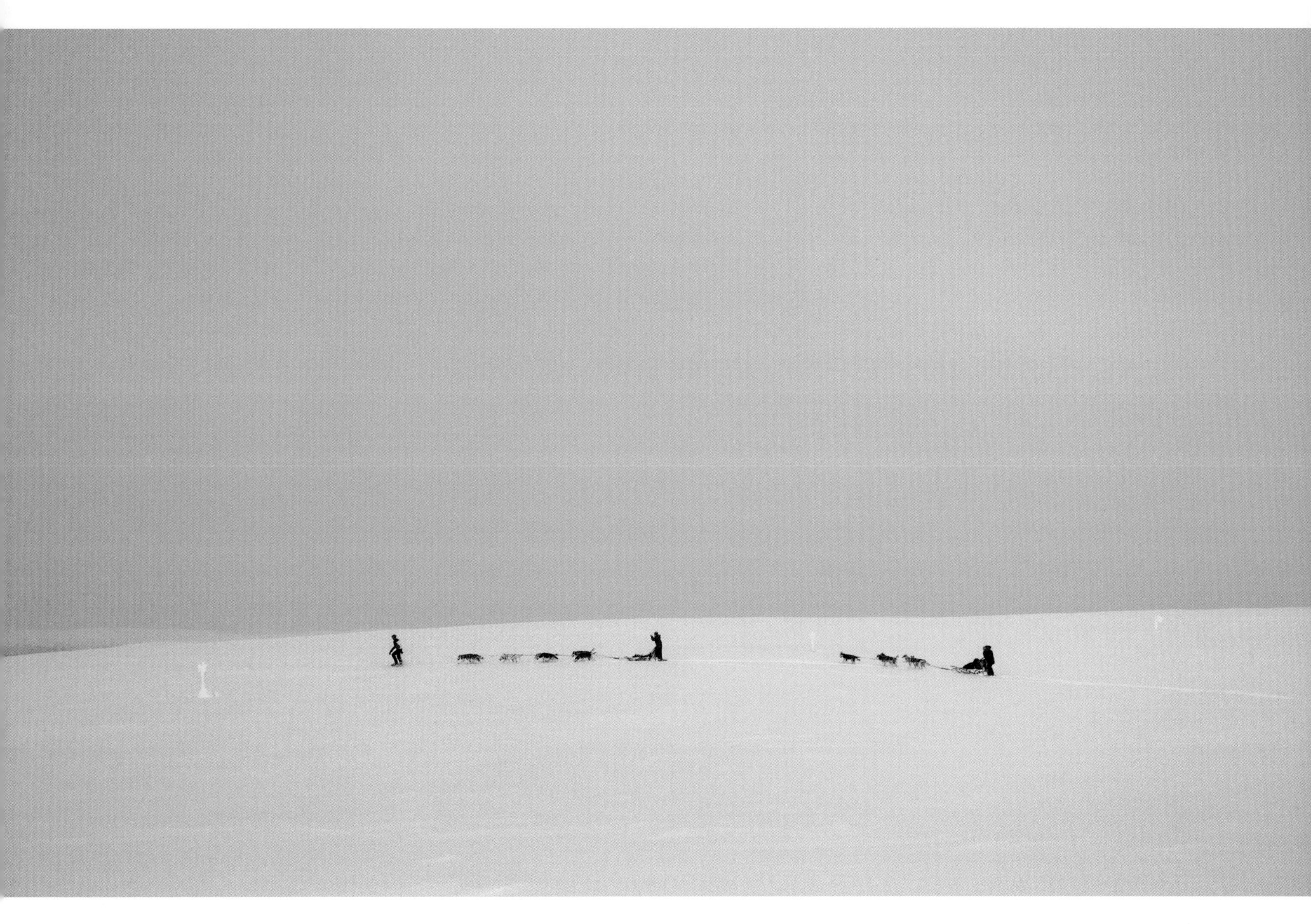

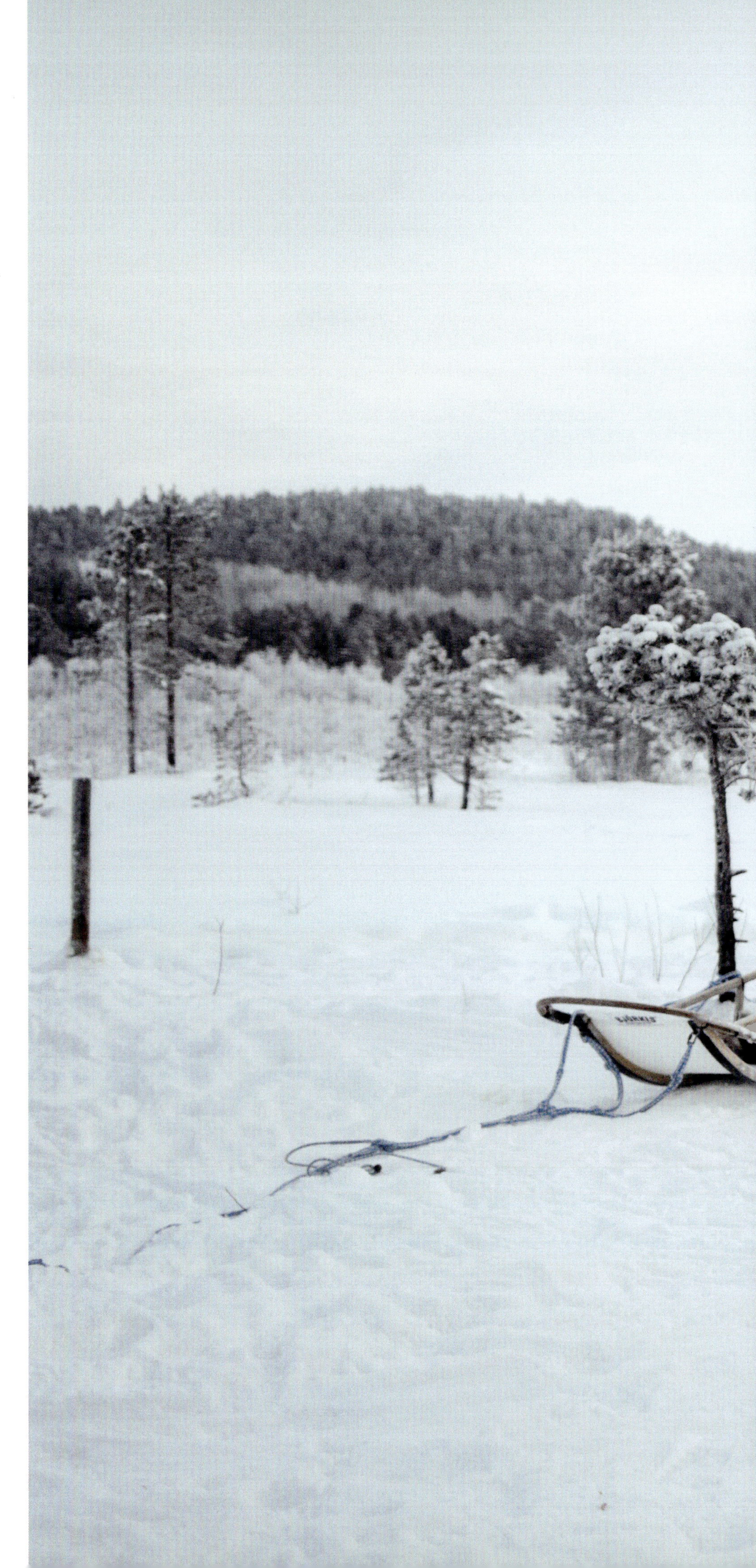

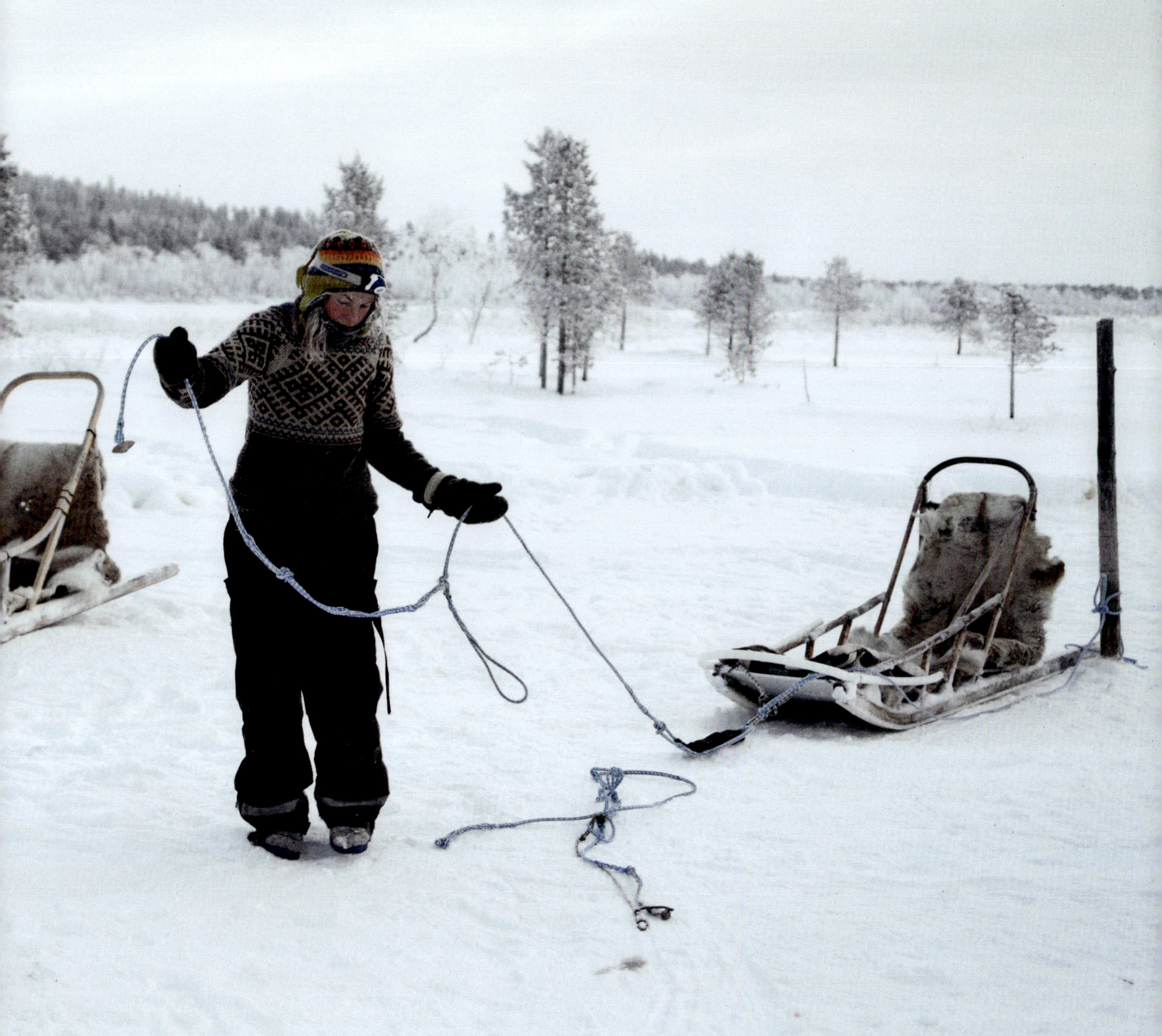

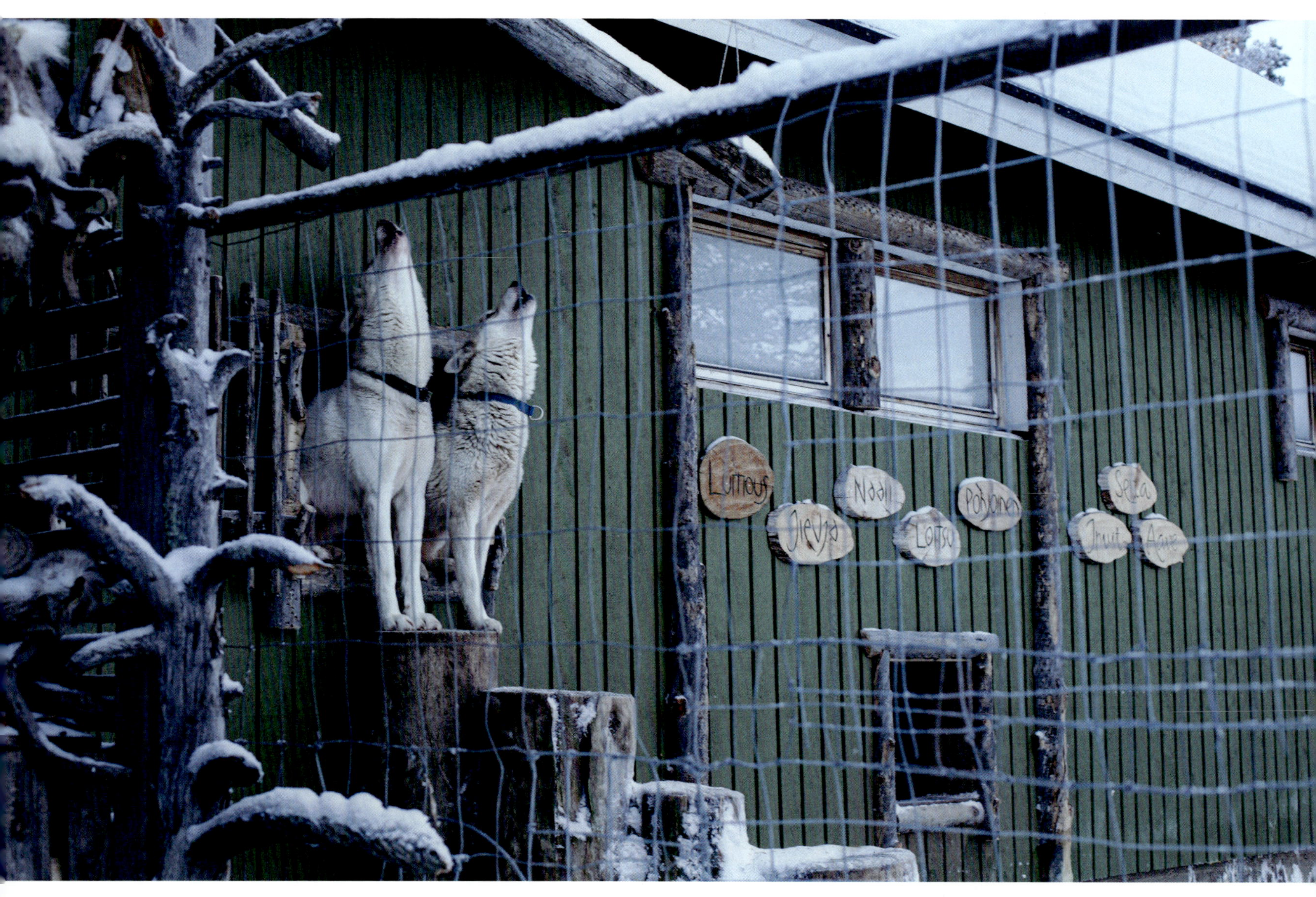

Lumous
Jievja
Naali
Loitsu
Pohjoinen
Setla
Inuit
Acara

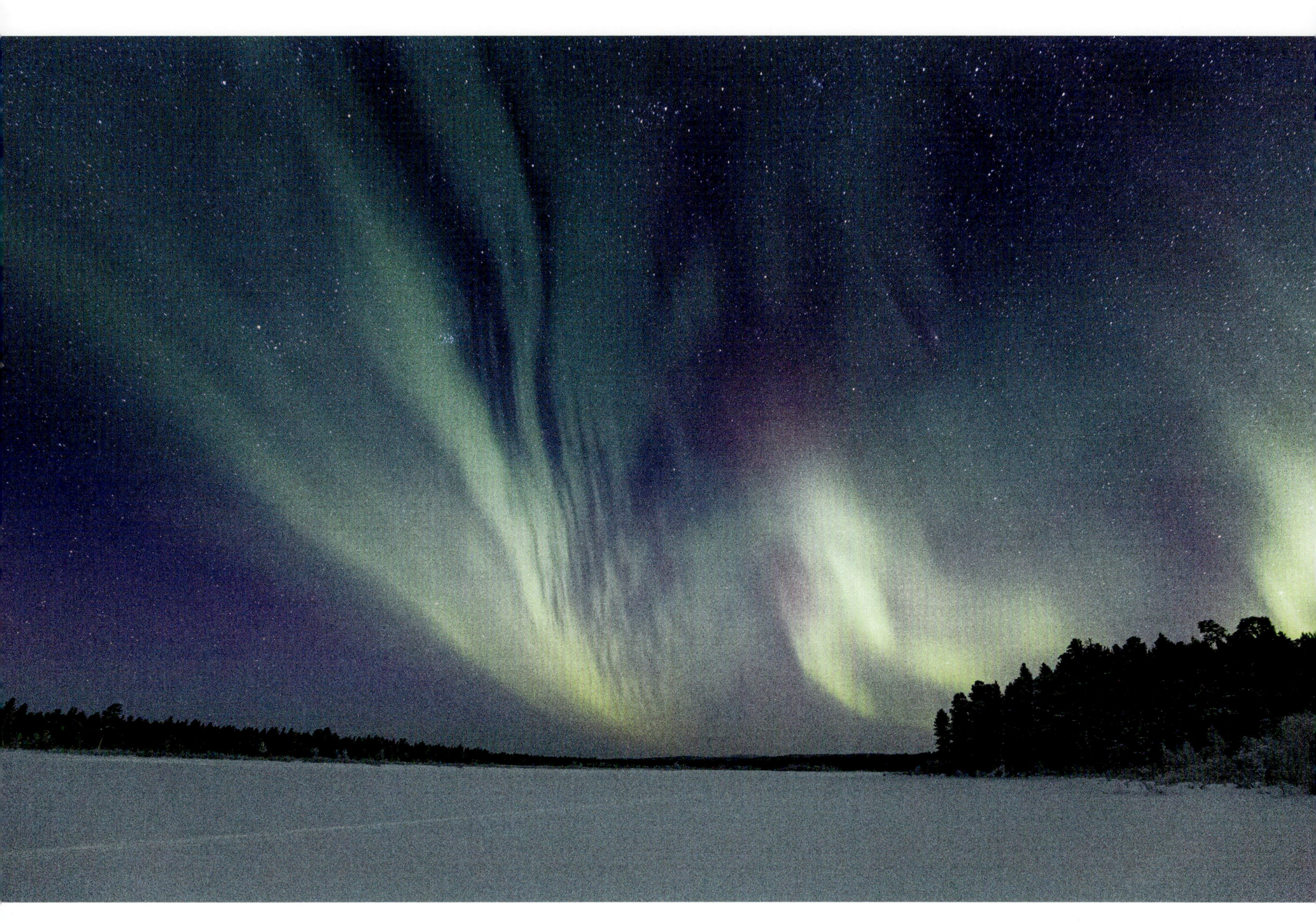

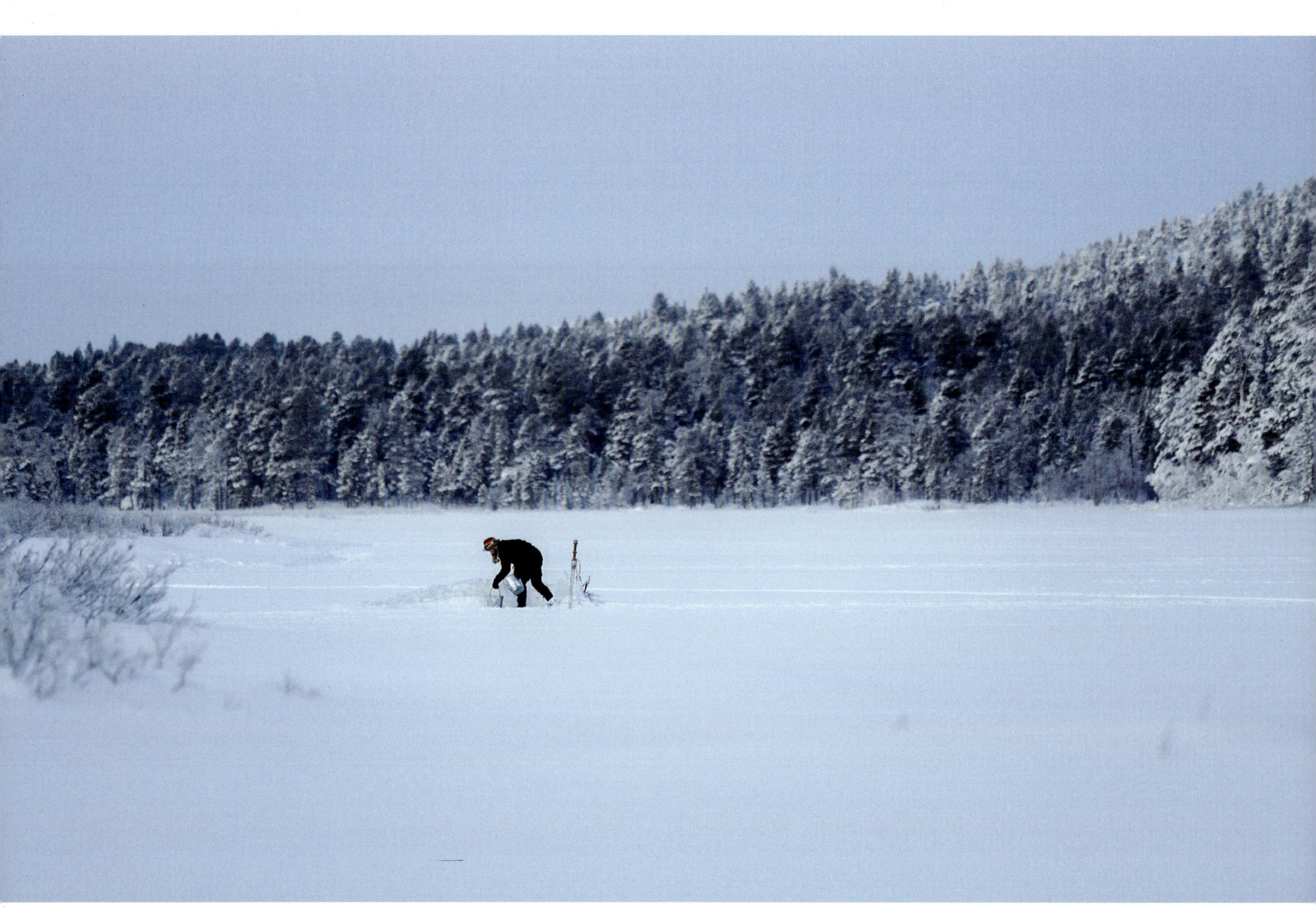

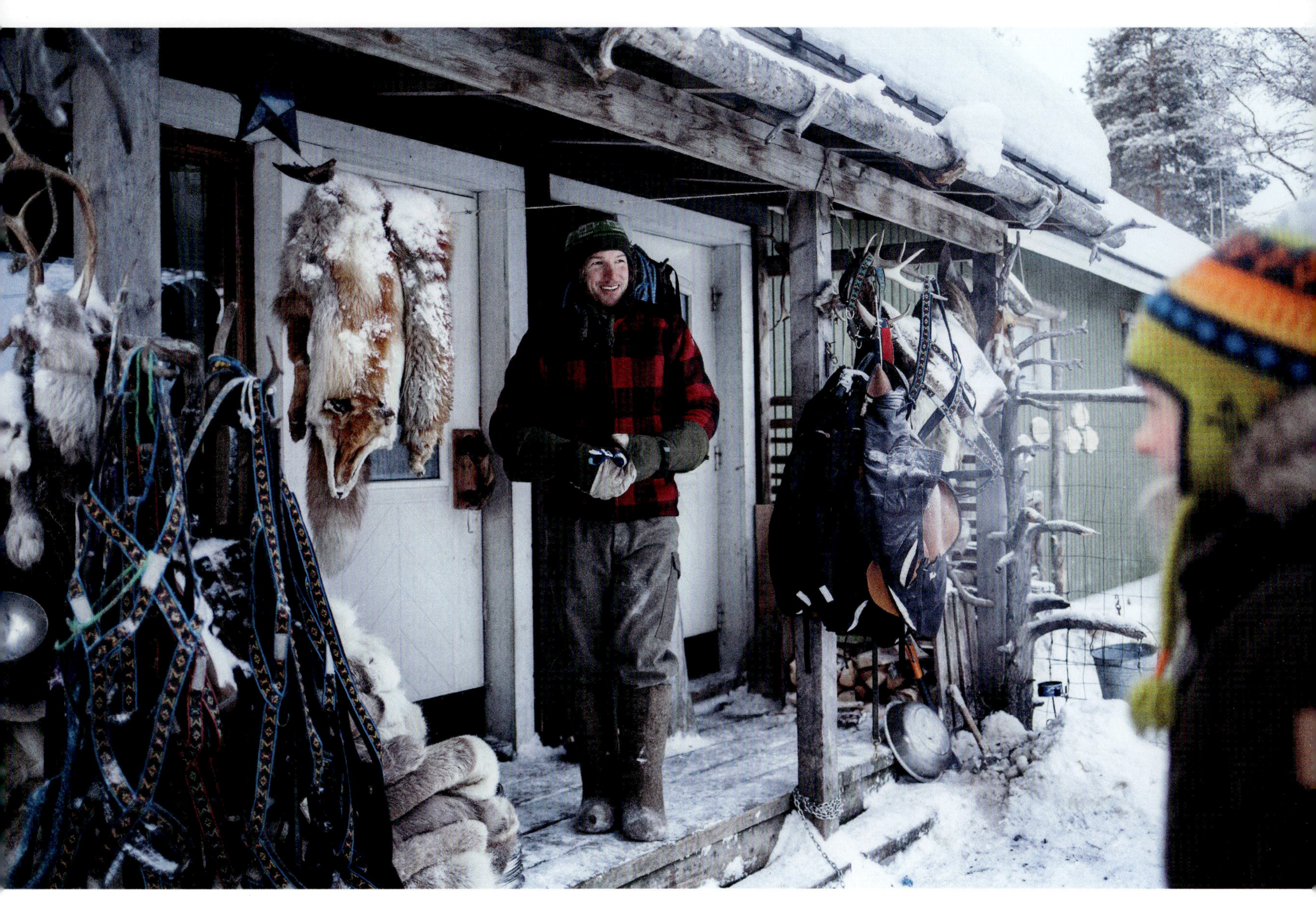

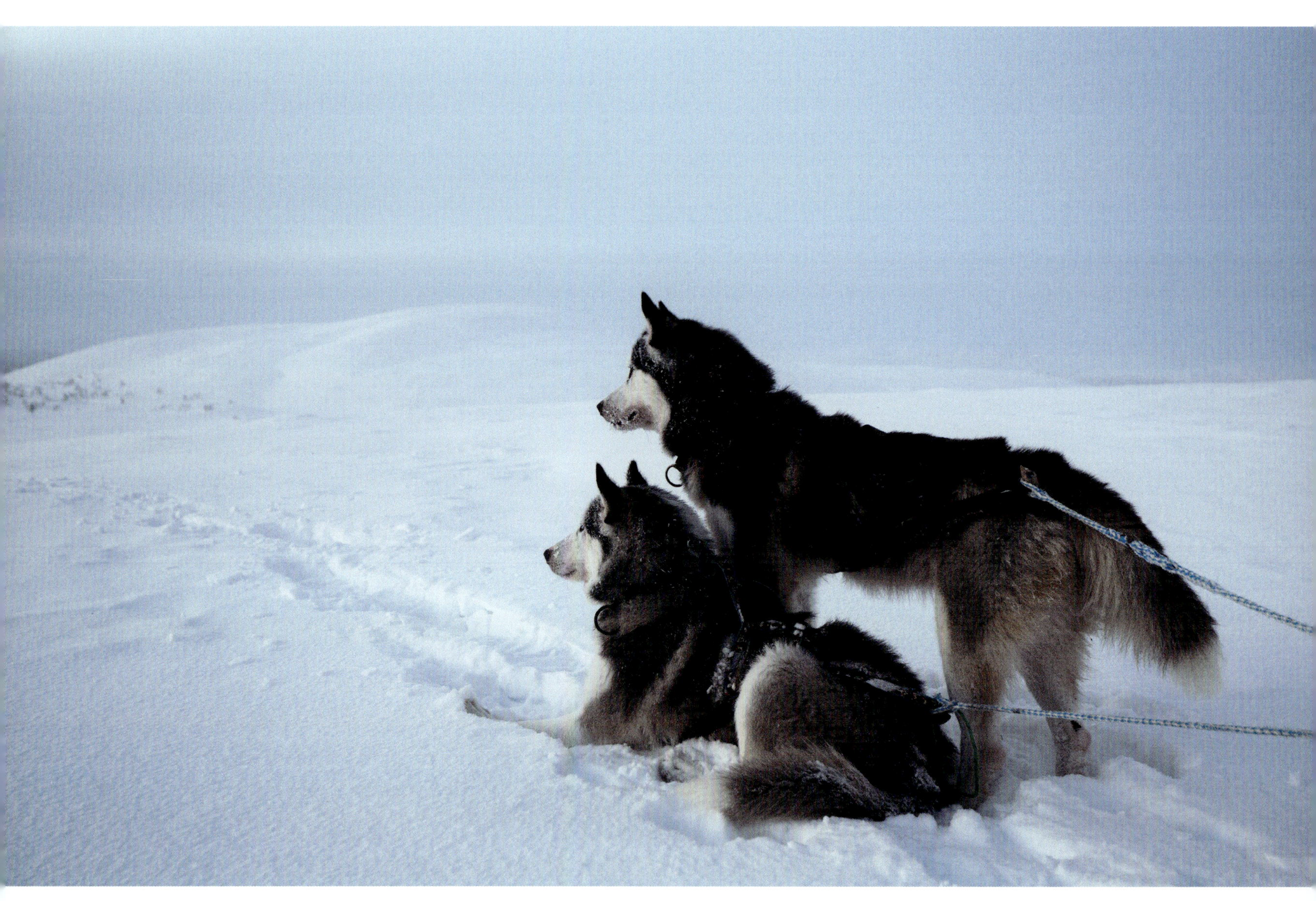

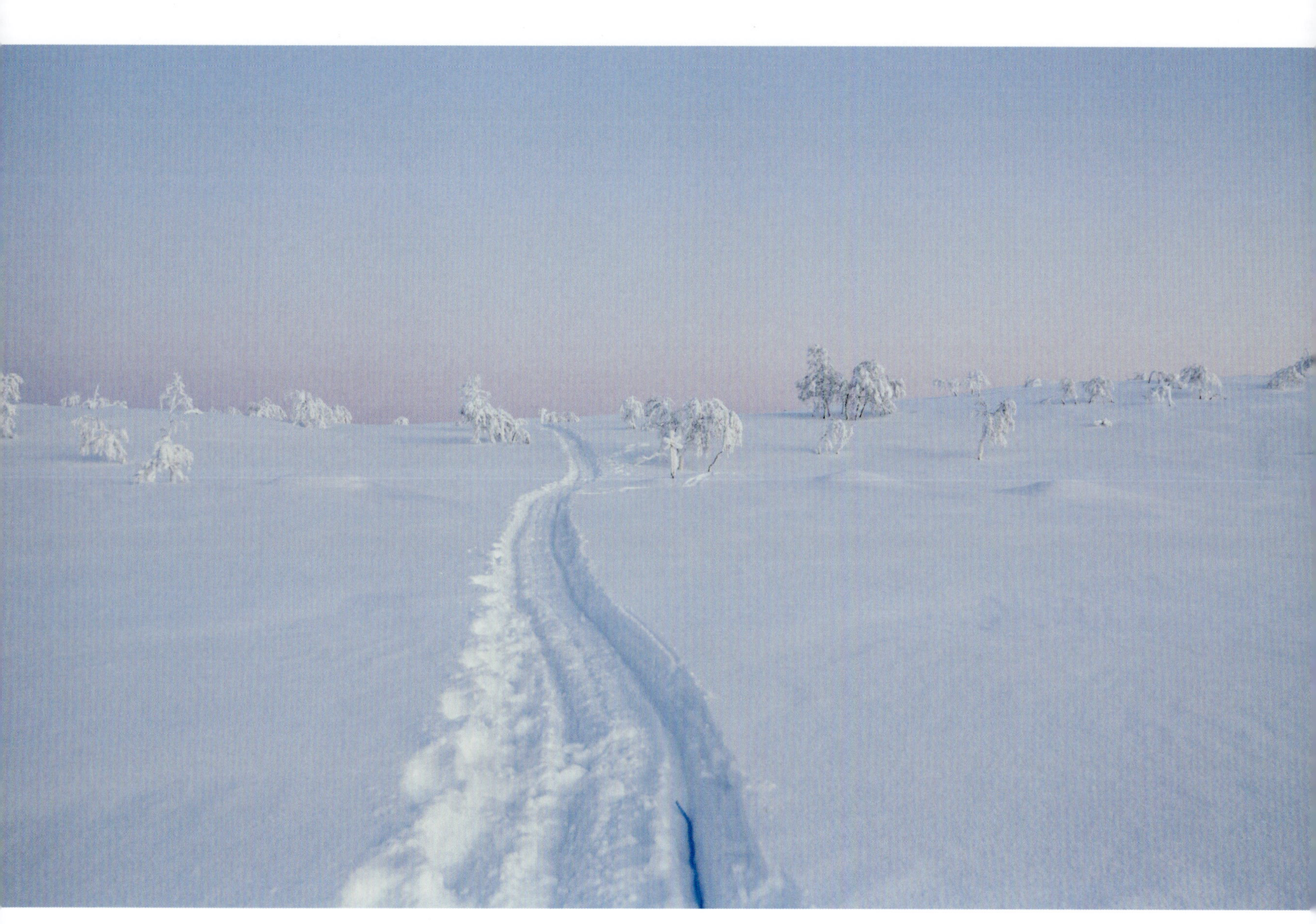

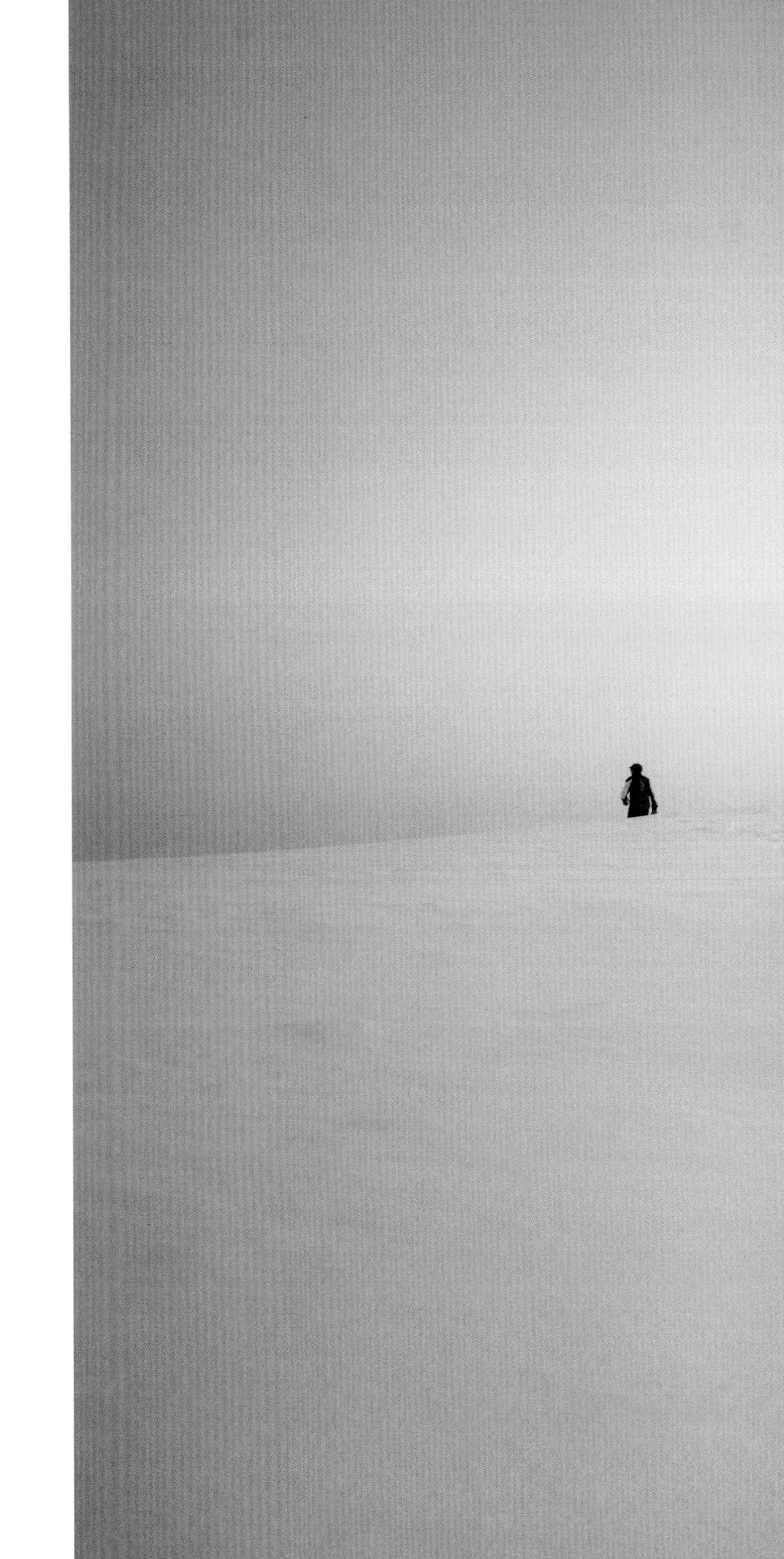

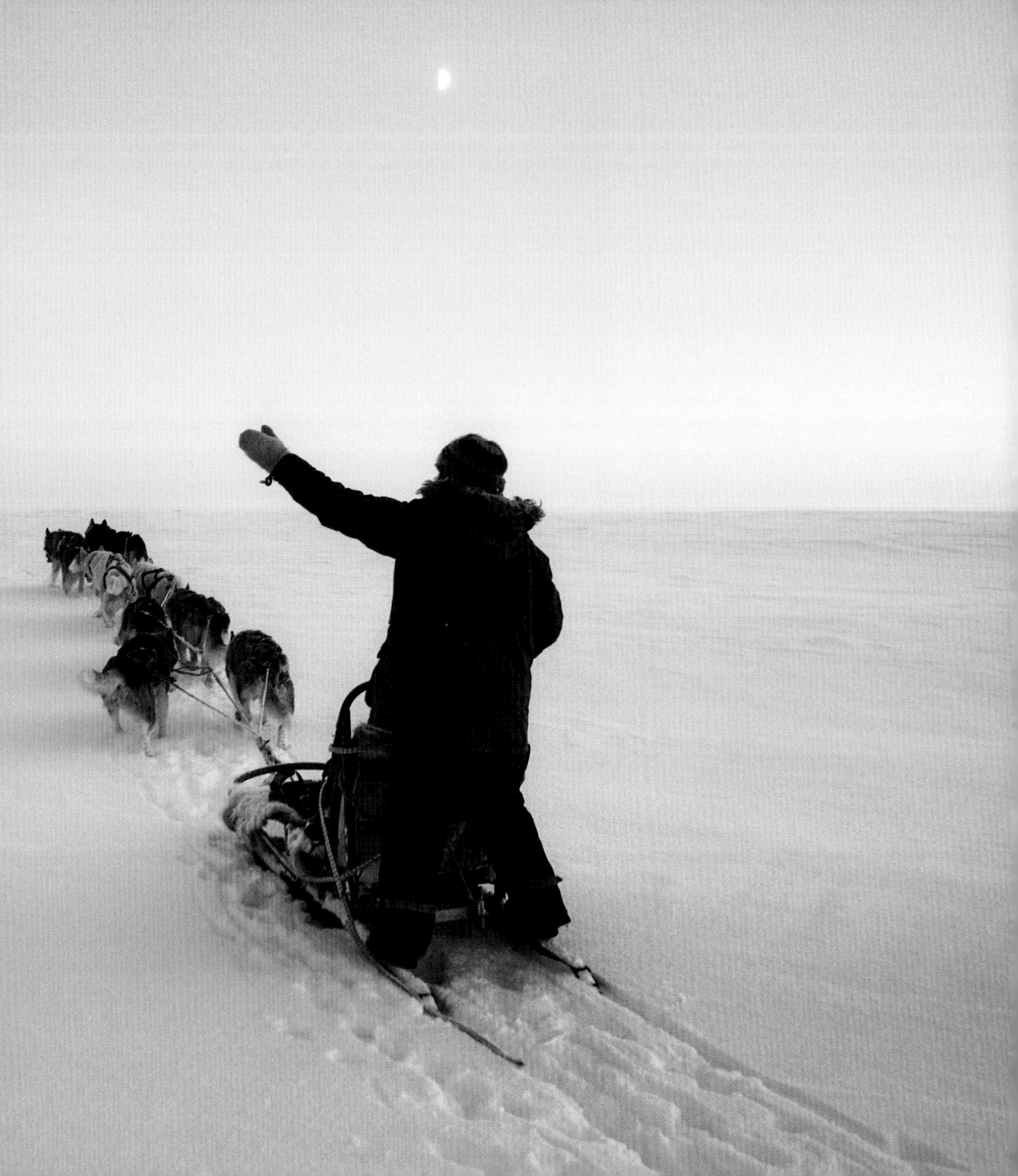

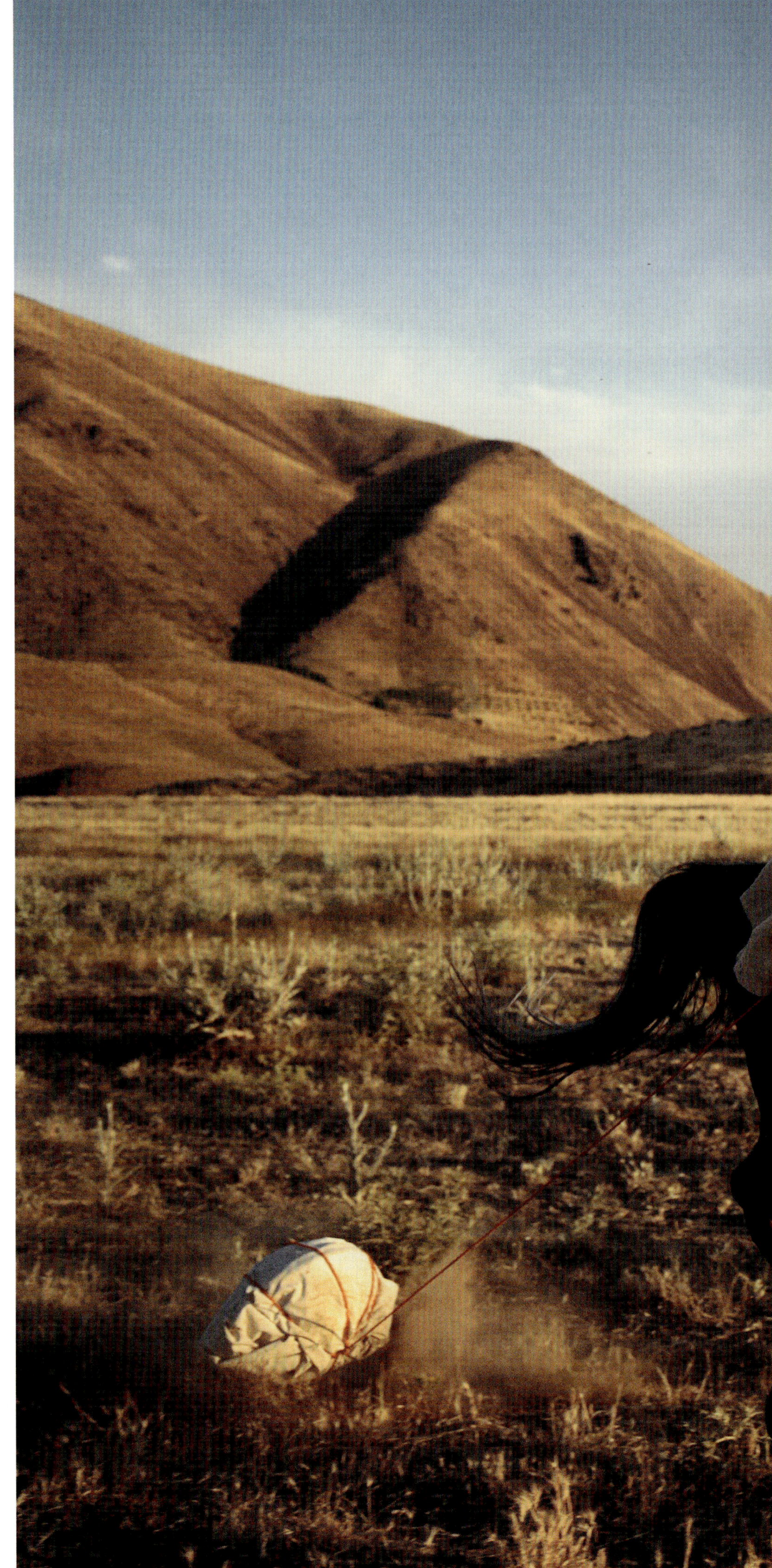

ALI

"THESE MOUNTAINS ARE MY KINGDOM; ON HORSEBACK, I CAN GO ANYWHERE I WANT."

„DIESE BERGE SIND MEIN KÖNIGREICH; ICH KANN REITEN, WOHIN ICH WILL."

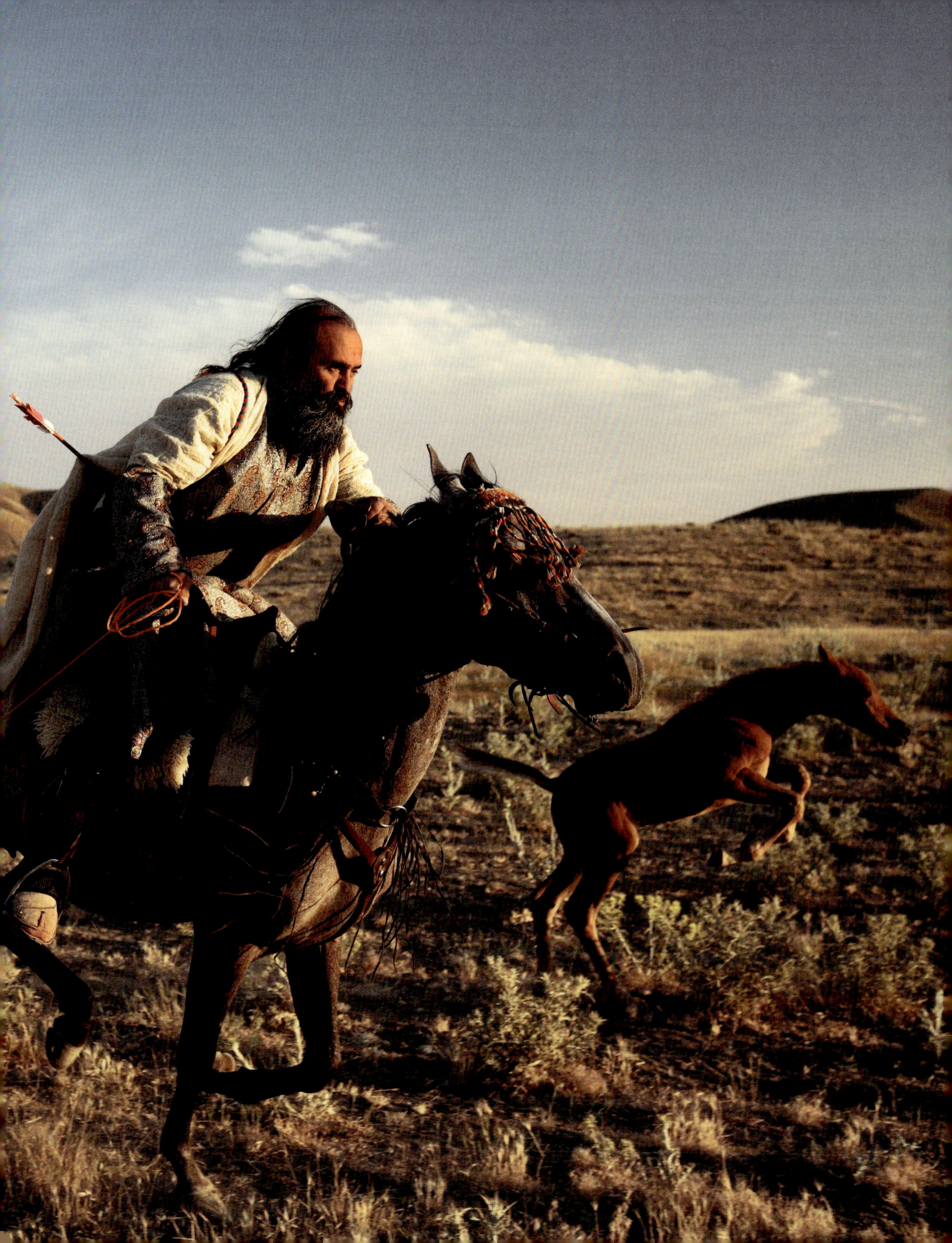

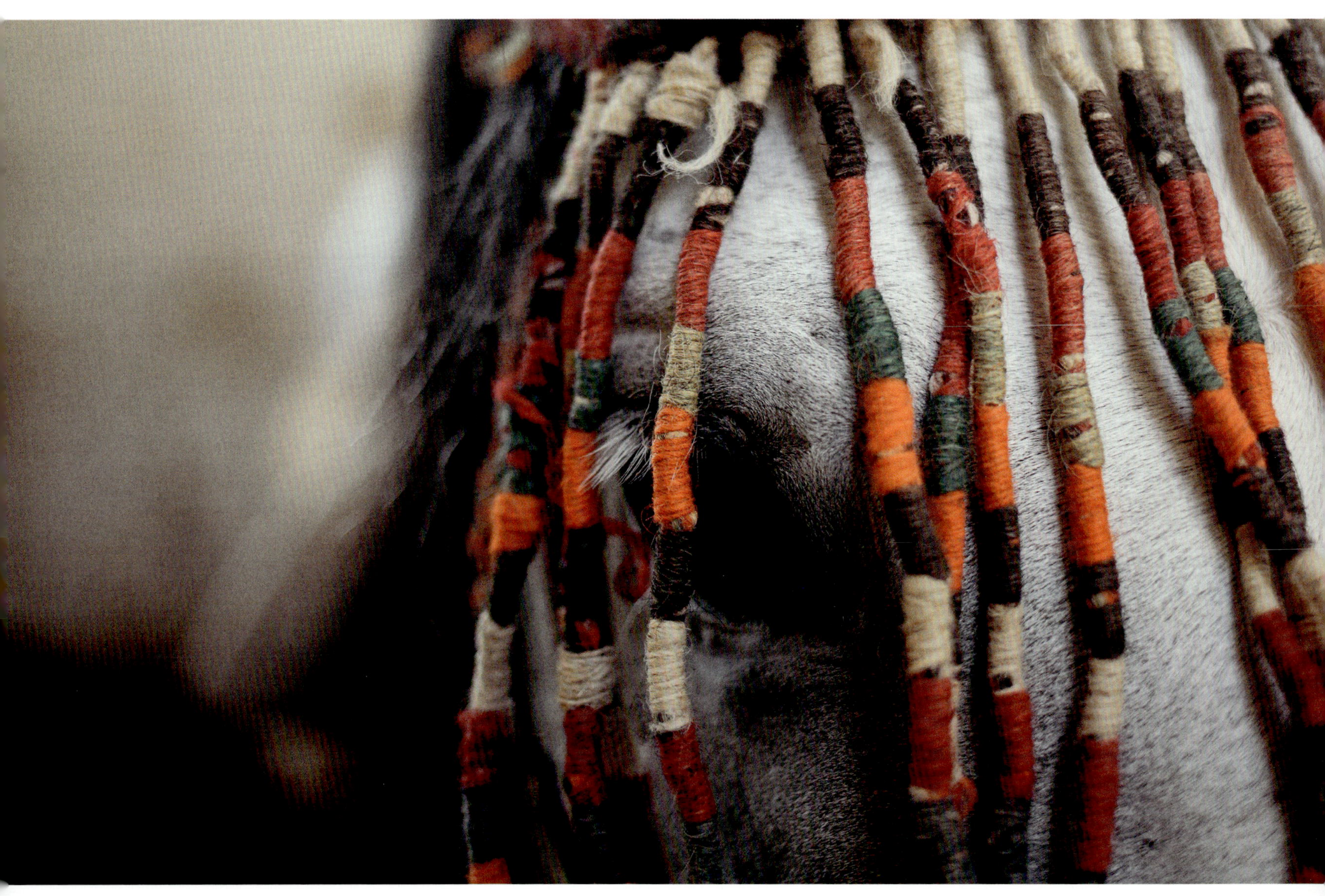

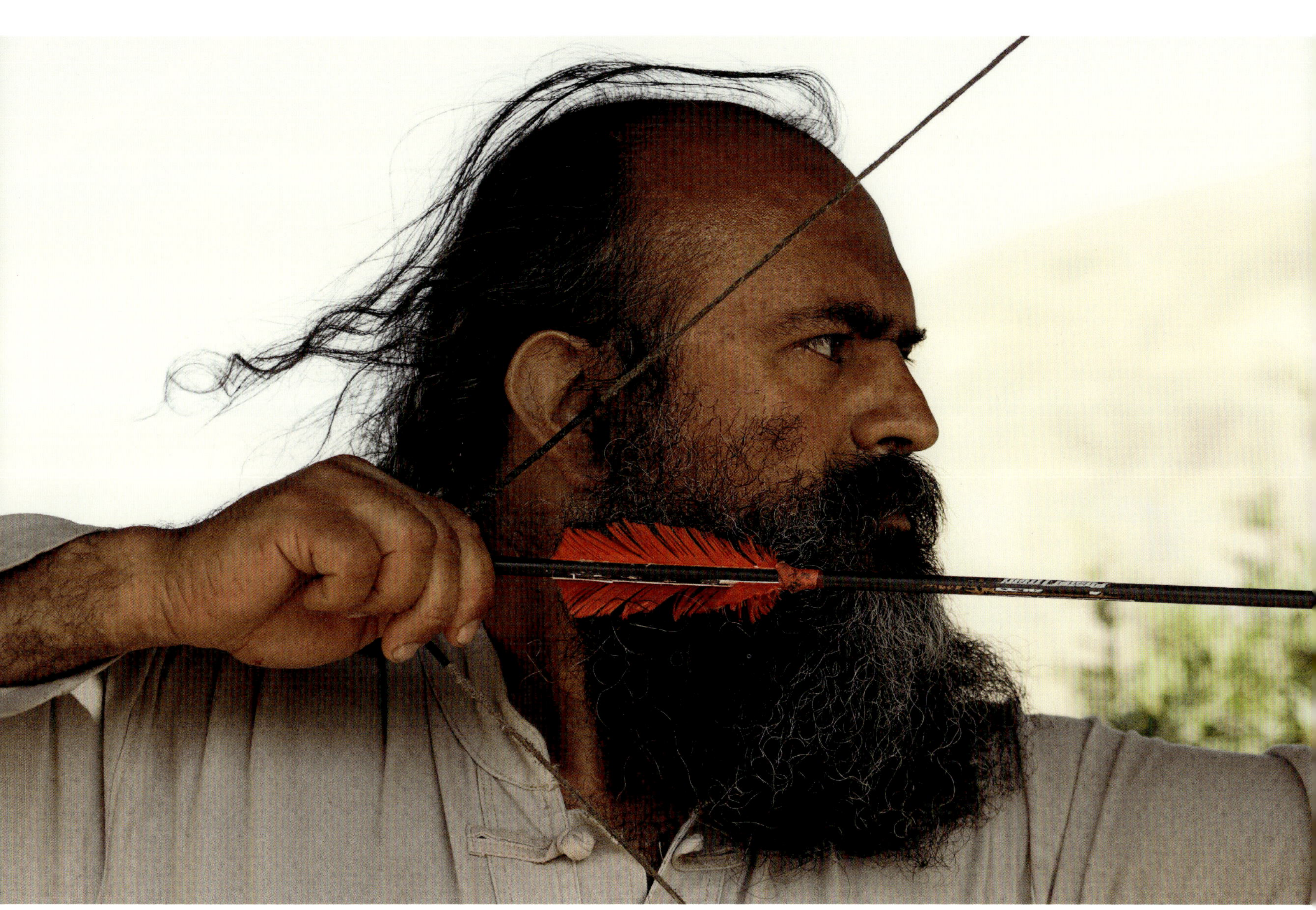

THE PERSIAN HORSE RIDER

KORDAN, IRAN

An outstanding horse rider, Ali decided to leave Tehran and change his life to live
out his passion for horseback archery at the foot of the Elburz mountains.

In his former life, Ali, whose long greying beard makes him look older than his age, was a professor of art at the University of Tehran. Until one day, he had had enough – enough of not being able to devote his time to his passion for horses and Persian martial arts, enough of sitting around for hours on end in traffic jams in the Iranian capital.

After learning to ride as a child, Ali dreamed of being able to get on a horse every day and spend his time out in nature. He finally took the plunge in 2014 after years of putting his dreams on hold, leaving behind the city, his job, his family and his friends to work in the stables at the foot of the Elburz mountains.

"When I left Tehran, many of my friends wrote me off. My family wanted me to leave the horses and come back to Tehran to lead a normal life. My new life was too unconventional for them and they couldn't understand how important it was for me. [...] But now I'm closer than ever to my real friends. When one of them calls me 'brother', I know they really mean it."

In the foothills of this long mountain range, peaking at over 5,600 metres, wealthy individuals from Tehran board their horses in these stables – regardless of whether they know how to ride them or not. This is because in Iran, owning a purebred Arabian horse is a sign of wealth, but mounting these hot-blooded stallions with their lively yet nervous energy is not something every horse rider is capable of.

Ali is tasked with looking after around forty horses with the help of half a dozen employees, most of whom from neighbouring Afghanistan. He receives board in return. As soon as he finishes work, he sets off into the mountains, sometimes for several days at a time. "These mountains are my kingdom; on horseback I can go anywhere I want. For me, this is how I get the most out of life."

He wakes up at dawn, completing his training before 10 o'clock and then getting back on the saddle at 5 o'clock in the evening. When the sun is at its highest, with temperatures frequently exceeding 40 °C in the summer, Ali, like everyone else here, takes a siesta in the shade of the fruit trees. Gusts of wind pick up the dark, arid soil, swirling it around in clouds of dust. The raking light makes you feel as though you are in a painting, as though the fading heat had frozen the landscapes and vegetation in place. The stables where Ali works are made up of several long buildings, hiding within them a small oasis. Only the sound of the leaves rustling on the trees breaks the silence. From time to time, an unripened apricot falls from its tree, driven to the ground by the high temperatures. The shade offered by the surrounding trees is the safest bet for staying cool during this heavy heat.

Luckily, the nights are cool and the food served is delicious. Breakfast consists of large round loaves of sesame bread, butter, honey and fresh fruit served with piping hot black tea. Meals often revolve around rice served with aubergine fried in garlic, lamb skewers and goats' milk yoghurt. A real delight for the palate.

Does Ali ever feel tempted to return to Tehran and his social life? "Sometimes I miss the city, but at the end of the day there's nothing for me to do there." The sprawling Iranian capital may seem suffocating to those who like big, open spaces. Ali speaks little of the trauma of his past. Born in Tehran in 1974, the

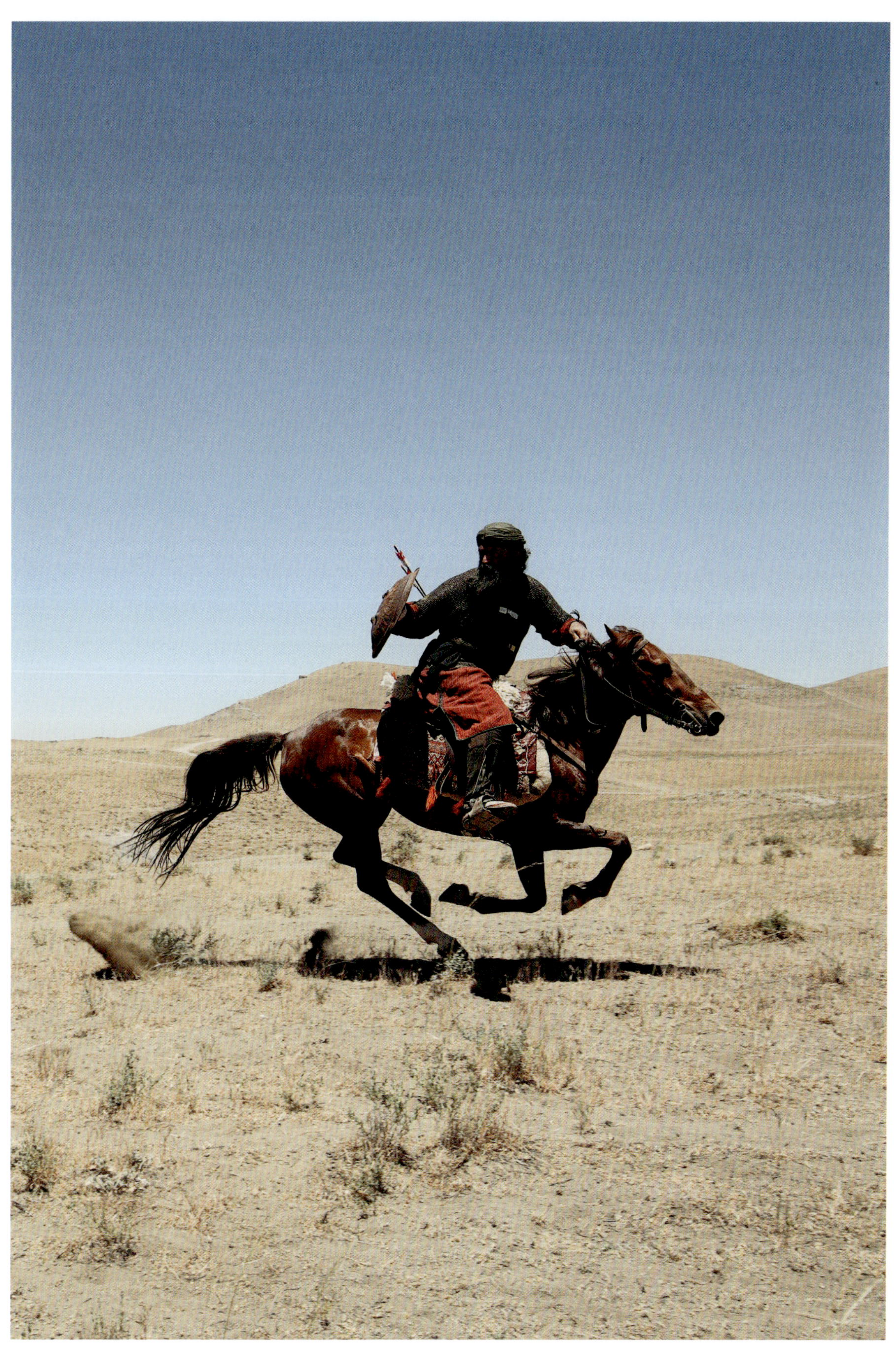

former professor grew up during the Iran–Iraq war, which lasted from 1980 to 1988. This time left him with nightmares, which sometimes come back to haunt him even now. Though he keeps this period of his life to himself, it is evident that it shaped the horse rider in a huge way.

In Kordan, the village he now calls home, Ali lives in very basic comfort and rarely ventures into town. Sometimes you cannot help but wonder whether the horse rider is living in another era, in a completely different time. In summer, he often sleeps under the stars, on a Persian rug on the floor or on a wooden bed. From time to time, some of his musician friends stop by from town and the rhythms of their Persian music liven up the night, sounds to which the men and horses dance until the early hours of the morning.

The nights are short and Ali has little time to rest between his night-time horse rides and dawn training sessions for the World Championship, held annually in South Korea. As president of the Persian Horseback Archery Association, Ali, a double world champion in 2011 and 2012, actively takes part in the event. Besides training every day on a dry riverbed, which offers him a long straight track on which to practise, the horseback archer focuses his energy on promoting the discipline. The sport, which had long remained unknown, is now becoming increasingly popular–much to his delight.

Ali, fiercely passionate about Persian martial arts, is helping to keep alive this ancestral tradition that fills him with such pride as a Persian himself. The discipline dates back to the 9th century BC in Central Asia, and has been intensively studied by Ali to ensure that he performs every aspect of the ancient art correctly. Horseback archery comprises multiple activities, all of which he takes part in, but the showpiece event consists of a long straight track with three targets that must be hit while galloping hell for leather. Seeing Ali so at ease on his thoroughbred, it is clear that the traditional Persian fighting spirit has not entirely vanished. This autumn, Ali will ride to the high isolated pastures located at the summit of the Elburz mountains, standing at an altitude of 2,500 metres. There, he plans to capture a falcon or eagle, which he will train. Together, they will hunt rabbits and foxes over the winter, under the watchful, distant eye of the wolf, before Ali releases the bird of prey back into the wild the following spring. Then, he will waste no time in jumping back on his horse to continue living out his dreams – free.

DER PERSISCHE REITER

KORDAN, IRAN

Ali, ein herausragender Reiter und ehemaliger Kunstprofessor, hat Teheran verlassen und ein neues Leben begonnen, um seine Leidenschaft für das berittene Bogenschießen am Fuße des Elburs-Gebirges auszuleben.

In seinem früheren Leben war Ali, dessen langer grauer Bart ihn ein wenig älter erscheinen lässt, als er ist, Kunstprofessor an der Universität Teheran. Irgendwann hatte er genug. Genug davon, seine Leidenschaft für Pferde und persische Kampfkunst nicht ausleben zu können. Genug davon, stundenlang in den Staus der iranischen Hauptstadt festzustecken.

Ali, Reiter von Kindesbeinen an, träumte davon, täglich aufs Pferd zu steigen und Zeit in der Natur zu verbringen. Nach jahrelangem Zögern geht er das Wagnis ein und verlässt 2014 die Stadt, seinen Beruf, seine Familie und seine Freunde, um in den Pferdeställen am Fuß des Elburs-Gebirges zu arbeiten.

„Als ich Teheran verließ, brachen viele Freunde den Kontakt ab … Meine Familie bat mich, die Pferde aufzugeben und wieder ein normales Leben in der Stadt zu führen. Sie fanden das alles zu seltsam und konnten sich nicht vorstellen, wie wichtig mir dieses Leben war. [...] Heute habe ich zu meinen wahren Freunden eine engere Beziehung. Wenn mich einer von ihnen ‚Bruder‘ nennt, weiß ich, dass er das ernst meint.“

In den Ausläufern dieser langen, bis auf 5600 Meter ansteigenden Gebirgskette liegen die Ställe, in denen die Reichen Teherans ihre Pferde in Pension geben – ob sie sie nun reiten können oder nicht. Im Iran gilt es zwar als Zeichen von Reichtum, Vollblut-Araber zu besitzen, aber es ist nicht allen Reitern gegeben, diese heißblütigen, lebhaften und sehr nervösen Hengste zu bändigen.

Ali kümmert sich mit Hilfe einer Handvoll Mitarbeiter, die meisten aus dem benachbarten Afghanistan, um vierzig Pferde.

Dafür darf er vor Ort wohnen. Sobald die Arbeit getan ist, bricht er auf in die Berge, manchmal für mehrere Tage. „Diese Berge sind mein Königreich; ich kann reiten, wohin ich will. Für mich ist dieses Leben der beste Weg, das auszunutzen.“

Er steht im Morgengrauen auf, trainiert bis 10 Uhr morgens und steigt erst nach 17 Uhr wieder aufs Pferd. Wenn die Sonne am höchsten steht, steigen die Temperaturen im Sommer über 40 °C und zwingen Ali, wie alle hier, eine Siesta im Schatten der Obstbäume zu halten. Windböen wirbeln die dunkle, trockene Erde als Staub in die Luft. Im Streiflicht fühlt man sich wie auf einem Gemälde, als hätte die Hitze Landschaft und Vegetation erstarren lassen.

Der Pferdestall, in dem Ali arbeitet, besteht aus mehreren langen Gebäuden, die eine kleine, in sich geschlossene Oase bilden. Nur das Blätterrauschen in den Bäumen durchbricht die Stille. Hin und wieder lässt ein Aprikosenbaum wegen der Temperaturen eine noch grüne Frucht fallen. Trotzdem bietet der Schatten der Bäume den besten Schutz vor der drückenden Hitze.

Zum Glück sind die Nächte frisch und das Essen köstlich. Große Sesambrote, Butter, Honig und frisches Obst bilden das Frühstück, zu dem man glühend heißen Schwarztee trinkt. Zu den Mahlzeiten gehört viel Reis, serviert mit gegrillten Auberginen, Knoblauch, Lammspießen und Ziegenjoghurt. Ein Festschmaus. Verlockt ihn das nahe Teheran mit seinem Sozialleben denn nie? „Manchmal fehlt mir die Stadt, aber schon eine Stunde später habe ich nichts mehr mit ihr zu tun.“ Die krakenartige iranische Hauptstadt muss jedem erstickend vorkommen, der die Weite liebt. Von Wunden der Vergangenheit spricht Ali selten. Der

1974 in Teheran geborene Ex-Professor war noch ein Kind, als 1980 bis 1988 der Erste Golfkrieg wütete. Diese Zeit hat Alpträume hinterlassen, die ihn bis heute manchmal heimsuchen. Auch wenn er keine Einzelheiten erzählt, ist unübersehbar, dass der Krieg diesen riesenhaft wirkenden Reiter geprägt hat.

In dem Dorf Kordan führt ein Ali ein sehr einfaches Leben; Ausflüge in die Stadt sind selten. Manchmal fragt man sich, ob er in einer anderen Epoche lebt, jenseits der Zeit. Im Sommer schläft er oft unter den Sternen, auf einem Perserteppich, den er am Boden oder auf einem Holzbett ausrollt. Manchmal kommen ein paar Musikerfreunde aus der Stadt vorbei, deren persische Rhythmen durch die Nacht klingen und Menschen wie Pferde bis zum Morgengrauen tanzen lassen.

Die Nächte sind kurz; nach seinen nächtlichen Ausritten hat Ali nur wenig Zeit zum Ausruhen, bis er bei Tagesanbruch aufsteht, um sich auf die Weltmeisterschaft vorzubereiten. Sie findet jedes Jahr in Südkorea statt, und als Präsident der persischen Vereinigung für berittenes Bogenschießen ist der Weltmeister von 2011 und 2012 sehr aktiv dabei.

Neben dem täglichen Training in einem ausgetrockneten Flussbett, das ihm eine lange, gerade Strecke bietet, konzentriert Ali seine ganze Energie darauf, seine Disziplin bekannter zu machen. Sie war lange unbekannt, nimmt aber zu seiner Freude an Popularität zu.

Als leidenschaftlicher Freund der persischen Kampfkunst trägt Ali zum Erhalt einer altehrwürdigen Tradition bei, von der er als Perser mit großem Stolz spricht. Sie entstand schon im 11. Jahrhundert v. Chr. in Zentralasien; Ali hat lange Recherchen dazu angestellt, um seinen Sport nach allen Regeln der Kunst zu praktizieren. Zum berittenen Bogenschießen gehören verschiedene Übungen, die er alle beherrscht, aber die Königsdisziplin besteht aus einer langen, geraden Bahn, von der aus im Galopp drei Zielscheiben getroffen werden müssen. Wenn man sieht, wie wohl er sich auf seinem Vollblut fühlt, hat man das Gefühl, dass die Seele der persischen Krieger noch nicht verschwunden ist.

Im Herbst reitet Ali bis zu den Gipfeln des Elburs-Gebirges und fängt auf den einsamen Hochwiesen in 2500 Metern Höhe einen Falken oder Adler, den er dressiert. Zusammen jagen sie den ganzen Winter über Kaninchen und Füchse, unter den wachsamen, fernen Blicken der Wölfe; im folgenden Frühjahr lässt Ali den Raubvogel wieder frei. Dann kehrt er ungeduldig zu seinen Pferden zurück, um erneut seine Leidenschaft auszuleben.

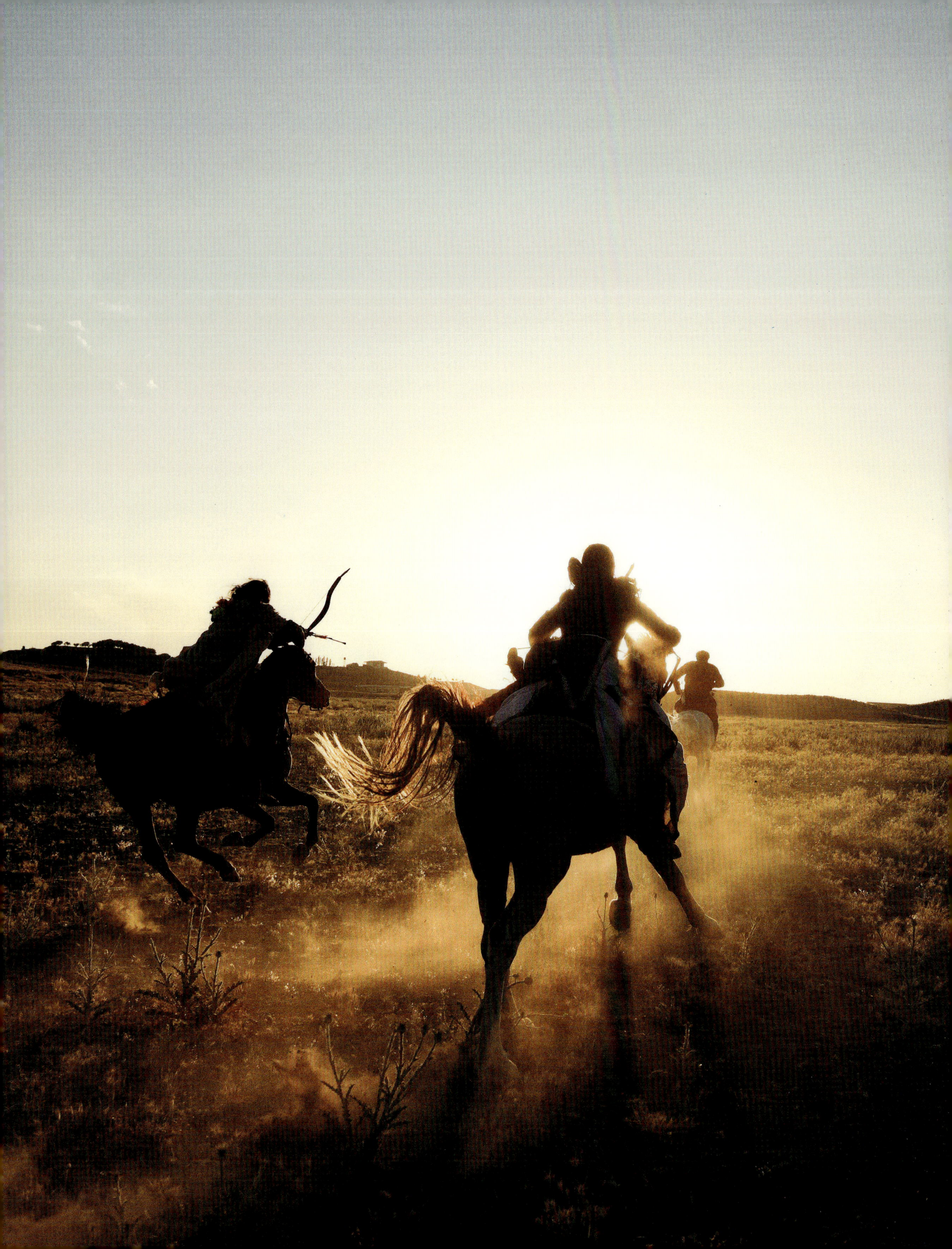

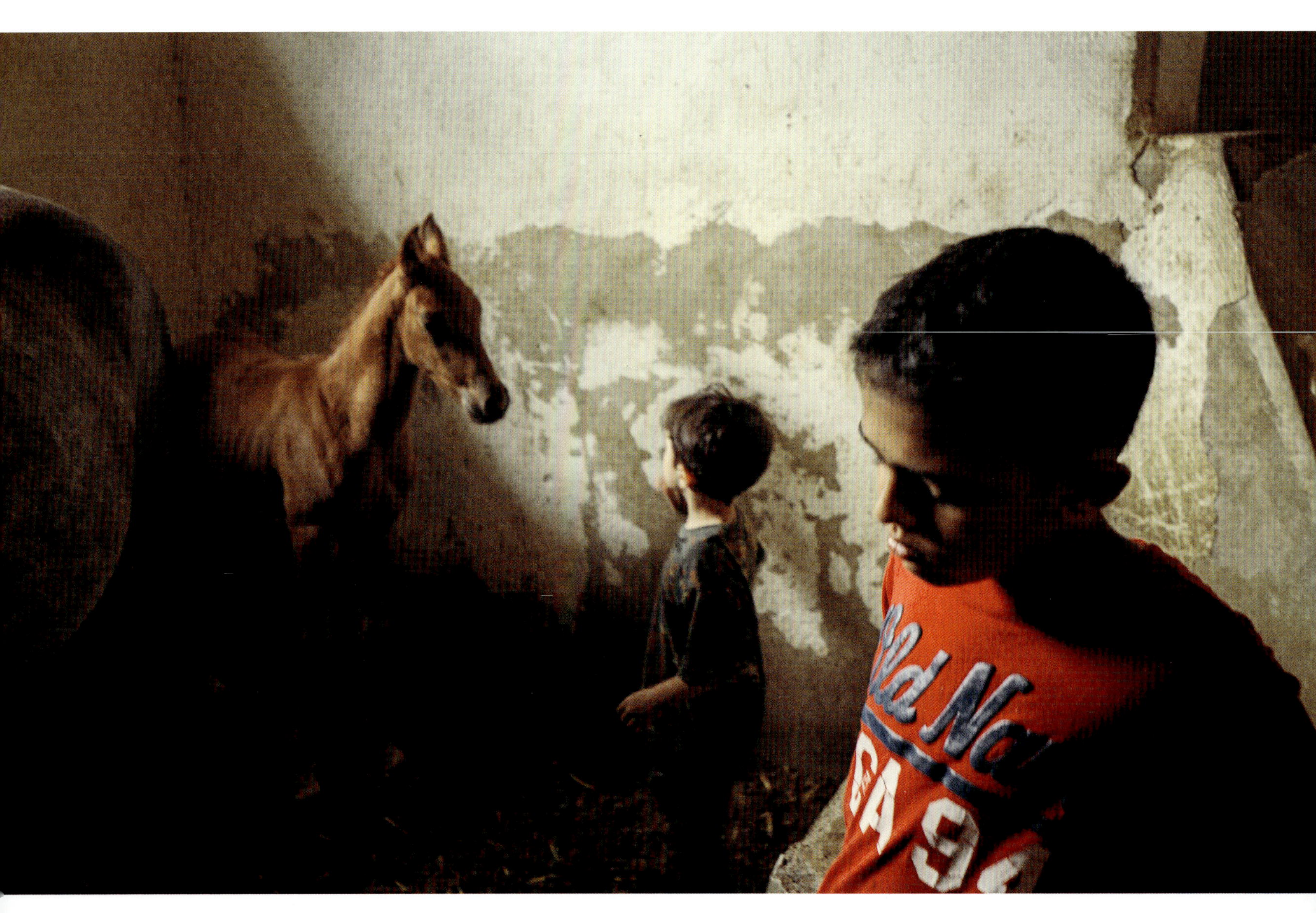

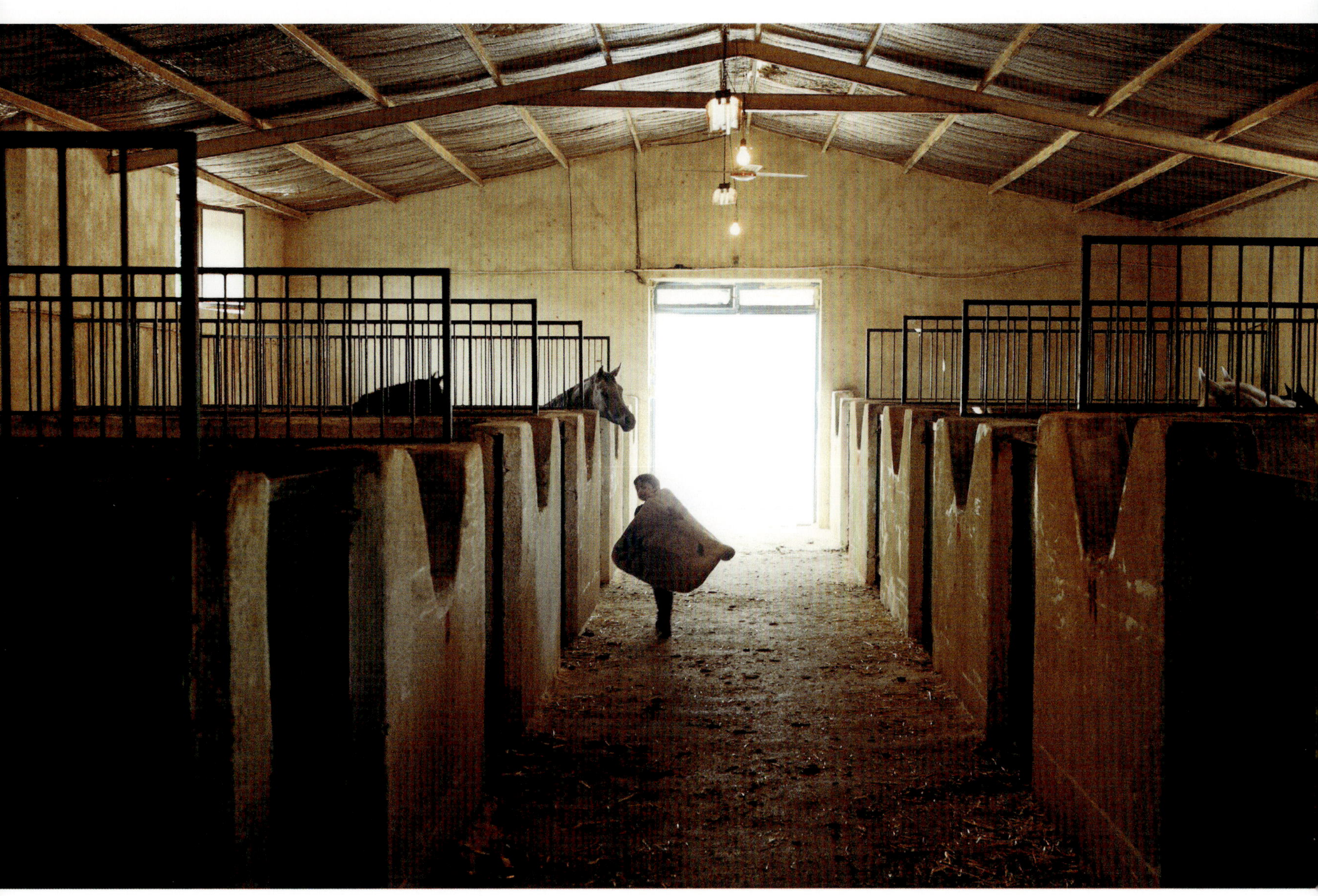

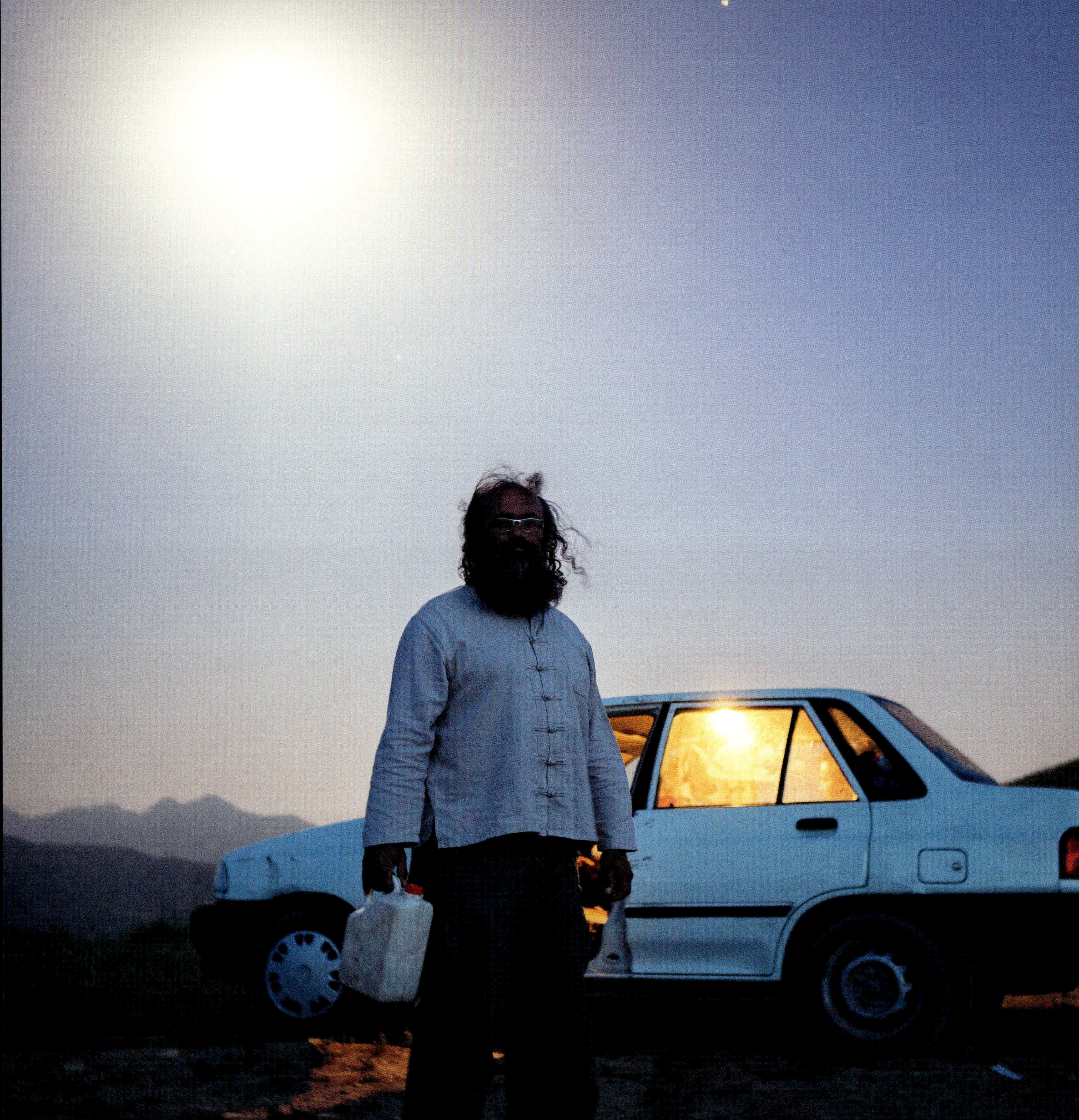

"If a man does not keep pace
with his companions,
perhaps it is because he hears
a different drummer.
Let him step to the music which he hears,
however measured or far away."

HENRY DAVID THOREAU
Walden; or, Life in the Woods

„Wenn jemand mit seinen
Gefährten nicht Schritt hält,
so tut er es vielleicht deshalb nicht,
weil er einen anderen Trommler hört.
Lasst ihn zu der Musik marschieren,
die er hört, ungeachtet ihres Takts
und ihrer Entfernung."

HENRY DAVID THOREAU
Walden oder Leben in den Wäldern

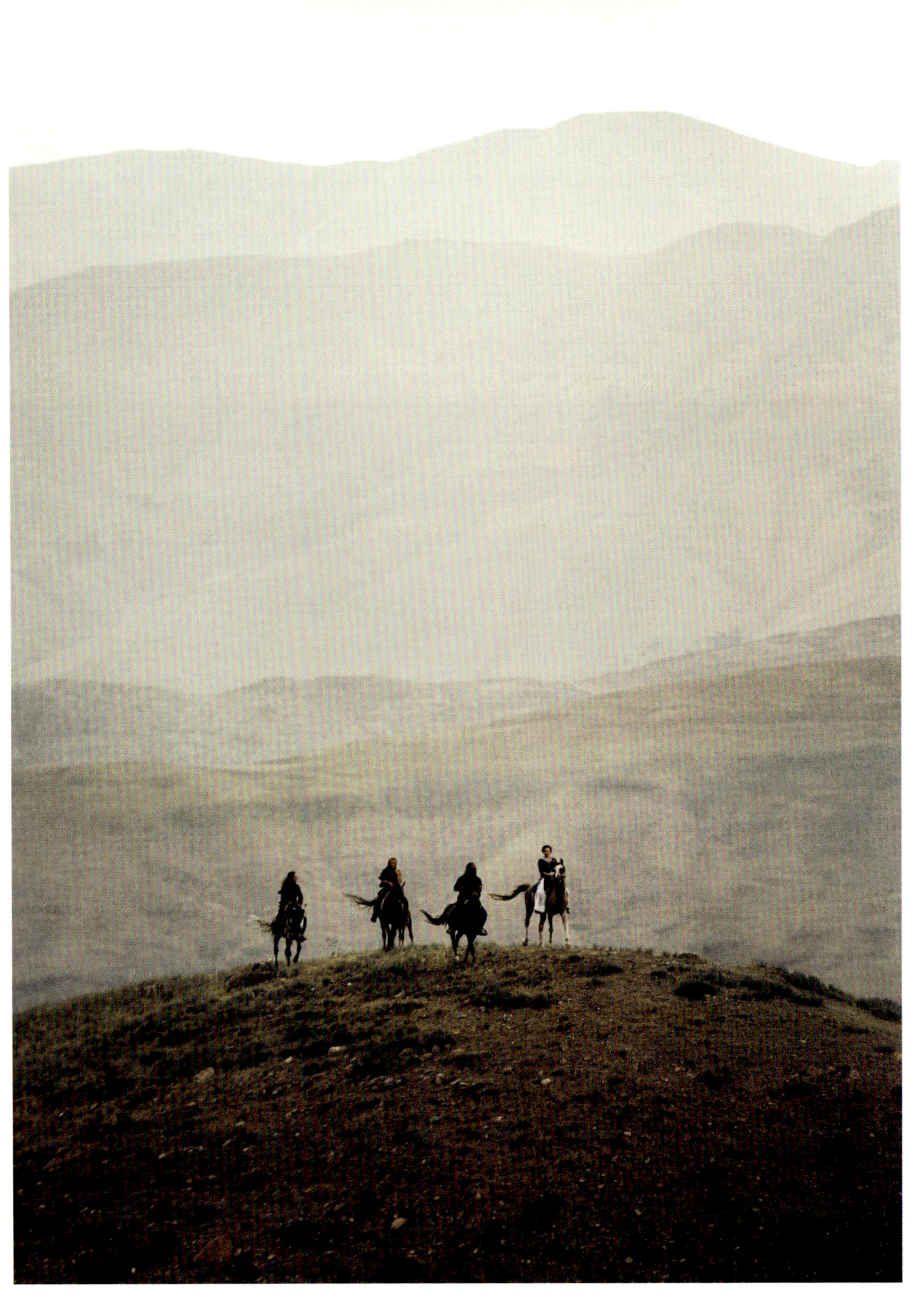

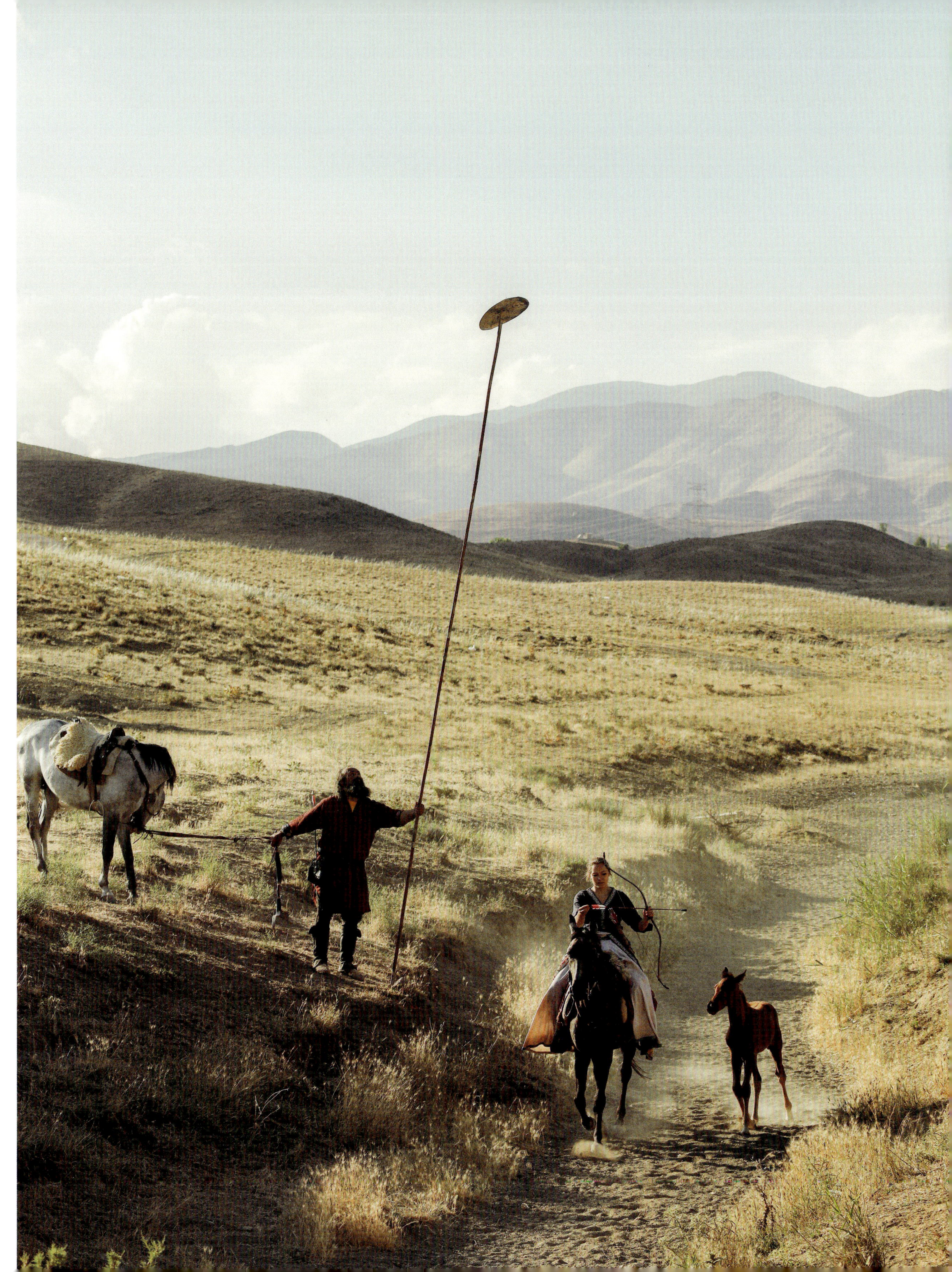

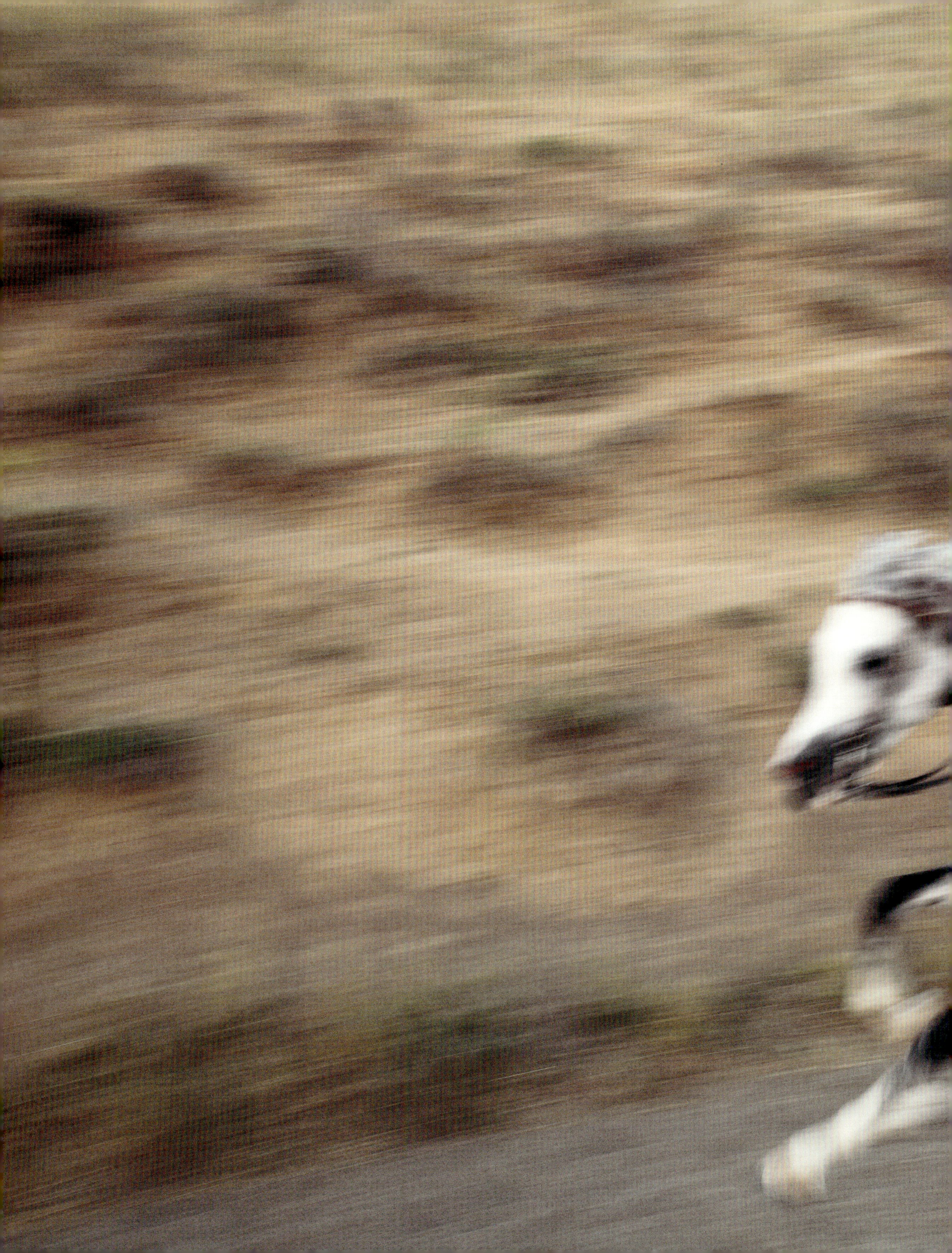

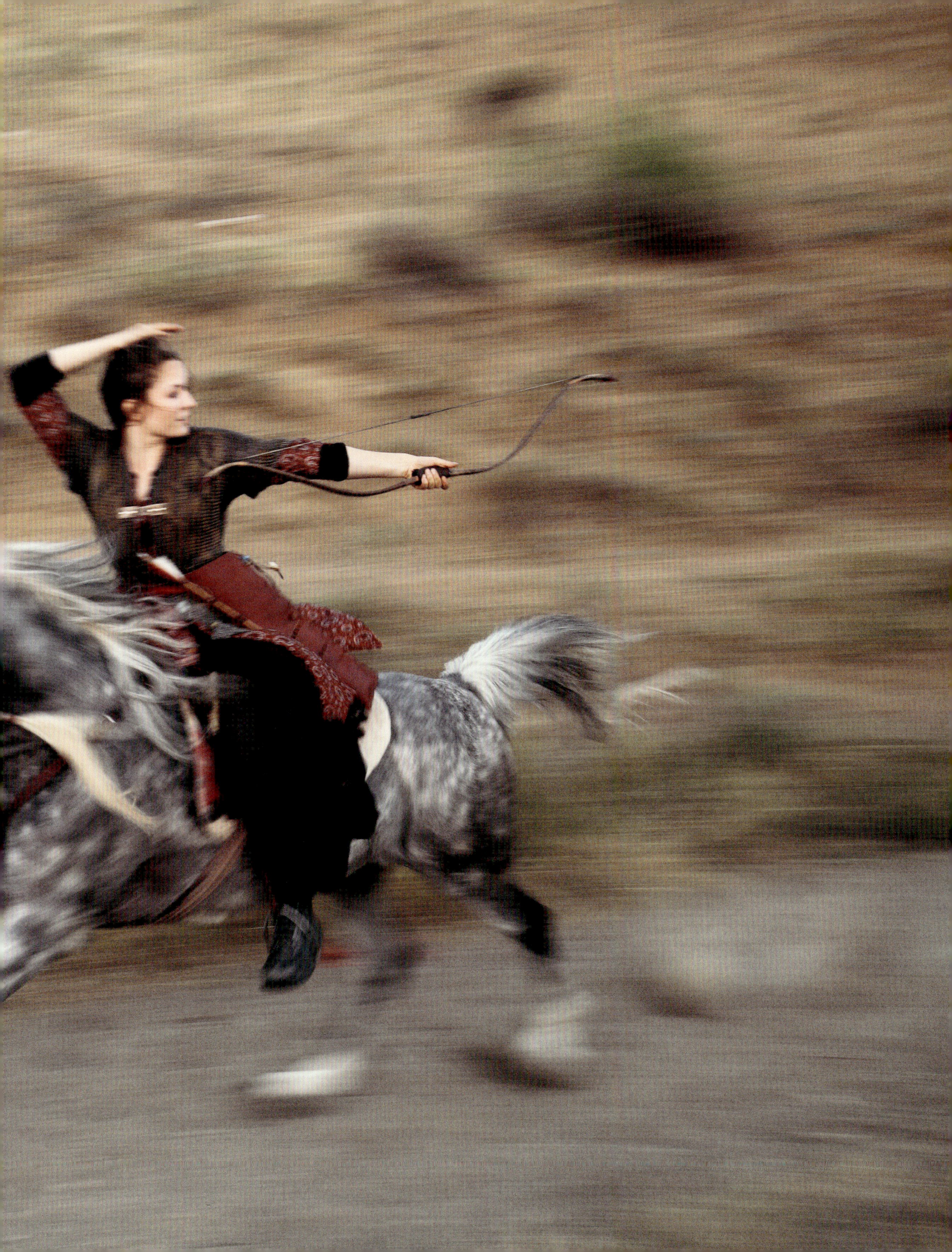

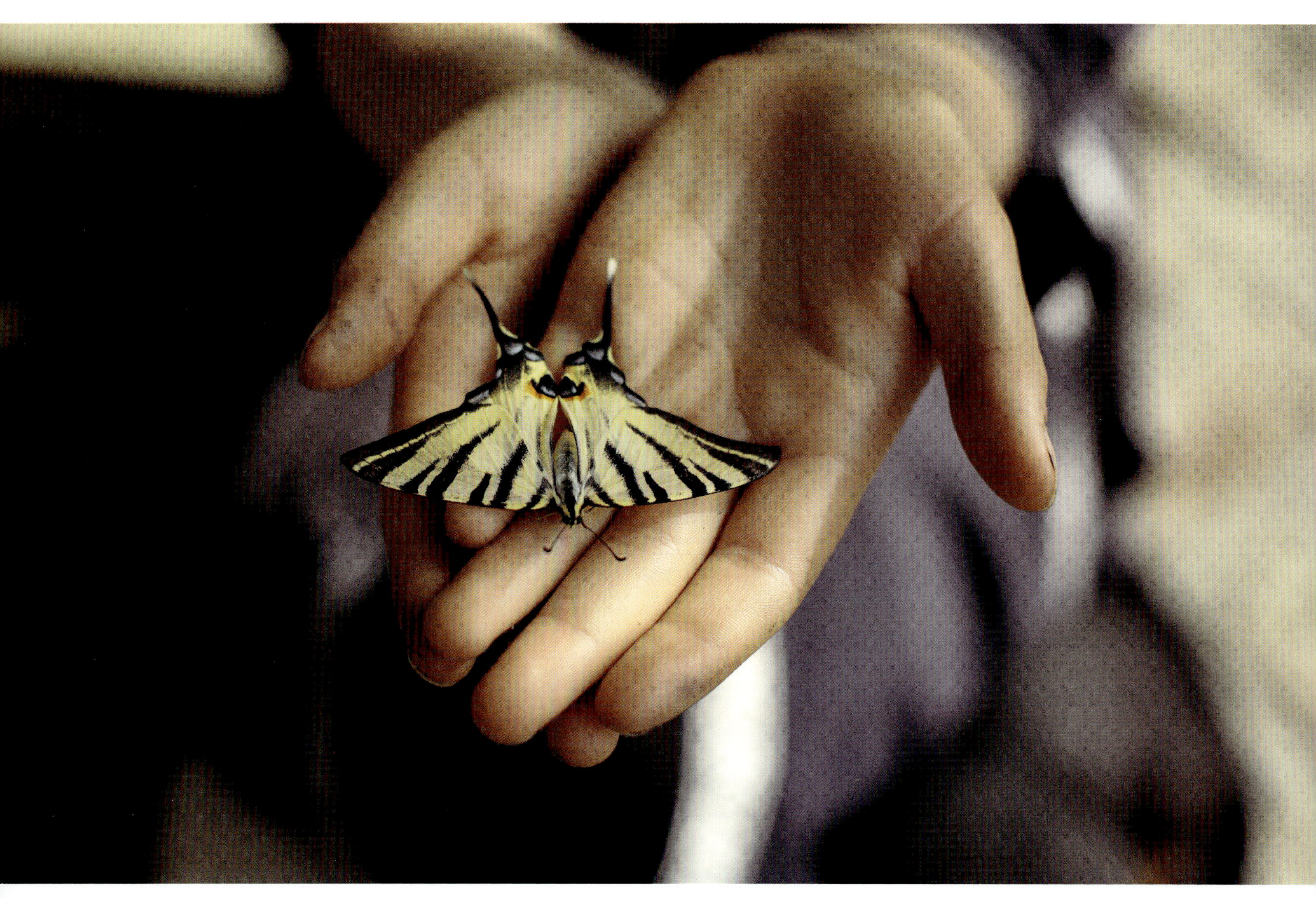

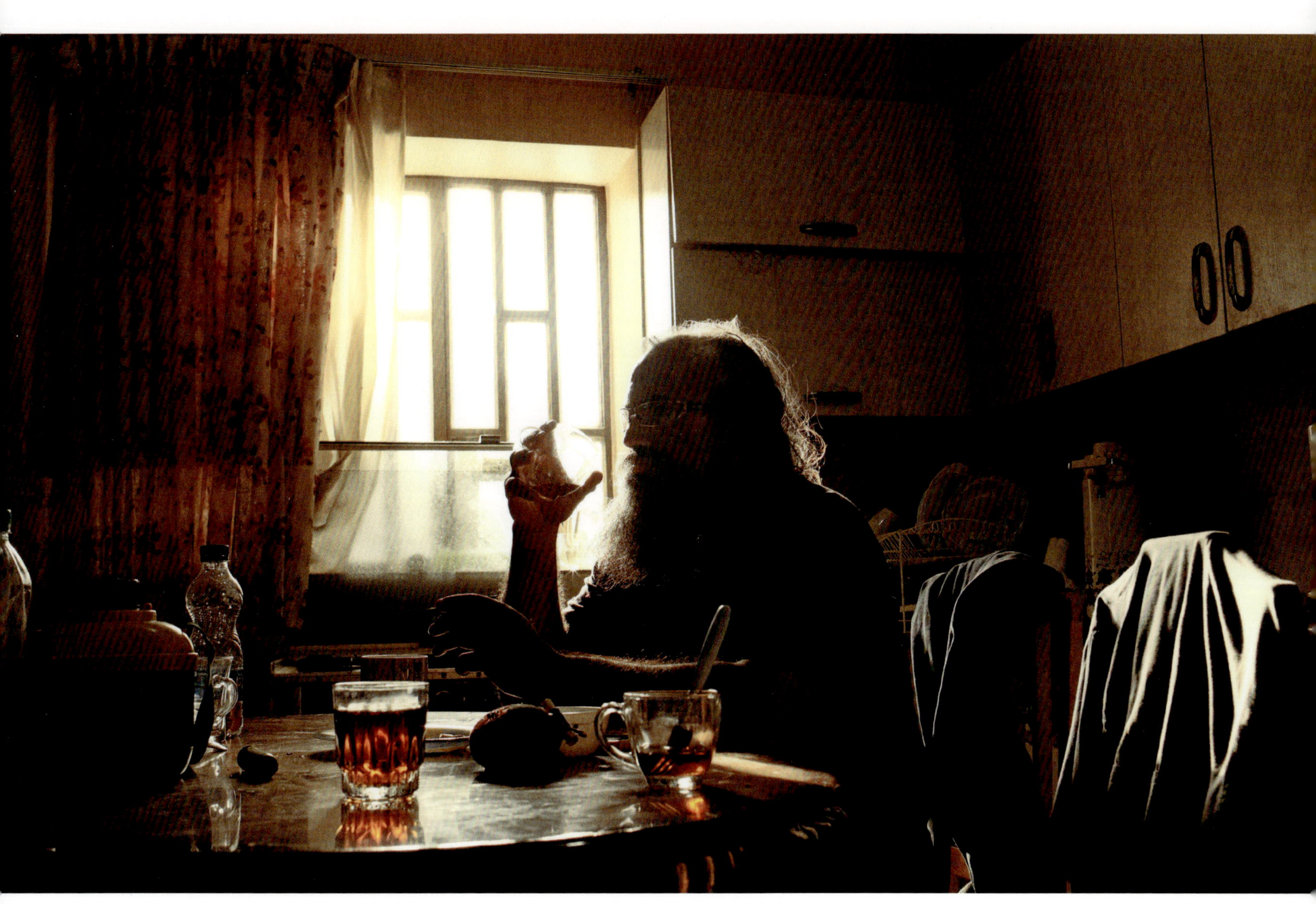

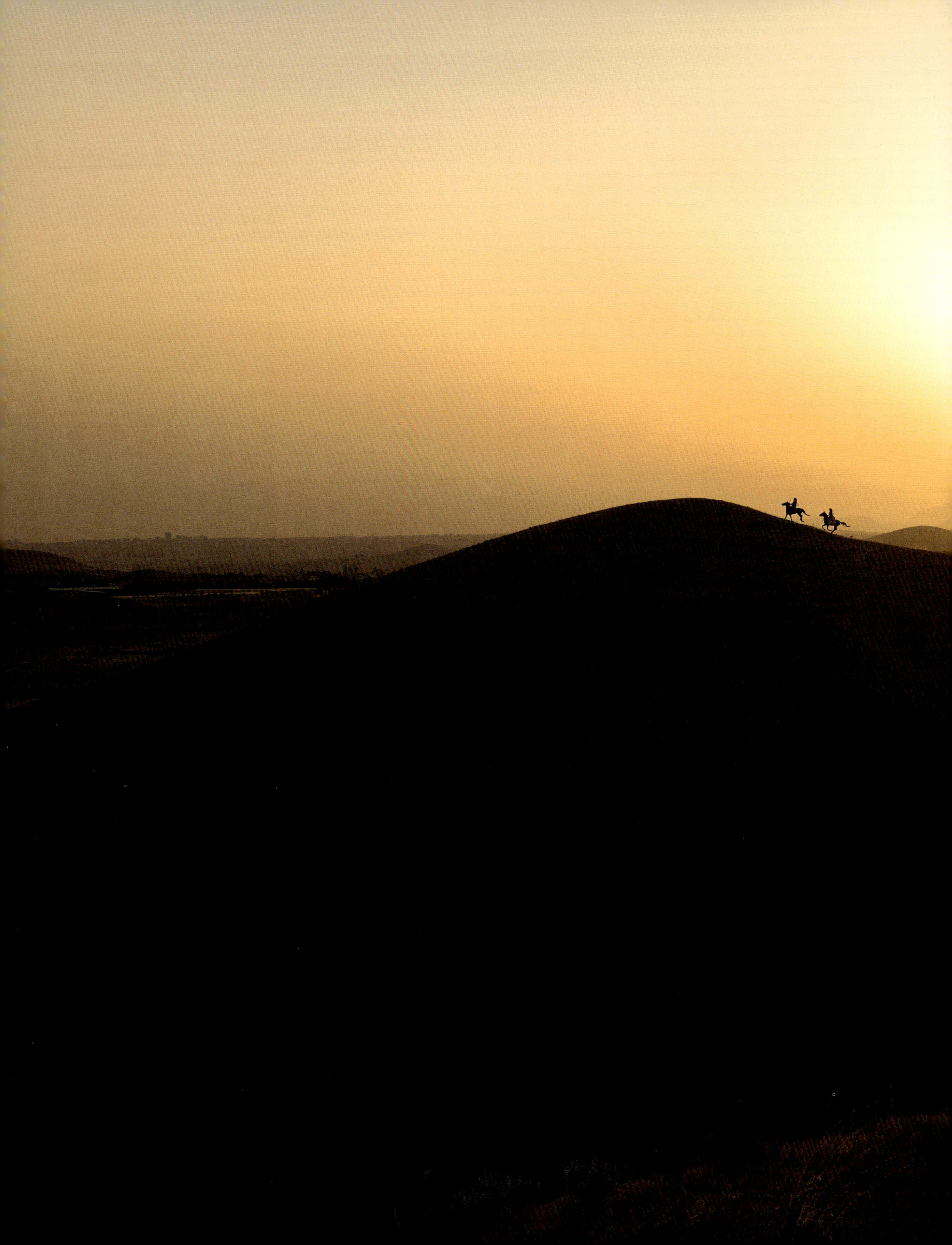

BARNY

"I WAS HAPPIER TO GIVE UP SOME LUXURIES AND COMFORTS THAT I COULD DO WITHOUT RATHER THAN MY TIME AND MY LIFE."

„ICH HABE LIEBER EIN WENIG VERZICHTBAREN LUXUS UND KOMFORT GEOPFERT ALS MEINE ZEIT UND MEIN LEBEN."

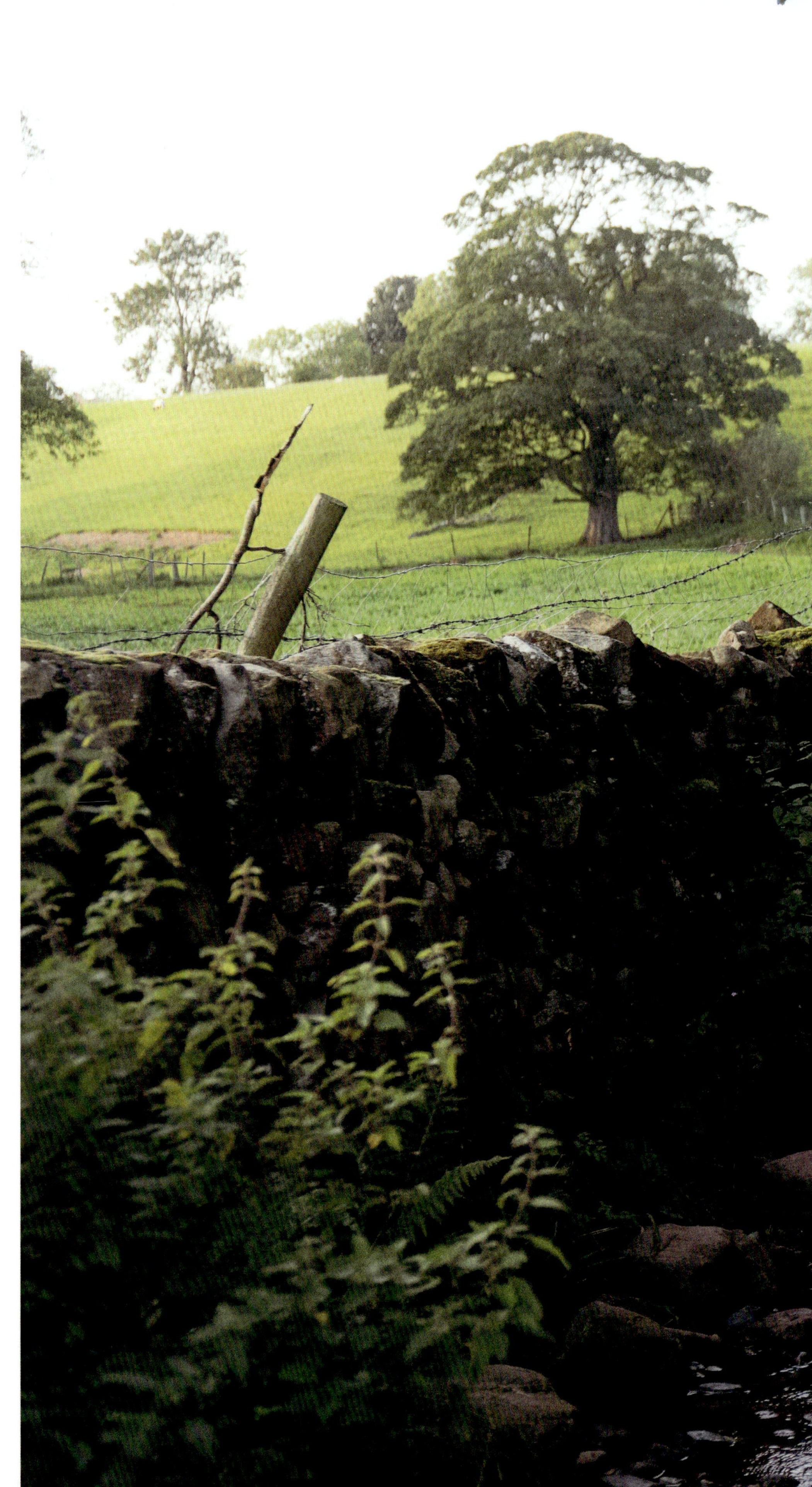

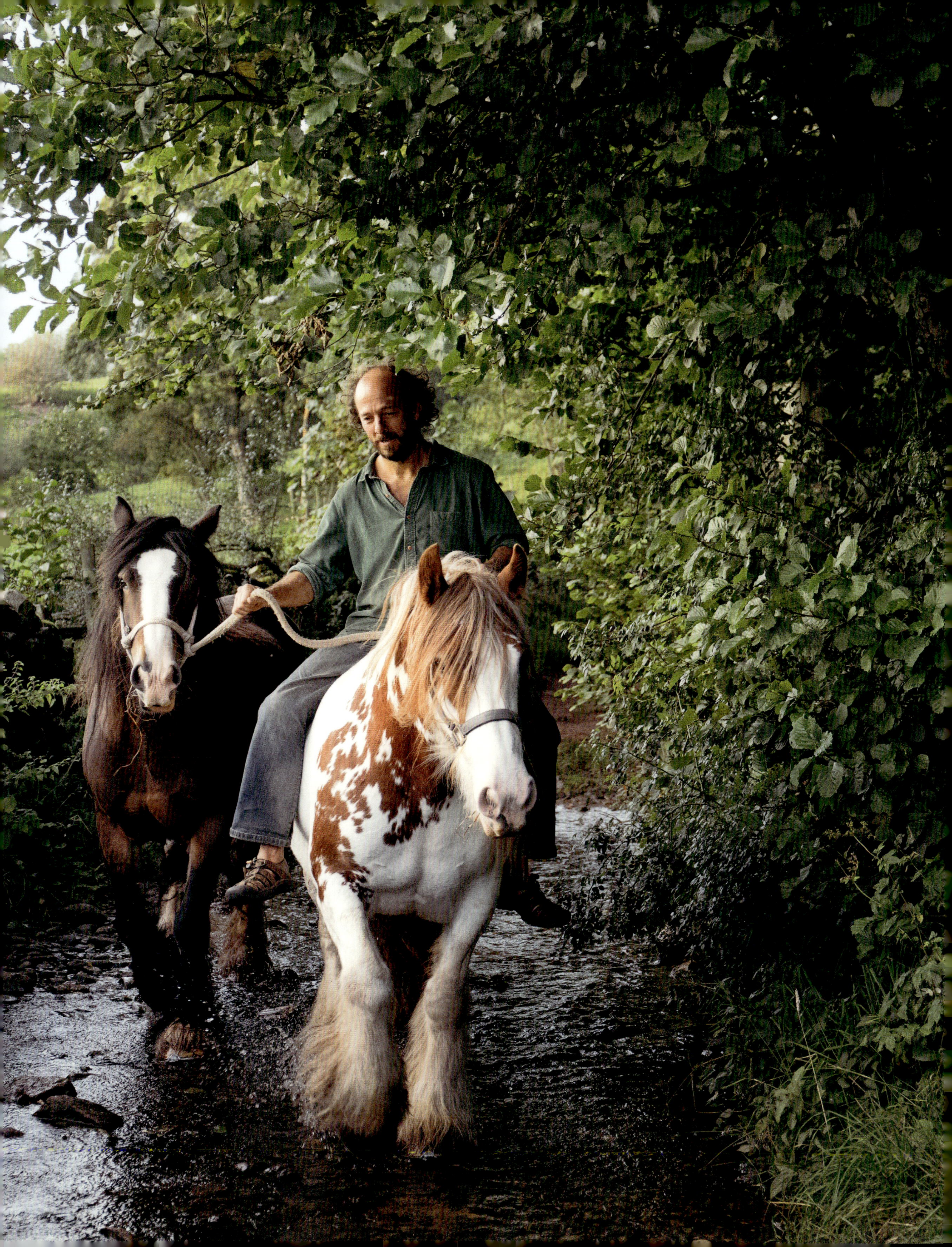

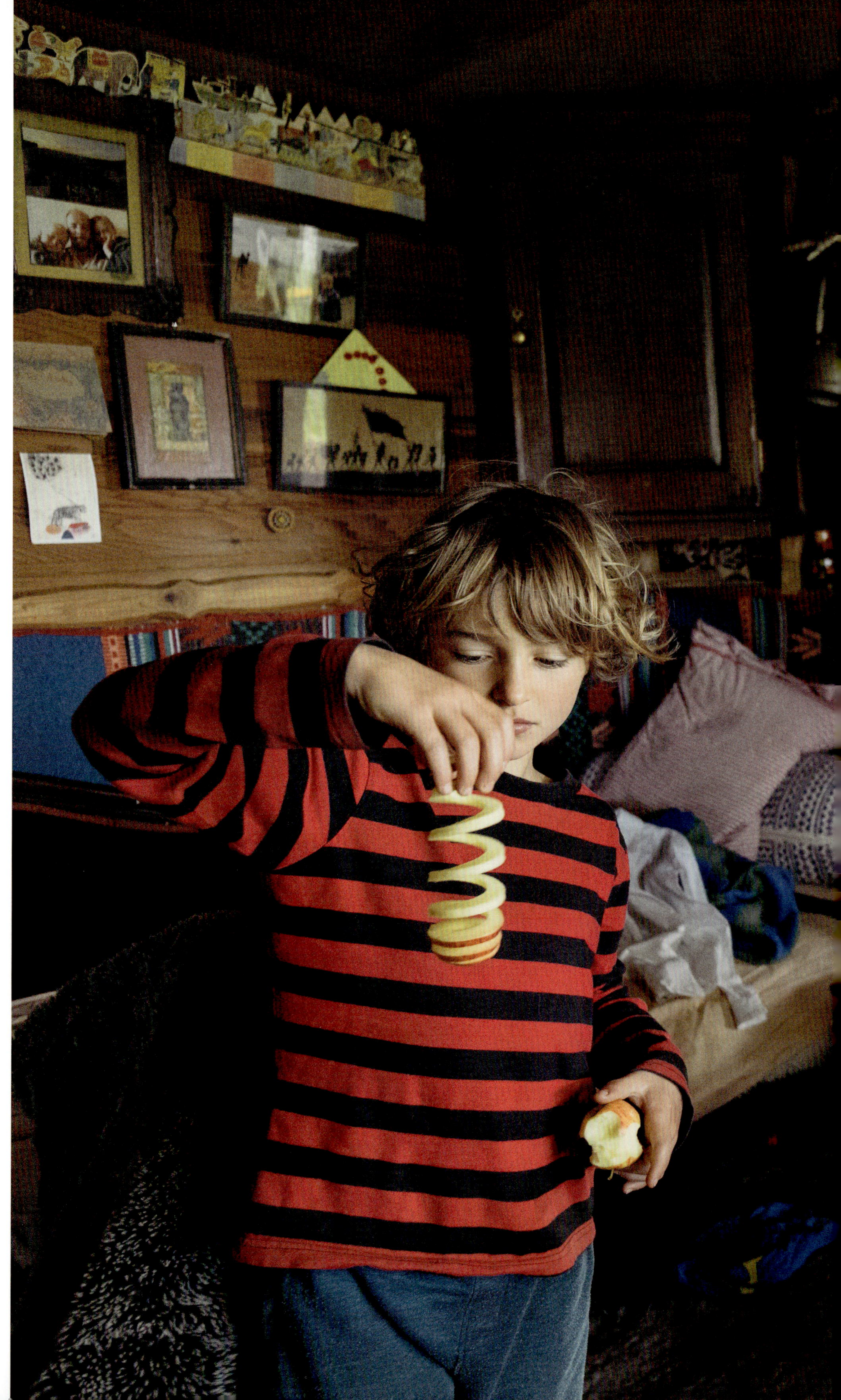

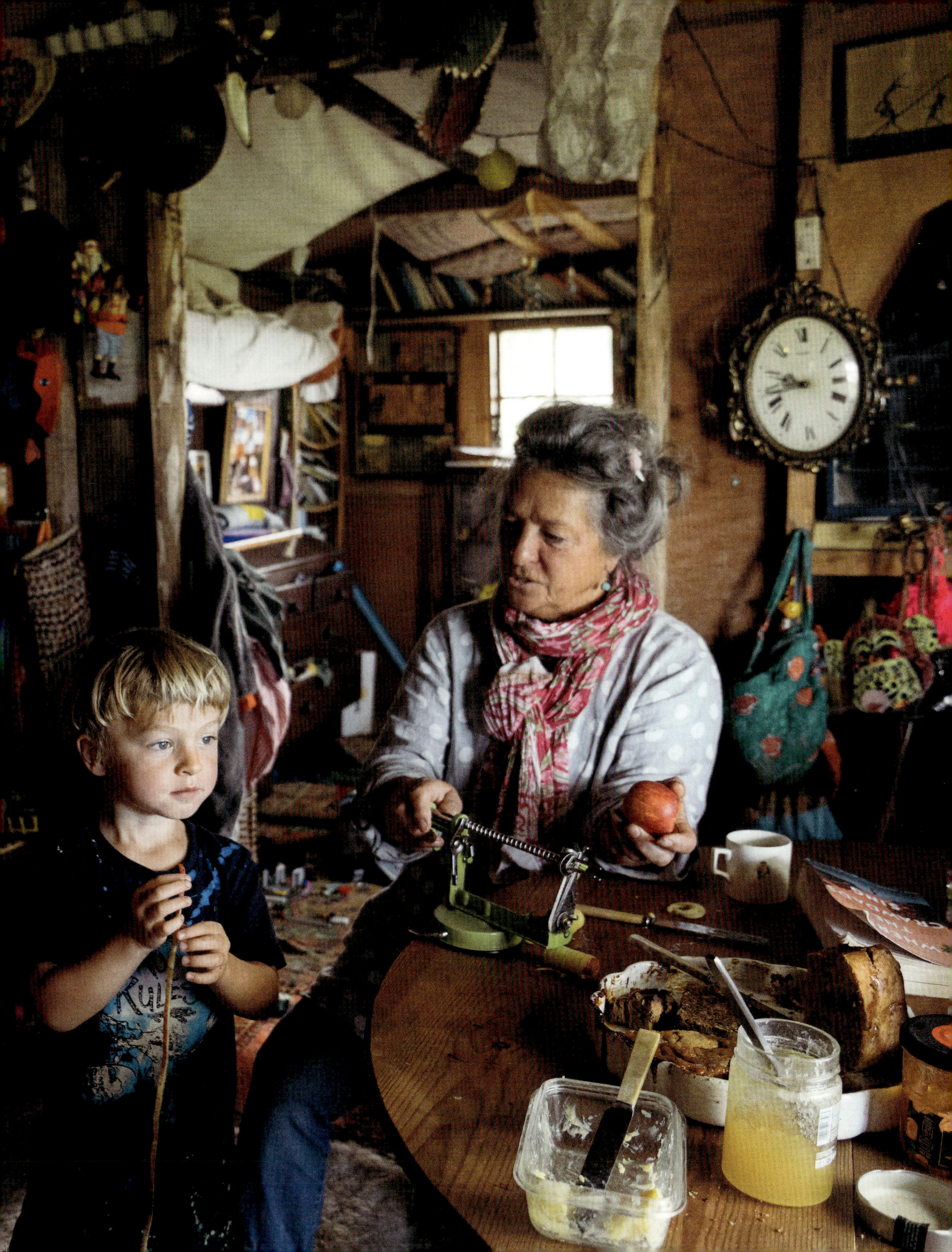

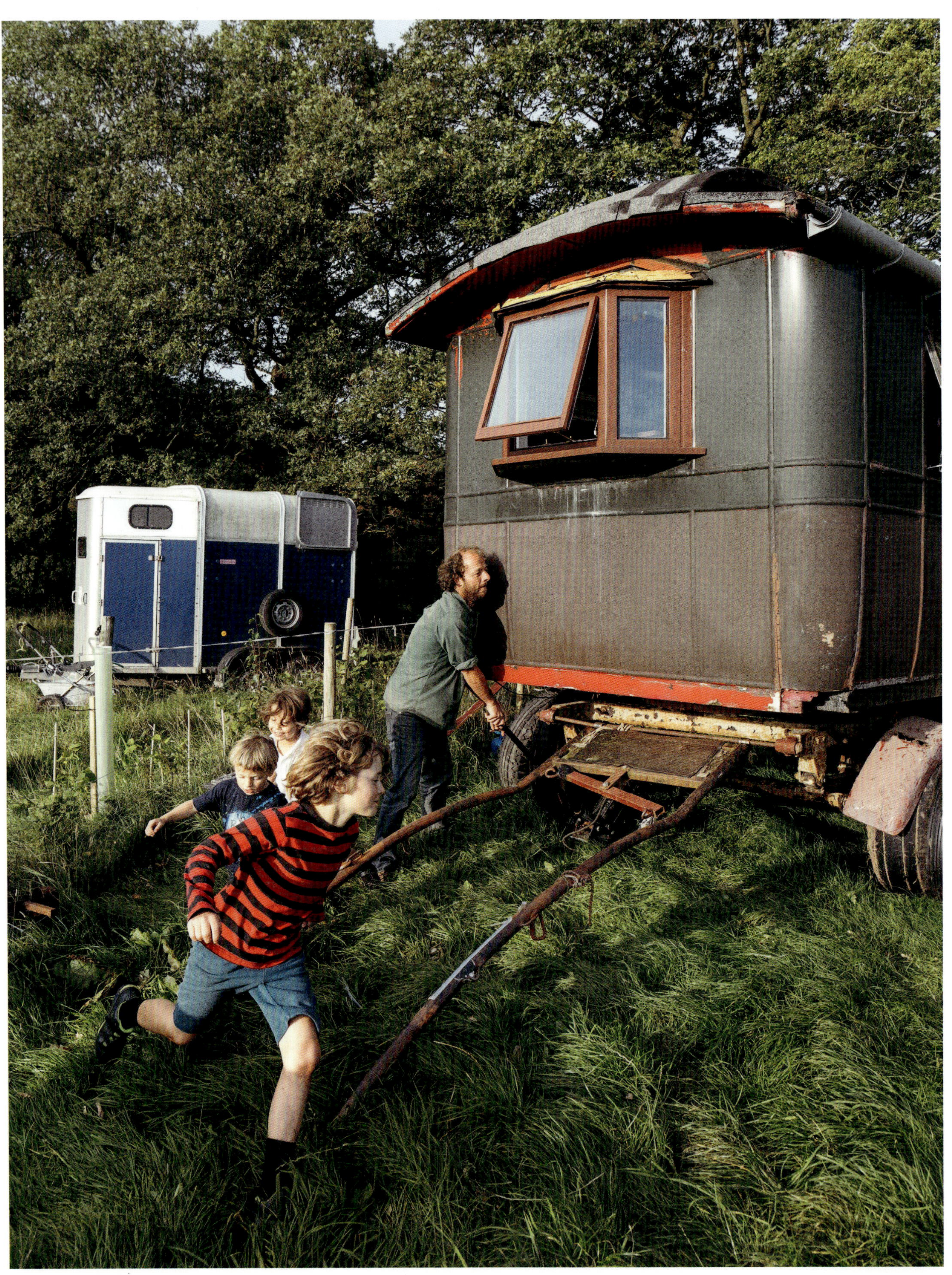

LIFE IN THE SLOW LANE

CUMBRIA, ENGLAND

A former trapez artist in England's biggest circuses, Barny parked his caravan in the northern English countryside after tiring of life on the road and time flying by. He has lived there with his family ever since, without water or electricity, occasionally taking to the road with his horses for short journeys in his caravan across the English countryside.

The little wooden house is cobbled together with recycled materials, surrounded by numerous caravans. There is no running water and the electricity is powered by solar panels. "No bills, no stress," says Barny amid hens, sheep, a cat, his two draft horses and a pony. The Englishman has lived like this for years. And he has never been happier or felt more peaceful since setting up in the verdant Cumbrian countryside in the north of England. "Barny? When he was little and climbing up the hill with his friends, he'd always stop along the way because he'd seen a grasshopper!" his mother reminisces, as though confiding that he had always been different.

At the age of sixteen, Barny ran away with a circus that was passing through his town to satisfy his natural curiosity and escape a routine that terrified him. He started out in the ticket office, before constructing the circus tents and eventually becoming a trapeze artist. He spent months on the road in caravans, giving his life to the company. "Working in a circus is like being in the army. There's never any time for yourself. There's nowhere or no opportunity to spend money. I worked for major circuses – the Moscow State Circus, Mongolian State Circus and Chinese State Circus – breaking my back, seven days a week without a single day off in nine months. Until I couldn't do it anymore." The only break in this exhausting nomadic routine was a few weeks in winter when he would spend his savings on trips to faraway places. From India to Central America via Europe, he took his chance to see the world.

After eight years on the road, Barny fled once again, leaving the circus to work with horses. He headed north to the Isle of Arran

in Scotland where he organised horse and cart rides with caravans he built himself, as a long-time enthusiast. Accompanied by his faithful cob, he also drew wood out of forests.

"It was a huge change to leave the circus and live in a caravan on this island. But I wanted to settle down somewhere." It was there that Barny realised that an unconventional existence was possible. "I never felt comfortable in a house and, at some point, I realised that I didn't need all these things I had got used to. I was happier to give up some luxuries and comforts that I could do without rather than my time and my life."

His aim? To set up somewhere and find his slice of paradise. Barny succeeded. His Eden is called Melmerby, a little village with 200 inhabitants in … Eden District! "I bought the land and built my hut a year later. Then I went travelling again for two years and came back to finish my house and settle down for good."

Later, he completely restored and converted the caravan to host tourists, and another life began. A life shaped by a slow pace, contemplation and discoveries along the way. In this life, meat is grilled on the hearth, water is drawn from the river, a vegetable garden provides the whole family with healthy food, neighbours and friends barter – cabbage and potatoes for game – and tea is drunk at any time of day, around the fire or in the shade of the lofty oak trees.

Life is abundant here, where togetherness with other humans is all you need. Full of dreams for the future, Barny loves nothing more than the idea of sharing and passing this on to his many friends, artists, teachers, farmers and employees. The crazy discussions stretch into the evening in the glimmer of the candlelight. Raised with their hands and feet in the earth, his two children, Madog and Malinki, are a pair of Robinsons, travelling to school in a cart pulled by Jet, the pony. Life in Melmerby is exciting, fun and vibrant.

Settled though he may be, Barny remains something of a nomad. He describes his journeys along French roads, especially when his wife Katus was several months' pregnant. "We left Melmerby for Saintes-Maries-de-la-Mer in Camargue with the caravan and horses, stopping off at my mother's place in Drôme so Katus could give birth to Madog. We crossed France using the back roads. It was a hell of an adventure!"

Barny chose his path unconsciously. "It's not to be part of a clan or a tribe. I've always operated differently, somewhat on the margins of life."

And in his voluntary and very social exile, he has regular visitors who come to have fun experiencing his unconventional day-to-day, which is also his livelihood.

"Sharing this way of life with all these people validates my choices and gives them a legitimacy. Because you lose confidence sometimes and question yourself. In the traditional school system, we're constantly told that this isn't possible. Over time, I learnt that this system limits our horizons rather than broadening them. I like to inspire people with different dreams, whatever they may be, and give them a little spark to get them dreaming too."

Do not listen to those who criticise another way of life without ever having dared start over. Barny does not let himself judge, though he himself is sometimes treated like a crazy guy in his caravan. "I simply live how I decided to. It's a personal choice. I don't think someone's wrong to live the way they do. I'm just not meant to live in a house. I like my life as it is." Happy are they who, like Barny, have travelled long and far and finally settled down.

DAS ENTSCHLEUNIGTE LEBEN

CUMBRIA, ENGLAND

Einst trat Barny als Trapezkünstler unter den größten Zirkuskuppeln Englands auf. Von dem hektischen Leben auf der Straße erschöpft, zog er mit seinem Planwagen in den Norden des Landes. Seitdem lebt er mit seiner Familie ohne Strom oder Wasser; manchmal unternimmt er heute noch mit Pferden und Planwagen kurze Reisen durchs Land.

Ein kleines, aus Fundstücken zusammengeschustertes Holzhaus, umgeben von Planwagen. Kein fließendes Wasser, nur Strom aus Solarpaneelen: „Keine Rechnungen, kein Stress", bilanziert Barney inmitten von Hühnern, Schafen, einer Katze, seinen beiden Zugpferden und einem Pony. Schon vor Jahren hat der Engländer beschlossen, so zu leben. Seit er in der grünen Landschaft von Cumbria in Nordengland lebt, fühlt er sich so glücklich und ruhig wie nie zuvor.

„Barny? Schon als kleiner Junge blieb er auf halbem Weg stehen, wenn er mit seinen Freunden auf einen Hügel stieg, weil er einen Grashüpfer gesehen hatte!", erinnert sich seine Mutter, als wolle sie mir verraten, dass er immer schon etwas Besonderes war.

Mit sechzehn brennt Barny mit einem in der Stadt gastierenden Zirkus durch – aus Neugierde und um einer Routine zu entfliehen, die ihn erschreckt. Anfangs verkauft er Eintrittskarten, dann arbeitet er sich hoch in die Zirkuskuppel und wird schließlich Trapezkünstler. Monatelang ist er unterwegs, lebt nur für die Truppe. „In einem Zirkus ist es wie in der Armee. Man hat nie Zeit für sich. Keinen Raum, keine Gelegenheit, sein Geld auszugeben. Ich habe für die größten Zirkusse gearbeitet: Moskauer Staatszirkus, Mongolischer Staatszirkus, Chinesischer Staatszirkus … Ich habe sieben Tage die Woche geschuftet, neun Monate ohne einen einzigen Tag Urlaub. Bis ich nicht mehr konnte."

Die einzige Atempause in dieser anstrengenden Nomadenroutine: einige Winterwochen, in denen er sein Erspartes für Fernreisen von Indien über Europa bis nach Mittelamerika nutzt, um die Welt zu entdecken.

Nach acht Jahren des Reisens brennt Barny ein zweites Mal durch; er verlässt den Zirkus, um mit Pferden zu arbeiten. Auf der Insel Arran im Norden Schottlands organisiert er Touren in selbst gebauten Planwagen, die er schon seit langem liebt. Und er arbeitet mit seinem treuen Pferd im Wald, als Holzrücker.

„Es war eine enorme Veränderung in meinem Leben, den Zirkus zu verlassen und auf dieser Insel in einen Wohnwagen zu ziehen. Aber ich wollte mich irgendwo niederlassen." Im Norden erkennt Barny, dass eine Existenz jenseits der Norm möglich ist. „In Häusern habe ich mich nie wohlgefühlt, und irgendwann erkannte ich, dass ich die ganzen Dinge, an die ich mich gewöhnt hatte, gar nicht brauchte. Ich habe lieber ein wenig verzichtbaren Luxus und Komfort geopfert als meine Zeit und mein Leben."

Sein Ziel: sich irgendwo niederlassen und das eigene Stück Paradies entdecken. Schließlich findet er es. Sein Garten Eden heißt Melmerby, ein kleines Dorf mit 200 Einwohnern im … Eden District! „Ich habe das Grundstück gekauft und ein Jahr später meine Hütte gebaut. Dann war ich zwei Jahre auf Reisen, kam zurück, baute das Haus fertig und ließ mich endgültig nieder."

Ein Planwagen, den er komplett restauriert und ausbaut, um ihn an Touristen zu vermieten, wird zum Beginn eines neuen Lebens – voller Langsamkeit und Kontemplation, voller Fundstücke am Wegesrand. Eine Existenz, bei der man Fleisch über dem Feuer grillt und Wasser aus dem Fluss schöpft, bei der ein Gemüsegarten ausreicht, um die ganze Familie gesund zu ernähren, bei der Tauschgeschäfte mit Nachbarn und Freunden stattfinden – Kohl und Kartoffeln gegen Wildbret – und man den ganzen Tag Tee trinkt, am Feuer oder im Schatten hoher Eichen.

In diesem erfüllten Leben gibt es keine weiteren Bedürfnisse als das Zusammensein mit anderen Menschen: Barny steckt voller Träume und liebt nichts mehr, als sie mit seinen zahlreichen Freunden zu teilen – Künstlern, Lehrern, Bauern und Büroangestellten. Die wilden Debatten erstrecken sich über lange Abende bei Kerzenschein. Seine beiden Kinder Madog und Malinki, zwei kleine Robinsons, die auf und mit dem Land großgeworden sind, fahren mit einer Kutsche zur Schule, die ihr Pony Jet zieht. Melmerby ist voller Energie, voller Lachen, voller Leben.

Auch wenn Barny sich niedergelassen hat, sehnt sich ein Teil von ihm noch nach dem Nomadendasein. Er erzählt von seinen Fahrten auf den Landstraßen Frankreichs, vor allem von der Reise, auf der seine Frau Katus schwanger war. „Wir fuhren von Melmerby bis nach Saintes-Maries-de-la-Mer in der Camargue, mit Pferden und Planwagen, und machten bei meiner Mutter im Département Drôme eine Pause, damit Katus Madog auf die Welt bringen konnte … Wir durchquerten ganz Frankreich auf Nebenstraßen, ein ganz schönes Abenteuer!“

Barny hat sich seiner Natur folgend für diesen Weg entschieden. „Ich tue das nicht, um zu irgendeinem Klan oder Stamm zu gehören. Tatsächlich war ich immer schon ein bisschen anders, irgendwie am Rand der Gesellschaft.“

Er lebt in einem freiwilligen, sehr geselligen Exil und empfängt regelmäßig Besucher, die seinen ungewöhnlichen Alltag, der auch sein Broterwerb ist, gerne mitleben.

„Meinen Lebensstil mit all diesen Leuten zu teilen, gibt meinen Entscheidungen einen Wert und legitimiert sie. Manchmal verliert man nämlich das Selbstvertrauen und stellt sich infrage. Im traditionellen Ausbildungssystem wird uns immer wieder beigebracht, dass all dies hier unmöglich ist. Im Lauf der Zeit habe ich gelernt, dass dieses System unseren Horizont verengt, statt ihn zu erweitern. Ich liebe es, Leute zu inspirieren, die andere Träume haben, welcher Art auch immer – ihnen jenen kleinen Funken zu liefern, der sie auch zum Träumen bringt.“

Dabei hört er nicht auf diejenigen, die es selbst nie gewagt haben auszusteigen, aber eine andere Lebensweise dennoch kritisieren. Barny selbst erlaubt es sich nicht, über andere zu urteilen, selbst wenn man ihn mit seinem Wohnwagen manchmal einen Verrückten nennt. „Ich lebe ganz einfach so, wie ich es mir ausgesucht habe. Das ist eine persönliche Entscheidung. Ich lehne andere Lebensweisen nicht ab. Aber ich bin schlicht nicht dafür gemacht, in einem Haus zu leben. Mein Leben gefällt mir so.“ Glück ist, wie Barny nach einer langen Reise endlich anzukommen.

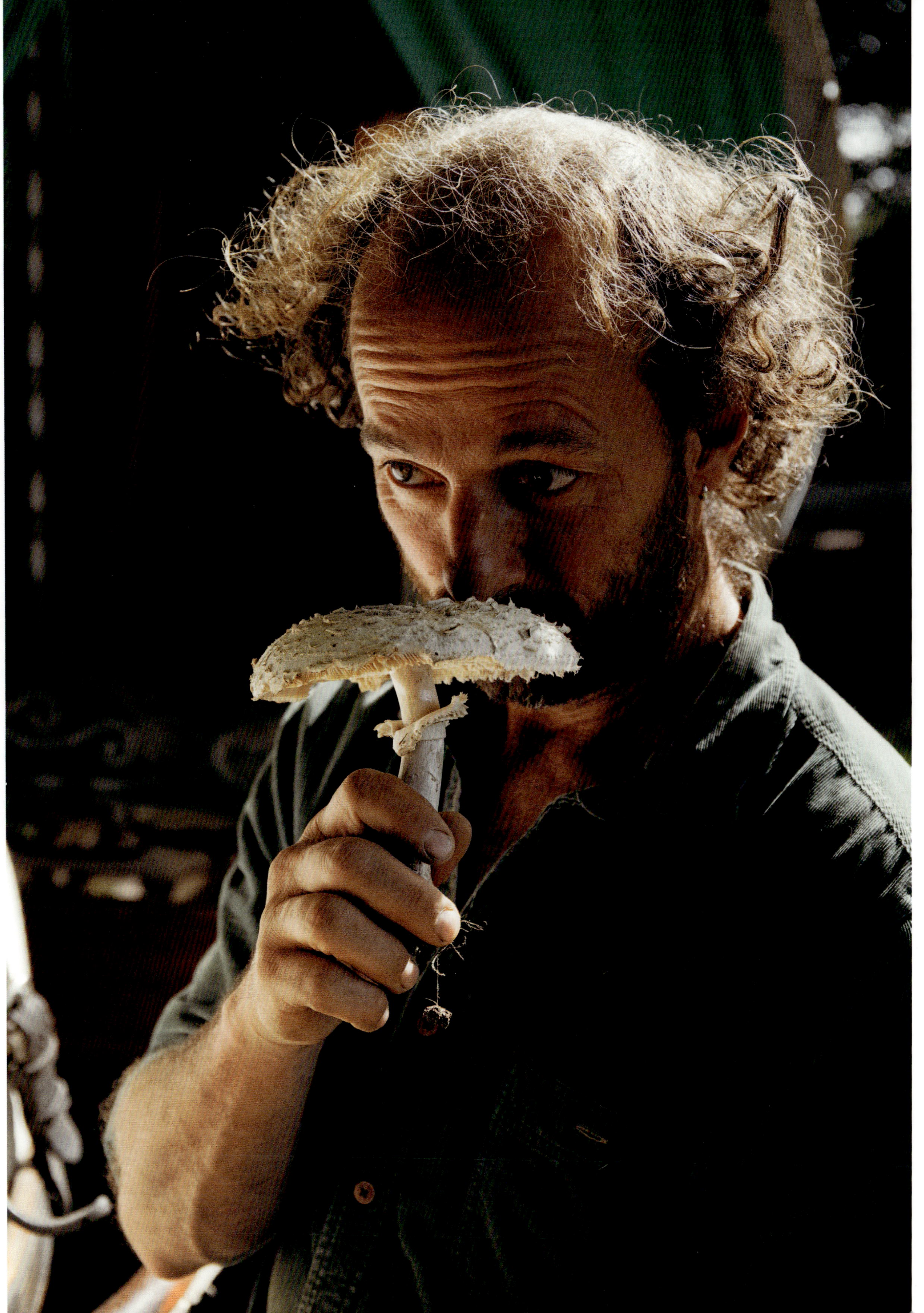

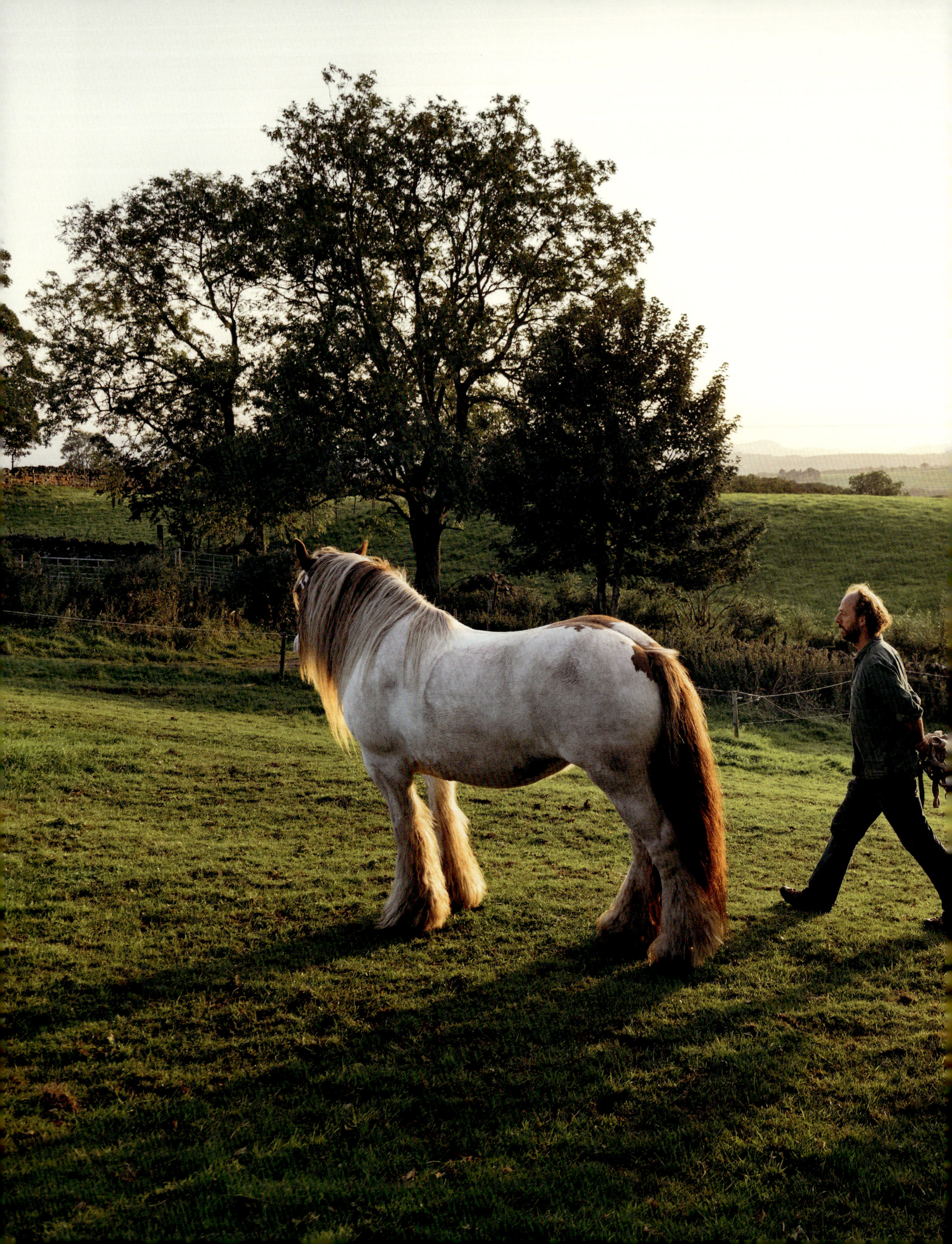

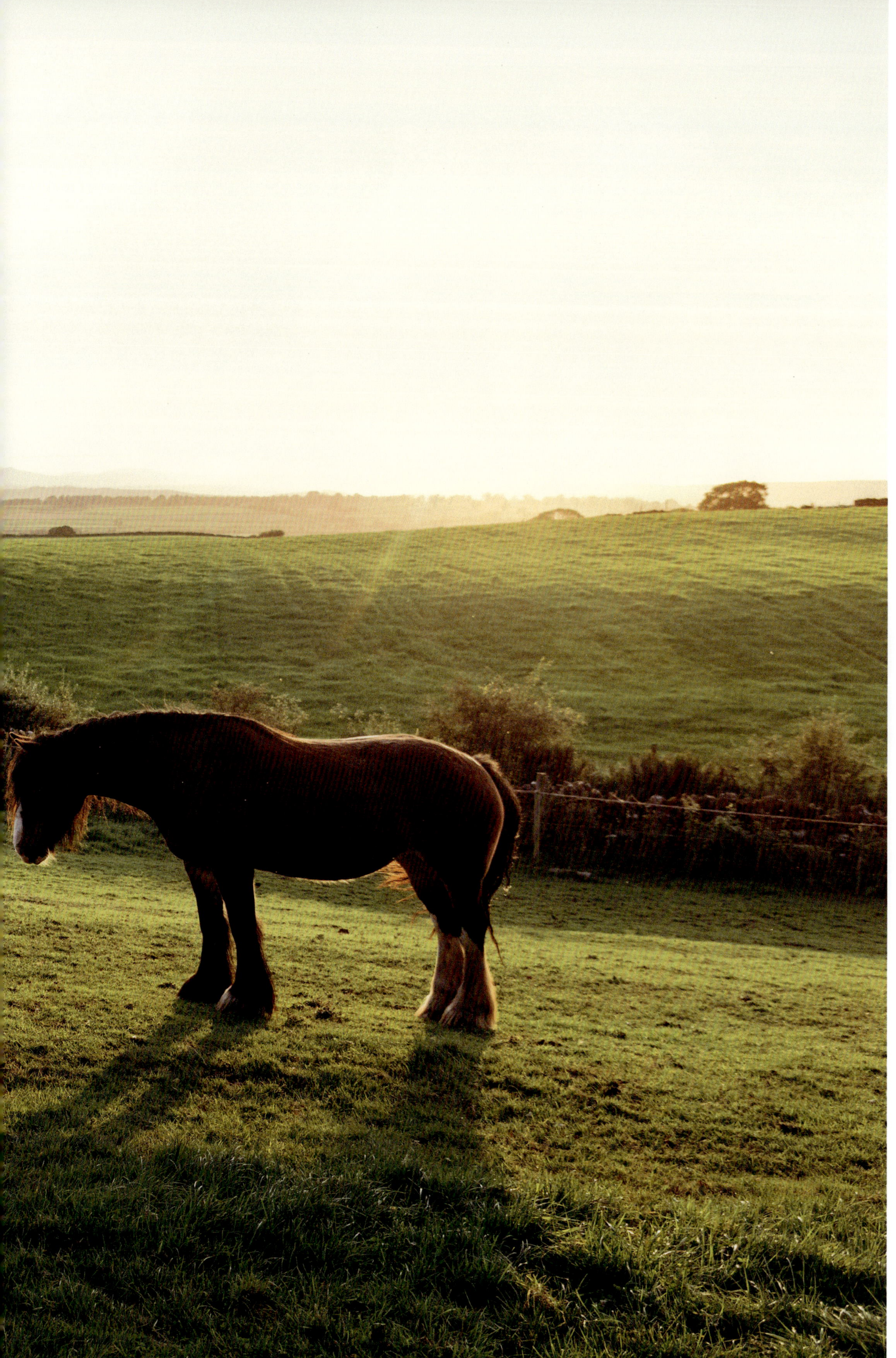

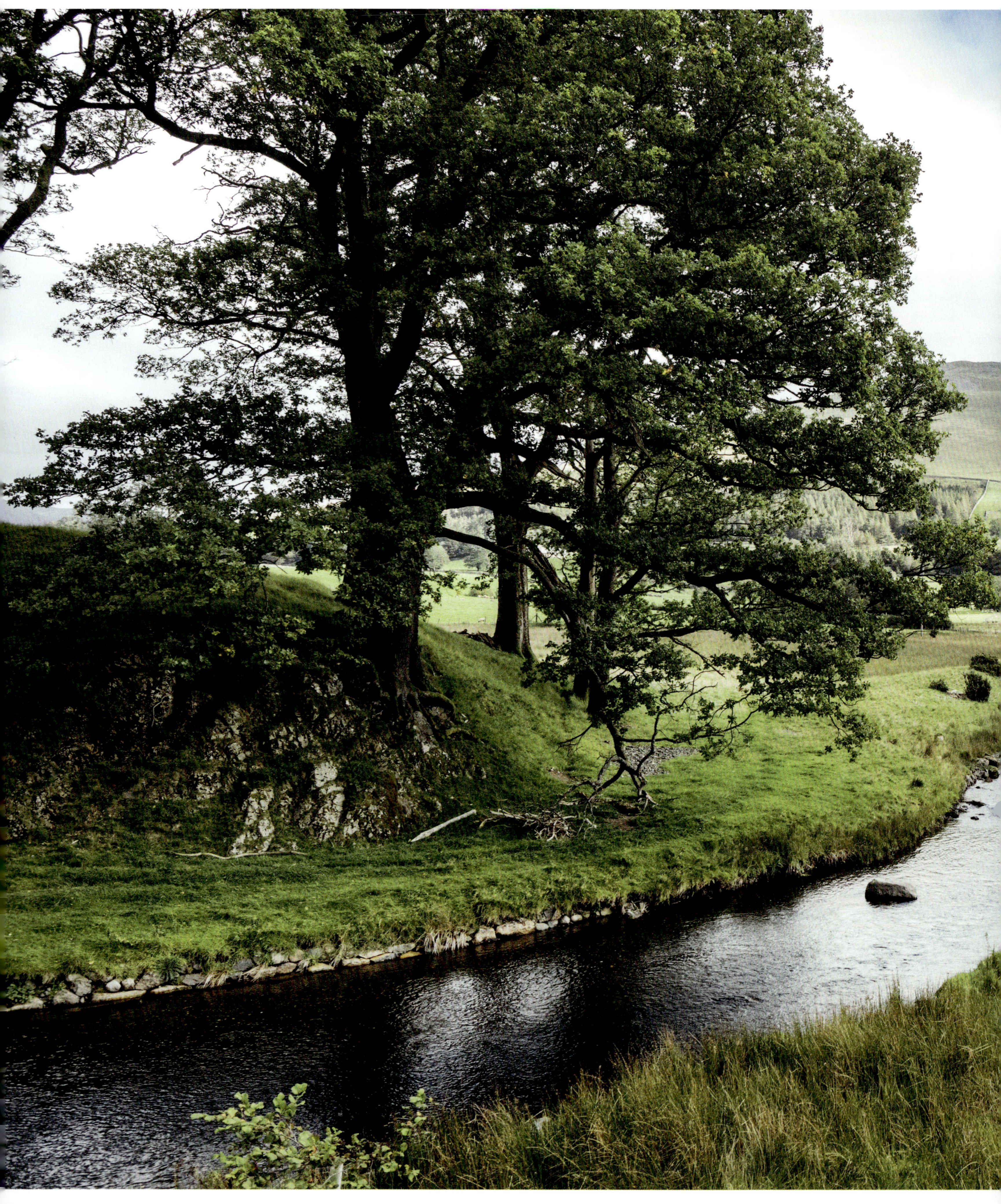

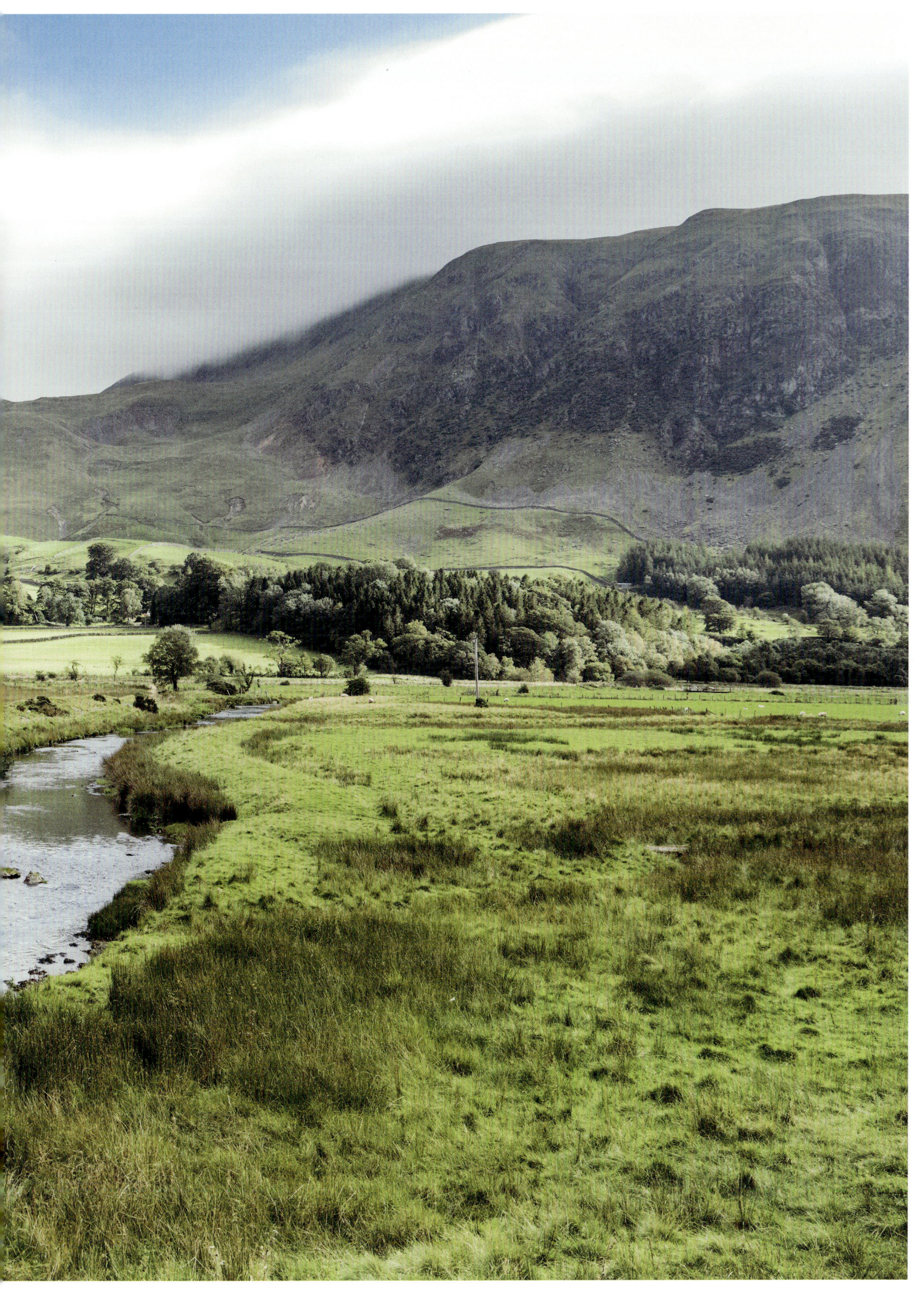

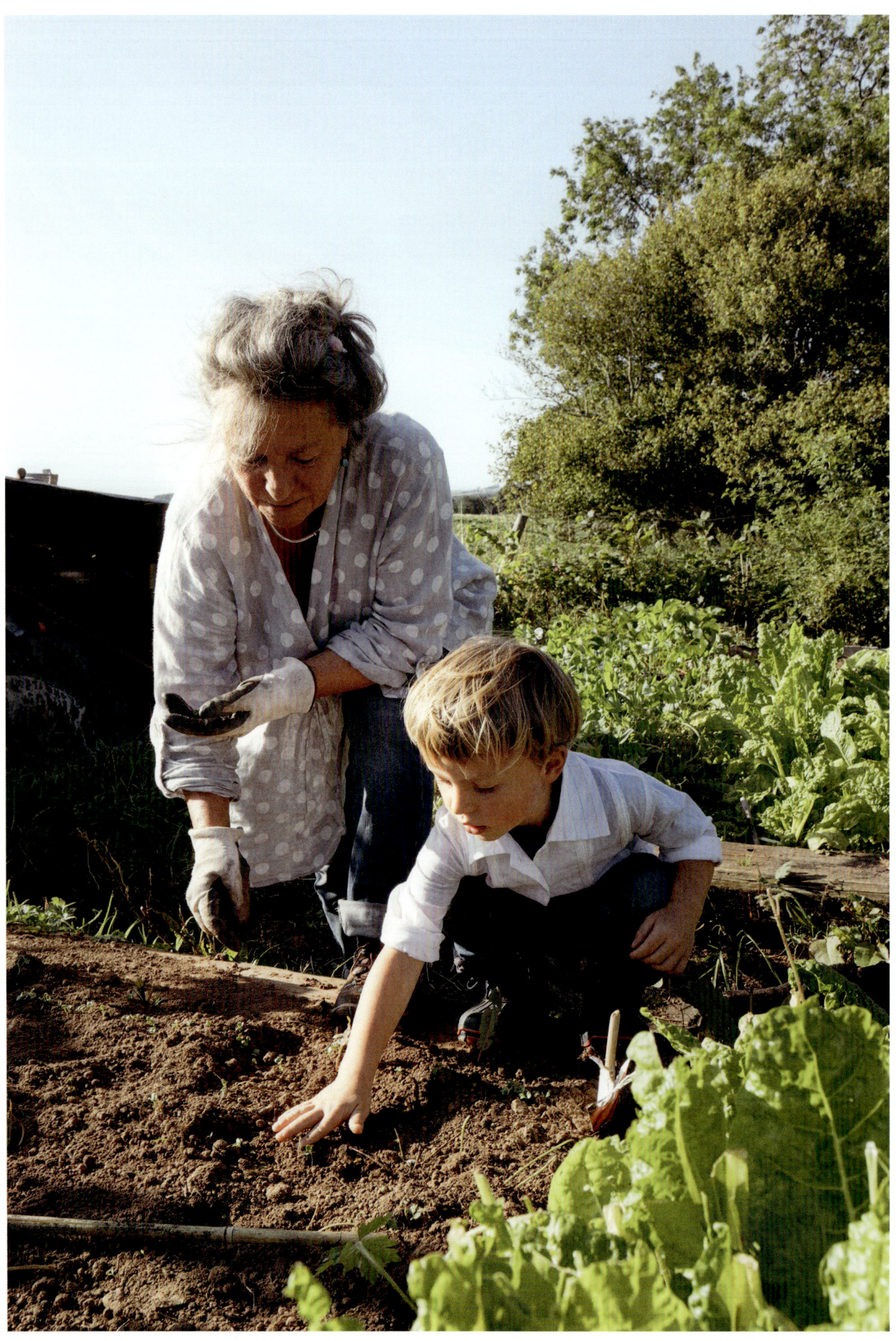

"The cost of a thing is the amount of what I will call life which is
required to be exchanged for it, immediately or in the long run.
As I preferred some things to others, and especially valued my
freedom, as I could fare hard and yet succeed well, I did not wish
to spend my time in earning rich carpets or other fine furniture,
or delicate cookery …"

HENRY DAVID THOREAU
Walden; or, Life in the Woods

„Der Preis einer Sache aber ist das, was ich von dem, was ich
Leben zu nennen pflege, sogleich oder im Lauf der Zeit dafür
austauschen muss. [...] Da ich manche Dinge anderen vorzog und
besonders meine Freiheit schätzte, da ich hart leben und mich
doch wohl befinden konnte, so wollte ich nicht meine Zeit
damit verbringen, kostbare Teppiche oder hübsche Möbelstücke
oder feine Kost zu verdienen."

HENRY DAVID THOREAU
Walden oder Leben in den Wäldern

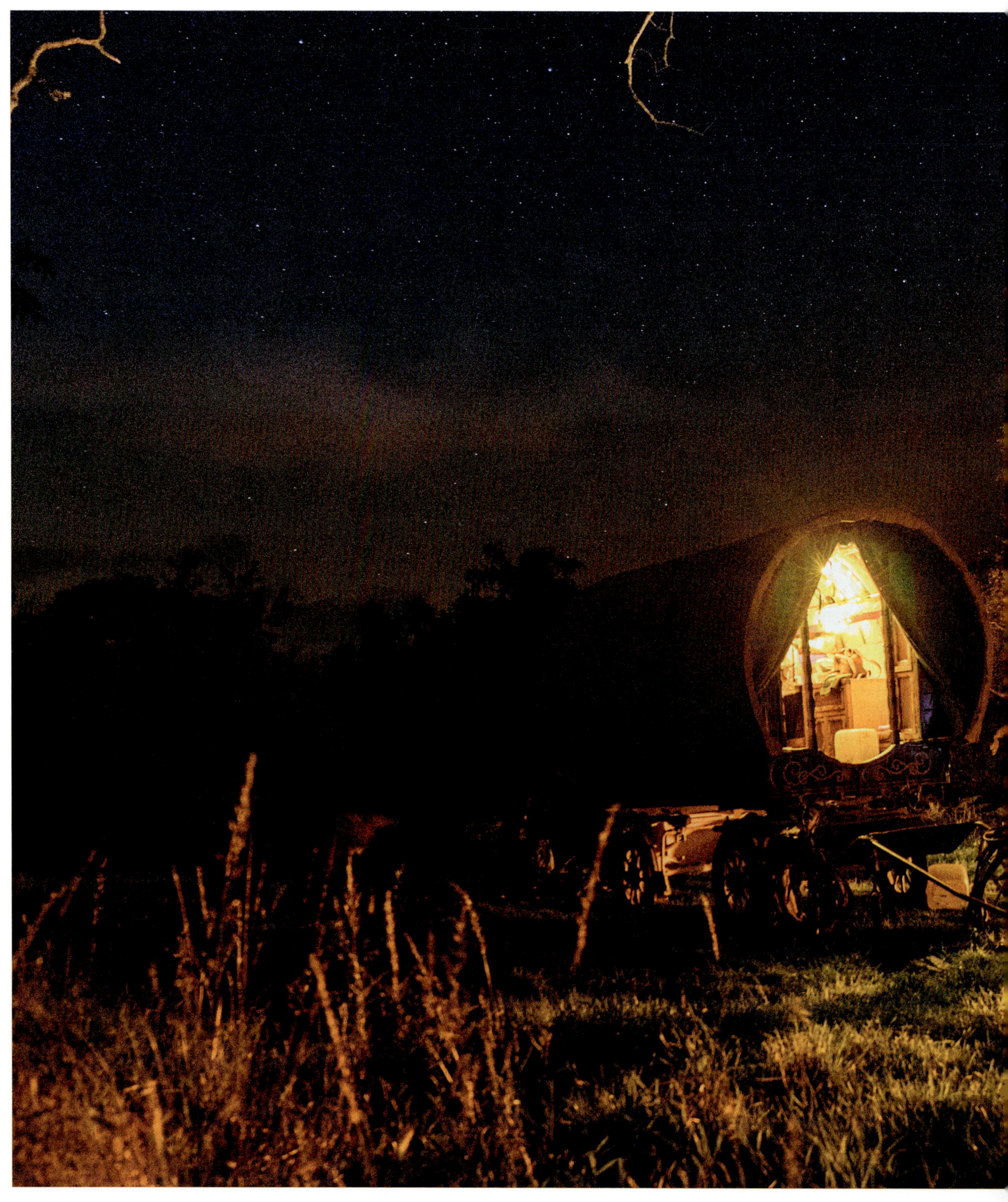

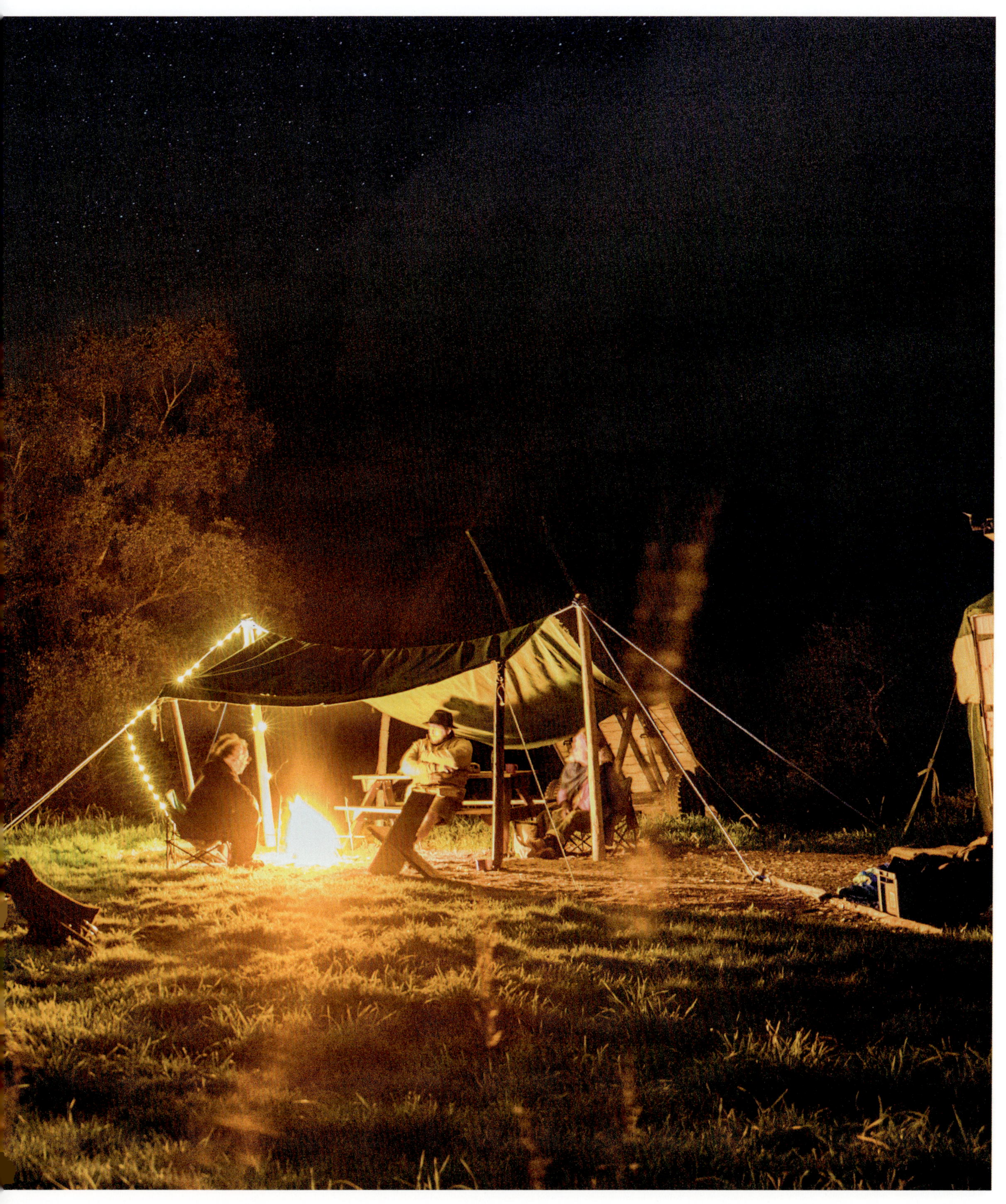

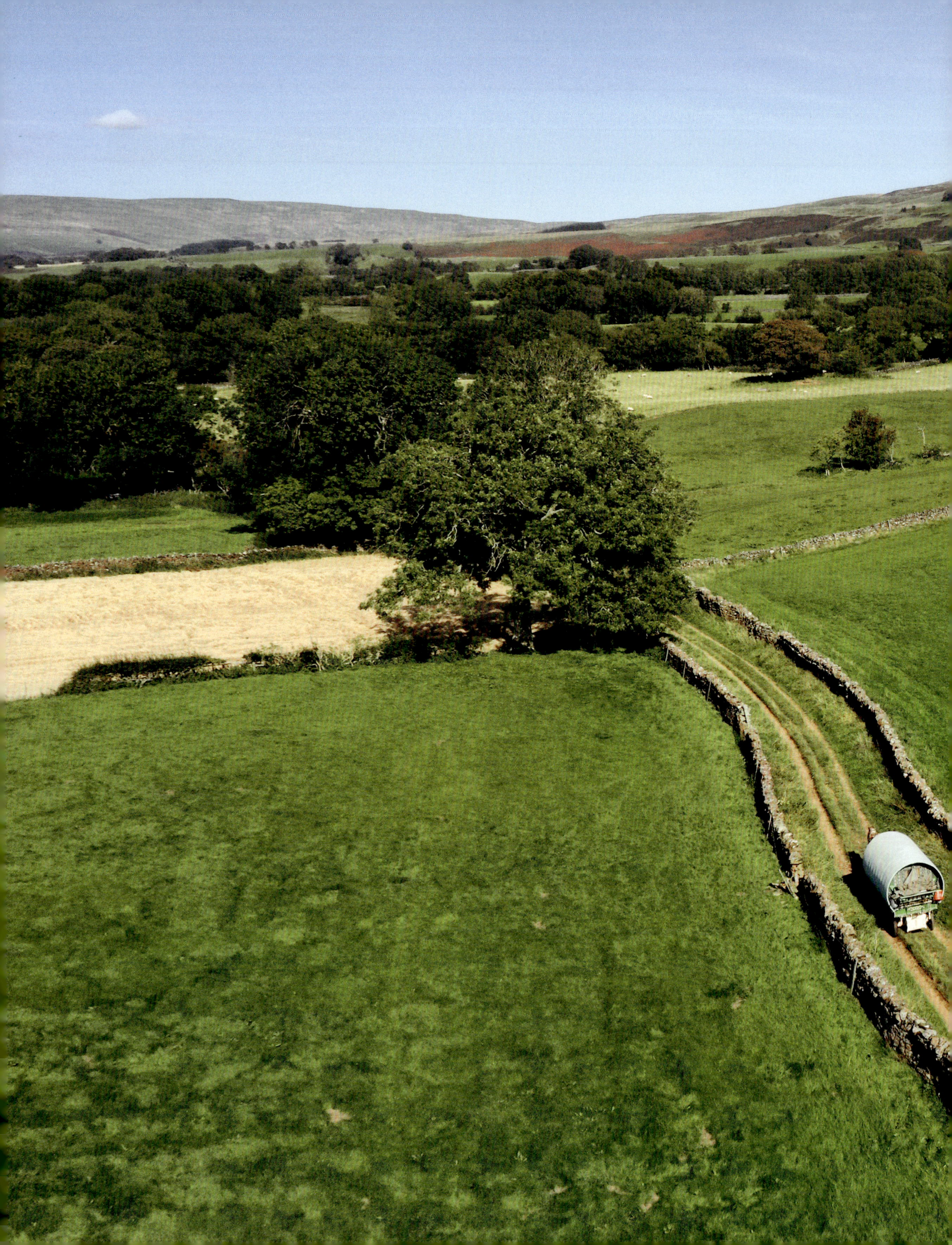

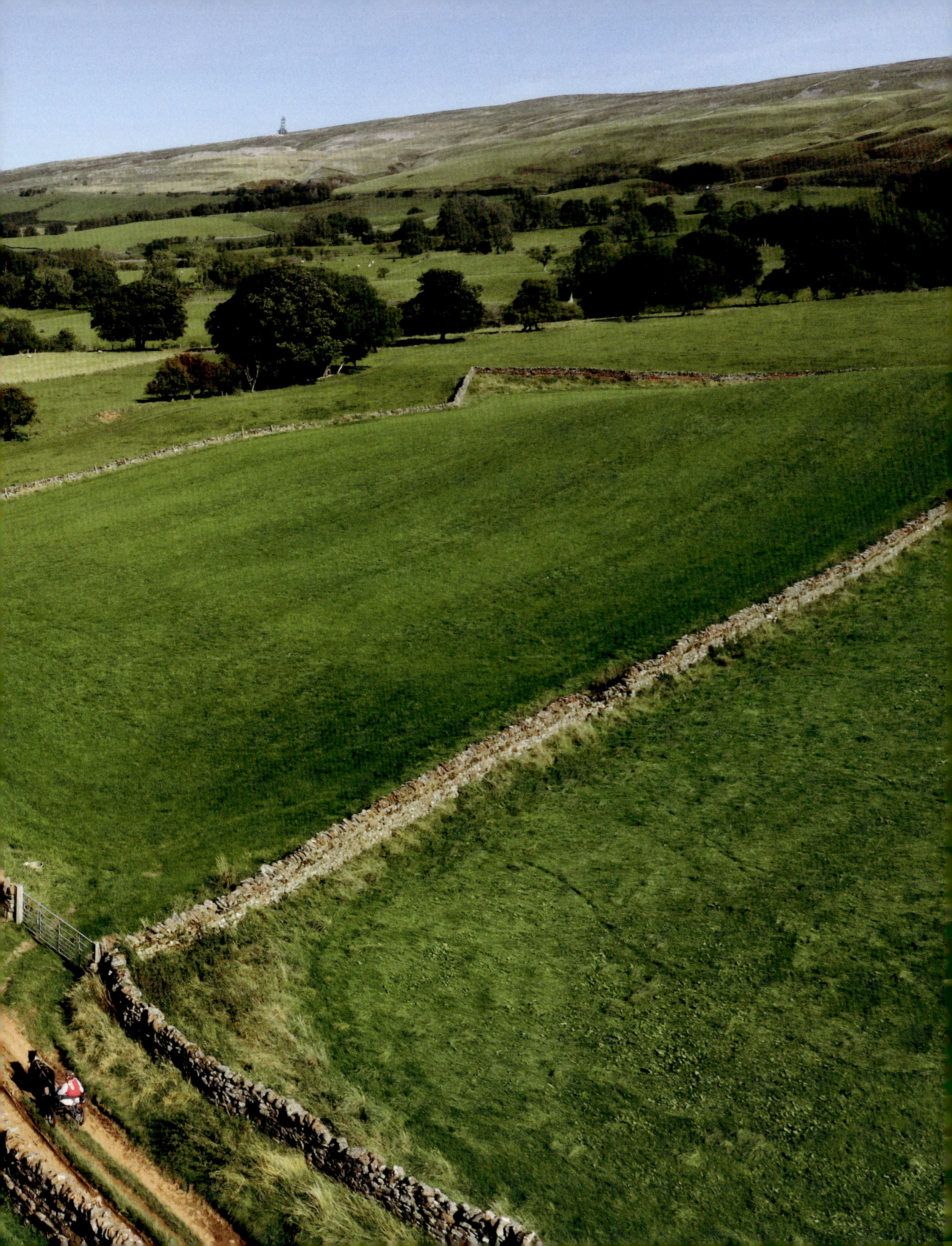

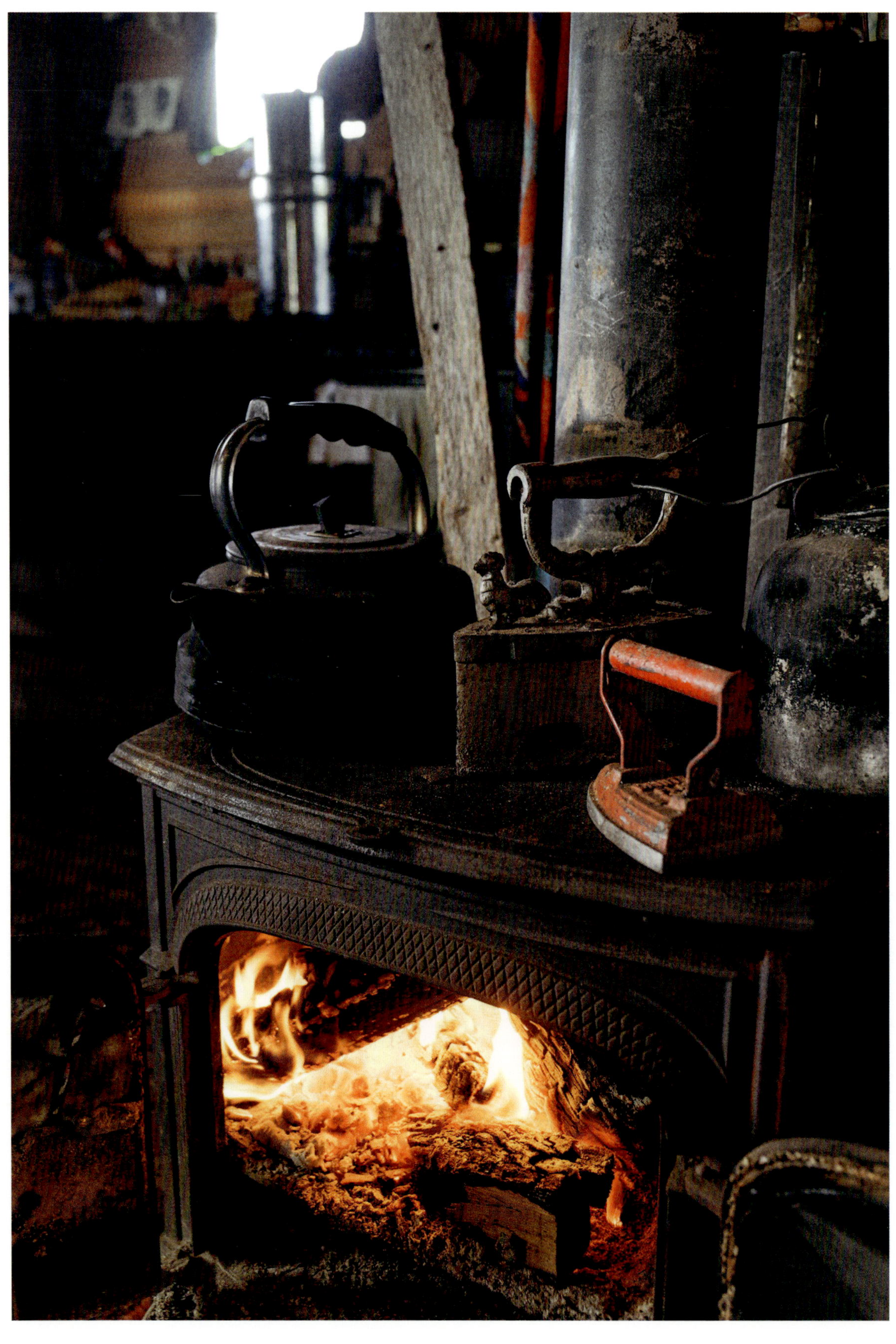

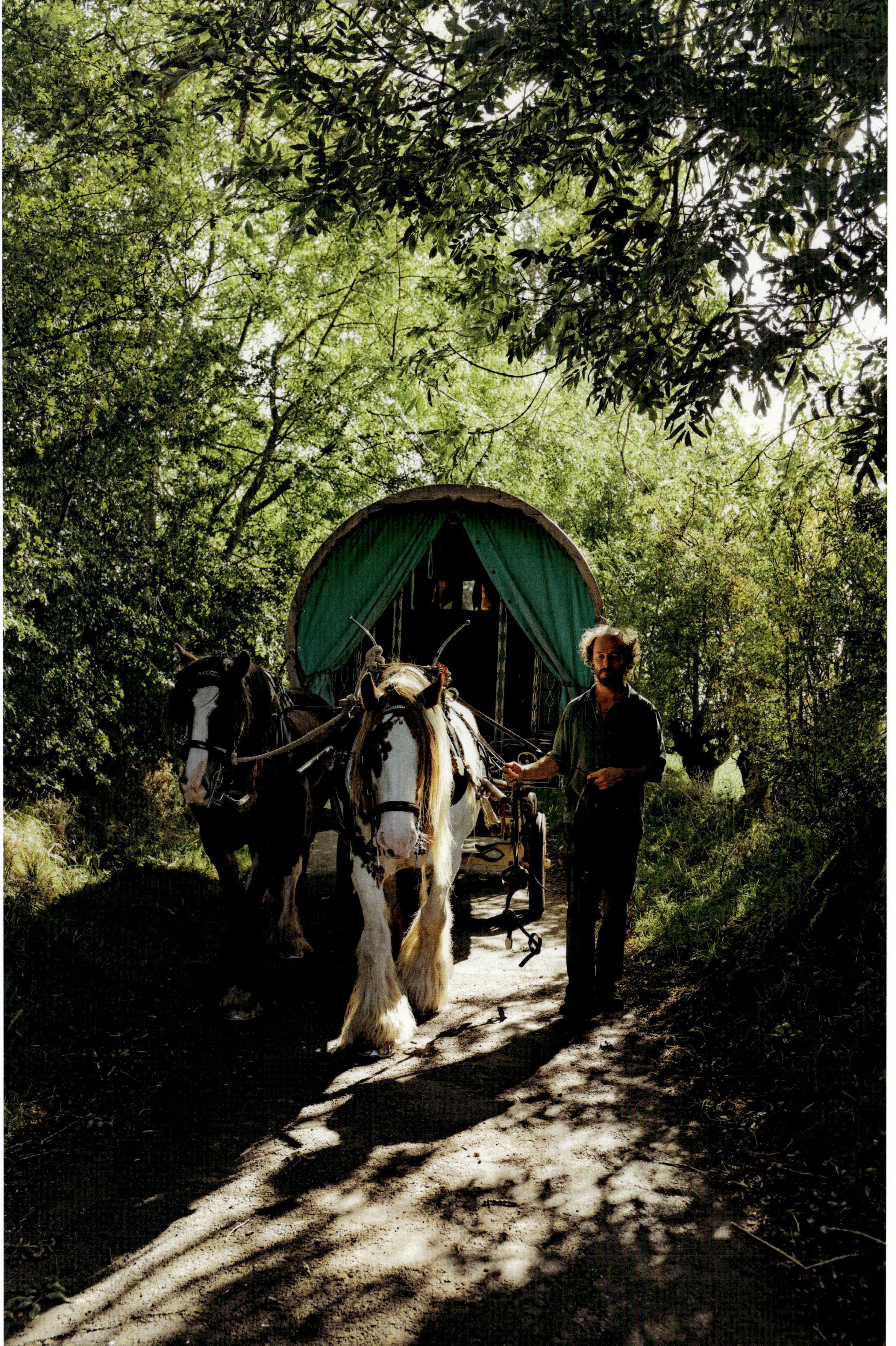

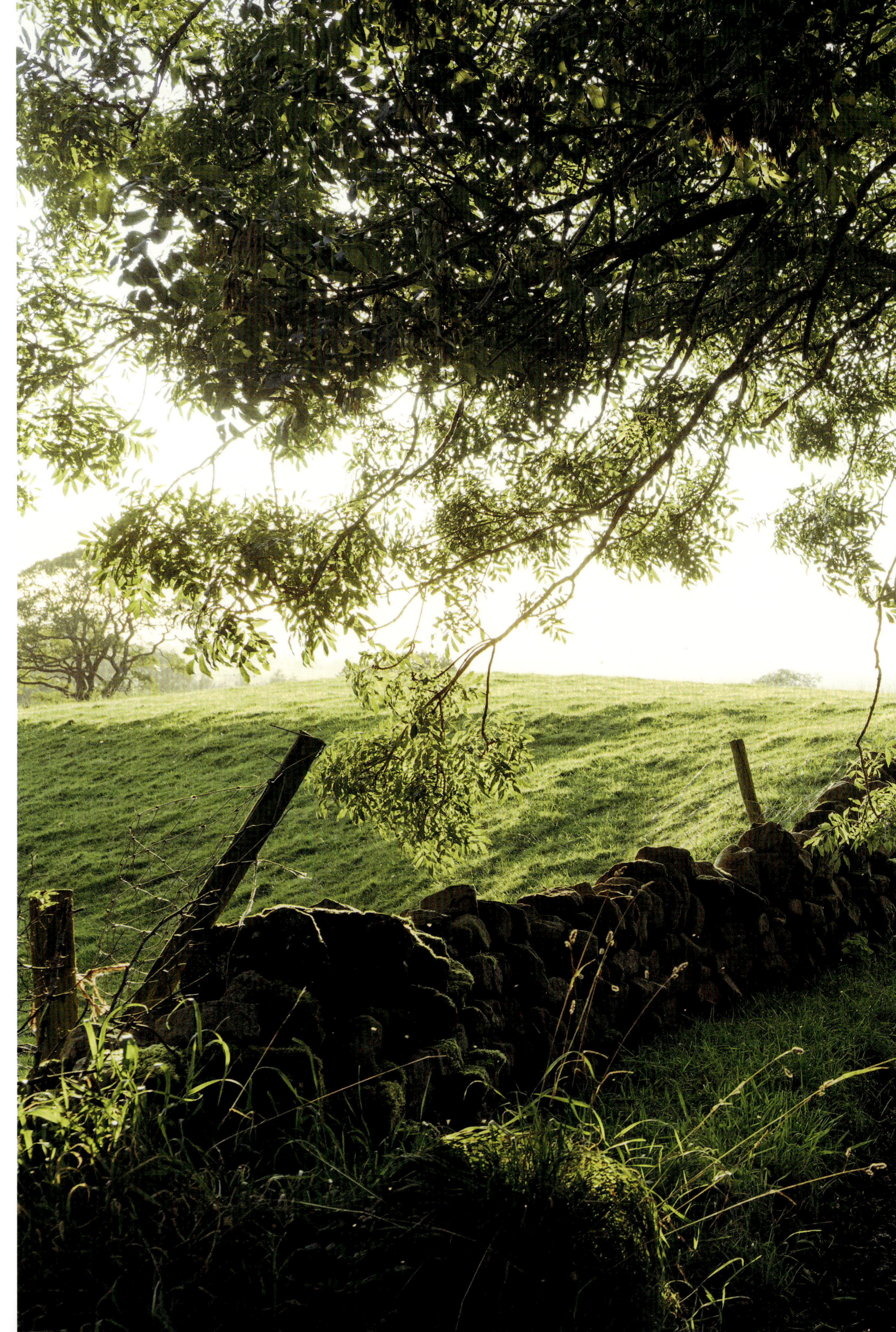

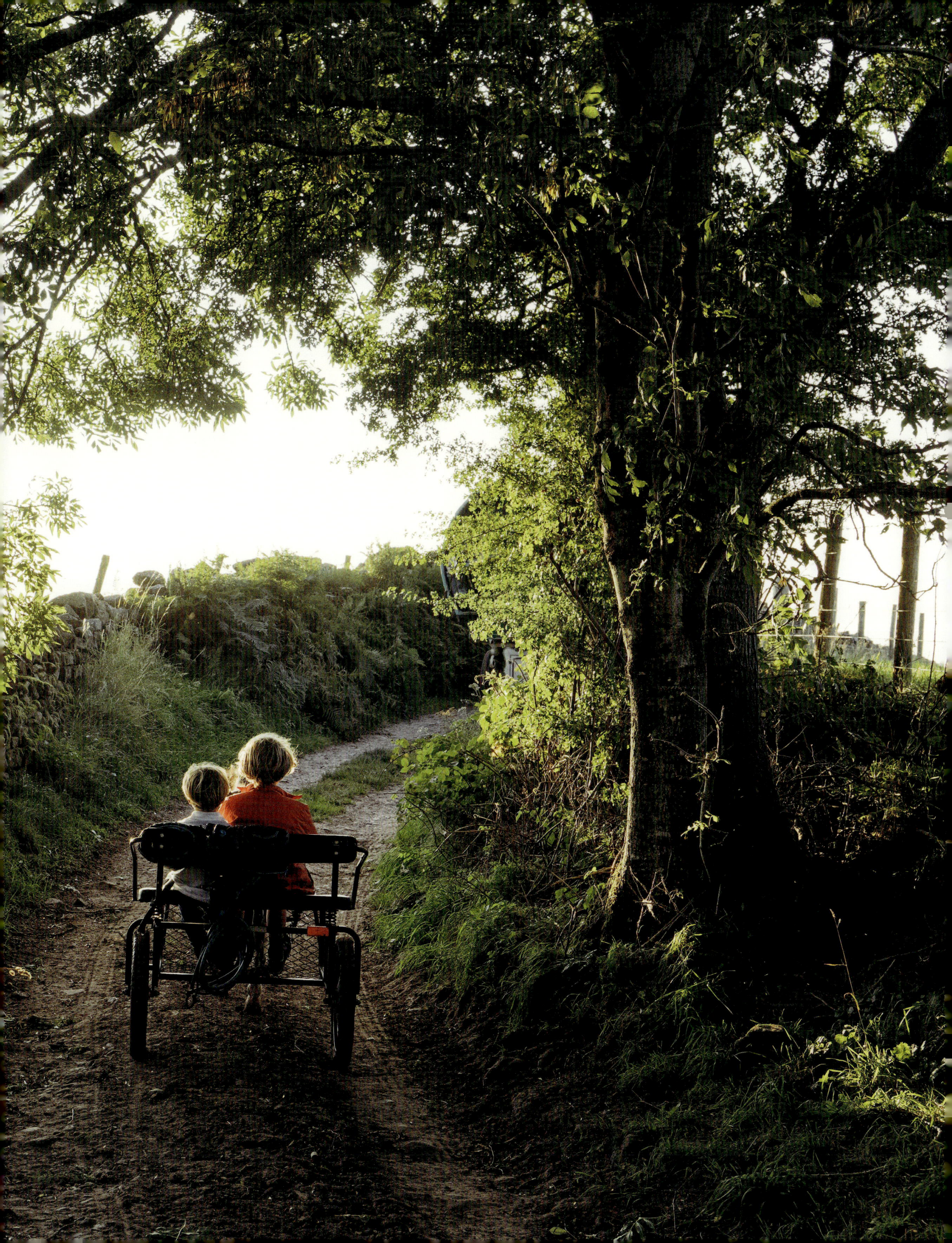

ZAYA

"I DON'T DISMISS OR
REGRET MY PAST LIFE.
BUT I'M SO HAPPY TO BE
WHERE I AM TODAY."

„ICH LEHNE MEIN FRÜHERES
LEBEN WEDER AB NOCH
BEREUE ICH ES.
ABER ICH BIN HIER UND
JETZT VOLLKOMMEN
GLÜCKLICH."

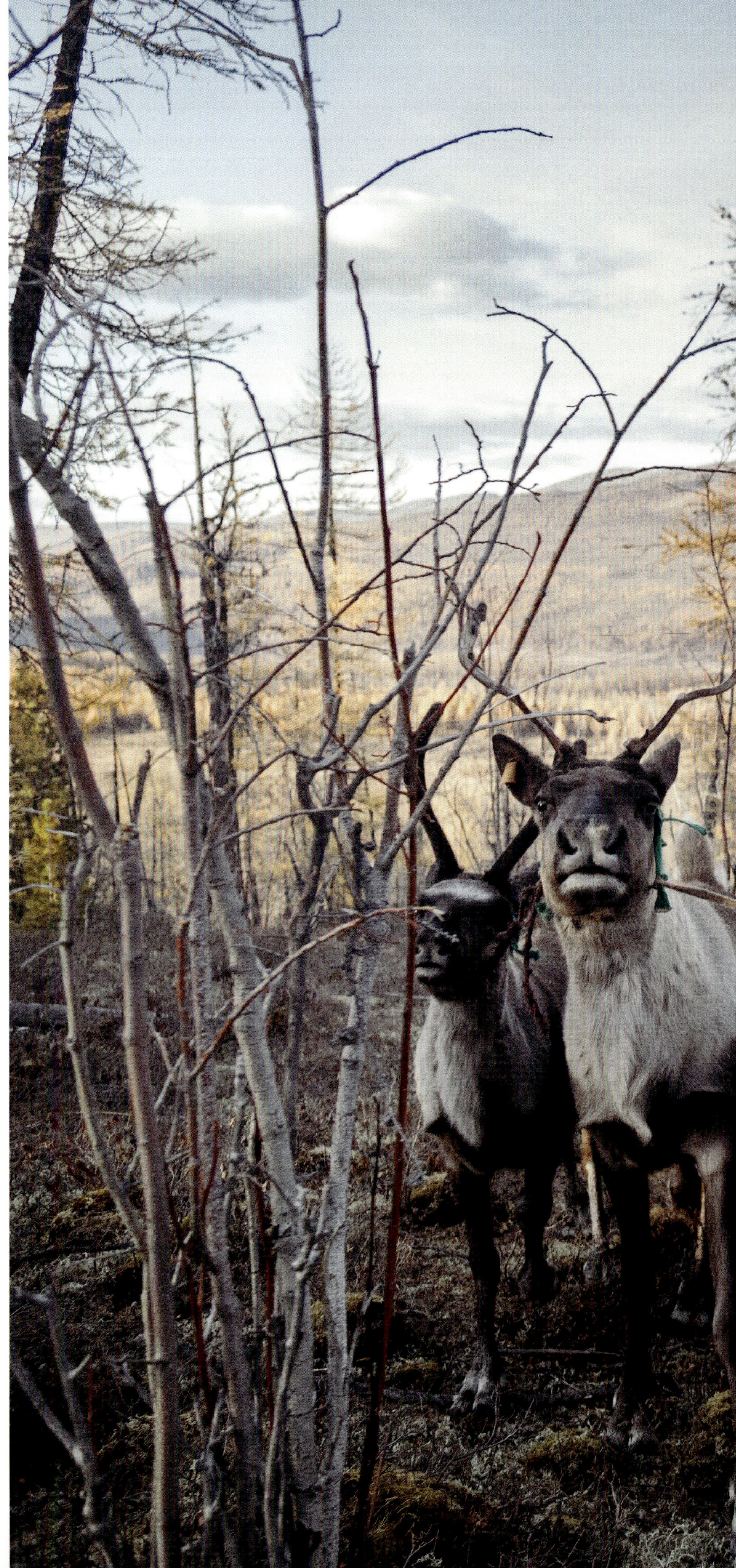

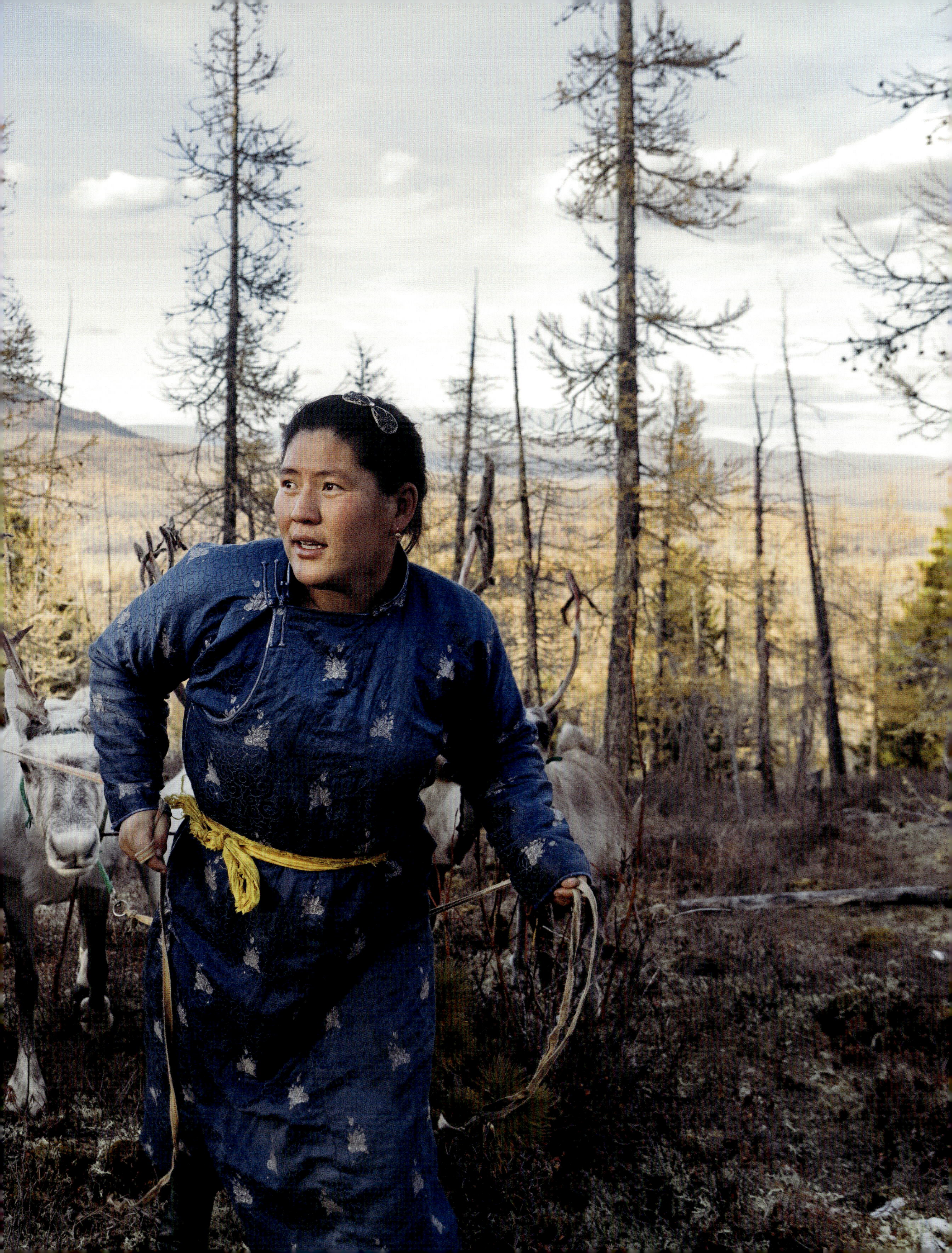

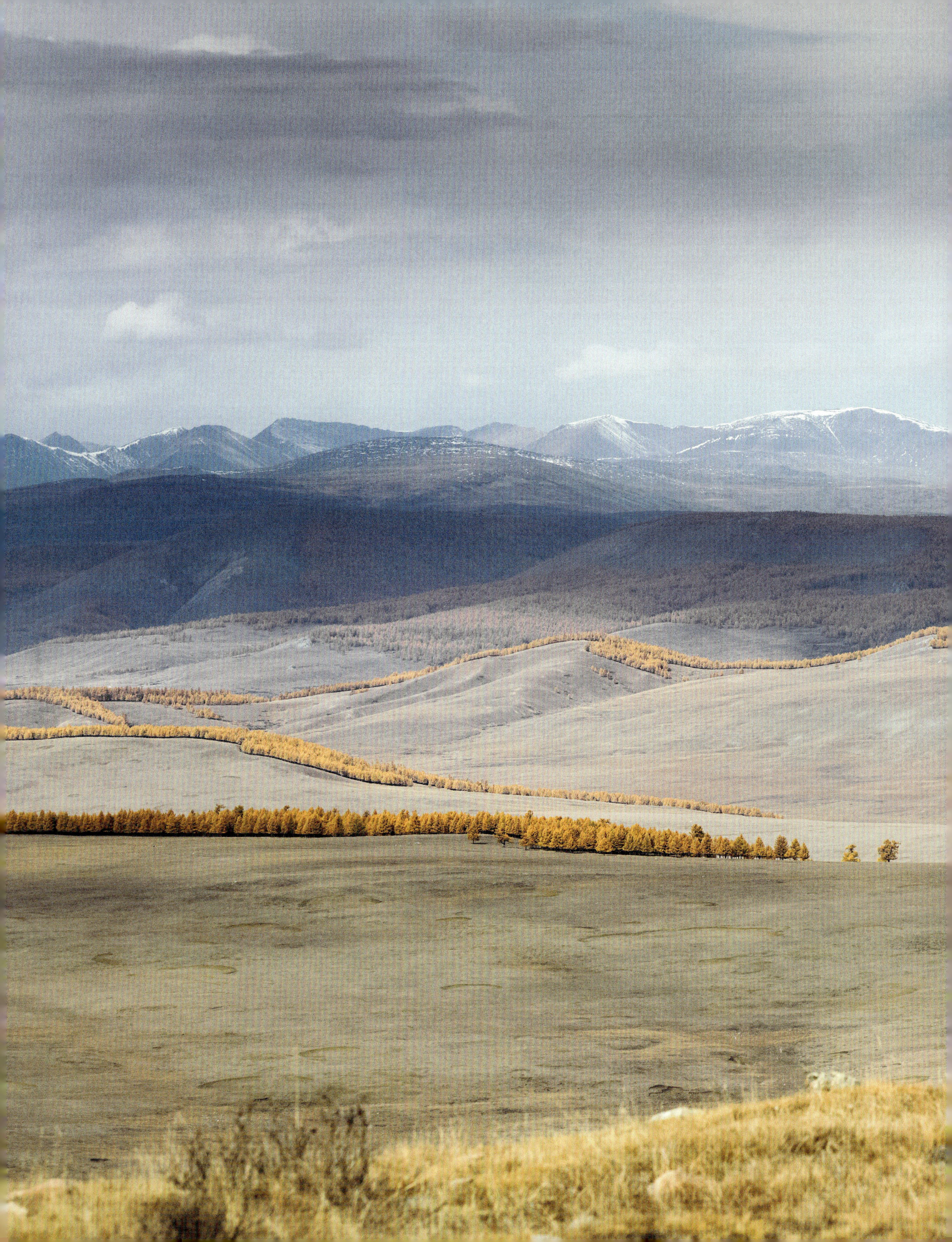

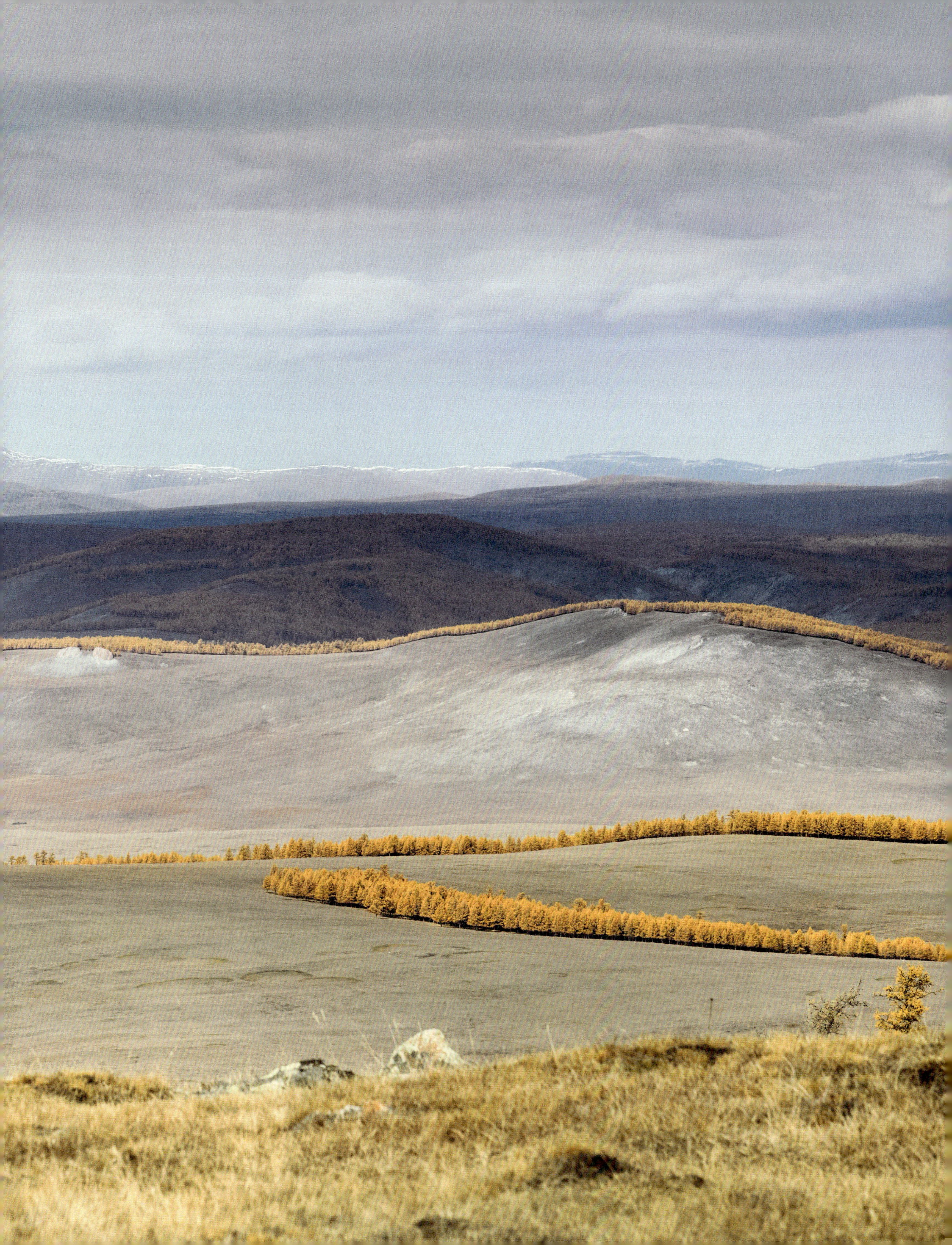

THE REINDEER HERDER

DARKHAD VALLEY, MONGOLIA

After growing up in the USA and studying in China, Zaya took the decision to return to her native Mongolia. There she met a Tsaatan reindeer herder and embraced a new nomadic way of life with him and his herd in the taiga.

"When I arrived here in the valley in 2006, I was transported back in time – to a period when people still lived in tepees. I didn't even know that reindeer really existed, let alone that people herded them. I was a city girl. I just couldn't believe my eyes." From the age of six to sixteen, Zaya was your typical American schoolgirl, growing up in the city of Boulder in Colorado. From a young age, she felt drawn to nature and the sounds and smells of the natural world, but never did she imagine that one day she would embrace it so completely. At sixteen, Zaya received a grant to study international relations in Shanghai in China. Four years later, her qualification complete, she started looking for a job which would allow her to spend time in the great outdoors, and even return to her home country of Mongolia, which, aside from the capital Ulaanbaatar, she barely knew.

"I felt drawn to the steppe grasslands and vast open spaces. I wanted to explore the natural world of my home country. And thanks to a job with an NGO, I got my wish."

Zaya returned to the country of her birth – this time to the heart of the taiga and the vast swampy forests of the Darkhad Valley. Located in the north of Mongolia, this dead-end valley lies sandwiched between the Russian border, the Sayan Mountains and the stunning Lake Khövsgöl – the little brother to its crystal-clear neighbour Lake Baikal. Zaya spent two years in this remote region working for a foreign NGO helping to protect the nomadic Tsaatan tribe. For a girl who had only ever known city life, it was a truly eye-opening experience.

When the programme finished, Zaya did not leave. By then, she had already met Ultsan, her future husband. She moved into his tepee and together they started tending a herd of reindeer in the taiga, much to the surprise of locals, who thought she must be mad to make such a decision. But little by little, Zaya got used to the rigours of life outdoors, where nature rules supreme. Over the years she has become part and parcel of this small nomadic community and they, in turn, have welcomed her with open arms.

"There's no postal service and we only got mobile phone reception in 2009. When I first arrived with my mobile phone, the people here had never seen one before. That seems incredible in the 21st century. But here in the extreme north of Mongolia, change comes very slowly because we're so isolated. And yet despite this, I knew almost immediately that there was nowhere else I'd rather live."

"You have to get used to certain things living out here, not least living in a tepee. It's really hard at first because the wind whips all around and the winters are long. For seven months of the year, temperatures can fall to below -50°C. You're outside all the time tending the reindeer. Snow gets in your boots and your feet feel like blocks of ice. But the warmth of the people around you makes up for it. People talk more when there's no internet. Here, people respect their elders as a source of knowledge and as a role model."

Time flies by at the camp, which is home to up to 130 people in summer, including around 30 children. There is simply no time to get bored. The seasons roll on: babies are born, the reindeer are prepared for winter, the herd put out to graze, or their antlers cut to stop them being injured when they attempt to rut. "Your perception of time is different here in the taiga. Here, there is always something to do, so the days pass much quicker than in the city," Zaya explains.

As summer draws to a close, the pace of life slows slightly ahead of the arrival of winter. At this time of year, the larch trees are resplendent in shades of gold and crimson and the first dusting of snow can be seen on the surrounding summits. Inside the

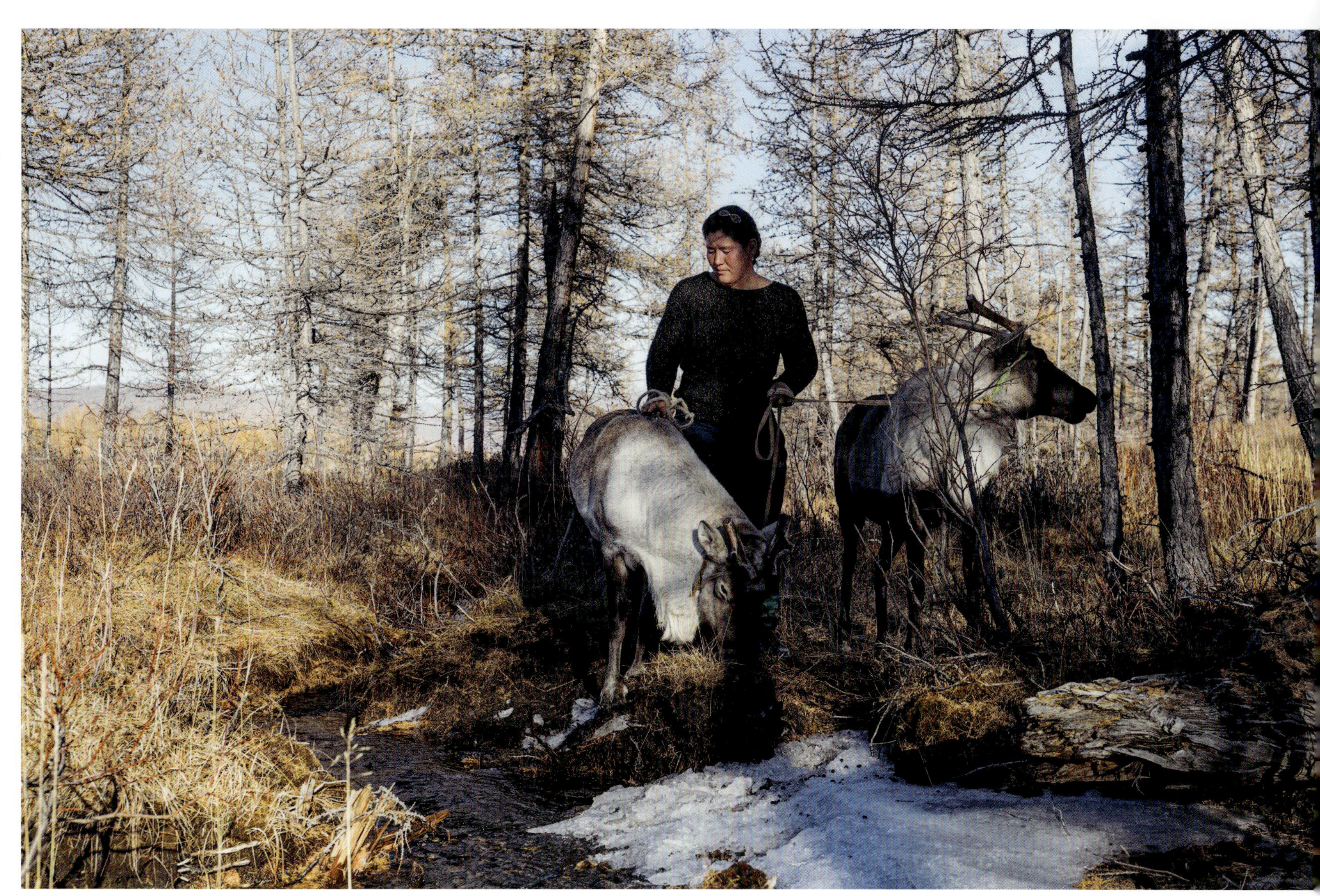

forest, every sound is muffled, as if absorbed by the lichen and wild bilberry bushes – the silence broken only by the frequent barking of the dogs from the camp.

As you walk through the taiga's thick boggy forest, you'll occasionally spot the remains of an old camp. Left alone, nature is slowly reclaiming the old tepee supports but Zaya and her community will return, once the lichen, so vital for preparing the reindeer for winter, has had enough time to grow back. "Reindeer herding is a form of subsistence farming. The reindeer essentially provide us with a source of milk. We only eat their meat when they are old and their teeth are starting to fall out, which means they will soon die of hunger. The reindeer also help us carry all our possessions, our tepee canvases and our wood-fired stove when we move camp."

The reindeer are semi-wild, which means at night they are tethered close to the camp to prevent them from escaping or being attacked by the many wolves that roam the region – a source of fear for all. The Tsaatans source their food from the village of Tsagaannuur and rely on foraging. Until 2011, they also hunted in the mountains but hunting was banned when the area was designated as a nature reserve, a decision that has created significant challenges for the community and their daily lives. As the community goes about their day-to-day tasks in the mild autumn air, you see that this is life at its most simple. The toilets? A tree trunk with two planks marked with an axe to help you locate it in the forest. The bath? A small metal bowl shared between neighbours, which you bend over and wash yourself in using river water heated over the fire. "We use wood-fired stoves for heating and for cooking, but we also have a small solar panel connected to a car battery which we use to power a light in the evening." It is a rare concession to the modern world in their simple, and often fragmented, nomadic lifestyle, which sees them moving camp five or six times every year.

When asked about city life, Zaya says that she has no plans to return. "I'm not a city person anymore, but I go back to visit my parents in Ulaanbaatar for the festive season at the end of each year. My husband finds it hard to cope with the pollution and noise in the city. It makes him cough. But I find it easier. It must be in my genes!" The journey to Mongolia's capital city (home to half of the country's three million inhabitants) is certainly an expedition, requiring no less than three days' travel by horse, motorbike, 4x4 and finally a bus.

The recent arrival of their baby son, Temuulen, will naturally open up questions about his education. Like the other children from the camp, he will probably board in the village of Tsagaannuur and spend weekends and holidays with his parents back at the camp. Right now, Zaya is clearly relishing her life as a nomadic reindeer herder, working alongside her husband and brother-in-law, who also helps manage the herd. Their first few reindeer have now expanded to a healthy herd of forty.

"I'm just so happy to be here in the taiga with my reindeer, my dogs and my horses. No money in the world could buy me this. We only have one life and for me it's so important to trust your instincts... I don't dismiss or regret my past life. But I'm so happy to be where I am today."

DIE RENTIERZÜCHTERIN

DARKHAD-TAL, MONGOLEI

Nach einer Kindheit in den USA und einem Studium in China kehrt Zaya in ihr Geburtsland, die Mongolei, zurück. Dort lernt sie einen Tsaatan-Rentierzüchter kennen und übernimmt seine Art zu leben, im Rhythmus der Herdenwanderungen durch die Taiga.

„Als ich 2006 in diesem Tal ankam, fühlte ich mich, als wäre ich plötzlich in eine andere Zeit versetzt worden – eine Epoche, in der die Menschen noch in Tipis lebten. Ich wusste nicht, dass Rentiere wirklich existieren, und erst recht nicht, dass man sie züchten kann. Als jemand, der aus der Stadt kam, traute ich meinen Augen nicht.“

In Boulder, Colorado, wo die sechs- bis sechzehnjährige Zaya aufwächst, ist sie eine junge Amerikanerin wie jede andere. Sie liebt zwar die Natur mit ihren Düften und Geräuschen, kann sich aber nicht im Entferntesten vorstellen, sich eines Tages mit Leib und Seele hineinzustürzen. Mit sechzehn erhält sie ein China-Stipendium, um in Shanghai Internationale Beziehungen zu studieren. Vier Jahre später hat Zaya ihr Diplom in der Tasche und sucht eine Arbeit, bei der sie Zeit im Freien verbringen und in die Mongolei zurückkehren kann, von der sie als Kind nur Ulan-Bator gesehen hat.

„Die Steppe und die großen Weiten lockten mich sehr; ich hatte Lust, die Natur meines Landes zu entdecken. Dank einer NGO fand ich schließlich, was ich suchte.“

So kehrt die junge Frau in ihr Geburtsland zurück, diesmal allerdings in die schöne Welt der Taiga mit den großen Sumpfwäldern des Darkhad-Tals. Dieses Sackgassental im Norden der Mongolei liegt zwischen der russischen Grenze, dem Sajan-Gebirge und dem prächtigen Khuvsgul-See, der mit seinem klaren Wasser wie der kleine Bruder des benachbarten Baikalsees wirkt. In dieser abgelegenen Region arbeitet Zaya zwei Jahre lang für eine ausländische Organisation, die das Nomadenvolk der Tsaa-

tan schützen möchte – eine echte Entdeckung für sie, die immer in einem urbanen Umfeld gelebt hatte.

Als das Programm endet, reist Zaya nicht wieder ab. Sie hat Ultsan kennengelernt, ihren zukünftigen Ehemann, zieht in seinem Tipi ein und hütet mit ihm eine Rentierherde in der Taiga – zur großen Überraschung der Mongolen, die fest davon überzeugt sind, sie müsse verhext worden sein. Nach und nach gewöhnt sich Zaya an das raue Leben im Freien, bei dem jeder Moment von der Natur diktiert wird, und wird im Lauf der Jahre ein vollwertiges Mitglied der kleinen Nomadengemeinschaft, die sie warmherzig aufnimmt.

„Es gibt keine Post; Mobiltelefone erst seit 2009. Als ich mit meinem Handy hier ankam, hatten die Leute so etwas noch nie gesehen. Das kommt einem im 21. Jahrhundert unglaublich vor. Im hohen Norden der Mongolei passiert alles sehr langsam, weil wir so isoliert sind. Trotzdem habe ich mich schon bald gefragt: Kann es einen besseren Ort zum Leben geben?“

„Man muss sich an vieles gewöhnen, und sei es nur an das Leben im Zelt. Am Anfang ist das sehr schwer, weil der Wind hineinfegt und die Winter lang sind. Sie dauern sieben Monate, und die Temperaturen können unter -50 °C fallen. Mit den Rentieren ist man die ganze Zeit draußen. Irgendwann dringt der Schnee in die Stiefel und lässt die Füße gefrieren. Aber die Wärme der menschlichen Beziehungen gleicht das wieder aus. Die Menschen reden mehr miteinander, wenn es kein WLAN gibt … Hier respektiert man die Älteren; sie bewahren das Wissen und kennen die richtige Art, sich zu verhalten.“

Im Lager, wo im Sommer bis zu 130 Menschen leben, darunter etwa 30 Kinder, vergeht die Zeit im Nu – es gibt keine Langeweile. Die Jahreszeiten wechseln, Kinder kommen auf die Welt, die Rentiere müssen auf den Winter vorbereitet oder auf die Weide getrieben werden, man muss ihre Geweihe kürzen, damit sie sich beim Kämpfen nicht verletzen … „Die Zeitwahrnehmung ist in der Taiga anders; man ist ständig beschäftigt und die Tage vergehen viel schneller als in der Stadt", erklärt Zaya.

Gegen Ende des Sommers, wenn sich der Rhythmus ein wenig verlangsamt, bevor der Winter einsetzt, wechseln die Lärchen zu Gold- und Purpurtönen, und auf den nahen Gipfeln fällt der erste Schnee. Im Wald klingen alle Geräusche gedämpft, als würden sie von den Flechten und wilden Heidelbeerbüschen verschluckt. Dieses Schweigen wird regelmäßig vom Gebell der Hunde im Lager durchbrochen.

Manchmal stößt man in den dichten Sumpfwäldern der Taiga auf die Spuren eines ehemaligen Lagers: Reste von Tipis, die nach und nach von der Natur verschluckt werden. Bis Zayas Gemeinschaft sich wieder hier einrichtet, werden die Flechten, die für die Rentiere im Winter sehr wichtig sind, nachgewachsen sein.

„Die Rentierhaltung ist eine Subsistenzwirtschaft, die uns vor allem Milch liefert, manchmal auch Käse. Das Fleisch essen wir nur sehr selten, wenn die Rentiere schon alt sind und ihnen die Zähne ausfallen, wodurch sie zum Hungertod verurteilt wären. Außerdem helfen uns die Rentiere, unsere Sachen zu transportieren, wenn wir den Lagerplatz wechseln – die Zeltplanen und den Holzofen."

Die halbwilden Rentiere werden jeden Abend in der Nähe des Lagers angebunden. Anderenfalls könnten sie ausreißen oder Wolfsangriffen zum Opfer fallen, die in dieser Gegend sehr häufig sind und von allen gefürchtet werden. Ihre Nahrung kaufen die Tsaatan im Dorf Tsagaannuur ein oder sammeln sie in der Wildnis. Bis 2011 jagten sie in den Bergen, aber seit diese zum Naturschutzgebiet erklärt wurden, ist die Jagd verboten, was den Alltag der Gemeinschaft deutlich komplizierter macht. Momentan findet die Alltagsarbeit in der milden Herbstluft statt.

Ein häusliches Leben, das sich aufs Einfachste beschränkt. Die Toiletten? Ein Baumstamm und zwei Planken im Wald, mit einem Axthieb markiert. Das Badezimmer? Eine kleine, mit den Nachbarn geteilte Metallwanne, in die man sich hockt, um sich mit auf dem Feuer erwärmtem Flusswasser abzuspülen. „Zum Heizen und Kochen benutzen wir Holzöfen, aber wir haben auch eine kleine, an eine Autobatterie angeschlossene Solarzelle, die am Abend eine Lampe speist." Eine der wenigen Zugeständnisse an die Moderne in der ländlichen Routine, die fünf bis sechs Mal im Jahr durch die notwendigen Ortswechsel des Nomadenlebens unterbrochen wird.

Auf die Stadt angesprochen, erklärt Zaya, dass sie nicht dorthin zurückkehren wird. „Ich bin keine Städterin mehr, aber an den Festtagen zum Jahreswechsel besuche ich meine Eltern in Ulan-Bator. Die Umweltverschmutzung und der Lärm in der Stadt sind für meinen Mann schwer erträglich; er fängt dort an zu husten. Für mich ist es einfacher, das sind wohl meine Gene!" Um in die Hauptstadt zu gelangen, muss man eine wahre Expedition unternehmen: Drei Tage dauert die Reise per Pferd, Motorrad, Geländewagen und zuletzt im Bus nach Ulan-Bator, wo die Hälfte der drei Millionen Landesbewohner lebt.

Seit vor kurzem ihr Sohn Temuulen geboren wurde, müssen die beiden an eine Schule denken. Wie die anderen Kinder aus dem Lager wird er vermutlich eine Pensionsschule im Dorf Tsagaannuur besuchen und seine Eltern nur am Wochenende und in den Ferien sehen. Inzwischen sind die anfangs wenigen Rentiere auf eine gesunde Herde von vierzig Tieren angewachsen, und Zaya blüht in ihrer Rolle als nomadische Viehzüchterin auf, mit ihrem Mann und ihrem Schwager, die sich ebenfalls um die Herde kümmern.

„Es ist ein unglaubliches Glück, in der Taiga zu sein, mit meinen Rentieren, meinen Hunden, meinen Pferden. Das lässt sich mit keinem Geld der Welt erkaufen. Wir haben nur ein einziges Leben, und ich glaube, es ist wichtig, dem eigenen Instinkt zu folgen … Ich lehne mein früheres Leben weder ab noch bereue ich es. Aber ich bin hier und jetzt vollkommen glücklich."

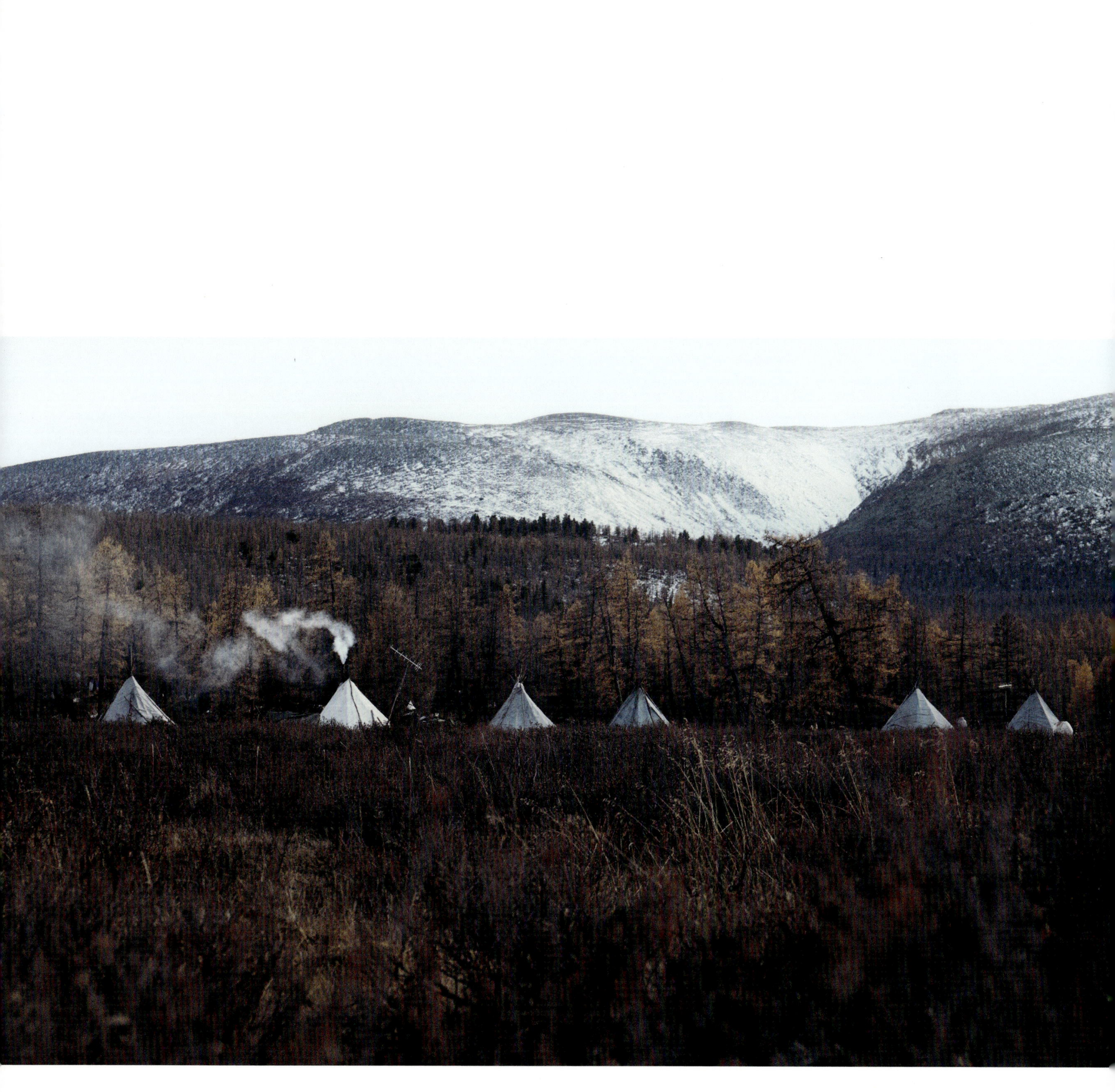

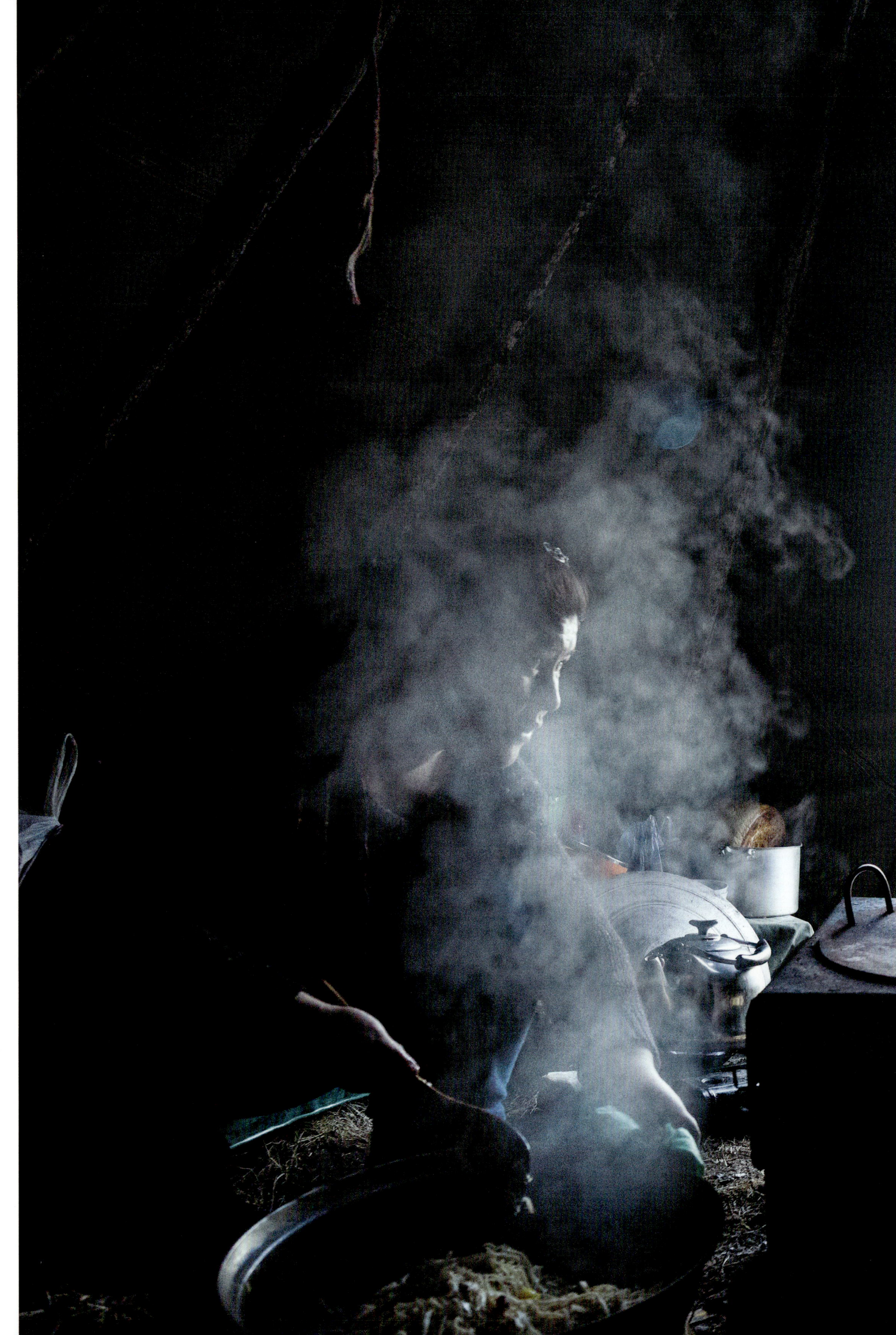

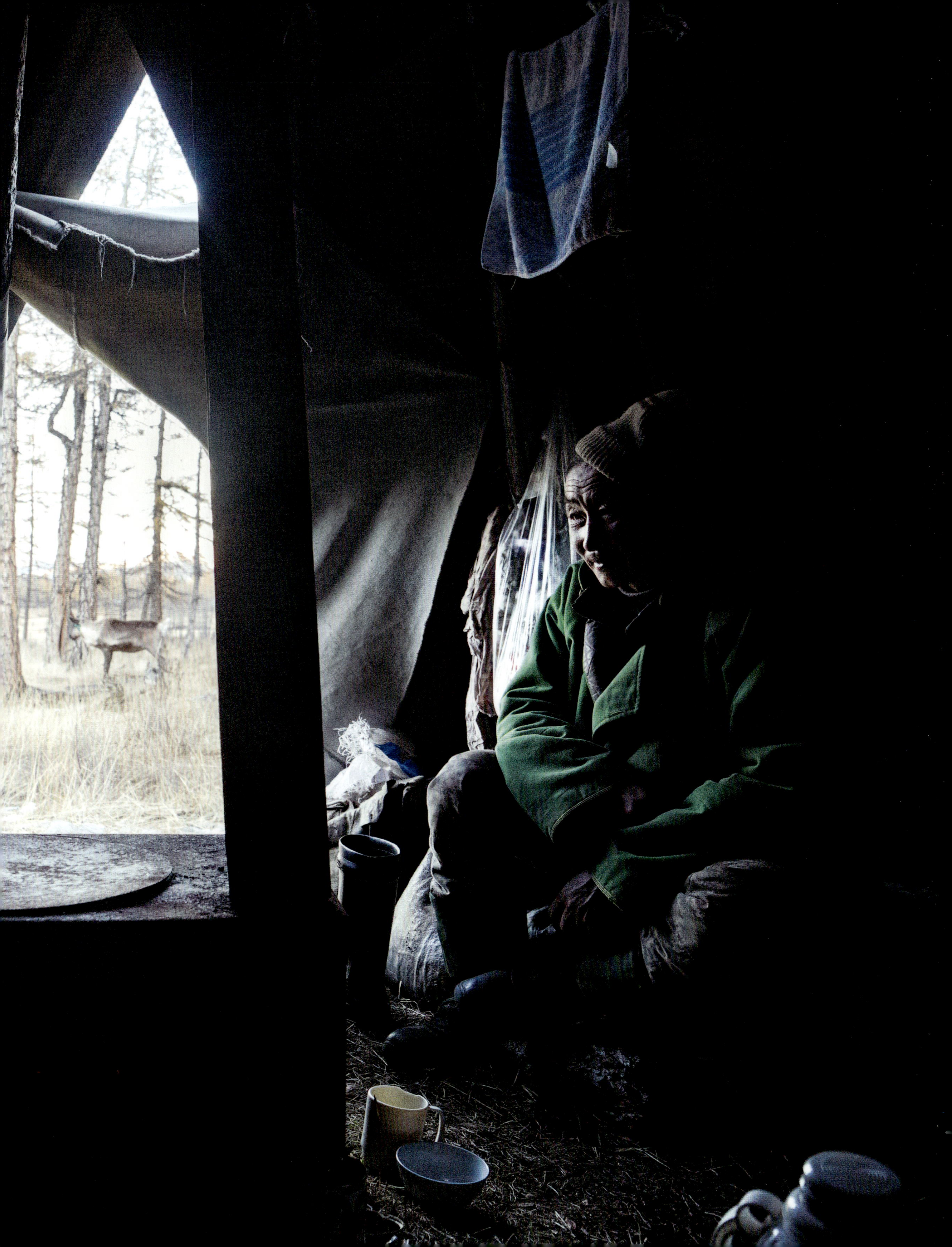

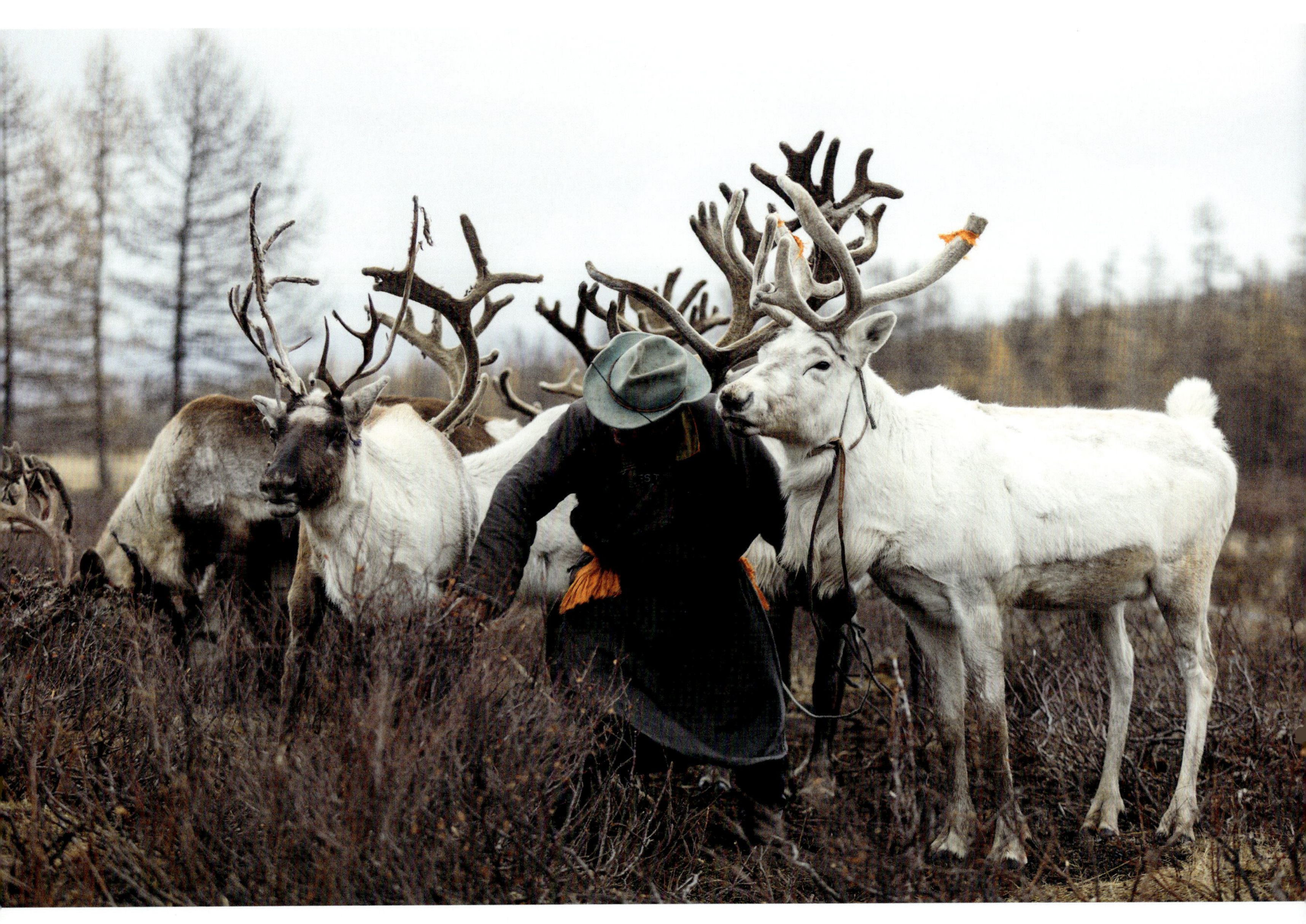

"It is remarkable how easily and insensibly we fall into a particular route, and make a beaten track for ourselves. I had not lived there a week before my feet wore a path from my door to the pond-side; and though it is five or six years since I trod it, it is still quite distinct … The surface of the earth is soft and impressible by the feet of men; and so with the paths which the mind travels. How worn and dusty, then, must be the highways of the world, how deep the ruts of tradition and conformity!"

HENRY DAVID THOREAU
Walden; or, Life in the Woods

„Es ist merkwürdig, wie leicht und unmerklich wir auf eine spezielle Route geraten und daraus eine Routine herstellen. Ich hatte noch keine Woche dort gewohnt, als meine Füße schon zum Teichufer einen Pfad ausgetreten hatten, und obgleich das fünf bis sechs Jahre her ist, ist er immer noch deutlich sichtbar. [...] Die Oberfläche der Erde ist weich und nimmt leicht die menschlichen Fußabdrücke an; ebenso ist es mit den Pfaden, auf denen der Geist wandert. Wie abgenutzt und schmutzig müssen dann die Landstraßen der Welt sein, wie tief die Geleise der Tradition und Konformität!"

HENRY DAVID THOREAU
Walden oder Leben in den Wäldern

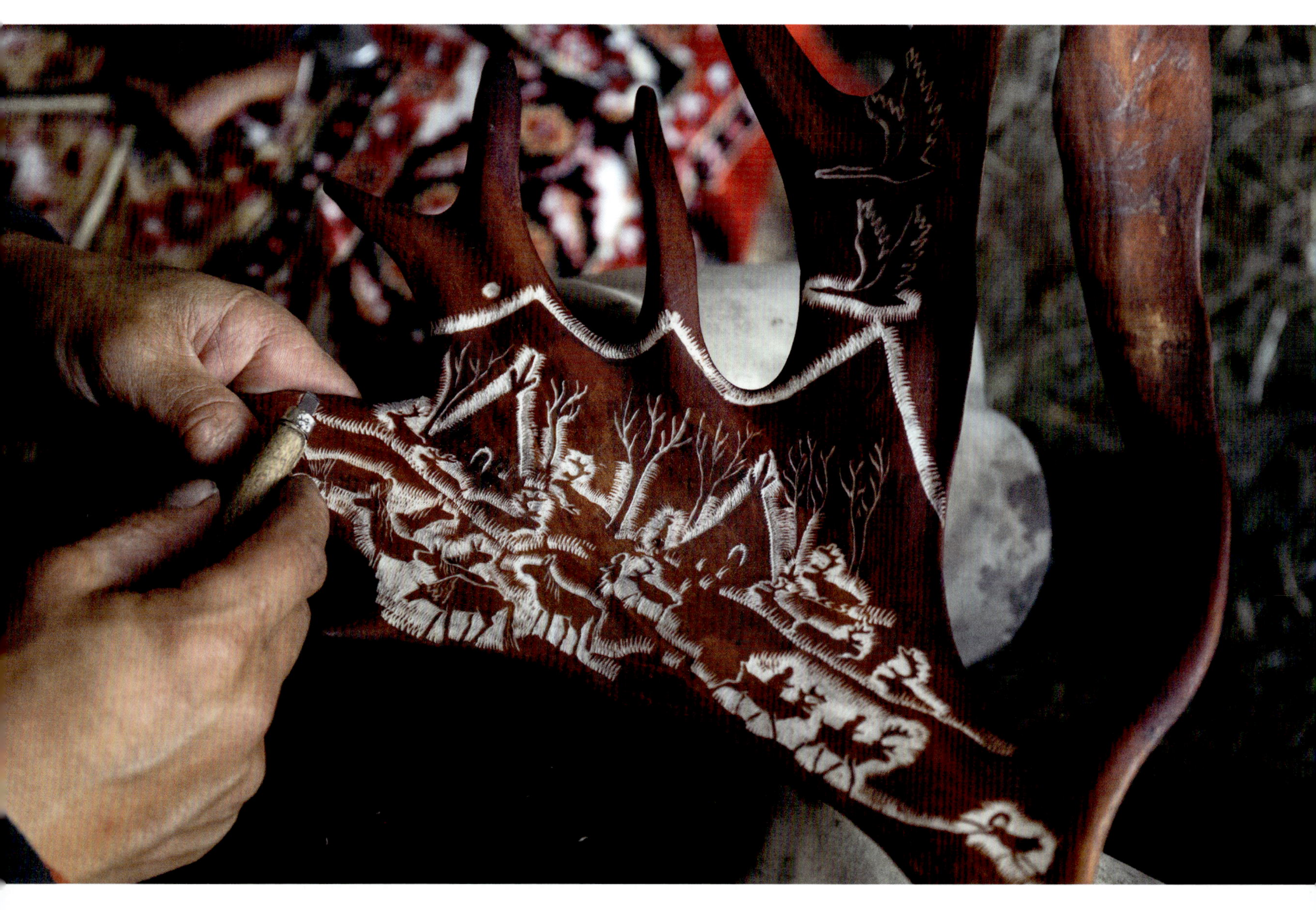

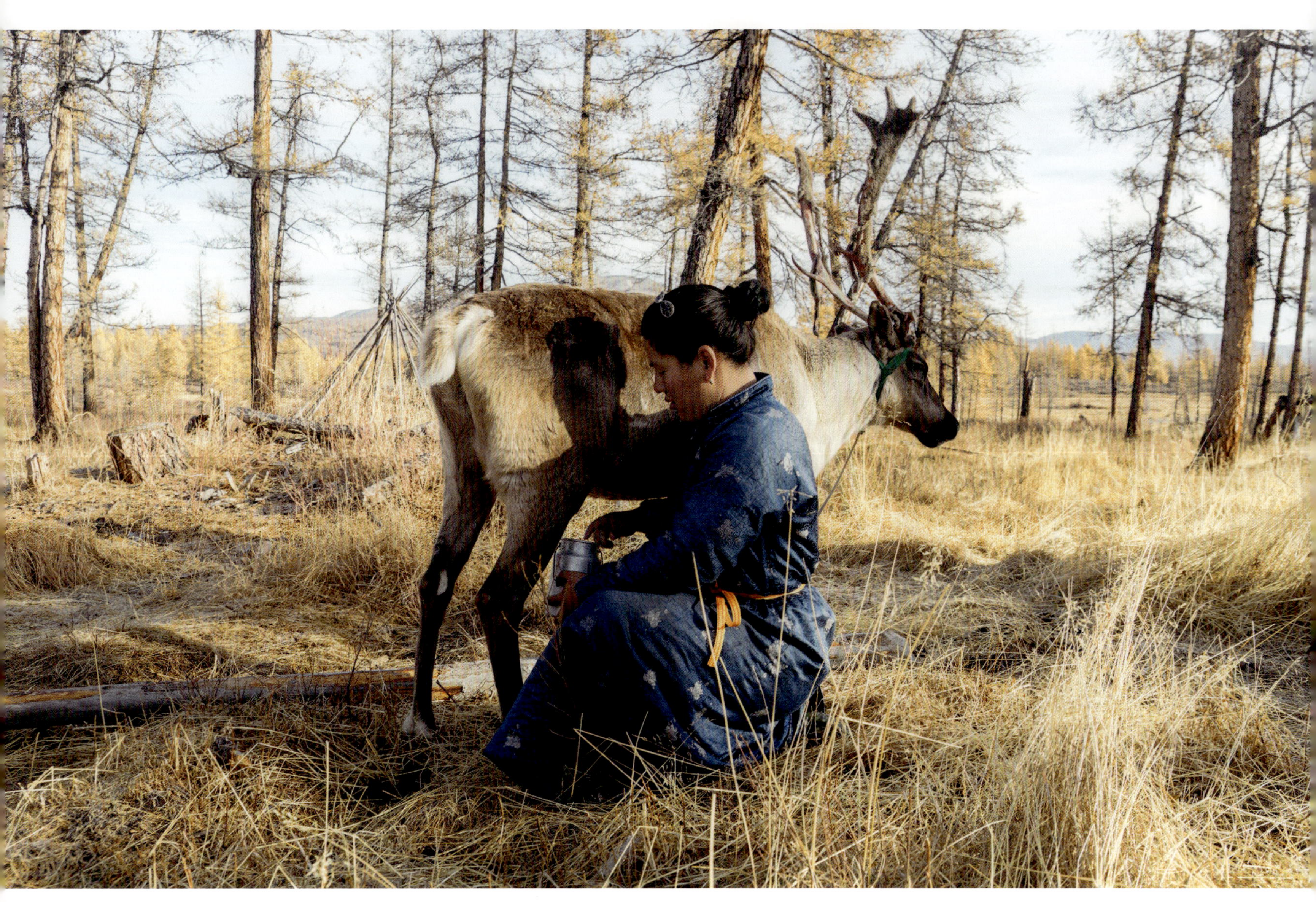

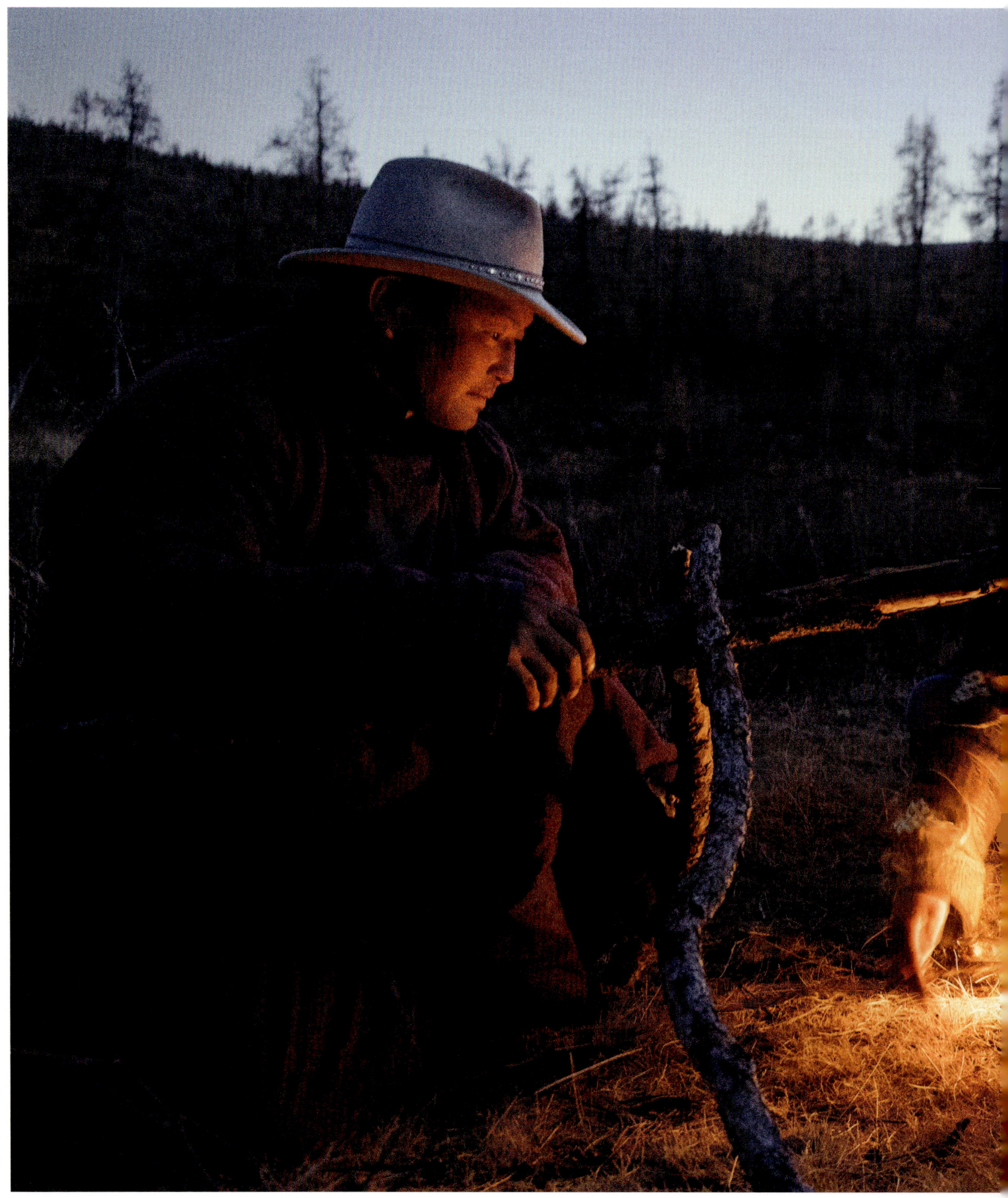

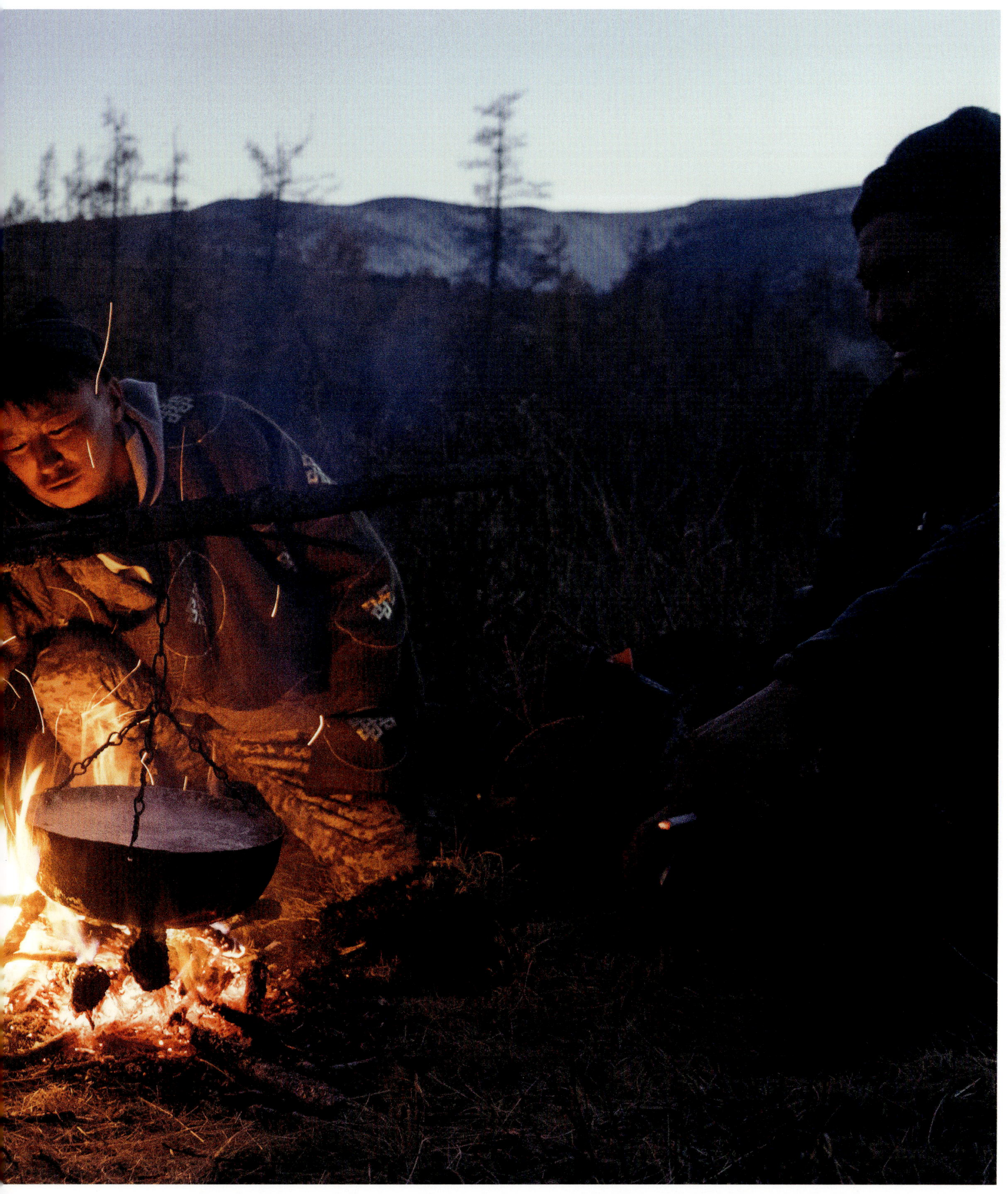

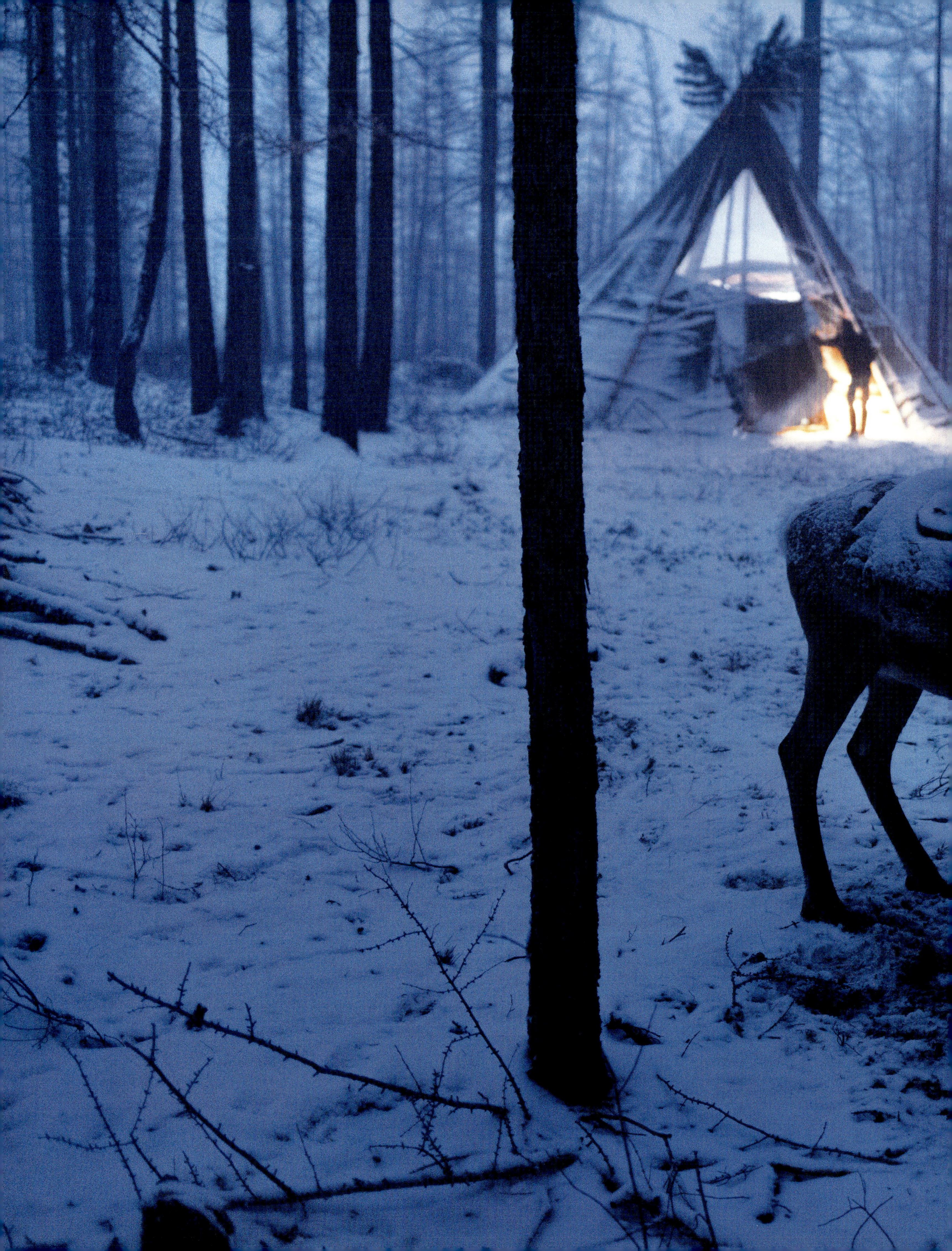

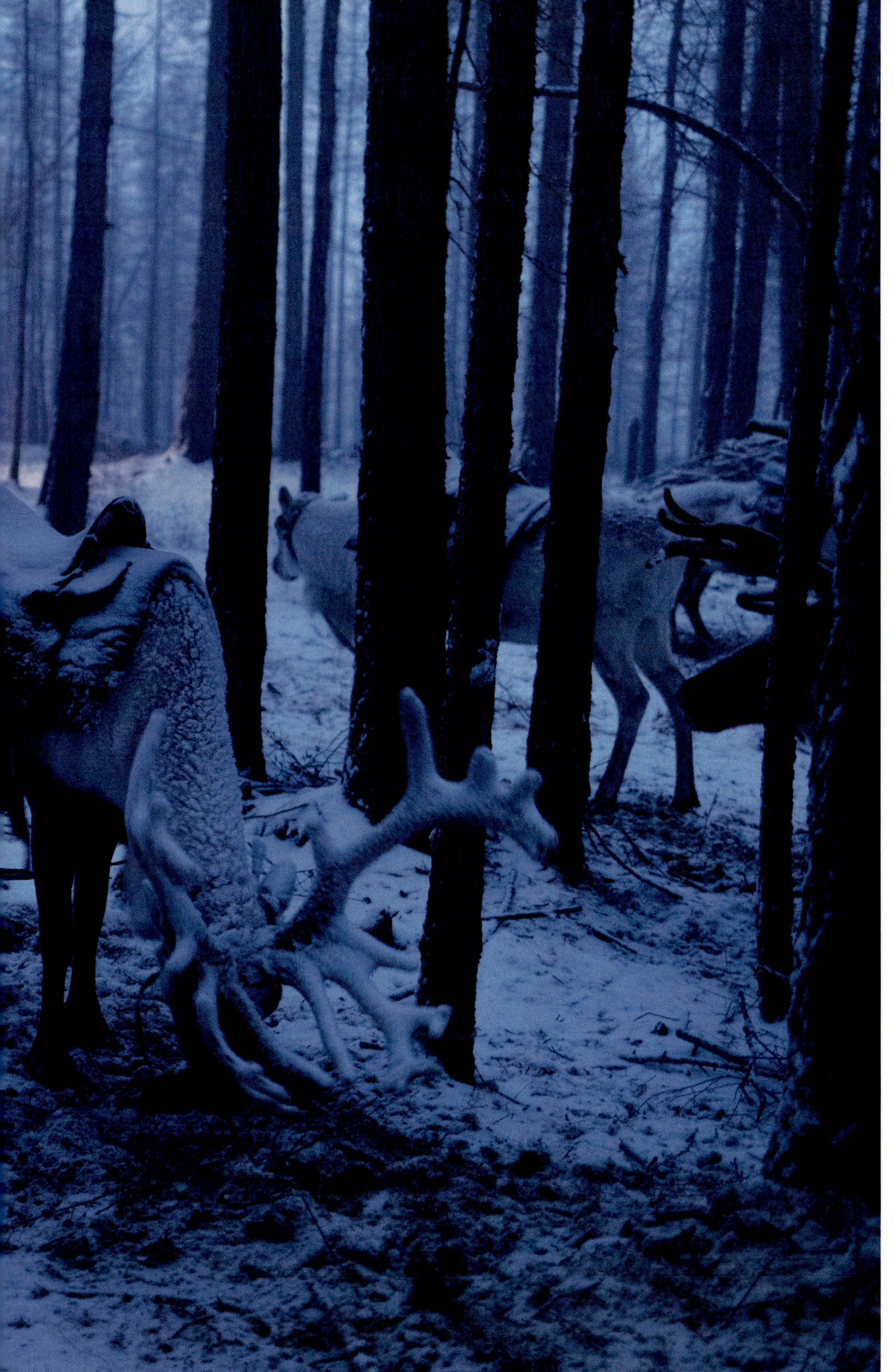

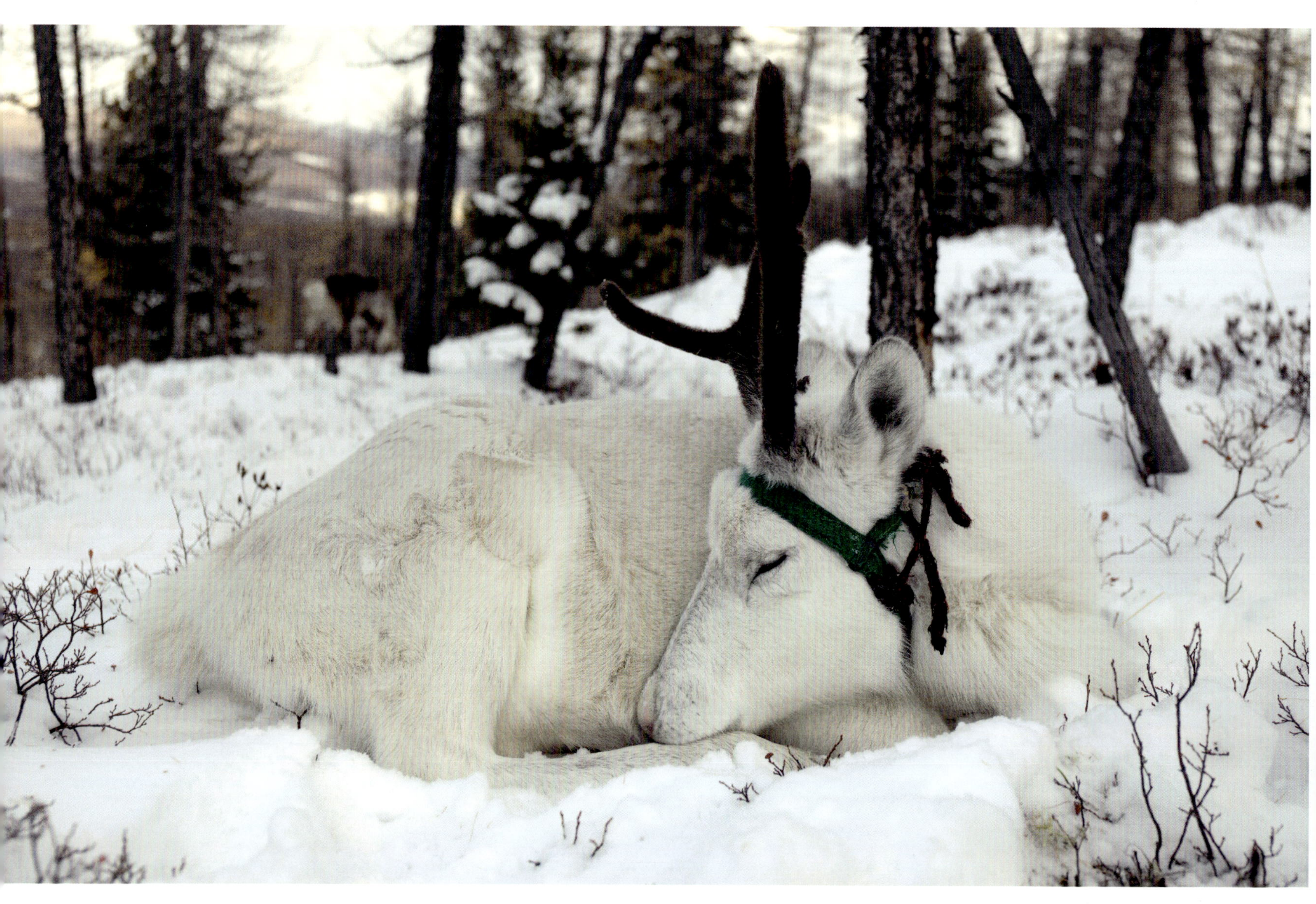

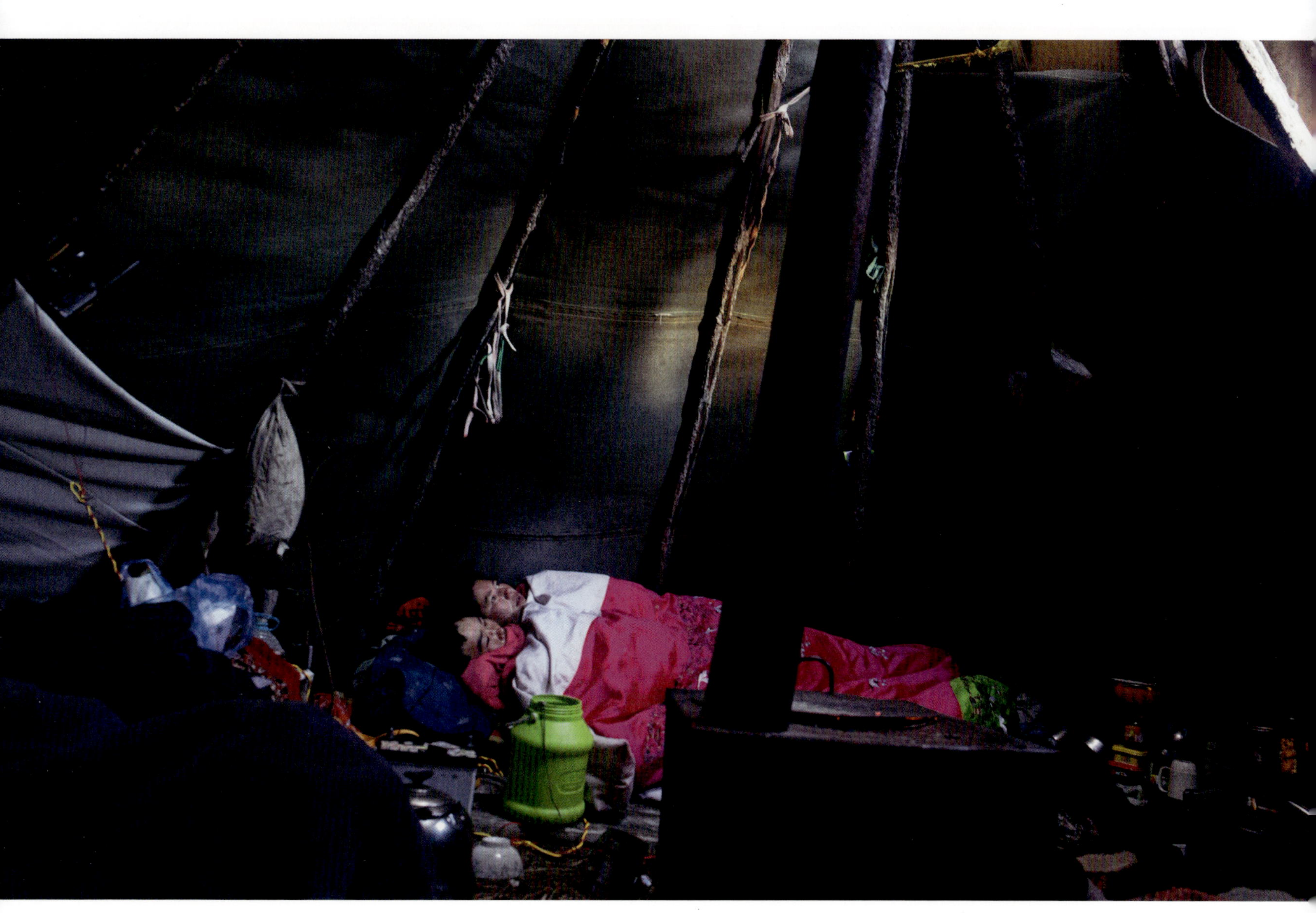

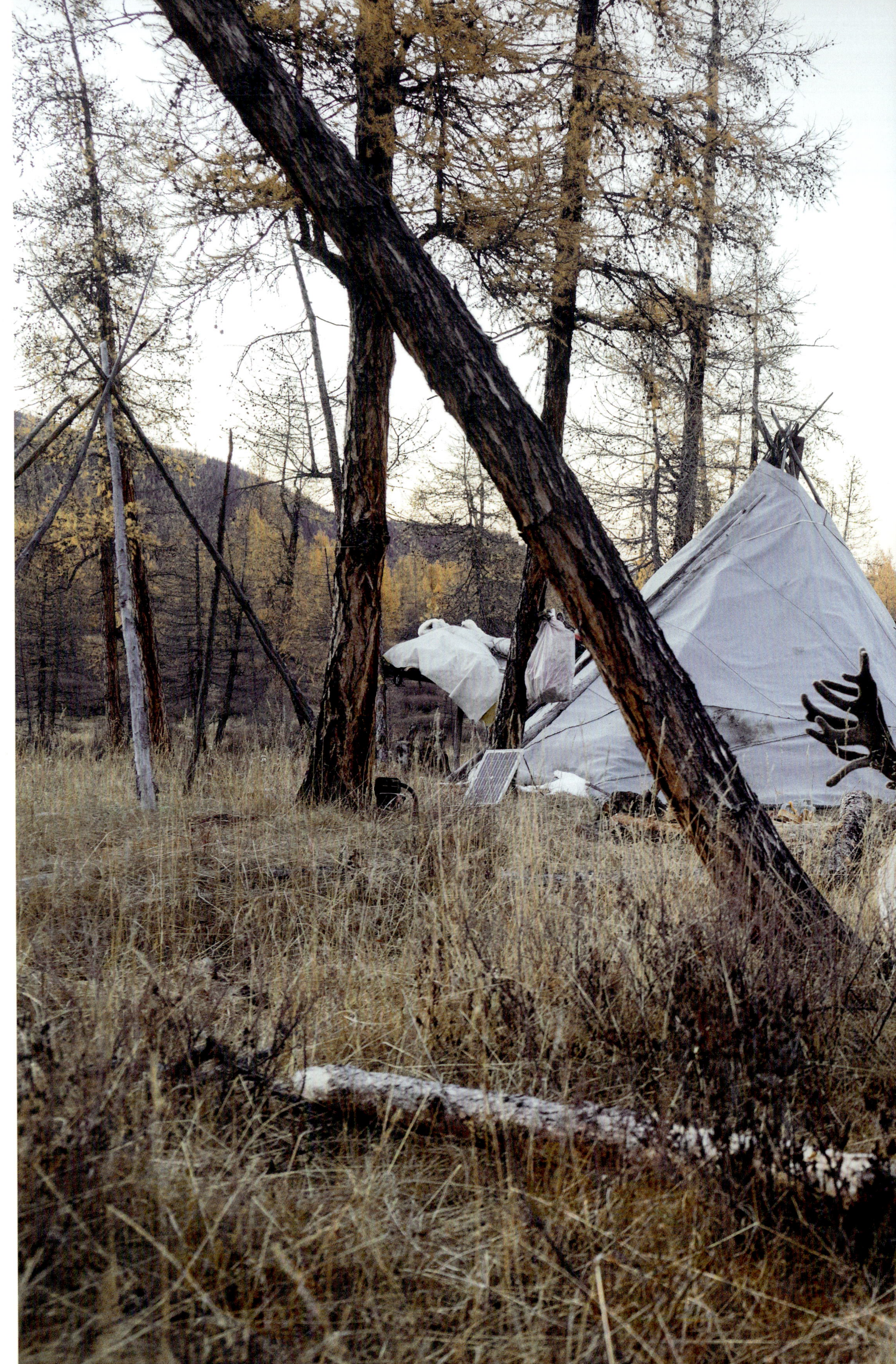

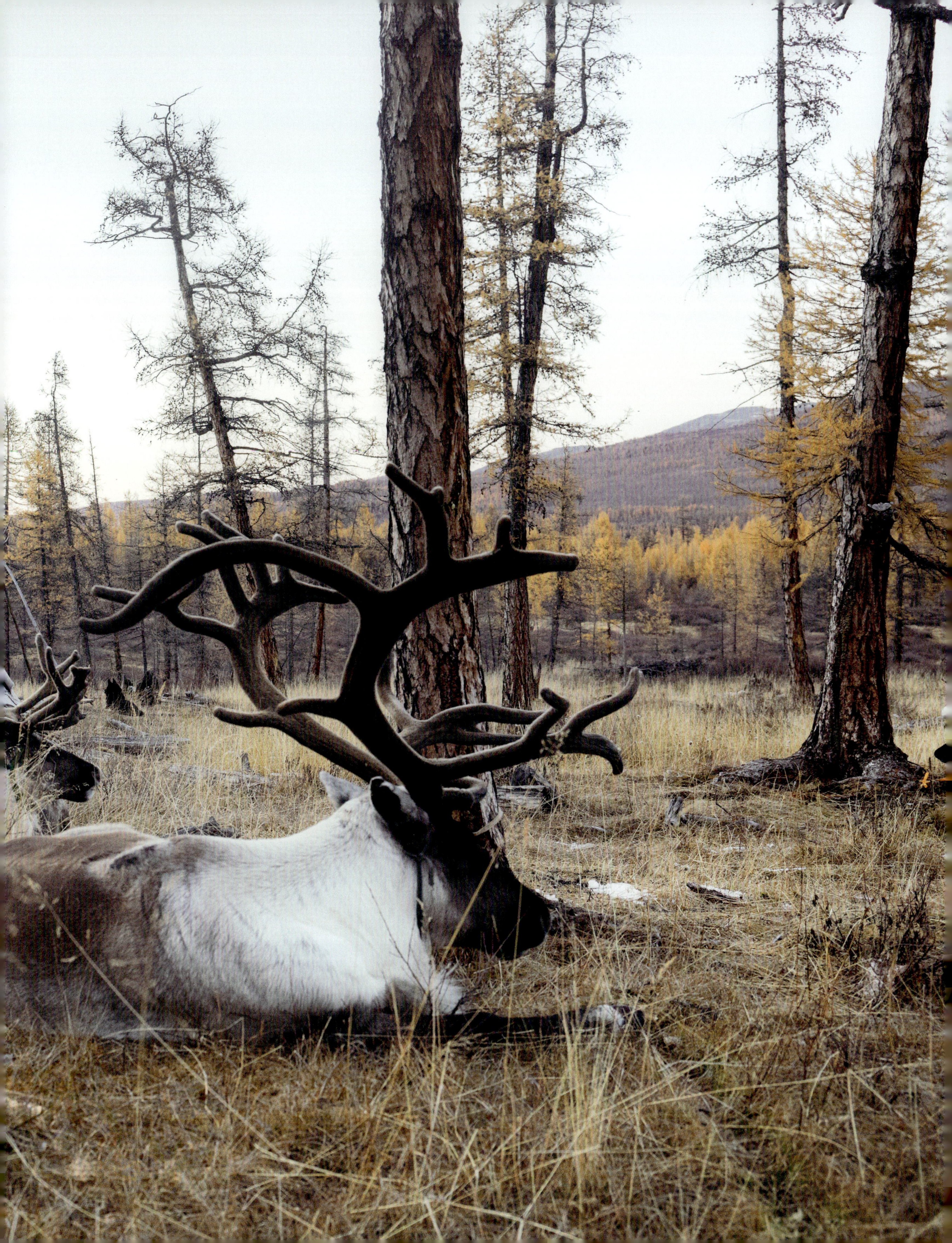

GEORGE

"HERE, THERE IS A SENSE OF
IMMEDIACY TO EVERYTHING
I DO: CHOPPING WOOD,
GROWING VEGETABLES …"

„HIER SPÜRE ICH,
DASS ALLES, WAS ICH TUE,
EINEN UNMITTELBAREN
SINN HAT: HOLZ SCHLAGEN,
GEMÜSE ANBAUEN …"

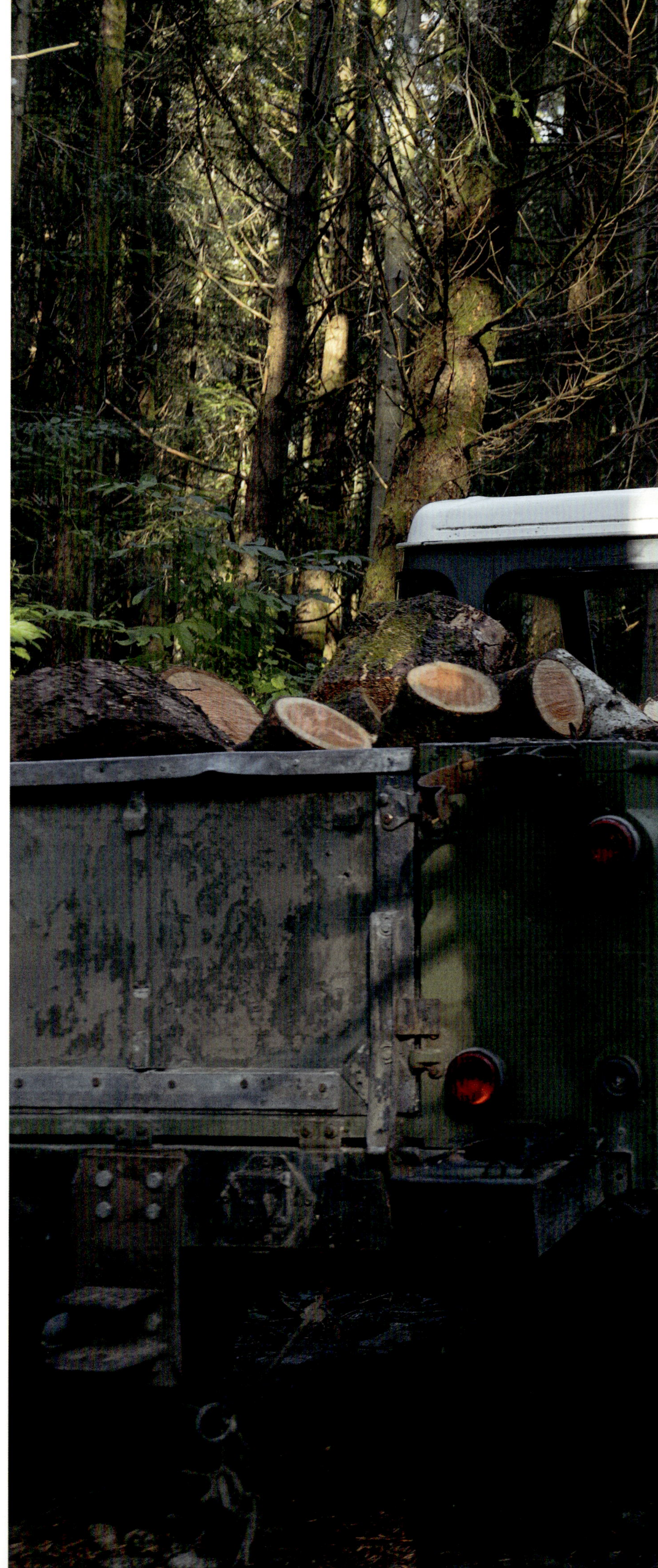

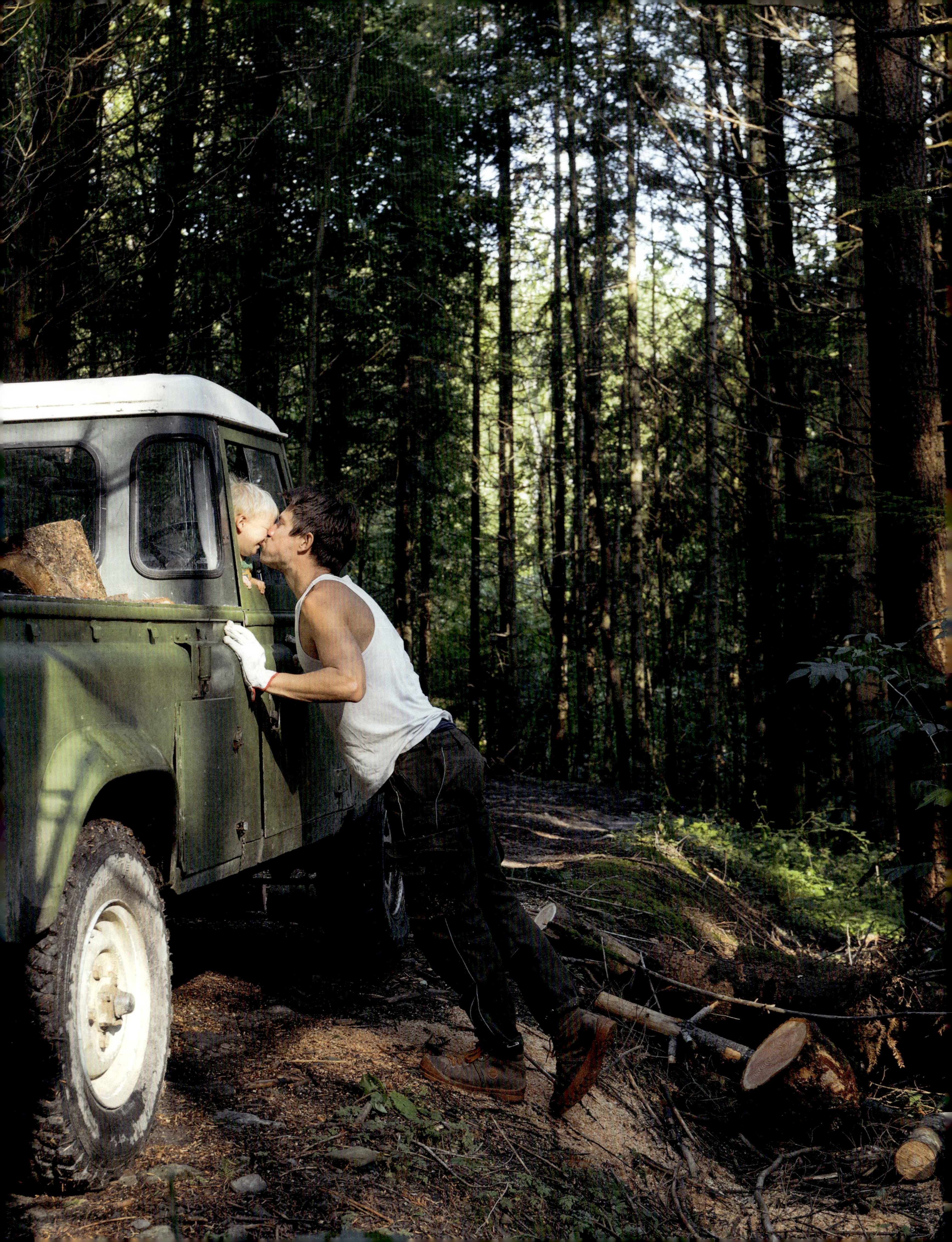

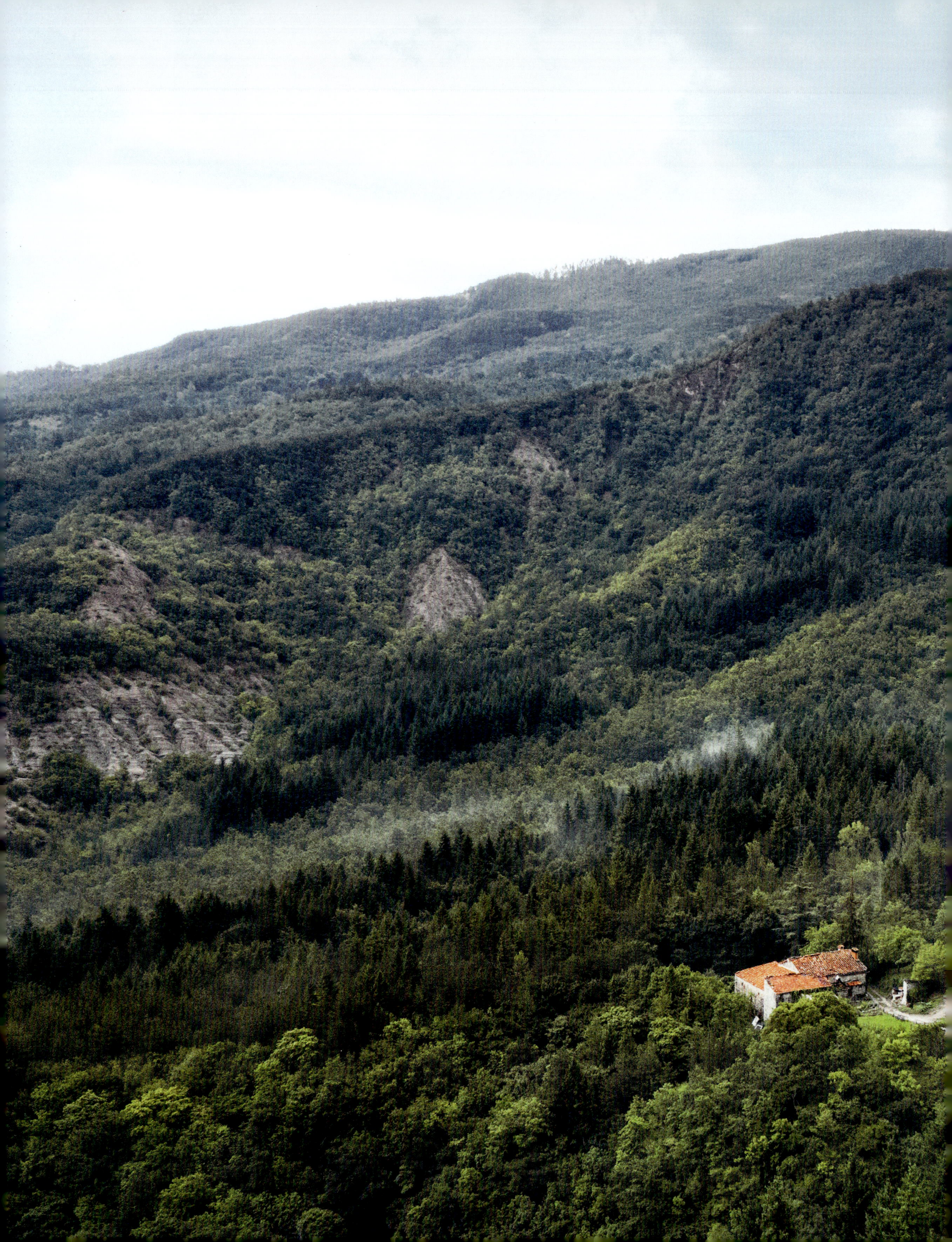

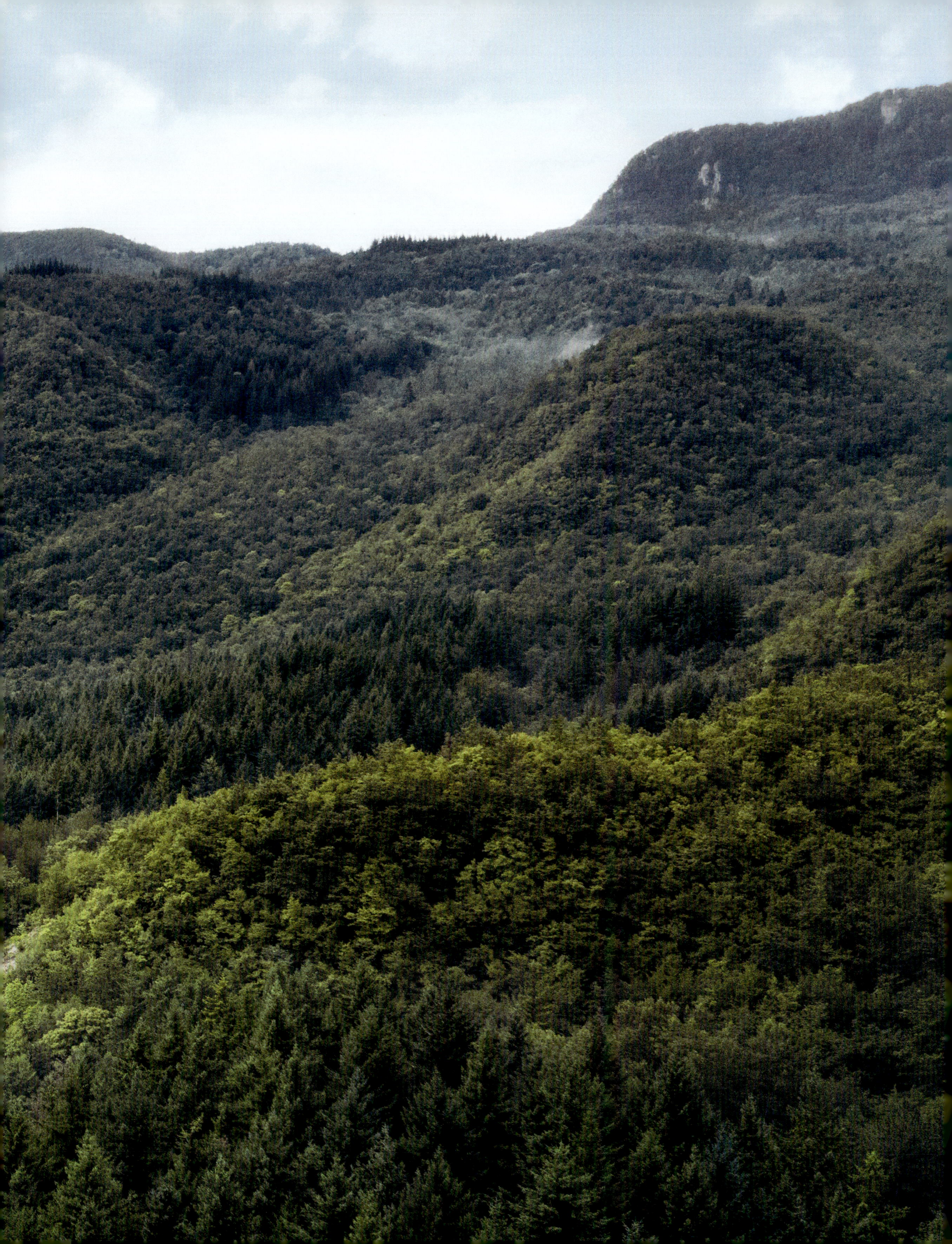

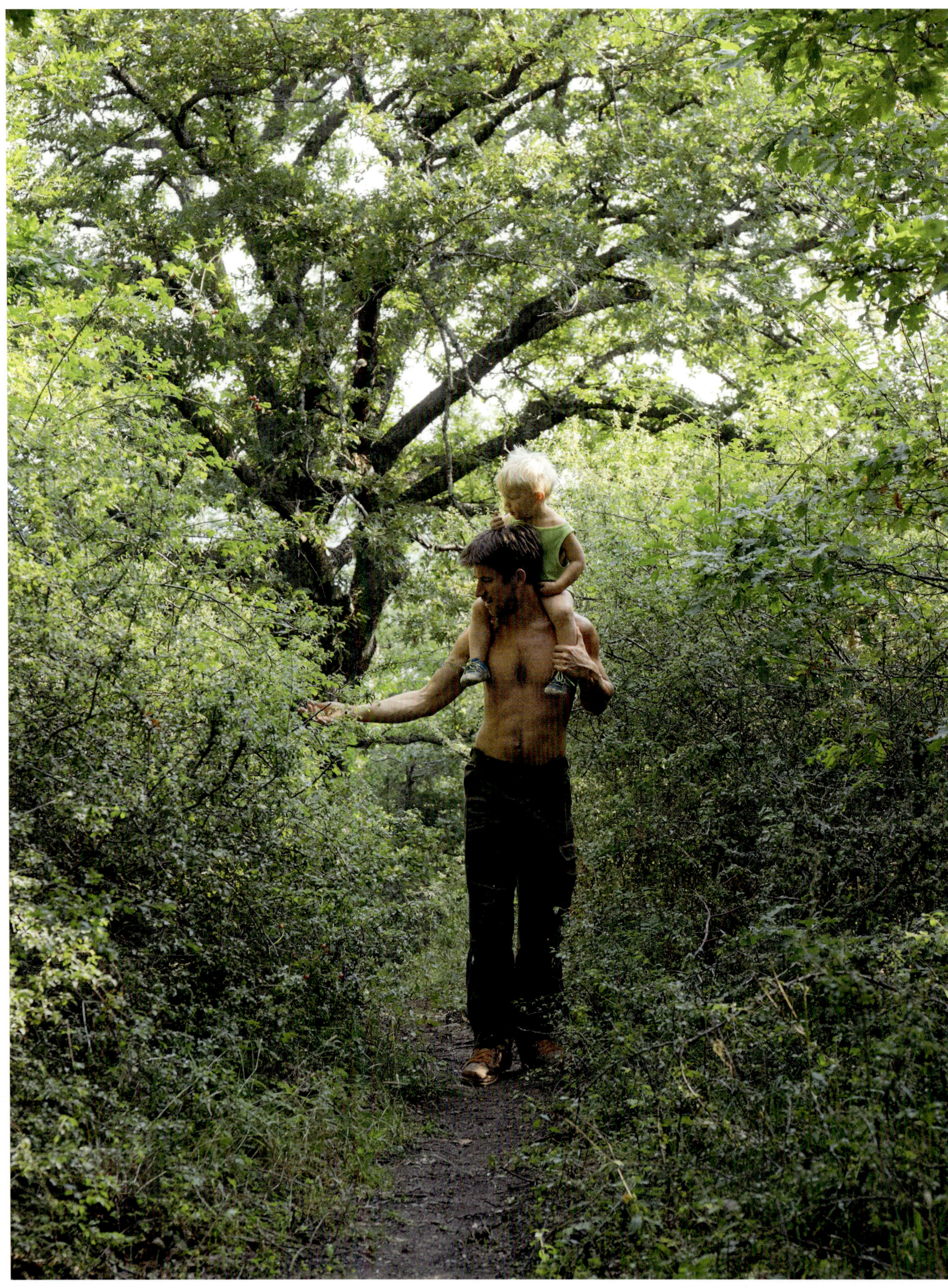

IN THE WILD FORESTS

TUSCANY, ITALY

George left the United Kingdom as soon as he reached adulthood to live on a small farm in disrepair a few hours from Florence. He set to work renovating it over the next few years before starting a family and watching his children grow up in this timeless place.

"As a child, all I wanted was to be surrounded by nature, to be free. School and I never really got on. It felt like a prison, and I dreamed of living completely in the wild. I would dream of being an Indian and living in a tepee. Later, as a teenager, I was a bit of a hippie with an interest in survivalism."

Back then, every time George came to this 17th century Italian farm his father was looking after, he would get a new lease of life. "I have been coming here since I was little. When I was at the farm I felt free. It was a time of not only doing what I wanted but also knowing where things like my food, water and heating were coming from – all the things you take for granted in modern life."

The story goes that wolves, on the brink of extinction, hid out here, in the dense forests of the Apennines, during the 19th century. At the age of eighteen, two years after leaving school and working small jobs here and there, George, who is now in his early thirties, made the move to this hillside house in Tuscany. Being in close contact with nature, having a garden and working around the house and land gave him a purpose in life and he fell irrevocably in love with the area.

"When I was younger and living in Norwich in the east of England, I struggled to find a purpose. I was lost." By the time George moved here, five kilometres from the small village of Rimbocchi, the old farm had fallen into ruin. But the leaky roof, the glacial winters and the lack of home comforts – which, by George's own admission, plunged him straight into a more primitive way of life – didn't deter him. Little by little, George set to work restoring the farm, adding solar panels, building a clay bread oven and, to round it all off, carving out a vegetable patch, in the hope of sharing its beauty with others.

Despite the farm's isolated location, there is a friendly atmosphere at George's table. Home-grown vegetables sit alongside sourdough bread and delicious local charcuterie, all ready to be washed down with a glass of Chianti. The water is sourced directly from the hillside, home to numerous springs, transforming the valley's northern slope into a damp, green forest. With no fridge or washing machine in the traditional sense, clothes are washed by turning a drum by hand and fresh produce is kept in the cellar or in a small reservoir that collects spring water. And the only place to find a bit of signal is at the top of the hill.

This is George's slice of mountainside life, 800 metres above sea level, surrounded by countless ghost towns and magnificent churches, those too in ruin. A rural exodus emptied the surrounding area of most of its population, bar the local farmers, causing time to stand still. There are some monks living nearby in the sanctuary of La Verna, where Saint Francis of Assisi is said to have received the stigmata. Along the hiking path that passes in front of the house, pilgrims have been known to mistake the farm for a shop. George is no stranger to finding the occasional visitor in his kitchen, casually helping themselves to a cup of coffee in the middle of the afternoon.

For fourteen years, he has made a living offering bed and board. In the summer, with the help of friends and volunteers, he welcomes groups of tourists for yoga, meditation or capoeira retreats before returning to his reclusive lifestyle in the winter. He gets his travel kicks from his foreign visitors, who give him advice and share their knowledge. In fact, it was a German visitor who taught George how to make such a good sourdough bread.

It was during one of these summers that he met his wife Sophie, also from England, who had come to work as a volunteer but ultimately ended up staying for much longer than she originally intended. They are now raising their two young children, India and Kayo, here. Their daily routines revolve around the farm. They wake up early as the sun rises, before almost immediately starting work in the vegetable patch and then attending to the ovens. George is currently restoring another house a little further up the hill and is also required to look after an area of the forest under his ownership obligations. In the sweltering heat of the summer, the family sometimes heads down to the river that flows through the valley to cool off.

"Here, there is a sense of immediacy to everything I do: chopping wood to cook with or heat the house, growing vegetables to prepare healthy meals and going for a walk when the mood strikes me. For me and my family, living here was the obvious choice." It may be an ideal existence, but things are not always as easy as they seem. "Every way of life has its advantages and disadvantages. Living in the middle of nature means sacrificing home comforts, your social life, shopping with ease, visiting a museum or going to a concert. But life is difficult no matter which life you choose for yourself."

For George, the thing he finds the most difficult is adapting to the contrasting rhythms of the different seasons. During the summer months, he spends a lot of time socialising, which can make the isolation of winter feel unbearable. "Not seeing anyone else for days or weeks at a time is difficult after being used to seeing so many people during the summer."

The young man rarely ventures into town. "Sometimes, I miss the comforts of modern life, even simply popping to a shop to buy some milk. But I don't really miss going out, apart from concerts... And also walking on flat ground! Out here, even the shortest trip out of the house involves a lot of climbing up and down hills. Everything is very steep. Whenever I go back into town, I enjoy it for a few days, but then become tired of it very quickly. That way of life is not sustainable. When I was younger, I would sometimes ask myself: Am I running away from something? Or am I chasing after something? It's definitely a bit of both!"

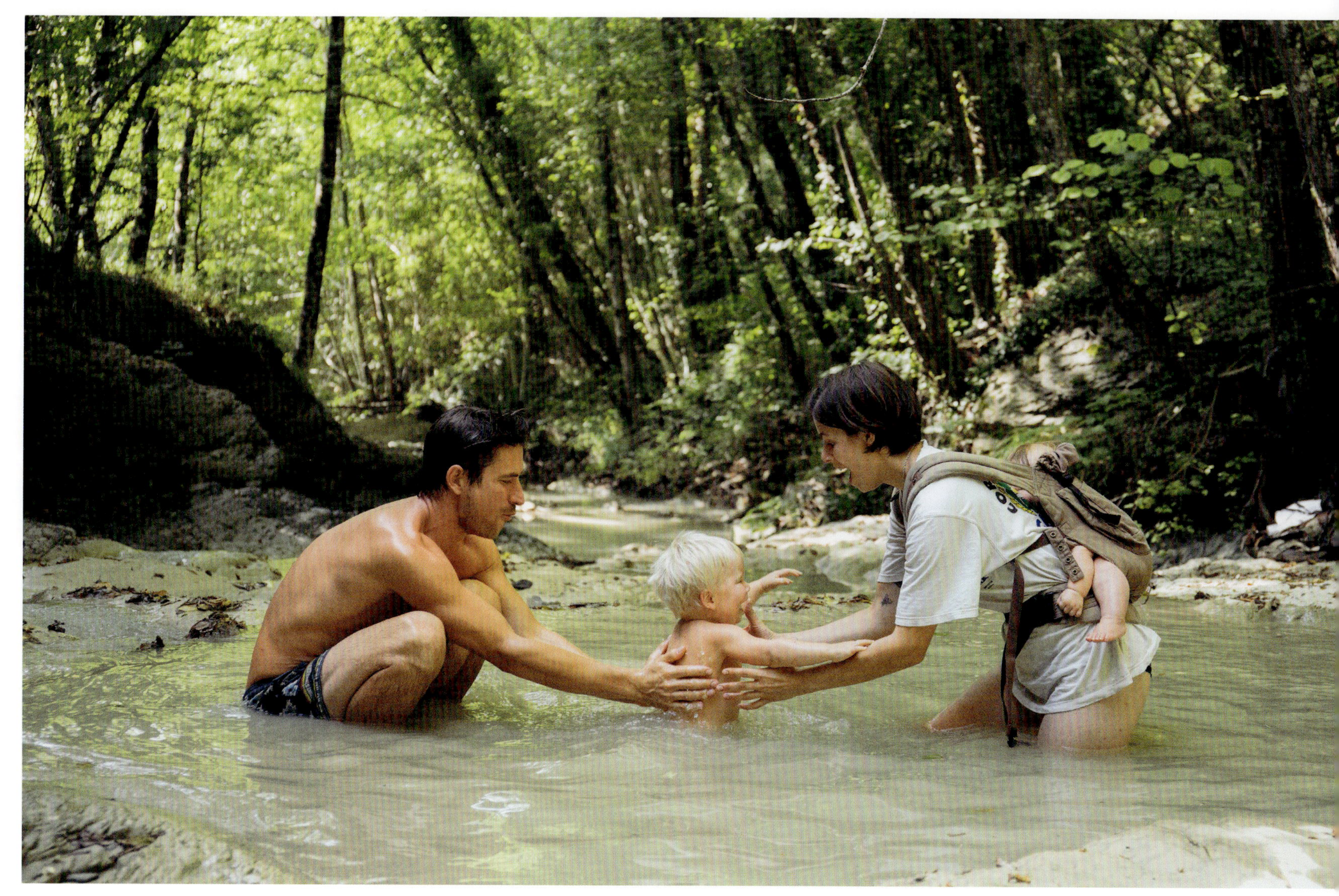

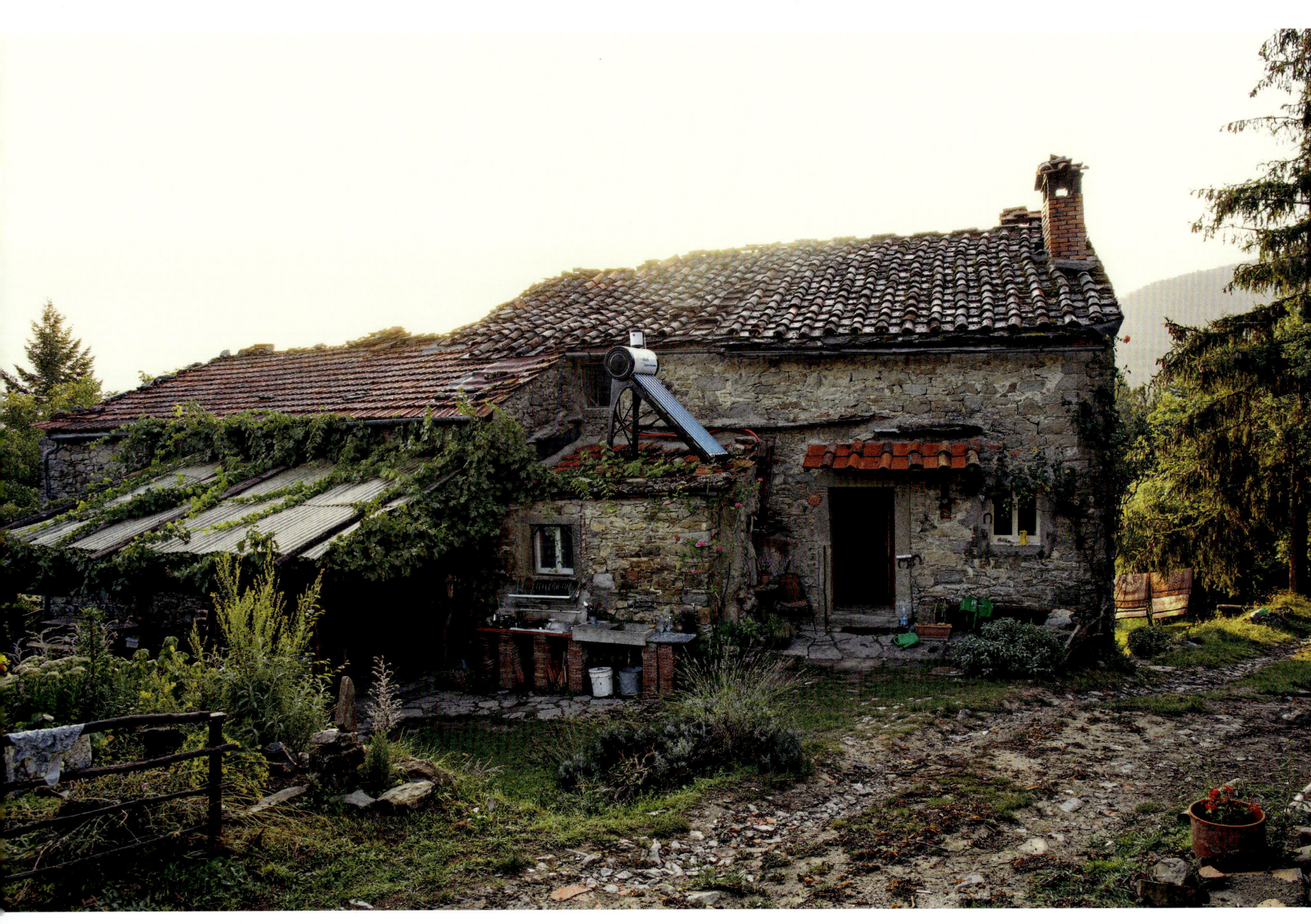

IN DEN WILDEN WÄLDERN

Kaum volljährig, verlässt George Großbritannien und lässt sich auf einem kleinen, verfallenen Bauernhof nieder, ein paar Stunden von Florenz entfernt. Im Lauf der Jahre renoviert er ihn, gründet eine Familie und zieht seine Kinder an diesem Ort außerhalb der Zeit auf.

„Als Kind wollte ich immer nur draußen in der Natur sein, frei. Mit der Schule funktionierte es nicht so richtig. Ich fühlte mich wie im Gefängnis und träumte von einem vollkommen wilden Leben, am liebsten als Indianer in einem Tipi. Später, als Jugendlicher, war ich auf dem New-Age-Trip, ein bisschen Hippie, und interessierte mich für Survival-Training …"

Damals hat George jedes Mal das Gefühl aufzuleben, wenn er bei diesem italienischen Bauernhof aus dem siebzehnten Jahrhundert ankommt, um den sich sein Vater kümmert. „Ich war schon als kleiner Junge dort. Die Zeit, die ich hier verbrachte, war für mich das Synonym von Freiheit – nicht nur tun zu können, was ich wollte, sondern auch zu wissen, wo mein Essen, mein Wasser, das Material zum Heizen herkam … All die Dinge, die man im modernen Leben als gegeben hinnimmt."

Es heißt, hier in den dichten Wäldern der Apenninen hätten sich die letzten Wölfe versteckt, die im neunzehnten Jahrhundert nur knapp der Ausrottung entgingen. Mit achtzehn – zwei Jahre nach seinem Schulabschluss und nach einer Reihe von Nebenjobs – beschloss George, der heute um die dreißig ist, sich in diesem toskanischen Haus im Hügelland niederzulassen. Die Nähe zur Natur, ein Garten und die Arbeit darin genügen ihm als Lebensinhalt, und er verliebt sich endgültig in die Gegend.

„Als Jugendlicher lebte ich in Norwich, im Osten Englands, und fand keinen Sinn in meinem Leben. Ich war völlig verloren." Als George hier einzieht, fünf Kilometer von dem Dörfchen Rimbocchi entfernt, ist der alte Hof eine Ruine. Aber das löchrige Dach, die eisigen Winter und der komplette Mangel an Komfort stören den Eigentümer kaum, der sich, wie er zugibt, direkt in die Wildnis geworfen fühlt. Um deren Schönheit mit anderen zu teilen, renoviert George den Hof nach und nach, schließt Solarpaneele an, baut einen Lehmofen zum Brotbacken und ergänzt das Ganze um einen Gemüsegarten.

Trotz der Abgeschiedenheit des Ortes geht es an Georges Tisch gastfreundlich zu. Gemüse aus dem Garten gesellt sich zu Sauerteigbrot und den herrlichen Wurstwaren der Gegend, dazu gibt es Chianti. Das Wasser stammt direkt aus dem Berg, wo zahlreiche Quellen entspringen und den Nordhang des Tals in einen feuchten, grünen Wald verwandeln. Es gibt weder Kühlschrank noch Waschmaschine – die Wäsche wird in einer Trommel von Hand gedreht, und frische Lebensmittel lagern im Keller oder in dem kleinen Becken, wo sich das Quellwasser sammelt. Und wenn man ein wenig Netzempfang erhaschen möchte, muss man zum Gipfel des Hügels hinaufsteigen.

So findet sich George an seinem Berghang in 800 Metern Höhe wieder, umzingelt von zahlreichen Geisterdörfern und wunderbaren, ebenfalls zerfallenen Kirchen. Die Landflucht hat die Gegend entvölkert und die Zeit angehalten; nur die Bauern bringen weiterhin ihre Ernten ein. Im nahen Kloster von La Verna leben Mönche – genau dort, wo Franz von Assisi angeblich die Wundmale Christi empfing. Ein Wanderweg verläuft vor dem Haus, und es kommt vor, dass Pilger diesen Ort für ein Lebensmittelgeschäft halten: George hat schon Besucher in seiner Küche angetroffen, die sich am helllichten Nachmittag in aller Ruhe einen Kaffee zubereiteten.

Seit vierzehn Jahren ernährt er sich davon, Kost und Logis anzubieten. Im Sommer empfängt er mit Hilfe von Freunden und Freiwilligen Touristengruppen zu Yoga-, Meditations- oder Capoeira-Kursen, bevor er im Winter wieder zum Eremiten mutiert. Die ausländischen Besucher erzählen ihm von ihren Reisen, geben ihm Ratschläge und teilen ihr Wissen. Einem deutschen Gast ist es zu verdanken, dass George so gutes Sauerteigbrot backt.

So hat er auch seine Frau Sophie kennengelernt, eine Engländerin, die als Freiwillige kam und länger blieb als geplant. Inzwischen sind sie eine Familie, mit ihren kleinen Kindern India und Kayo. Ihr Alltag kreist um den Bauernhof. Morgens mit der Sonne aufstehen, fast sofort in den Gemüsegarten, dann an den Herd. George ist dabei, ein weiteres, etwas höher gelegenes Haus zu renovieren, und kümmert sich um ein Waldstück, was zu seinen Verpflichtungen als Grundbesitzer gehört. Im Sommer flieht die Familie manchmal vor der Hitze und badet im Fluss, unten im Tal.

„Hier spüre ich, dass alles, was ich tue, einen unmittelbaren Sinn hat: Holz schlagen, um zu kochen oder das Haus zu heizen, Gemüse anbauen, um gut zu essen, Spazieren gehen, wenn ich Lust dazu habe. Für mich ist es etwas Selbstverständliches, hier mit meiner Familie zu leben." Dieses traumhafte Leben ist allerdings nicht so einfach, wie es scheint. „Jede Lebensweise hat ihre Vor- und Nachteile. Mitten in der Natur zu leben bedeutet, den eigenen Komfort zu opfern, das Sozialleben, die Möglichkeit, einfach einzukaufen, ins Museum oder in ein Konzert zu gehen. Aber das Leben ist immer hart, wie es auch aussehen mag."

Für George liegt die größte Schwierigkeit darin, sich an die unterschiedlichen Rhythmen der Jahreszeiten anzupassen. Im Sommer nehmen soziale Beziehungen den ganzen Tag ein, im Winter bedrückt ihn manchmal die Abgeschiedenheit. „Tage- und wochenlang keinen Menschen zu sehen, ist schwierig, wenn man sich im Sommer daran gewöhnt hat, so viele Leute um sich zu haben."

Der junge Mann fährt nur selten in die Stadt. „Manchmal fehlt mir der Komfort des modernen Lebens, und sei es nur, Milch in einem Lebensmittelgeschäft zu kaufen. Aber das Ausgehen fehlt mir eigentlich nicht, von Konzerten abgesehen … Und das Gehen auf ebenen Flächen! Hier gibt es schon beim kleinsten Spaziergang Steigungen, alles ist sehr steil. Deshalb bin ich ein paar Tage lang glücklich, wenn ich zurück in die Stadt komme, aber ich habe auch schnell wieder genug, weil dieser Lebensstil nicht nachhaltig ist. Als ich jünger war, habe ich mich manchmal gefragt: Laufe ich vor etwas weg? Oder jage ich hinter etwas her? Bestimmt ein wenig von beidem!"

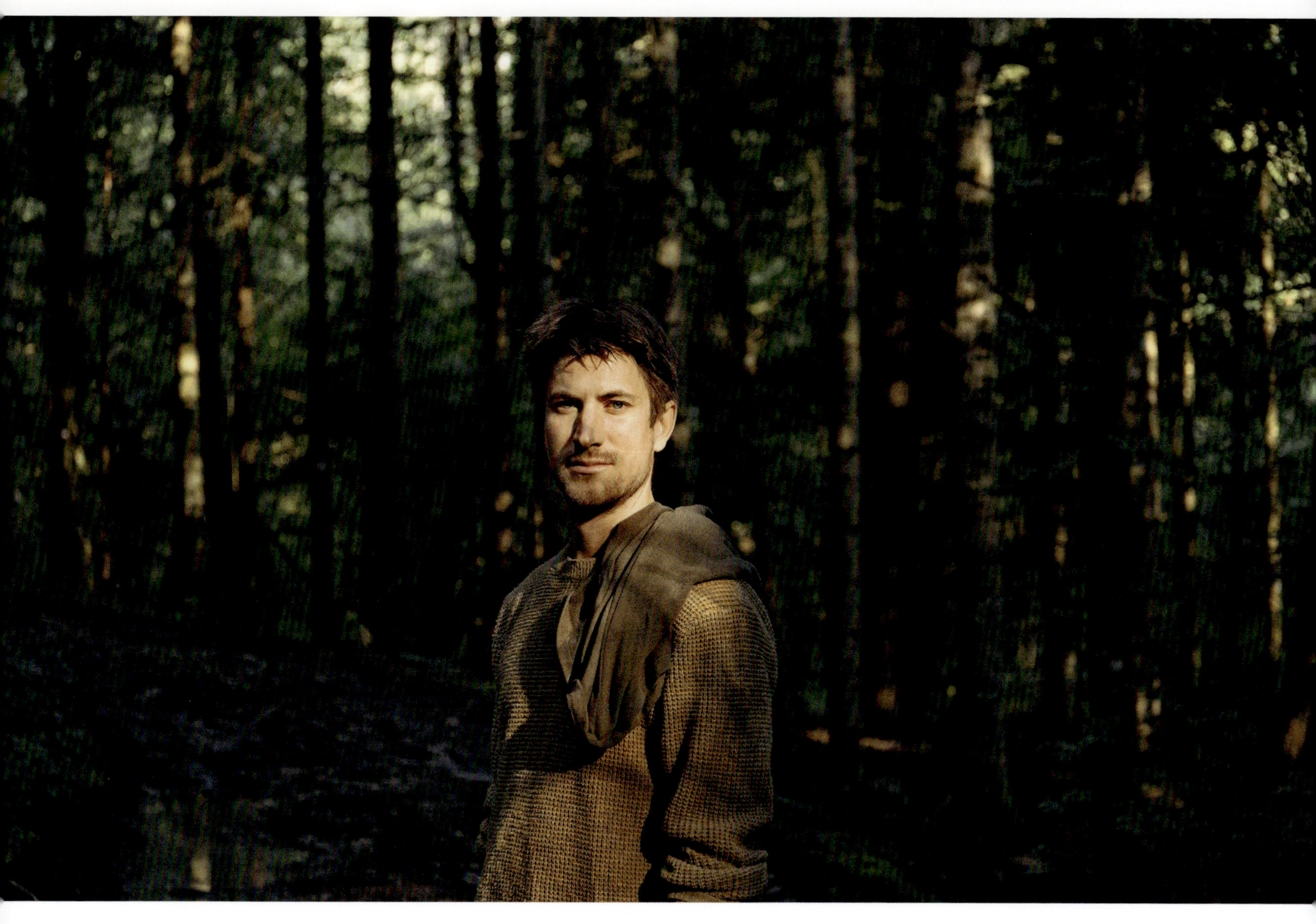

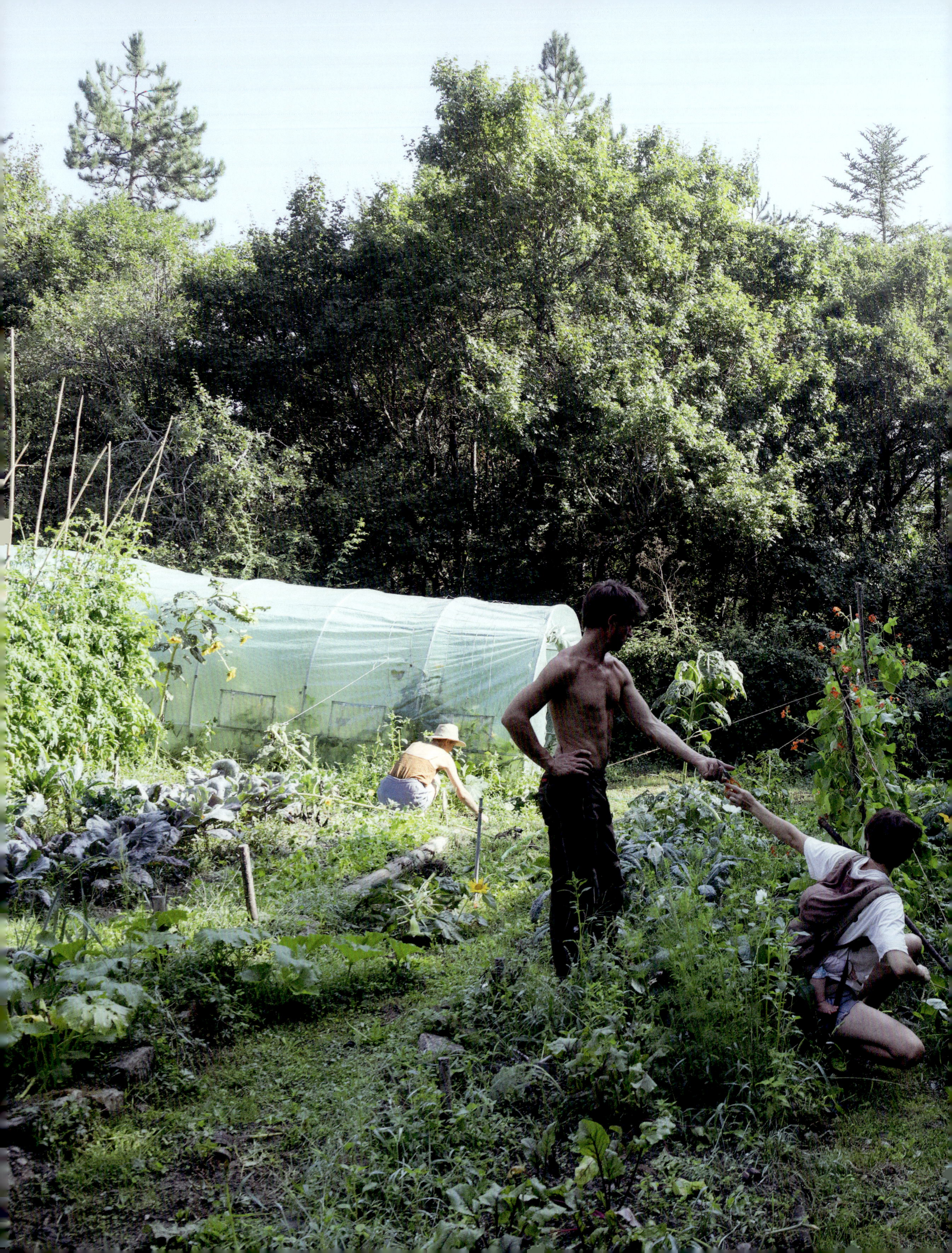

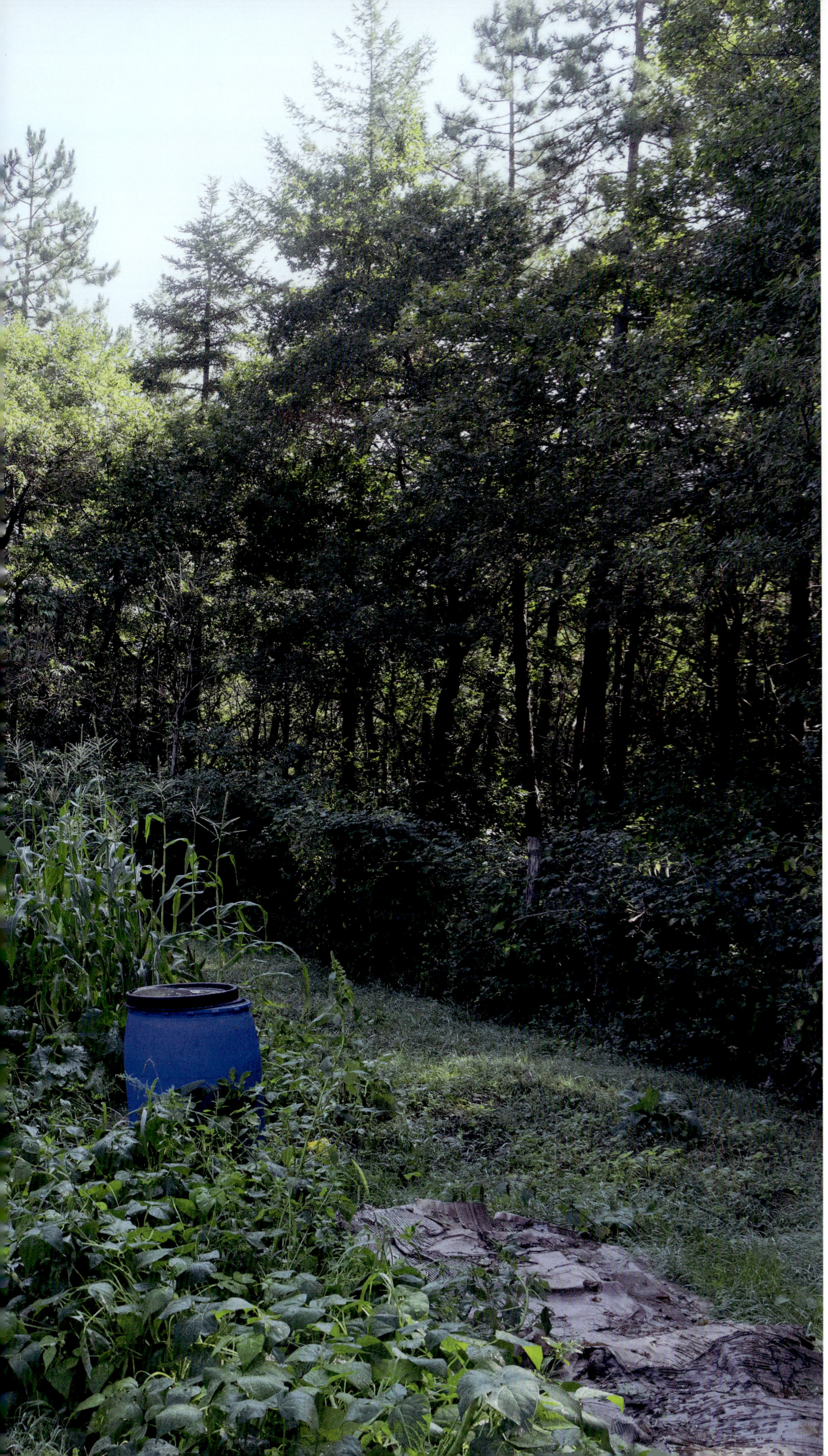

"Every child begins the world again, to some extent, and loves to
stay outdoors, even in wet and cold. It plays house, as well as
horse, having an instinct for it. Who does not remember the
interest with which, when young, he looked at shelving rocks, or
any approach to a cave? It was the natural yearning of that
portion, any portion of our most primitive ancestor which still
survived in us."

HENRY DAVID THOREAU
Walden; or, Life in the Woods

„Jedes Kind fängt in gewissem Sinn wieder die Welt von vorn an
und ist am liebsten im Freien, selbst bei Nässe und Kälte. Seinem
Instinkt folgend, spielt es „Haus" und „Pferd". Wer erinnert sich
nicht daran, mit welchem Interesse er in seinen jungen Tagen
ausgehöhlte Felsen ansah, oder alles, was nur im entferntesten
Ähnlichkeit mit einer Höhle hatte? Es war die natürliche
Sehnsucht unserer frühesten Vorfahren,
von der ein Teil noch in uns lebte."

HENRY DAVID THOREAU
Walden oder Leben in den Wäldern

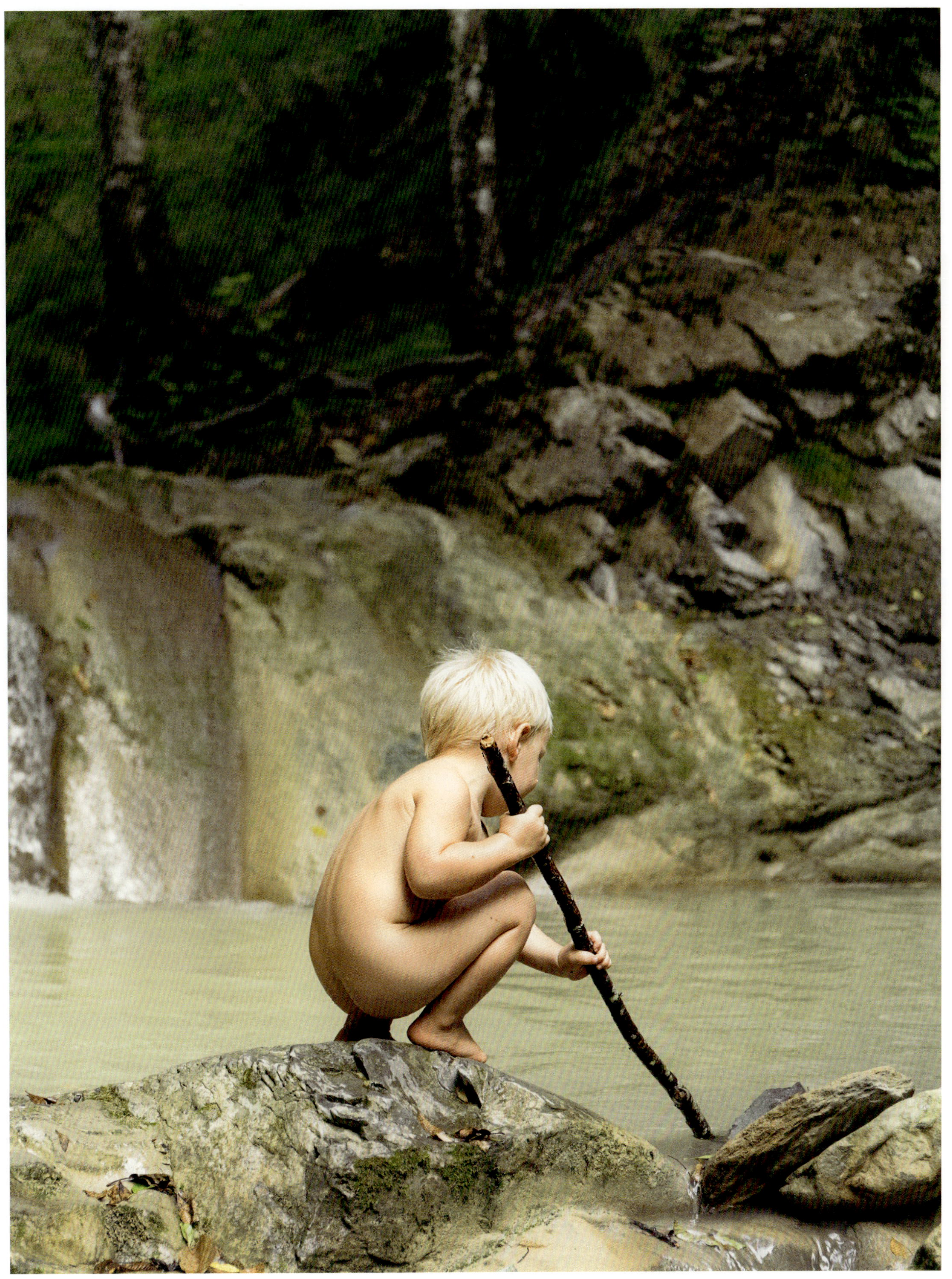

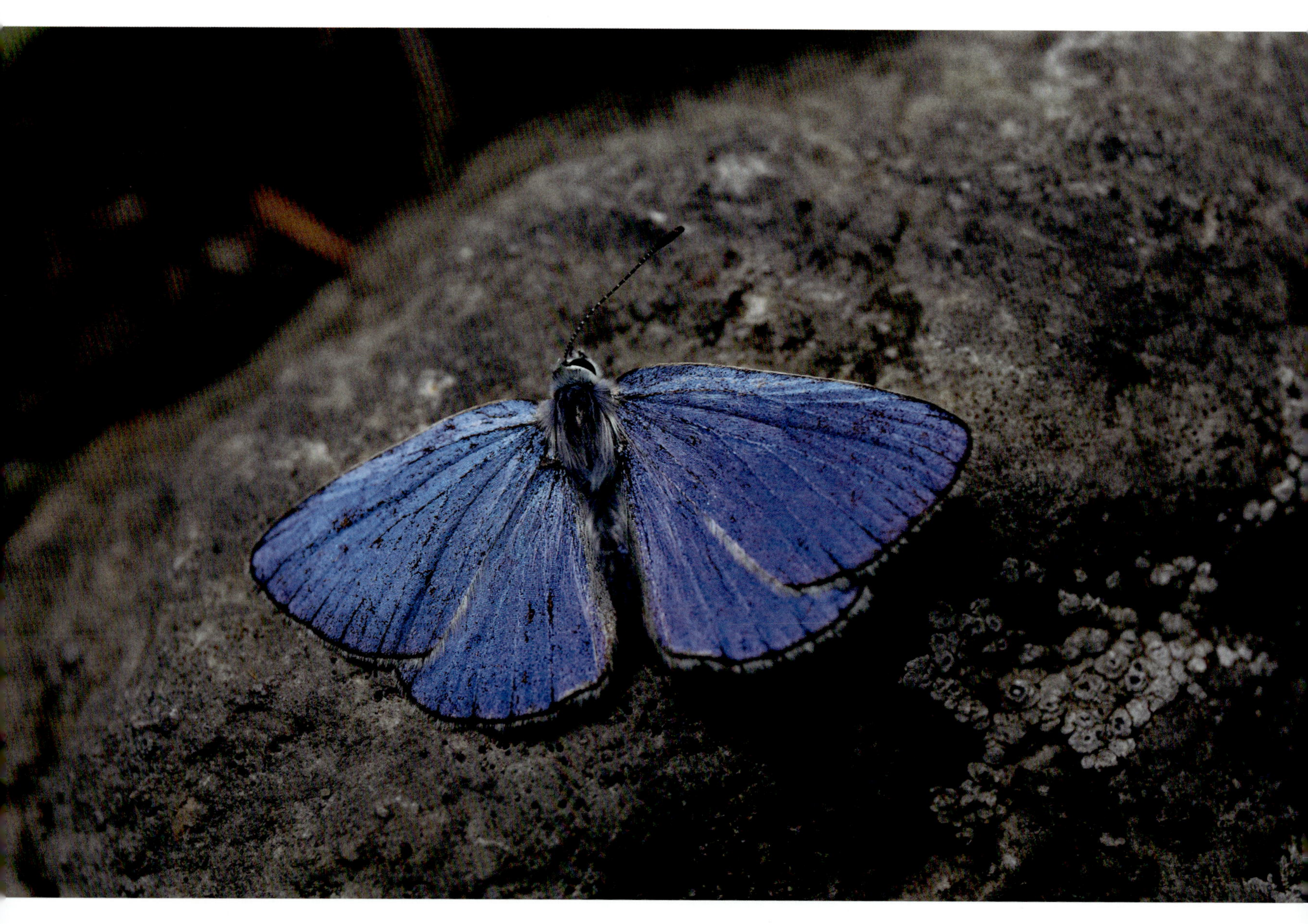

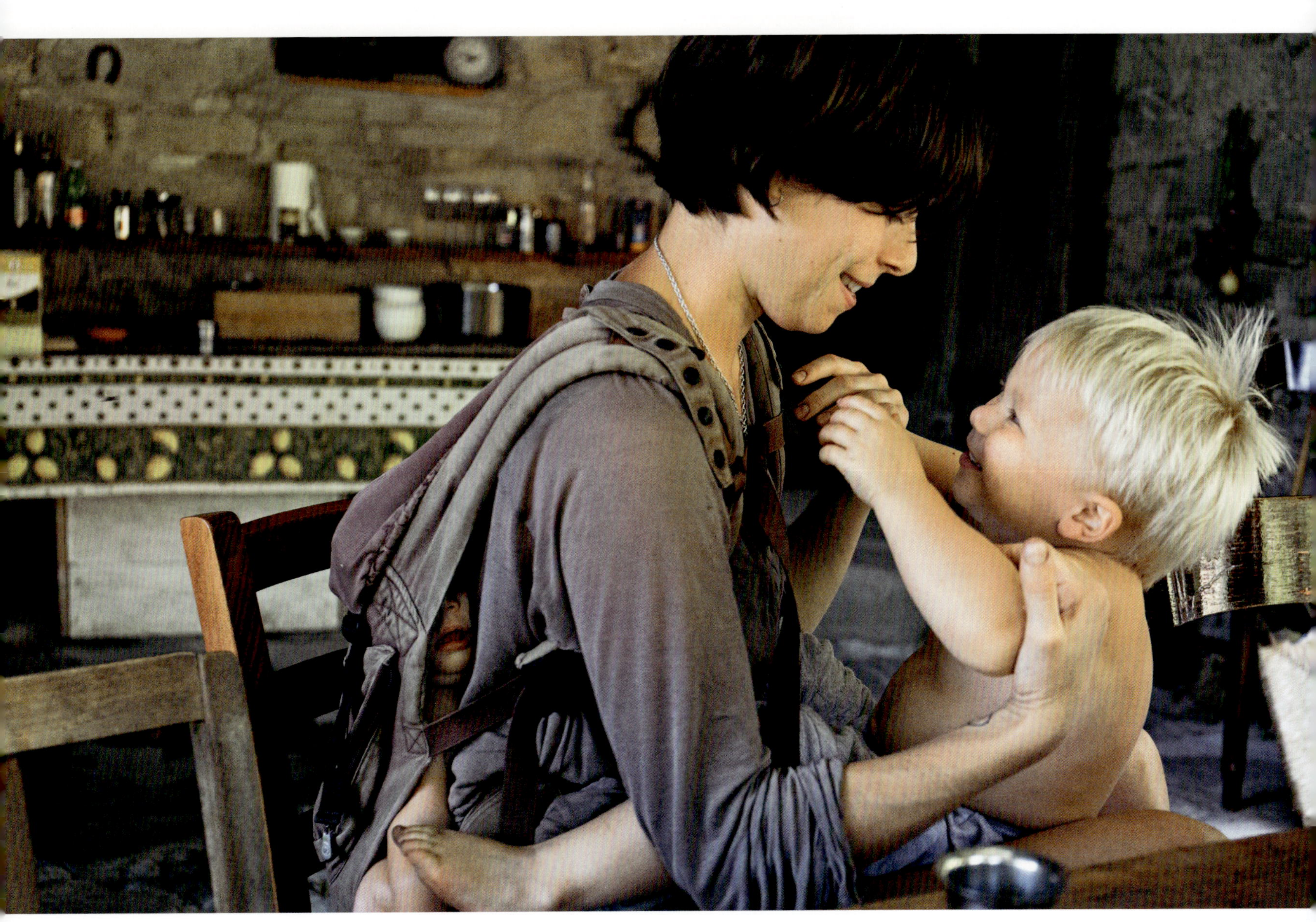

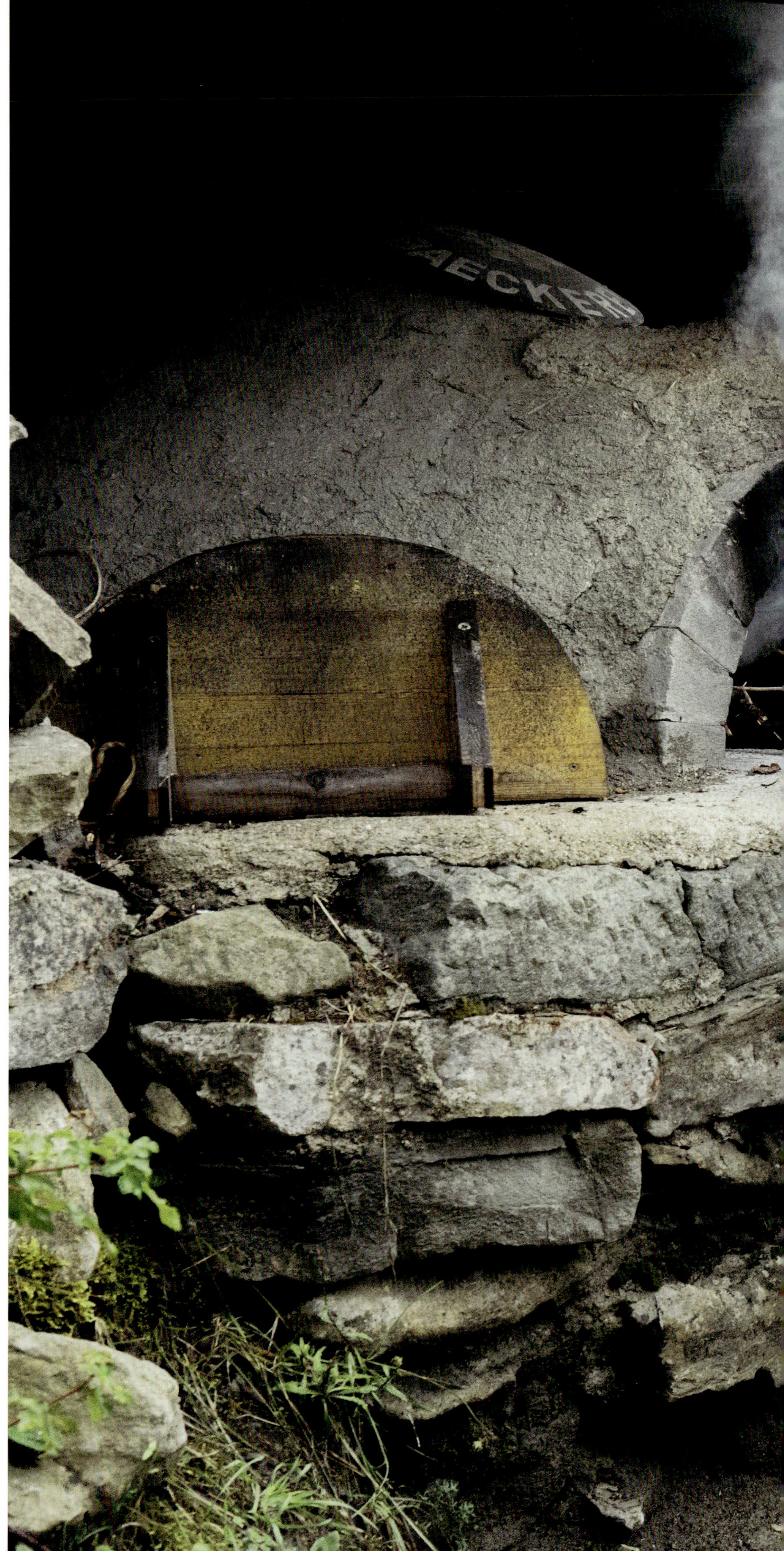
AECKERE

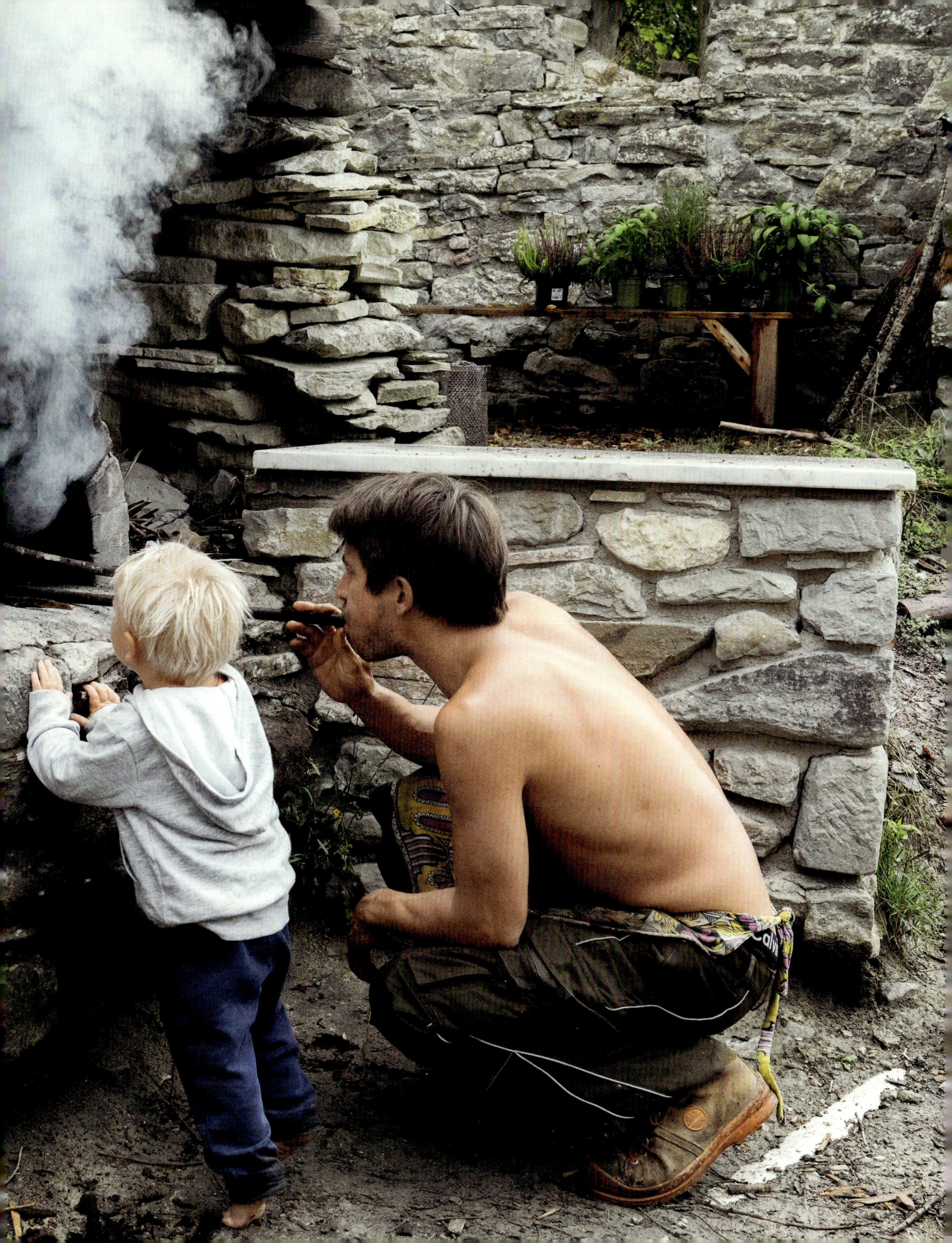

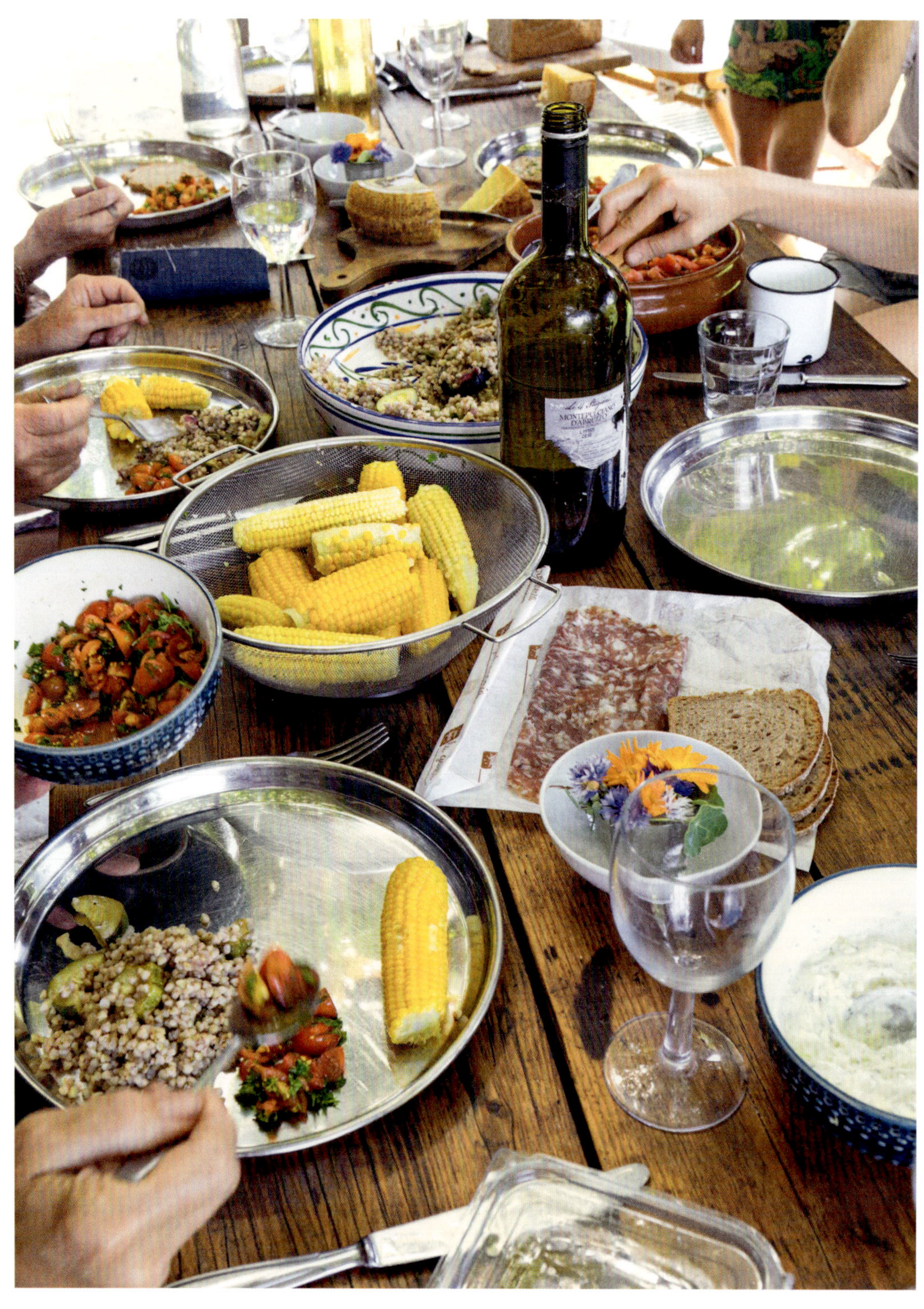

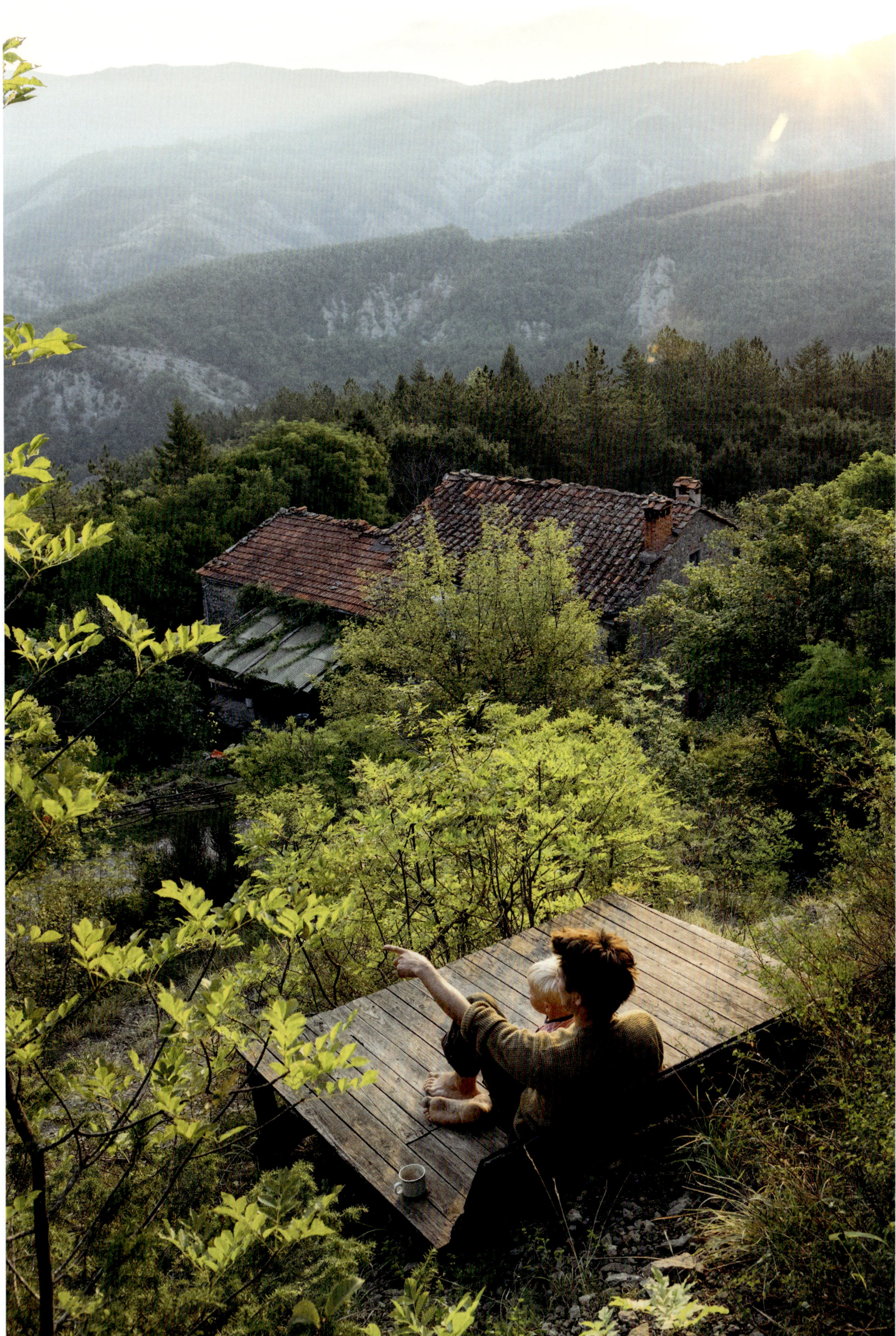

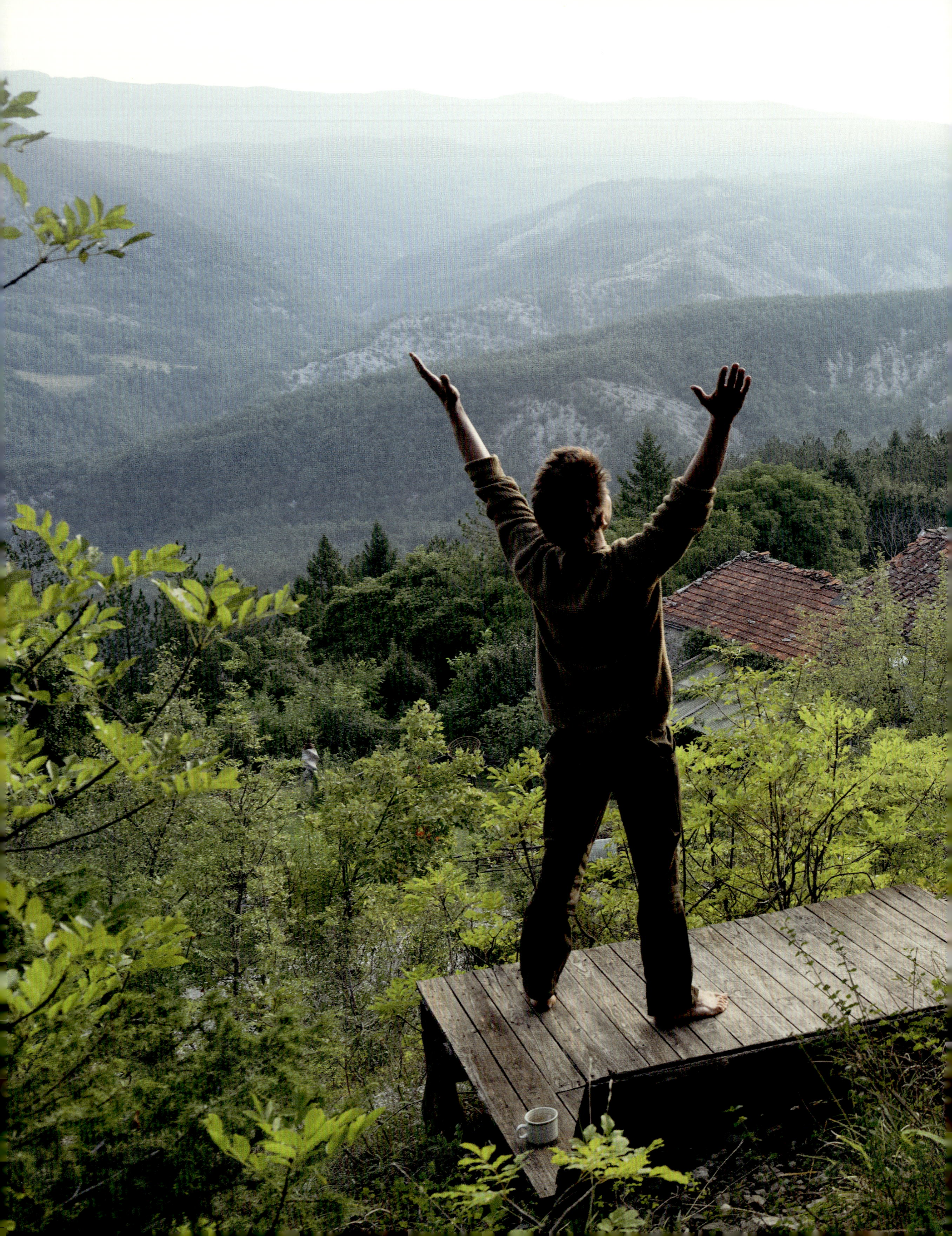

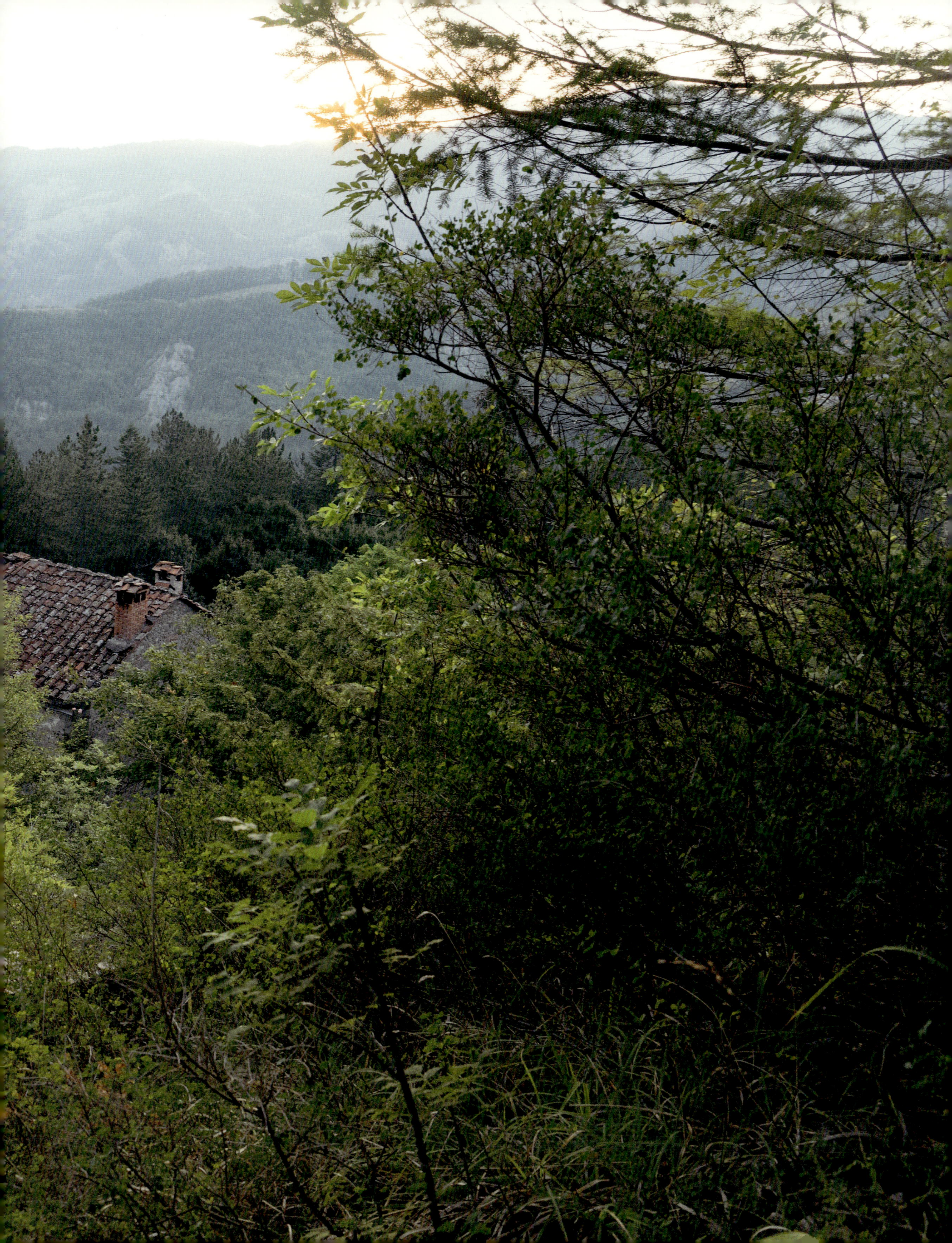

SYLWIA

———

"THIS PLACE HAS REALLY
GROUNDED ME. [...] FOR THE
FIRST TIME, I FEEL THAT I'M
FINALLY GETTING TO KNOW
MYSELF."

———

„DIESER ORT VERWURZELT
MICH UNGEMEIN. [...] ZUM
ERSTEN MAL HABE ICH
DAS GEFÜHL, MICH SELBST
KENNENZULERNEN."

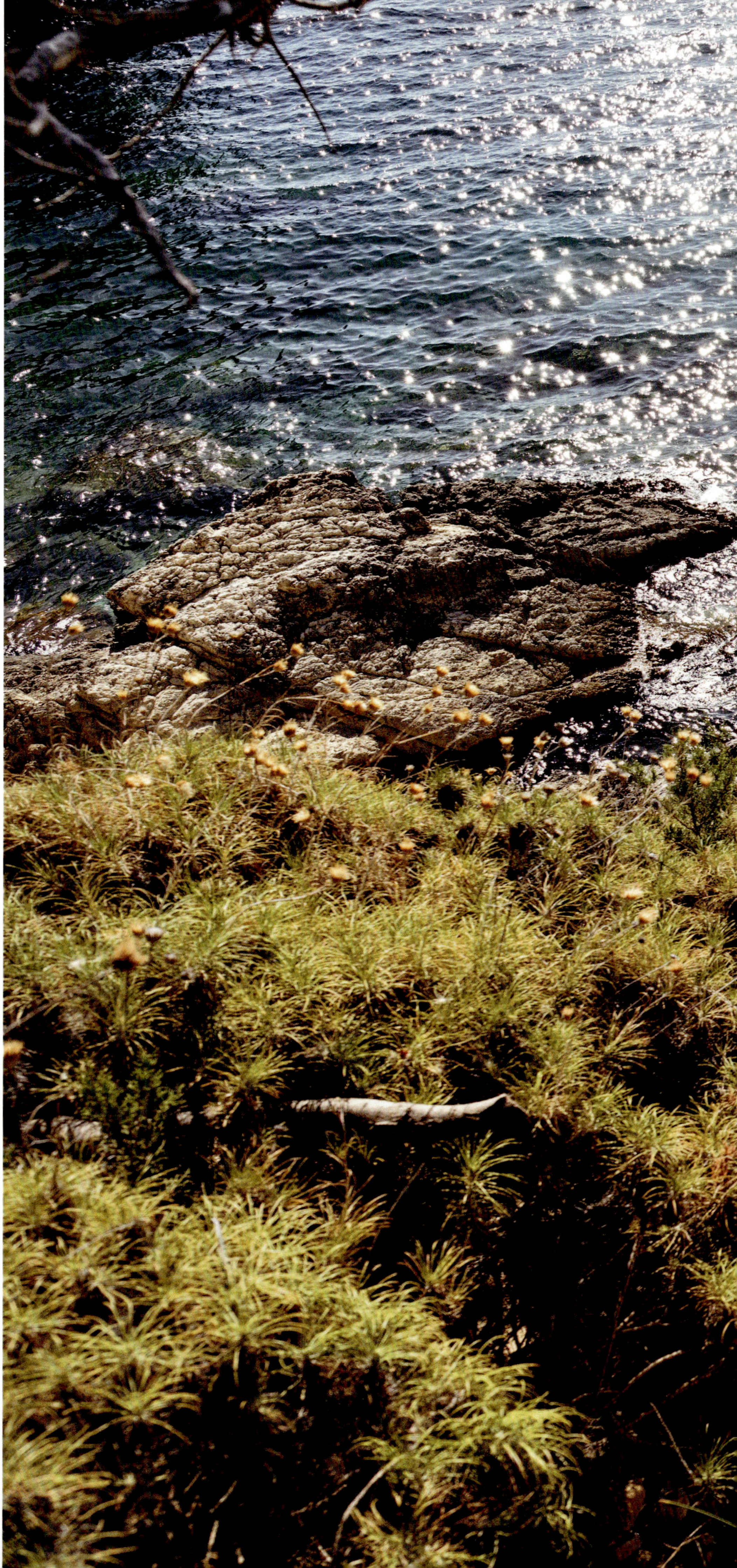

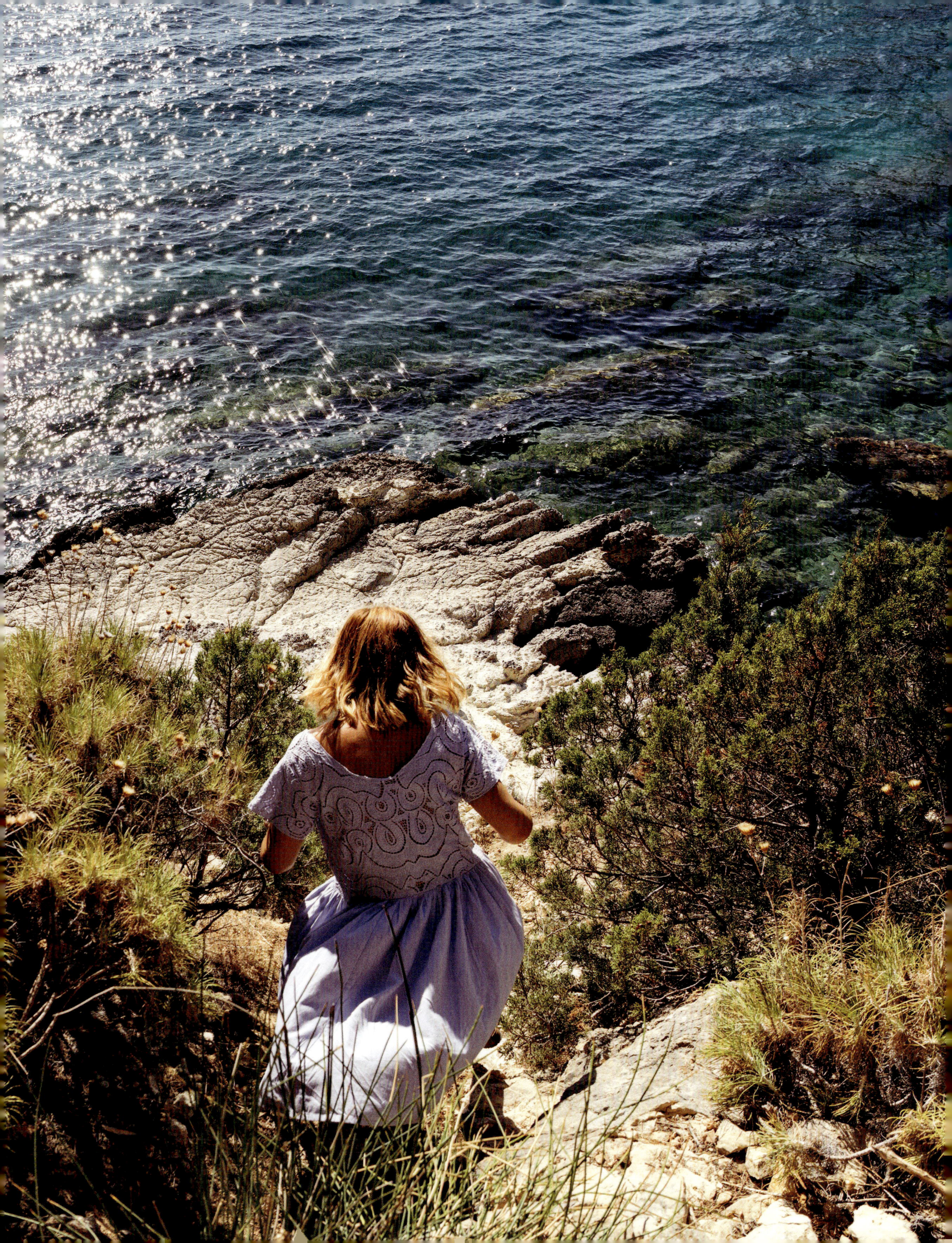

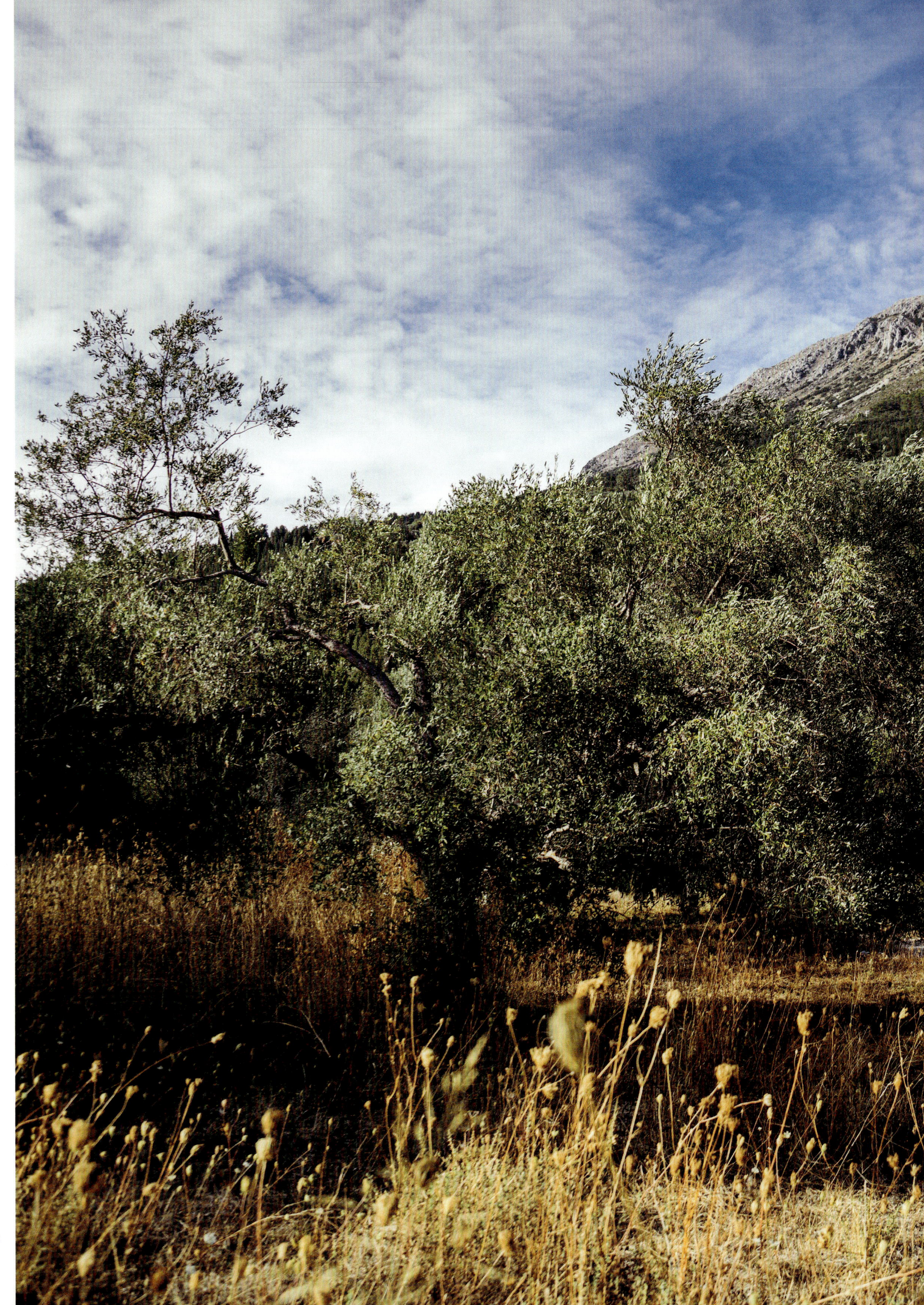

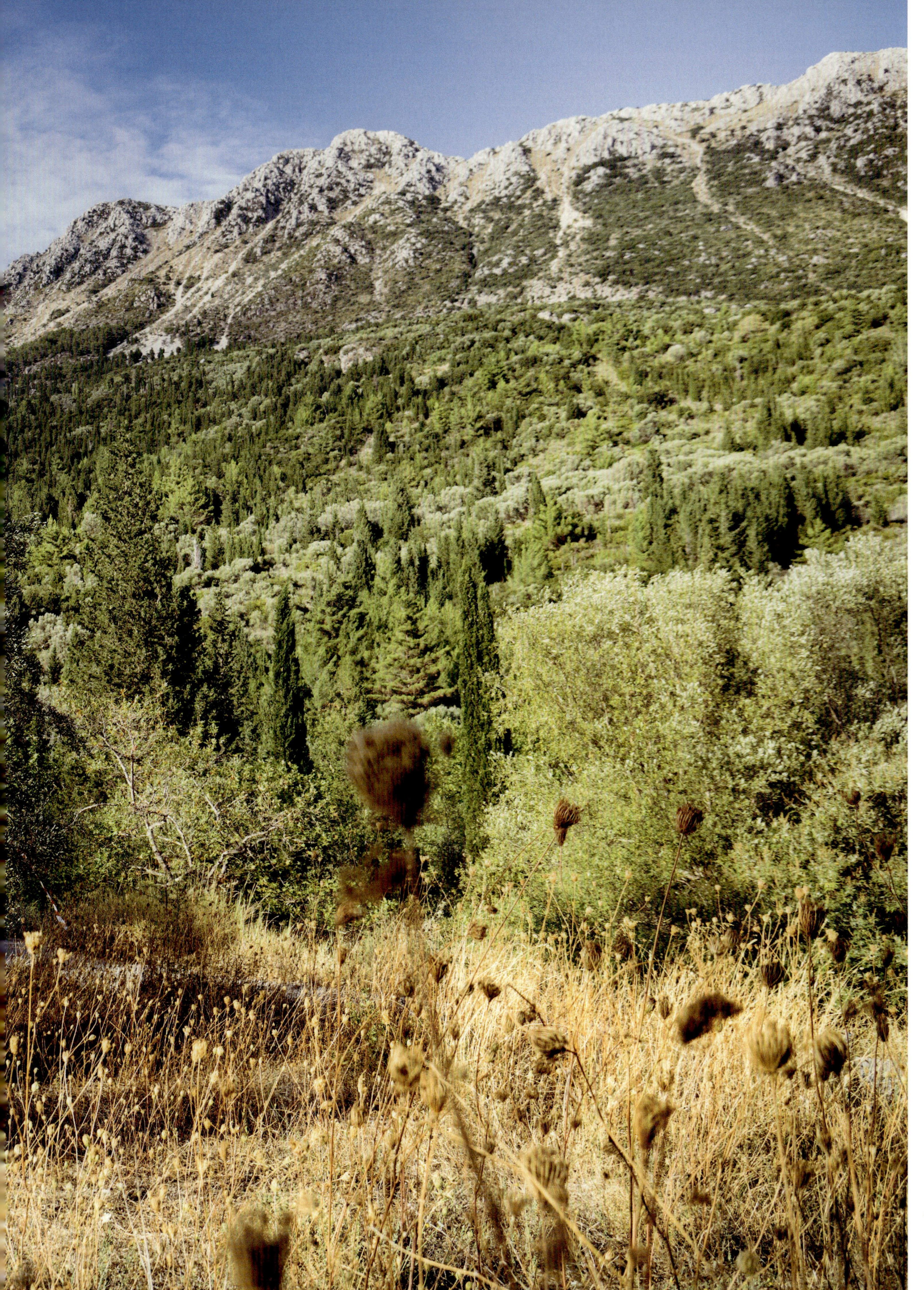

THE GREEK ISLAND

LEFKADA, GREECE

Having grown up in rural Poland during the communist era and spent several years in New York, Sylwia knows what it is like to live in two vastly different worlds. Some time ago, she and her partner decided to buy a ruined property on a Greek island and make it their home.

To find Sylwia on her Greek island, you have to cross salt marshes, skirt round the coast and then follow a small valley up into the mountains. As you round the bend at the end of a minor road overgrown with vegetation, the village of Roupakias comes into view nestled among the olive groves. This is where Sylwia lives with her partner Mariusz – the sole inhabitants of this small Greek village abandoned in the 1970s, after the village was moved further up the hill because it proved too costly to install phone and electricity lines. Life in the village slowly ebbed away, as the villagers each took their leave, first the baker, then the butcher and finally the school teacher. Today most of Roupakias lies hidden under ivy, vines, trees and other bushes, as bit by bit nature has slowly reclaimed the land where the village once stood.

For 42-year-old Sylwia, it has been a long and difficult journey, full of twists and turns, to reach this small Greek village. She grew up in rural Poland, but as soon as she was old enough she left, ultimately emigrating to the USA where she worked as an au pair for a wealthy family from the Upper East Side and East Hampton. Mariusz, who is 43, also left Poland for the USA and got a job as a broker on Wall Street. Their paths eventually crossed in the city of Boulder in Colorado. They decided to travel around Europe together and spent several years living life on the road until they arrived on the island of Lefkada to the south of Corfu. Here they found work and sometime later discovered Roupakias, their hidden gem, where they bought first one abandoned ruin, and then several more.

Roupakias was their chance to say goodbye to their hectic and stressful former lives and the endless quest to do more. "I never felt truly content. You couldn't really see it from the outside, but I felt it in my heart. There was never any time to waste. Every minute had to be filled with something exciting, but I was never really present. My spirit was elsewhere. There were times when I managed to stand still, to stop running and take stock, but I

never found the right balance. Even so, during those fleeting moments of calm, I realised that I needed to build myself a nest – a home – and I needed to do it my way. I needed to pour all my love into it and feel its warmth in return, rather than running around collecting nothing but little crumbs of happiness." Arriving in Roupakias, Sylwia felt like a weight had been lifted. Here was a new life – an exciting opportunity to create a new home with very limited funds, and to start rebuilding her life from the ruins of a difficult past.

"Life in Poland was very hard. I hated growing up on the farm, working myself to the bone. There was nothing there for me, certainly nothing I enjoyed. As soon as I was old enough to make my own decisions, I got as far away as I could. When I was sixteen, I went to study in a small town and as soon as I finished my course I left Poland for the USA." Sylwia was only too pleased to swap rural communist Poland for capitalist America."

"I was delighted to find myself in this materialistic world. And I embraced the lifestyle in every way. I dressed in expensive clothes, ate in overpriced restaurants and travelled extensively. It was a ball! Back then, I thought that if I didn't have expensive branded clothes, then I wouldn't be as attractive as the other girls. And then one day I realised that none of it mattered. But I really needed to go through the process to understand that and to grow as a person." Years later, Sylwia got up one day and promised herself that from then on she would live her life in pursuit of one thing – happiness. Roupakias became her magical retreat away from the world – her eulogy to life in the slow lane. "My soul really needed it. That's what drew me here. I needed to be surrounded by nature, to set down roots, to keep making plans, but to do so very consciously. This place has really grounded me. It fills me with calm and allows me to feel at one with myself. For the first time, I feel that I'm finally getting to know myself. Ten years earlier, there was no way I could've abandoned everything I knew. I was so

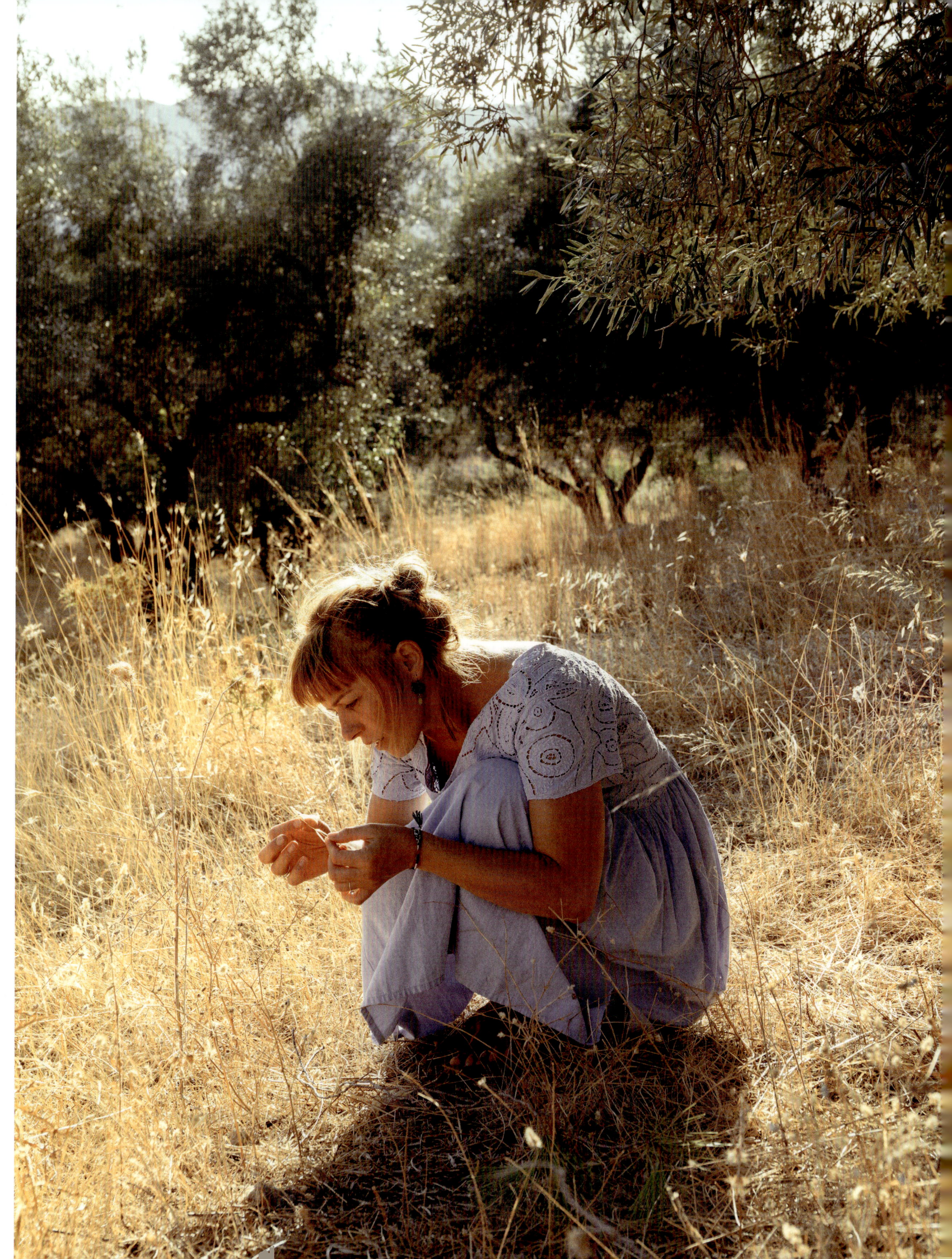

hergeführt. Von Natur umgeben zu sein, sich nicht mehr zu verzetteln, weiterhin ein Projekt nach dem anderen anzustoßen, aber ganz bewusst. Dieser Ort verwurzelt mich ungemein. Er beruhigt mich und bringt mich mit mir selbst in Einklang. Zum ersten Mal habe ich das Gefühl, mich selbst kennenzulernen. Vor zehn Jahren hätte ich nicht alles aufgeben können. ‚Zeit ist Geld‘ – davon war ich so fest überzeugt, dass ich das Leben hier als Zeitverschwendung betrachtet hätte.

Für mich ist die Entscheidung für ein Leben mit der Natur kein Rückschritt, sondern im Gegenteil ein Schritt voran – der Fortschritt liegt in der Erkenntnis, dass wir die Natur für eine höhere Lebensqualität brauchen. Wir können komplett in der heutigen Gesellschaft leben und gleichzeitig der Natur nahe sein; es ist nicht nötig, sich für eine der beiden Optionen zu entscheiden und alle Freuden des früheren Lebens aufzugeben, im Gegenteil. Nur weil ich in einem verlassenen Dorf mitten in der Wildnis wohne, muss ich doch nicht aufs Internet verzichten!“

Sylwia ist damit vertraut, sich neuen Umständen anzupassen, und gewöhnt sich schnell an ihr neues Leben. „Unsere Überzeugungen ändern sich ständig. Ich bin ein vollkommen anderer Mensch als vor zehn oder zwanzig Jahren, oder selbst vor zwei Jahren. Vor zehn Jahren wusste ich nur die Hälfte der Dinge über mich selbst, die ich heute weiß.“ Aber das Alltagsleben in Roupiakas ist mehr als ein langer ruhiger Fluss. Bei ihrer Ankunft sahen sich Sylwia und Mariusz mit einer ungeheuren Last dringend zu erledigender Aufgaben konfrontiert. Allmählich wird Sylwia bewusst, dass es nicht so einfach ist, ohne die Gesellschaft Gleichgesinnter an einem so abgeschiedenen Ort zu leben …

Nach und nach strukturiert sich der Alltag. Der Tag beginnt gegen acht Uhr mit einem Frühstück im Schatten des großen Feigenbaums, in Gesellschaft von Criket der Katze und Rudy dem Hund. Es fehlt nicht an Projekten: Verputzen, Zimmermannsarbeiten, Schreinern … Nicht zu vergessen den Gemüsegarten und eine Runde durchs Dorf, um Früchte von den Bäumen zu ernten, die frühere Bewohner gepflanzt haben. Sylwia pflückt köstliche weiße Trauben, Zitronen, Mandeln, Äpfel. „Es gibt hier eine solche Fülle an Obst und Gemüse, zu jeder Jahreszeit! Die Zeit des wilde Spargels ist zu Ende, wenn die des Knoblauchs beginnt, dann kommen die Maulbeeren, Feigen, Granatäpfel, Oliven, Orangen … Die Natur würde beinahe ausreichen, um uns zu ernähren, allerdings mit einer sehr eintönigen Diät …!“ Ein Paradies für Sylwia, die es liebt, in den verlassenen Häusern nach vergessenen Schätzen zu suchen.

Die Trägheit des Ortes hat den anfänglich straffen Rhythmus beruhigt. Nach dem Mittagessen hält das Paar oft eine Siesta, um der Nachmittagshitze zu entgehen. Die beiden haben zahlreiche Freundschaften geknüpft, und die Bewohner der umlie-

genden Dörfer kommen regelmäßig zu Besuch. Sie treffen sich auch an der Quelle, die inmitten eines undurchdringlichen Dschungels entspringt und an deren Fuß eine riesige Platane emporragt. Manchmal kommen abends Inselbewohner vorbei und ernten Tomaten auf den Grundstücken, die sie bewirtschafteten, als sie noch hier lebten. Jedes Jahr im Spätherbst helfen Sylwia und Mariusz den ehemaligen Nachbarn, mit denen sie Kontakte geknüpft haben, bei der Olivenernte. Als Gegenleistung bekommen sie einen Teil des Öls, mit dem sie das ganze Jahr lang großzügig ihr Essen beträufeln.

Ihr Strom stammt aus einer Solaranlage mit Batteriespeicher; außerdem benutzt Mariusz einen Generator, wenn er Starkstrom für seine Werkzeuge braucht. Das Wasser kommt aus der berühmten Quelle, an die sie einen Schlauch angeschlossen haben; den Rest erledigt die Schwerkraft. Die beiden denken darüber nach, eine Turbine im benachbarten Fluss zu installieren, um die Kraft des im Winter reichlich fließenden Wassers zur Stromgewinnung zu nutzen.

Das ganze Jahr über, auch im Winter, baden Sylwia und Mariusz im Fluss mit seinen natürlichen Becken und Wasserfällen: Sylwia hält das Wasser für magisch – es wasche ihre Probleme buchstäblich weg. „Statt Ibuprofen zu nehmen, springe ich in den Fluss, und wenn ich herauskomme, weiß ich nicht einmal mehr, was mir gefehlt hat. Er gibt mir eine unglaubliche Energie.“ Im Sommer, wenn die Hitze an den Kräften zehrt und der Fluss austrocknet, gehen sie im kristallklaren Wasser des Ionischen Meeres baden.

Seit sie hier lebt, zehrt Sylwia auch schöpferisch von ihrer Umgebung. Sie hat die Ruinen in ein Künstleratelier verwandelt, das später auch als Galerie, Konzertsaal, Theater und Wohnraum dienen soll – eine Premiere in der Gegend. „Ich habe in Colorado an einer Kunstschule studiert. Bildhauerei hat mir immer gefallen, aber dafür braucht man einen Raum, um die Gießformen zu machen und die Skulpturen zu brennen. Ich habe während unserer großen Reise durch Europa damit aufgehört und stattdessen mit Zeichnungen und kleinformatiger Malerei begonnen, was leichter zu transportieren ist.“

Inzwischen gehen ihre künstlerischen Ausdrucksformen wieder über das Zeichenpapier hinaus. „Etwas Schönes herzustellen, macht mich glücklich. Stufen aus Zement zu bauen, bereitet mir keine Freude – sie aus Stein zu hauen, schon. Auch Mariusz lernt viel, indem er Dinge auf die althergebrachte Art tut. Wenn wir es schaffen, unseren Lebensunterhalt zu verdienen und weiterhin so zu leben, wäre es unser Traum, auch anderen Menschen beizubringen, wie man kreative Vorhaben umsetzt. Und wie man glücklich lebt – so wie wir!“, sagt Sylwia und bricht in Gelächter aus.

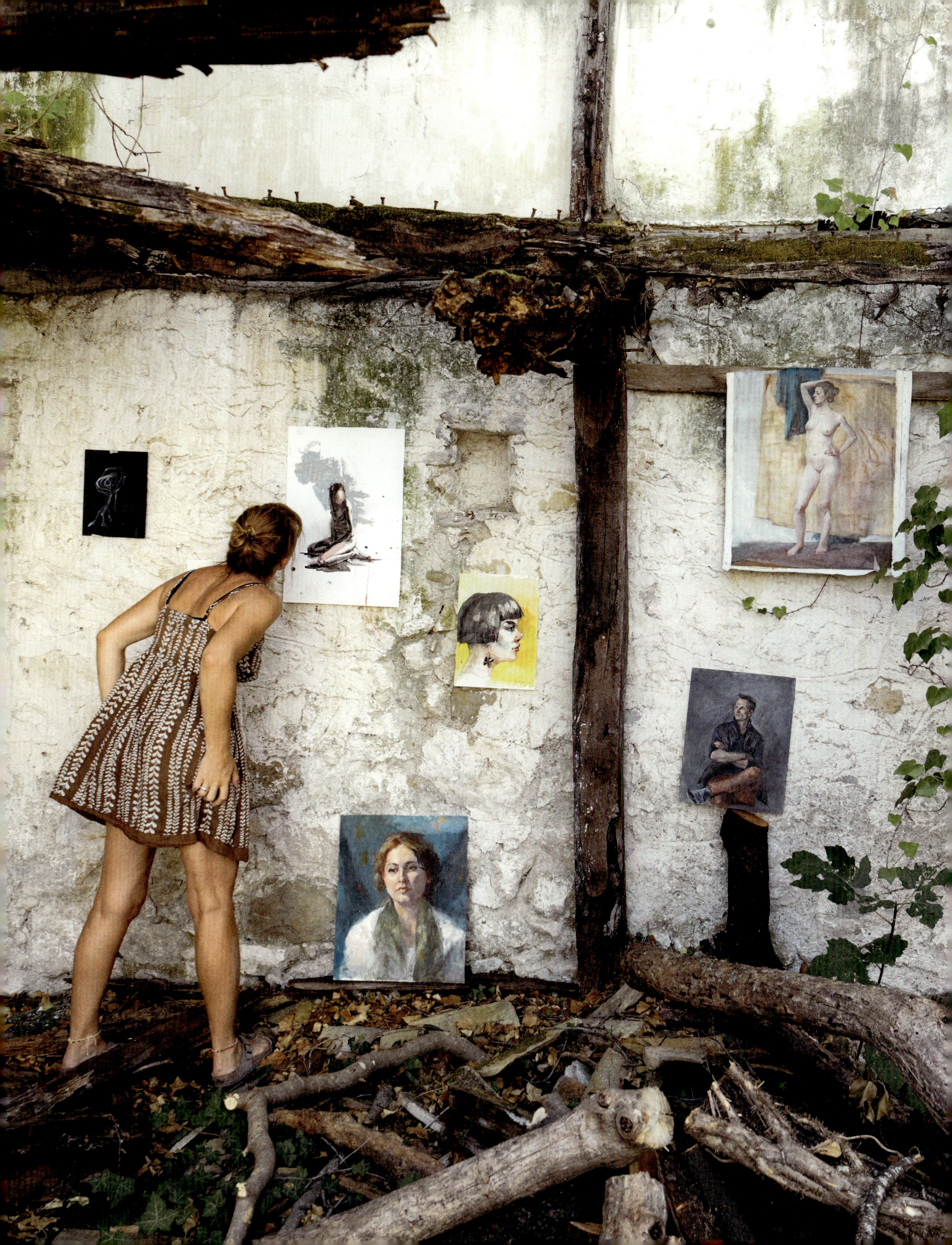

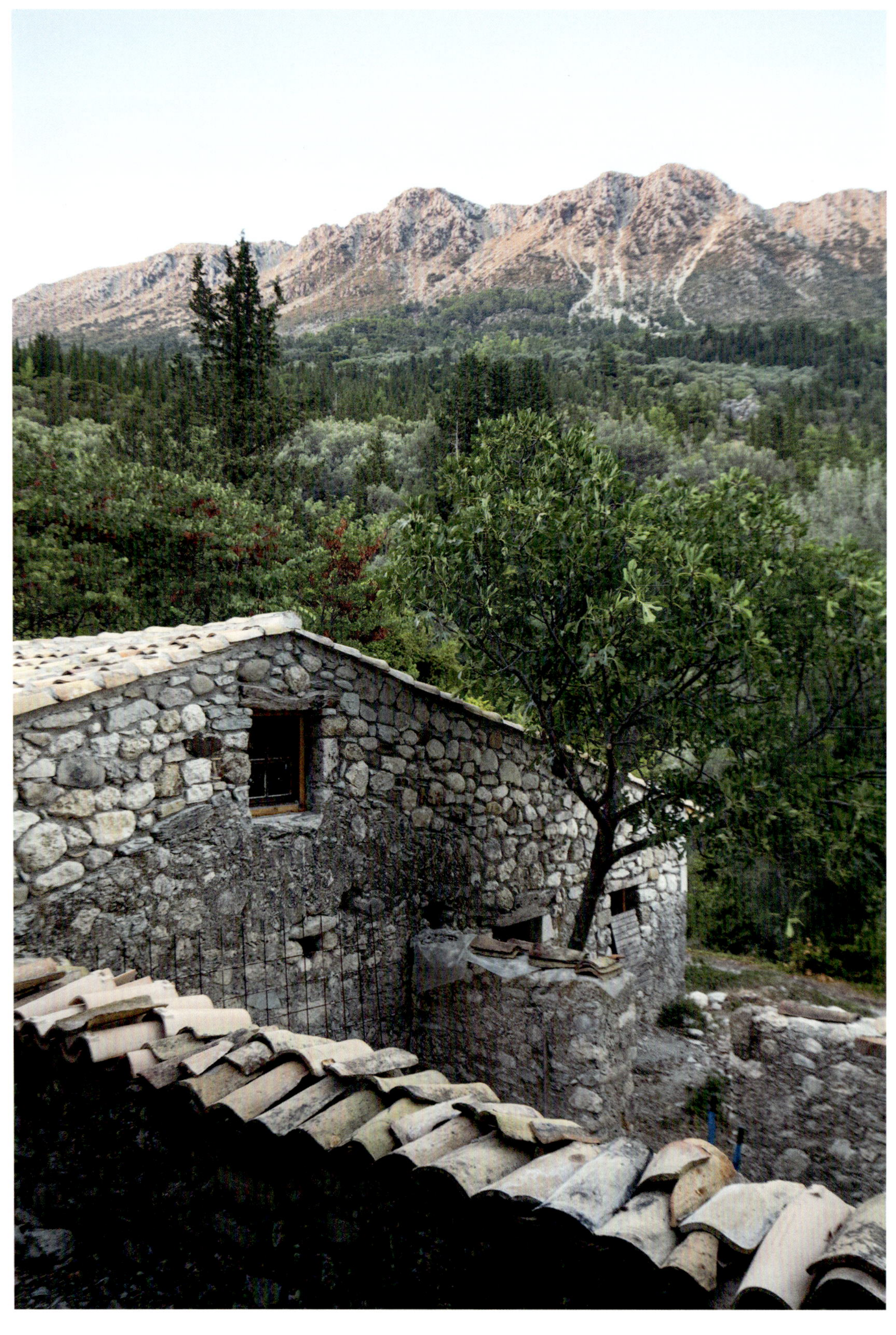

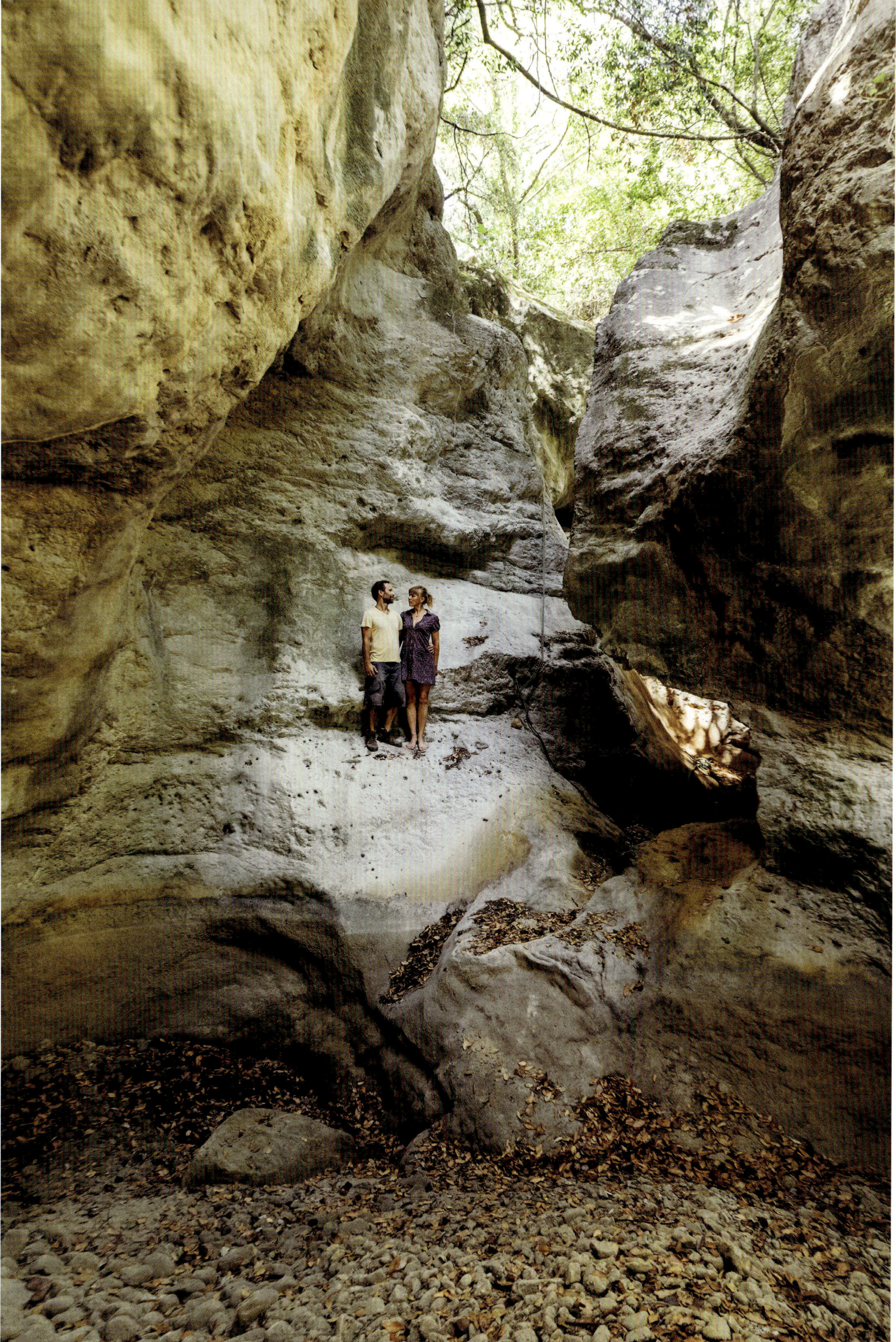

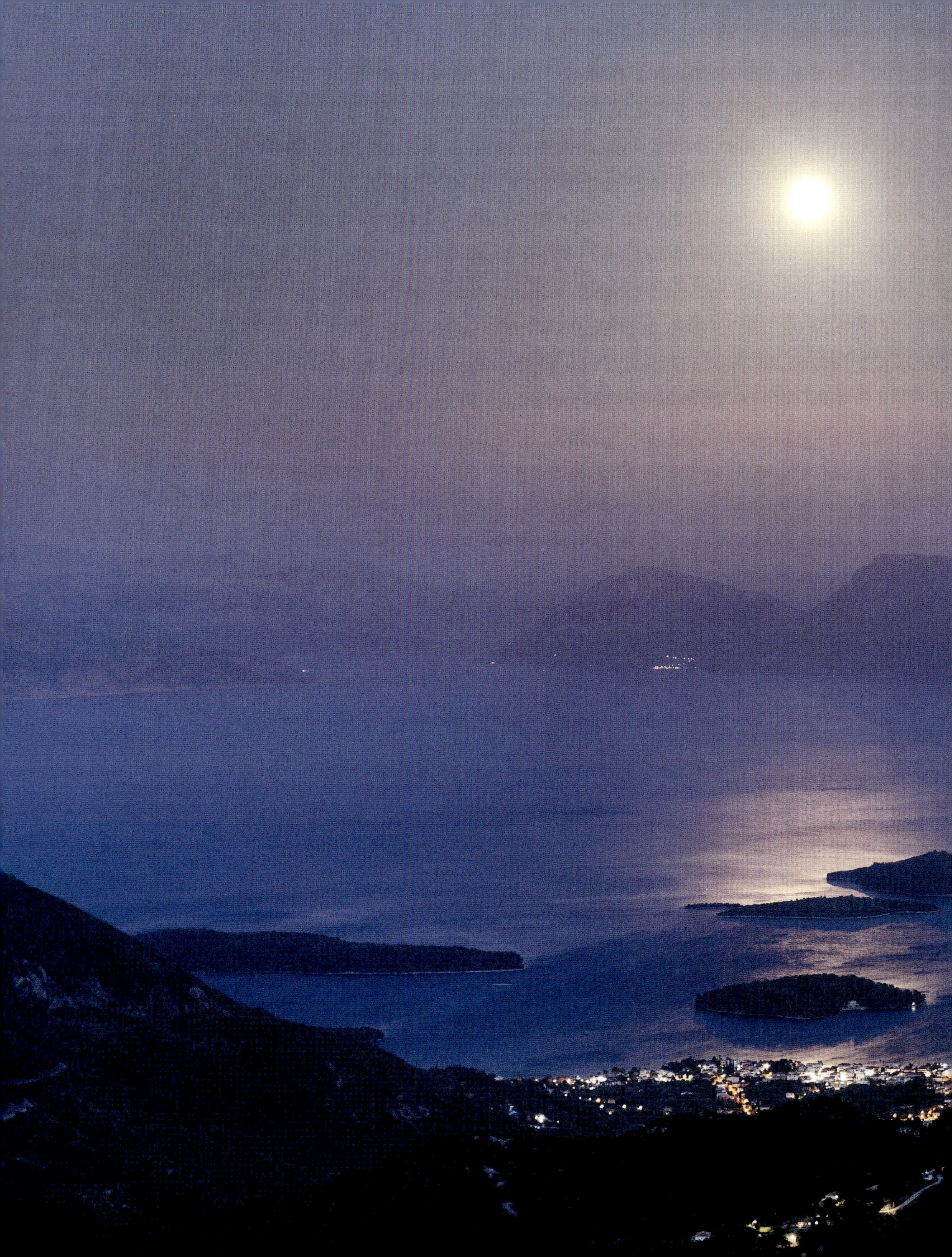

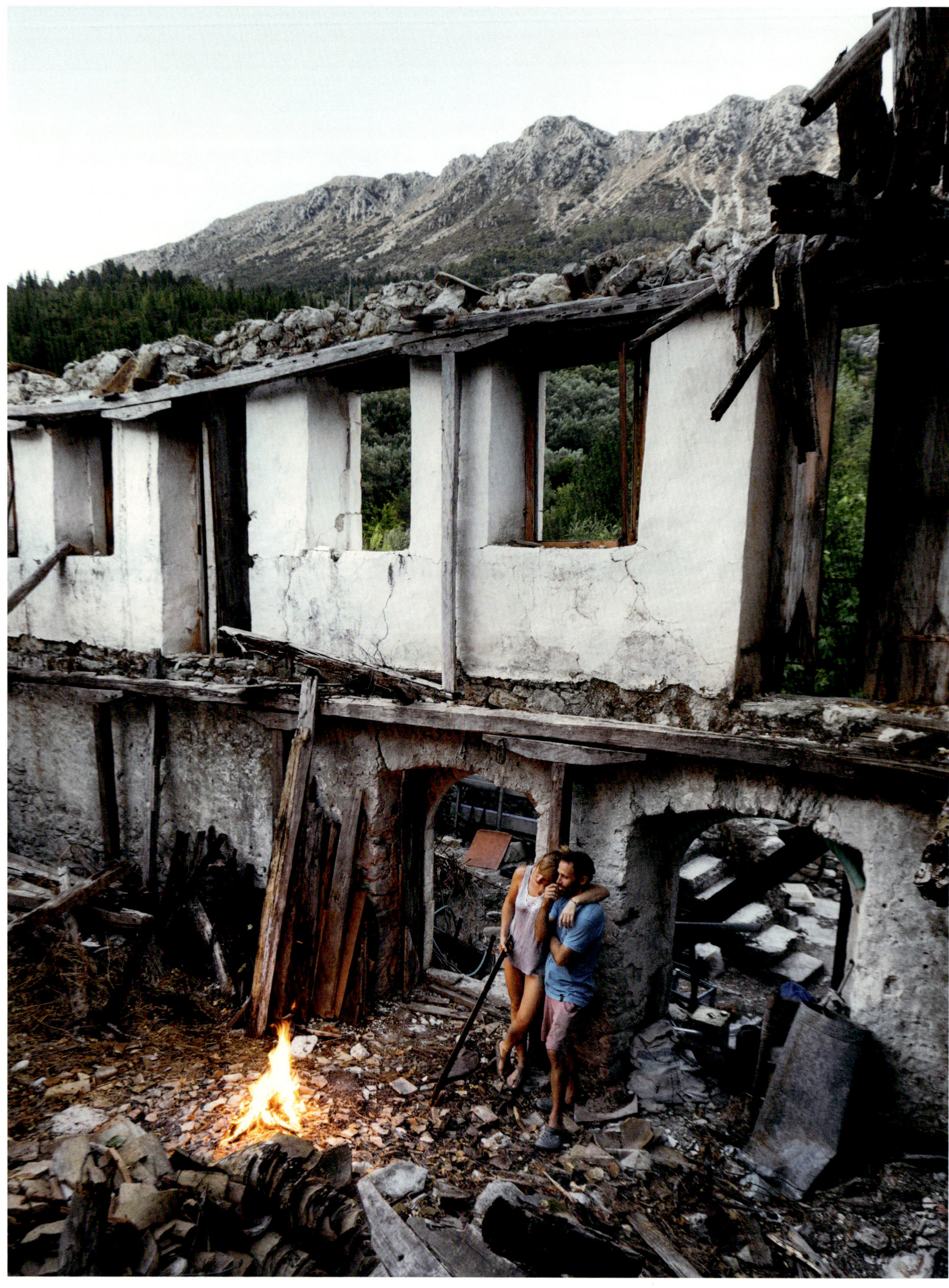

"Why do you stay here and live this mean moiling life, when a glorious existence is possible for you? Those same stars twinkle over other fields than these."

HENRY DAVID THOREAU
Walden; or, Life in the Woods

„Was bleibst du hier und führst dieses durchschnittliche, mühselige Leben, wo dir ein glorreiches Dasein möglich ist? Die Sterne da oben leuchten noch über anderen Feldern als diesen.“

HENRY DAVID THOREAU
Walden oder Leben in den Wäldern

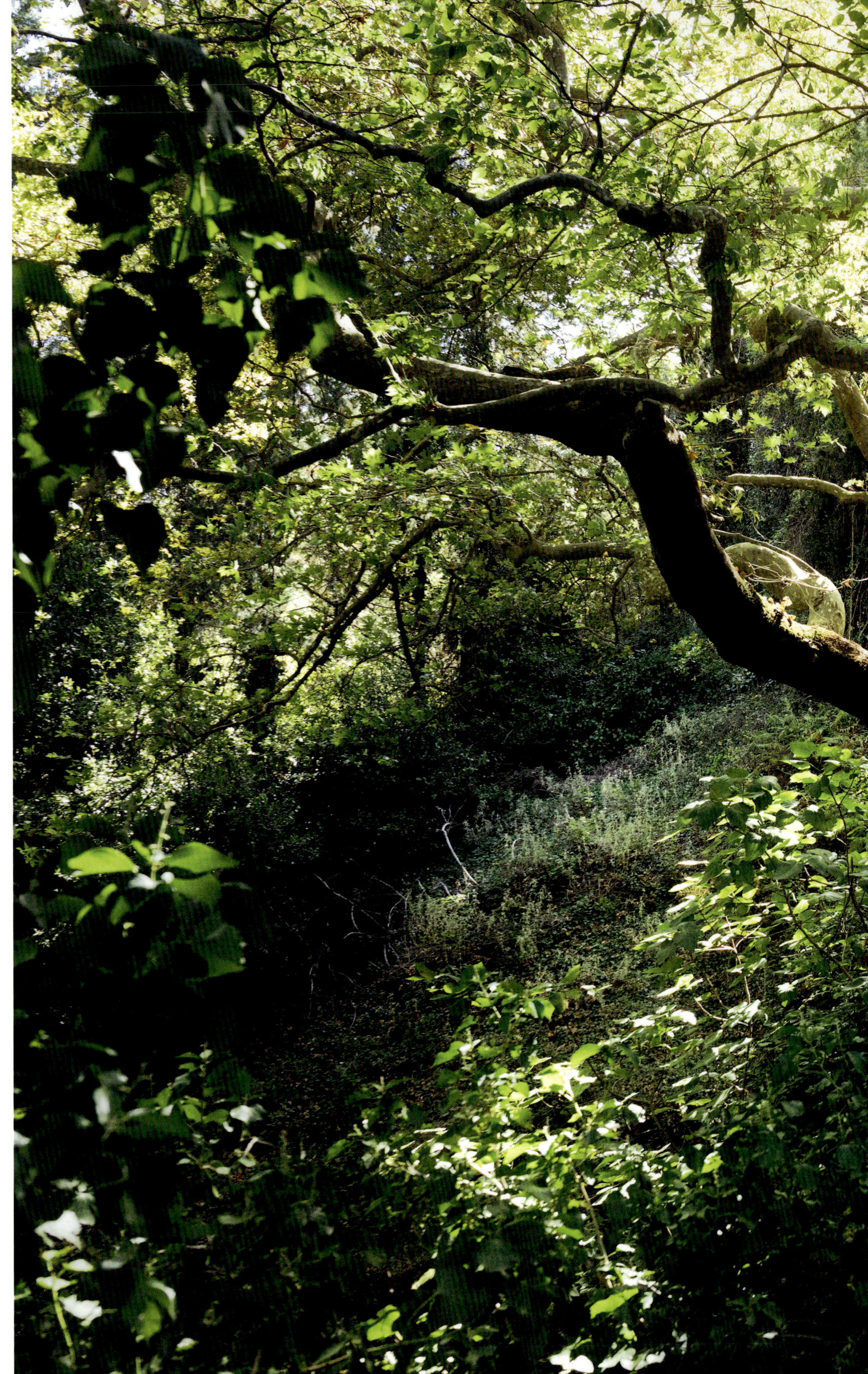

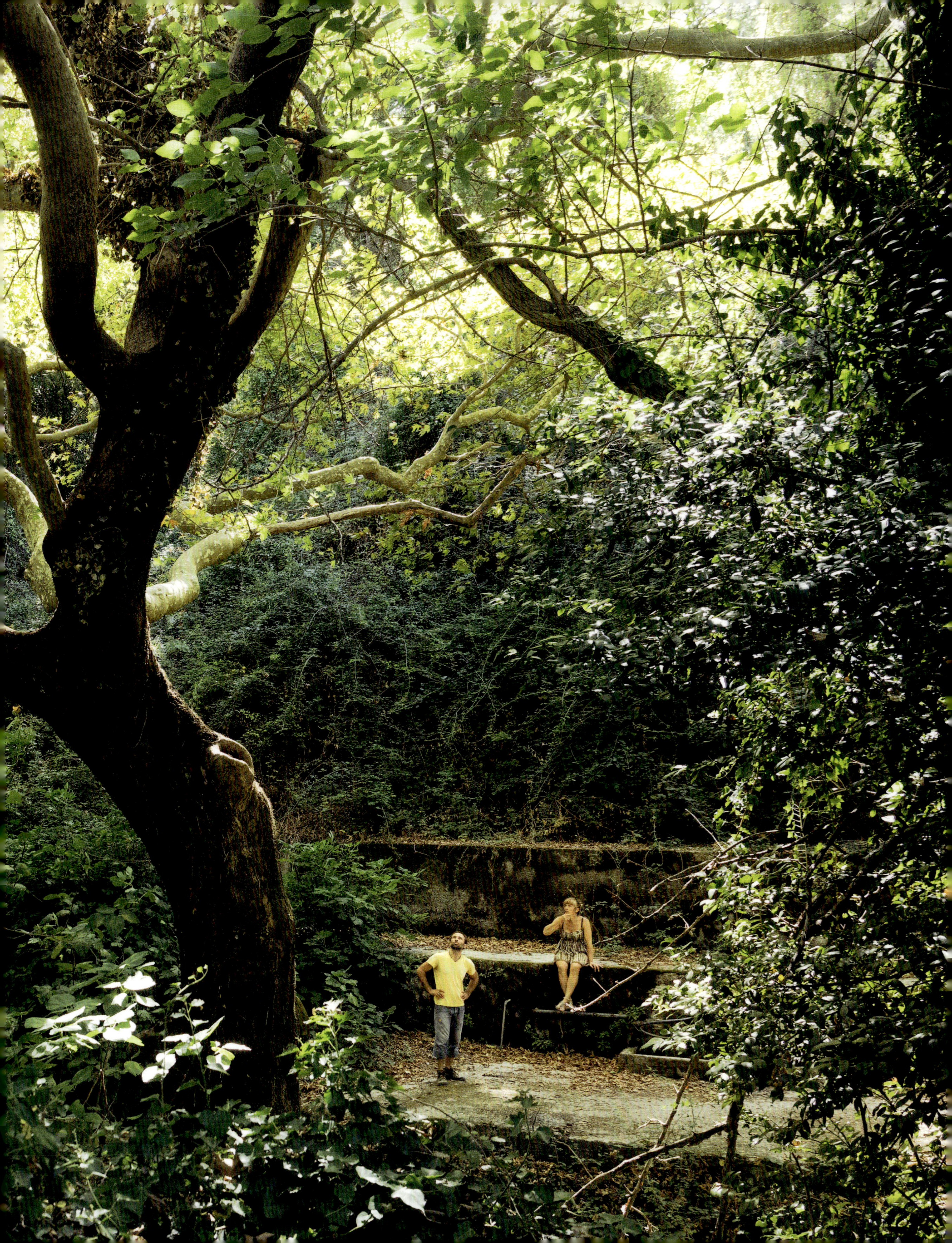

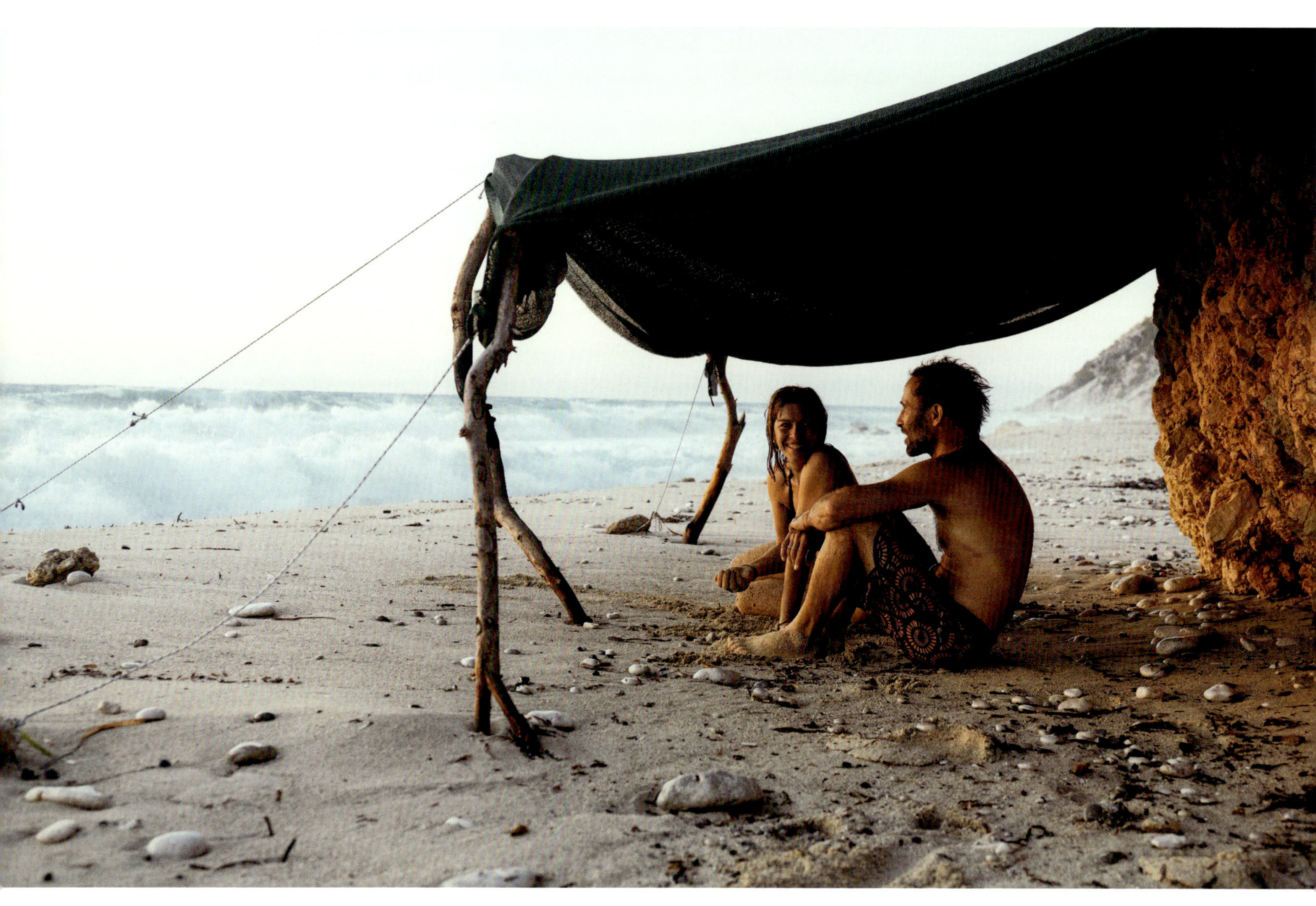

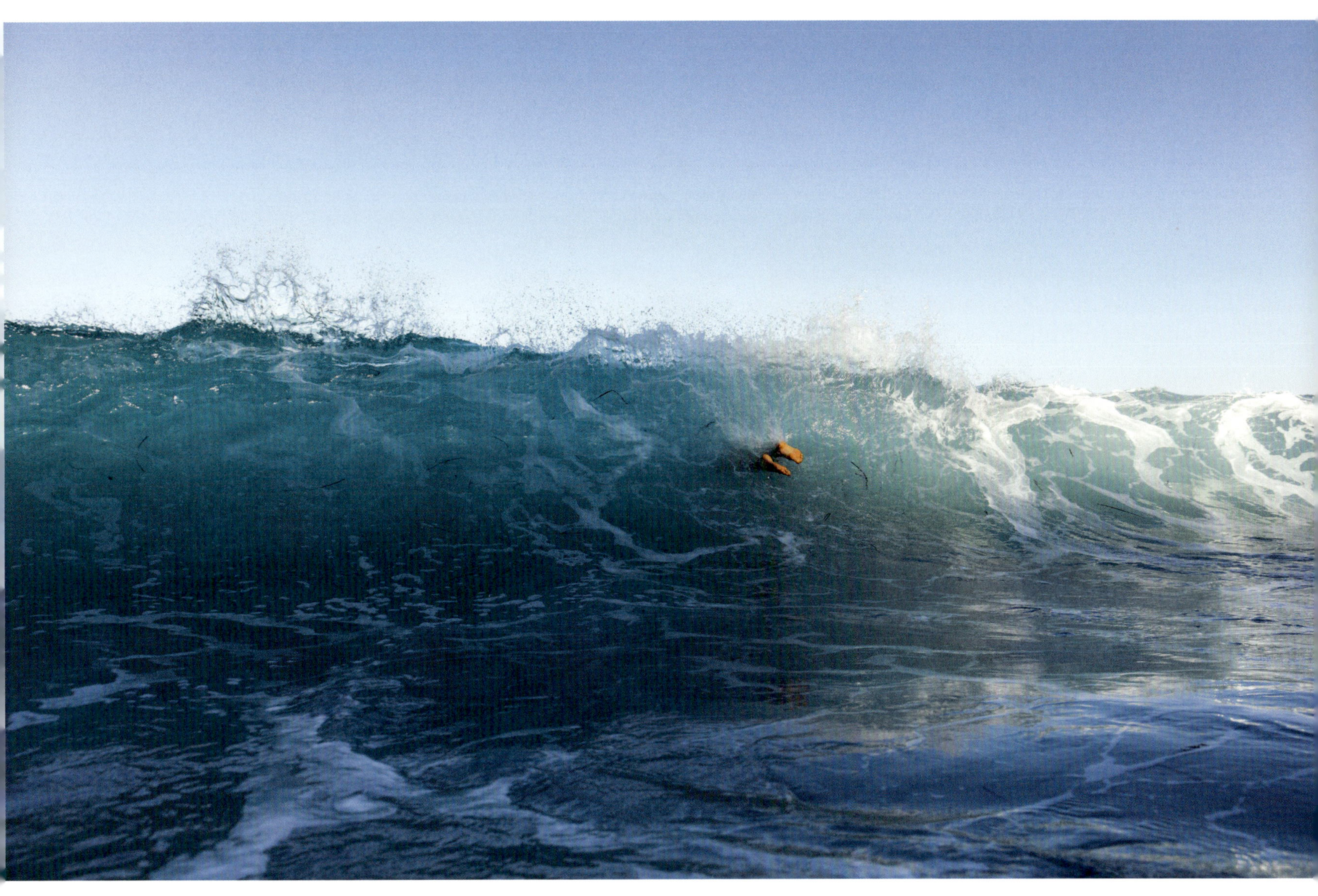

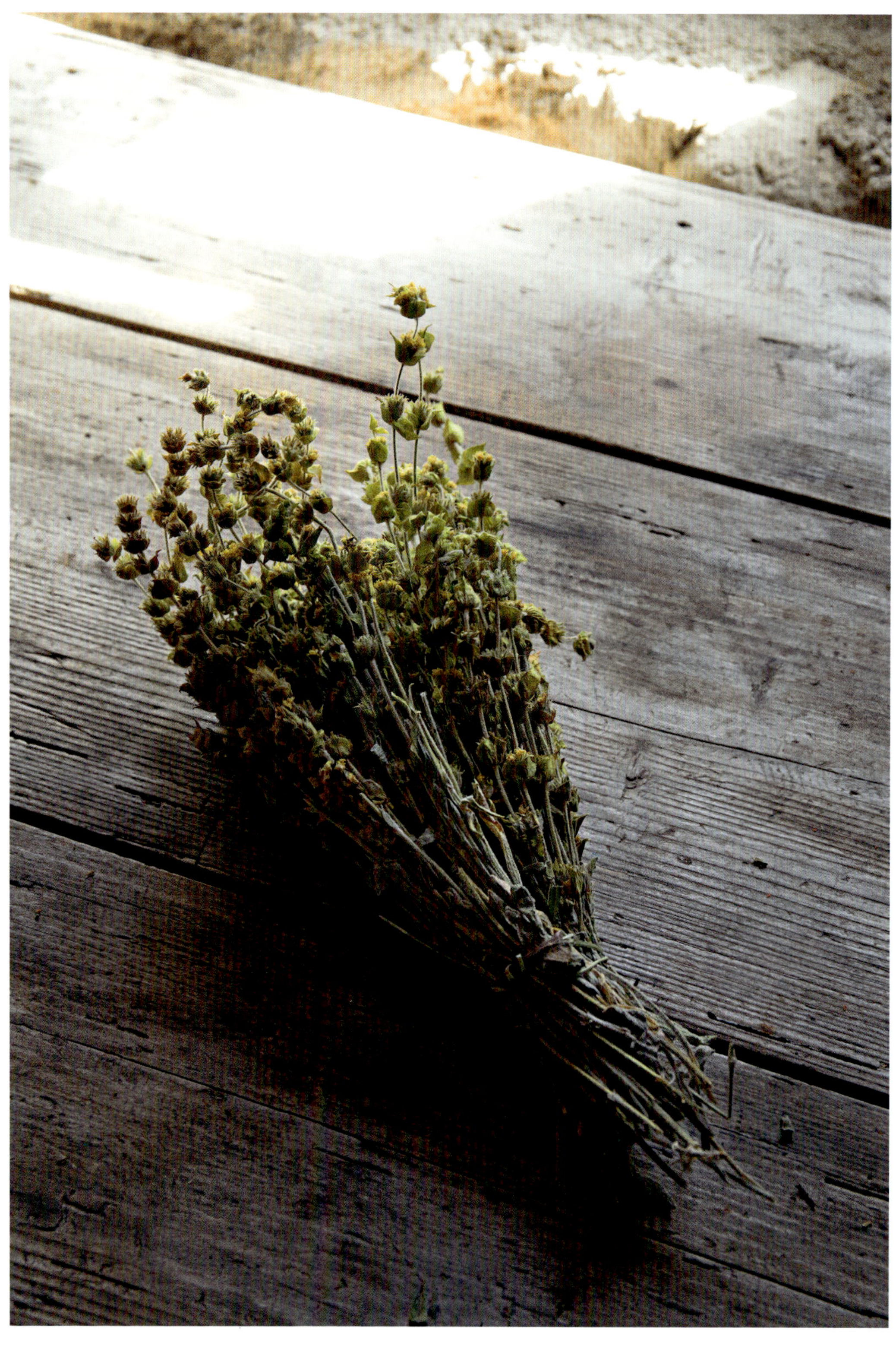

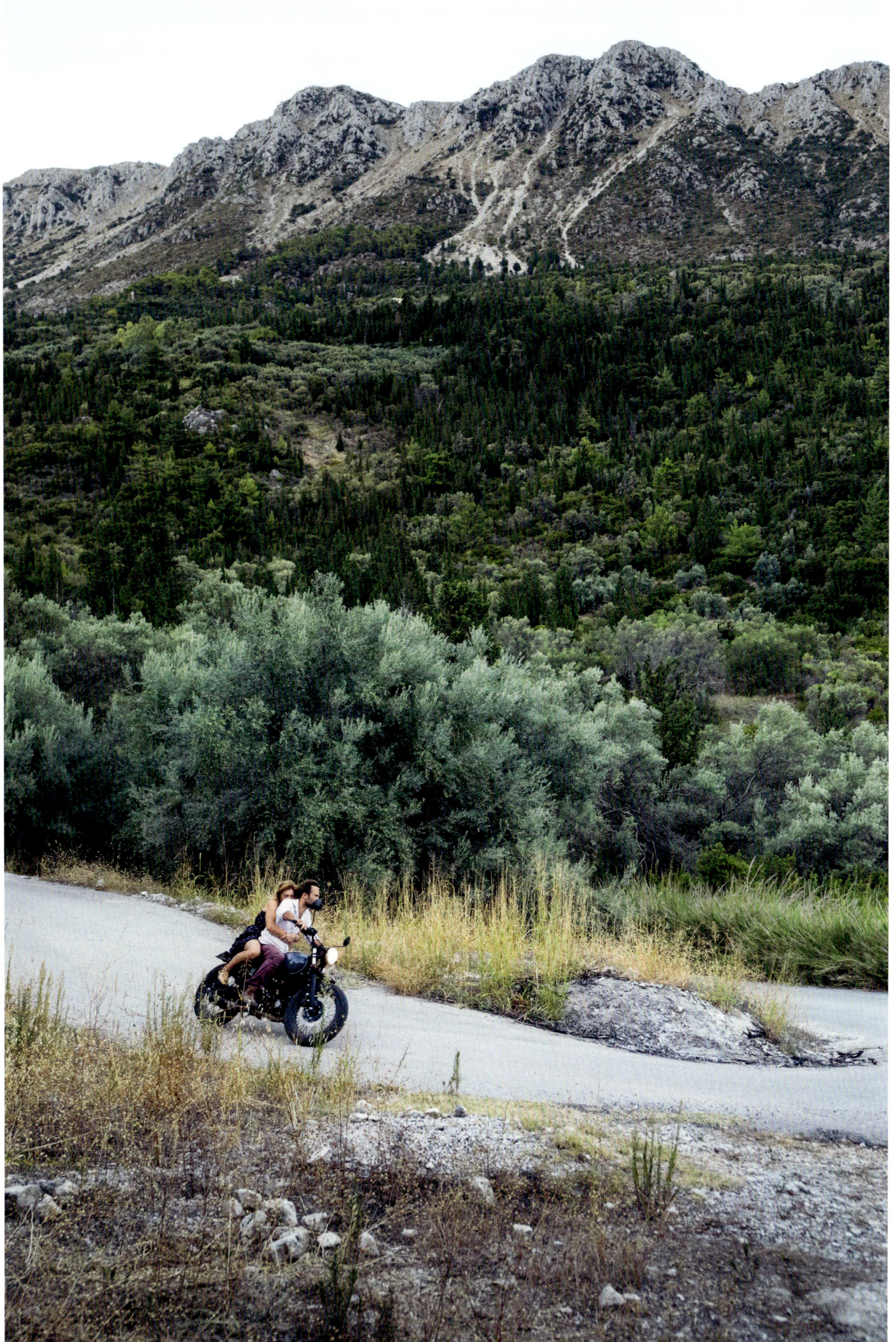

SKY

———

"IT WOULD BE SO STRANGE
TO LIVE SOMEWHERE
WITHOUT THE SOUND OF THE
HENS CACKLING OR BIRDS
SINGING."

———

„ES WÄRE SO EIGENARTIG,
IRGENDWO ZU LEBEN,
WO MAN DIE HÜHNER NICHT
GACKERN UND DIE VÖGEL
NICHT SINGEN HÖRT."

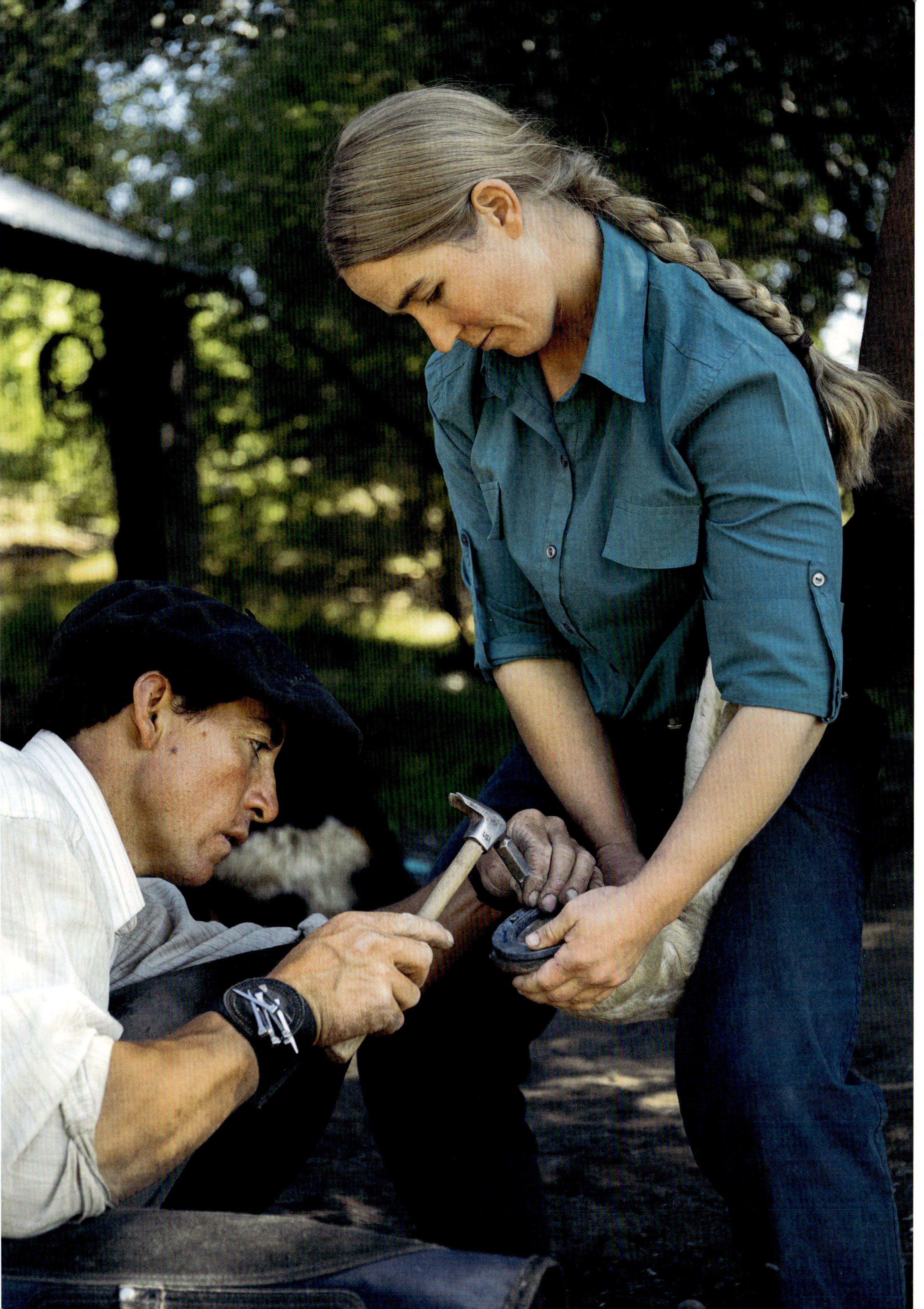

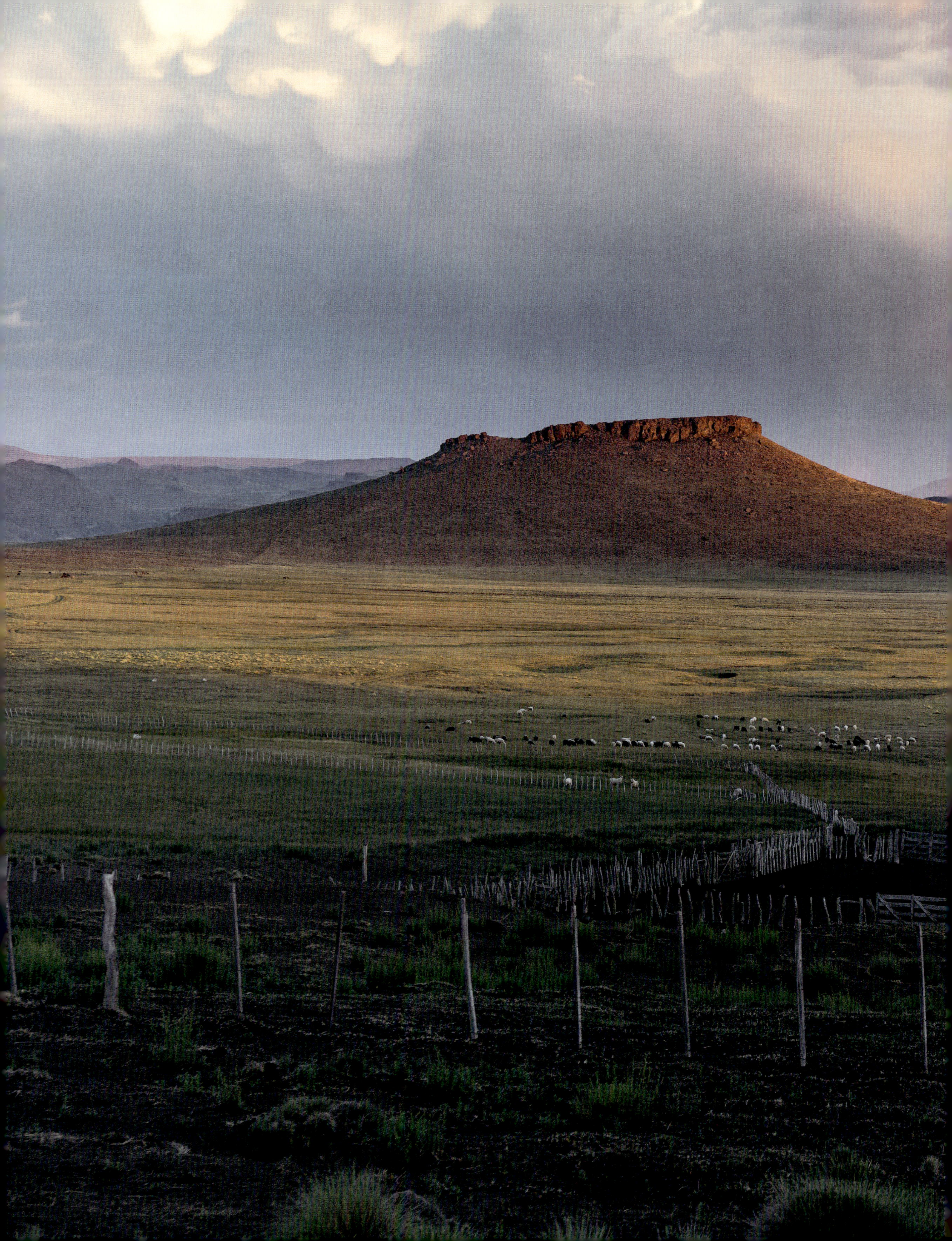

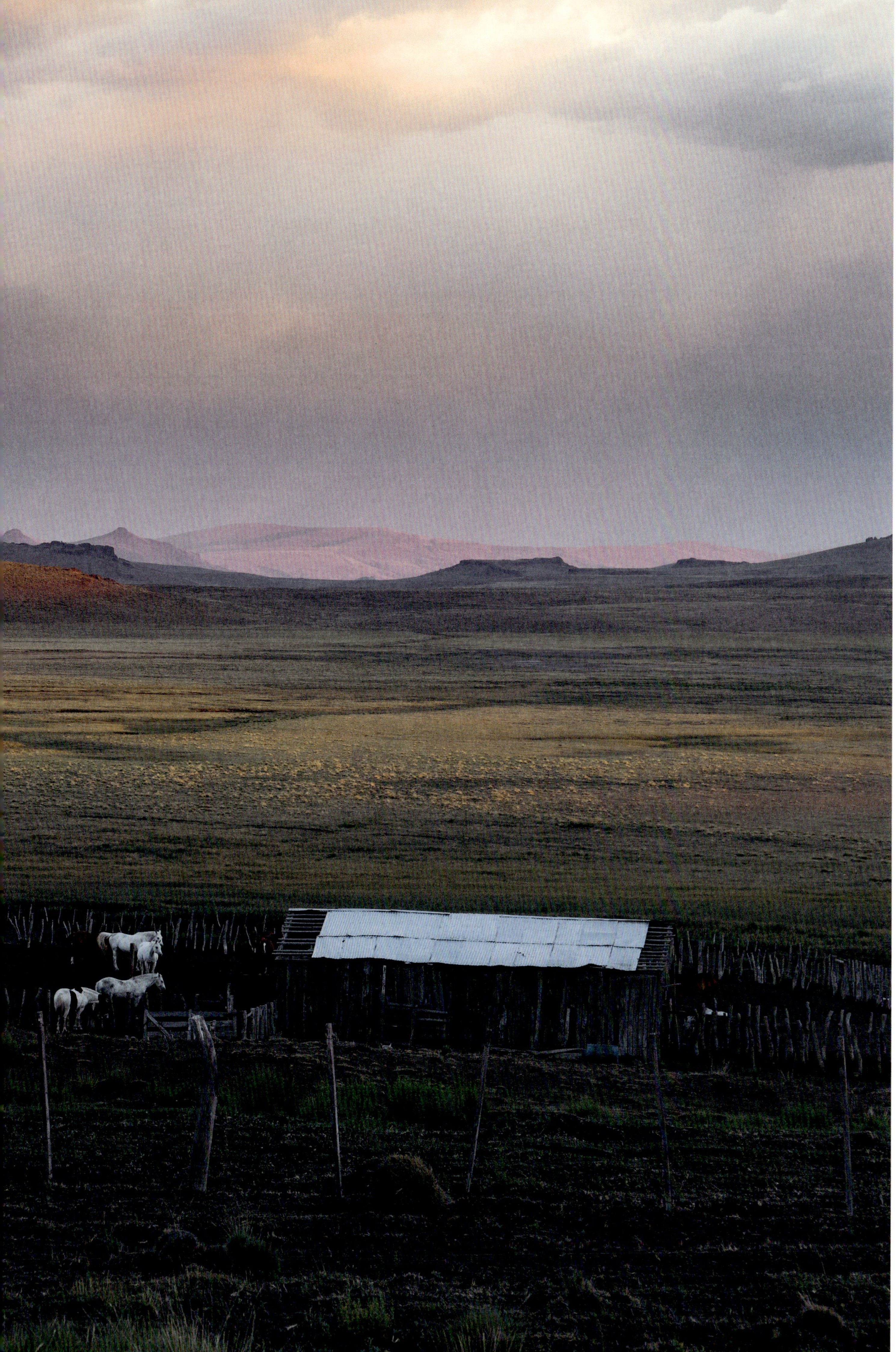

THE GAUCHO OF PATAGONIA

PROVINCE OF NEUQUÉN, ARGENTINA

A reserved and introverted teenager, Sky's passion for horses was so strong
that she decided to move to an isolated little farm in northern Patagonia to breed livestock
with her husband Chano and their son Léo.

Sky's little farm sits at the foot of the Andes mountain range, on high plateaux battered by unceasing Patagonian winds. Born in 1988 in Aspen, Colorado, to a family of wealthy hippies, she grew up between the USA and Argentina where her father had acquired an estancia after a life of thrilling journeys and adventure. "I would spend the summer in Colorado and California. In winter, my parents went to Argentina and I would join them there. I was home-schooled, an only child, a loner and shy, with few friends. Growing up, I became passionate about horses and decided to make a career out of it."

At eighteen, Sky started working on ranches and in equestrian centres. After a lifetime immersed in the equestrian world, a passion inherited from her mother Ginny, an artist and painter, Sky changed direction at the age of 26. She chose to live in Argentina full-time and become a gaucho, ready to overturn a few traditions. Because, here, few women work with livestock. Along with her husband, Chano, a gaucho from the region, she started up her own farm.

"I always wanted to work with horses but I realised while working on ranches that the horses I was training would never belong to me. In Argentina, I had the opportunity to channel all my heart and energy into something that could be mine. And it is now! It's very satisfying."

The couple put in long days to make it work. "I get up early every morning to milk my cows. I don't look at the time. My only pointers during the day are the sun's position, the changes in the weather and the rhythm of the livestock's movements. Our entire life revolves around the animals. We have 600 to 700 if we count the goats, sheep and cows. We do all our work on horseback, from checking on the animals with our dogs to maintaining our kilometres of fencing."

When the heat gets too much in summer, it is time for the major summer migration, known as transhumance. The couple and their large herd travel for three days on horseback to their destination – a high plateau at 2,000 metres' altitude where a number of gauchos leave their livestock in Raúl's care. A reclusive shepherd, Raúl lives in a little hut made up of three low stone walls and a piece of blue tarpaulin that flaps in the wind. He spends the summer months alone and keeps a close eye on the animals in his charge.

As they journey to meet him, the Patagonian mountains unfurl along with their magic. The nature teems with strange animals, armadillos and rheas, cousins of the ostrich, as well as hares and pheasants which scurry away at the sound of the hoofs. This wild abundance brings a beauty to this cowboy life in a remote and unspoilt region. The group of riders cross valleys and rivers to the mountains; an equestrian epic with a heavy- and slow-moving herd that kicks up clouds of dust which settle in the lines of tired faces reddened by the sun.

Though exhausting for the gauchos, this transhumance is essential for the herd. This gruelling outdoor life pushes young generations to live in cities and do easier, better-paid jobs. The rural

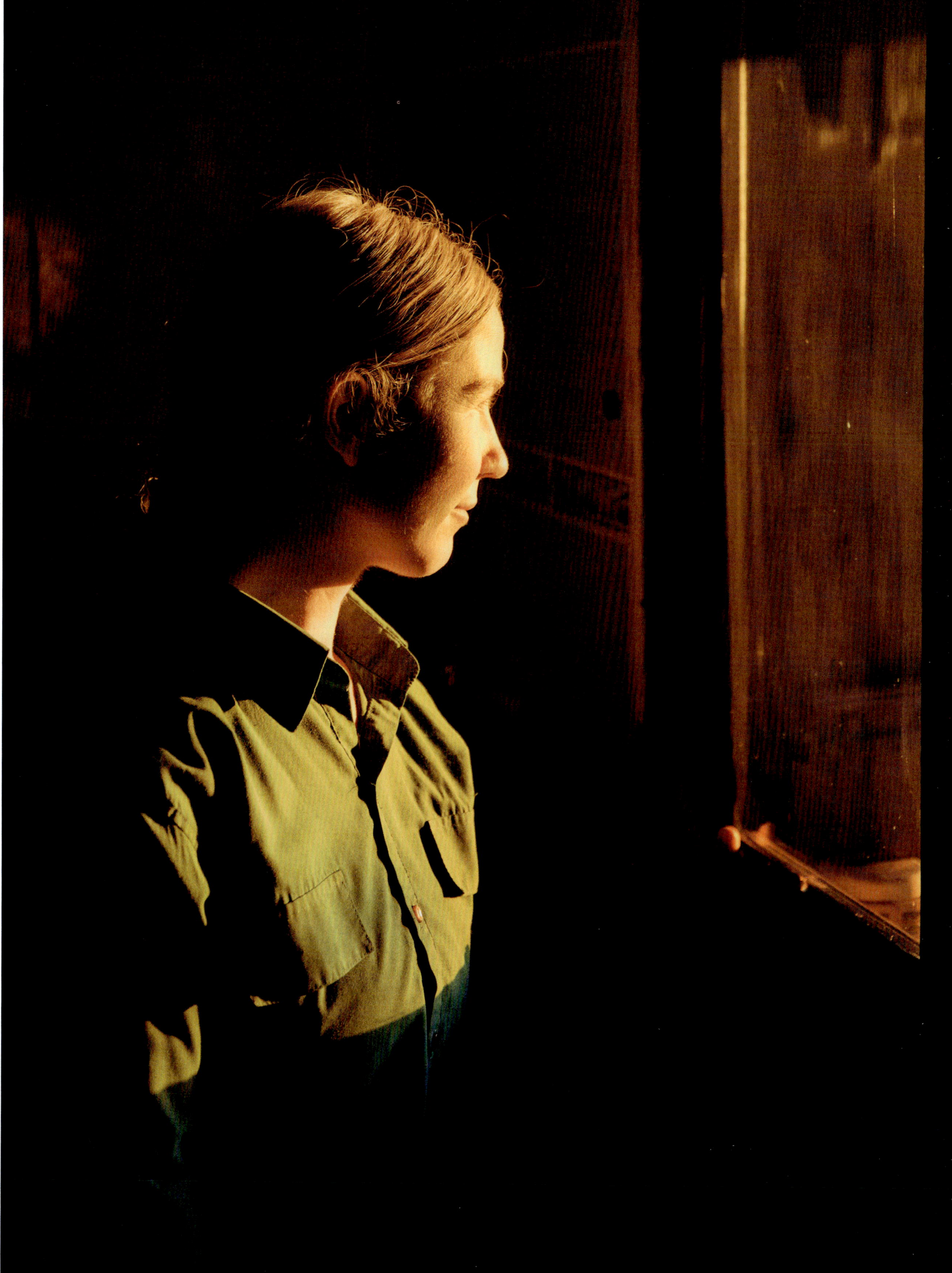

exodus is slow but sure, proven by the many poplars they encounter along the way – the only vestiges of the little farms that once stood in the mountains.

Sky has never been back to her home country. Here, she has few needs; perhaps a little burst of electricity in the evening, captured by the solar panels during the day. No TV, no internet. To make a phone call, she has to crest the windy hill behind the ranch to get the beginnings of a signal. Since Léo was born, she has taken something of a she-wolf approach to parenting, always overseeing the transhumance but staying away from the farm for shorter periods of time. Léo cannot yet ride unassisted and Sky is waiting for him to master his horse before resuming all her duties on the ranch. There is her mother Ginny too who suffers with multiple sclerosis and on whom she checks regularly – Ginny now lives with her for much of the year.

The closest neighbours are 45 minutes down the track, which is in such poor condition that it is faster by horse than by car. Despite this, she has made her choice and embraces it joyfully in the abundant nature, however not without a little concern for the future. "We're lucky to have water sources that never run dry, which we use to irrigate all our pastures. The water is very good quality and tastes good. But one day, a volcanic eruption affected the water for a few days. We were very worried."

Such is her attachment to this immense region, Sky cannot imagine leaving. "Every time I go to the city, I feel a huge emptiness. This shows me how connected I am to nature and this life. It would be so strange to live somewhere without the sound of the hens cackling or birds singing." But she also knows that she is completely dependent on the climate and how it evolves.

"We know that this can't last. It gets warmer every year and we're afraid that episodes of drought may occur. A large livestock farm may not be the most sustainable solution for the future." By then, her son Léo will be grown up and may also live life on horseback, either here or elsewhere.

EINE GAUCHO IN PATAGONIEN

Sky, die als Jugendliche zurückhaltend und introvertiert war, ist von einer solchen Leidenschaft für Pferde beseelt, dass sie sich mit ihrem Mann Chano und ihrem Sohn Léo auf einer abgelegenen Farm im Norden Patagoniens niedergelassen hat, um Rinder zu züchten.

Auf den Hochebenen am Fuß der Anden, von den unaufhörlichen Winden Patagoniens gepeitscht, steht Skys kleiner Bauernhof. Sie wurde 1988 in Aspen, Colorado als Tochter einer Familie wohlhabender Hippies geboren und wuchs in den USA und Argentinien auf, wo ihr Vater nach einem Leben voller Fernreisen und Abenteuer eine Estancia gekauft hatte. „Die Sommer verbrachte ich zwischen Colorado und Kalifornien. Im Winter reisten meine Eltern nach Argentinien, und ich ging mit. Ich wurde zu Hause unterrichtet und war ein Einzelkind, einsam, schüchtern, mit wenigen Freunden. Als ich größer wurde, begeisterte ich mich für Pferde und beschloss, sie zu meinem Beruf zu machen.“

Mit achtzehn Jahren beginnt Sky, auf Ranches und in Reitsportzentren zu arbeiten. Die junge Frau, die immer im Reitermilieu gelebt hat – eine von ihrer Mutter, der Malerin Ginny, geerbte Passion –, ändert mit 26 Jahren ihr Leben. Sie beschließt, ganzjährig in Argentinien zu bleiben und Gaucho zu werden, auch wenn das einige Traditionen über den Haufen wirft, weil hier nur wenige Frauen mit den Rindern arbeiten. Gemeinsam mit ihrem Mann Chano, einem aus der Gegend stammenden Gaucho, gründet sie ihre eigene Zucht.

„Ich wollte immer etwas mit Pferden machen, aber bei der Rancharbeit wurde mir bewusst, dass die Pferde, die ich trainierte, mir nie gehören würden. In Argentinien hatte ich die Chance, mein Herz und meine Energie in etwas Eigenes zu stecken … Und jetzt ist es da! Das ist sehr befriedigend.“

Das Paar kommt zurecht, allerdings um den Preis langer Tage. „Jeden Morgen stehe ich früh auf, um meine Kühe zu melken.

Ich schaue nicht auf die Uhr, meine einzigen Anhaltspunkte für den Tageslauf sind Sonnenstand, Wetter und die Ortwechsel der Rinder. Unser ganzes Leben hier dreht sich um die Tiere. Wir haben 600 bis 700 Ziegen, Schafe und Kühe. Die Tiere mit unseren Hunden zu überwachen, kilometerlange Zäune zu unterhalten … All diese Arbeiten erledigen wir zu Pferd.“

Im Sommer, wenn die Hitze zu groß wird, kommt die Zeit des großen Viehtriebs. Diese Reise mit der großen Herde dauert drei Tagesritte. Sie führt zu einem Hochplateau in über 2000 Metern Höhe, wo mehrere Gauchos ihre Rinder dem Hirten Raúl anvertrauen. Er lebt wie ein Eremit in einer kleinen Hütte aus drei Steinwänden und einer blauen, im Wind flatternden Plane und hütet in den Sommermonaten allein und aufmerksam die ihm anvertrauten Rinder.

Im Lauf dieser langen Reise offenbaren sich die Berge Patagoniens in ihrem ganzen Zauber. Die Natur ist voller seltsamer Wesen: Gürteltiere und Nandus, Cousins der Strauße, aber auch Hasen und Fasane, die vor dem Stampfen der Hufe fliehen. Eine wilde Vielfalt, die das Cowboyleben in dieser unberührten, abgeschiedenen Gegend reicher macht. Die Reitergruppe durchquert auf dem Weg in die Berge Täler und Flüsse – ein reales Reiterepos, in dessen Verlauf die Herde in langsamem, schwerem Schritt vorwärtstrottet und Staubwolken aufwirbelt, die sich in den Falten der erschöpften, von der Sonne geröteten Gesichter absetzen.

Dieser Viehtrieb mag für die Gauchos anstrengend sein; für die Herde ist er lebenswichtig. Übrigens ist es genau diese Härte des Lebens im Freien, die die jüngere Generation dazu treibt, sich in der Stadt leichtere, besser bezahlte Berufe zu suchen. Die Landflucht verläuft langsam, aber wahrnehmbar. Die zahlreichen Pappelhaine am Wegesrand zeugen davon – sie sind die letzten Spuren kleiner Farmen, die einst in den Bergen existierten.

In ihr Heimatland ist Sky nie zurückgekehrt. Hier braucht sie zum Leben nur wenig: einen kurzen Moment der Elektrizität am Abend, tagsüber von Solarpaneelen eingefangen. Kein Fernsehen, kein Internet. Um zu telefonieren, muss man auf den windigen Hügel hinter der Ranch steigen, um Spuren eines Signals einzufangen. Seit Léos Geburt verhält sie sich ein wenig wie eine Wolfsmutter; sie begleitet immer noch die Viehtriebe, entfernt sich aber nicht mehr so lang vom Haus. Léo steigt noch nicht allein aufs Pferd, und Sky möchte abwarten, bis er sein Reittier meistert, bevor sie wieder voll auf der Ranch mitarbeitet. Außerdem kümmert sie sich regelmäßig um ihre Mutter Ginny, die einen Großteil des Jahres bei ihr verbringt, seit sie an multipler Sklerose erkrankt ist.

Die nächsten Nachbarn wohnen 45 Minuten entfernt, allerdings ist die Straße so schlecht, dass man zu Pferd schneller dort ist als mit dem Auto. Aber das macht nichts. Die Entscheidung ist getroffen, sicher und freudig inmitten einer großzügigen Natur, auch wenn das Ganze manchmal von leisen Zukunftssorgen überschattet wird. „Wir haben das Glück, über Wasserquellen zu verfügen, die nie versiegen und mit denen wir all unsere Weiden bewässern können. Das Wasser ist hochwertig und schmeckt gut. Aber einmal hat ein Vulkanausbruch das Wasser tagelang getrübt. Wir waren sehr besorgt.“

Sky liebt dieses riesige Gebiet so sehr, dass sie sich nicht vorstellen kann, es je zu verlassen. „Jedes Mal, wenn ich in die Stadt fahre, spüre ich eine große Leere. Daran erkenne ich, wie stark ich mit der Natur und diesem Leben verbunden bin … Es wäre so eigenartig, irgendwo zu leben, wo man die Hühner nicht gackern und die Vögel nicht singen hört.“

Aber sie weiß auch, dass sie vollkommen vom Klima und dessen Entwicklung abhängig ist. „Uns ist bewusst, dass es nicht so weitergehen kann. Jedes Jahr wird es heißer, und wir haben Angst vor Dürreperioden. Vielleicht ist eine große Rinderfarm nicht die nachhaltigste Lösung für die Zukunft …“ Bis dahin wird ihr Sohn erwachsen sein und sein Leben vielleicht auch zu Pferd verbringen – hier oder anderswo.

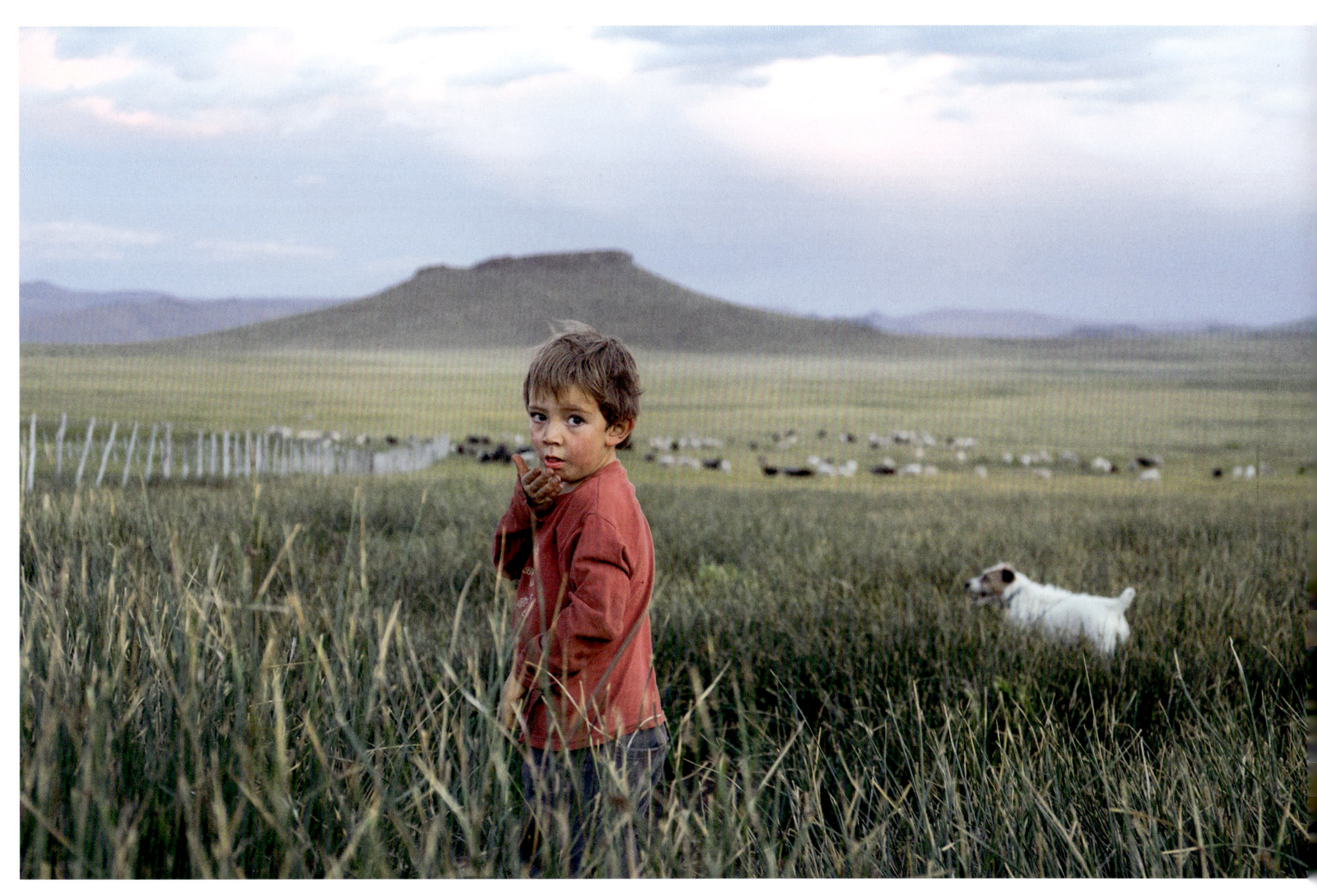

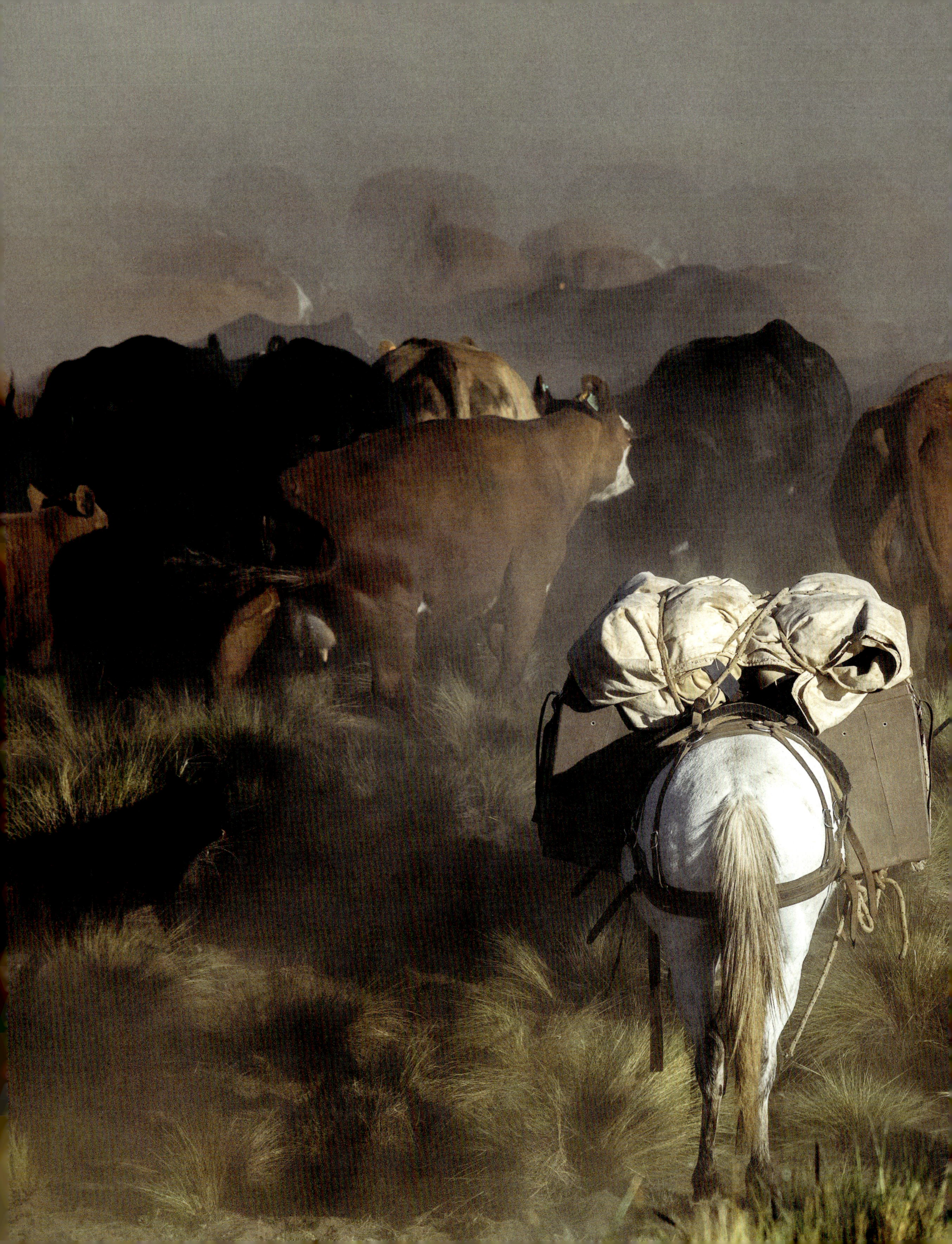

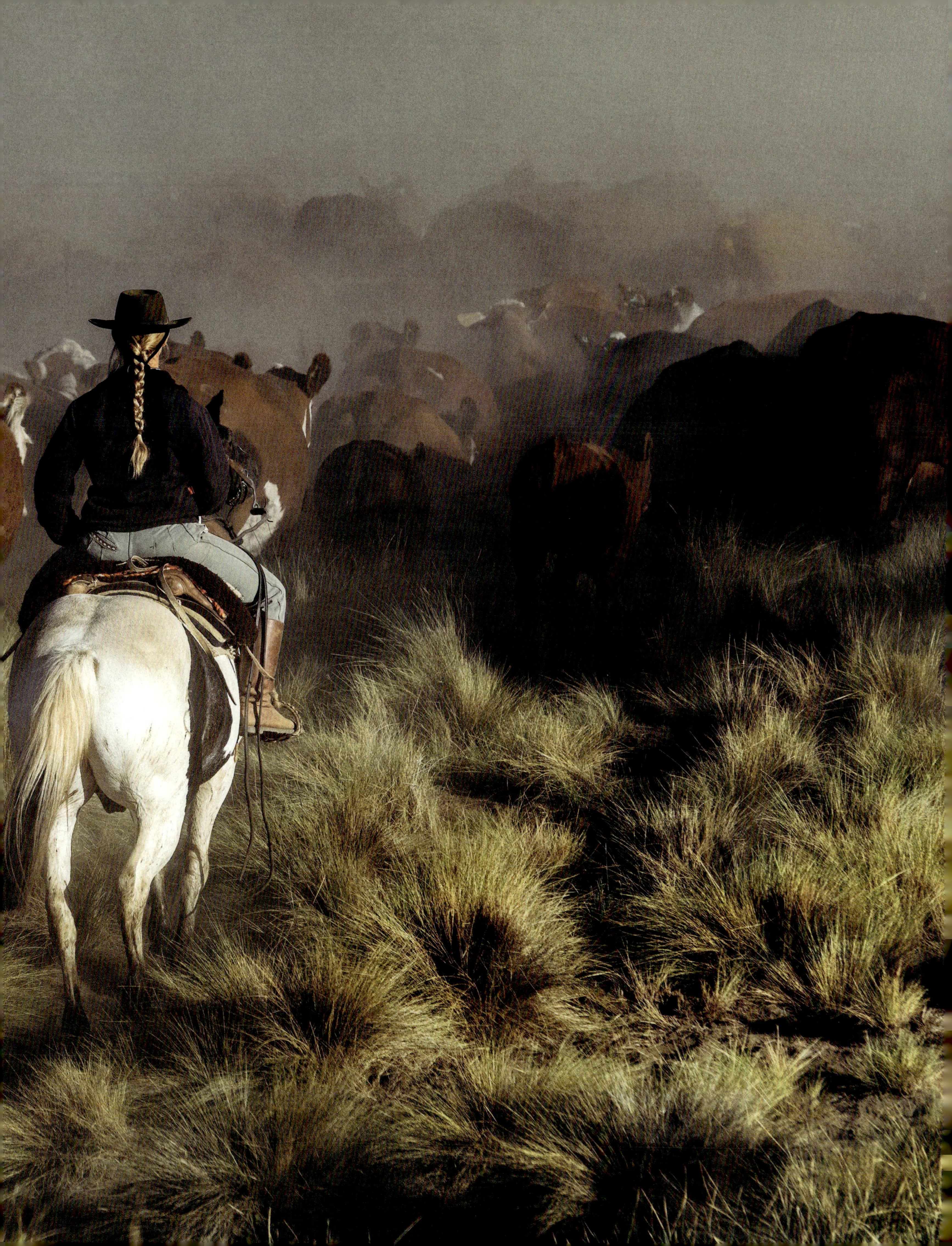

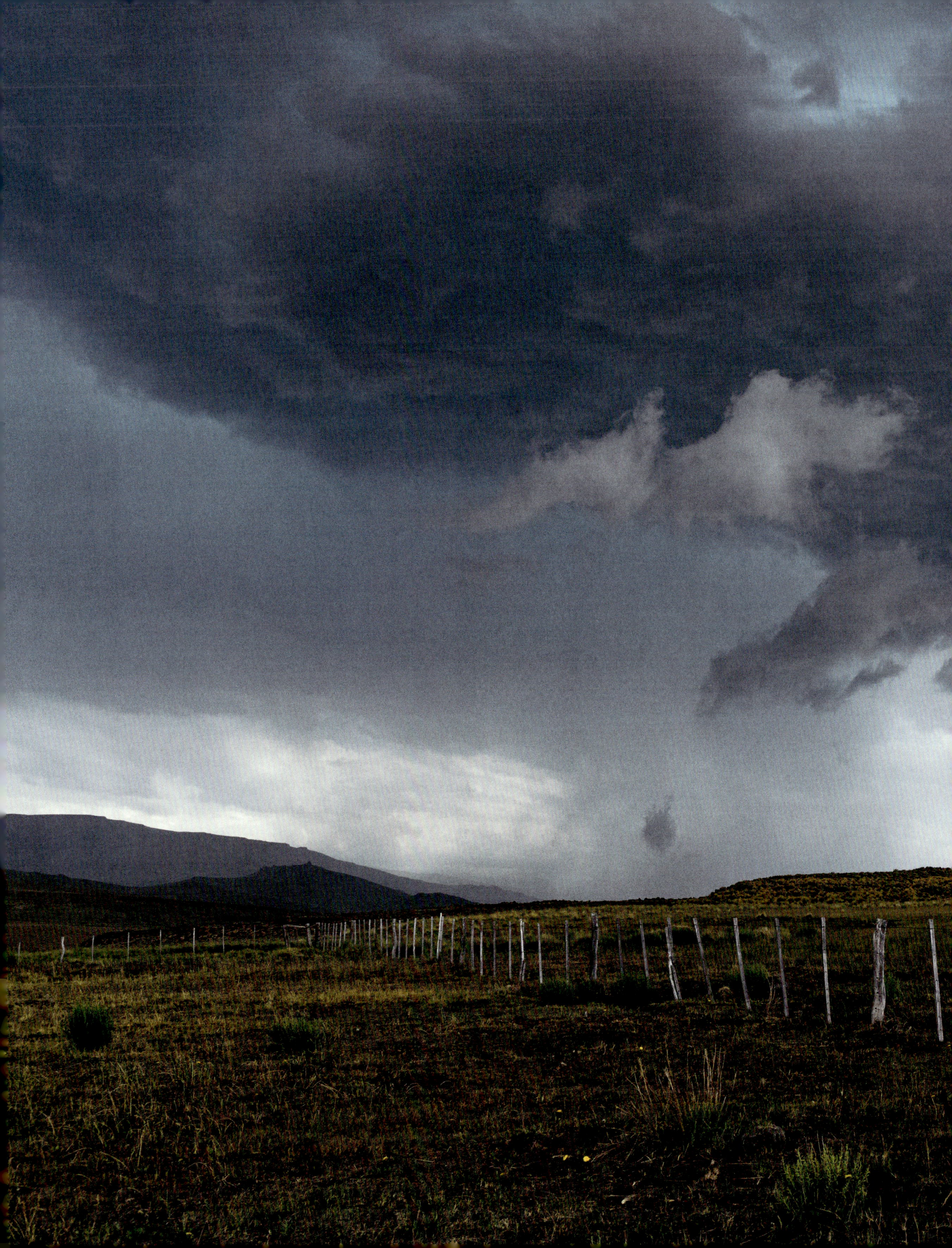

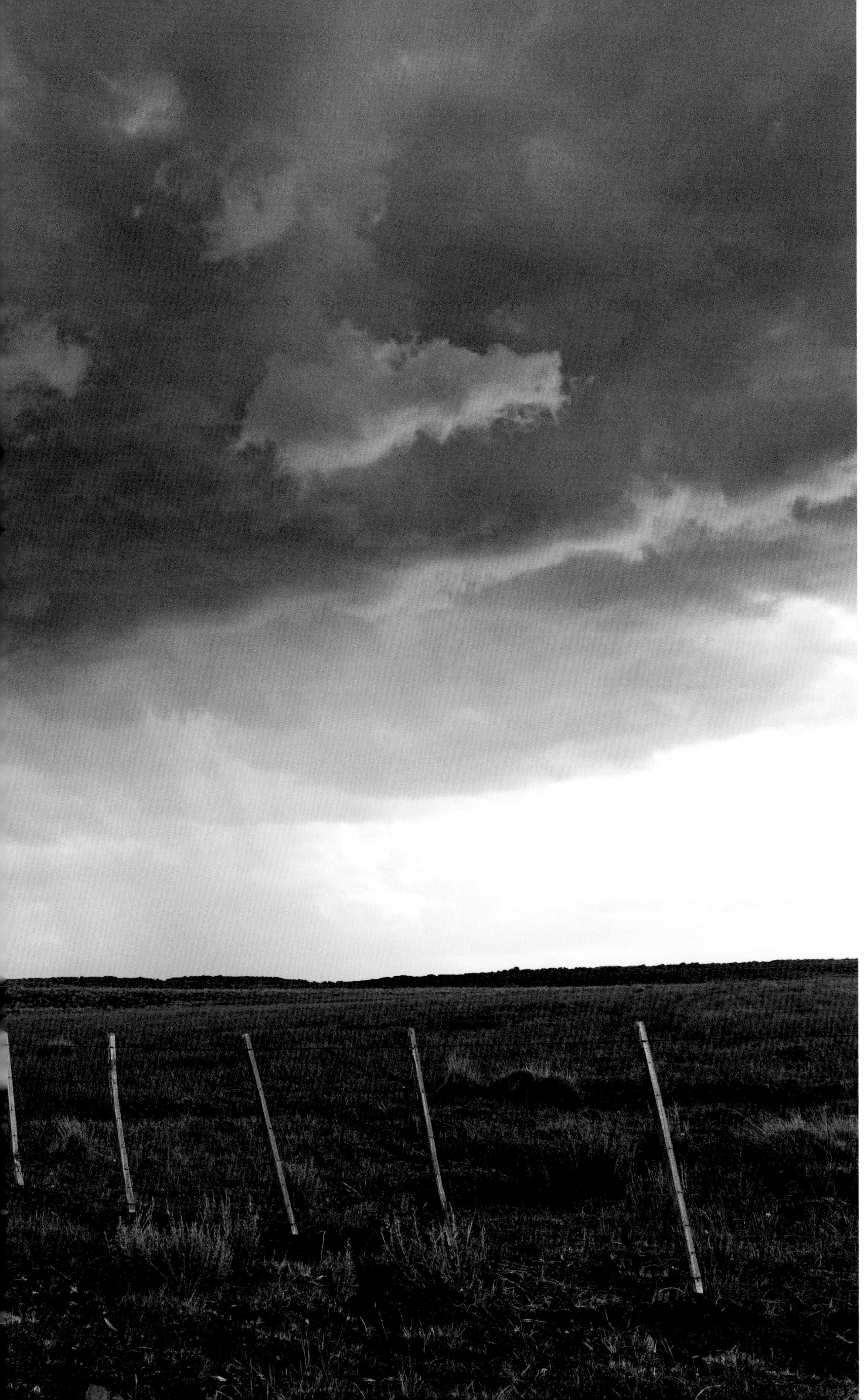

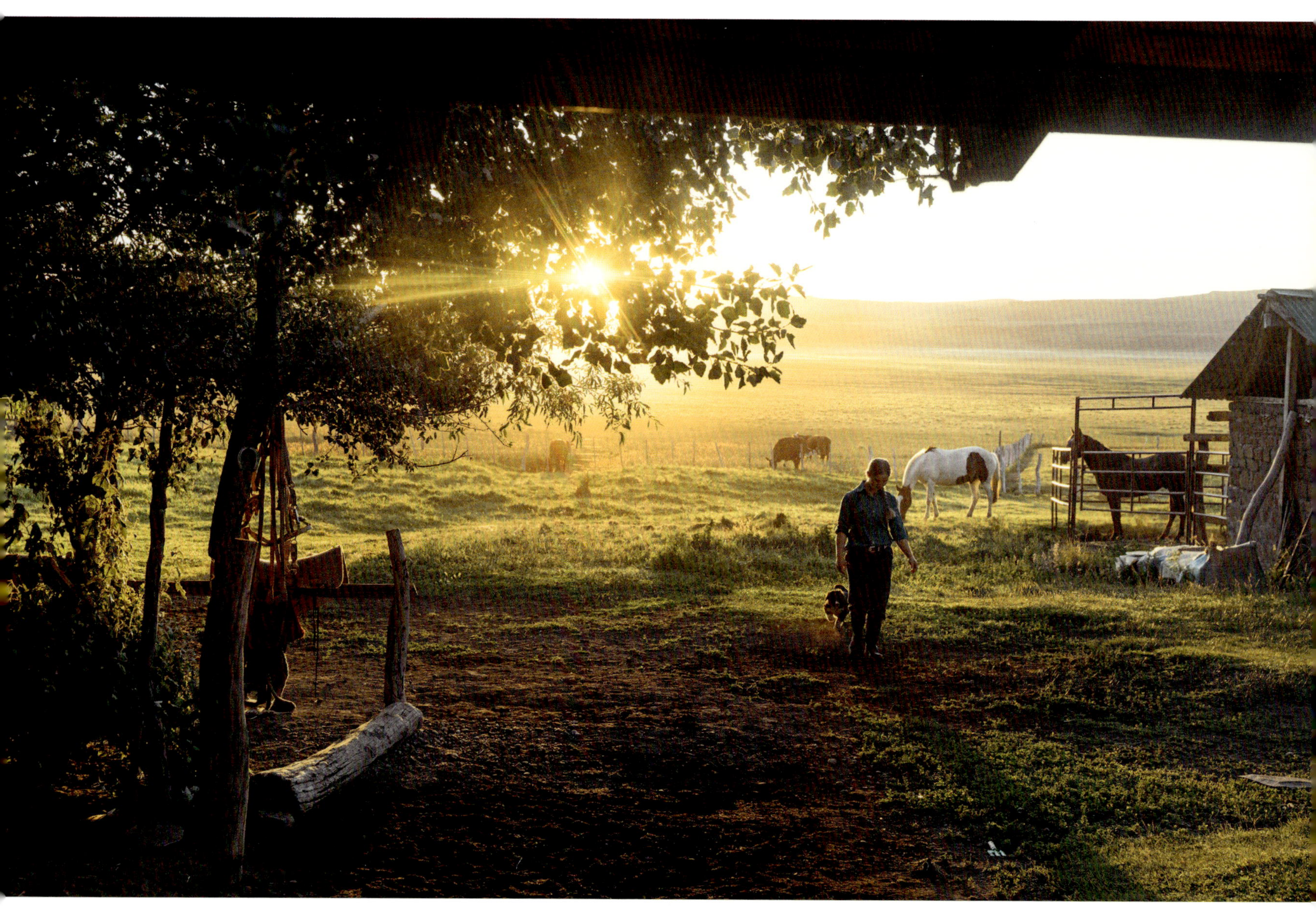

"Perhaps the facts most astounding and most real are
never communicated by man to man. The true
harvest of my daily life is somewhat as intangible and
indescribable as the tints of morning or evening. It is
a little star-dust caught, a segment of the rainbow
which I have clutched."

HENRY DAVID THOREAU
Walden; or, Life in the Woods

„Vielleicht erzählen sich die Menschen nie die
staunenswertesten, wirklichsten Tatsachen.
Die wahre Ernte meines Lebens ist etwas so
Unbegreifliches und Unbeschreibliches wie die Farbe
des Morgen- und Abendhimmels. Ein wenig
eingefangener Sternenstaub, ein bisschen
Niederschlag von dem Regenbogen, den ich
umklammert hielt."

HENRY DAVID THOREAU
Walden oder Leben in den Wäldern

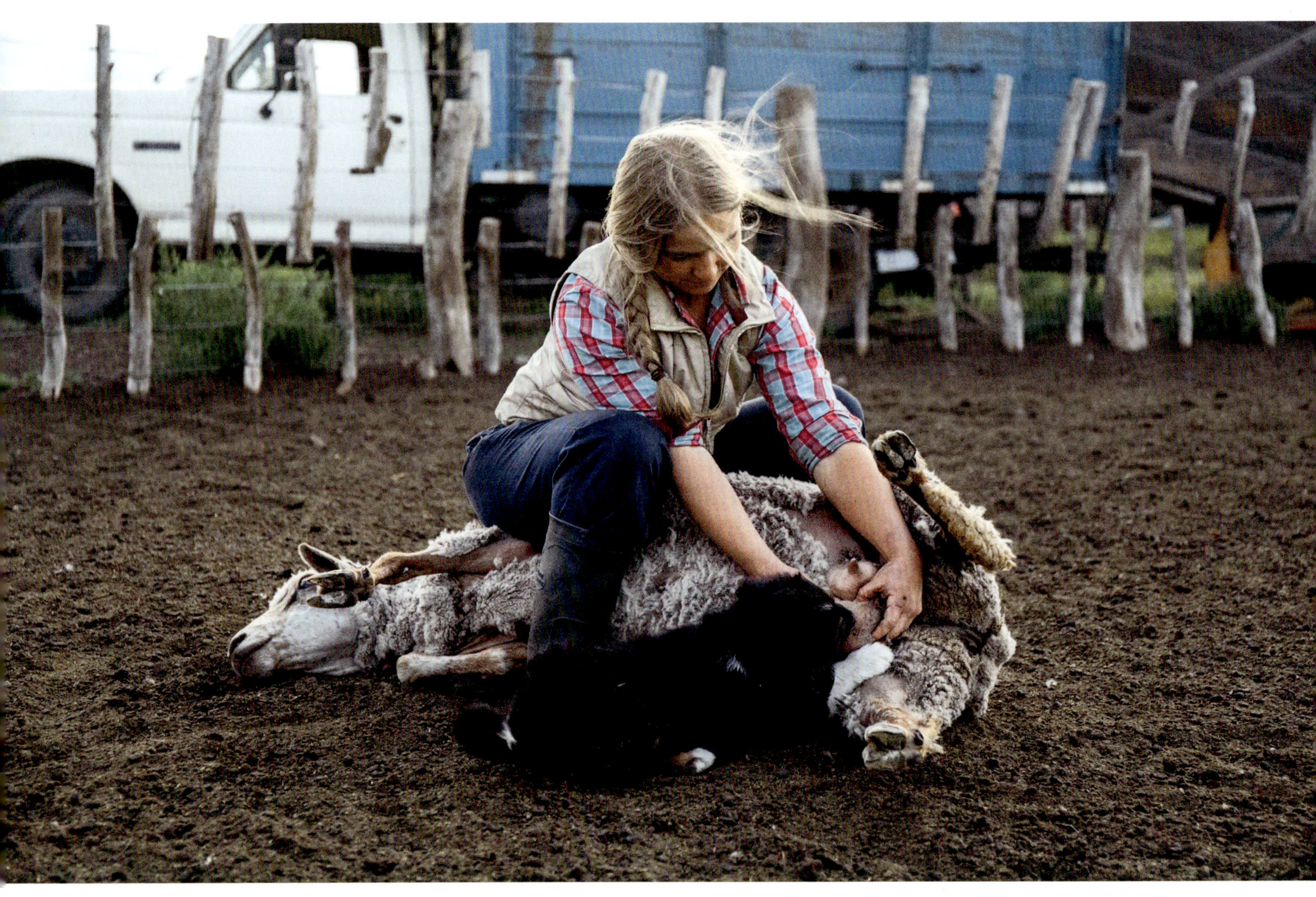

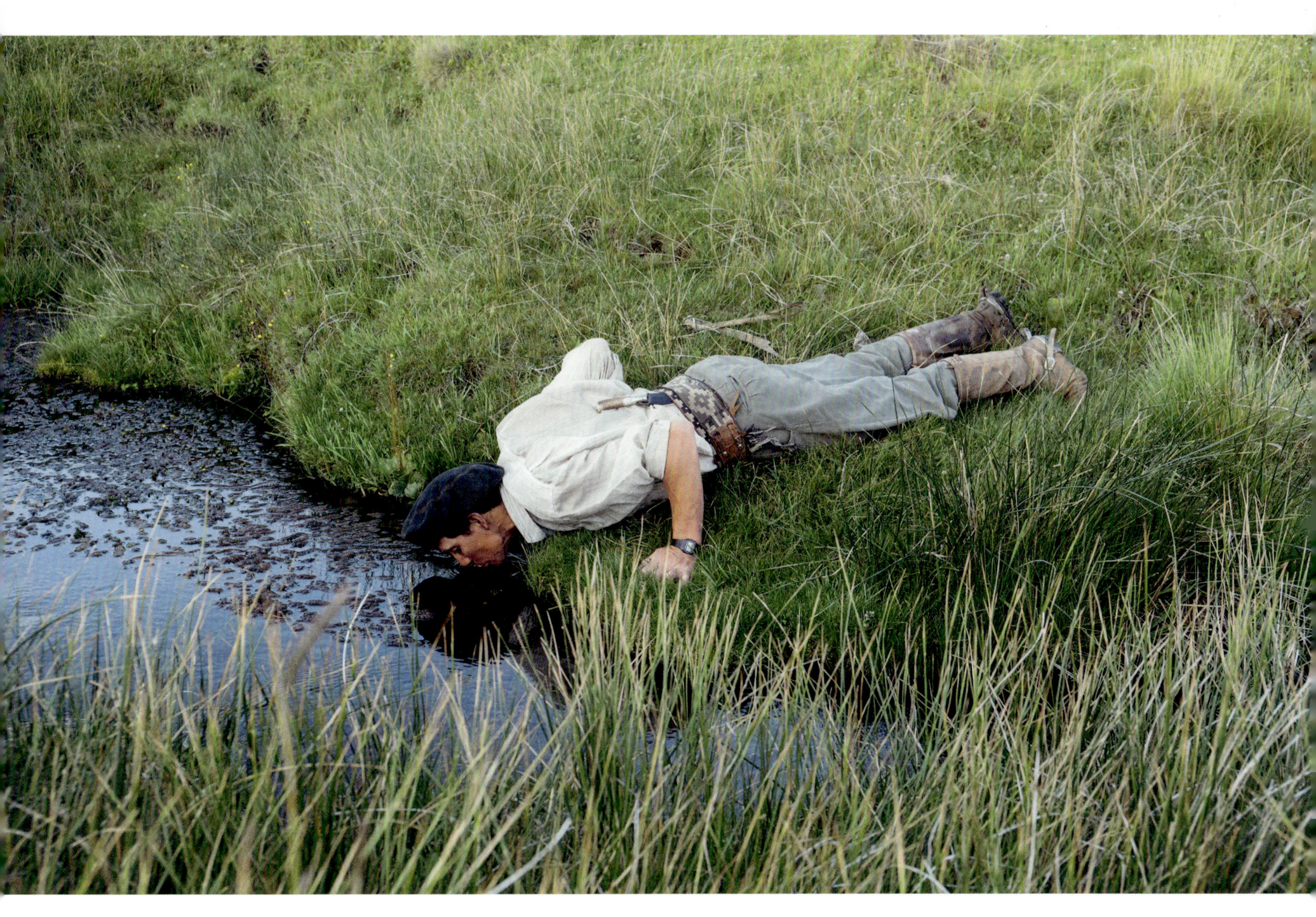

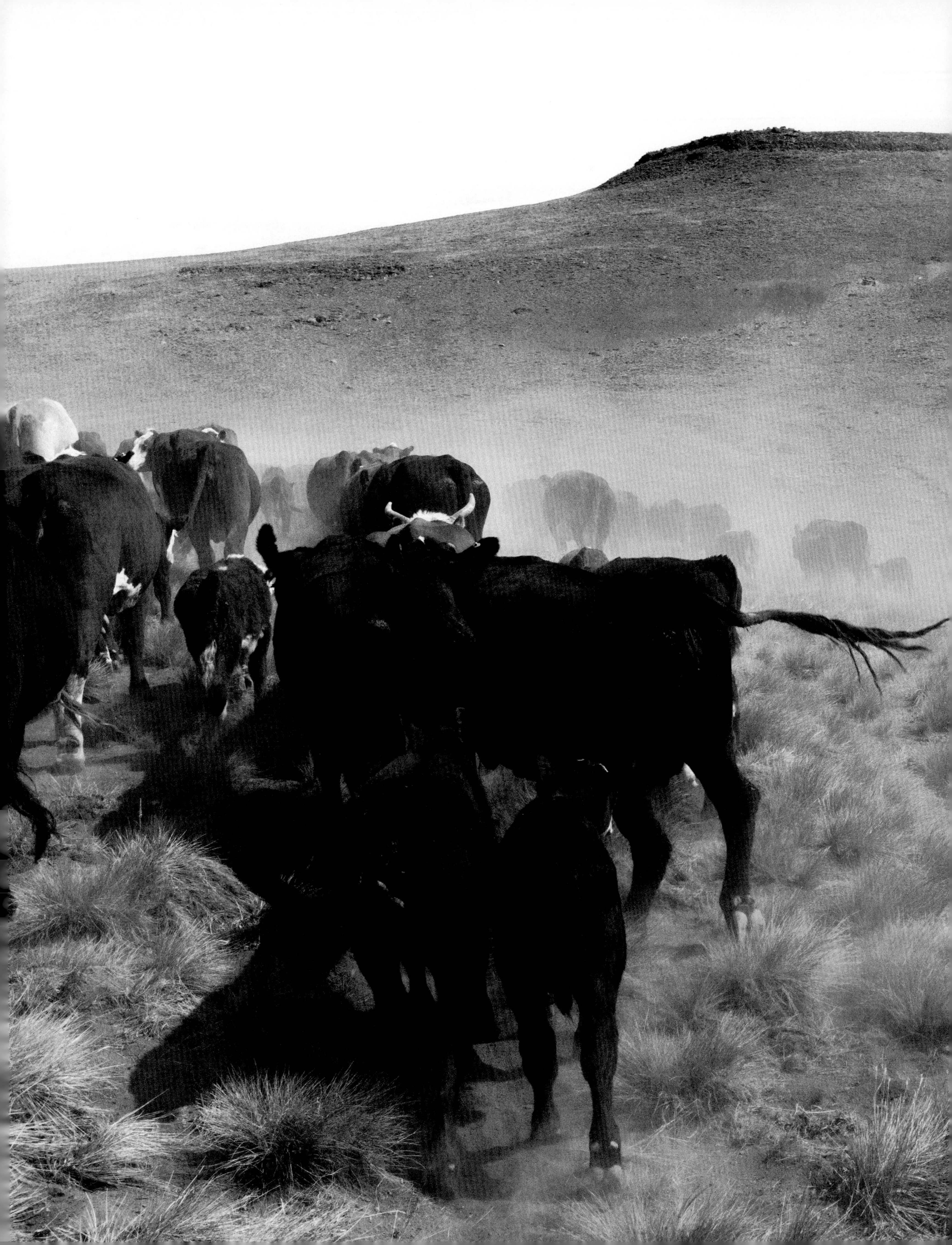

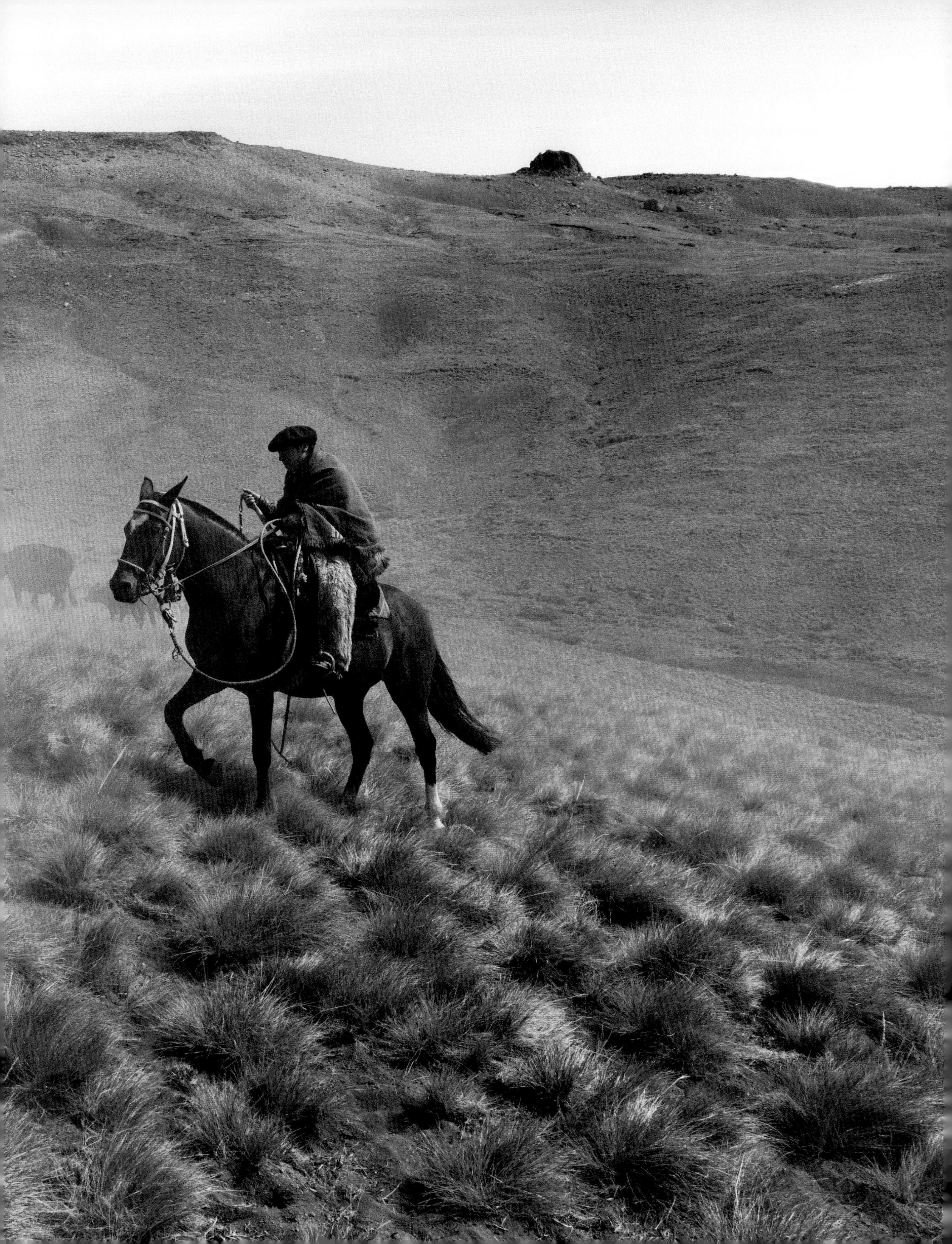

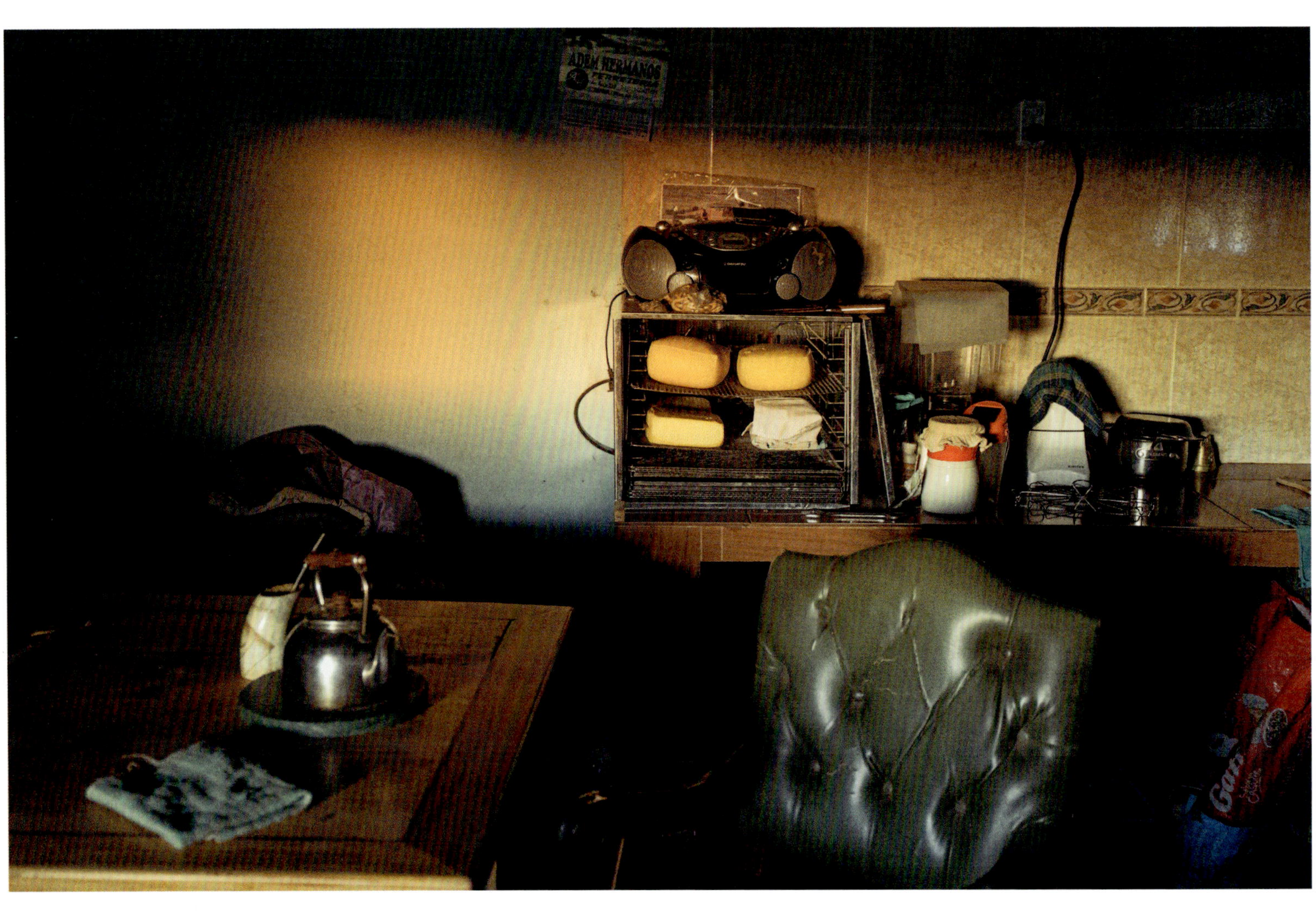
ADEM HERMANOS
CERVEZA

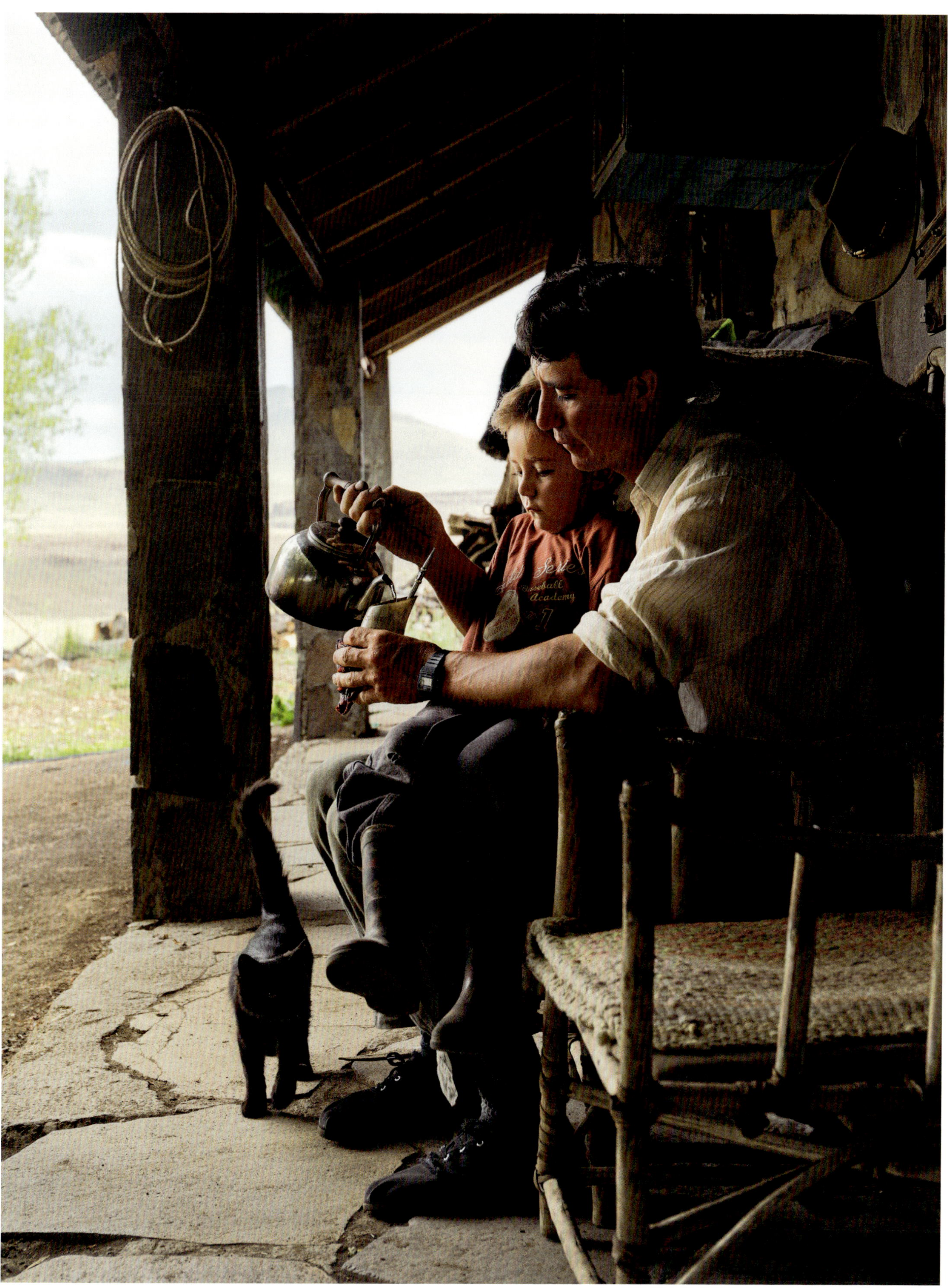

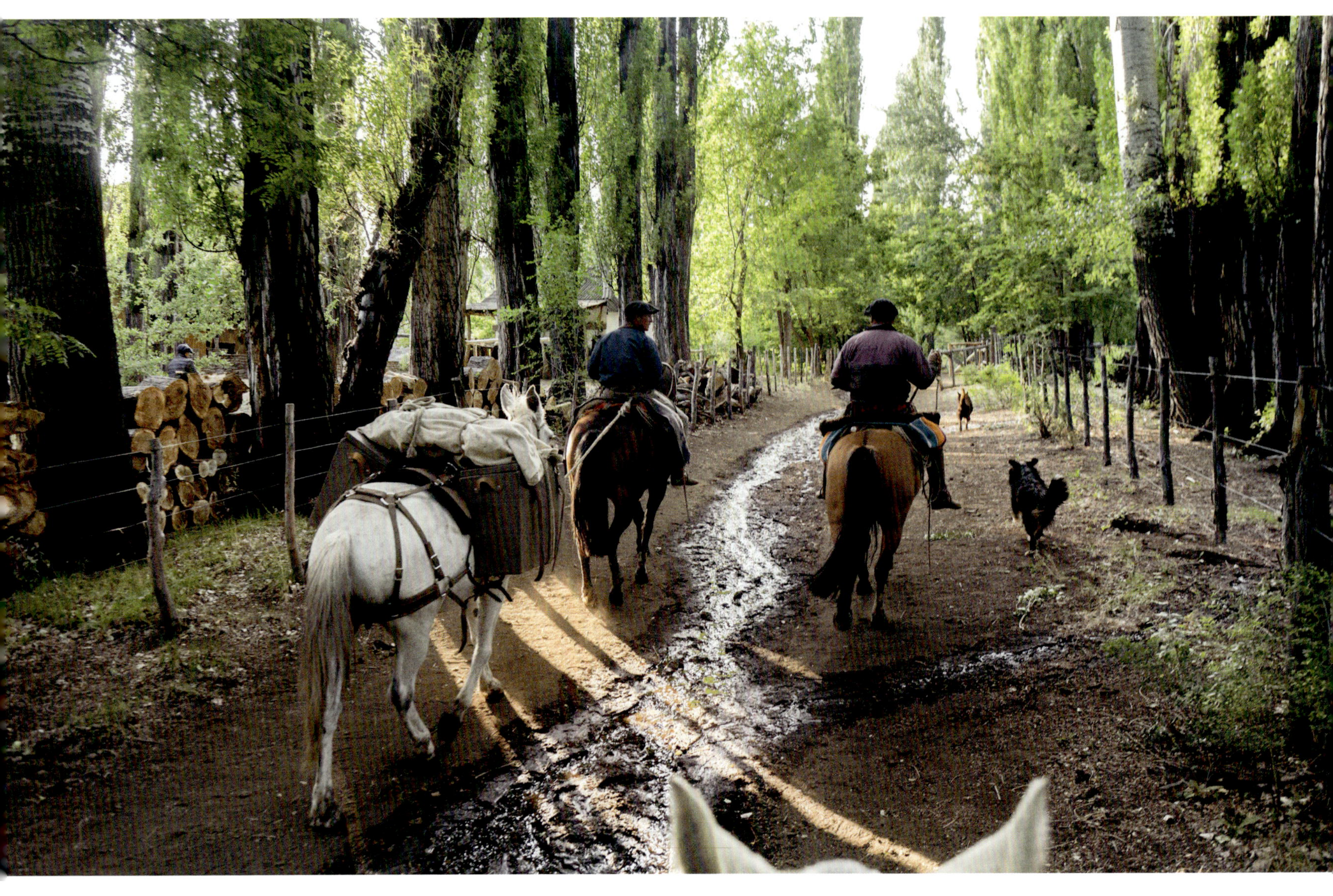

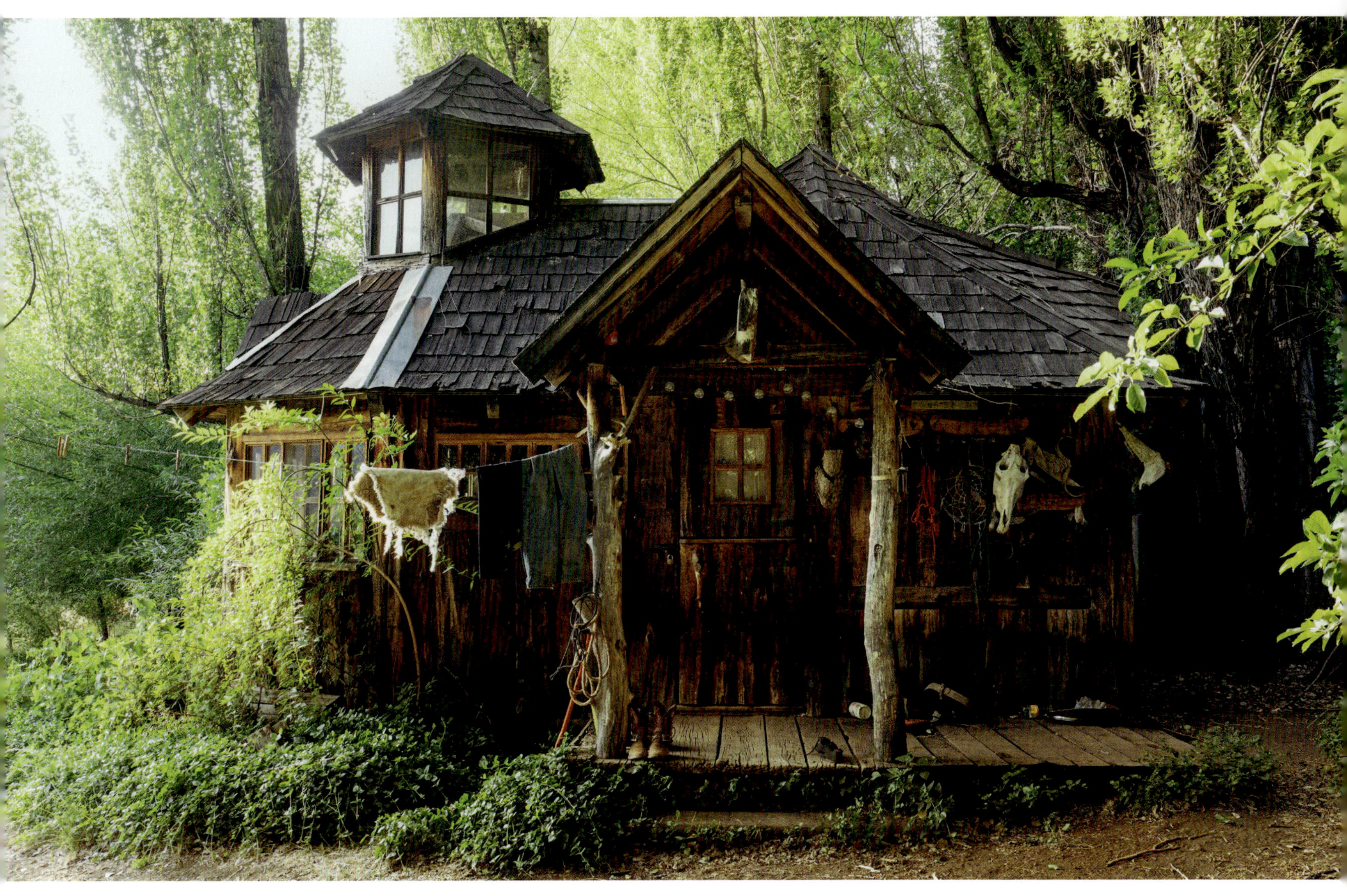

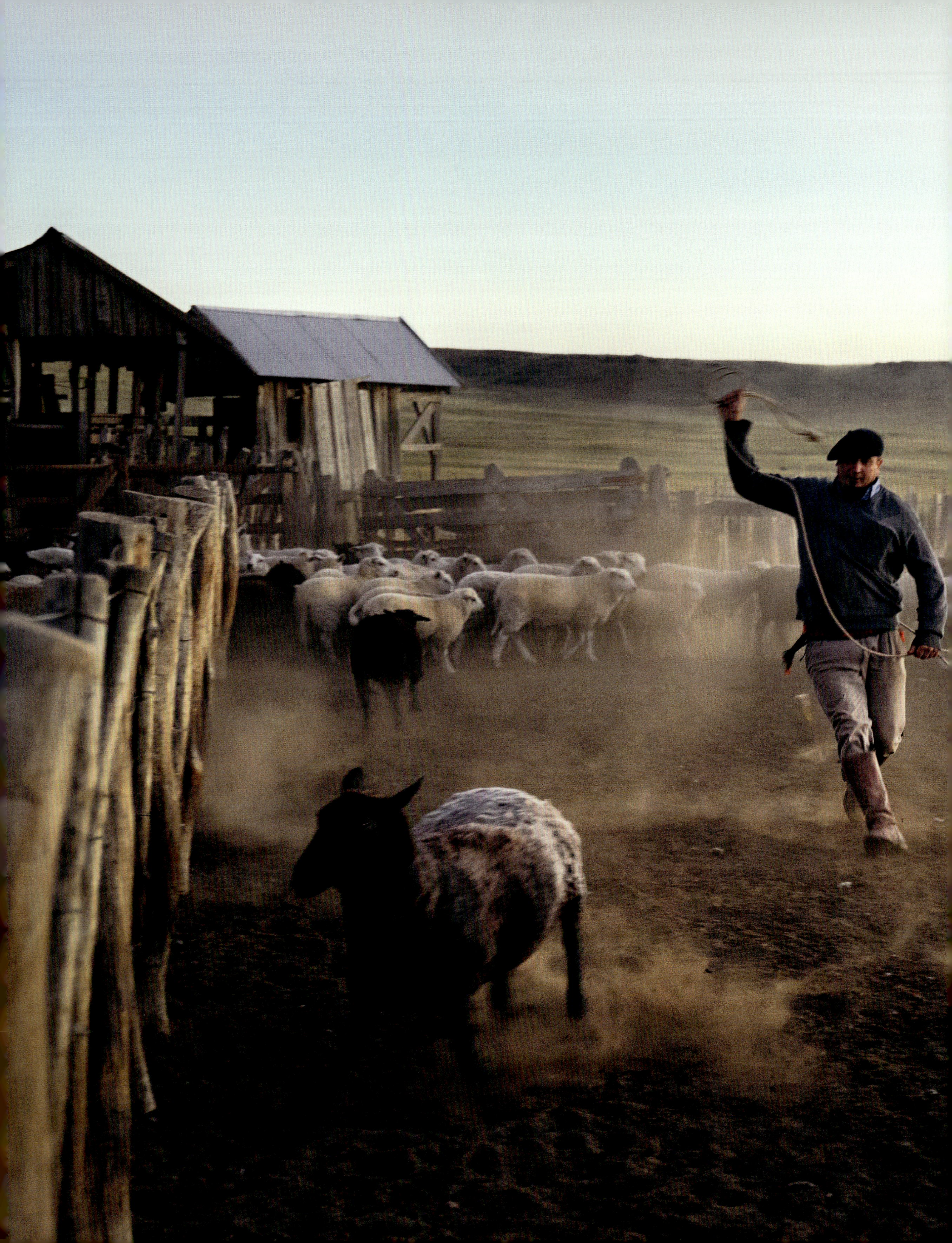

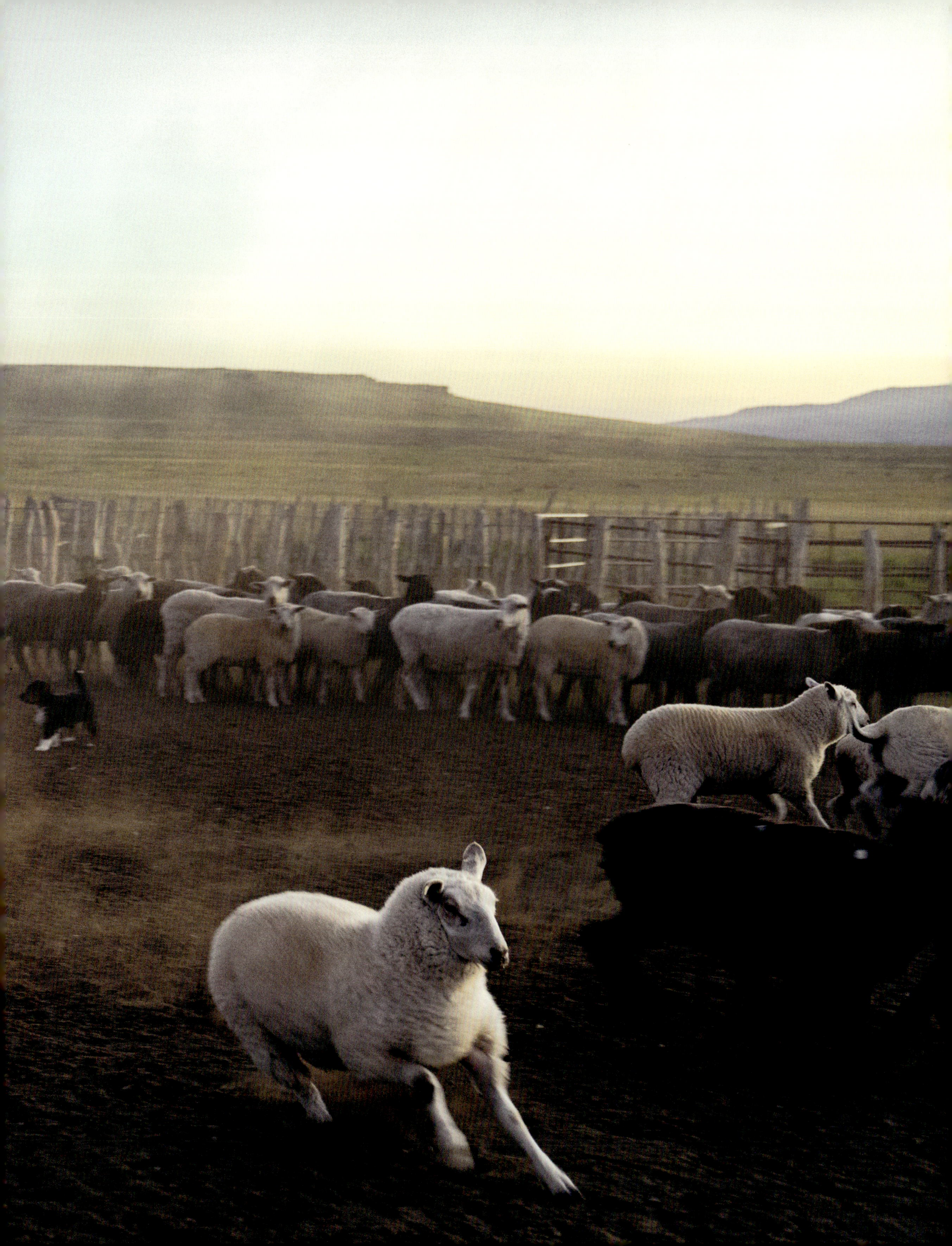

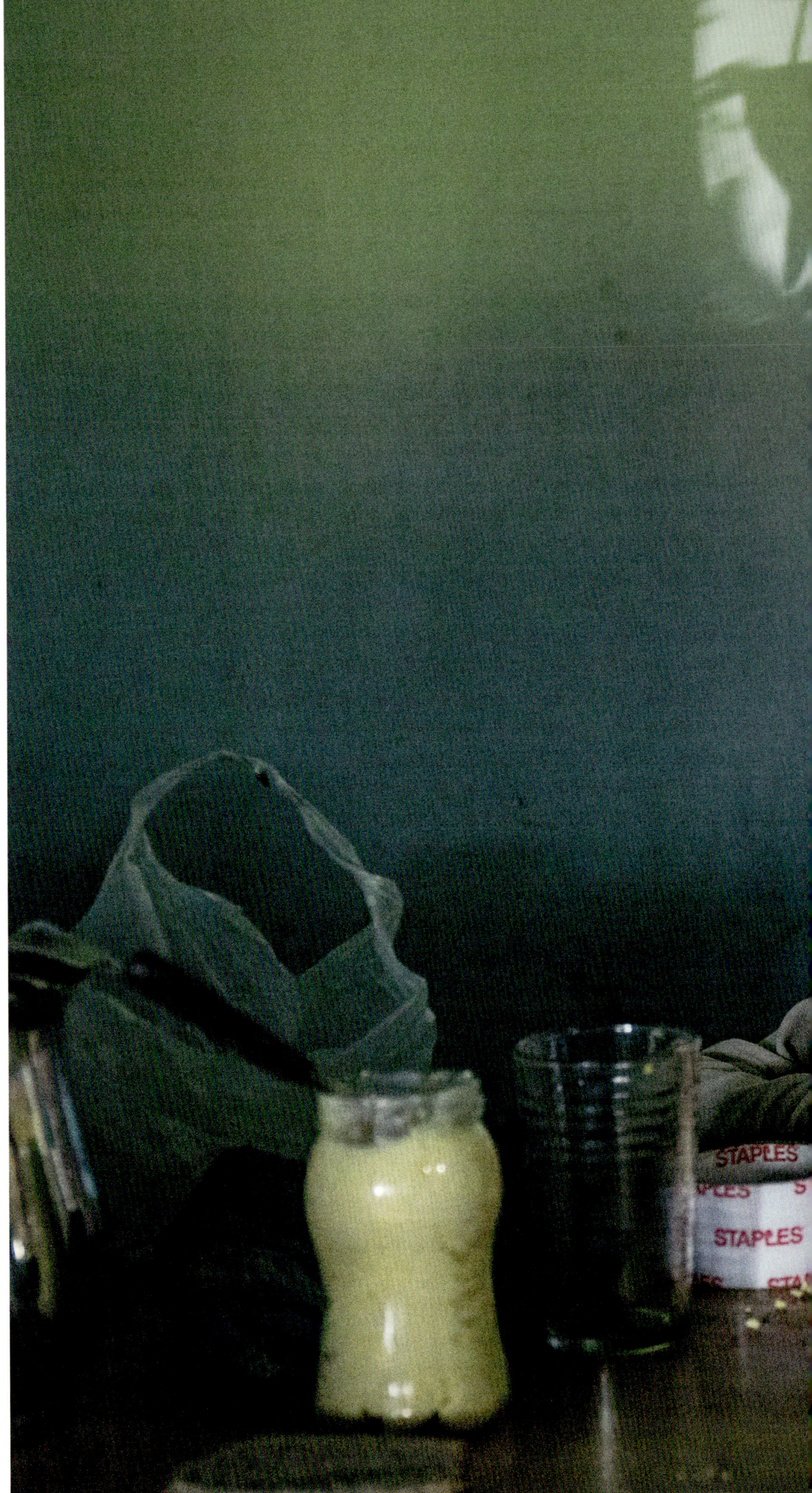
STAPLES
STAPLES
STAPLES

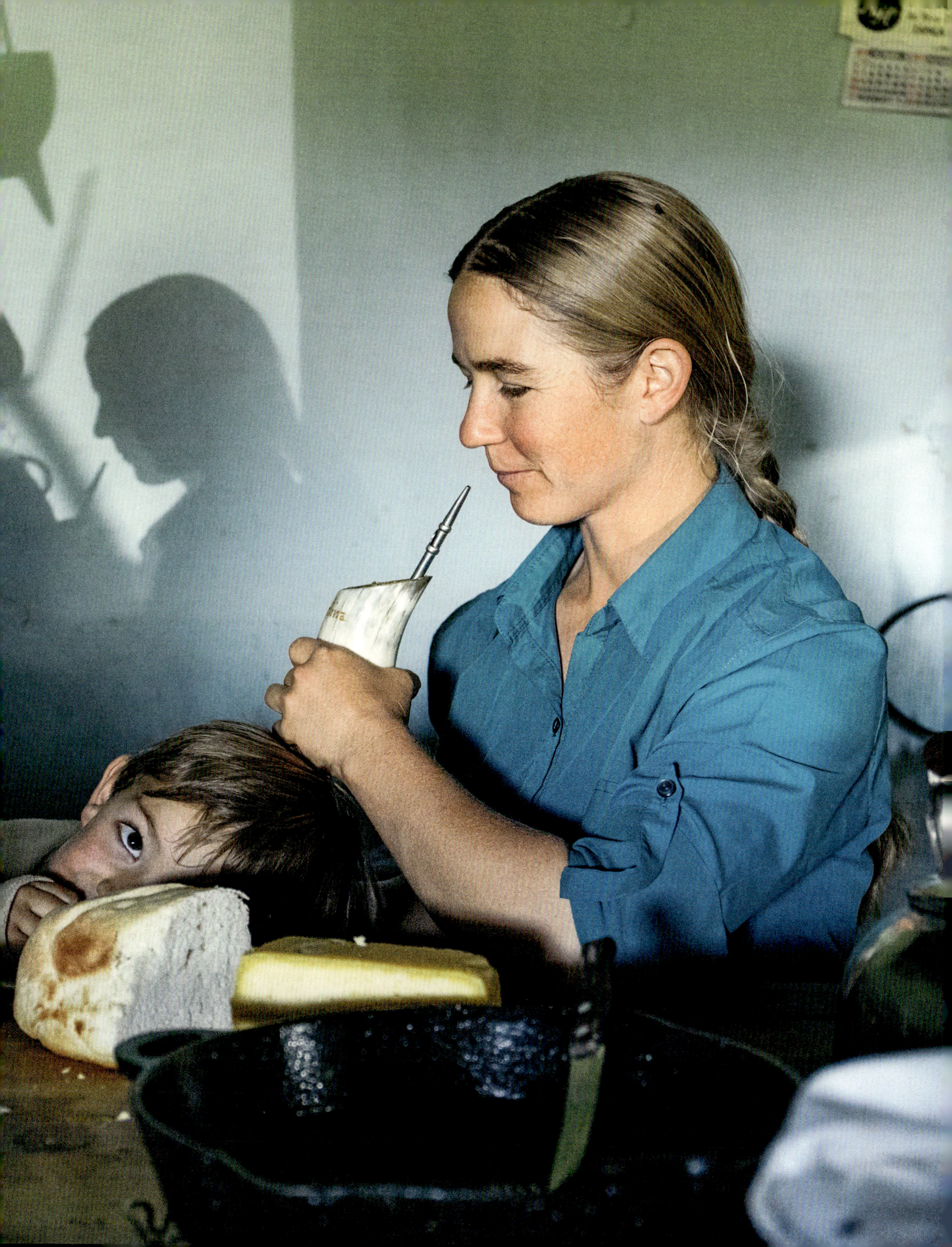

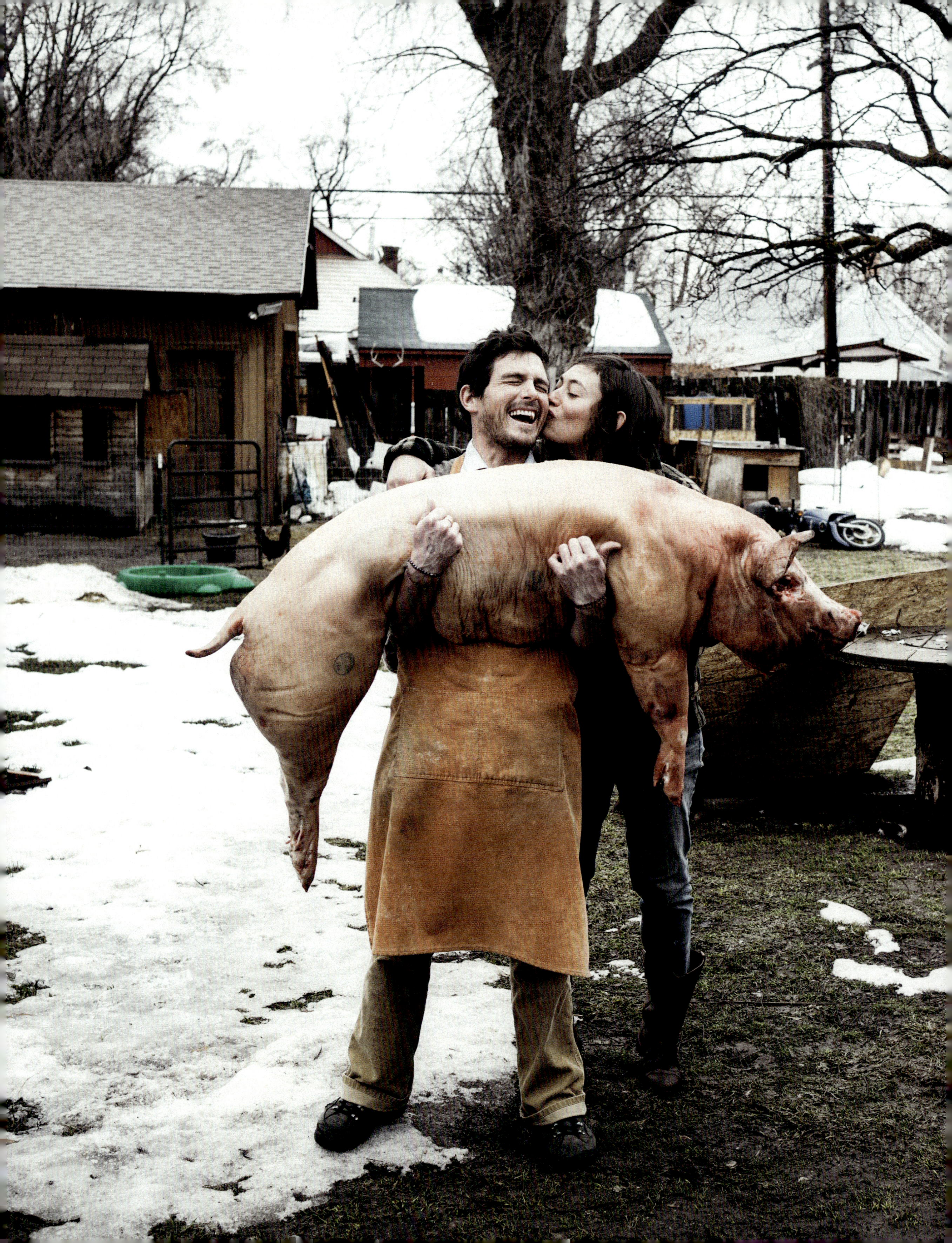

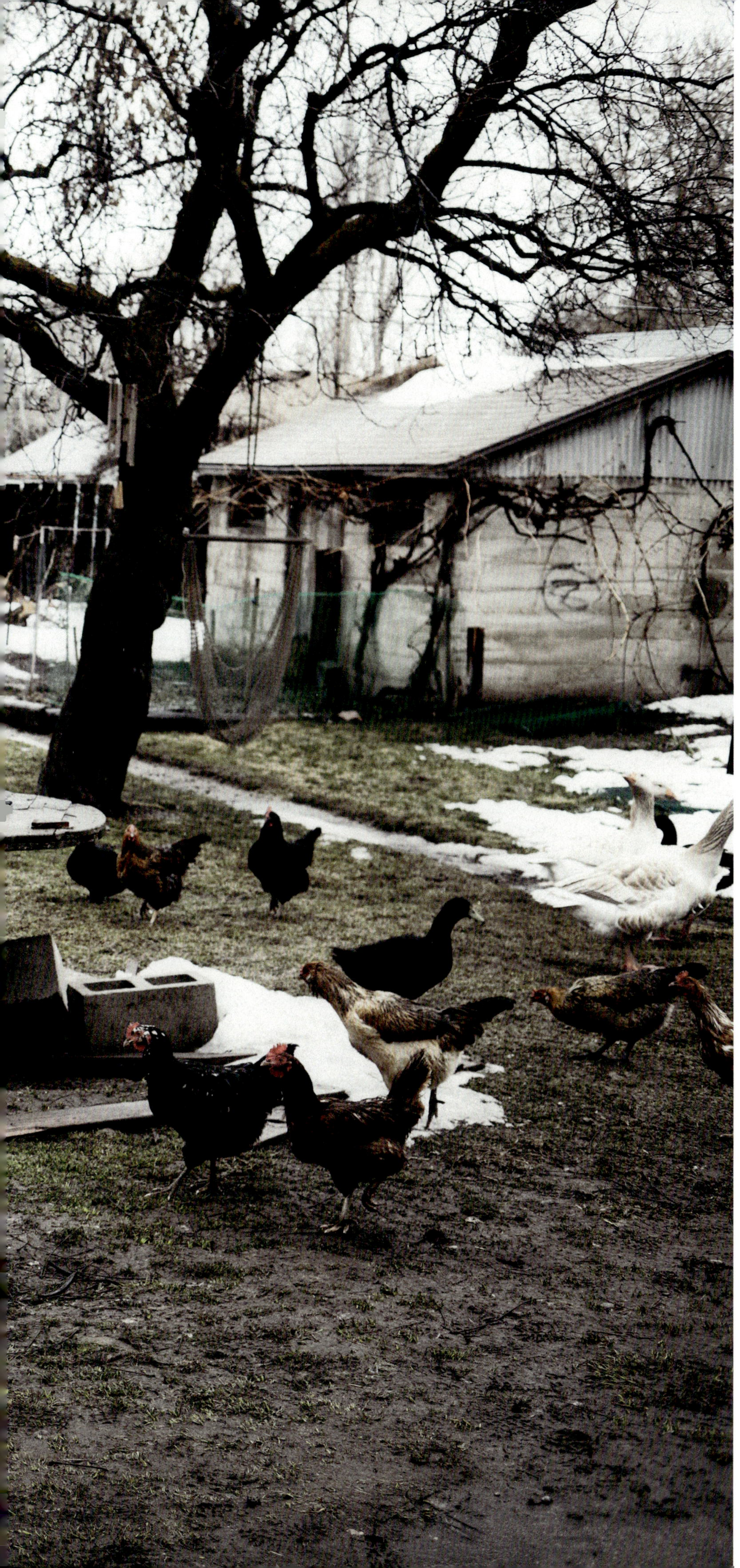

BEN

"WHY IS IT THAT I'M NOT HUNGRY AFTER WALKING FOR 25 KILOMETRES IN THE FOREST BUT WHEN I SPEND THE DAY IN FRONT OF THE COMPUTER, I'M STARVING? IT MAKES NO SENSE!"

„WIE KOMMT ES, DASS ICH NACH 25 KILOMETERN FUSSMARSCH DURCH DEN WALD KEINEN HUNGER VERSPÜRE, ABER NACH EINEM TAG AM COMPUTER VOLLKOMMEN AUSGEHUNGERT BIN? DAS ERGIBT GAR KEINEN SINN!"

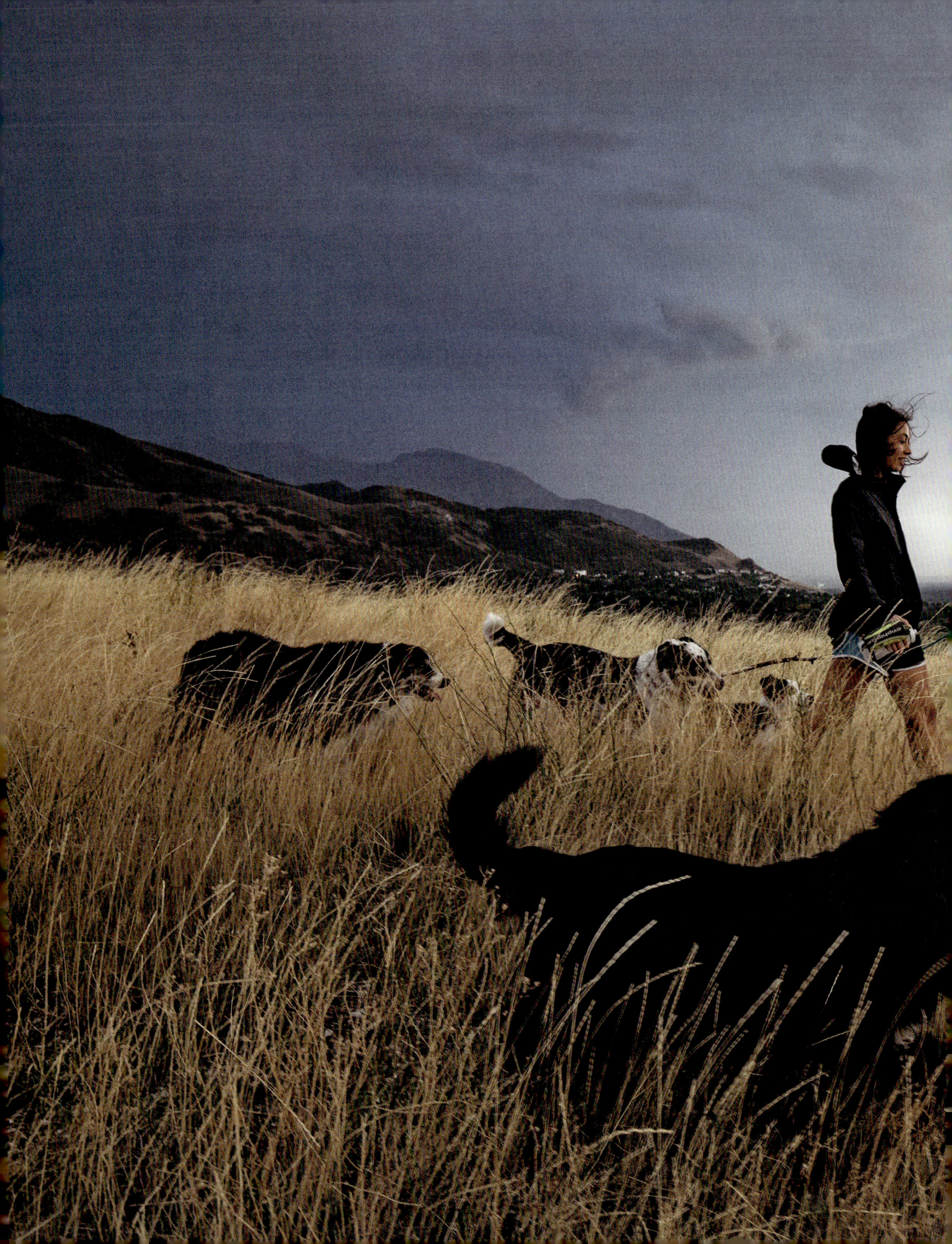

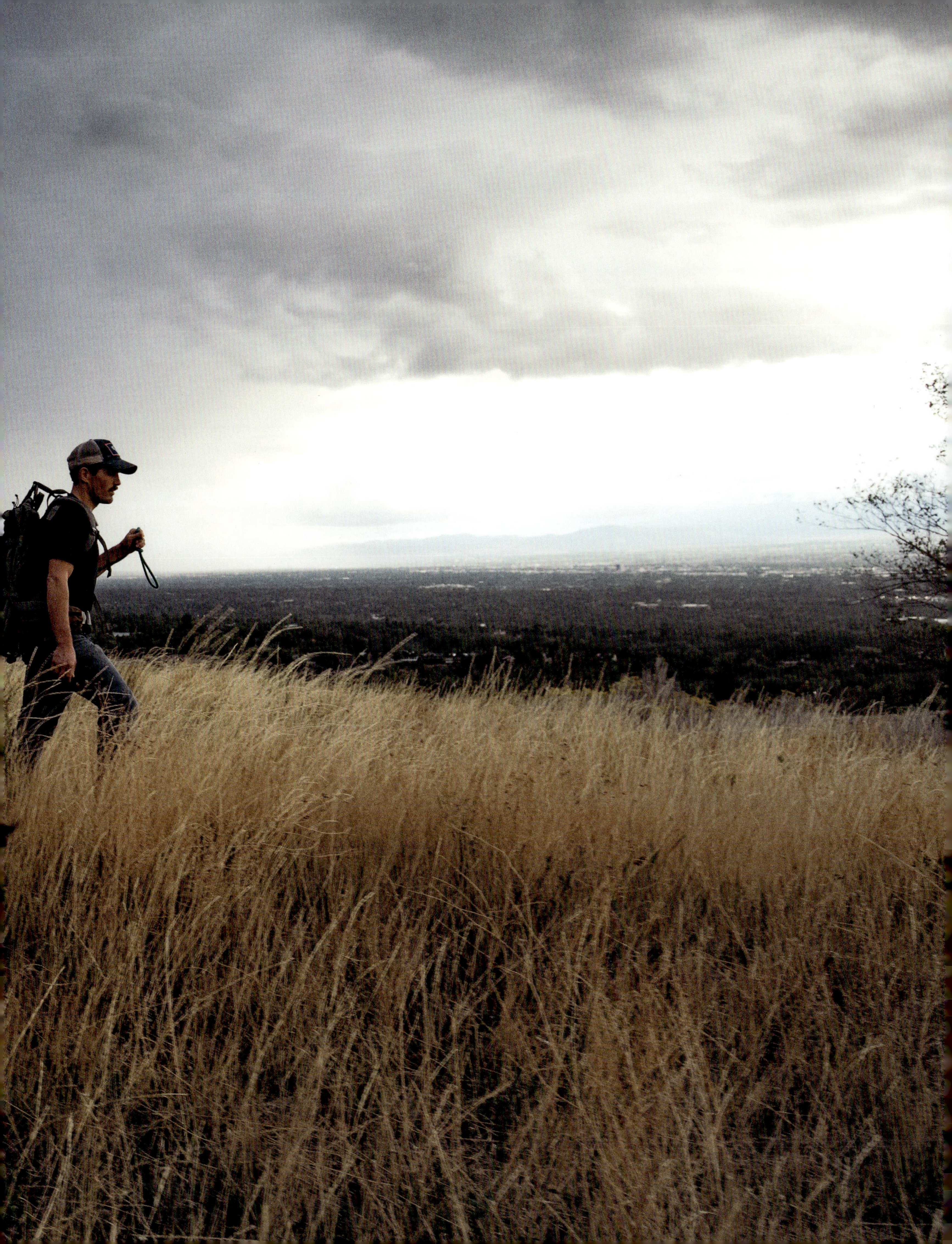

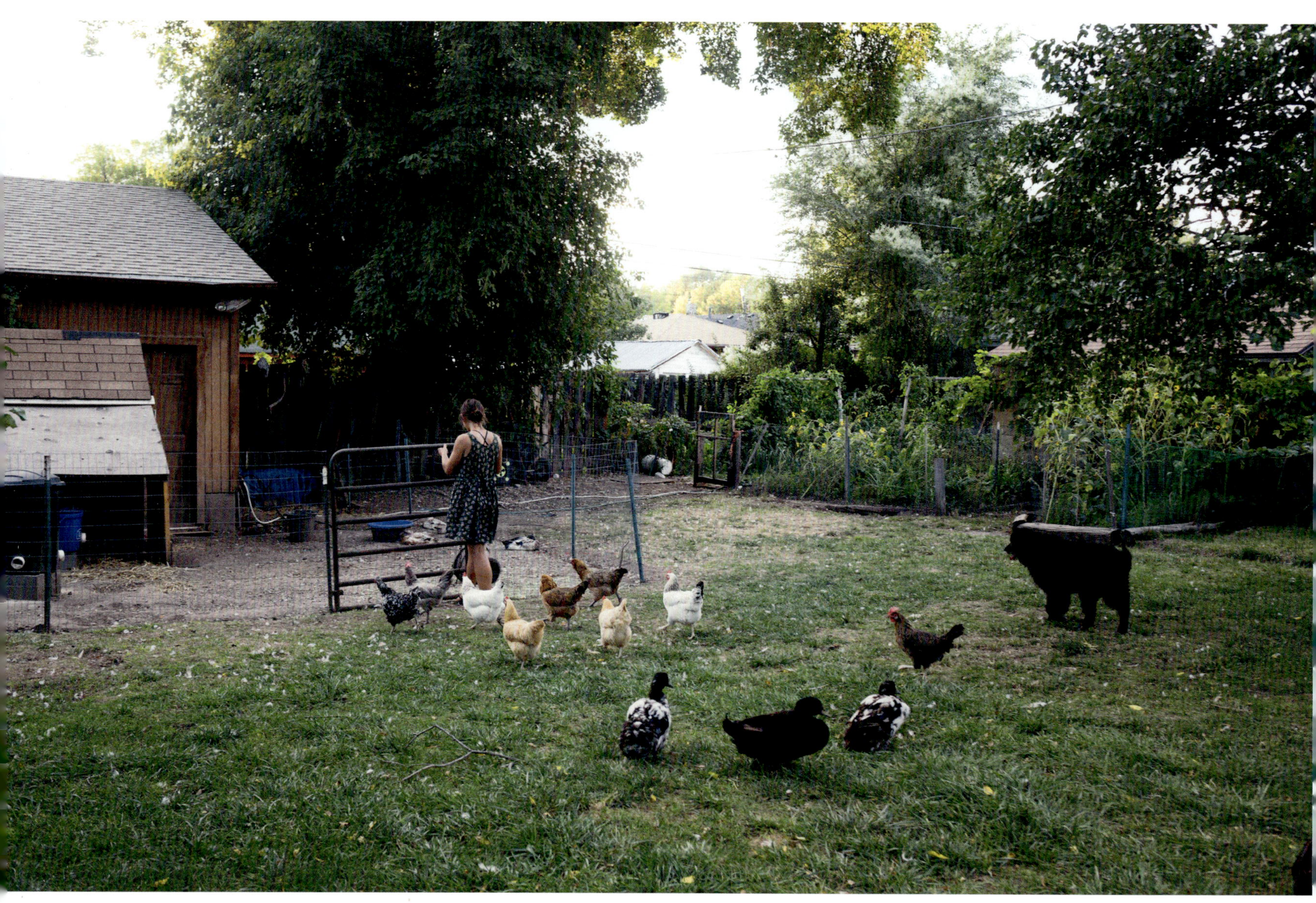

THE SELF-SUFFICIENT LIFE

UTAH, USA

Faced with American agri-food industry, Ben embarked on a search for meaning, deciding to produce almost all his own food. He has transformed his kitchen into a butcher's, his garden into a vegetable patch and enters the mountains of the American West every autumn to hunt elk, ensuring his meat supply for the year to come.

Ben long dreamt of living in tune with the values he has held since early childhood: self-sufficiency, improvisation, mastery of traditional techniques, etc. Growing up in an America where healthy eating can be a struggle, his desire for authenticity and more honest food grew until breaking point. One day, he decided to make a change and produce almost all his own food.

"I eventually felt really guilty about eating industrial meat. I was a vegetarian for three years, then I focused more specifically on the source of my food and how it was produced. That was the beginning of me growing my own vegetables and hunting my own food. It immediately felt more natural and more logical."

To realise his old dream of self-sufficiency, Ben and his wife Katherine breed hens, geese and ducks in their garden, and grow a wide variety of fruit and vegetables in their vegetable patch. During this time, bacon dries in their cellar while cider, beer and wine ferment. At home, chores are evenly allocated: Katherine produces the vegetables while Ben takes care of the meat. And then in autumn, after the first snow, Ben journeys into the Ashley national forest on horseback to set up camp at an altitude of 3,400 metres.

Ben goes into wild mode up there, immersing himself in a hunter mindset, ultra-focused, at one with nature and immune to all other concerns. Crouching in the woods, he hunts down elk in the dense forests and high fen, existing alongside the cougars and black bears that inhabit this wild and uninhabited region. From dawn to dusk, in the pure and sharp autumn light, he weaves in and out of the white scree, among the birch trees whose golden leaves rustle in the wind under a deep blue sky.

At this altitude, headaches and nausea are not unusual but Ben acclimatised long ago and is able to move without getting out of breath. On his return home several days later, he brings only his horses loaded with game. "It's very gratifying to get home with meat that I hunted myself."

"During this week, I lose between four and six kilos, my mind is clear and my body is in excellent shape. When I hunt, everything has meaning: every movement has its use and no energy is wasted."

Once home, he slips on his butcher's apron and cuts up the various parts of the animal. This precise and meticulous work can take several days. And just like that, the couple have a year's supply of cured meat, sausages and fillets. "Someone could do this for me but I take great satisfaction in producing my own food."

When they are not adventuring in the wide open spaces of the American West, Ben and Katherine spend most of their free time in a kitchen full of recipe books. "A lot of people watch TV when they get home from work. Our hobby is cooking together. Living like this brings us closer to nature and each other."

To prepare for this hunt for food, Ben trains relentlessly all year long. He regularly goes into the mountains and follows an intense physical training plan. When he is not on horseback, he practises archery and shooting. While he lives near the city, his proximity to nature, at home and in the mountains, has profoundly influenced his character, paving the way for future, more radical changes. To prepare for a life closer to the wilderness, Ben forces himself to manage without heating until late autumn, works standing up in a 16 °C office and swims in icy rivers. Strong and assured, he is tough on himself but true to his values.

"I'm normally quite scattered but when I'm in the woods, my mind is more intensely calm than ever, in a way I can't compare to anything else. Not even exercise gives me this feeling! When I hunt, I have a mission to accomplish: if I return empty-handed, that means I'm incapable of meeting my family's needs. So I train really hard throughout the year for this hunting week."

For Ben, this way of life in a turbulent America is also a way of responding to the absurdity of the world he grew up in. "Why is it that I'm not hungry after walking for 25 kilometres in the forest but when I spend the day in front of a computer, I'm starving? It makes no sense! I think our bodies are lost and angry. We're simply not meant to sit in front of a screen all day long. I think our western lifestyle is sick," says Ben, thoughtfully. "I mean honestly 'diseased', I'm not just tossing that word out."

The last I heard, Ben now hunts with his wife Katherine and the couple have welcomed their son Sebastian. Nearing fourty, Ben has officially traded his gun for bow – a much more difficult and demanding form of hunting, bringing him ever closer to the animal. One step closer to his quest for authenticity.

LEBEN ALS SELBSTVERSORGER

UTAH, USA

Auf der Suche nach dem richtigen Weg angesichts der US-amerikanischen Lebensmittelindustrie, beschließt Ben, praktisch all seine Nahrungsmittel selbst zu produzieren. Er verwandelt seine Küche in eine Metzgerei, sein Grundstück in einen Gemüsegarten und steigt jeden Herbst im Westen der USA in die Berge, um Wapiti-Hirsche zu jagen und seinen Fleischvorrat für das kommende Jahr zu sichern.

Seit langem träumte Ben davon, in Einklang mit den Werten zu leben, die er schon seit seiner Kindheit in sich trägt: Autarkie, Ideenreichtum, Beherrschung traditioneller Fertigkeiten … Während er in den USA aufwächst, wo es manchmal schwierig ist, sich gesund zu ernähren, wird seine Sehnsucht nach Authentizität und ehrlicheren Nahrungsmitteln immer stärker, bis es zum Bruch kommt: Eines Tages beschließt er, den entscheidenden Schritt zu tun und die Nahrung, die er zu sich nimmt, praktisch komplett selbst zu produzieren.

„Wenn ich Industriefleisch aß, habe ich mich zuletzt richtig schuldig gefühlt. Ich war drei Jahre lang Vegetarier, dann begann ich mich für die genaue Herkunft meines Essens und die Produktion unserer Nahrungsmittel zu interessieren. So habe ich angefangen, mein Gemüse selbst anzubauen und mich von der Jagd zu ernähren … Das erschien mir plötzlich natürlicher und offensichtlicher.“

Um ihren alten Traum vom Selbstversorgertum zu verwirklichen, halten Ben und seine Frau Katherine im Garten Hühner, Gänse und Enten; in ihrem Garten ziehen sie zahlreiche Obst- und Gemüsearten. Speck trocknet im Keller, wo auch Cidre, Bier und Wein gären. Im Haus sind die Aufgaben gerecht verteilt: Katherine kümmert sich um den Gemüseanbau, Ben um das Fleisch. Dafür reitet er jeden Herbst nach dem ersten Schnee in den Ashley National Forest und schlägt in 3400 Metern Höhe sein Lager auf.

Dort oben wird Ben zu einem wilderen Menschen; er fällt in den Jagdmodus, extrem konzentriert, im Einklang mit der Natur und taub für alles andere. Geduckt folgt er den Spuren des Wapiti-Hirschs durch dichte Wälder und Hochmoore, nicht weit von den Pumas und Schwarzbären, die dieses wilde, menschleere Gebiet bevölkern.

Von der Morgen- bis zur Abenddämmerung schlängelt er sich im klaren, durchdringenden Herbstlicht auf den weißen Geröllhalden zwischen Birken hindurch, deren goldene Blätter unter einem tiefblauen Himmel rascheln. In dieser Höhe leidet man nicht selten unter Kopfschmerzen und Übelkeit, aber Ben ist schon lange akklimatisiert und bewegt sich, ohne außer Atem zu kommen. Einige Tage später bringt er nur die mit Wildbret beladenen Pferde nach Hause. „Es ist ein sehr befriedigendes Gefühl, mit selbst erjagtem Fleisch heimzukommen.

In dieser einen Woche verliere ich vier bis sechs Kilo, mein Geist ist klar, mein Körper in Hochform. Wenn ich jage, hat alles einen Sinn: Jede Bewegung ist zweckgerichtet, keine Energie wird verschwendet.“

Zu Hause angekommen, streift er seine Metzgerschürze über und zerlegt das Tier in Einzelteile – eine präzise, zeitraubende Tätigkeit, die mehrere Tage in Anspruch nehmen kann. Danach werden Trockenfleisch, Würste und Filets das Paar ein ganzes Jahr lang ernähren. „Diese Arbeit könnte jemand für mich übernehmen, aber ich empfinde es als sehr befriedigend, mein Essen selbst zu produzieren.“

Wenn sie sich nicht in die Weiten des amerikanischen Westens hinauswagen, verbringen Ben und Katherine den Großteil ihrer Freizeit in der Küche, die voll ist mit Kochbüchern. „Viele Leute setzen sich vor den Fernseher, wenn sie von der Arbeit nach Hause kommen. Unser Hobby ist es, zusammen zu kochen. Durch dieses Leben kommen wir nicht nur der Natur, sondern auch einander näher."

Um sich auf seine Essensjagd vorzubereiten, trainiert Ben das ganze Jahr über pausenlos. Regelmäßig macht er in den Bergen intensive körperliche Übungen. Wenn er nicht aufs Pferd steigt, schießt er mit Bogen oder Gewehr. Obwohl er in der Nähe einer Stadt wohnt, hat die Nähe zur Natur, zu Hause wie in den Bergen, seinen Charakter zutiefst geprägt und den Boden für radikalere Veränderungen bereitet. In Erwartung eines zukünftigen Lebens näher an der Wildnis zwingt Ben sich dazu, bis in den Spätherbst ohne Heizung zu leben, arbeitet in seinem Büro im Stehen bei 16 °C und badet in eiskalten Flüssen. Dieser starke, selbstsichere Charakter fordert sich selbst viel ab, stets im Einklang mit den eigenen Werten.

„Normalerweise bin ich ziemlich zerstreut, aber im Wald beruhigt sich mein Geist auf unvergleichliche Weise und in unvergleichlichem Ausmaß. Selbst der Sport kann mir das nicht bieten! Beim Jagen habe ich eine Mission: Wenn ich mit leeren Händen zurückkomme, heißt das, dass ich nicht für den Unterhalt meiner Familie sorgen kann. Deshalb trainiere ich das ganze Jahr über wirklich hart, für diese eine Woche der Jagd."

Ein solches Leben inmitten der krisengeschüttelten USA zu führen, ist für Ben auch eine Antwort auf die Absurdität der Lebensweise, mit der er aufgewachsen ist. „Wie kommt es, dass ich nach 25 Kilometern Fußmarsch durch den Wald keinen Hunger verspüre, aber nach einem Tag am Computer vollkommen ausgehungert bin? Das ergibt gar keinen Sinn! Ich glaube, unsere Körper sind verwirrt und zornig. Wir sind einfach nicht dafür gemacht, den ganzen Tag vor dem Bildschirm zu sitzen." Nachdenklich offenbart Ben: „Ich glaube, unser westlicher Lebensstil ist krank … Wirklich krank, ich verwende das Wort nicht einfach so."

Mittlerweile hat Ben berichtet, dass er inzwischen mit seiner Frau Katherine jagen geht; außerdem hat das Paar einen Sohn bekommen, Sebastian. Aber der knapp vierzigjährige Vater hat endgültig sein Gewehr durch Pfeil und Bogen ersetzt – eine viel schwierigere, anspruchsvollere Form der Jagd, bei der man dem Tier noch näher kommen muss. Ein weiterer Schritt auf seinem Weg zur Authentizität.

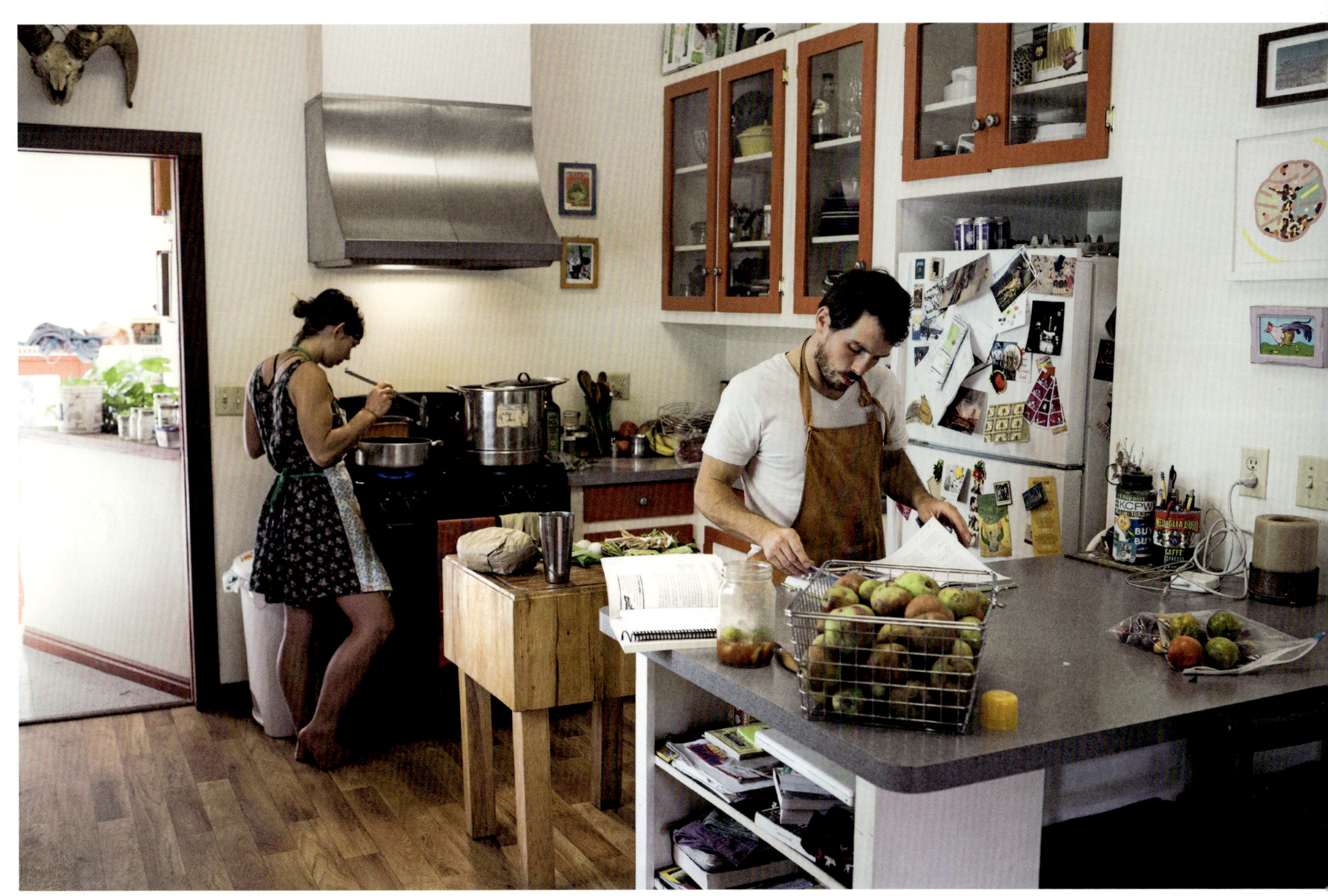

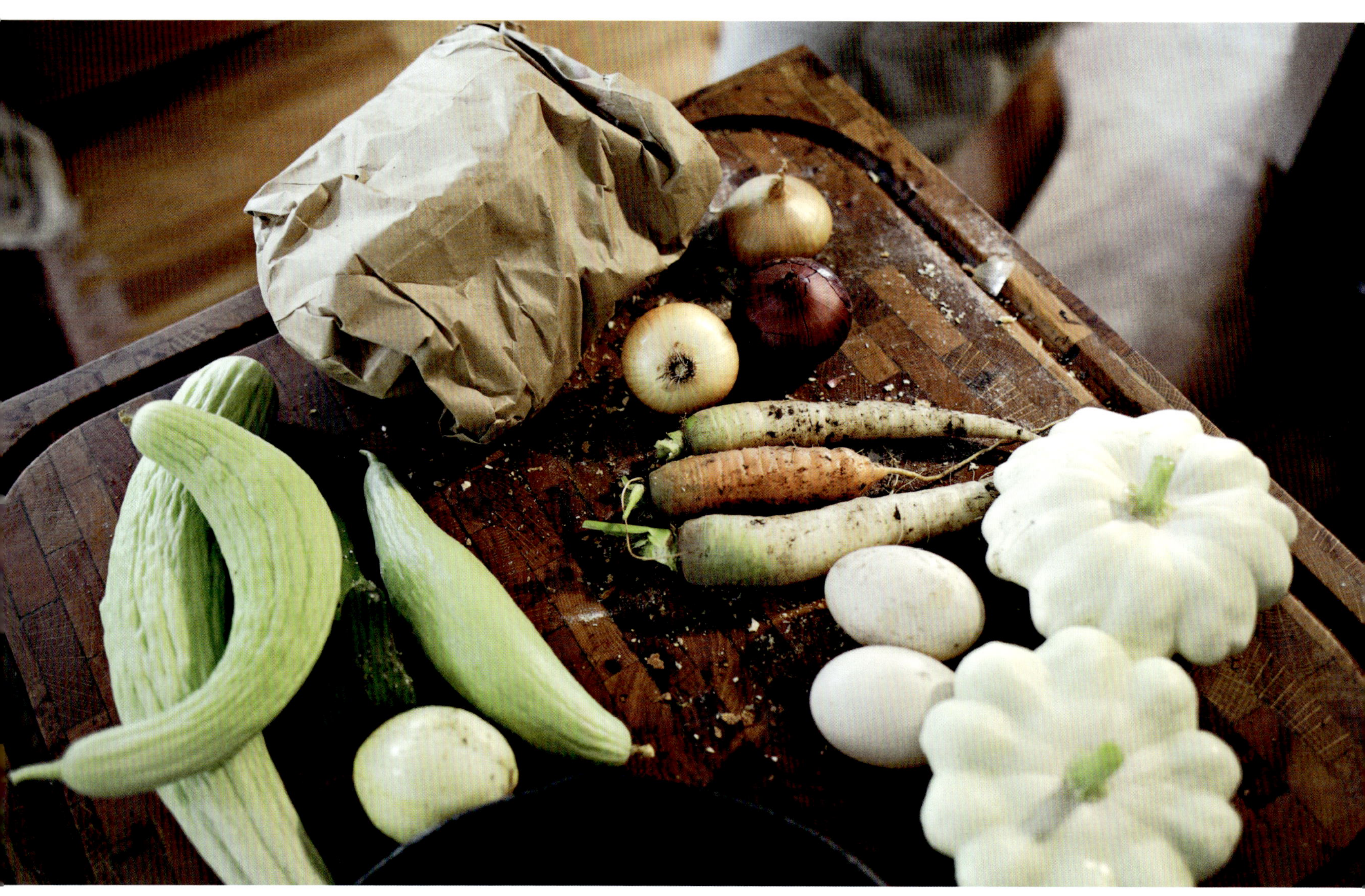

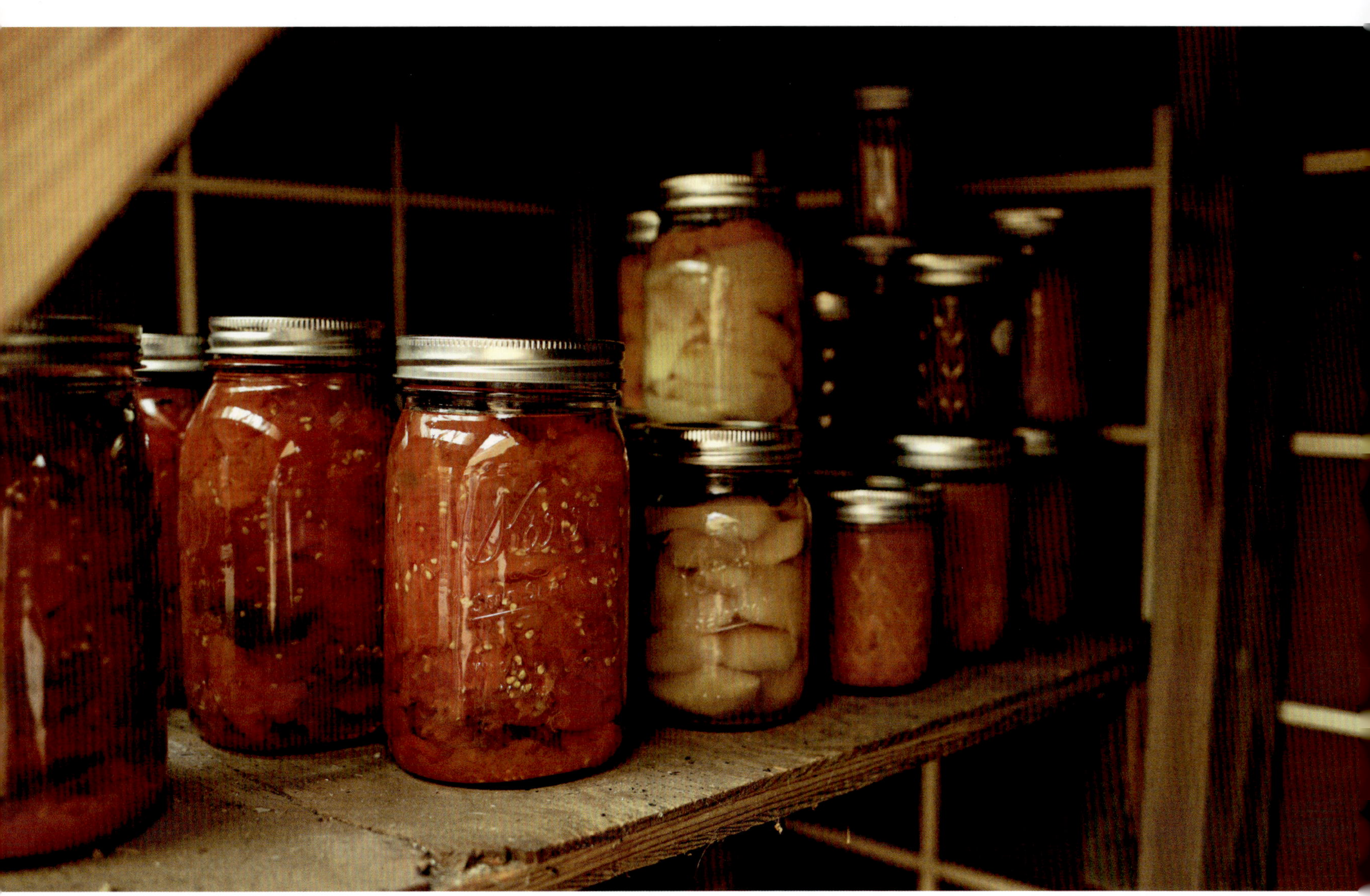

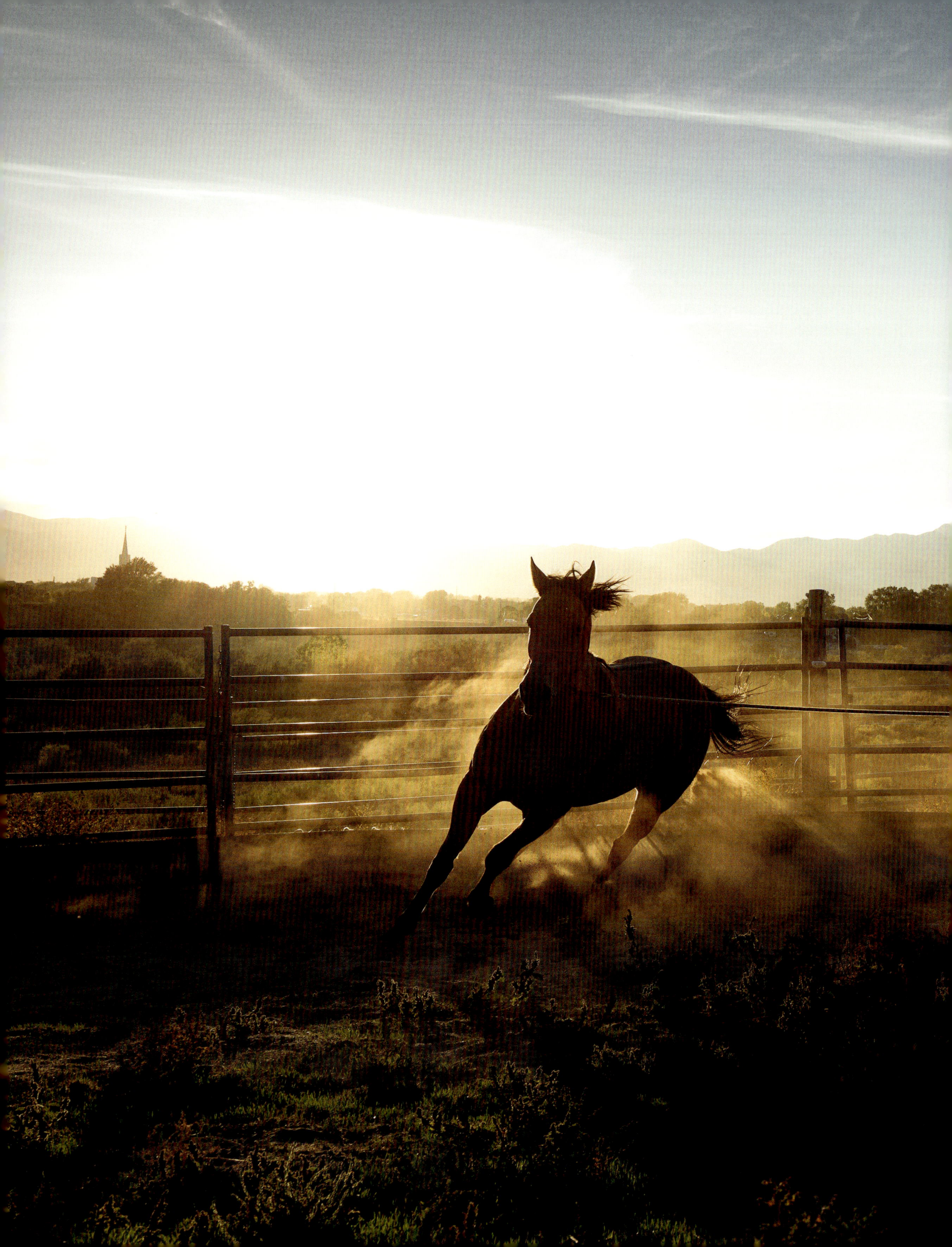

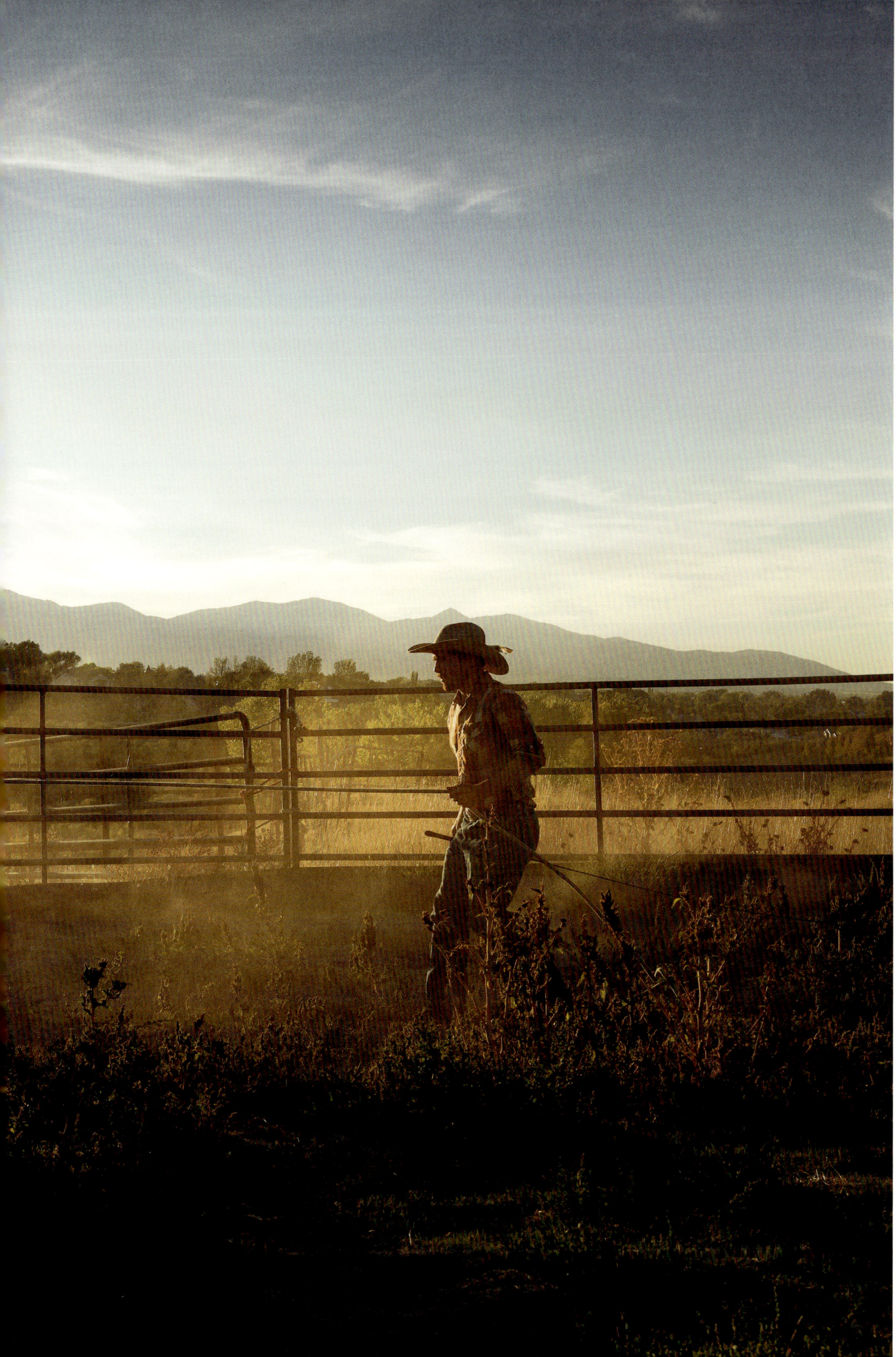

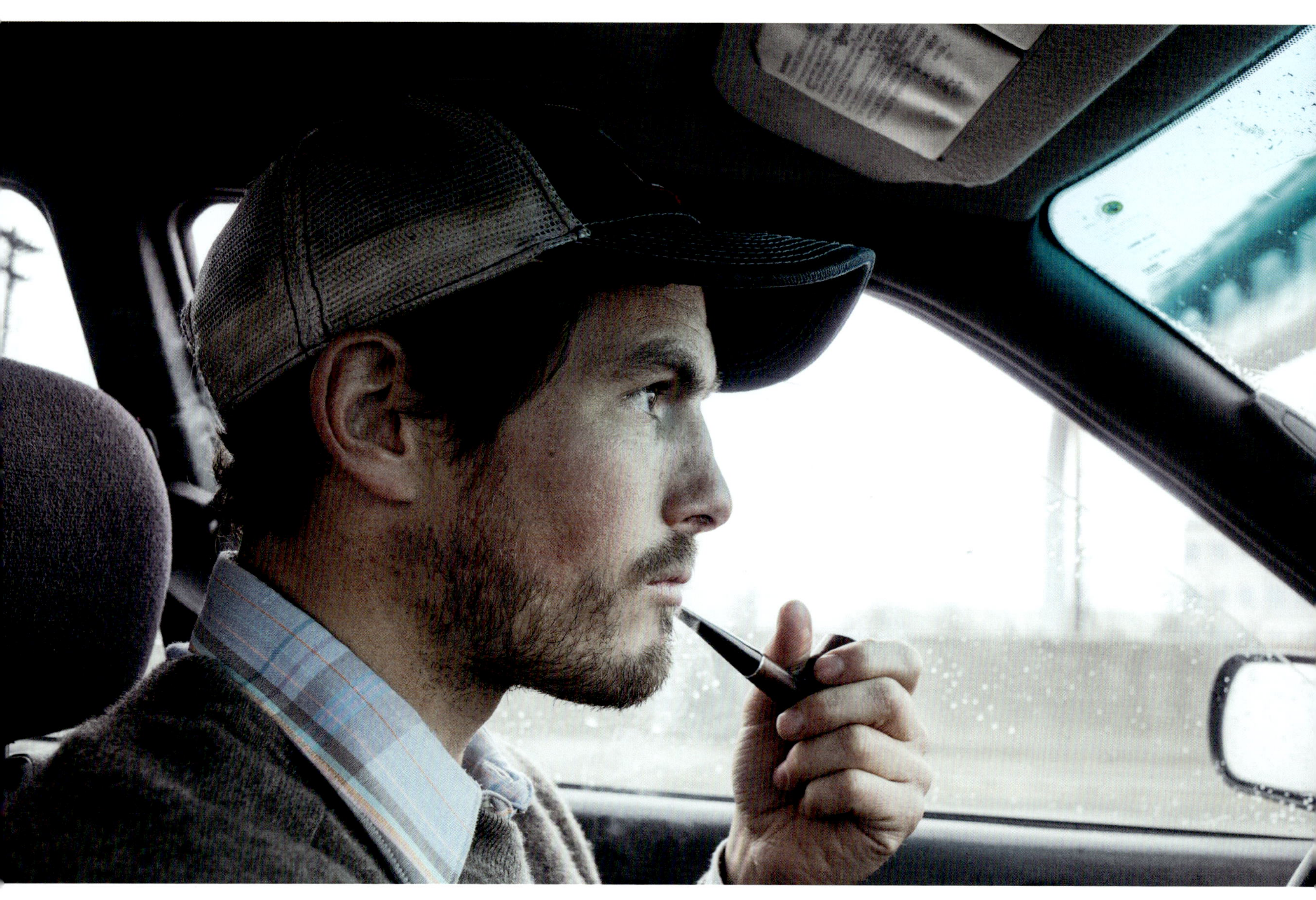

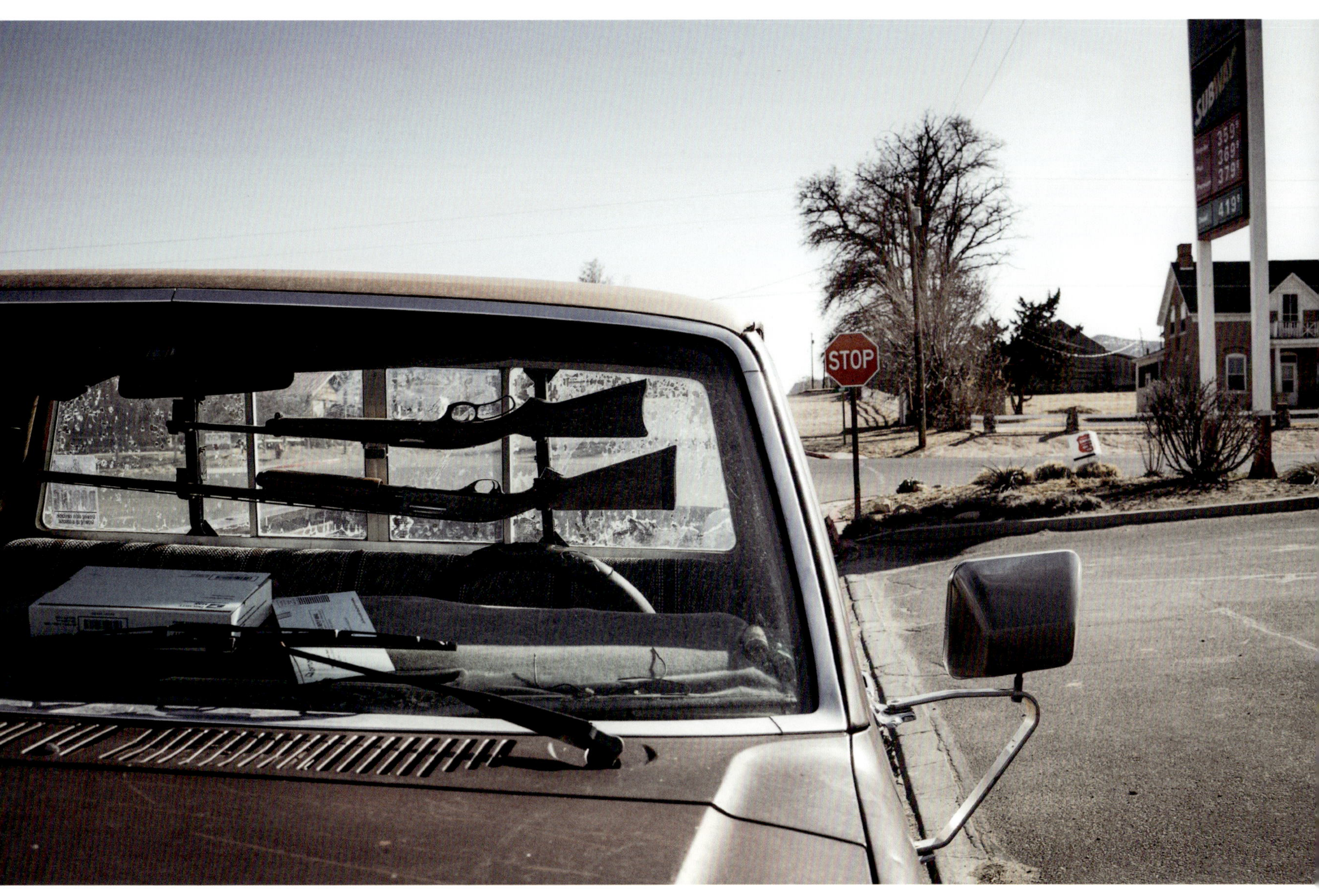

STOP
SUBWAY

"I learned from my two years' experience that it would cost incredibly little trouble to obtain one's necessary food, even in this latitude; that a man may use as simple a diet as the animals, and yet retain health and strength."

HENRY DAVID THOREAU
Walden; or, Life in the Woods

„Ich lernte aus meiner zweijährigen Erfahrung, dass es selbst in diesem Breitengrad unglaublich wenig Mühe bereitet, sich seine Nahrung zu beschaffen, und dass der Mensch eine so einfache Diät wie das Tier befolgen und doch Gesundheit und Kraft bewahren kann."

HENRY DAVID THOREAU
Walden oder Leben in den Wäldern

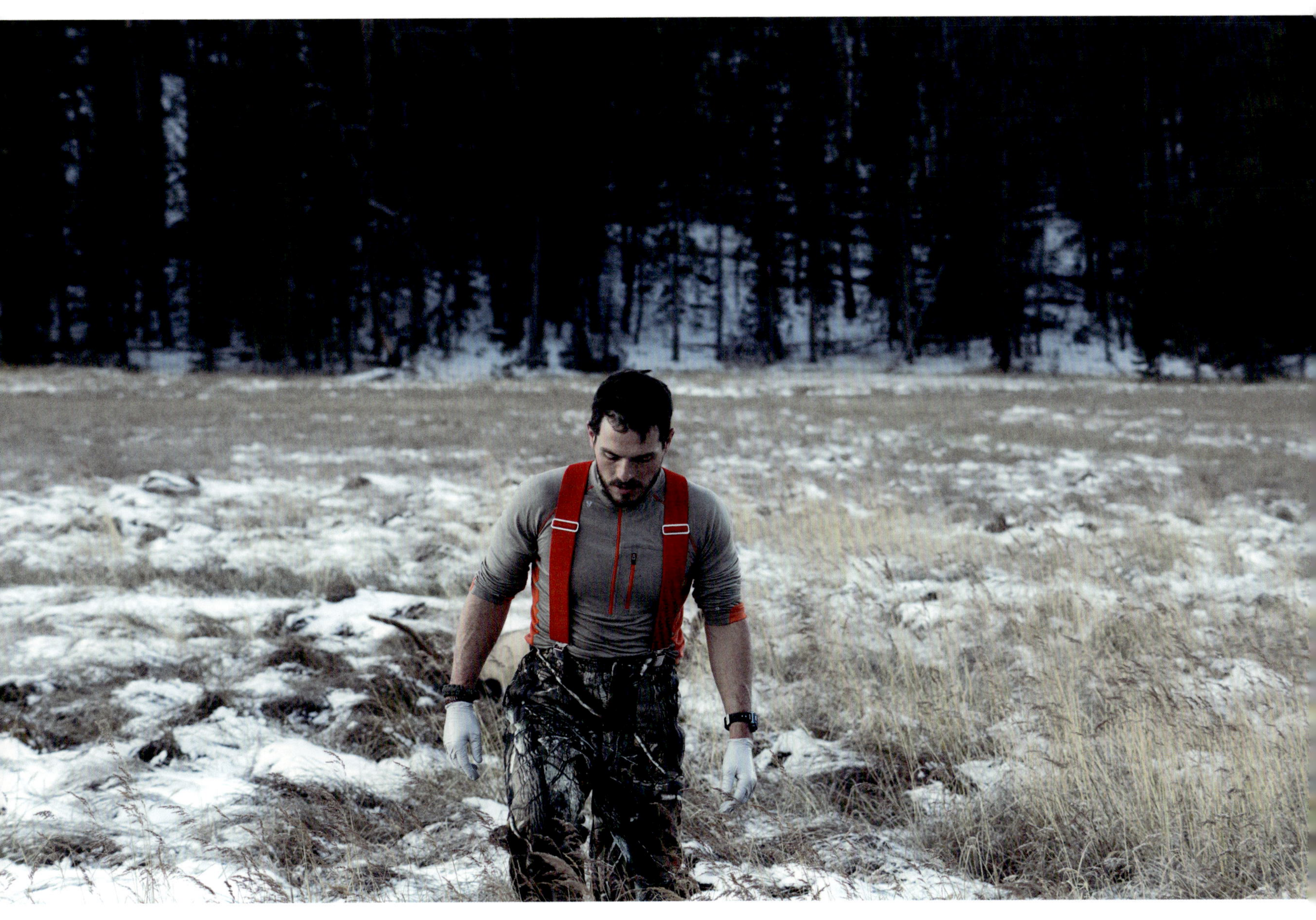

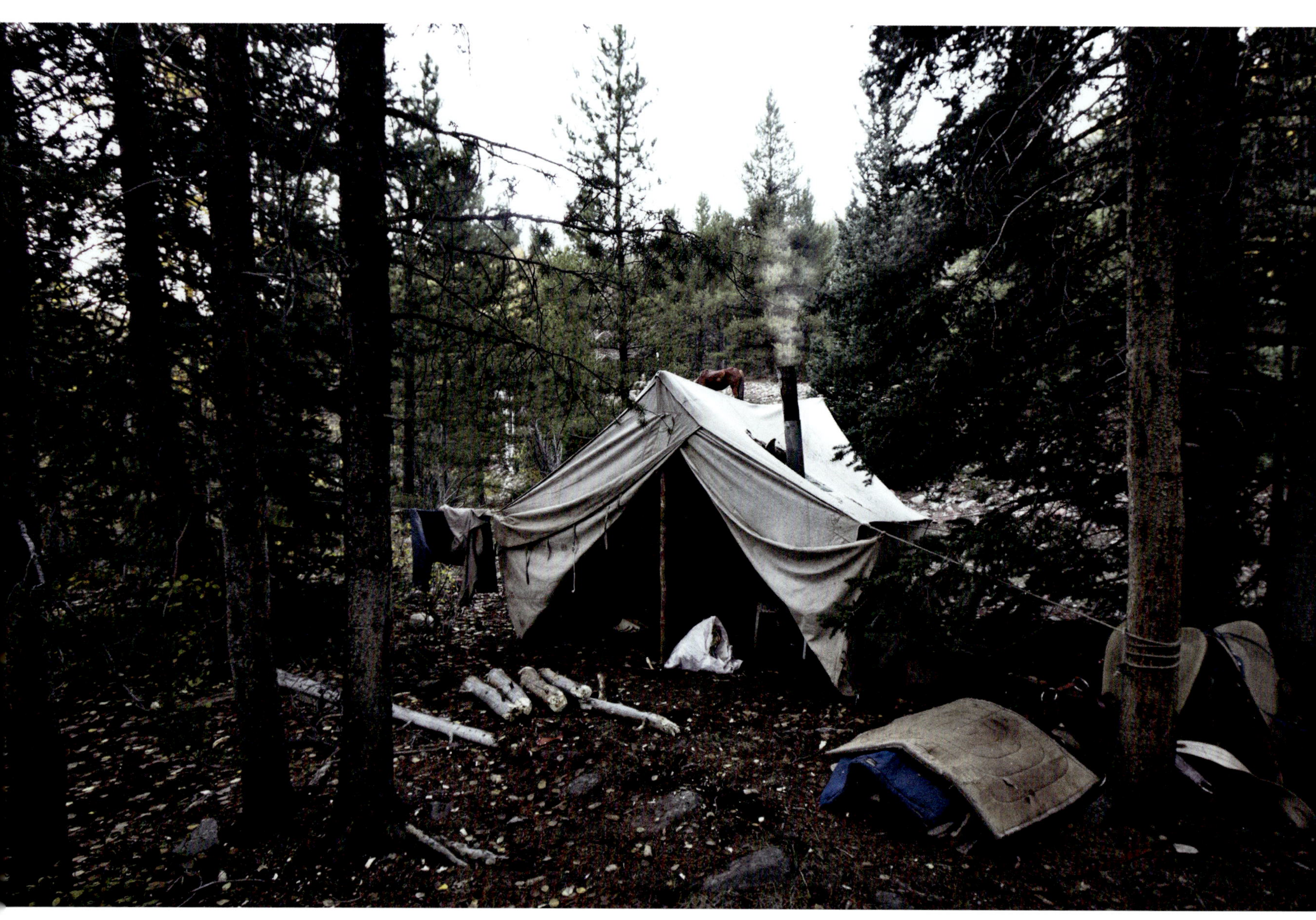

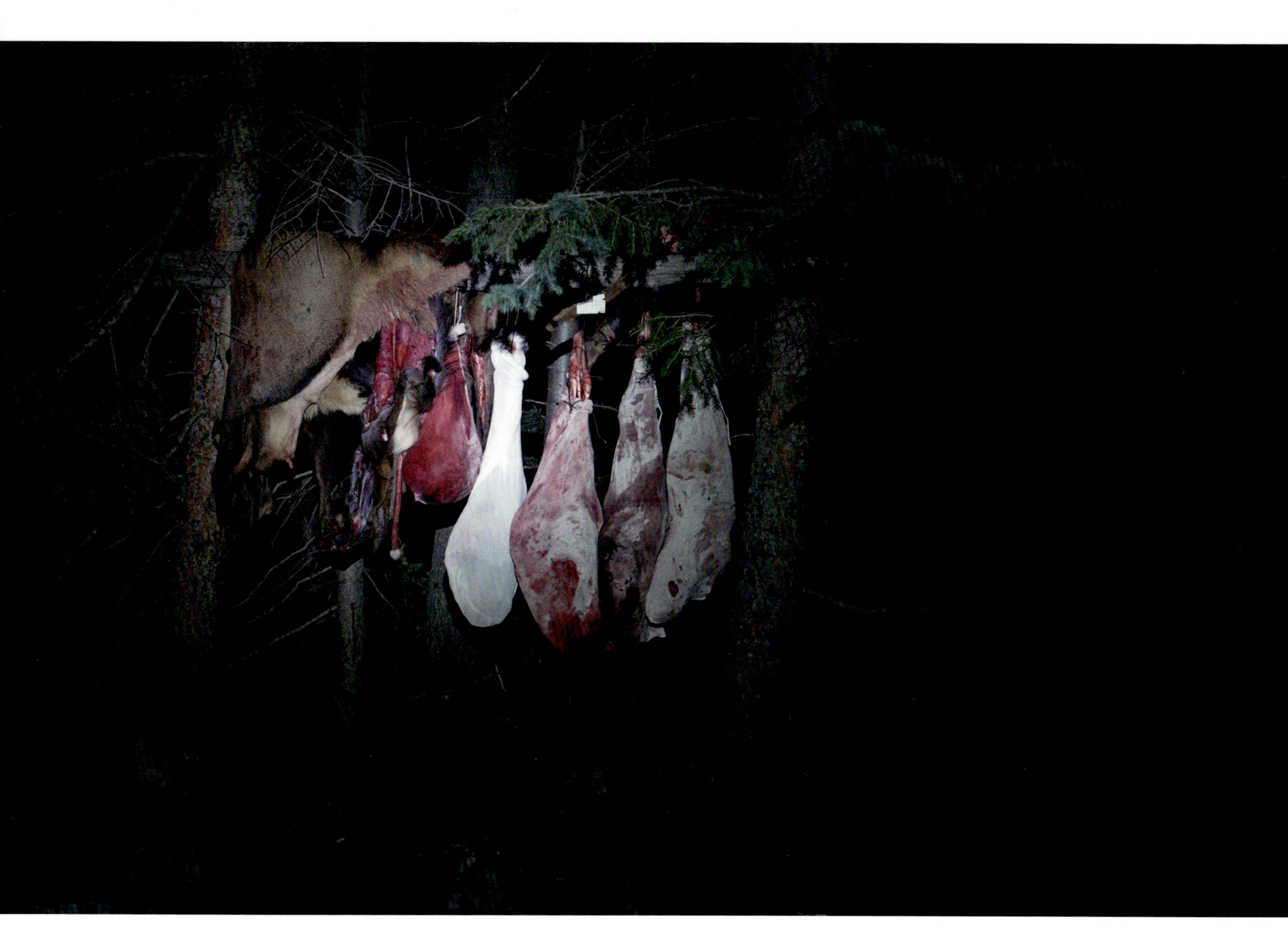

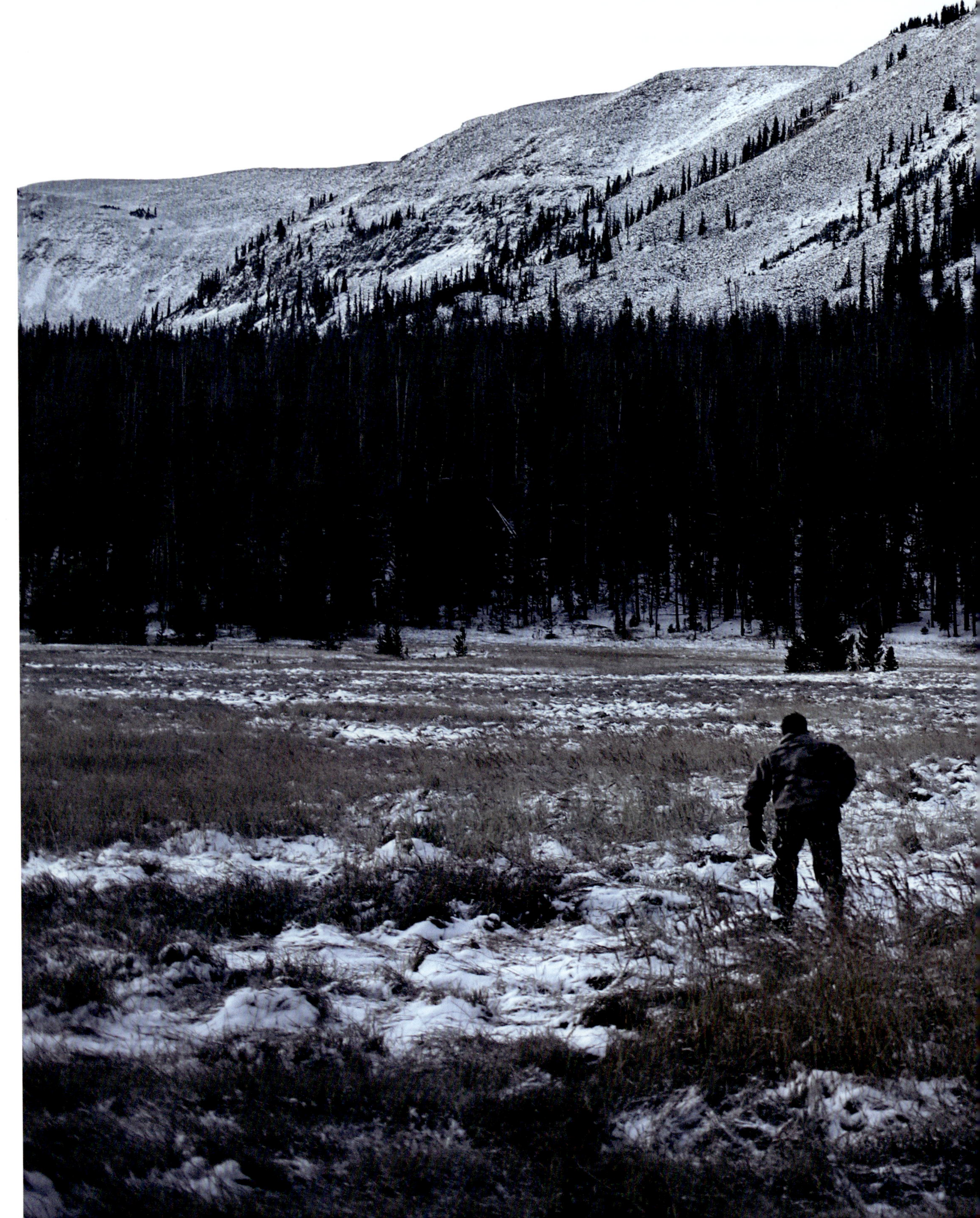

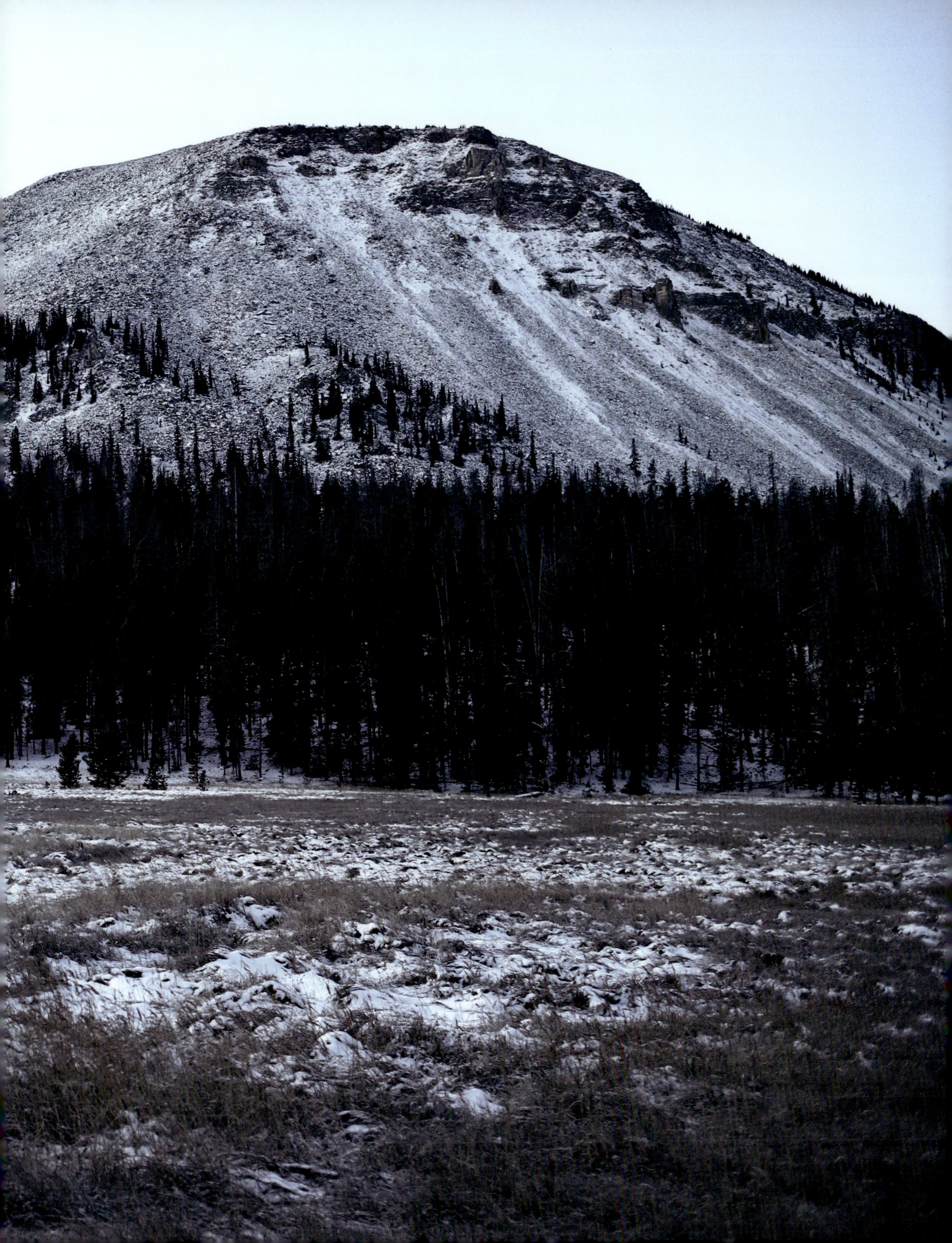

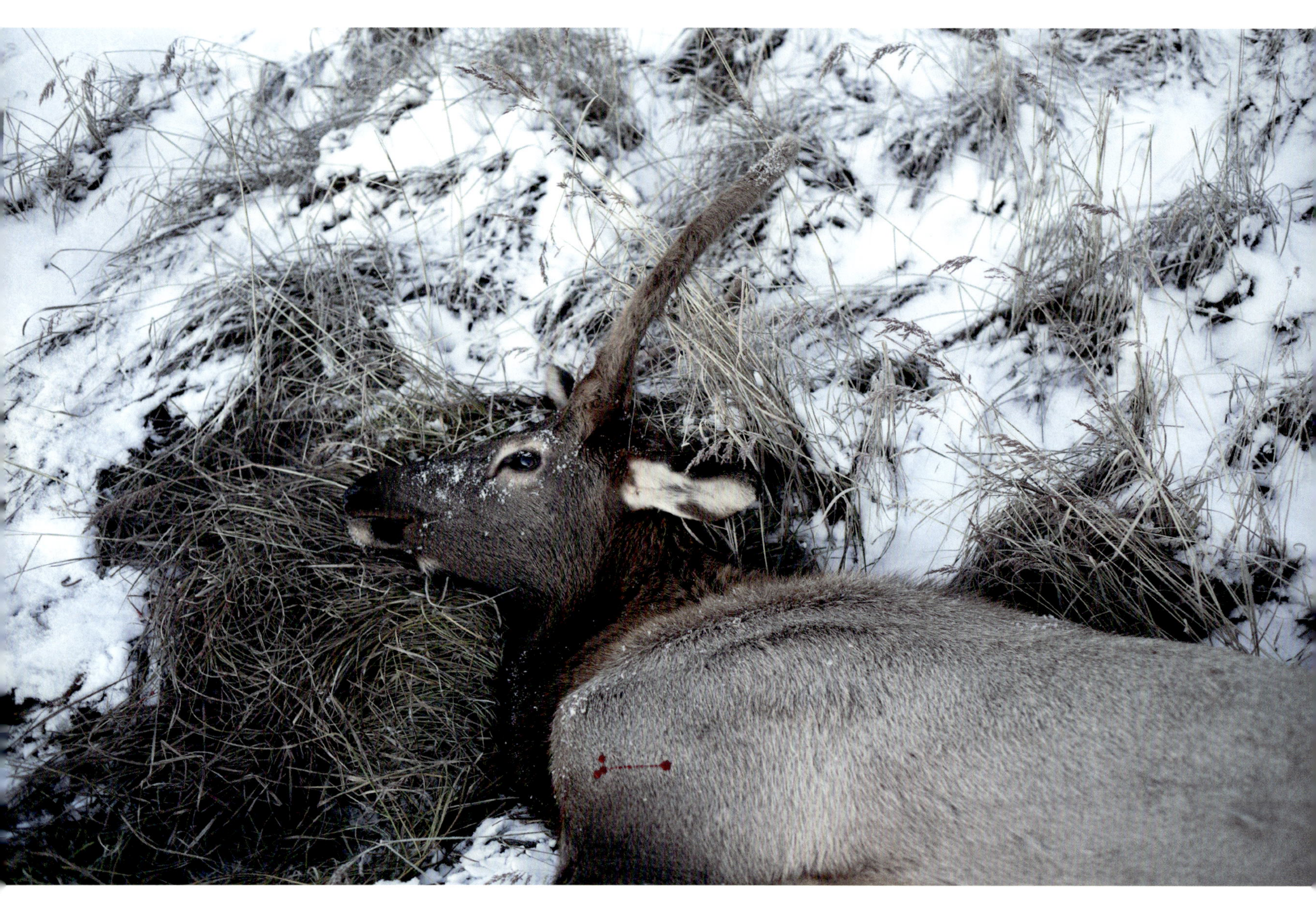

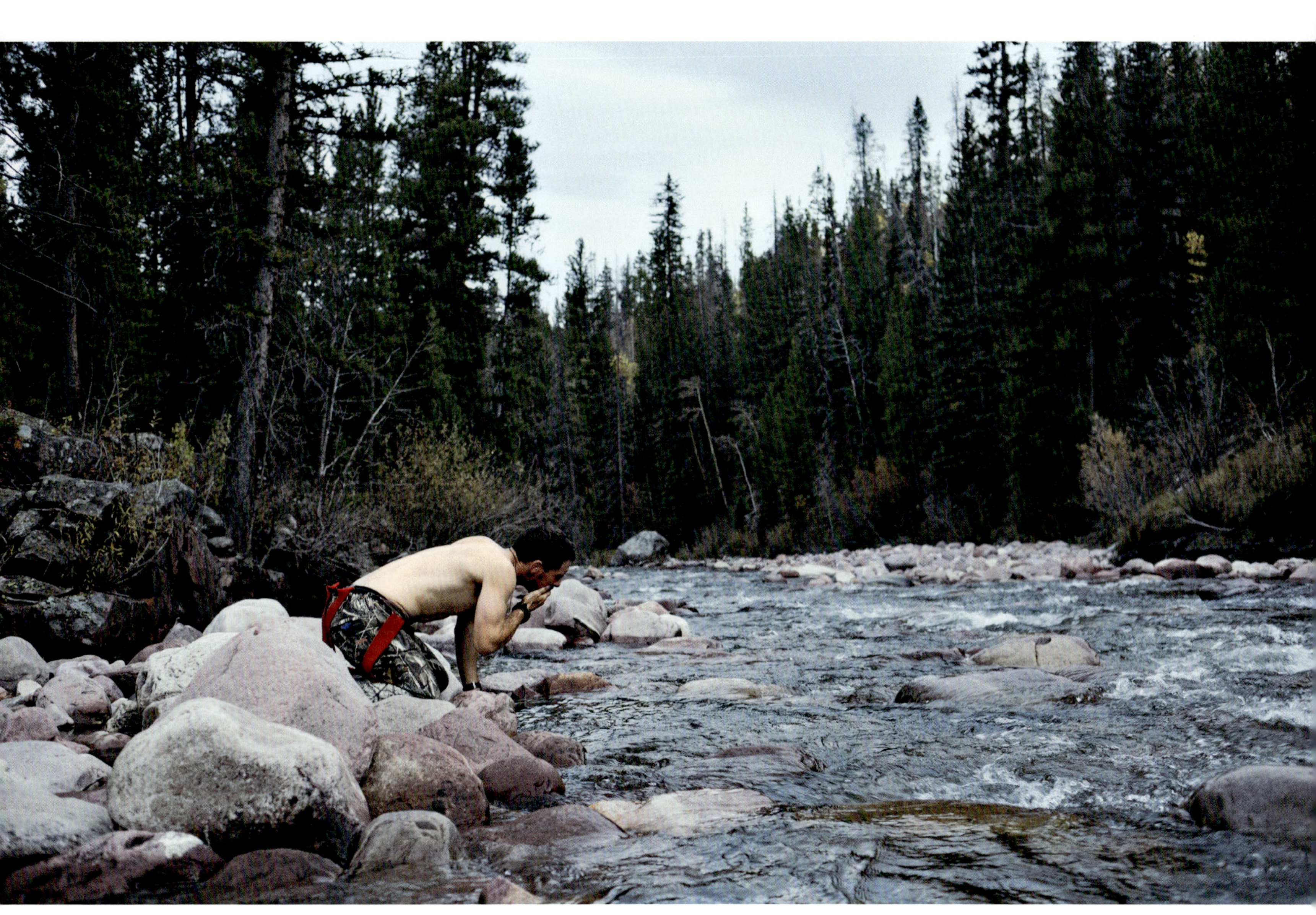

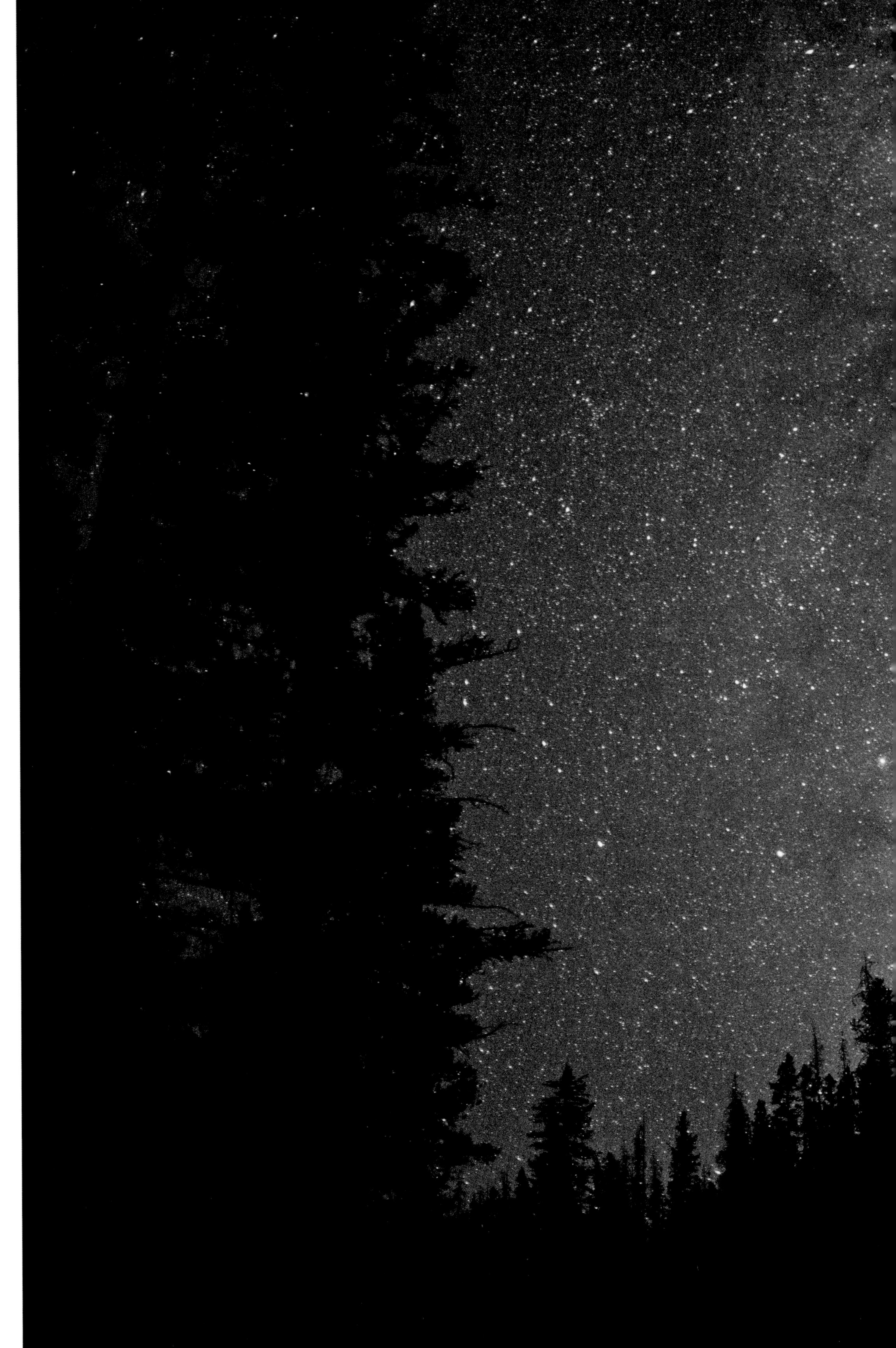

JERRY

"PEOPLE TELL ME I'M LUCKY TO LIVE THIS LIFE. BUT THE TRUTH IS THAT ANYONE CAN COME AND LIVE HERE. YOU JUST HAVE TO BE PREPARED TO WORK HARD TO STAY HERE."

„DIE LEUTE SAGEN MIR, MEIN LEBEN SEI EIN GLÜCKSFALL, ABER JEDER KANN HIERHER KOMMEN UND SO LEBEN. MAN MUSS SCHLICHT BEREIT SEIN, HART ZU ARBEITEN, UM HIER ZU WOHNEN."

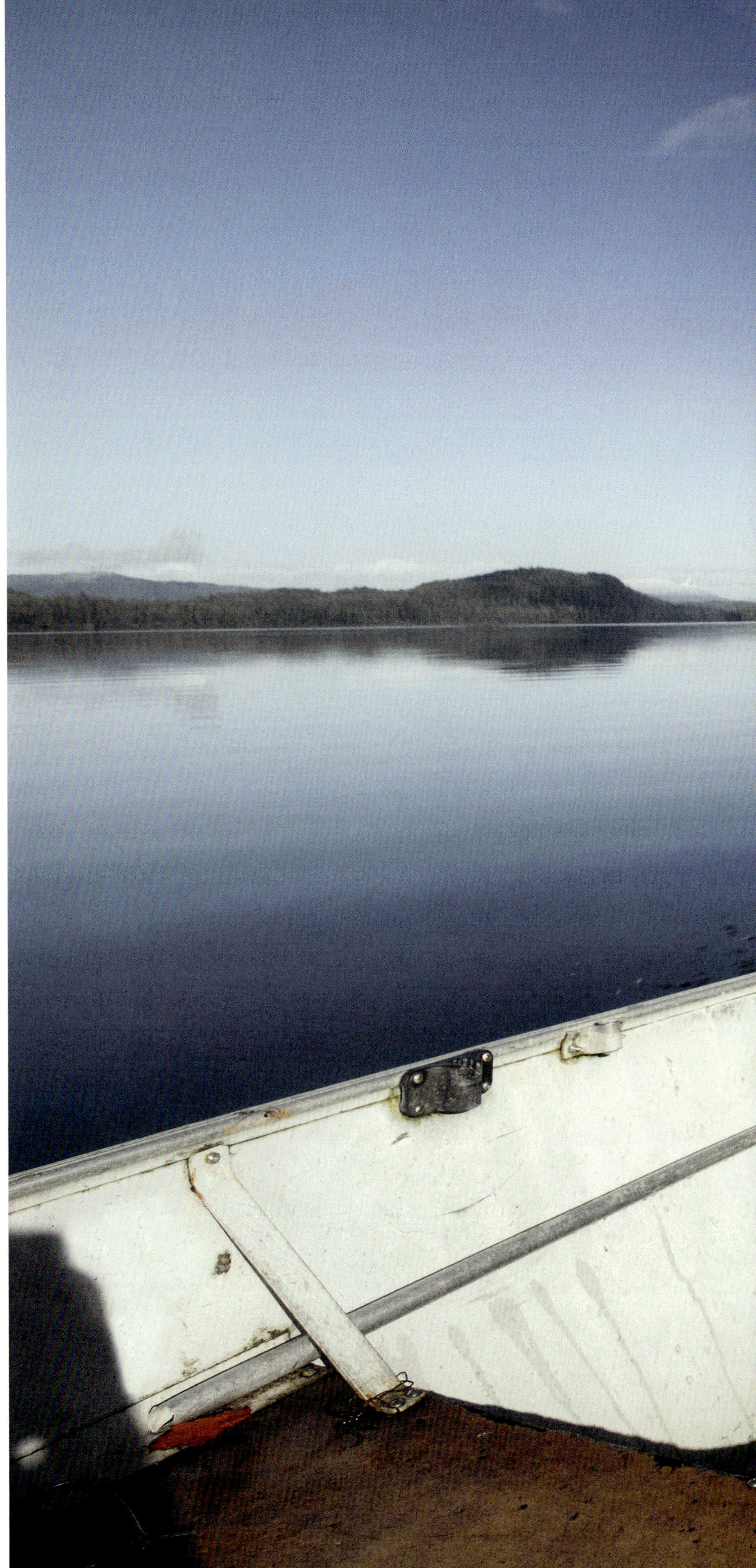

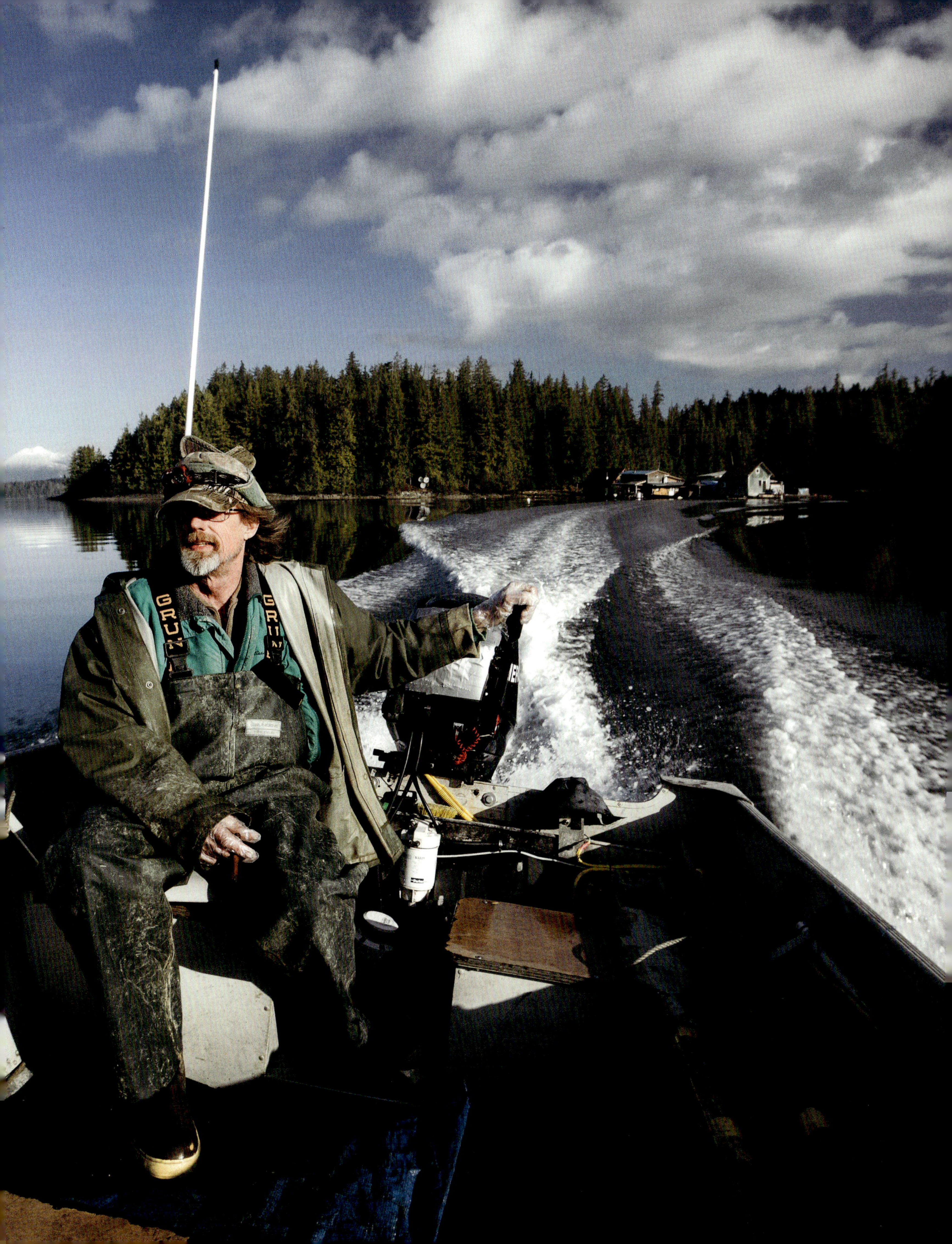

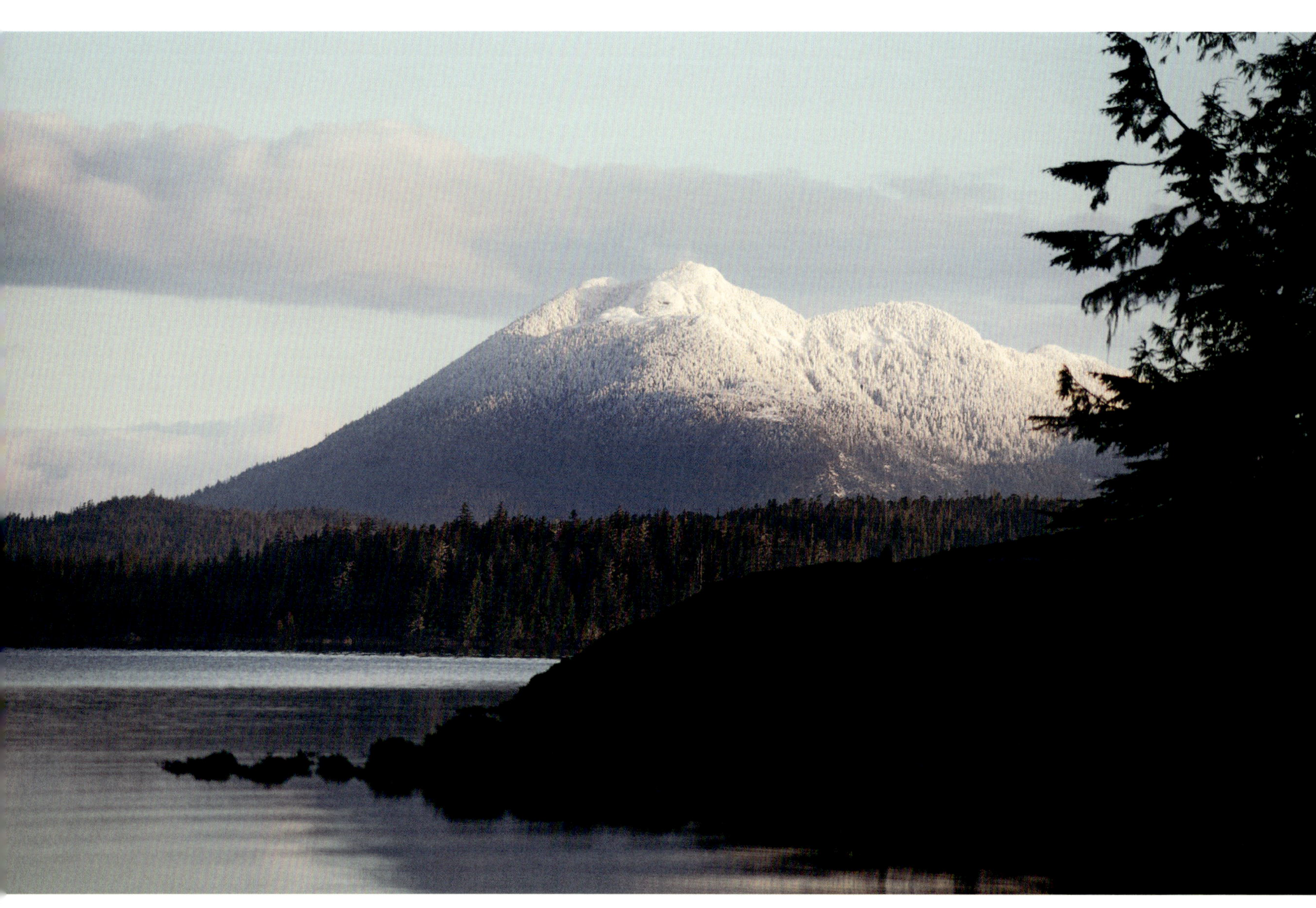

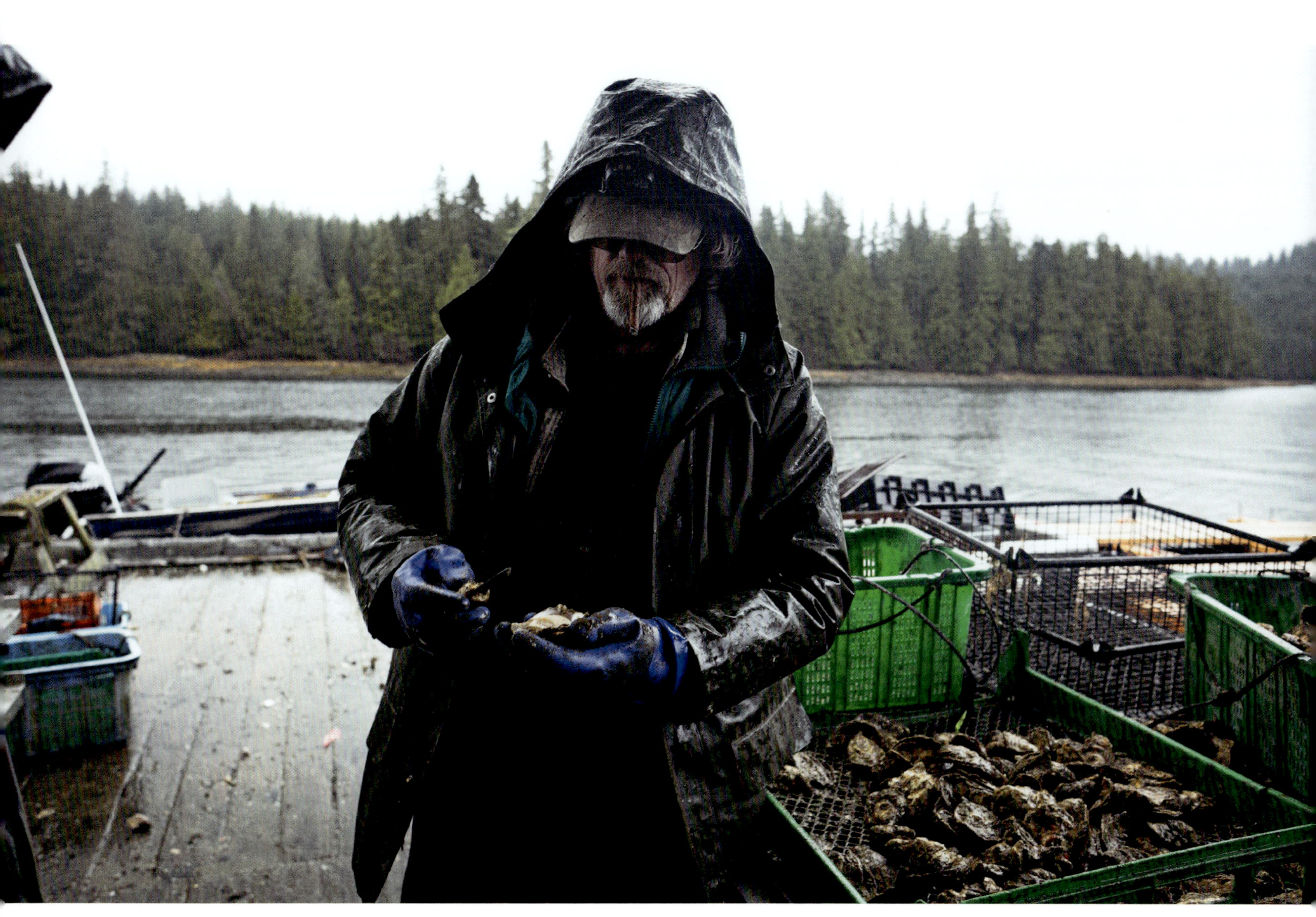

IN SEARCH OF FREEDOM

ALASKA, USA

Burnt from a career as an estate agent, Jerry moved to Alaska where he became
an oyster farmer. He has since enjoyed life in a small, isolated cove surrounded
by unspoiled wilderness.

Jerry's story is one of radical change. In another life, he was an estate agent in Michigan, in the northeast of the USA. Back in 2007 when the subprime mortgage crisis was brewing, Jerry was making business deals with expert ease: "My focus was buying and selling property. It was much easier than oyster farming. I was earning lots of money, I was single and constantly on the go, with four telephone lines and a fax line in my office. Everything piled up, all of these worries and minor details, and I just cracked. I left that ridiculous life behind and drove all the way to Alaska, 5,000 kilometres away."

After several months in Ketchikan, a small port town in the southeast of Alaska, Jerry caught wind of a good business opportunity: a man heading for prison looking to get rid of all of his possessions before being locked up. A businessman at heart, Jerry jumped at the chance and soon found himself with a boat and oyster farm, both in decent condition. The only catch was that he knew nothing about oyster farming – the idea had never even really been on his radar.

But none of that mattered to Jerry, who likes a challenge, and he decided to teach himself the art of oyster farming. He set himself up on Prince of Wales Island, a one-and-a-half-hour seaplane journey from Ketchikan. There, he moored his new home in a deserted cove – far away from his worries as an estate agent. He was now in the heart of the Alaskan rainforest, in an incredibly wild and unspoiled region. Here, Jerry has no neighbours – just his dog Brick a.k.a. "The Boy" for company.

The former businessman adapted quickly to his new life in the great wide open. As the son of a gamekeeper, and a seasoned hunter himself since his teenage years, he may well have been destined for this life in the great outdoors. His passion for the wilderness and fishing in particular were what prised him away from the comforts of urban living that his peers see as the only possible way of life. "People tell me I'm lucky to live this life," Jerry says. "But the truth is that anyone can come and live here. You just have to be prepared to work hard to stay here."

While the pace of life is calm over winter, Jerry works relentlessly as soon as spring arrives, working hour after hour, day after day. In the early morning hours, he drinks his coffee on the wooden pontoon, watching the eagles catching fish in the bay, before slipping on his oilskins and jumping into his small aluminium boat. Throughout the morning, he very carefully arranges the oysters in cardboard boxes, disregarding the occasional backache he feels – which is getting worse as the years go on, the result of pulling up 25-kilo oyster traps submerged underwater. "Each oyster sells for at least 80 cents and there are around 30,000 of them in the water. They're the reason I'm able to live here!"

Then, while he is grilling some oysters on a make-shift BBQ, the radio suddenly crackles, signalling the imminent arrival of the seaplane. A few moments later, the pilot lands in the bay and moors up to the small oyster farm to collect the oysters. These will be sold 120 kilometres away to the restaurants in Ketchikan, which in normal times welcomes over a million cruise passengers every year.

Saturday is "wood day", a key part of Jerry's routine. He finds a dead, but still standing, cedar tree – a sure indication of a really dry wood – and then cuts it down with a chainsaw, before taking to it with an axe. The repetitive sound of the tool striking the wood echoes around the mossy forest, scarcely disturbing the peace and quiet of the surroundings. Rays of sunshine pierce the canopy and a thin mist hovers among the trees. At ground level, tree trunks slowly decompose, creating a layer of incredibly fertile humus, home to countless insects and small animals. This

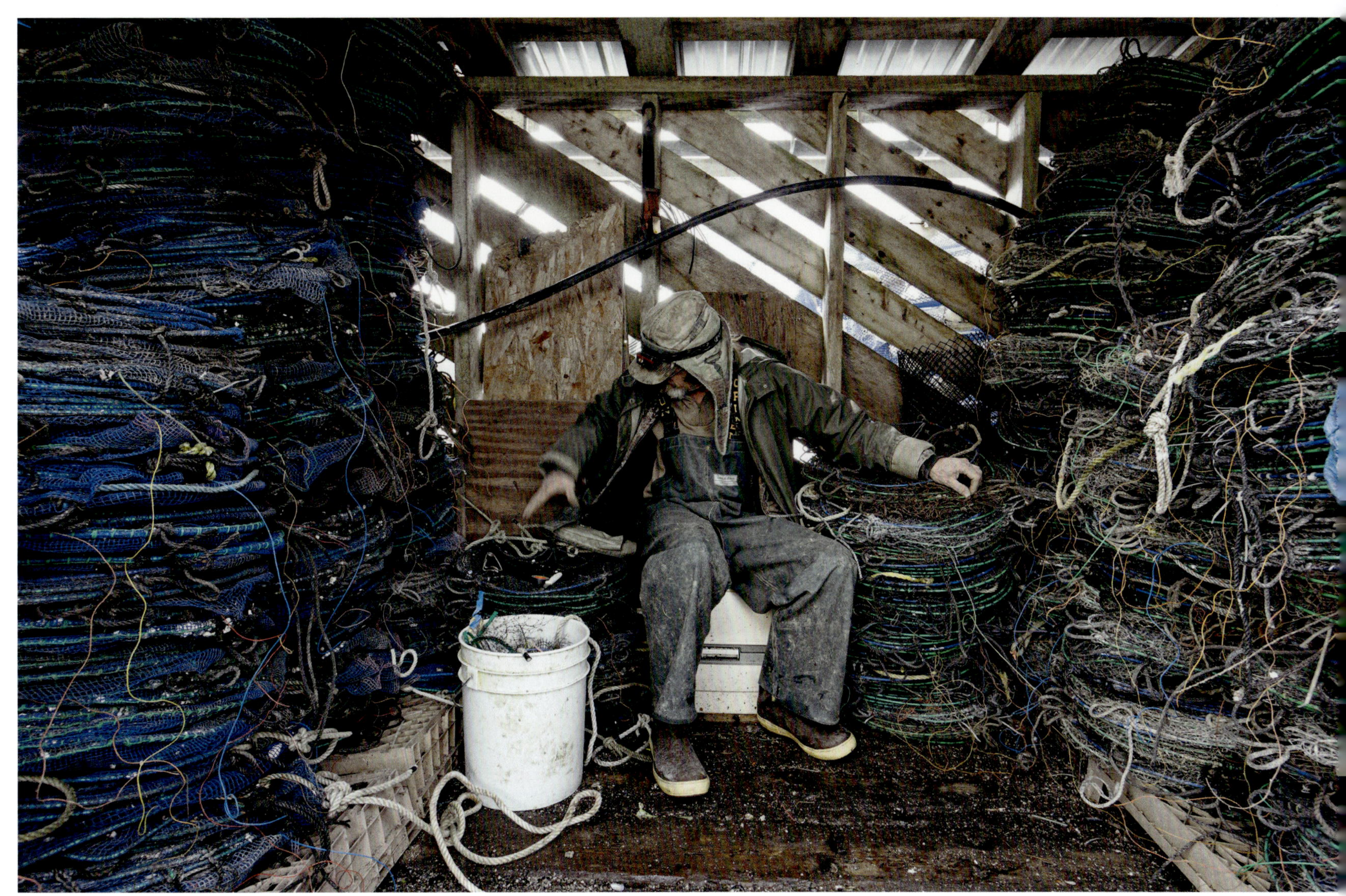

uneven terrain may very well prevent humans from moving around these forests, but the numerous animal tracks running through it are evidence of the teeming life made possible by this precious ecosystem.

The overall dexterity and agility with which Jerry moves around the forests, steers his boat or gets up at 4 o'clock in the morning to embark on a whirlwind fishing trip, fuelled by a swig of cheap whisky that passes for breakfast, are proof that this is where he is meant to be. He was built for this life off the grid, detached from the outside world, with no electricity or running water – a life that quenches his deep thirst for freedom and independence, bar, paradoxically, his dependence on petrol to run his boat and work his chainsaw.

At 58 years of age, Jerry lives a life of minimum comfort, and the rainy winter days are often spent watching TV with the wood-burning stove crackling alongside him. The water barely freezes over in this region of Alaska, but the winter is dark and damp, and so it is essential to have a comfortable, warm place in which to wait out the cold season until spring arrives. For the internet, Jerry's best bet is to wake up early and try to find a signal between 4 and 6 o'clock, when the satellite connection is the most reliable. Jerry also receives radio signals through his satellite dish, but he now hardly bothers to tune into the songs played daily over and over in the same old order.

Like many Americans, he believes that America is run by a group of incompetent people and that chaos is just around the corner. He also sees his self-sufficient life as a way to protect himself from problems in a world he thinks – a thought shared by many – is heading towards ruin. All of this – his deep love of fishing and the outdoors combined with his instinct to survive in the face of the constantly changing landscape of a divided America – make Alaska the perfect home for him in every respect. When it comes to fishing in particular, Alaska is a dream come true. The large bay where Jerry lives is home to huge halibut, while the adjoining river teems with salmon. Every summer when they swim upstream to spawn, Jerry grabs his fishing rod and jumps into his boat to try his luck in the mouth of the river. In summer, the region's wildlife shows itself in all its glory: from eagles fishing along the surface of the ocean to sea otters nibbling on clams. In the distance, black bears emerge from the forest to dine on the young shoots of grass lining the water's edge before feasting on salmon to bulk up for the win-

ter. These nutrient-rich waters are the perfect fishing grounds for animals and humans alike.

Living in complete isolation, Jerry sustains himself through fishing, of course, but also through hunting, foraging for berries and mushroom picking. Two or three times a year, he makes the long journey into Ketchikan to stock up on supplies. He travels by boat rather than by seaplane – a longer journey, but the cheaper option. This is the most economical way of shopping when you consider that an apple costs two dollars from the local grocery store, "local" here meaning an hour away by boat. He makes the most of his trip into civilisation by taking a long hot shower and filling up at an all-you-can-eat buffet. But he never stays in town for too long: too many people, too much noise. Back home, the wood-fired stove stays ablaze all day long and Jerry's shotgun hangs on the wall beside a two-person saw, ready to take the place of the chainsaw should the petrol ever run out. Living in a sometimes hostile environment, Jerry needs to remain vigilant at all times, taking care on wet and slippery pontoons, avoiding cold 8 °C waters, navigating unpredictable weather conditions and watching out for unexpected visitors. In addition to black bears, numerous wolves roam the region, their majestic howling reverberating in the forest – all too close by. Jerry sometimes catches a glimpse of them when they come to quietly observe his abode from the shoreline.

The arrival of summer is when nature truly comes to life. From his home, Jerry can admire the procession of orcas and whales come to feast on herring in the bay. They've been known to put on a memorable show for the fishers, all of a sudden propelling their monolithic bodies out of the water in a cloud of spray, rotating subtly in the air and then crashing back down onto the surface of the ocean, causing huge ripples. Just like the wolves and the black bears, this extraordinary feat of strength is one example of the legends of the Tlingit tribe, the "people of the tides" that has inhabited this fertile region of south-east Alaska for millennia.

These encounters never cease to amaze Jerry, and they reconfirm the choice he has made in coming to live here. "With such an abundance of nature and animals around me, every day is like a holiday. I left a ridiculous life behind in order to feel free, to work for myself and to live in the heart of Alaska. It's easy to fall in love with this place. There is so much freedom here. It is literally paradise."

AUF DER SUCHE NACH FREIHEIT

Der ehemalige Immobilienmakler Jerry erlebte einen Burnout und zog nach Alaska,
um Austernzüchter zu werden. Seitdem lebt er in einer abgeschiedenen kleinen Bucht,
umgeben von wilder, unberührter Natur.

Dies ist die Geschichte eines radikalen Bruchs. In einem anderen Leben war Jerry Immobilienmakler in Michigan, im Nordosten der Vereinigten Staaten. Im Jahr 2007, zu Beginn der Krise am US-Immobilienmarkt, ist Jerry ein harter Geschäftsmann: „Ich kaufte Häuser und verkaufte sie wieder; das war definitiv einfacher als die Austernzucht. Ich verdiente viel Geld, war ledig und ständig beschäftigt; in meinem Büro hatte ich vier Telefonleitungen und ein Fax. Alles häufte sich immer mehr auf, die ganzen Sorgen, lauter unwichtige Details, bis ich zusammenbrach. Ich ließ dieses absurde Leben hinter mir und fuhr bis nach Alaska, 5000 Kilometer weit."

Nach einigen Monaten in der kleinen Hafenstadt Ketchikan im Südosten Alaskas hört Jerry von einem guten Geschäft: Ein Mann, der ins Gefängnis muss, will vor seiner Haftzeit all seinen Besitz verkaufen. Als waschechter Geschäftsmann ergreift Jerry die Gelegenheit, verhandelt hart und erwirbt ein Boot und eine Austernfarm in gutem Zustand. Das einzige Problem: Er weiß nichts über die Austernzucht und hat sich auch nie wirklich dafür interessiert.

Aber das macht nichts; Jerry liebt Herausforderungen und beschließt, das nötige Wissen allein zu erwerben, als Autodidakt. Er lässt sich in anderthalb Wasserflugzeugstunden Entfernung von Ketchikan nieder, auf der Prince-of-Wales-Insel, wo er sein schwimmendes Haus in einer einsamen, wilden Bucht verankert, weit weg von den Sorgen eines Immobilienmaklers. Ohne Nachbarn, nur mit seinem Hund Brick alias „The Boy", lebt Jerry im Herzen der gemäßigten Regenwälder Alaskas, in einer unglaublich intakten, unberührten Region.

Der ehemalige Geschäftsmann passt sich schnell an sein neues Leben in den wilden Weiten an. Als Sohn eines Wildhüters ist er seit seiner Jugend ein abgehärteter Jäger, vielleicht prädestiniert für dieses Leben im Freien. Seine Leidenschaft für die Wildnis, insbesondere fürs Fischen, hat ihn vom bequemeren Leben in der Stadt abgebracht, das viele Menschen als einzig möglichen Weg sehen. Jerry bestätigt: „Die Leute sagen mir, mein Leben sei ein Glücksfall, aber jeder kann hierher kommen und so leben. Man muss schlicht bereit sein, hart zu arbeiten, um hier zu wohnen."

Und auch wenn der Rhythmus im Winter friedlich ist, arbeitet Jerry ab Frühjahrsbeginn unermüdlich, ohne die Stunden oder Tage zu zählen. Im Morgengrauen, nach einem Kaffee auf dem hölzernen Bootsanleger, von wo aus er die Adler beim Fischfang in der Bucht beobachten kann, zieht er sein Ölzeug an und springt in sein Aluminiumboot. Den ganzen Vormittag lang packt er sorgfältig Austern in Kisten und ignoriert dabei seine Rückenschmerzen, die sich im Lauf der Jahre verstärkt haben, um Reusen von 25 Kilo Gewicht aus dem Meer zu hieven. „Jede Auster wird für mindestens 80 Cent verkauft, und unter Wasser gibt es ungefähr 30.000 davon. Ihnen habe ich es zu verdanken, dass ich hier leben kann!" versichert Jerry.

Während er ein paar Austern über einem improvisierten Feuer grillt, knistert das Funkgerät und kündigt die Ankunft eines Wasserflugzeugs an. Wenige Augenblicke später wassert der Pilot auf der Bucht und vertäut seine Maschine an der kleinen Austernfarm. Das Verladen der Austern kann beginnen. Sie werden in 120 Kilometern Entfernung in den Restaurants von Ketchikan verkauft, wo normalerweise jedes Jahr mehr als eine Million Kreuzfahrt-Passagiere an Land gehen.

Samstags ist Holztag, ein Schlüsselmoment in Jerrys Alltag. Er sucht sich eine tote, aber noch aufrecht stehende Zeder aus, mit garantiert trockenem Holz, die er mit der Motorsäge fällt. Danach hört man das regelmäßige Geräusch von Axthieben in dem moosigen Wald; es stört die Stille der Umgebung kaum. Sonnenstrahlen dringen durchs Blätterdach, während zwischen den Bäumen zarter Dunst schwebt. Am Boden vermodern morsche Baumstümpfe und schaffen eine ungeheuer fruchtbare Humusschicht, in der zahlreiche Insekten und Kleintiere leben. Der unebene Boden mag zwar Menschen die Fortbewegung in diesen Wäldern erschweren, aber eine Vielzahl von Tierpfaden zeugt von dem Leben, das dieses kostbare Ökosystem bevölkert.

Die Geschicklichkeit, mit der sich Jerry durch den Wald bewegt, sein Boot steuert oder um vier Uhr morgens mit einem Schluck billigem Whisky als Frühstück zu einer wilden Angelpartie aufbricht, zeigt: Hier ist er am richtigen Ort. Er ist für dieses autarke Leben ohne Internetverbindung, ohne Strom und ohne fließendes Wasser geschaffen, mit seinem Hunger nach Freiheit und einem ausgeprägten Wunsch nach Unabhängigkeit, auch wenn er paradoxerweise extrem abhängig von Benzin für sein Boot und seine Motorsäge ist.

Mit 58 Jahren legt Jerry Wert auf ein Minimum an Komfort, und die regnerischen Wintertage verbringt er oft am prasselnden Holzofen vor dem Fernseher. Auch wenn der Frost in dieser Gegend Alaskas die Meeresoberfläche nicht gefrieren lässt, sind die Winter so dunkel und feucht, dass man ein gemütliches warmes Nest braucht, um den Frühling abzuwarten. Das Internet ist nur etwas für Frühaufsteher, weil die Satellitenverbindung zwischen vier und sechs Uhr morgens am besten funktioniert. Was das Radio angeht, das Jerry ebenfalls über seine Satellitenantenne empfängt, achtet er gar nicht mehr auf die Endlosschleife, die es jeden Tag in der gleichen Reihenfolge von sich gibt.

Wie viele US-Amerikaner ist Jerry davon überzeugt, dass die USA in den vergangenen Jahren von einer inkompetenten Bande regiert wurden und das Chaos unmittelbar bevorstand. Für ihn ist die Autarkie auch ein Mittel zum Selbstschutz gegen die Probleme einer modernen Welt, die – nach seiner Meinung und der vieler anderer – ins Verderben rennt. Alaska entspricht in jeder Hinsicht seinem Lebensideal; dort vereint sich seine Begeisterung fürs Fischen mit seinem Überlebensinstinkt angesichts der Veränderungen, die in den gespaltenen USA ständig drohen. Vor allem aber ist es ein Königreich der Fischer: In der großen Bucht, in der Jerry angelt, gibt es riesige Heilbutte, im benachbarten Fluss wimmelt es von Lachsen. Jeden Sommer, wenn sie ankommen, um flussaufwärts zu laichen, packt er seine Ausrüstung und springt ins Boot, um an der Flussmündung zu angeln. Um diese Jahreszeit zeigt sich die Tierwelt in ihrer ganzen Pracht: Adler fangen an der Wasseroberfläche Fische, während die Meerotter Venusmuscheln knacken. In der Ferne kommen Schwarzbären aus dem Wald und knabbern am Fluss junge

Kräuter, bevor sie sich mit einem Festmahl aus Lachs ihren Winterspeck anfressen. In diesen nahrungsreichen Gewässern ist das Fischen immer lohnend, für Tiere wie für Menschen.

In seiner glücklichen Einsamkeit ernährt sich Jerry natürlich von dem, was er fischt, aber auch von seiner Jagdbeute, vom Beeren- und vom Pilzesammeln. Zwei bis drei Mal pro Jahr fährt er in die Stadt Ketchikan, eher im Boot als per Wasserflugzeug, weil das zwar länger dauert, aber billiger ist. Eine lange Reise zum Großeinkauf. Das ist die sparsamste Option, wenn man bedenkt, dass ein Apfel im Lebensmittelladen um die Ecke – der auch eine Bootsstunde entfernt ist – zwei Dollar kostet. Er nutzt die Reise, um eine ausgiebige warme Dusche zu nehmen und sich in einem All-you-can-eat-Restaurant zu stärken. Aber er bleibt nie lang in der Stadt: zu viele Menschen, zu viel Lärm.

Bei ihm zu Hause brennt der Holzofen den ganzen Tag, und das Gewehr hängt an der Wand bereit, neben einer Zweimannsäge, die im Fall von Benzinmangel die Motorsäge ersetzen könnte. In dieser manchmal feindseligen Welt ist ständige Wachsamkeit vonnöten, gegenüber ungebetenen Besuchern, glitschigen Holzstegen über 8 °C kaltem Wasser, unvorhersehbarem Wetter und einer Vielzahl wilder Tiere … Neben den Schwarzbären gibt es in der Gegend auch zahlreiche Wölfe, und von Zeit zu Zeit klingt ihr majestätisches Heulen in unmittelbarer Nähe durch den Wald. Manchmal entdeckt Jerry sie, wenn sie sich diskret nähern, um sein Haus am Ufer zu beobachten.

Wenn der Sommer kommt, setzt ein grandioses Naturschauspiel ein. Von seinem Haus aus kann Jerry das Ballett der Orcas und Wale beobachten, die zu einem Festmahl aus Heringen in die Bucht kommen. Manchmal liefern sie den Fischern unvergessliche Auftritte, wenn sie ihre monolithischen Körper ohne Vorwarnung aus dem Wasser katapultieren, in der Luft von Wasserfontänen begleitete Drehungen vollführen und dann mit ihrem ganzen Gewicht in einem unglaublichen Getöse auf die Meeresoberfläche krachen. Ein überwältigender Anblick, der sich – wie die Wölfe und Schwarzbären – durch die Legenden des indigenen Volkes der Tlingit zieht, dem „Volk der Gezeiten", das seit Jahrtausenden diese reiche Region im Südosten Alaskas bewohnt.

Für Jerry, den diese Begegnungen nach wie vor entzücken, bestätigen sie seine Entscheidung wieder einmal. „Wenn ich diese Fülle an Natur und Tieren sehe, habe ich den Eindruck, jeden Tag im Urlaub zu sein. Ich habe ein absurdes Leben verlassen, um frei zu sein, auf eigene Rechnung zu arbeiten und im Herzen Alaskas zu leben … Sich in diesen Ort zu verlieben, ist ziemlich einfach. Es gibt hier eine solche Freiheit, es ist buchstäblich das Paradies."

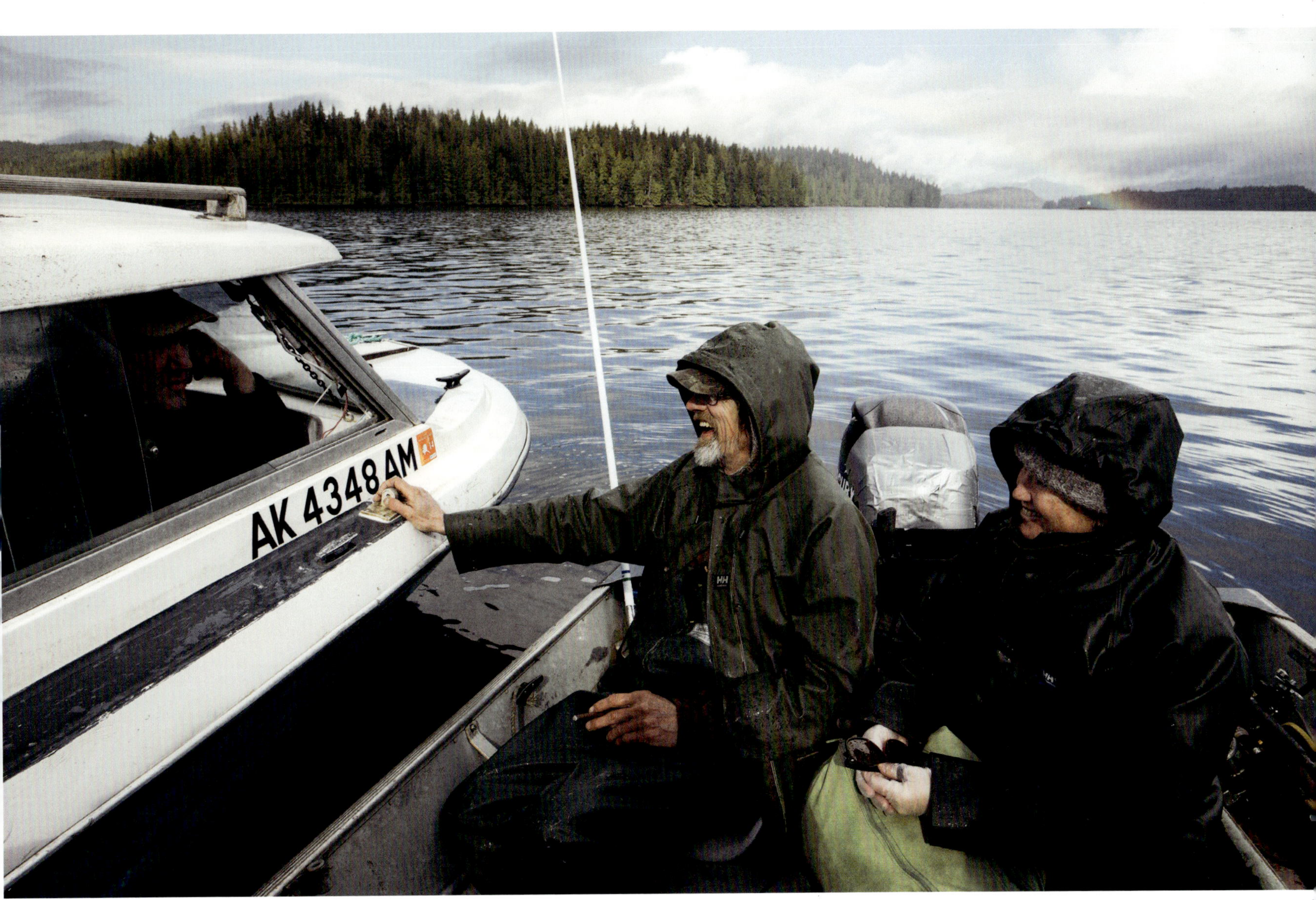

AK 4348 AM

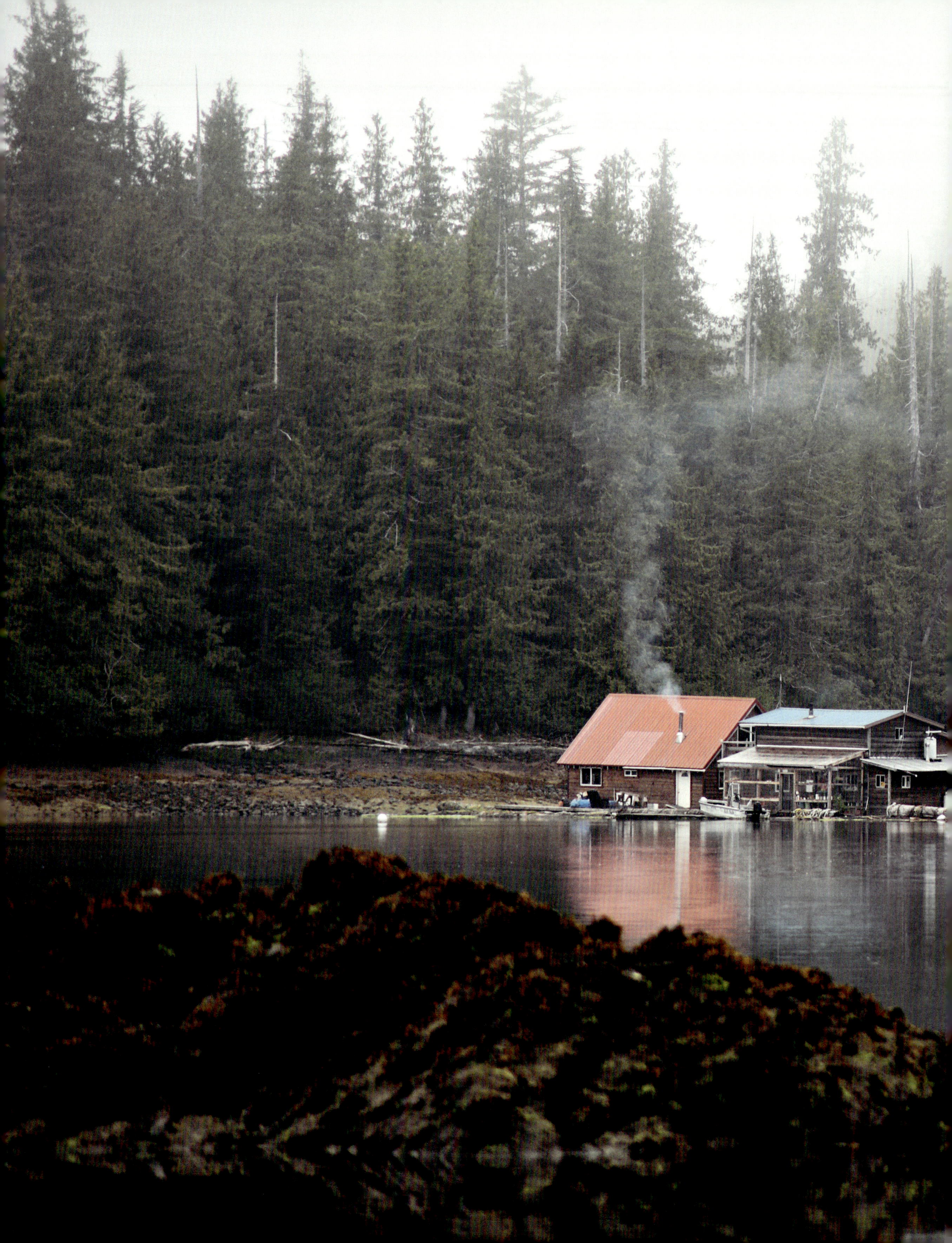

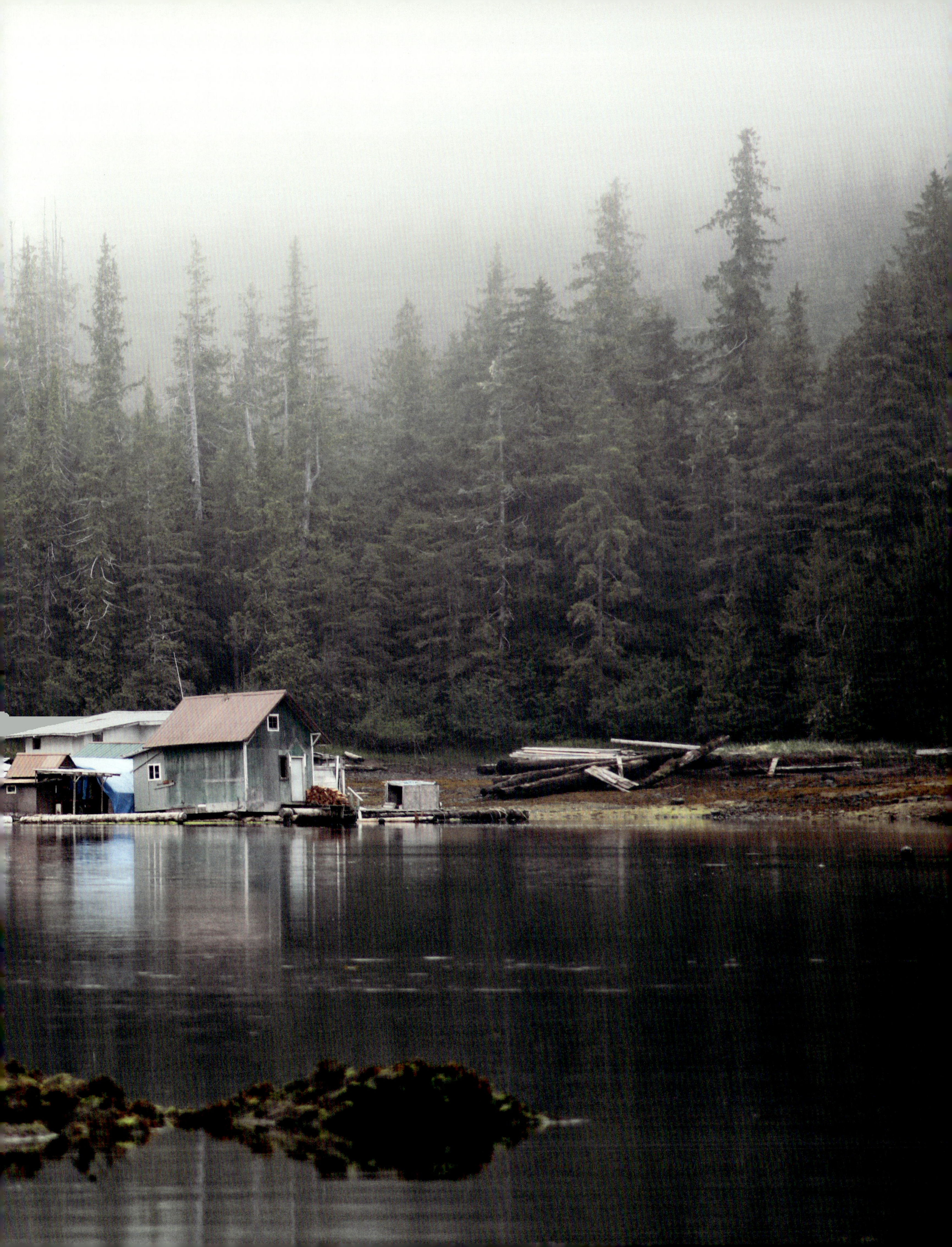

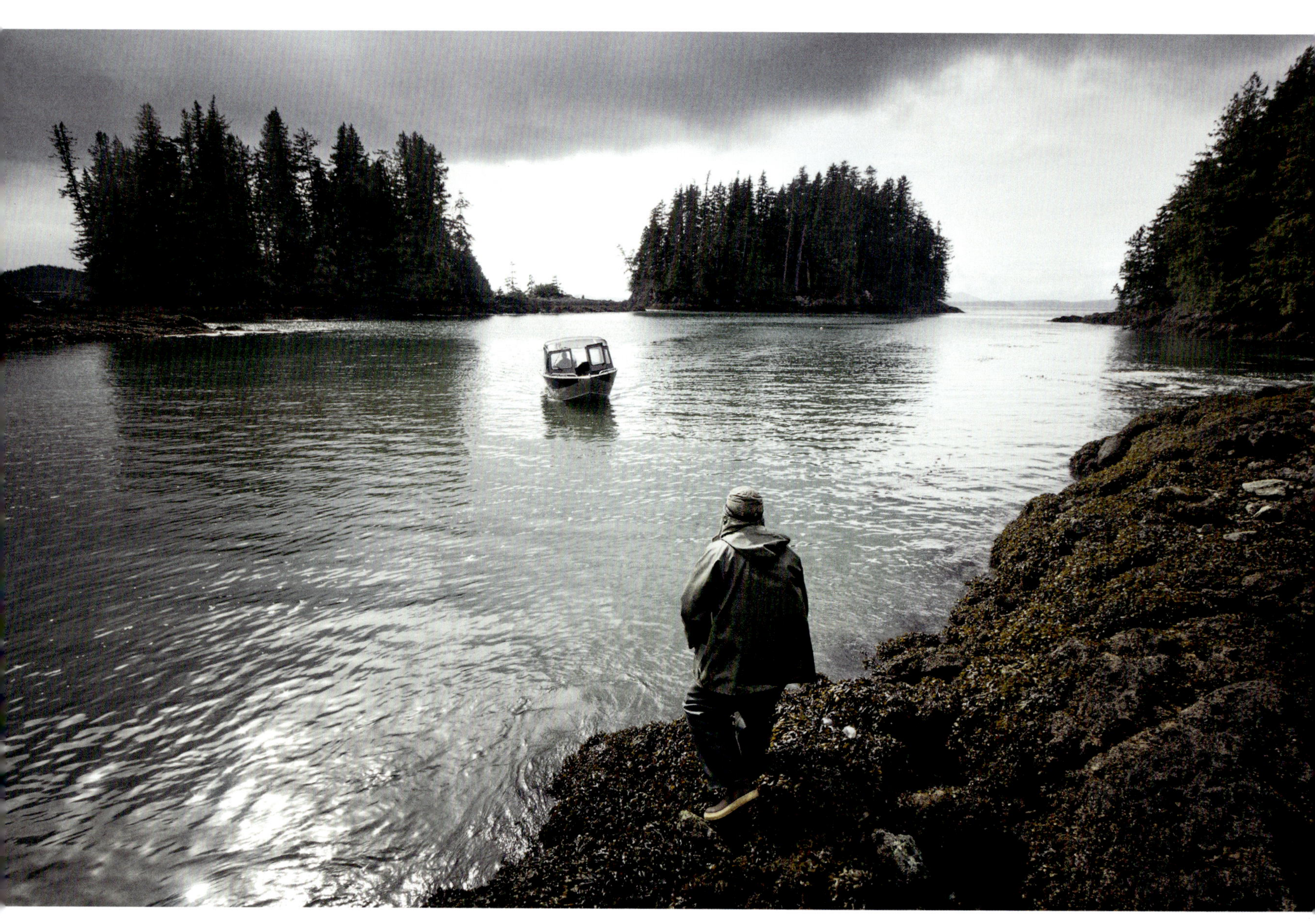

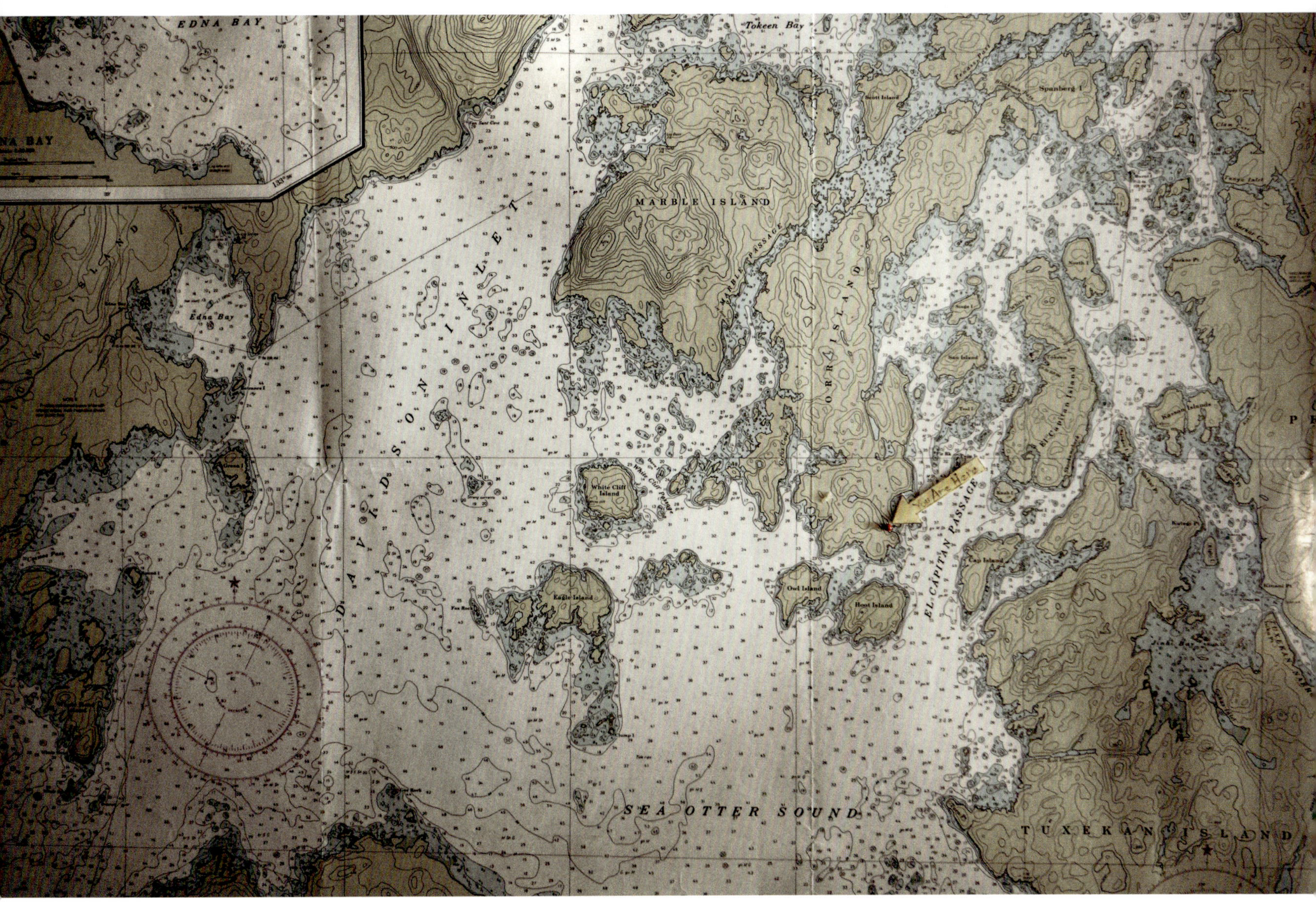

EDNA BAY
NA BAY
Tokeen Bay
Spanberg I
MARBLE ISLAND
DAVIDSON INLET
MARBLE PASSAGE
ORR ISLAND
White Cliff Island
EL CAPITAN PASSAGE
Eagle Island
Owl Island
Hoot Island
SEA OTTER SOUND
TUXEKAN ISLAND

"But men labor under a mistake. The better part of the man is soon ploughed into the soil for compost. By seeming fate, commonly called necessity, the are employed, as it says in an old book, laying up treasures which moth and rust will corrupt and thieves break through and steal. It is a fool's life, as they will find when they get to the end of it, if not before."

HENRY DAVID THOREAU
Walden; or, Life in the Woods

„Aber die Menschen laborieren unter falschen Voraussetzungen. Ihr besserer Teil ist bald als Dünger unter die Erde gepflügt. Infolge eines scheinbaren Verhängnisses, das man gewöhnlich Schicksal nennt, beschäftigen sie sich damit, Schätze zu sammeln, welche die Motten und der Rost fressen und denen die Diebe nachgraben, wie es in dem alten Buche heißt. Ein Narrenleben ist es, wie sie finden werden, wenn sie zu seinem Ende gelangen, wenn nicht schon früher."

HENRY DAVID THOREAU
Walden oder Leben in den Wäldern

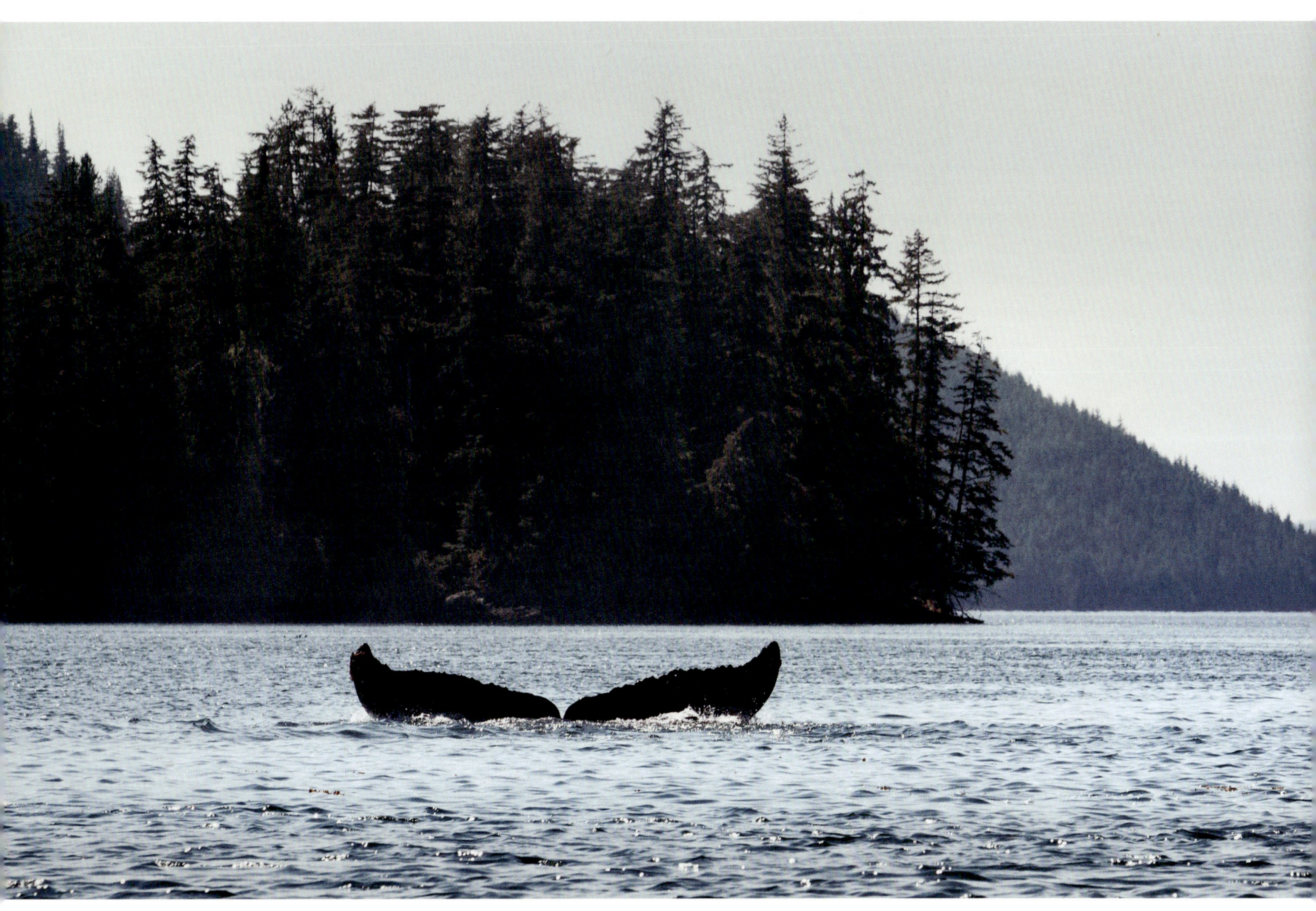

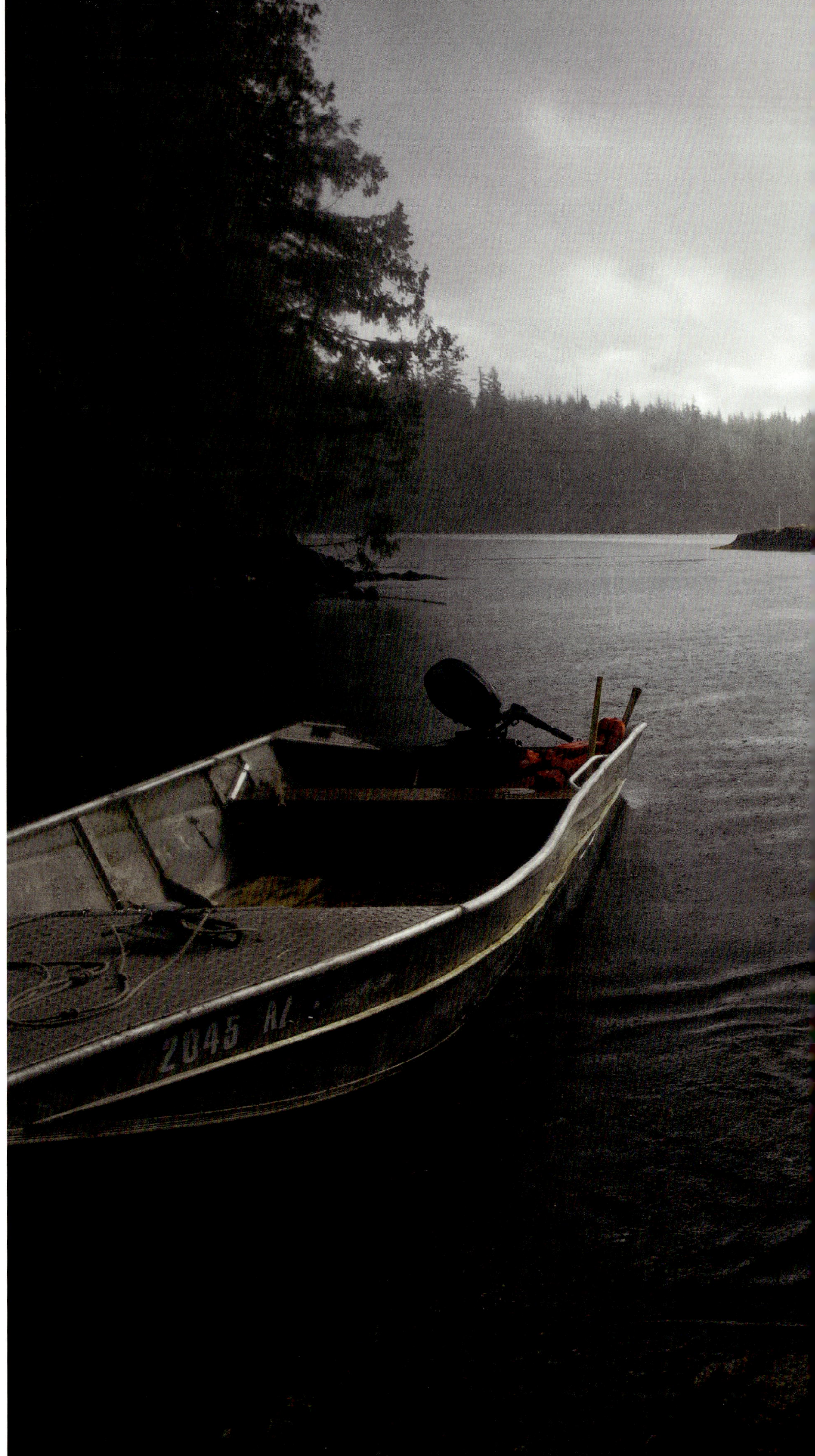

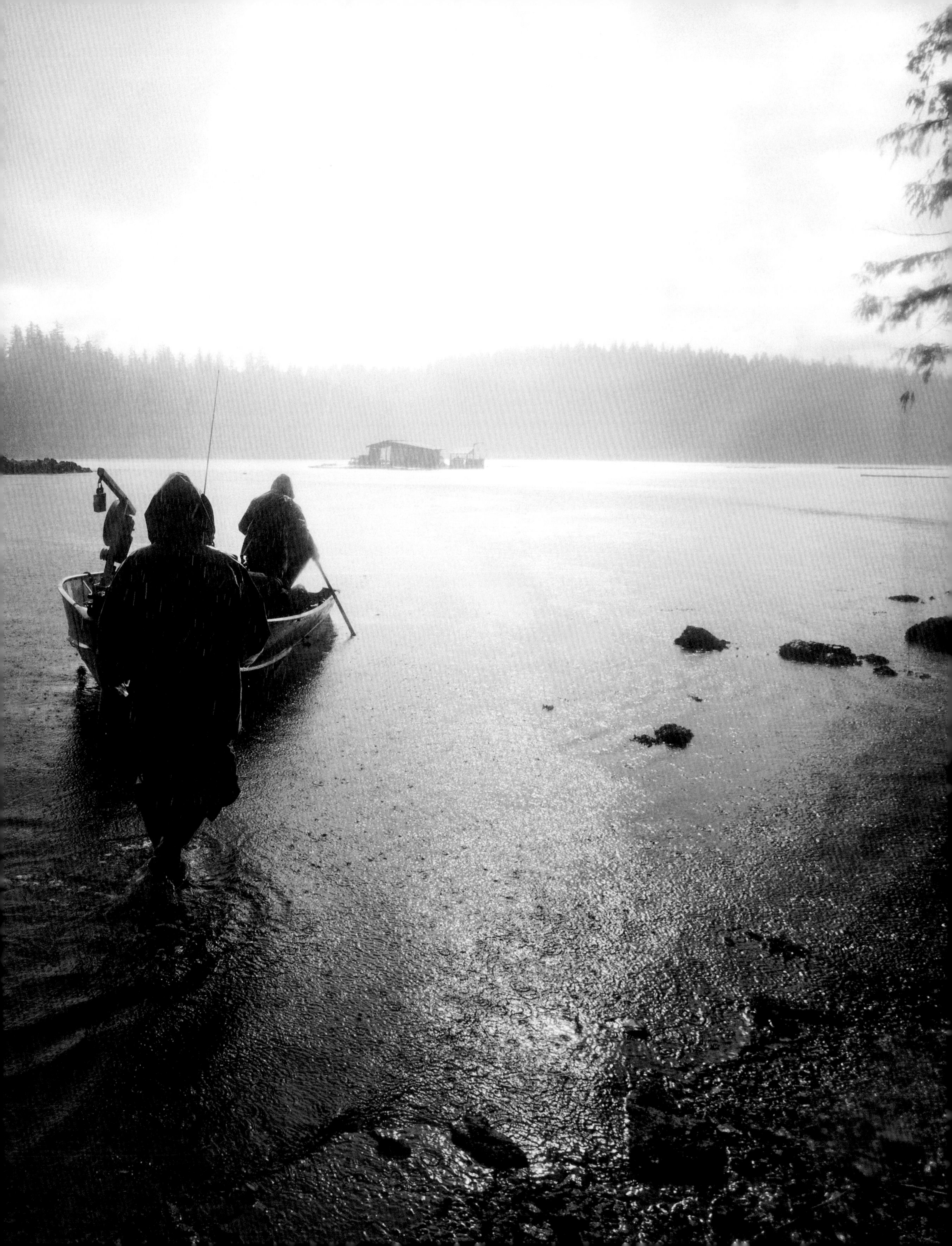

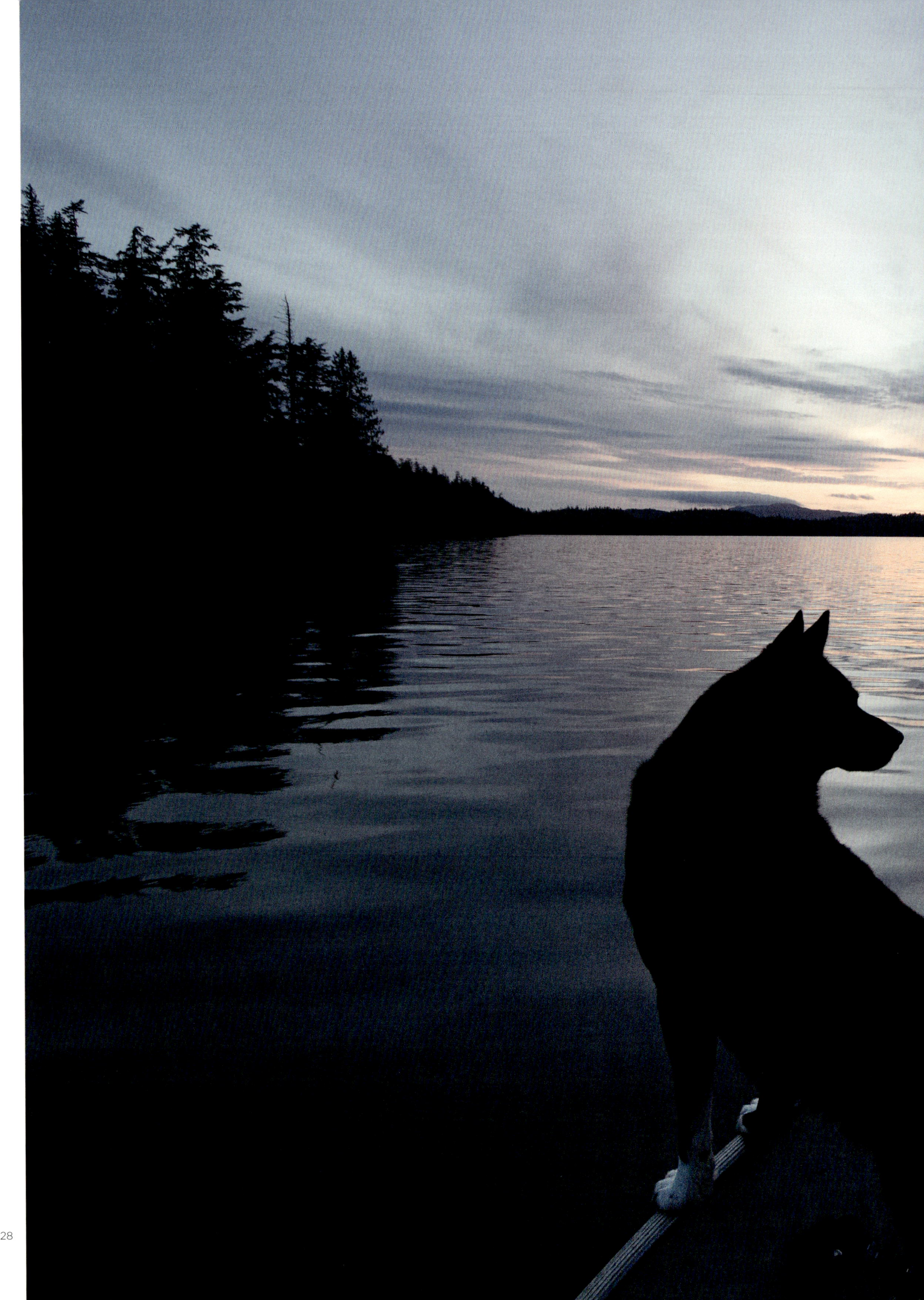

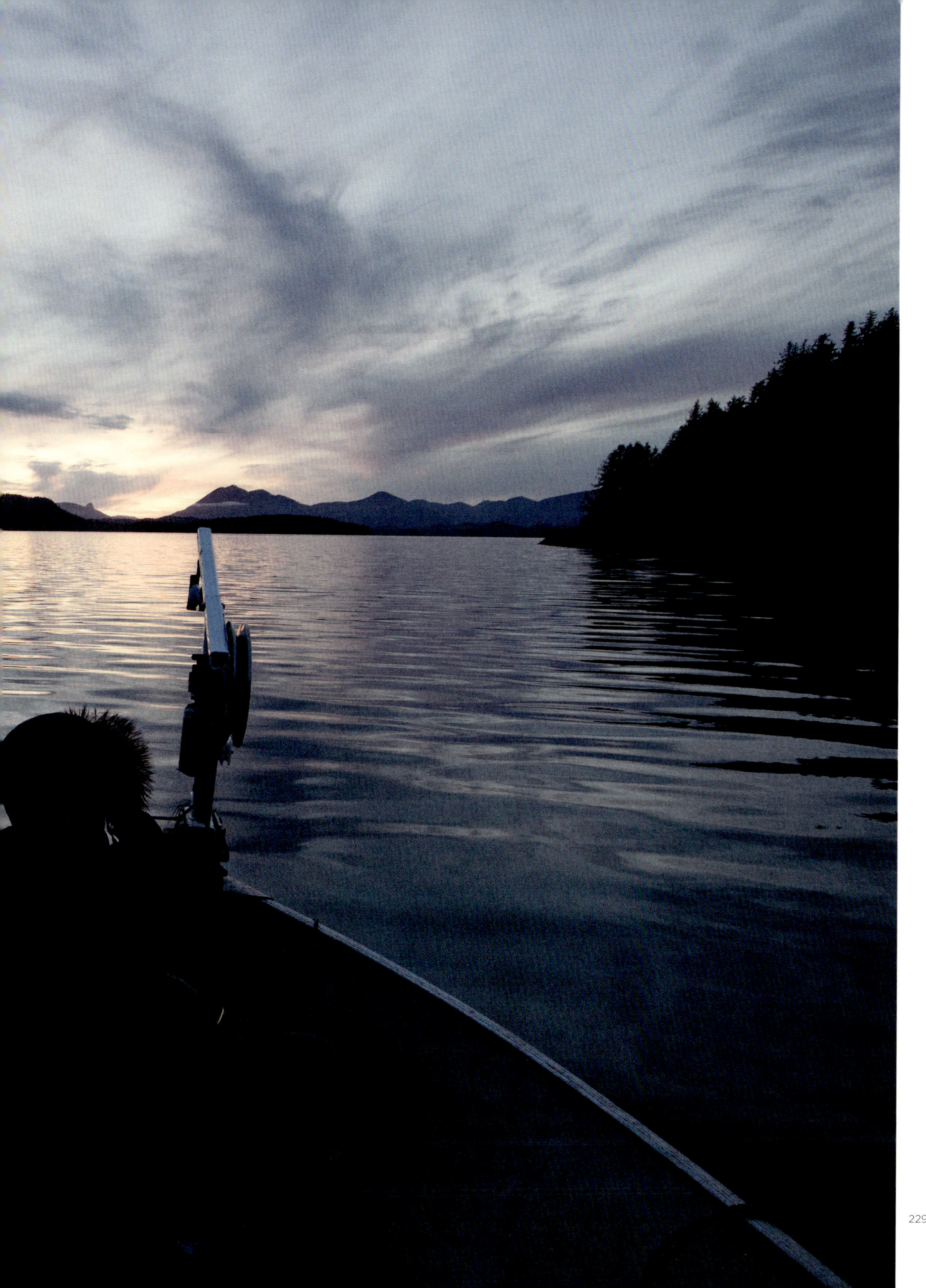

ELENA

„DIE NATUR GIBT MIR
UNGEHEUER VIEL; ICH
FÜHLE MICH STÄRKER,
WENN SIE SO NAHE IST."

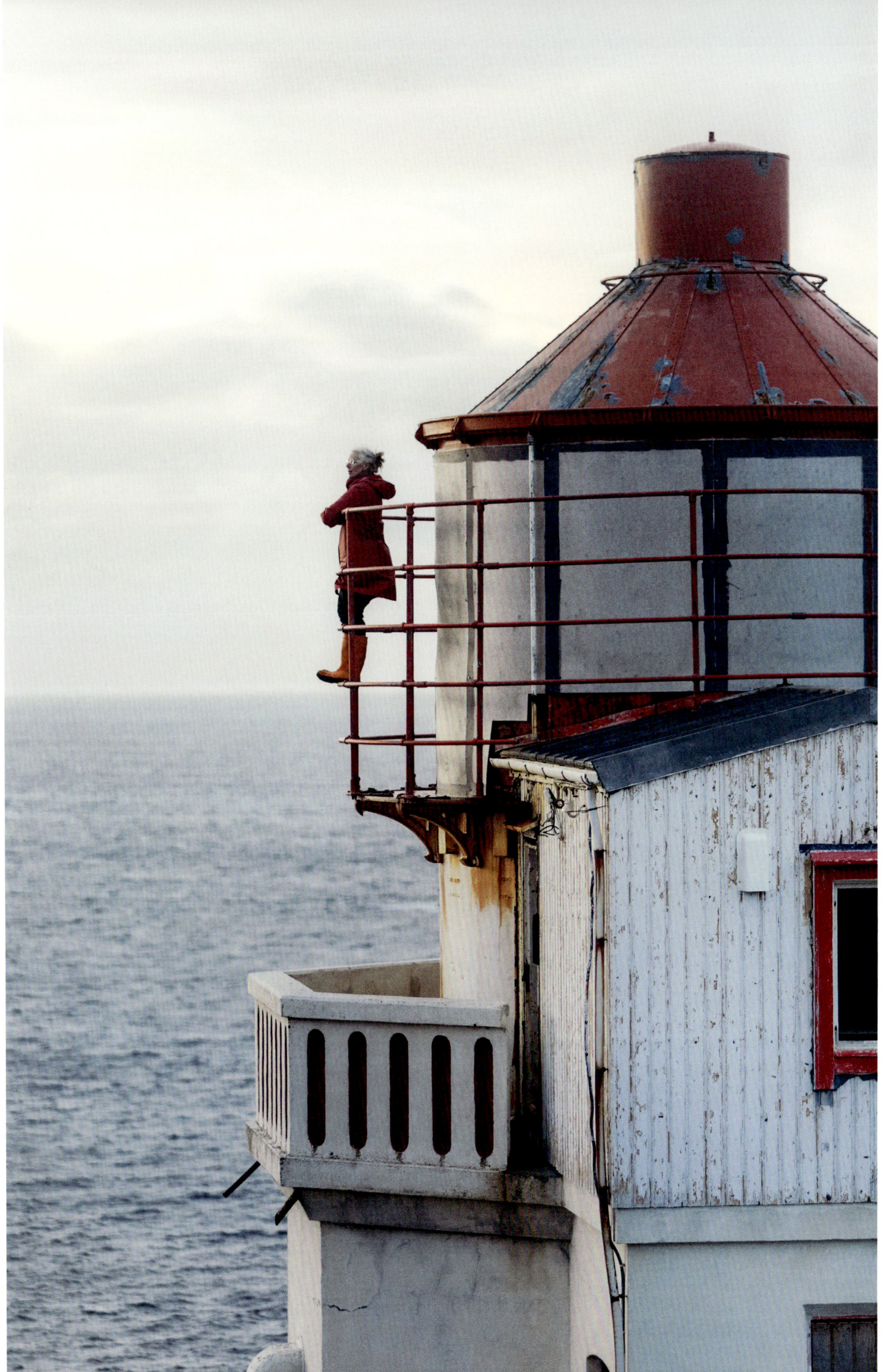

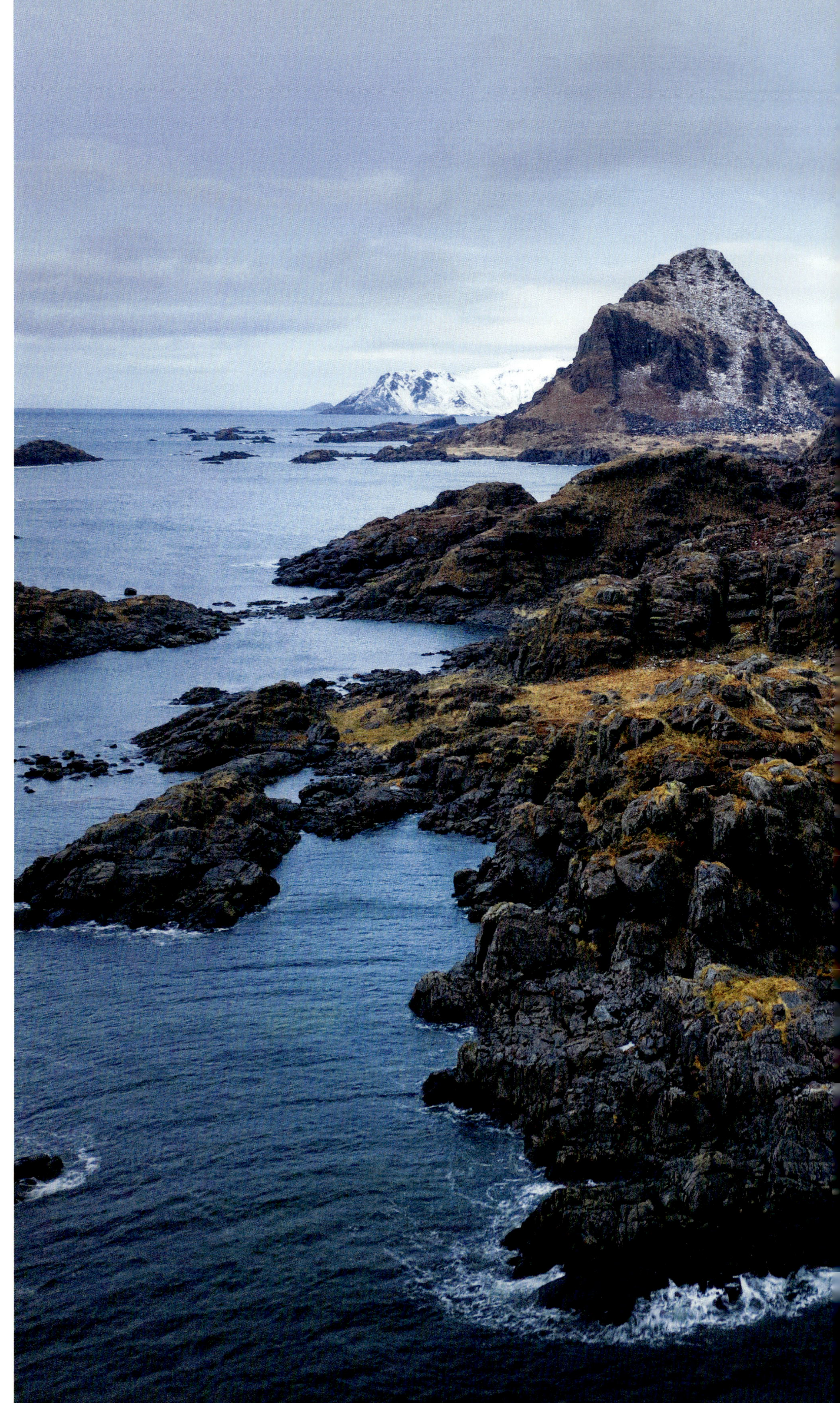

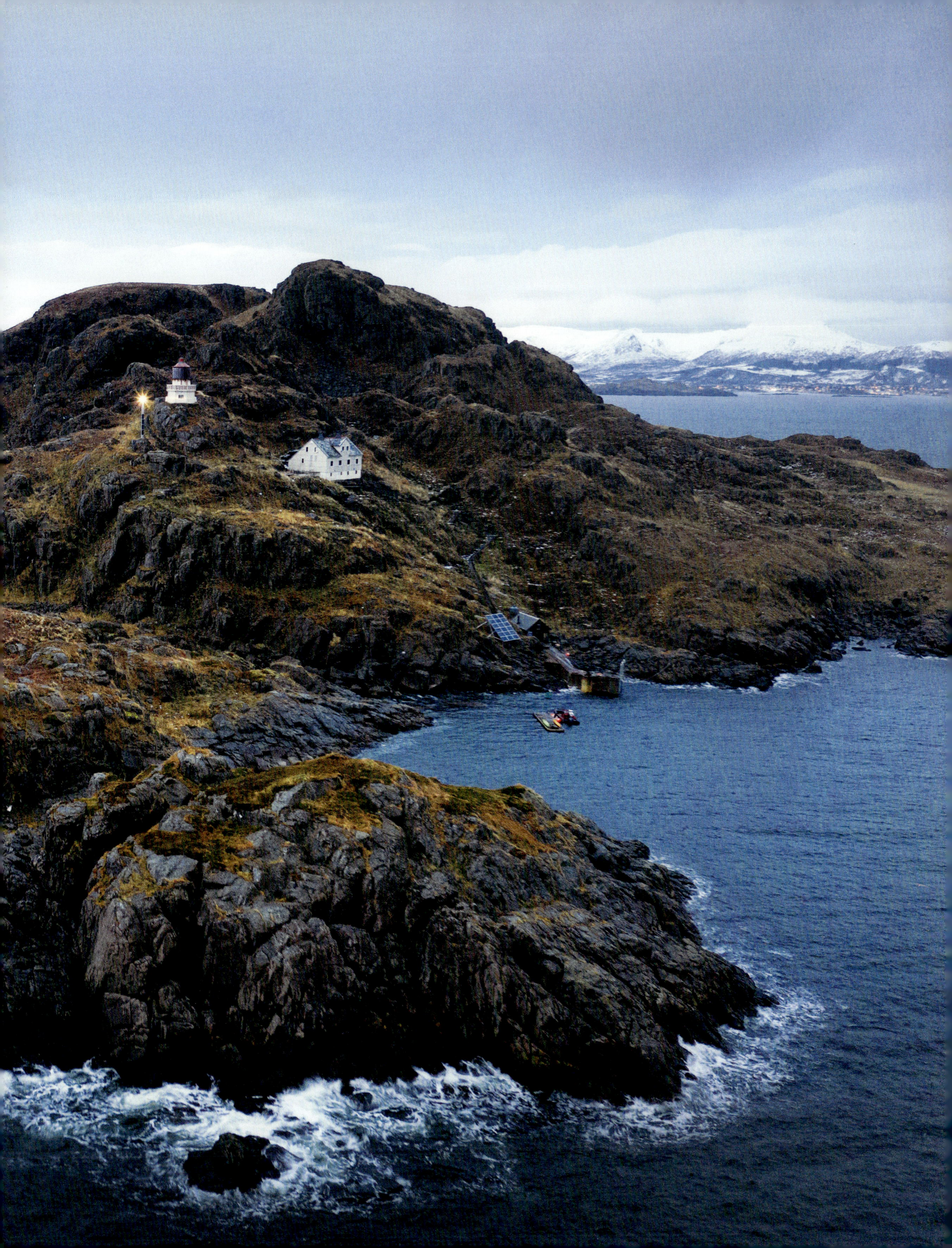

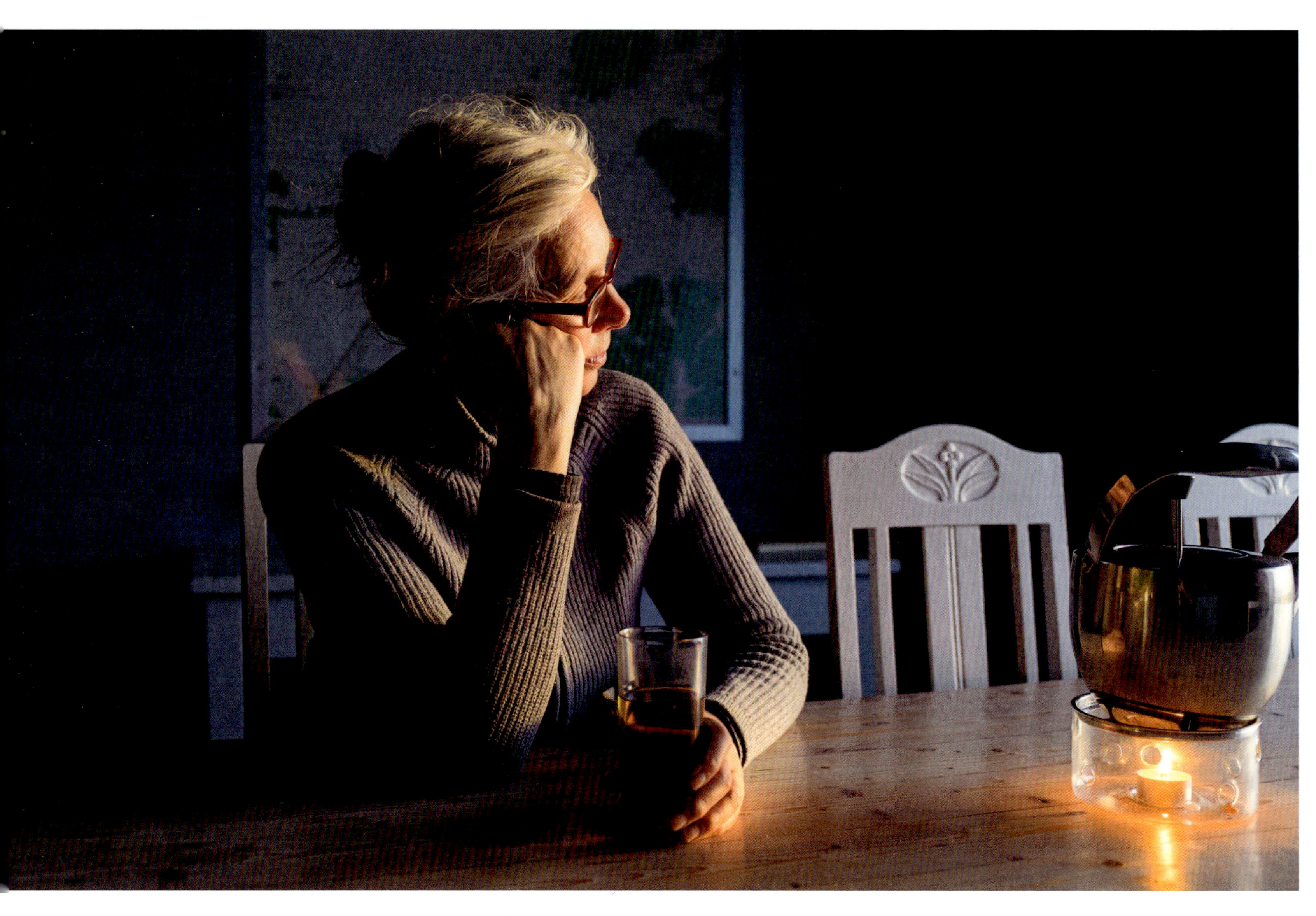

THE LIGHTHOUSE KEEPER

BØ I VESTERÅLEN, NORWAY

After a hectic life working in journalism, Elena left her career
and turned her dream into a reality, moving into a lighthouse on a small island
in the north of Norway, where she is the sole inhabitant.

Lighthouses feature in their fair share of legends and occupy a special place in the collective imagination. This is what inspired Elena in 2007 to leave the city lifestyle she had grown so tired of behind and give in to her longing to be close to the water. "I have always wanted to live as close to the sea as possible, but I never dared to follow this dream. I used to think that was a life reserved for the wealthy. But as the years went by, this idea always stuck in the back of my mind."

Elena grew up in Norway, and her father's job as a chef meant that the family moved a lot between different hotels and restaurants. As an adult, she continued to travel and lived in Oslo for many years, as well as in Paris, Jerusalem and Toronto.

"Back then, I was working as a Middle East correspondent. At a difficult time in my life, I decided to relocate to the far north. I ended up in the small village of Bø where I picked up a teaching job, and later a librarian job. Then one day I heard about a lighthouse that was up for sale."

And so Elena fulfilled her dream, snapping up this lighthouse at the very edge of the world with the intention of making it accessible to the public. The lighthouse is located in Litløya, pronounced Litleuya – literally "little island" in Norwegian. Eagles and cormorants inhabit the island's 67 hectares, which lies several nautical miles away from the Lofoten islands.

Built in 1912, the lighthouse was once one of the most powerful in Norway, its light dimmed somewhat by the installation of a solar-powered LED one at the start of the 21st century. Now it is less romantic, but more self-reliant as a result. Since then, there has been no need for two lighthouse keepers – who used to live along with their families in the large house reserved for them – and now it's Elena, with her cheerful, resolute outlook, who lives here. To reach the lighthouse, there are three hundred concrete steps to climb leading up from the boathouse. This small wooden cabin has been converted into accommodation, which is sometimes occupied by volunteers who have come to the island to lend a helping hand.

Litløya was full of life right up to the 1950s, counting up to 850 inhabitants at one point, and it even had its own prison cell. But the arrival of motorboats marked an end to the thriving island life and the fishers returned to Bø to be closer to the rest of the mainland. The village was completely dismantled and taken back to dry land, leaving only a few foundations still visible today. Little by little, the village's human population dwindled and eventually disappeared altogether – that is until Elena decided to breathe new life into this tiny island that is so small, it takes just an hour to walk around its perimeter.

It may be small, but the island of Litløya attracts many curious, adventurous visitors, who Elena ferries across the waters in her inflatable boat or who decide to brave the large Atlantic swell on their kayaks to make their own way to the island. These visitors come to the lighthouse, with its three bedrooms and infinite views of the horizon, to escape reality for a few nights, to bask in the glorious silence and breath in the clean Atlantic breeze, fresh and invigorating.

From the top of the lighthouse, the views of the ocean and Lofoten archipelago are spectacular. The island is completely cut off from the mainland – so much so that one visitor, so overwhelmed with a feeling of isolation, had to return to the rest of civilisation as a matter of urgency. The island is the ideal place for contemplation and reflection and Elena has found the perfect balance between spending time socialising and taking time for herself. "Nature is all around. I feel privileged to live here."

Her friends and family, however, could not believe her new way of life, where rain is collected for water, a wood-fired stove is used for heating and, with no trees on the island, wood has to be fetched from the mainland – where it is chopped and loaded into a boat before travelling across the sea to be carried up the three hundred steps to the lighthouse. "My mother always thought that I was a city person. She found it strange that I would want to live this life. But my decision to move here, at a time when I was worn out and lacking in energy, was the obvious choice, almost instinctive."

By the warmth of the wood-fired stove, Elena can sometimes spot pods of orcas or humpback whales heading up north to hunt shoals of herrings, or even eagles skimming past the towering lighthouse when the wind picks up. "Nature brings so much to my life. I feel stronger when I'm immersed in it. Looking around at the mountains, the sea and the sky, I feel a great sense of freedom."

It is a freedom that comes with some catches, however. Even in the 21st century, lighthouse keepers have their work cut out for them. "There is so much to do!" Besides welcoming visitors, Elena grows potatoes and even strawberries, gathers wild herbs for herbal tea, collects seaweed, does a bit of fishing and writes, but upkeep of the island takes up most of her time. The boat lift, for example, has to be repaired regularly so that she can keep her inflatable boat out of harm's way, sheltered from the frequent gales. She likes her life out here but has no intention of returning to the Stone Age. Elena wants to live in her own era, which is why she has a Wi-Fi connection and a small letterbox ashore where she regularly goes to pick up her post.

Isolated but not alone, Elena lives 5 kilometres from the Vesterålen islands and 25 kilometres from the Lofoten islands. "In the evening, when the lights arching off the mainland come on, I can feel my neighbours' presence. When you turn your back to the sea, you are at the edge of the world. But when you're facing it, it's like an open door to the rest of the world."

On this tiny island, Elena feels connected to the world. "The light changes all the time, like a kaleidoscope. And during winter, the northern lights keep me company. They truly take over the sky." She has no regrets about leaving city life. "When I was younger, I liked the rhythm of urban life but gradually it became too much for me and I couldn't handle it anymore. I enjoy going back every now and then but only for short periods of time."

Wild weather has now taken the place of pulsing city life, but the untamed elements do not frighten her. On the contrary, they have taught her self-control and patience. "Whenever there is a storm I wait for it to pass before venturing outside, unless I absolutely have to. I have fallen into the water a few times, but I am a good swimmer. I learnt to navigate my way around the island by boat as well as by kayak to get to know my limits and find out how bad the conditions can be for me to still go out and not be risking my life too much."

Elena also has her mind on the future. She is thinking of organising yoga retreats, transforming the lighthouse tower into an artists' residence, and finding a business partner to help develop her business further. "This place is perfect for me. I can soak everything in here. I don't necessarily have a slower pace of life because there is always lots of work to be done, but it's a different type of work, more physical."

"As someone who has moved around their whole life, I am really happy to have found this lighthouse. I feel truly at home here, like I've finally started putting down roots. I hope to spend the rest of my life here." Elena has found her place in life here in the lighthouse, now her very own guiding light at the edge of the world.

DIE LEUCHTTURMWÄRTERIN

BØ I VESTERÅLEN, NORWEGEN

Nach einem hektischen Leben beendet Elena ihre Karriere als Journalistin
und verwirklicht ihren Traum. Sie zieht in einen Leuchtturm im Norden Norwegens,
als einzige Bewohnerin einer kleinen Insel.

Um Leuchttürme ranken sich viele Legenden; sie spielen in unserer kollektiven Phantasie eine besondere Rolle. Aus genau diesem Grund beschloss Elena im Jahr 2007, des Stadtlebens müde und immer schon vom Meer angezogen, sich hier niederzulassen. „Ich wollte immer so nah wie möglich am Meer leben, wagte aber nicht, diesen Traum zu verwirklichen, weil ich dachte, ein solches Leben sei nur wohlhabenden Menschen möglich. Trotzdem behielt ich die Idee lange im Hinterkopf."

Elena wächst in Norwegen mit vielen beruflichen Umzügen ihres Vaters, eines Chefkochs, auf. Als Erwachsene reist sie weiterhin und lebt viele Jahre lang in Oslo, aber auch in Paris, Jerusalem und Toronto.

„Ich arbeitete als Journalistin und war auf den Nahen Osten spezialisiert. In einer schwierigen Lebensphase beschloss ich, in den hohen Norden zu ziehen. Ich ließ mich in dem kleinen Dorf Bø nieder, wo ich erst als Lehrerin, dann als Bibliothekarin arbeitete. Dort hörte ich eines Tages von einem Leuchtturm, der zu verkaufen sei …"

So verwirklicht Elena ihren Traum: Sie kauft den Leuchtturm am Ende der Welt, unter der Bedingung, ihn für Besucher zugänglich zu machen. Litløya, was sich „Litlöja" ausspricht und auf Norwegisch „kleine Insel" bedeutet, besteht aus 67 Hektar von Adlern und Kormoranen bewohnten Felsen, ein paar Seemeilen von den Lofoten-Inseln entfernt.

Der 1912 erbaute Leuchtturm gehört eine Zeitlang zu den leistungsstärksten in Norwegen, aber zu Beginn des 21. Jahrhundert wird die Lampe durch solarbetriebene LEDs ersetzt – weniger romantisch, aber unabhängiger. Seitdem wird der Leuchtturm nicht mehr von zwei Wärtern betreut, die mit ihren Familien in dem großen für sie vorgesehen Haus wohnen, sondern Elena,

eine robuste und fröhliche Frau um die fünfzig, lebt darin. Um hinaufzugelangen, muss man dreihundert Betonstufen erklimmen; sie beginnen am Bootshaus, einer kleinen Holzhütte, die zum Wohnraum umgebaut wurde und manchmal Freiwillige beherbergt, die auf der Insel helfen.

Bis in die 1950er-Jahre gab es auf Litløya reichlich Leben, mit bis zu 850 Einwohnern und sogar einer eigenen Gefängniszelle. Aber die Einführung von Motorbooten führt dazu, dass sich das Inselleben und die Fischerei nach Bø verlagern, näher am Rest des Kontinents. Daraufhin wird das Dorf komplett abgebaut und aufs Festland gebracht; heute sind nur noch ein paar Grundmauern zu sehen. Nach und nach verschwindet jede menschliche Präsenz … Bis Elena beschließt, diesen Felsen, der sich in einer Stunde umrunden lässt, zu neuem Leben zu erwecken.

Obwohl Litløya so klein ist, weckt es die Neugierde abenteuerlustiger Besucher, die Elena mit dem Schlauchboot abholt – falls es sich nicht um Kajakfahrer handelt, die der langen Dünung des Atlantiks trotzen und direkt auf der Insel landen. Der Leuchtturm heißt sie für einige Nächte fernab der Welt willkommen, mit drei Schlafzimmern und einem unendlich weiten Blick bis zum Horizont.

Hier ist Schweigen Gold, und die frische, belebende Meeresluft des Atlantiks reinigt die Atmosphäre. Von der Spitze des Leuchtturms aus hat man einen spektakulären Blick auf das Meer und die Inselgruppe der Lofoten. Die Abgeschiedenheit vom Kontinent ist so vollkommen, dass, wie Elena mir verrät, einmal ein Besucher unverzüglich aufs Festland zurückgebracht werden musste, weil ihn das Gefühl der Isolation vollkommen überwältigte. Die Insel eignet sich gut zur Kontemplation, und Elena hat für sich das perfekte Gleichgewicht zwischen einem erfreulichen Sozialleben und selbst gewählten Momenten der Einsamkeit gefunden. „Die Natur ist so nah, dass ich es als Privileg empfinde, hier zu leben."

Dennoch glaubte in ihrem Umfeld niemand an ihre neue Existenz, bei der das Wasser dem Regen entstammt, ein Holzofen zum Heizen dient und man mangels Bäumen mit dem Boot zum Festland fahren, dort Holz schlagen und es verladen muss, um es dann 300 Stufen zum Leuchtturm hinaufzutragen. „Meine Mutter dachte immer, ich wäre ein Stadtmensch und fand es seltsam, dass ich dieses Leben führen möchte. Aber die Entscheidung, in einer Phase hierher zu ziehen, in der es mir an Energie mangelte, traf ich ganz natürlich, fast instinktiv."

Von ihrem Platz am warmen Holzofen aus beobachtet Elena manchmal Gruppen von Orcas oder Buckelwalen, die nach Norden ziehen, um Heringsbänke zu jagen; manchmal sind es auch Adler, die um das große Gebäude streichen, wenn der Wind auffrischt. „Die Natur gibt mir ungeheuer viel; ich fühle mich stärker, wenn sie so nahe ist. Wenn ich die Berge betrachte, das Meer, den Himmel … Dann empfinde ich ein Gefühl großer Freiheit."

Eine Freiheit, die aber auch Zwänge auferlegt: Selbst im 21. Jahrhundert ist das Alltagsleben einer Leuchtturmwärterin keine reine Erholung. „Es sind so viele Dinge zu tun!" Elena beherbergt nicht nur Gäste, sie baut auch Kartoffeln und sogar Erdbeeren an, pflückt Wildpflanzen für Tee, sammelt Algen, fischt ein wenig, schreibt, kümmert sich aber vor allem um Instandhaltungsarbeiten: Der Bootslift, mit dem sie ihr Schlauchboot außer Reichweite der häufigen Sturmböen zieht, muss regelmäßig repariert werden. Aber obwohl sie das Leben im Freien liebt, geht es nicht um eine Rückkehr in die Steinzeit. Elena möchte mit der Zeit gehen. Sie hat etwas WLAN-Empfang und einen kleinen Briefkasten auf dem Festland, wo sie regelmäßig ihre Post abholt.

Abgeschieden, aber nicht einsam. Elena lebt 5 Kilometer von den Vesterålen-Inseln und 25 Kilometer von den Lofoten ent-

fernt. „Sobald abends auf dem Festland die Lichter angehen, spüre ich die Nähe meiner Nachbarn. Wenn man dem Meer den Rücken zukehrt, steht man am Rande der Welt. Wendet man sich ihm aber zu, ist es wie eine Tür, die sich zur Welt hin öffnet."

Auf ihrer winzigen Insel fühlt Elena sich mit der Welt verbunden. „Das Licht wechselt ständig, wie ein Kaleidoskop. Und im Winter begleiten mich die Nordlichter, sie sind eine echte Präsenz am Himmel." Die Stadt vermisst sie nicht. „Als ich jünger war, gab sie mir viel positive Energie, aber allmählich wurde diese zu stark und ich konnte sie nicht mehr ertragen. Ich fahre immer noch gern hin und wieder hin, aber immer nur für kurze Zeit."

Inzwischen sind die Stürme des Stadtlebens durch entfesselte Elemente ersetzt worden, die ihr keine Angst machen. Im Gegenteil – sie haben Elena Selbstbeherrschung und Geduld gelehrt. „Wenn es einen Sturm gibt, warte ich, wenn irgend möglich, drinnen ab, bis er vorbei ist. Ich bin schon einmal ins Wasser gefallen, aber ich bin eine gute Schwimmerin. Hier habe ich Kajak- und Bootfahren gelernt; ich kenne meine Grenzen und weiß, welches die schlechtesten Wetterbedingungen sind, bei denen ich noch hinausfahren kann, ohne mein Leben allzu sehr aufs Spiel zu setzen …"

Für die Zukunft zeichnen sich Projekte ab. Elena träumt davon, Yoga-Aufenthalte anzubieten, den Leuchtturm zum Künstleratelier umzubauen und Geschäftspartner zu finden, um ihre Aktivitäten ein bisschen weiterzuentwickeln. „Dieser Ort ist perfekt für mich; ich kann hier das Leben verdauen, das ich früher geführt habe. Mein Leben ist nicht unbedingt ruhiger, weil ich viel Arbeit habe, aber die Arbeit ist anders, eher körperlich.

Ich bin mein Leben lang so viel unterwegs gewesen, dass ich sehr glücklich bin, diesen Leuchtturm gefunden zu haben. Hier fühle ich mich wirklich am richtigen Ort, ich spüre, dass ich anfange, Wurzeln zu schlagen. Ich hoffe, bis ans Ende meiner Tage hier leben zu können." Der Leuchtturm am Ende der Welt ist zum Mittelpunkt ihres Lebens geworden.

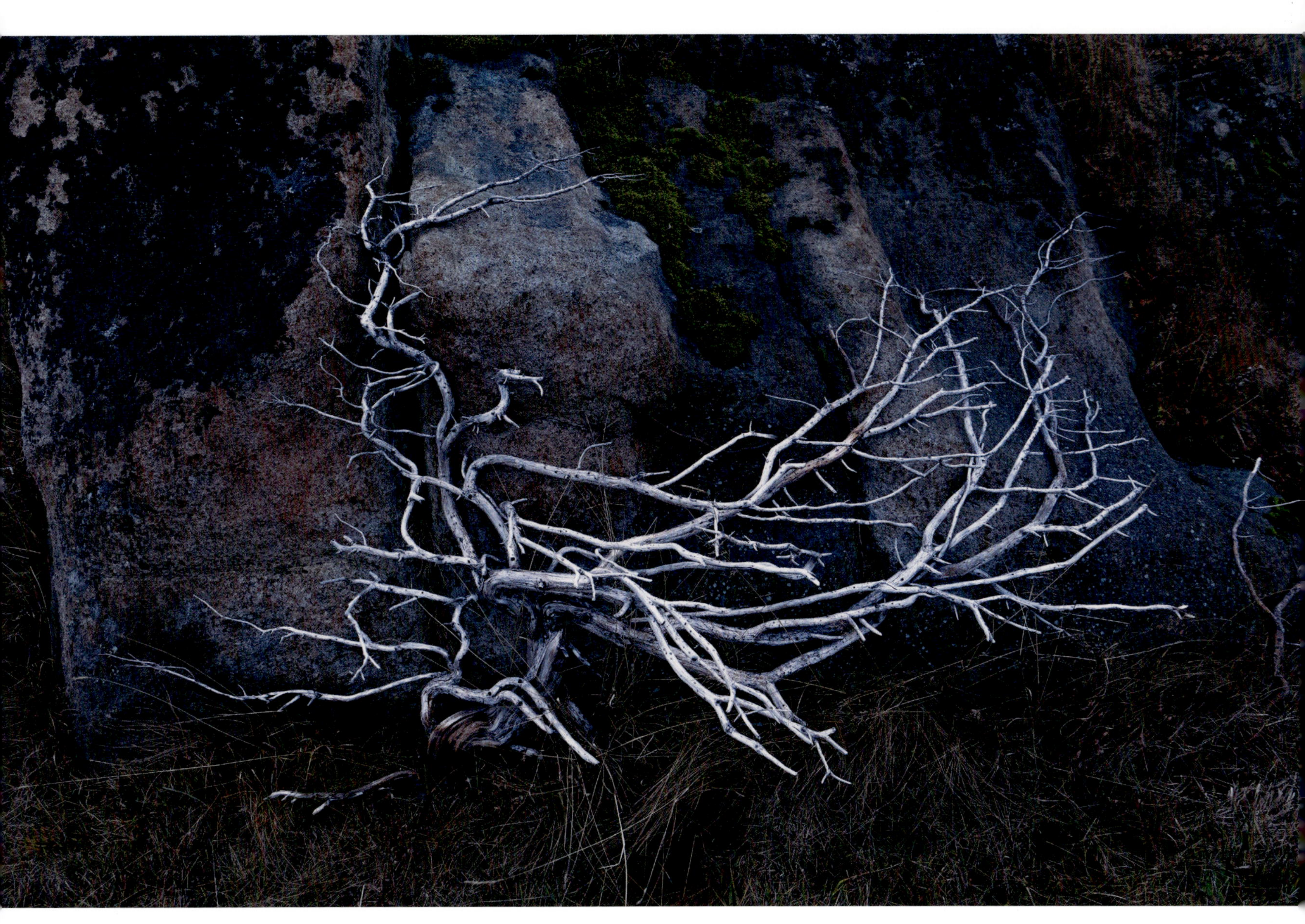

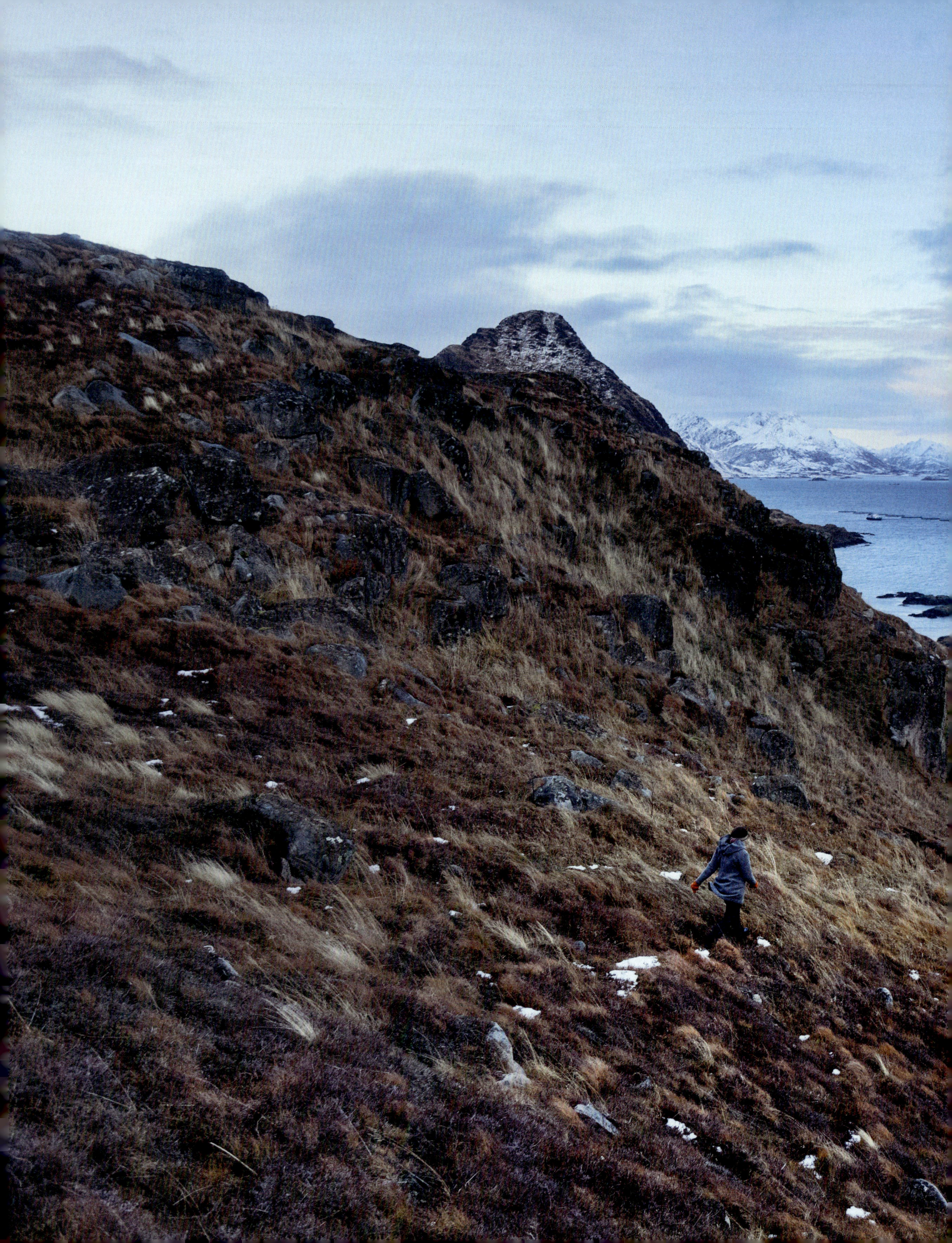

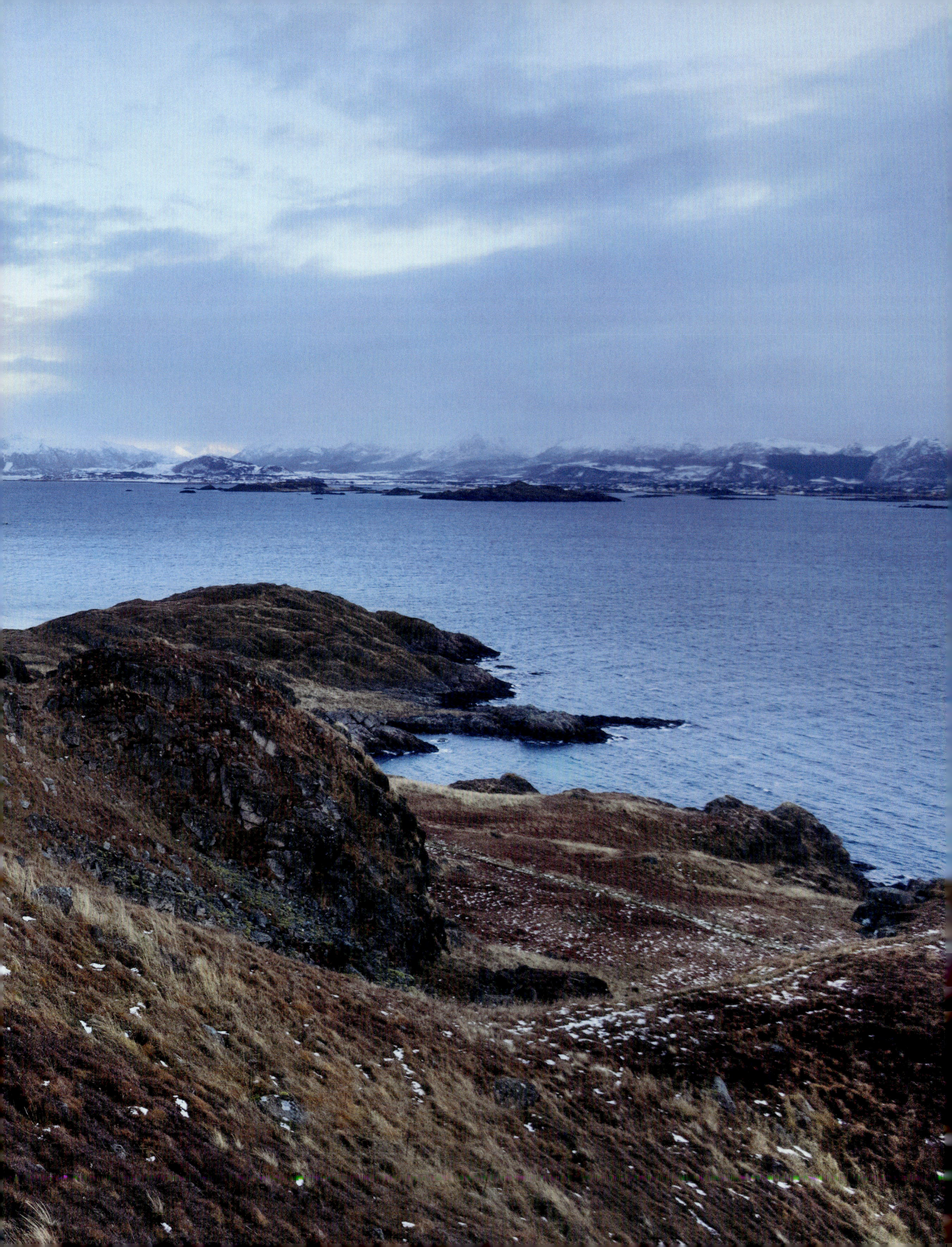

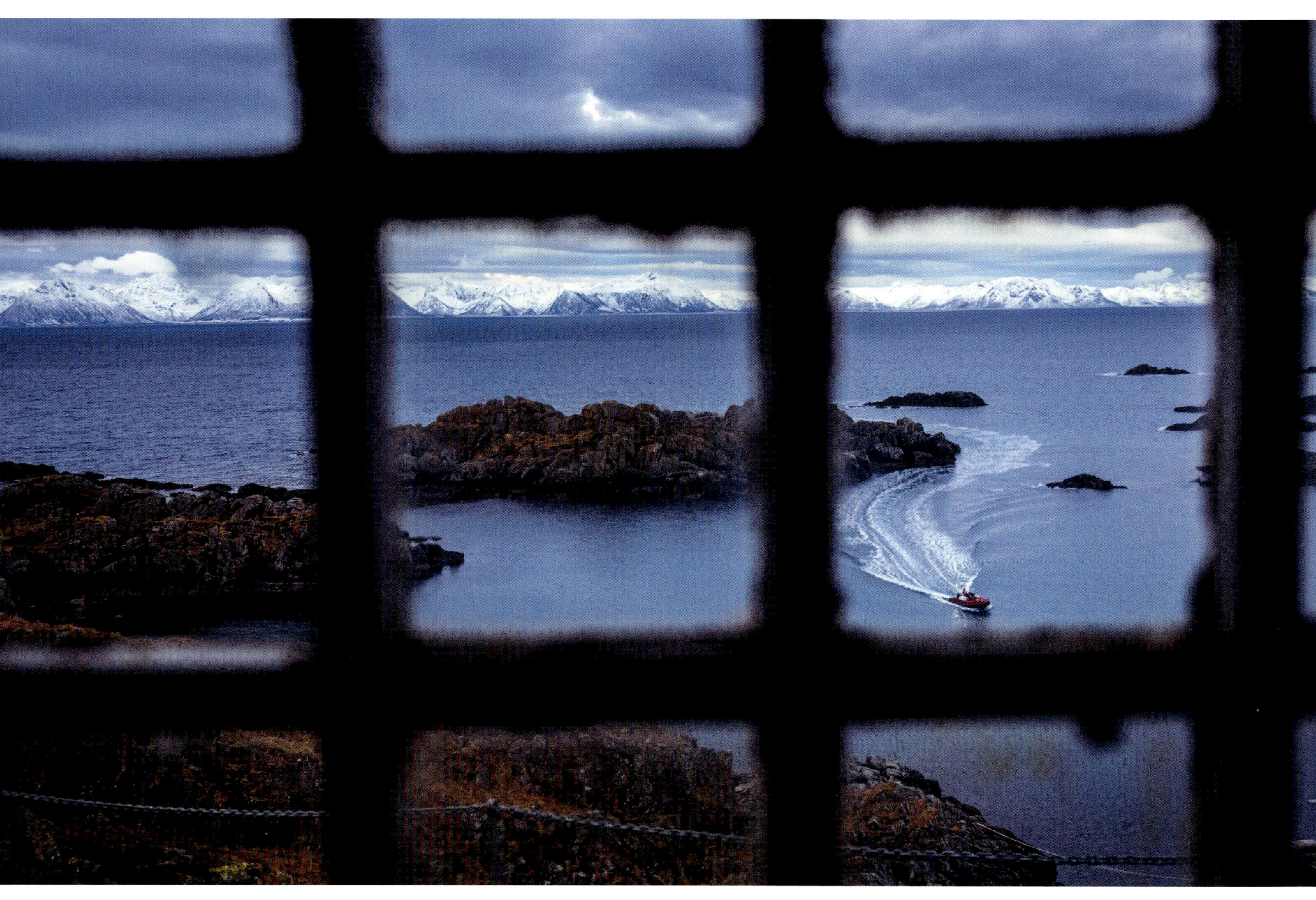

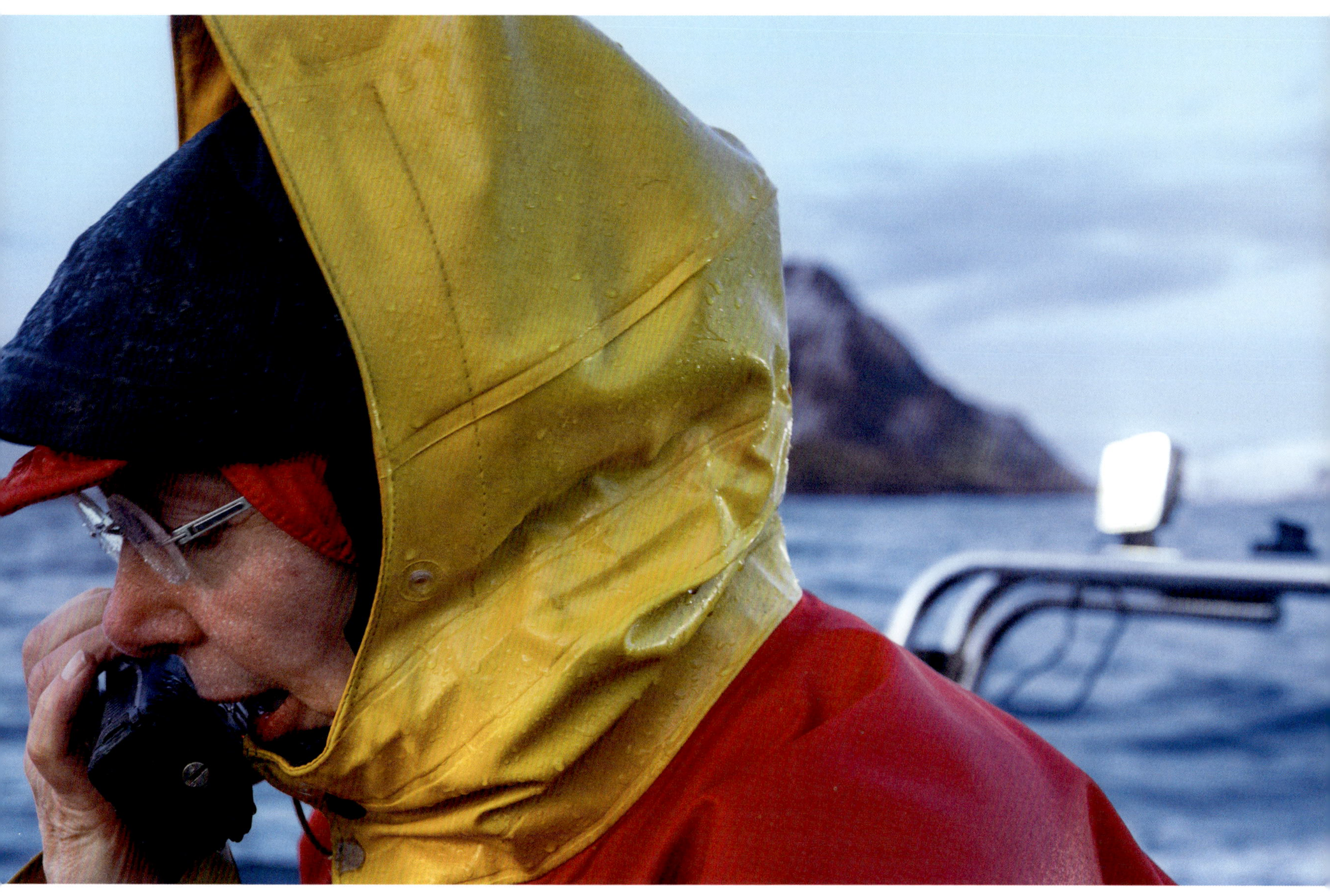

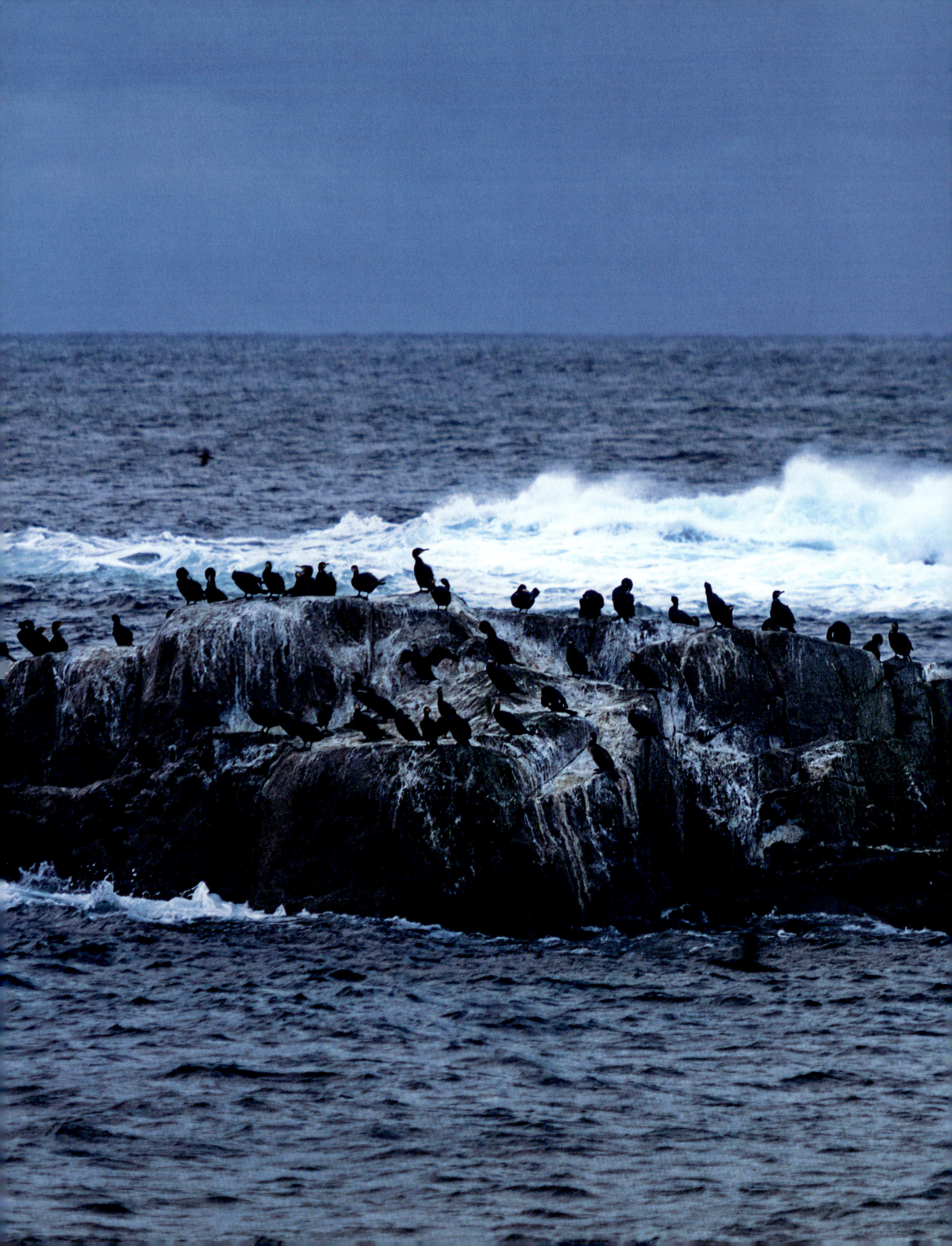

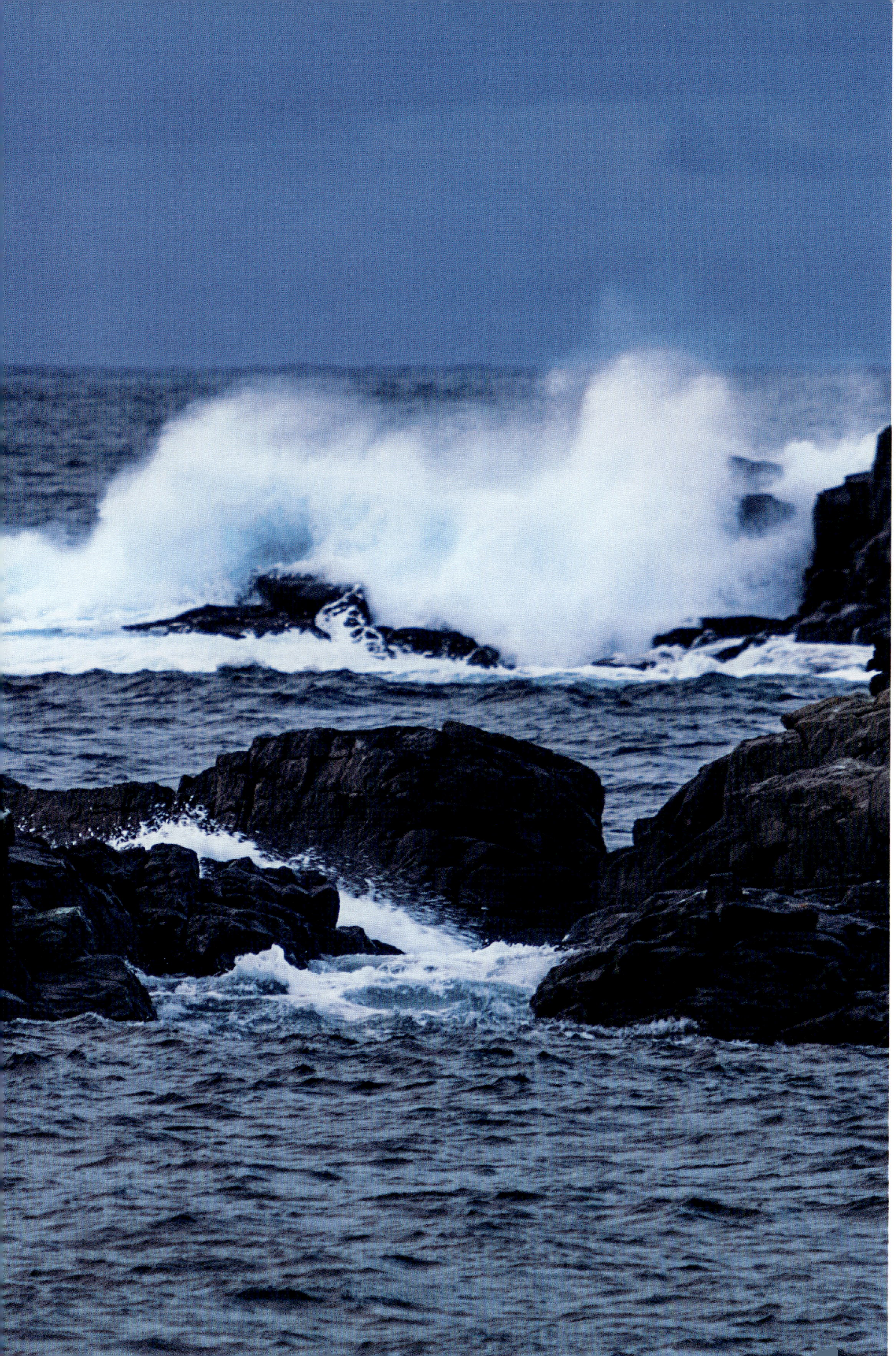

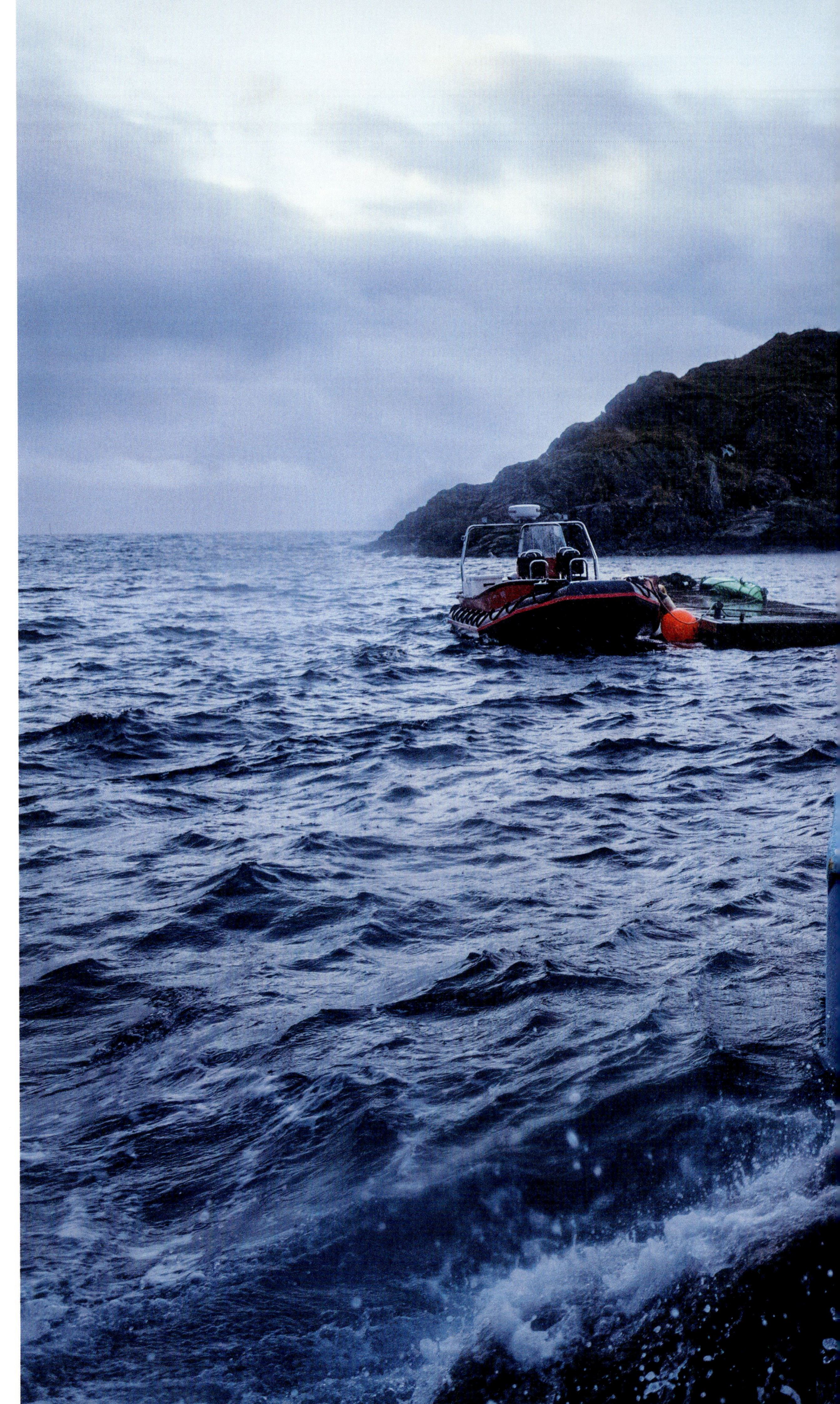

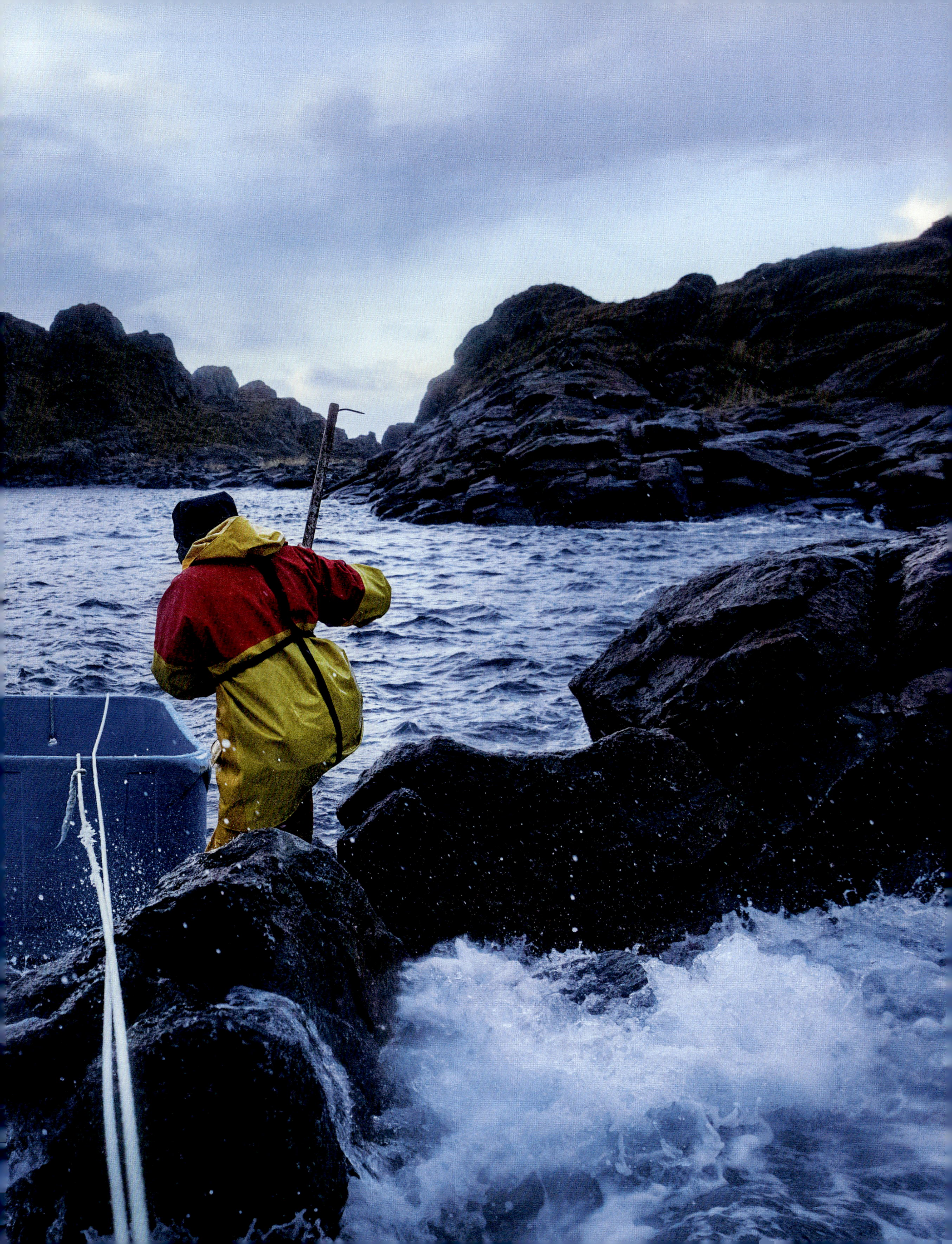

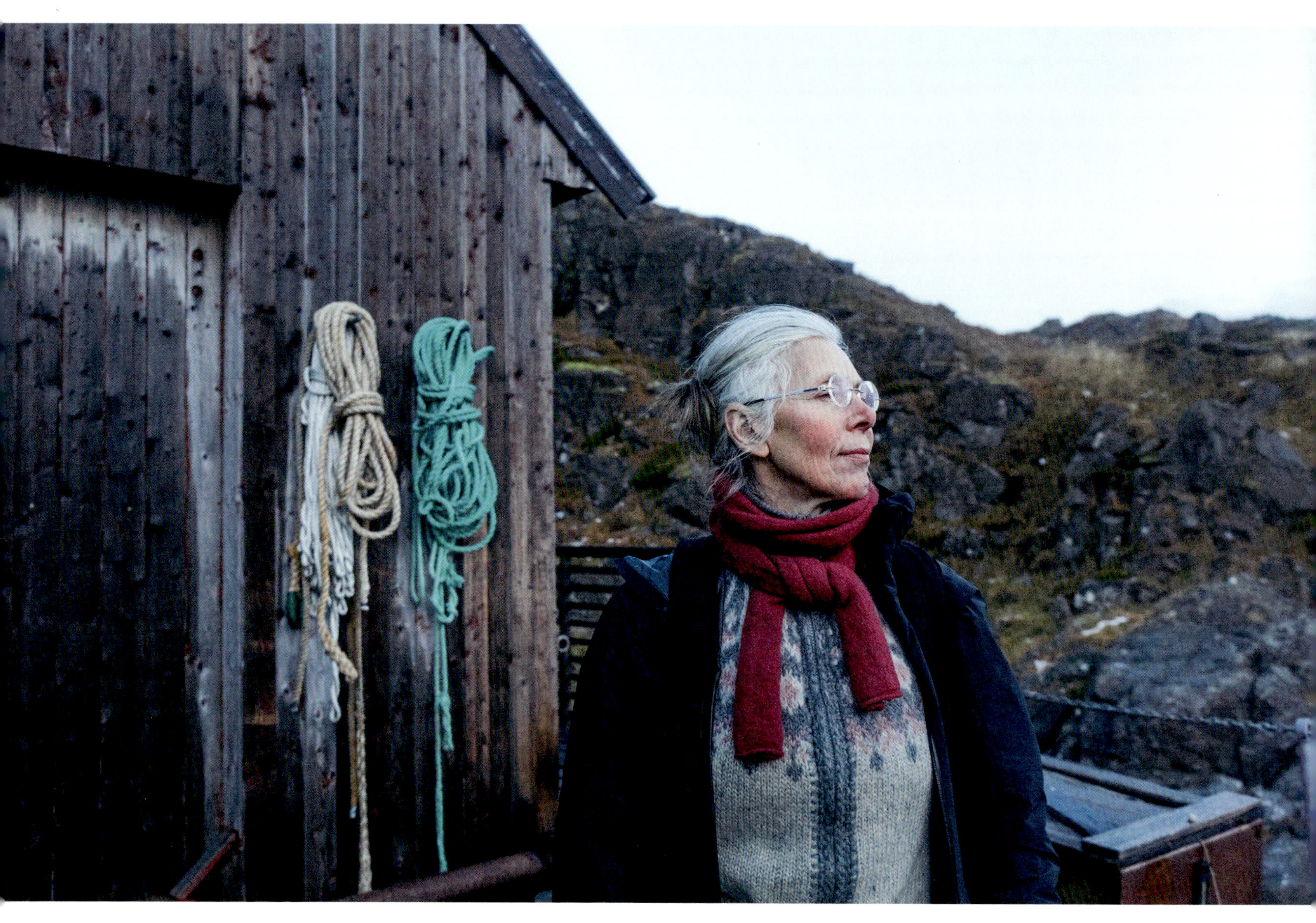

"If one advances confidently in the direction of his dreams, and endeavors to live the life which he has imagined, he will meet with a success unexpected in common hours. He will put some things behind, will pass an invisible boundary… If you have built castles in the air, your work need not be lost; that is where they should be. Now put the foundations under them."

HENRY DAVID THOREAU
Walden; or, Life in the Woods

„Wenn jemand zuversichtlich in Richtung seiner Träume vorwärtsschreitet und danach strebt, das Leben, das er sich vorstellte, zu leben, so wird er Erfolge haben, von denen er sich in gewöhnlichen Stunden nichts träumen ließ. Er wird mancherlei hinter sich lassen, wird eine unsichtbare Grenze überschreiten. […] Hast du Luftschlösser gebaut, so braucht deine Arbeit nicht verloren zu sein. Eben dort sollten sie sein. Jetzt lege das Fundament darunter!"

HENRY DAVID THOREAU
Walden oder Leben in den Wäldern

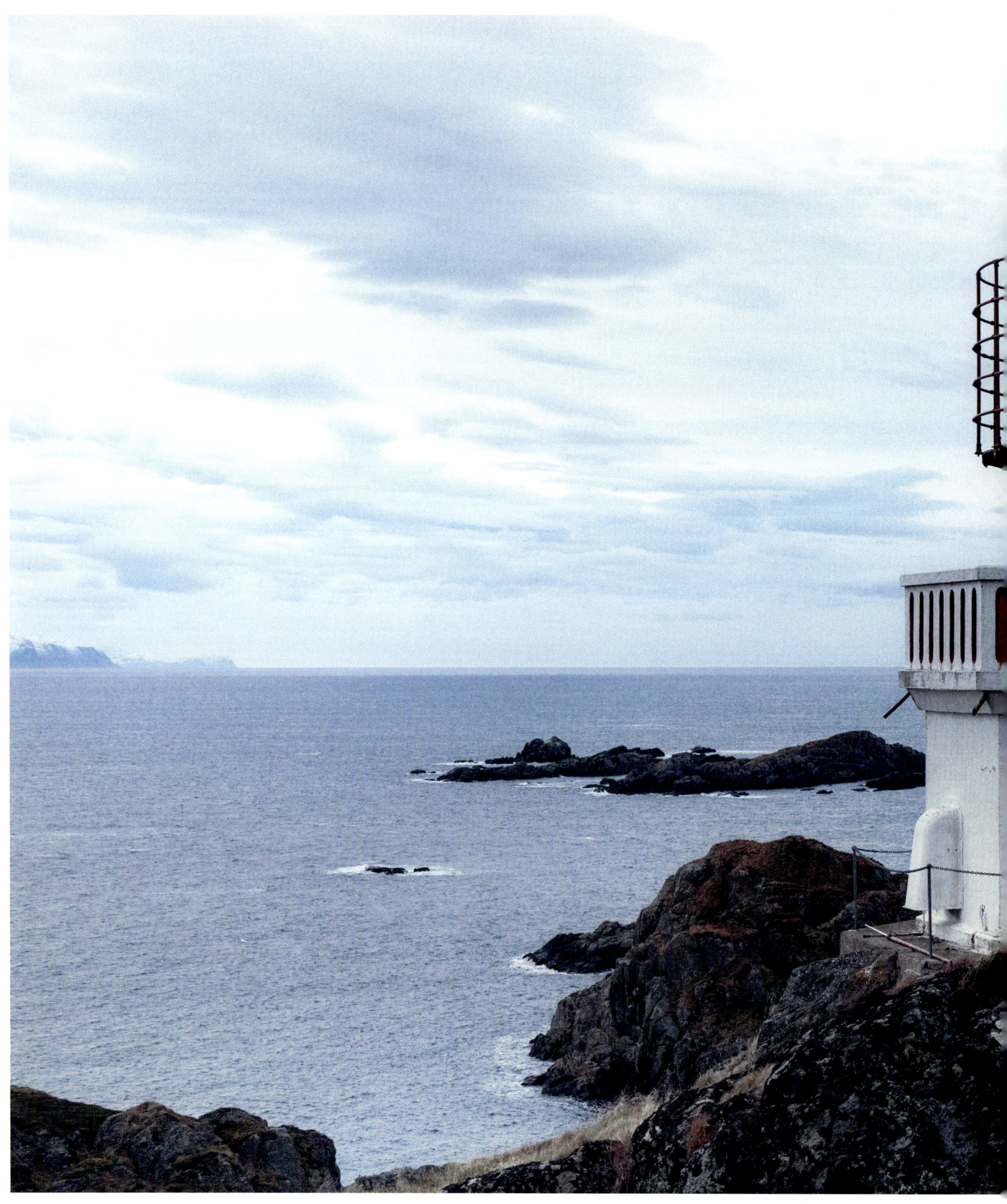

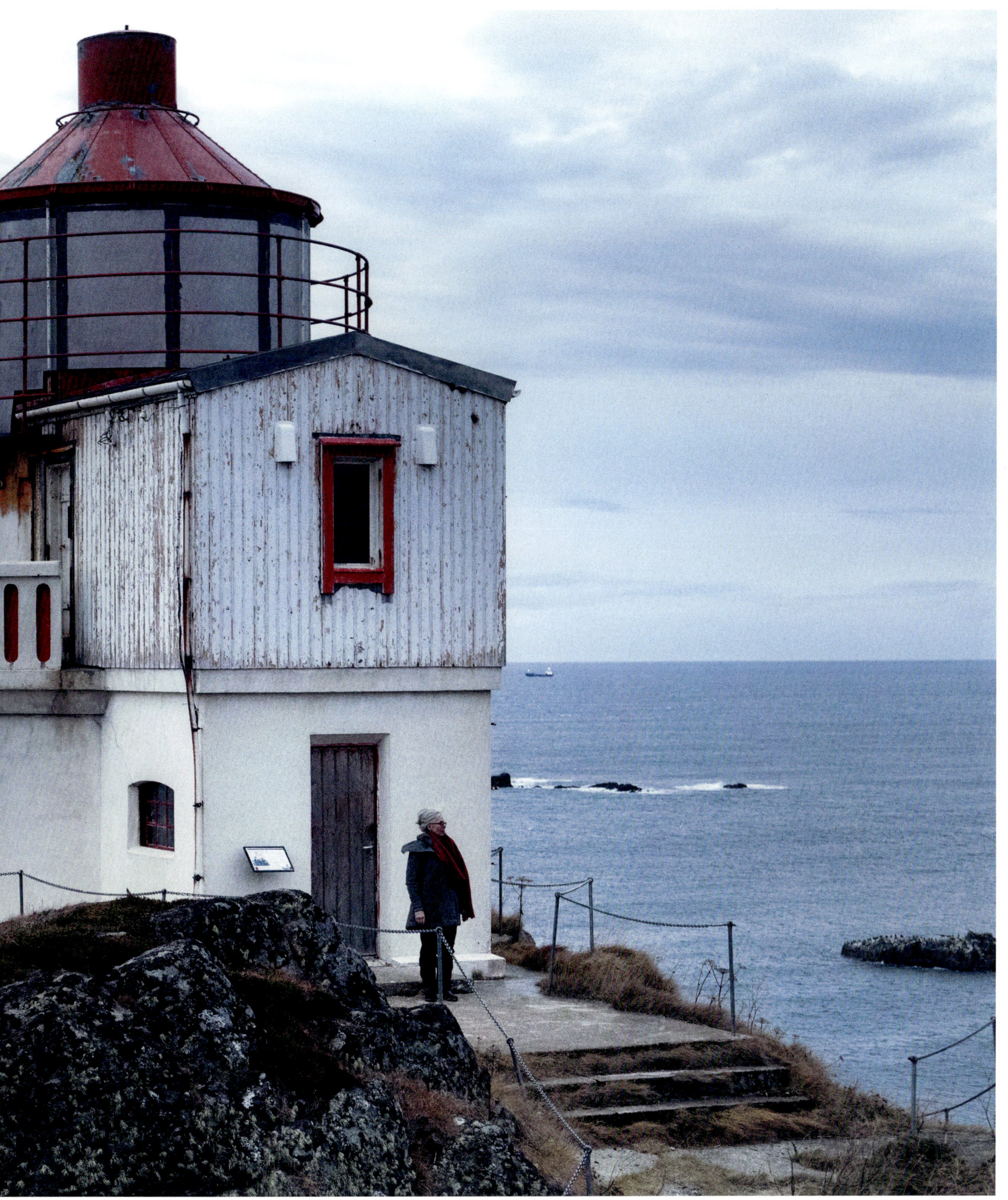

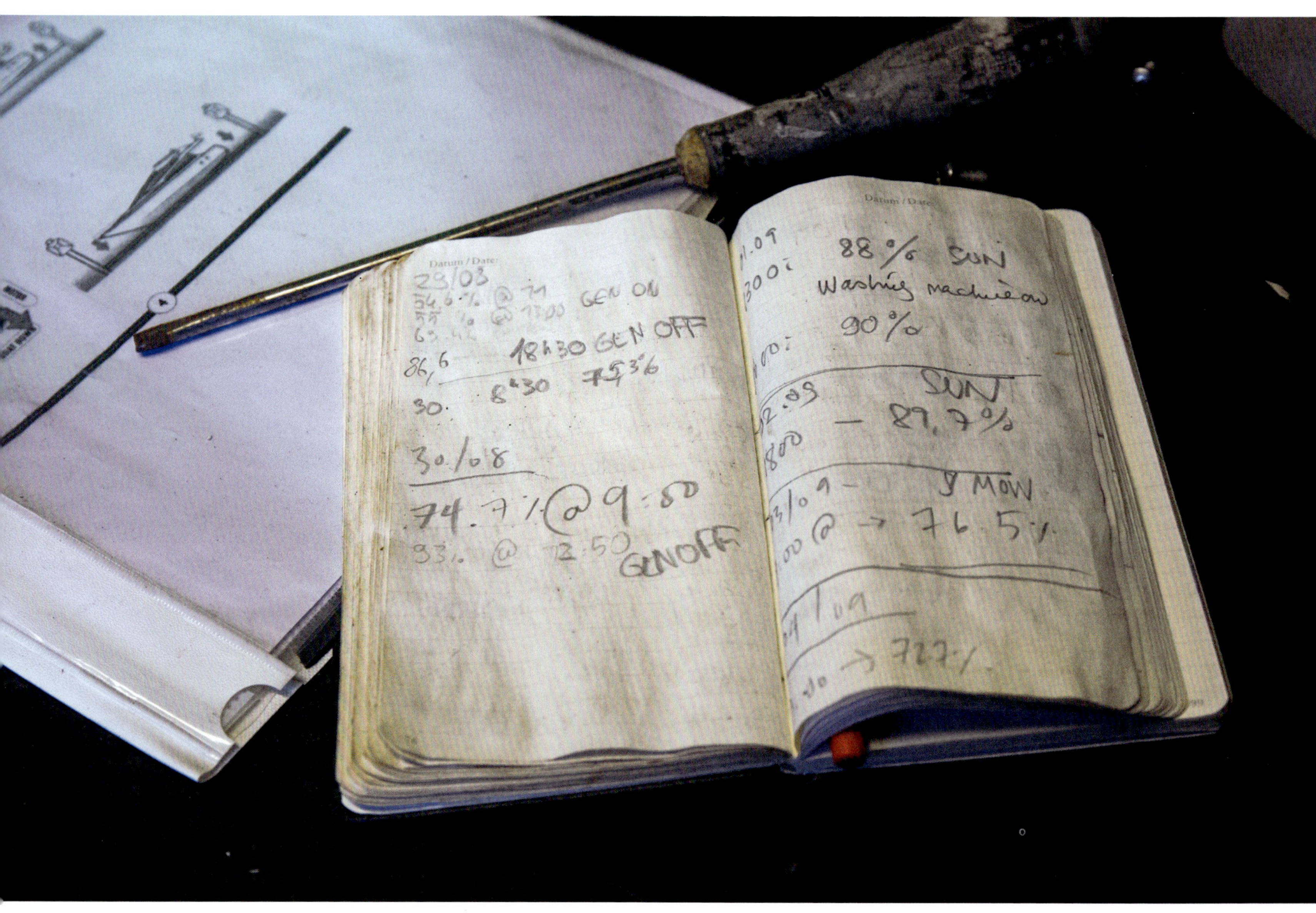

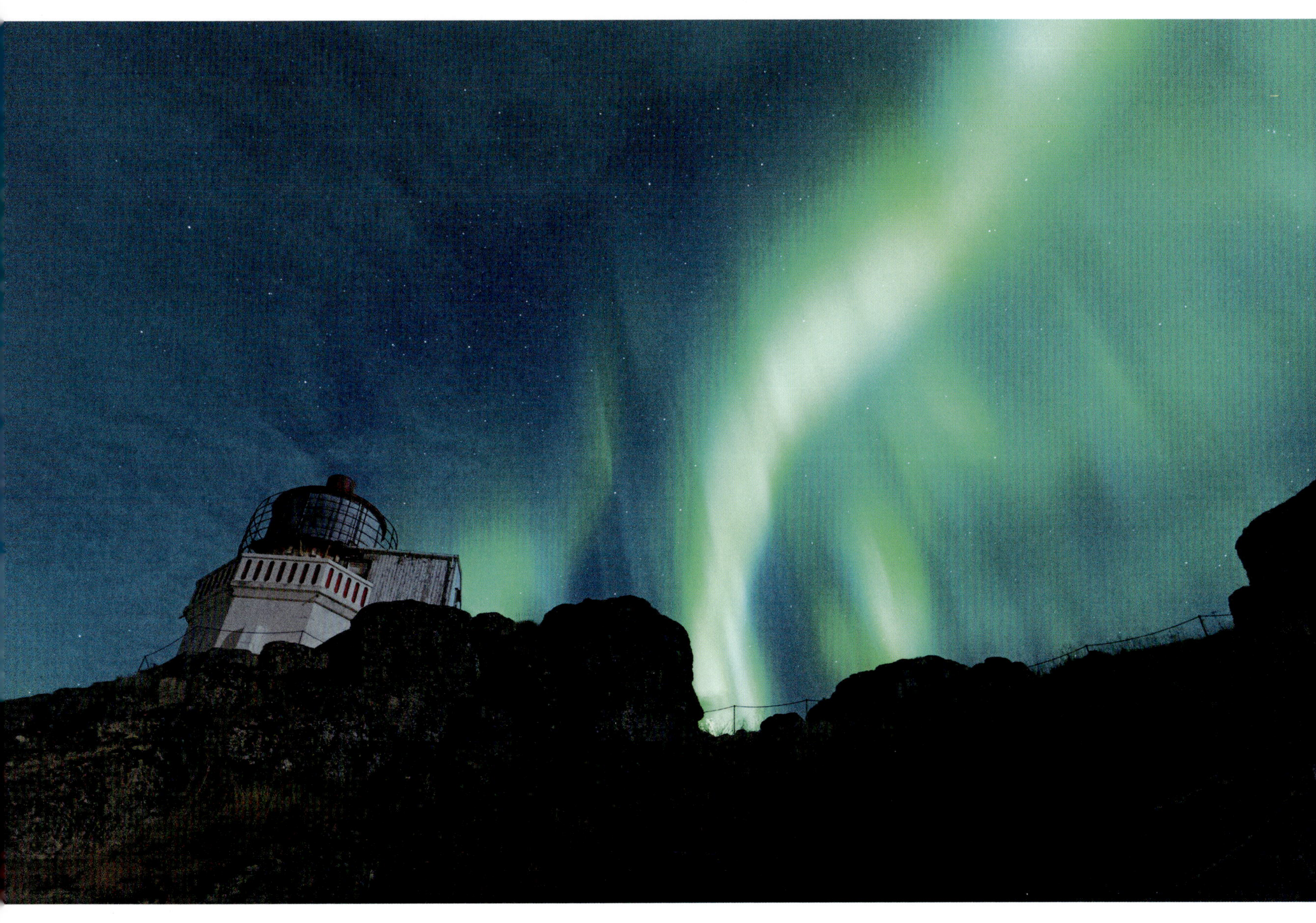

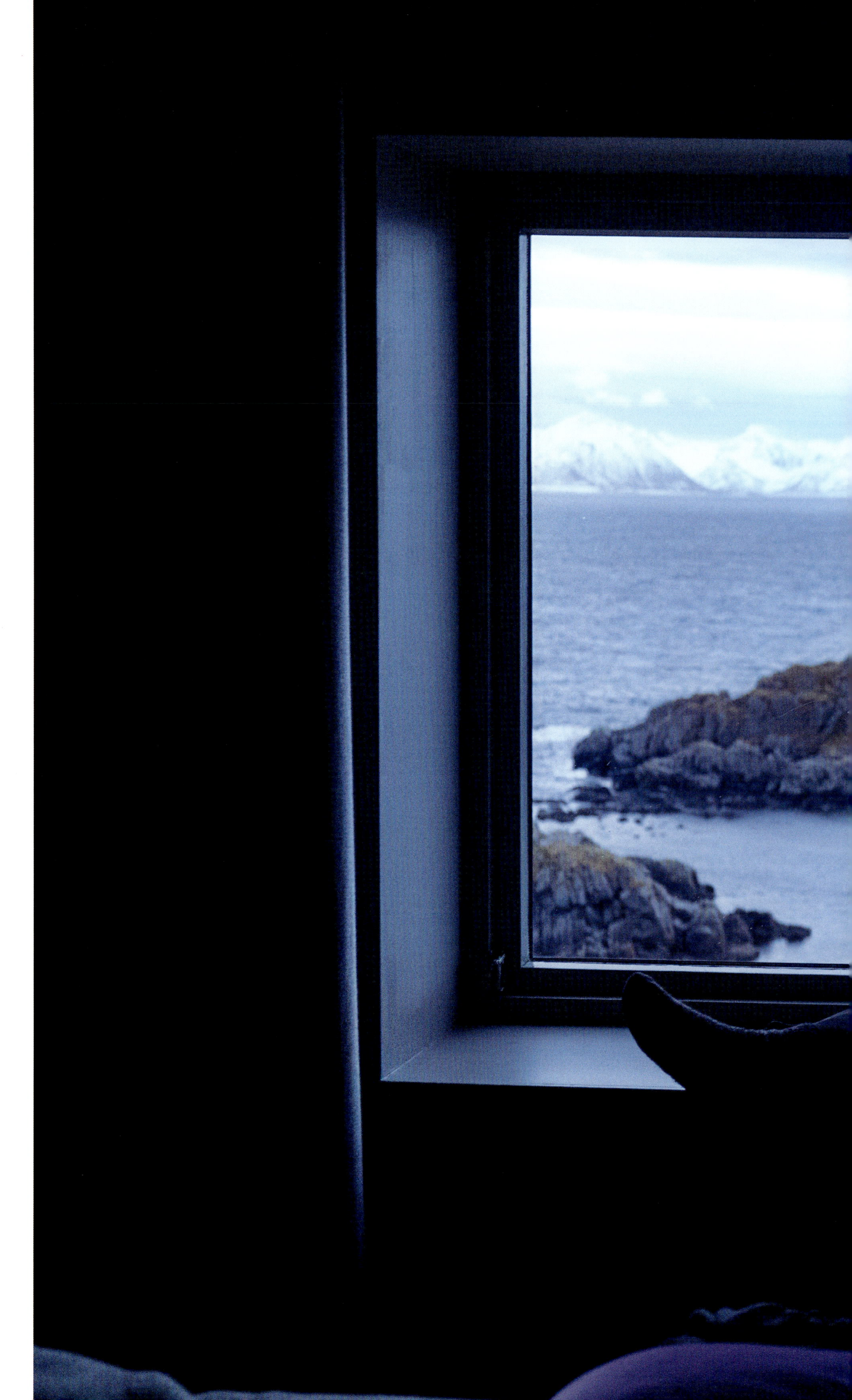

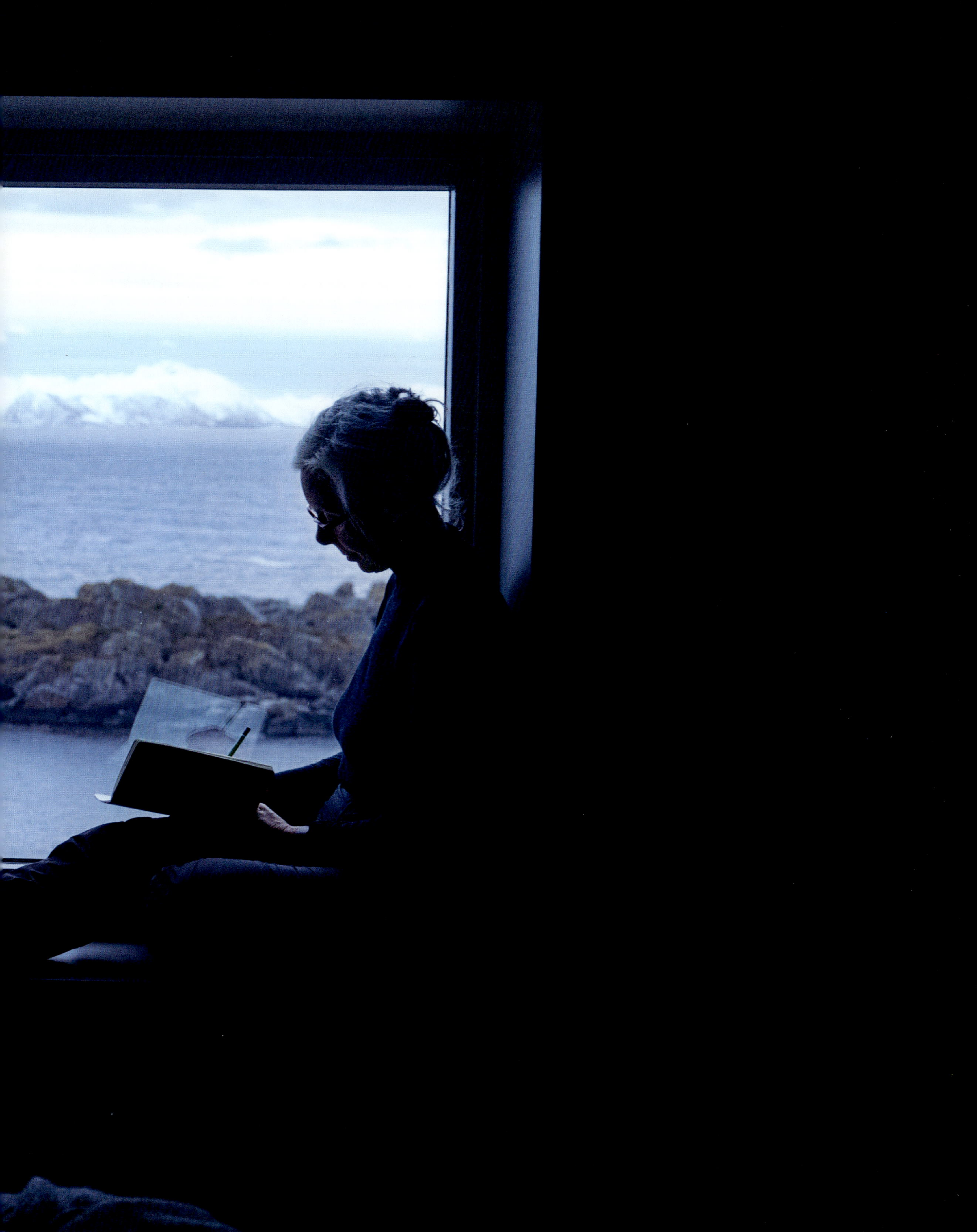

ABOUT THE AUTHOR
ÜBER DEN AUTOR

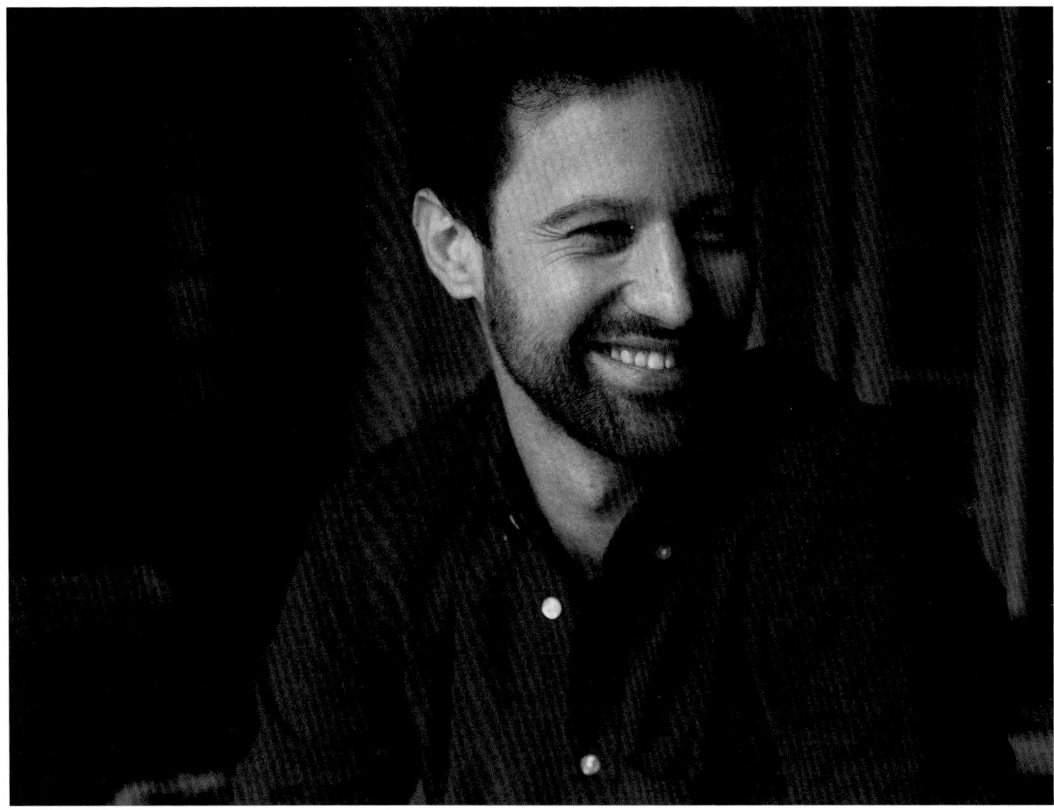

Born in 1991, Brice Portolano is a French photographer based in Paris. His work focuses on the relationship between man and nature in particular, and he enjoys documenting adventures in the wilderness. His work has appeared in *GEO Magazine, National Geographic, STERN, The Guardian* and *The Independent* among others. *No Signal* was a long-term project of his that he worked on from 2015–2020.

Brice Portolano, geboren 1991, ist ein französischer Fotograf mit Sitz in Paris. Seine Arbeiten konzentrieren sich besonders auf die Beziehung zwischen Mensch und Natur. Mit Vorliebe dokumentiert er Abenteuer in der Wildnis. Seine Aufnahmen wurden in zahlreichen Print- und Onlinemedien veröffentlicht, darunter *GEO Magazine, National Geographic, STERN, The Guardian* und *The Independent. Funkstille* war ein Langzeitprojekt von 2015-2020.

TRAVEL DIARIES
REISENOTIZEN

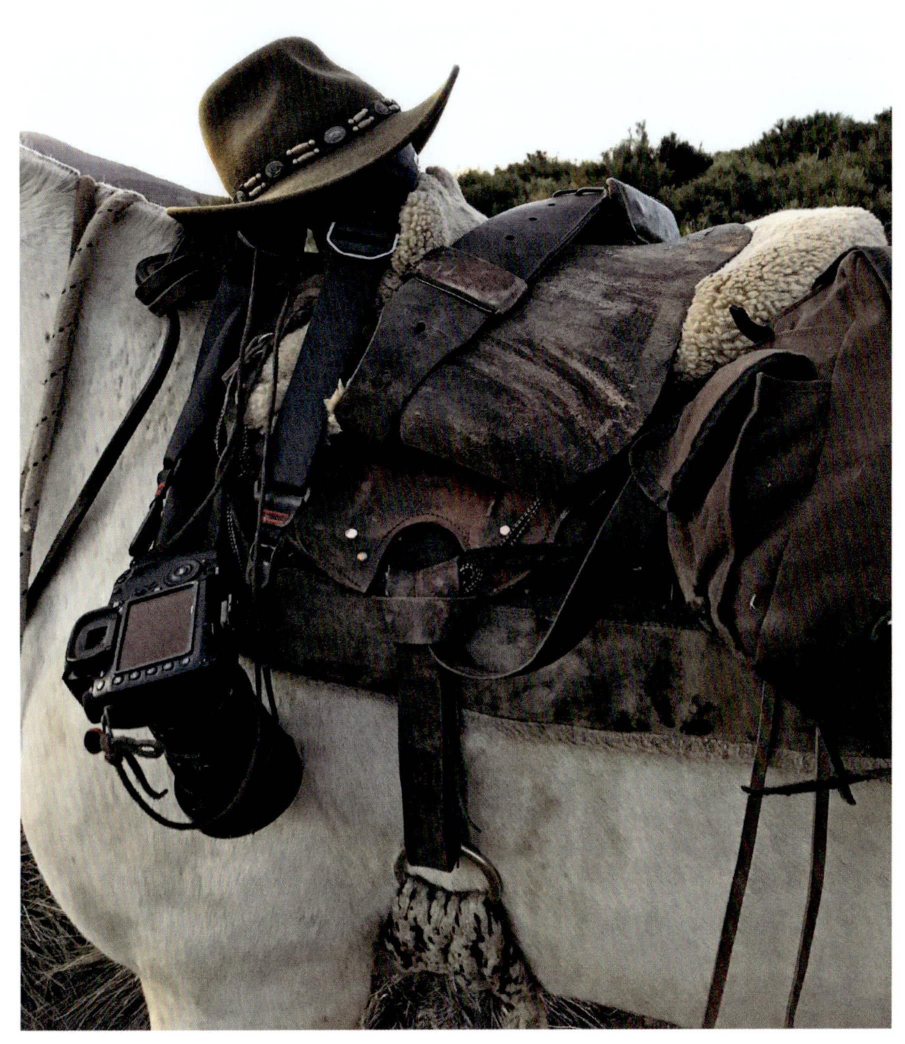

FINLAND | FINNLAND

During an afternoon with Tinja, I decide to take advantage of the departure of a group of tourists – who had come to pay her a flying visit – to travel to the village of Inari, 20 kilometres away. "Don't worry about how you'll get back. Hitchhiking works really well here and people always stop!" Tinja tells me.

Once I make it to the village, I find a cosy spot in the local restaurant, where I enjoy a hot meal and charge my camera. At around 6 o'clock in the evening, I set off, my rucksack brimming with provisions, and march optimistically out of the village, ready to hold my thumb out. But cars are rare here, and I quickly notice that all of them are travelling in the opposite direction. After walking for several kilometres into the night, it's time to face up to the facts: there are absolutely no cars travelling in my direction. By now, it's -35 °C and even a short break will send me into a state of hypothermia in a matter of minutes. I have to keep walking. A quarter-moon rises into the sky above, its faint glow accompanying me on my solitary walk. I take regular, mechanical strides to keep my body warm. With every step of the 20 kilometres making up this improvised pilgrimage, my survival instinct pushes me to continue, to stay the course and keep pace. A small group of reindeer silently disappear as I walk by. Turning off my headlamp, the bright glow of the moon, which has now firmly anchored itself into the sky, illuminates my snow-covered surroundings. After three hours of walking, I finally arrive at my small cabin, frozen, beard and hair completely iced over. I start a fire, before dining for the second time that night huddled in front of the wood-fired stove, slowly heating back up.

An einem Nachmittag bei Tinja nutze ich die Abreise einer Touristengruppe, die ihr einen kurzen Besuch abgestattet hat, um mitzufahren ins 20 Kilometer entfernte Dorf Inari. „Die Rückfahrt ist kein Problem, hier kommt man sehr gut per Anhalter voran, die Leute halten immer an!", wird mir gesagt.

Im Dorf angekommen, richte ich mich gemütlich in einem Eckrestaurant ein, um eine warme Mahlzeit zu mir zu nehmen und die Batterien meiner Kamera aufzuladen. Gegen 18 Uhr mache ich mich mit einem Rucksack voller Vorräte wieder auf den Weg und marschiere in optimistischem Schritt bis zum Dorfausgang, jederzeit bereit, den Daumen auszustrecken. Aber die wenigen Autos, die vorbeikommen, fahren alle in die Gegenrichtung. Nach einigen Kilometern im Dunkeln muss ich mir das Offensichtliche eingestehen: Kein einziges Auto fährt in meine Richtung. Die Temperatur beträgt -35 °C, und jede auch noch so kurze Pause würde innerhalb weniger Minuten zu Unterkühlung führen. Ich habe keine Wahl: Ich muss weitergehen. Ein Viertelmond geht auf, sein schwaches Licht begleitet mich auf meiner einsamen Wanderung. Ich falle in einen regelmäßigen, mechanischen Trott, der meinen Körper warm hält.

Im Lauf der 20 Kilometer dieser improvisierten Pilgerwanderung treibt mich der Überlebensinstinkt voran und verhindert, dass ich auch nur wenige Momente innehalte. Ein kleiner Trupp Rentiere verschwindet lautlos, als ich vorbeikomme. Ich habe meine Kopflampe ausgemacht, und das strahlende Licht des Mondes, der mittlerweile hoch am Himmel steht, erhellt die schneebedeckte Landschaft. Nach drei Stunden Marsch komme ich endlich bei meiner kleinen Hütte an, durchgefroren, Bart und Haare komplett von Reif überzogen. Ich mache ein Feuer an, bevor ich ein zweites Mal esse, an den Holzofen geschmiegt, der mich sanft aufwärmt.

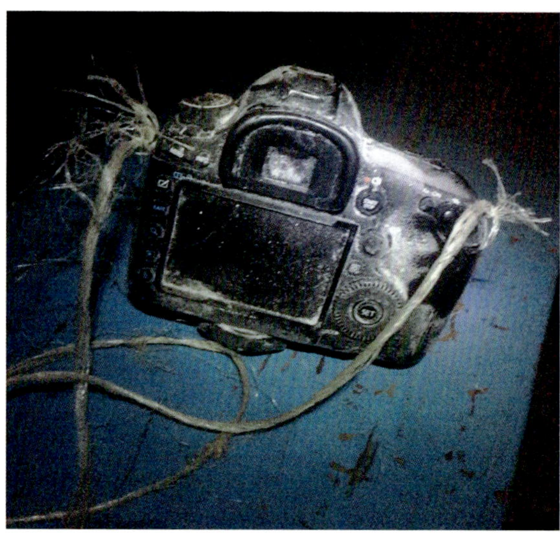

001 | After several hours at -30 °C, my camera is completely frosted over. I will wrap it up in a plastic bag before going back into my cabin to protect it from condensation caused by the temperature difference.

001 | Nach mehreren Stunden bei -30 °C bedeckt Reif meinen Fotoapparat. Vor meiner Rückkehr in die Hütte packe ich ihn in einen Plastikbeutel, um ihn vor Kondenswasser durch den Temperaturunterschied zu schützen.

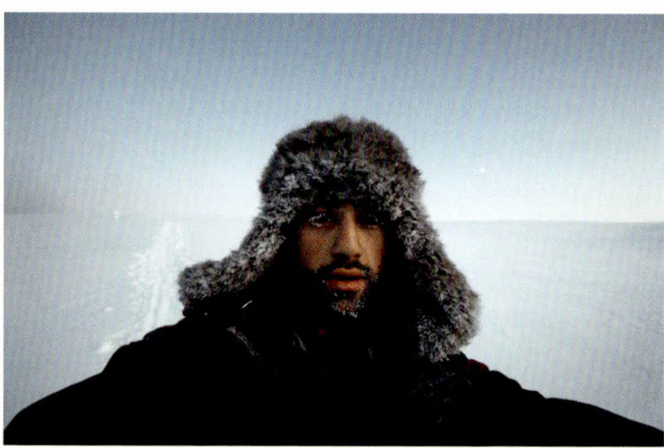

002 | At -38 °C, the moisture from my breathing freezes instantly and clings to my face. The air also freezes the insides of my nostrils and transforms my tears into small icicles at the end of my eyelashes.

002 | Bei -38 °C gefriert die feuchte Atemluft sofort auf meinem Gesicht. Auch in meinen Nasenlöchern setzt sich Reif ab, und meine Tränen verwandeln sich an den Spitzen meiner Wimpern in winzige Eiszapfen.

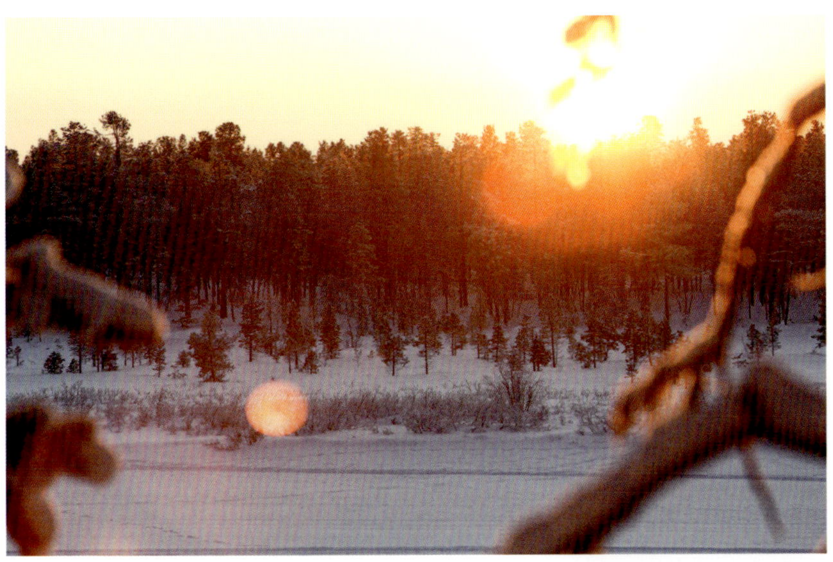

003 | At last! The sun returns after 45 days of Arctic night, a much-anticipated event in the far north.

003 | Endlich! Nach 45 Tagen Polarnacht ist die Rückkehr der Sonne ein Ereignis, auf das im hohen Norden alle warten.

004 | While fetching water at the river I spot the northern lights in the Arctic night – a beautiful spectacle of green, purple and white lights. Finnish legend has it that the lights are created by foxes dashing across the tundra and sending sparks up into the sky with their tails.

004 | Beim Wasserholen am Fluss sehe ich Nordlichter in der Polarnacht – ein echtes Spektakel in Grün-, Violett- und Weißtönen. Nach einer finnischen Legende sprühen die Füchse Funken, wenn sie durch die Tundra rennen, und erschaffen so die Nordlichter.

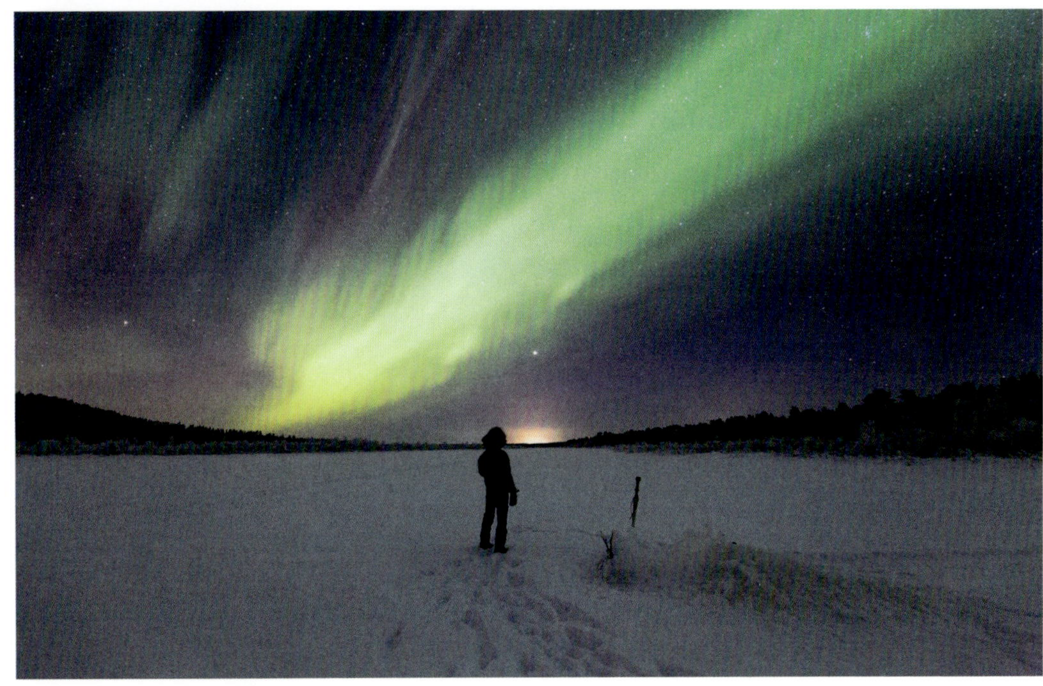

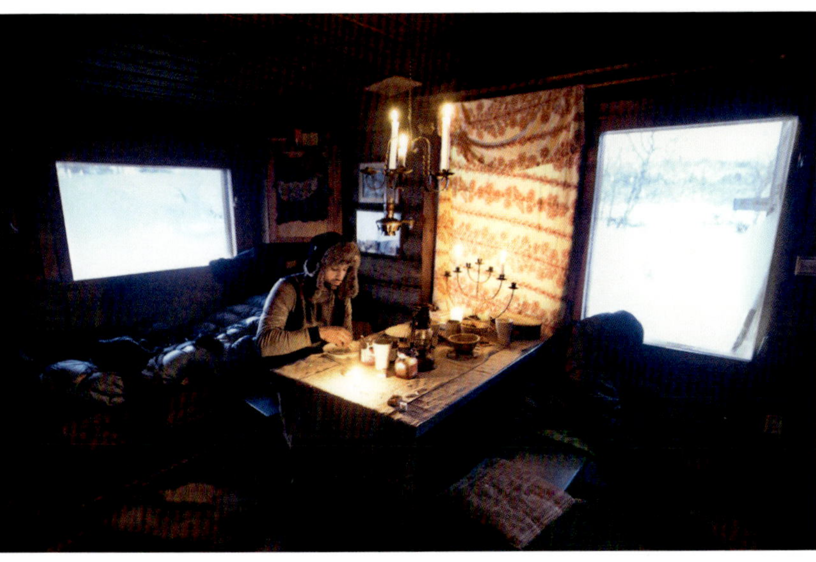

005 | It is -40 °C and the frost is creeping onto the windows of my cabin. With no electricity or running water, I light a candle and heat myself up in front of the wood-fired stove. The stove smokes dreadfully and it takes me two days to get it working properly. I eat a lot: rice, lentils, olive oil, sardines, chilli. The cold makes me hungry and I consume three times as much as I normally would. Cooking takes up a big chunk of my day.

005 | Bei -40 °C setzt sich Reif auf den Fenstern meiner Hütte ab. Ohne Strom und fließendes Wasser lebe ich bei Kerzenlicht und heize mit einem Holzofen. Er qualmt schrecklich, und ich brauche zwei Tage, bis er richtig funktioniert. Ich esse viel: Reis, Linsen, Olivenöl, Sardinen, Chilis. Kälte macht hungrig, und ich brauche dreimal so viel Nahrung wie sonst. In meinem Alltag nimmt das Kochen viel Raum ein.

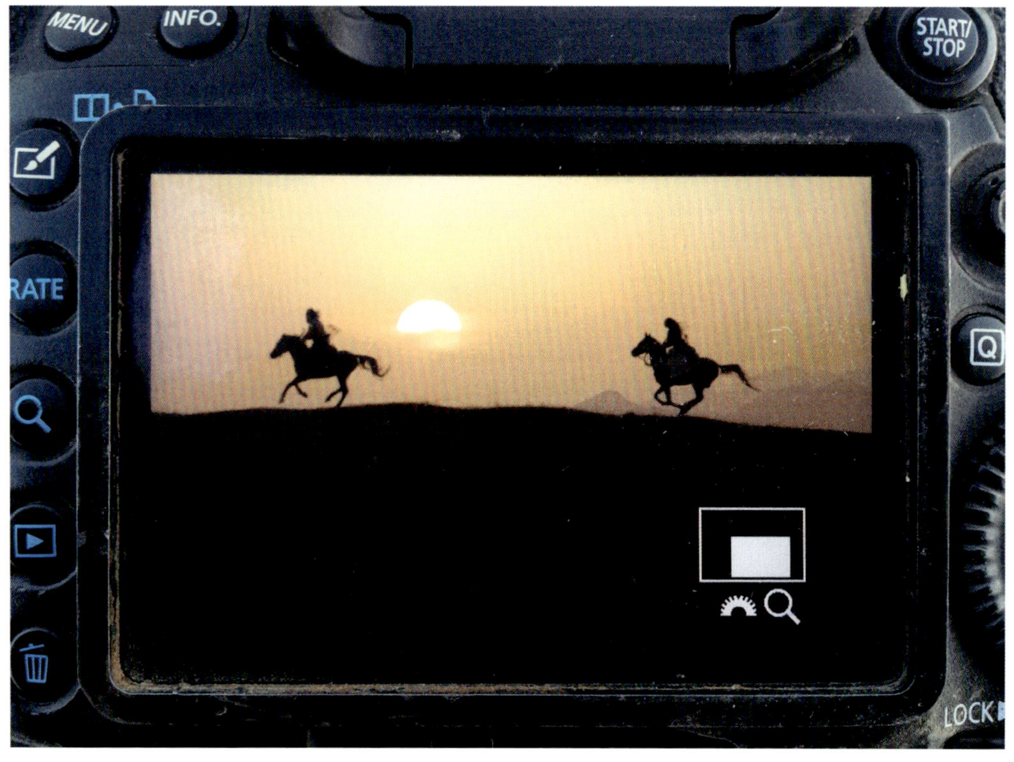

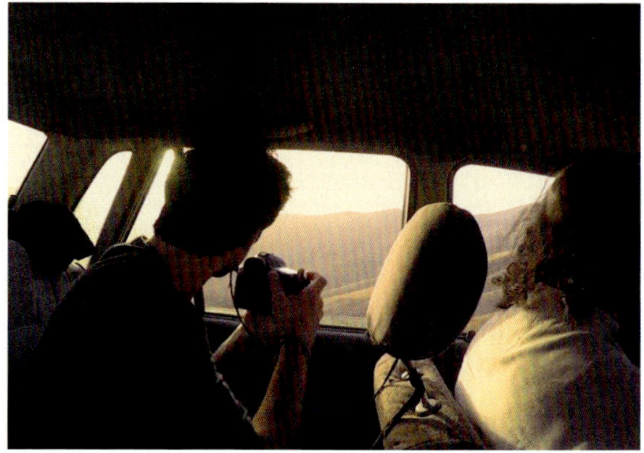

001 | Ali and Anna, one of his pupils, gallop at sunset along the hilltops in a misty atmosphere.

001 | Ali und Anna, eine seine Schülerinnen, galoppieren vor einem dunstigen Sonnenuntergang über die Hügel.

IRAN

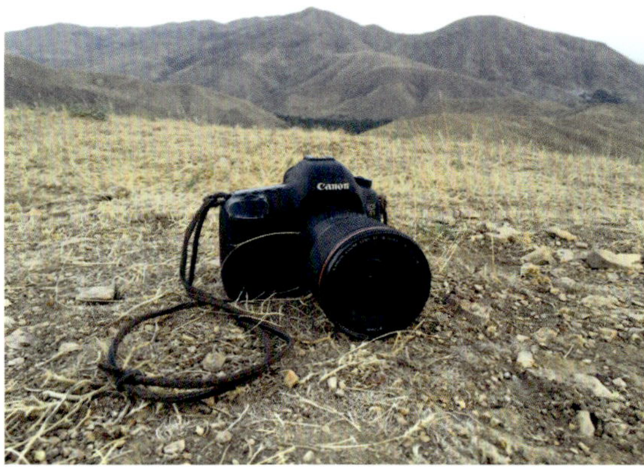

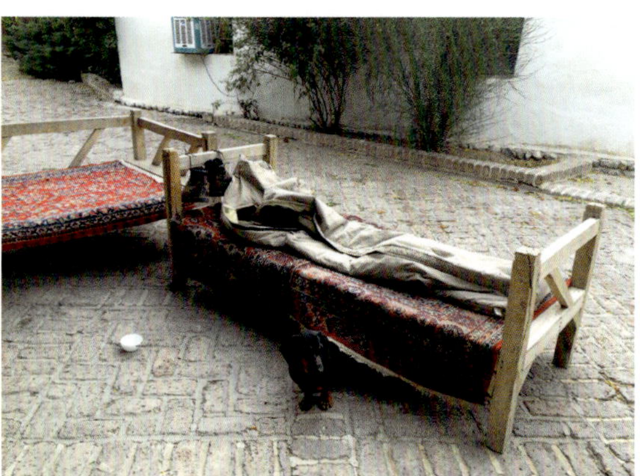

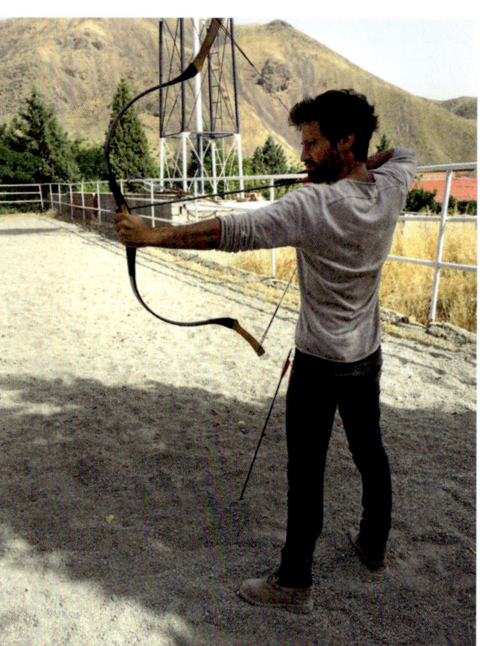

002 | I sometimes sleep under the stars on a wooden bench draped with a simple rug. The rest of the time, I spend my nights in a sort of very basic storeroom, wedged between the saddles, shields and armour, on a mattress on the floor.

002 | Manchmal schlafe ich unter den Sternen, auf einer Holzbank, die mit einem einfachen Teppich abgedeckt ist. Die übrigen Nächte verbringe ich in einer Art Abstellkammer zwischen Sätteln, Schilden und Rüstungen auf einer Matratze am Boden.

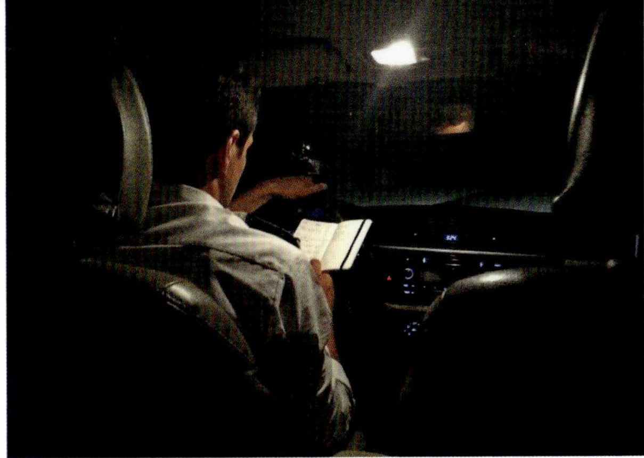

003 | The driver of the taxi taking me to the airport in Tehran reads the instructions that Ali has written for him on a notepad.

003 | Der Taxifahrer, der mich zum Teheraner Flughafen bringen soll, liest die Wegbeschreibung, die Ali ihm mitgegeben hat.

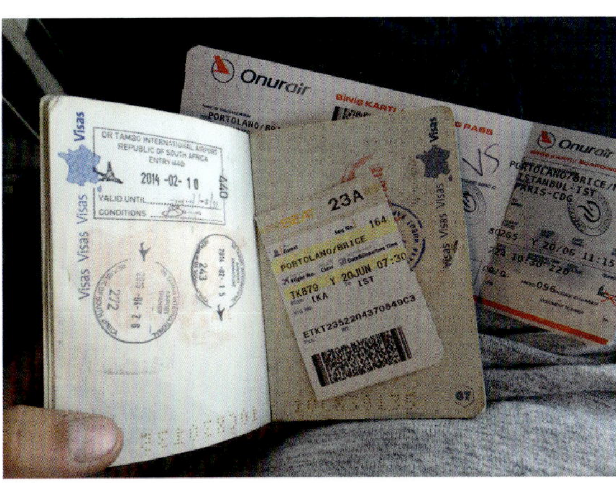

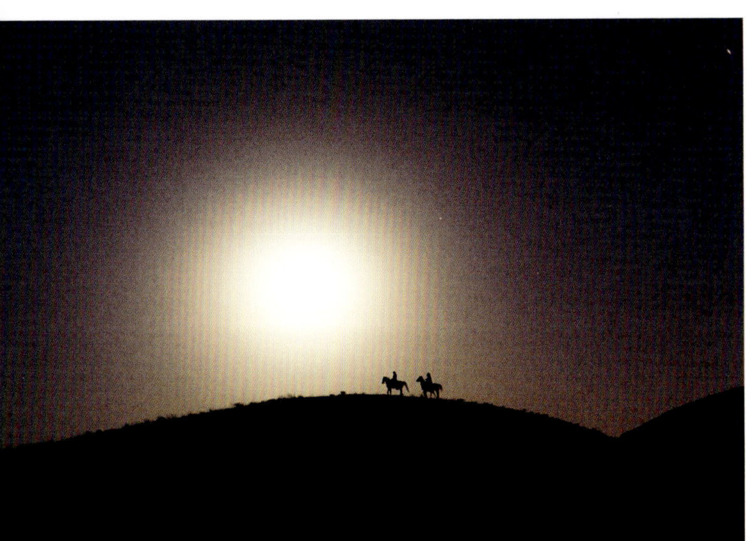

004 | Once night has fallen, we saddle the horses in preparation for our night-time outings in the moonlight. Accompanied by the sound of chirping crickets, we walk through the hills, feeling the temperatures change in the valleys, the air sometimes cooled down by the vegetation, sometimes heated up by the rocks that absorb heat over the course of the day.

004 | Sobald die Nacht anbricht, satteln wir die Pferde für Ausritte bei Mondlicht. Vom Zirpen der Grillen begleitet, streifen wir über die Hügel und spüren die wechselnden Temperaturen der Luft in den Tälern, die mal von der Vegetation gekühlt, mal von der gespeicherten Tageshitze der Felsen erwärmt wird.

005 | Ali teaches me his style of horse riding to make sure I am completely confident in my mount. This is something I will need to master before I will be able to let go of the reins and shoot arrows while galloping. He gets me to mount the horse backwards before bringing the horse, held by a red rope, to a gallop. I try to put Ali's lessons into practice. But it's going to take me quite a few attempts before I manage to hit the target.

005 | Ali bringt mir bei, meinem Reittier vollkommen zu vertrauen. Nur so kann man die Zügel loslassen und im Galopp mit dem Bogen schießen. Deshalb muss ich rückwärts aufsteigen, bevor er das Pferd an einer roten Longe im Kreis galoppieren lässt. Ich versuche, Alis Ratschlägen zu folgen, brauche aber trotzdem mehrere Versuche, bis ich die Scheibe treffe.

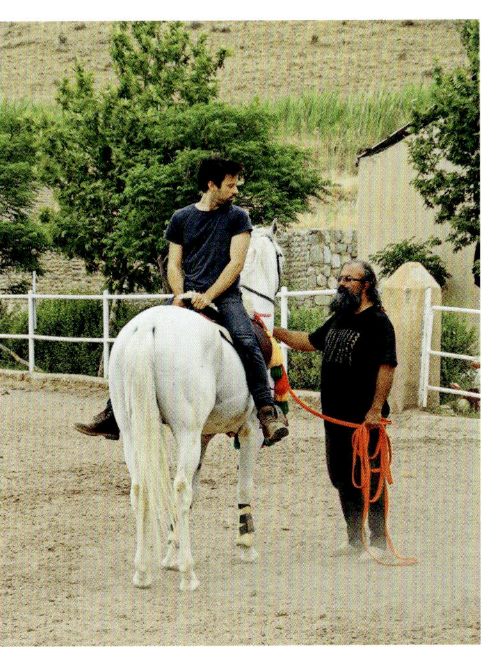

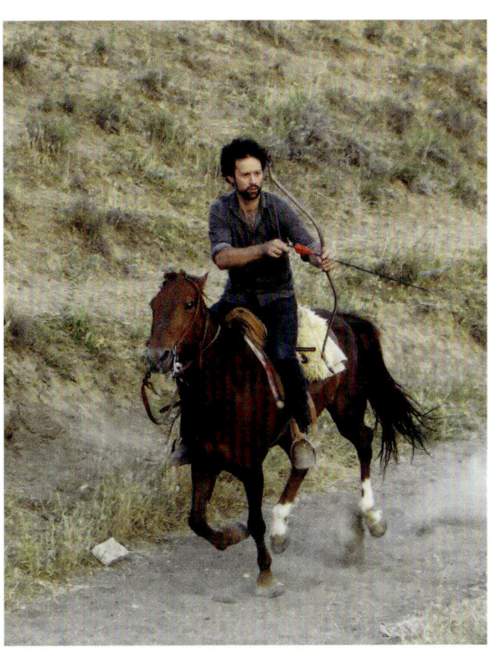

MONGOLIA | MONGOLEI

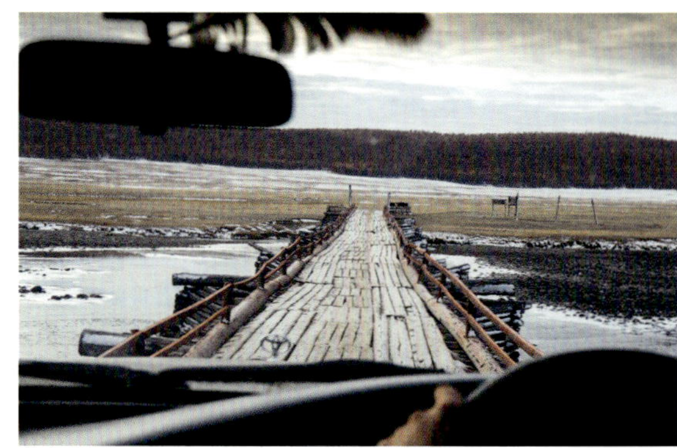

After a night flight over the forests of Siberia, I touch down in Ulaanbaatar, the capital of Mongolia. My lungs burning from the pollution, I look out of the taxi at the three coal-fired power plants located in the centre of town; a dystopian vision in one of the most polluted cities in the world. I then take a long bus journey over bumpy roads to reach the small town of Mörön in the centre of the country. I get off the bus and, in the dusty scramble for luggage, finally meet Zaya. We go out for dinner where we share genuine laughter, and I can already tell that we are going to get on well. At dawn, we set off once more with her husband Ultsan for a third day of travel, this time in a 4x4, on a rutted track at the mercy of the rainfall and seasons. We drive towards Tsagaannuur, Mongolia's northernmost village bordered by Lake Khövsgöl. The car shakes so much that it is impossible to sleep, and the top of my head frequently bumps against the roof of the car.

We spend the night in a basic cabin, eating mutton fritters that are, though I don't know this yet, the epitome of luxury. Because after this, I'll be eating tsuivan for almost all of my meals, a local dish of noodles with potatoes and meat, and sometimes a little spicy sauce.

On the fourth morning, I climb onto the back of a motorcycle with Ultsan to drive through the steppes and pick up our horses, on the border between the steppe and the taiga. En route, we stop several times to talk to acquaintances we meet by chance, and to drink a shot – sometimes several shots – of vodka before continuing on towards the mountains. Our journey back to camp will take four hours by horse. But before we have made it to our end destination, we are invited into a yurt for some tea to warm up.

I spot wolf tracks along the route and a change in the scenery around us. Up until this point, it had just been steppes as far as the eye could see, but now we are surrounded by snow-covered mountains. We set about tackling the taiga and its marshy tracks.

Nach einem Nachtflug über die Wälder Sibiriens lande ich in Ulan-Bator, der mongolischen Hauptstadt. Meine Bronchien schmerzen von der schmutzigen Luft, während ich durchs Fenster des Taxis die drei Kohlekraftwerke im Stadtzentrum betrachte; ein dystopischer Anblick in einer der am schlimmsten verschmutzten Städte der Welt. Es folgt eine lange Busreise über holperige Straßen, bis zur Kleinstadt Mörön im Zentrum des Landes. Als ich aussteige, lerne ich im staubigen Gedränge beim Ausladen des Gepäcks endlich Zaya kennen. Wir gehen zusammen essen, und an unseren freimütigen Späßen merke ich, dass wir uns gut verstehen werden. Im Morgengrauen brechen wir mit ihrem Ehemann Ultsan wieder auf zu einem dritten Reisetag, diesmal im Geländewagen, über eine ausgefahrene Piste, deren Verlauf sich mit den Regenfällen und Jahreszeiten ändert. Unser Ziel ist Tsagaannuur, das nördlichste Dorf der Mongolei, das am Khuvsgul-See liegt. Der Wagen holpert so, dass man unmöglich schlafen kann; mein Kopf stößt immer wieder gegen das Dach.

Wir verbringen die Nacht in einer einfachen Hütte und verdauen die Lammpasteten, die – was ich noch nicht weiß – einen absoluten Luxus darstellen. Von nun an wird es zu fast jeder Mahlzeit Tsuivan geben, ein lokales Nudelgericht, das mit Kartoffeln, Fleisch und manchmal ein wenig scharfer Soße serviert wird. Am vierten Morgen steige ich hinter Ultsan aufs Motorrad, um durch die Steppe zu unseren Pferden zu fahren, die an der Grenze zur Taiga warten. Unterwegs halten wir mehrfach an, um mit Bekannten zu plaudern, die wir zufällig treffen, und einen Schluck Wodka, oder mehrere, zu trinken, bevor wir weiterfahren Richtung Berge. Nach vier weiteren Stunden zu Pferd wird die Reise endlich beim Lager enden, aber vorher werden wir zum Tee in einer Jurte eingeladen, um uns aufzuwärmen.

Ich bemerke Wolfsspuren auf dem Weg, und einen Wechsel der Szenerie: Anstelle von Steppe, soweit das Auge reicht, sind wir nun von Bergen mit verschneiten Gipfeln umgeben. Die geografische Abgeschiedenheit kommt plötzlich. Wir nehmen die Taiga mit ihren sumpfigen Pfaden in Angriff.

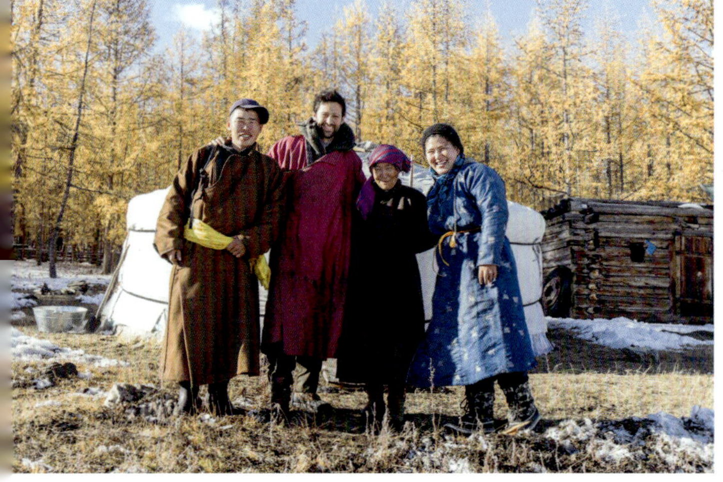

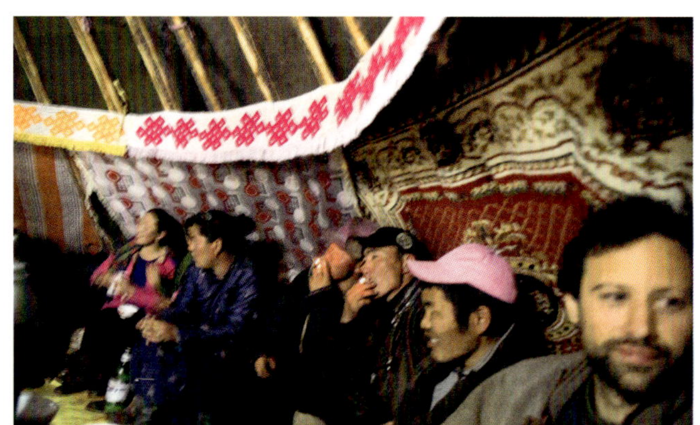

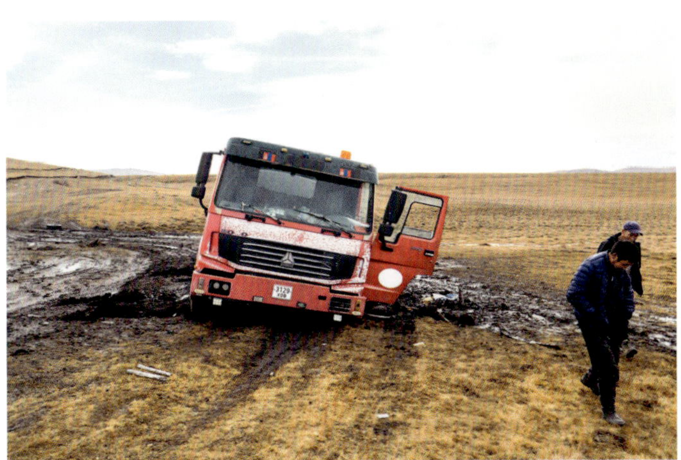

001 | En route between Mörön and Tsagaannuur. No chance. We offer our help to the unlucky people in this truck, but the vehicle is village-bound with a heavy load of fuel, making impossible to tow.

001 | Auf der Straße von Mörön nach Tsagaannuur. Wir bieten den verunglückten Fahrern unsere Hilfe an, aber der Lastwagen, der das Dorf versorgen sollte, transportiert eine wichtige Benzinladung und ist unmöglich abzuschleppen.

002 | The lodge acts as a living space, kitchen, dining room, bedroom and bathroom all in one. When the time for the weekly shower finally comes around, you have to squat down in a tiny aluminium basin to wash yourself in water from the river that has been heated on the wood-fired stove.

002 | Das Tipi dient als Wohnraum, Küche, Esszimmer, Schlafraum und Bad. Wenn die Zeit der wöchentlichen Dusche endlich gekommen ist, hockt man sich in eine winzige Aluminiumwanne und wäscht sich mit Flusswasser, das auf dem Ofen erwärmt wird.

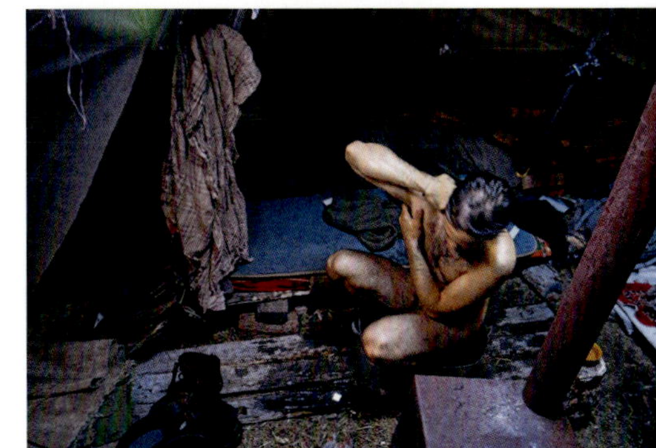

003 | I share the tepee with Zaya and her husband Ultsan, a small confined space measuring several square metres. The notion of privacy is completely relative: here, members of the community come into the tepees unannounced, without asking for permission to enter. It was a bit disconcerting the first few times it happened, but you quickly get used to it.

003 | Ich teile das Tipi, einen beengten Raum von wenigen Quadratmetern, mit Zaya und ihrem Mann Ultsan. Der Begriff der Intimität ist relativ: Nachbarn betreten das Tipi unangekündigt und ohne um Erlaubnis zu fragen. Als Besucher ist man anfangs verunsichert, gewöhnt sich aber schnell daran.

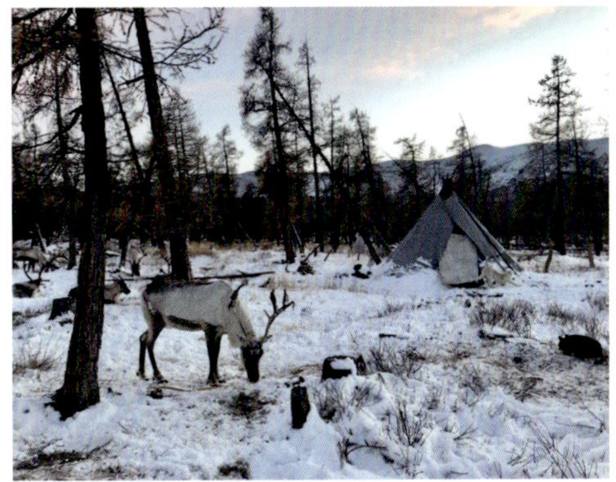

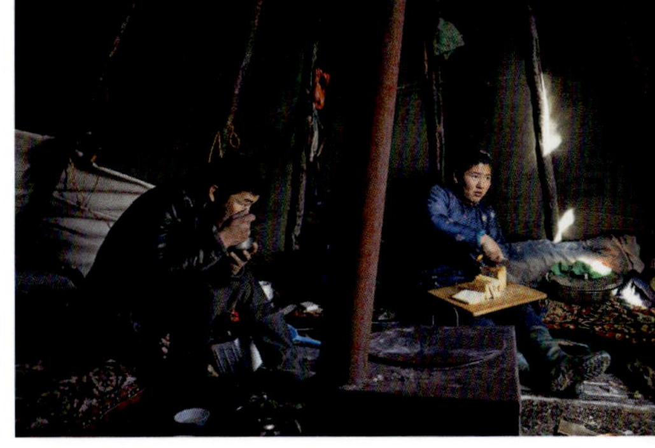

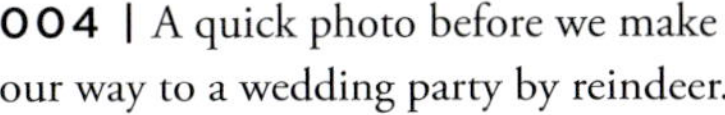

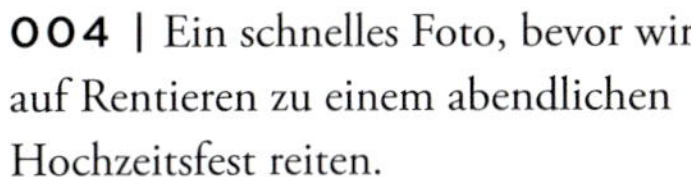

004 | A quick photo before we make our way to a wedding party by reindeer.

004 | Ein schnelles Foto, bevor wir auf Rentieren zu einem abendlichen Hochzeitsfest reiten.

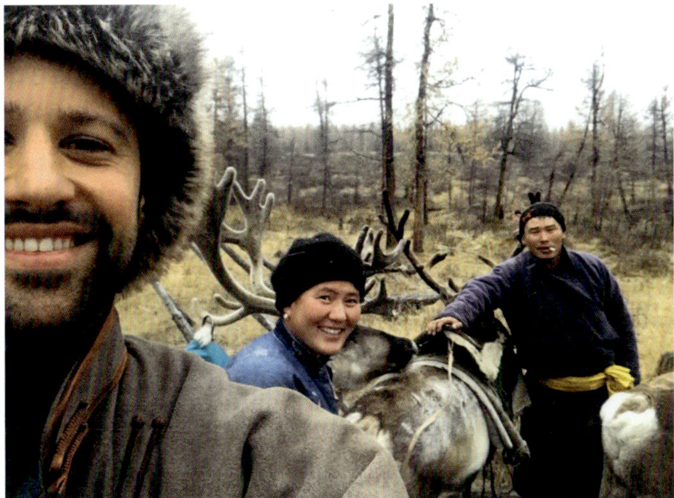

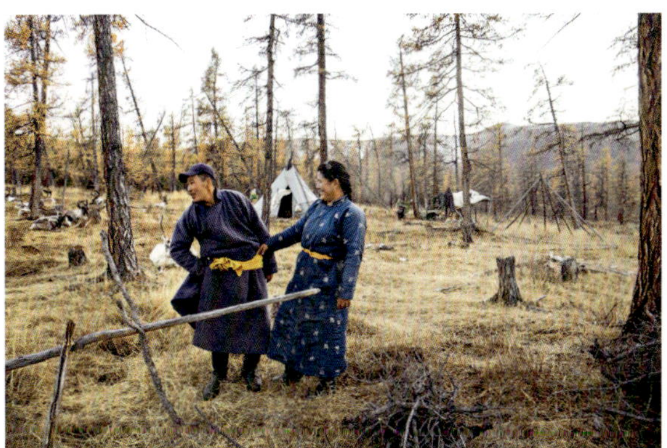

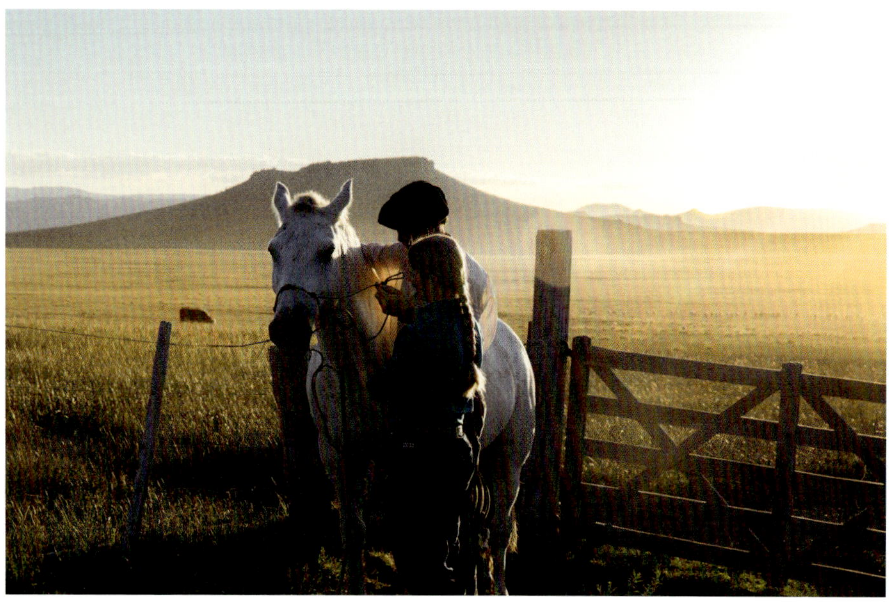

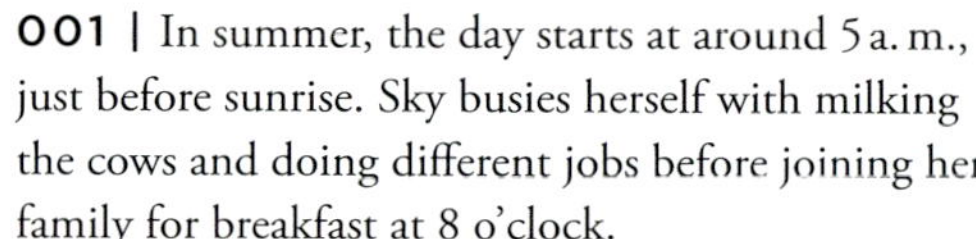

ARGENTINA
ARGENTINIEN

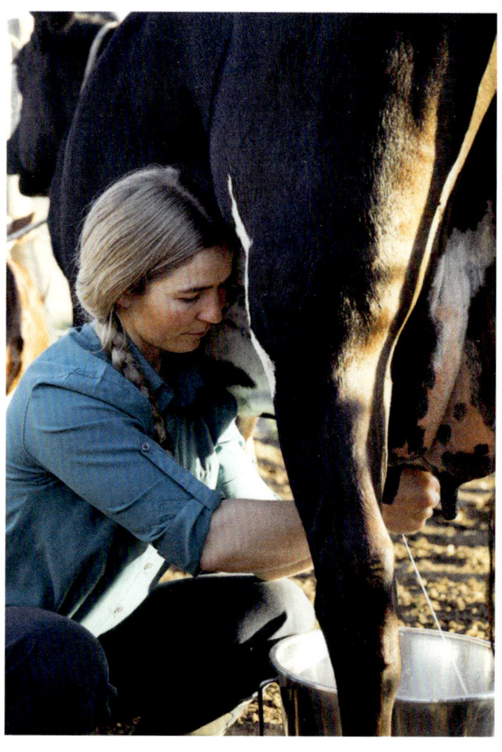

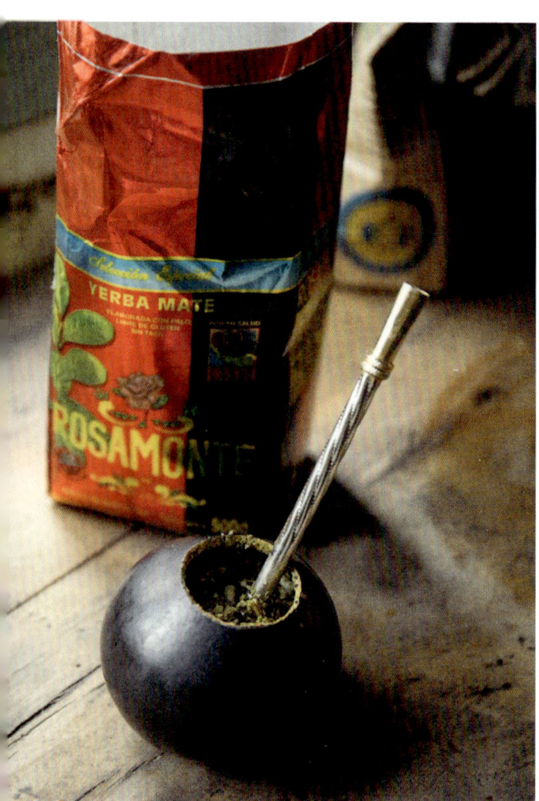

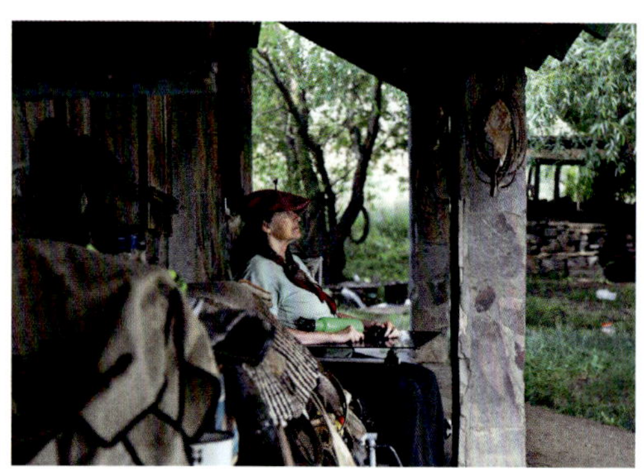

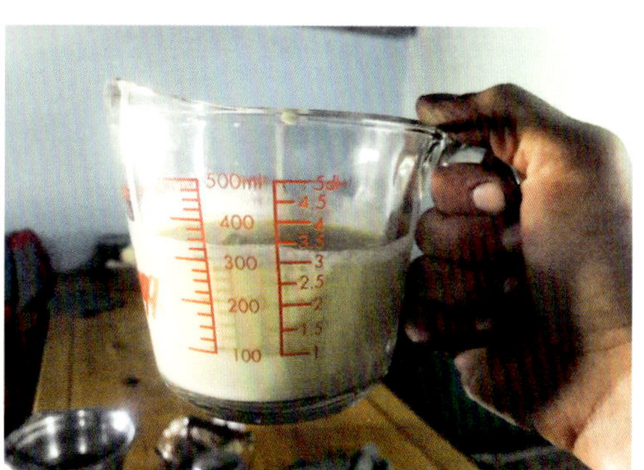

002 | Mate is a traditional South American
drink traced back to the Guaraní culture. Very
popular in Argentina, it has a bitter taste and is
consumed at all times of day.

002 | Mate-Tee ist ein traditionelles südamerika-
nisches Getränk, das der indigenen Guaraní-Kul-
tur entstammt. Es ist in Argentinien sehr beliebt,
schmeckt bitter und wird zu jeder Tageszeit
getrunken.

003 | Ginny, Sky's mother, watches the horses
galloping in the pastures. An artist and painter,
she has passed her love for horses down to her
daughter. But as a long-time sufferer of multiple
sclerosis, she hasn't been able to get on a horse
herself for several years.

003 | Skys Mutter Ginny schaut den Pfer-
den zu, die über die Weiden galoppieren. Die
Malerin hat ihrer Tochter die Liebe zu Pferden
vererbt, aber sie leidet an Multipler Sklerose und
kann seit Jahren nicht mehr selbst reiten.

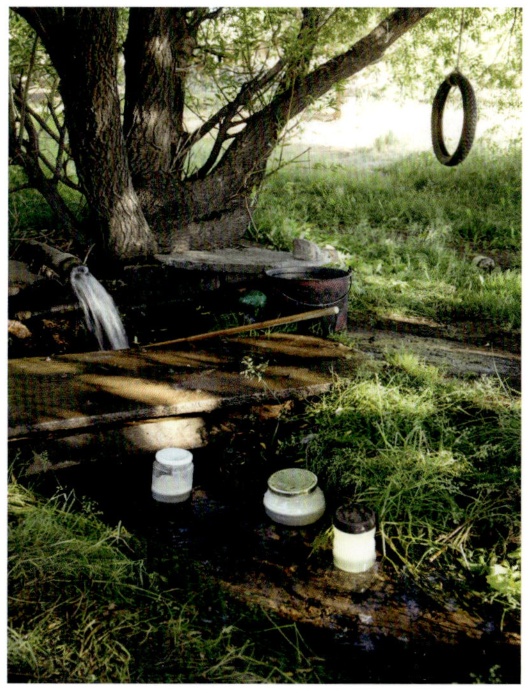

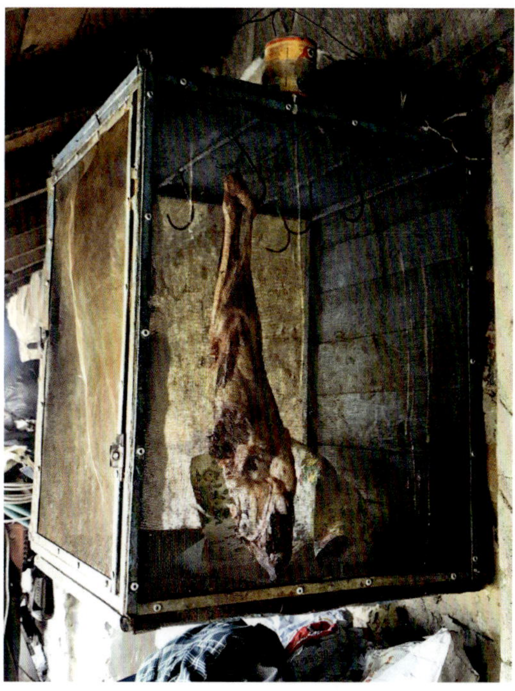

004 | Despite the abundance of milk and meat, Sky doesn't have a fridge. She stores her dairy products in glass jars submerged in the river, where the temperature remains stable at around 8 °C, while meat is suspended under the porch, a mosquito net protecting it from the unwanted insects.

004 | Trotz der Fülle an Milch und Fleisch hat Sky keinen Kühlschrank. Milchprodukte werden in Glasbehältern im Fluss versenkt, wo die Temperatur immer um 8 °C beträgt. Das Fleisch hängt unter dem Vordach, durch Gitter vor den Fliegen geschützt.

005 | The major summer migration known as transhumance starts at around 4:30 a. m. The stars are still twinkling overhead as we saddle the horses. I run around photographing Sky as she fixes the girth onto the mule, Leo as he wakes up and yawns in the first rays of sunshine or one of the gauchos as they catch a sheep with a lasso so that Pastor, a Shepherd puppy, can feed directly at its teat. And then we finally set off.
After lunch, while the gauchos are taking their siesta, I slip away to bathe in the river and wash off the dust. It's hot, and dragonflies perch on the rocks as I dry off in the sun. I notice huge nests built by the Andean condor – large scavengers with a wingspan of more than 3.20 metres – on the cliff overlooking the river. The next morning, after a short, cool night underneath the stars, we set off in the direction of high pastureland. Though the sun is high in the sky, the temperature is significantly colder at this altitude. The herd is travelling at a significantly slower pace than the day before and fatigue is setting in, but the gauchos continue to guide us with the invaluable assistance of their dogs. Many long hours later, we finally reach the end destination of our expedition: Raúl's cabin, the shepherd tasked with tending the herd until the end of the summer. We eat lunch together before retracing our steps, finally free from our herd.

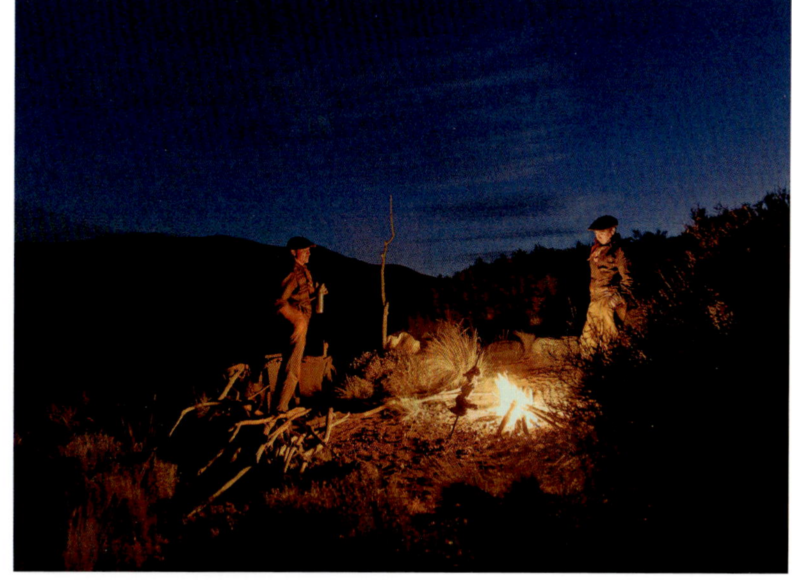

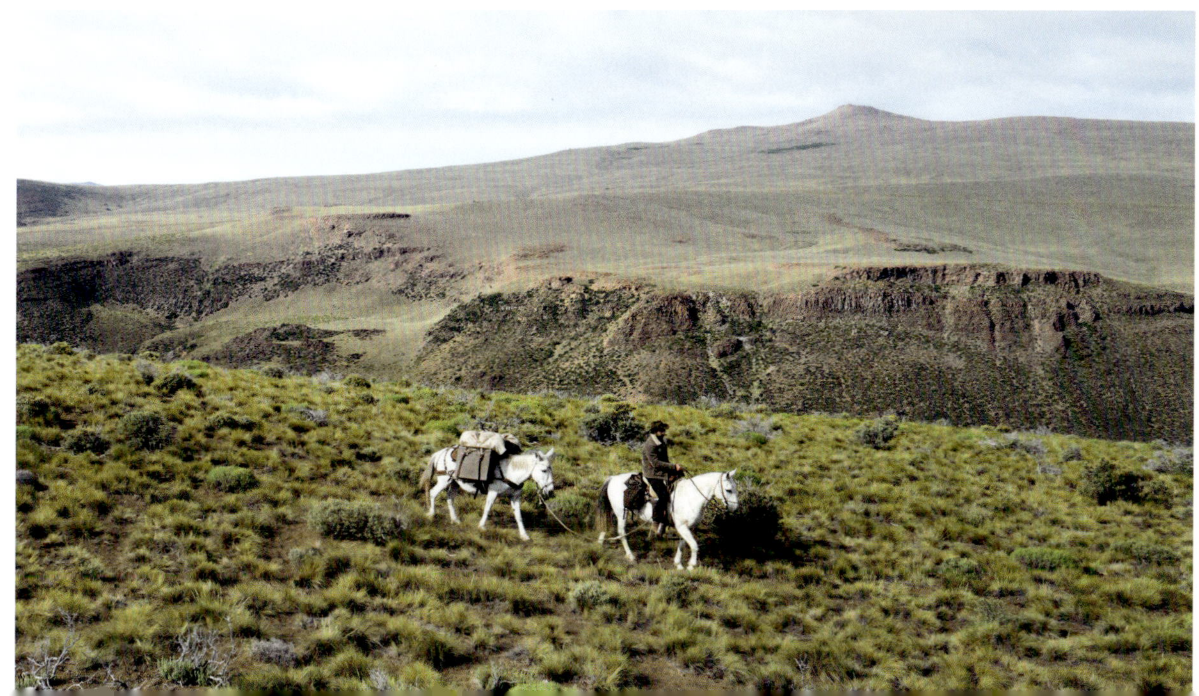

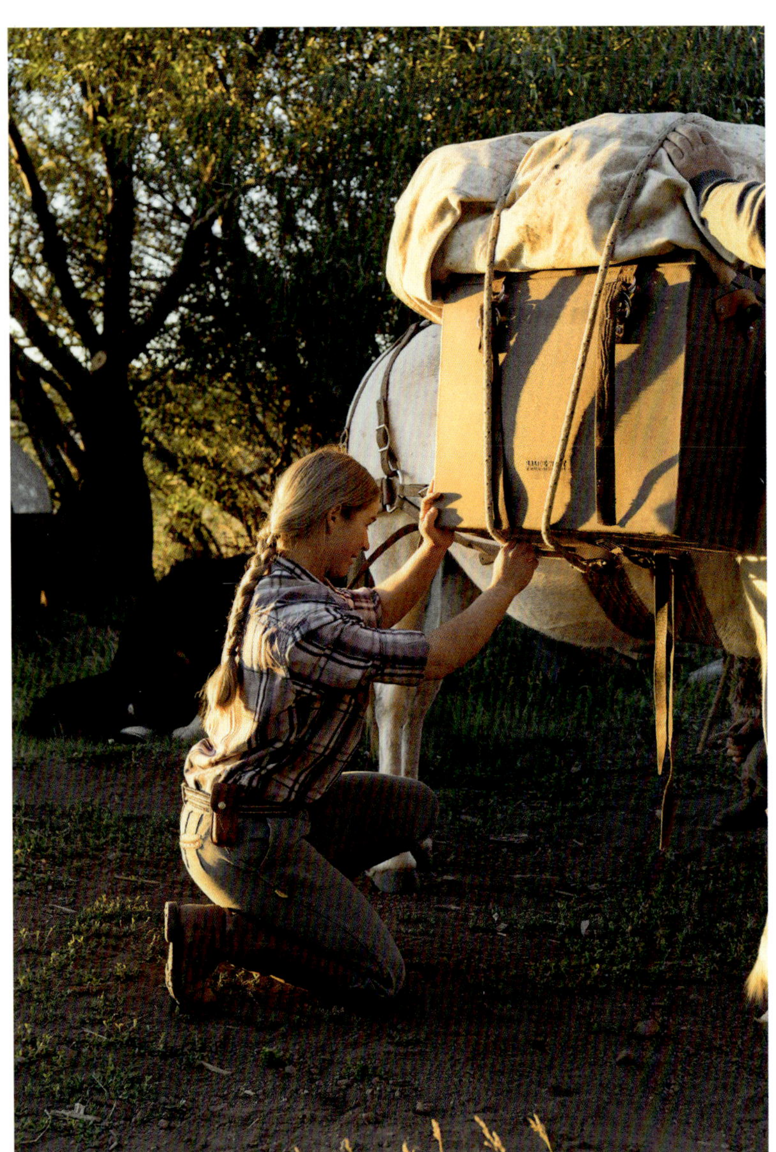

005 | Der Viehtrieb beginnt gegen halb fünf Uhr morgens. Die Sterne glitzern noch, als wir die Pferde satteln. Ich renne herum und fotografiere Sky beim Aufzäumen des Maultiers, den gerade erwachten, in die erste Sonne gähnenden Leo oder einen der Gauchos, der mit dem Lasso ein Schaf einfängt, damit der Hütehundwelpe Pastor an seinem Euter trinken kann. Endlich setzt sich die Karawane in Bewegung.

Nach dem Mittagessen halten die Gauchos Siesta, und ich wasche den Staub bei einem Bad im Fluss ab. Es ist heiß, auf den Felsen sitzen Libellen und ich lasse mich in der Sonne trocknen. Auf der Klippe über dem Fluss entdecke ich die riesigen Nester der Andenkondore. Diese großen Aasfresser mit ihrer Spannweite von über 3,20 Metern sehe ich oft in der Nähe von Skys Farm in den Aufwinden des Nachmittags kreisen.

Nach einer kurzen, kühlen Nacht im Freien brechen wir am nächsten Morgen wieder in Richtung Hochweiden auf. Ich bilde das Schlusslicht der Herde, die schweren Schritts vorantrottet und Staub aufwirbelt, den uns der Wind ins Gesicht bläst. Auch wenn die Sonne hoch am Himmel steht, ist die Luft dank der Höhe deutlich frischer. Die Herde kommt langsamer voran als gestern, die Müdigkeit ist spürbar, aber die Gauchos treiben die Tiere mit Hilfe ihrer Hunde voran. Lange Stunden später erreichen wir mit leerem Magen, Augen, Nasenlöcher und Fotoapparat voller Staub, das Ziel unserer Reise: die Hütte des Hirten Raúl, der die Herde den Sommer über hüten wird. Wir essen zusammen zu Mittag, bevor wir uns, endlich von der Herde befreit, auf den Rückweg machen.

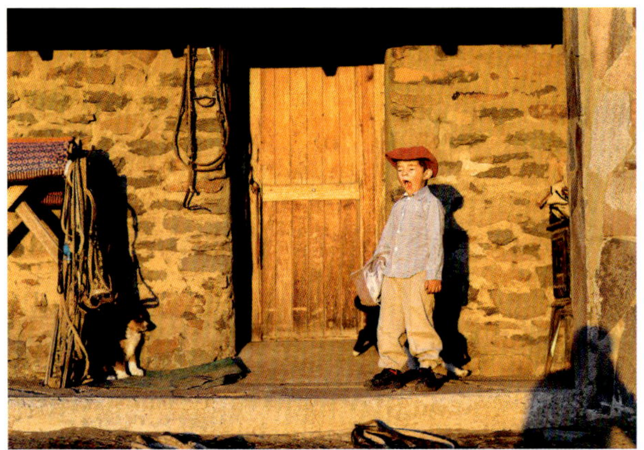

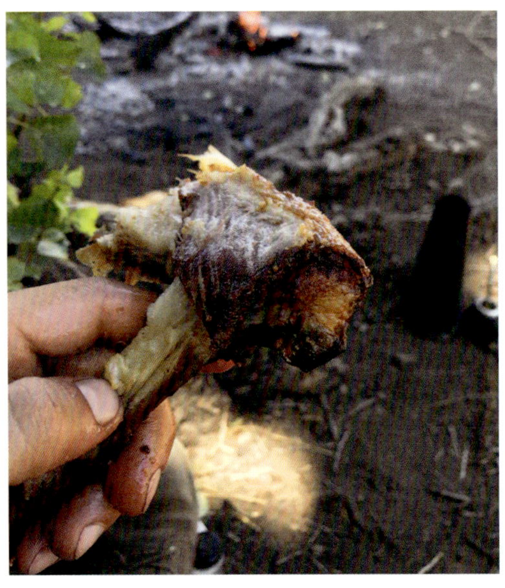

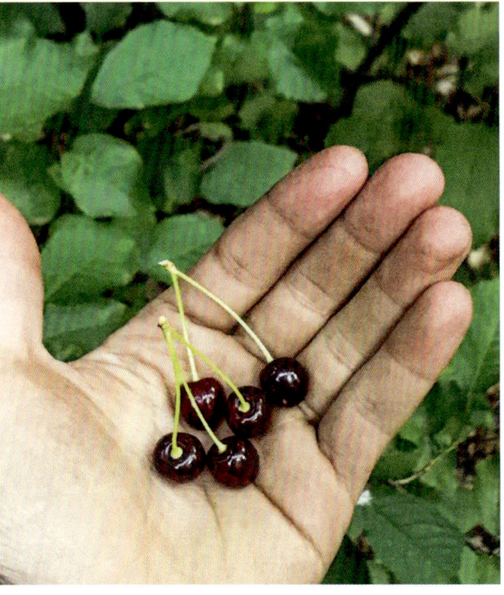

006 | During the three-day transhumance, we eat the same thing for all of our meals, including breakfast: grilled goat with a side of tortas, fritters fried in fat – goat fat, that is. The three precious apples stowed away in my bag and the wild cherries picked en route give me a little culinary diversity at least.

006 | Während des dreitägigen Viehtriebs gibt es zu allen Mahlzeiten, Frühstück eingeschlossen, das Gleiche zu essen: gegrillte Ziege mit Tortas, in (Ziegen-!) Fett ausgebackenen Teigfladen ... Drei kostbare, in meinem Beutel mitreisende Äpfel und am Wegrand gepflückte Wildkirschen liefern mir trotzdem ein wenig kulinarische Abwechslung.

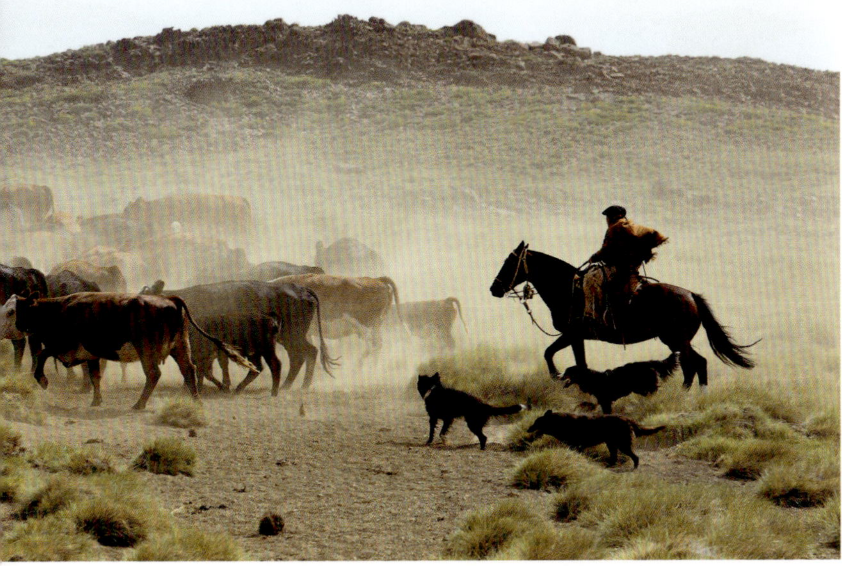

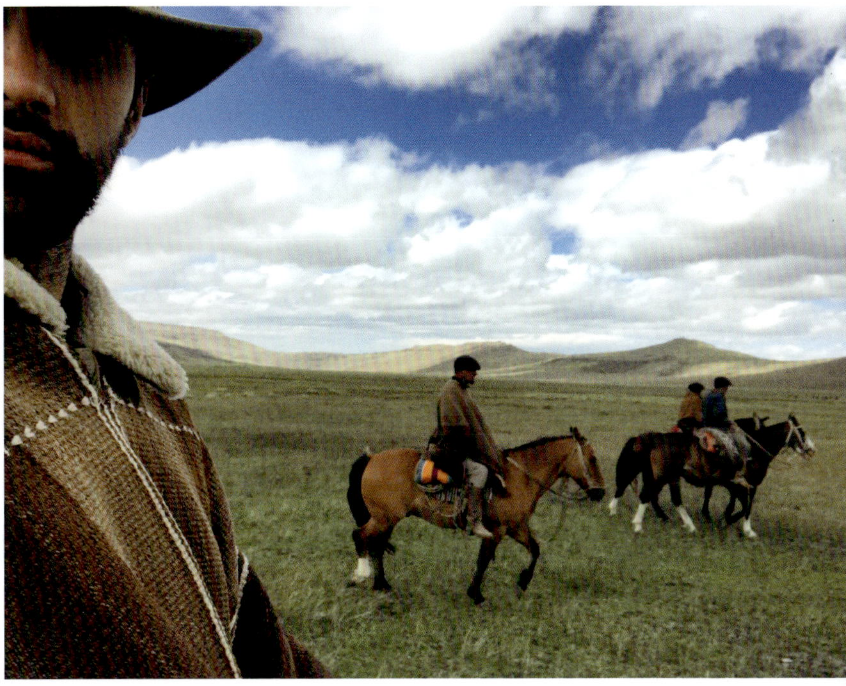

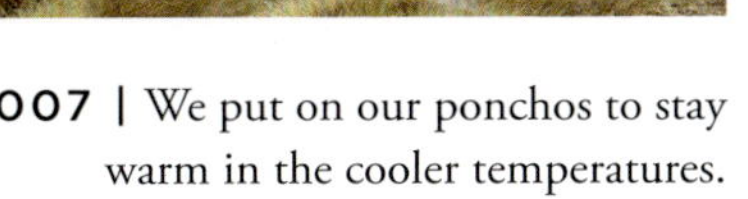

007 | We put on our ponchos to stay
warm in the cooler temperatures.

007 | Die Temperaturen fallen, und
wir hüllen uns in unsere Ponchos.

008 | It feels so good to live without any signal or internet,
not to be waiting for news from the outside world because you
know you're unreachable. I savour moments like these each
and every year, when everything is decided in the moment and
daily routines change with the weather. We are surrounded by
animals: cows, goats, sheep, cats and dog – not counting the birds
hiding in the small forest of trees surrounding Sky's farm, whose
chirping brightens up our mornings. I sometimes think that I was
born in the wrong era. I adore this simple life of cooking over a
wood fire and drinking water right from the source – it doesn't
get better than this!

008 | Wie gut es tut, ohne Telefon oder Internet zu leben,
nicht auf Nachrichten aus der Außenwelt zu warten, weil es kein
Netz gibt! Von Jahr zu Jahr weiß ich diese Momente mehr zu
schätzen. Dann regiert das Unmittelbare, und der Alltag richtet
sich nach dem Wetter. Wir sind von Tieren umgeben: Kühe,
Ziegen, Schafe, Katzen, Hunde ... Und Vögel, die sich in dem
Wäldchen rings um Skys Farm verstecken und mit ihrem Gesang
unseren Morgen erheitern. Manchmal kommt es mir vor, als
hätte ich mich im Zeitalter geirrt. Dieses einfache Leben – auf
dem Holzfeuer kochen, sich zum Trinken einfach an einer Quelle
auf den Boden legen ... Welch ein Glück!

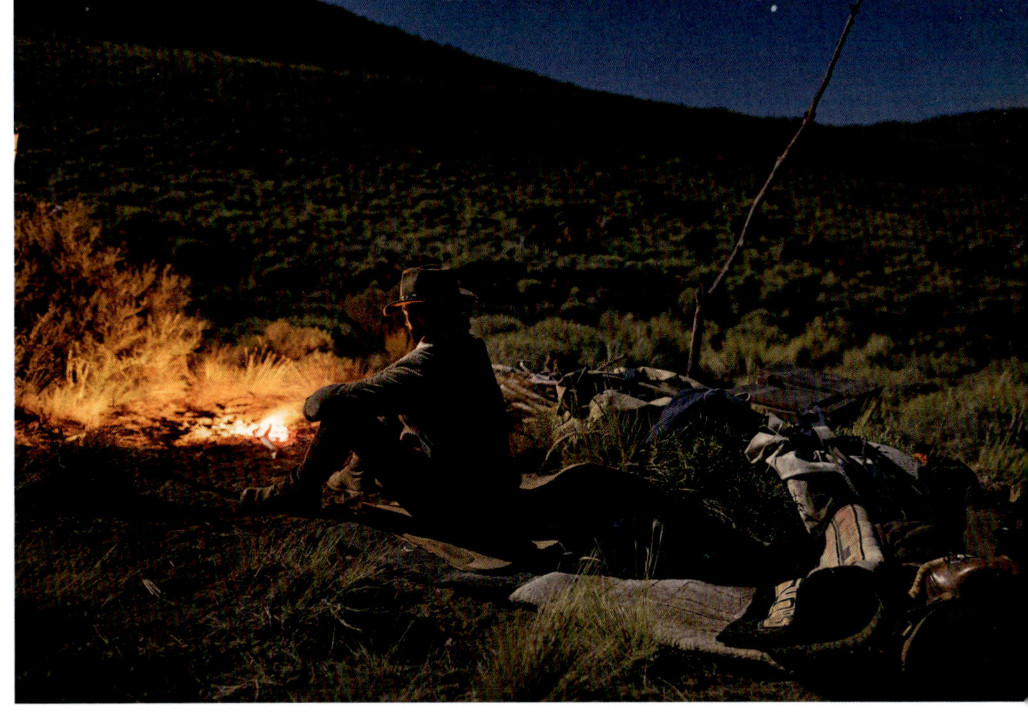

UTAH

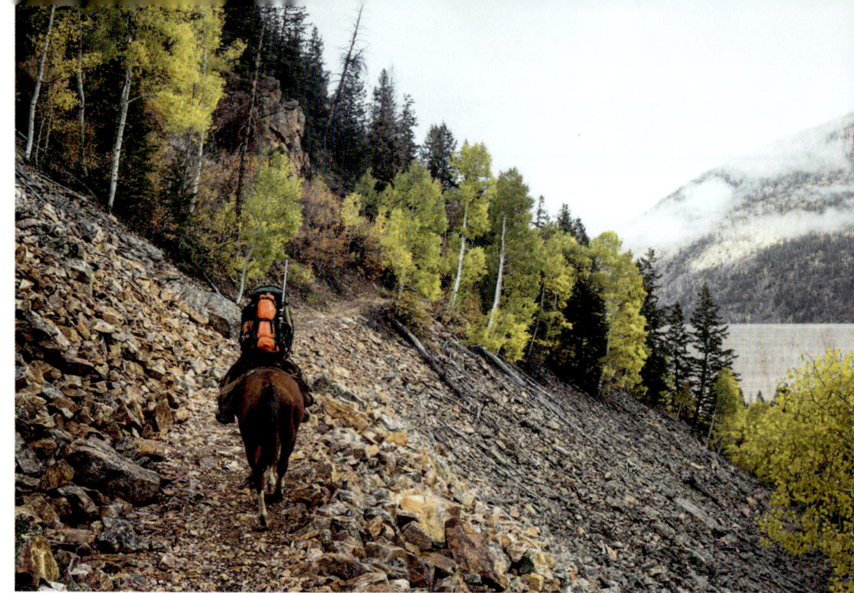

While staying with friends in Montréal, I get a message from Ben inviting me to meet him in Salt Lake City. "We've got a horse for you," he tells me. He plans to head into the mountains on horseback in forty-eight hours. In his email, he warns me that the conditions will be tough and glacial, the pace difficult to keep up with. Then he adds: "I would be delighted to have you join me. You're one of the rare people I've met in my life I would ask to accompany me on such an adventure."

I'm flattered, of course, though still a little worried. Am I really prepared or ready to set off on such an unexpected adventure? It's time to find out!

A few days later, I find myself sat on a horse in the north-eastern mountains of Utah, in the heart of Ashley National Forest, home to black bears and pumas. It has already been a long day and night falls while we still have quite a way to go. The autumn colours of our surroundings are gradually replaced by darkness. We are accompanied by a few snowflakes and the sound of horse hooves sliding on the smooth rocks, creating sparks in the dark night. Our toes numb from the cold, we finally reach a high plateau located 3,400 metres above sea level. We set up camp blind, unable to see our surroundings. Altitude sickness starts to set in and I'm hit by strong but short-lived headaches. At this altitude, the slightest step leaves you exhausted and setting up camp takes twice as long as usual.

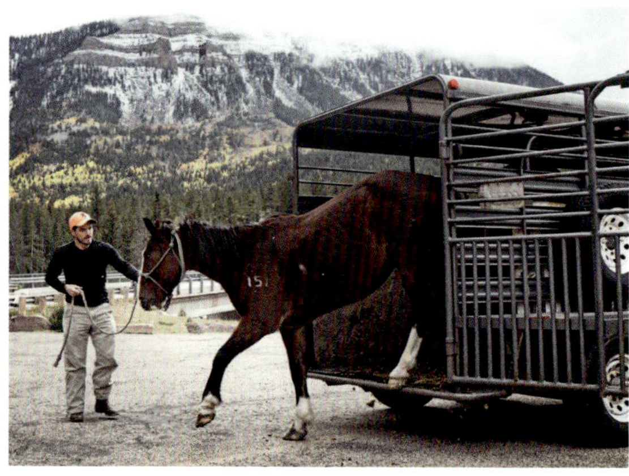

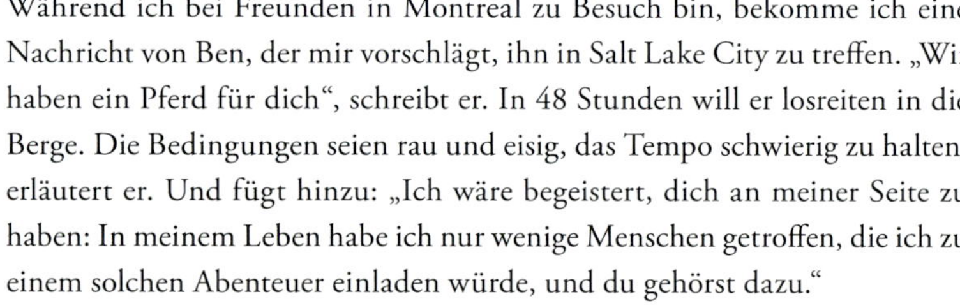

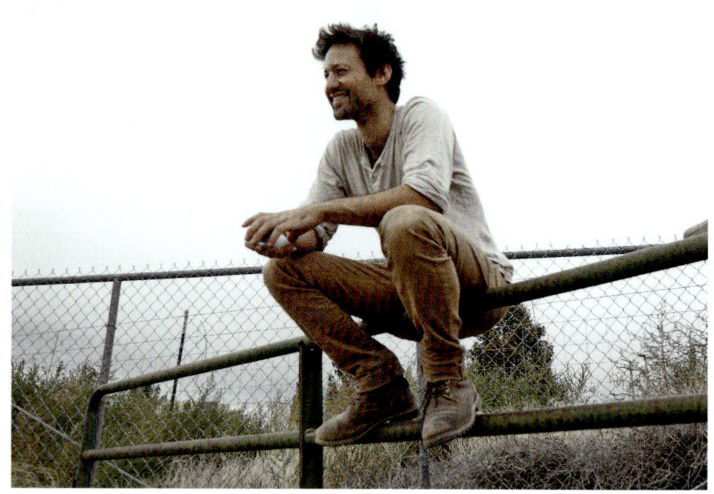

Während ich bei Freunden in Montreal zu Besuch bin, bekomme ich eine Nachricht von Ben, der mir vorschlägt, ihn in Salt Lake City zu treffen. „Wir haben ein Pferd für dich", schreibt er. In 48 Stunden will er losreiten in die Berge. Die Bedingungen seien rau und eisig, das Tempo schwierig zu halten, erläutert er. Und fügt hinzu: „Ich wäre begeistert, dich an meiner Seite zu haben: In meinem Leben habe ich nur wenige Menschen getroffen, die ich zu einem solchen Abenteuer einladen würde, und du gehörst dazu."

Ich fühle mich geschmeichelt, aber auch ein wenig besorgt ... Bin ich wirklich bereit, mich so improvisiert in ein solches Abenteuer zu stürzen? Das wird sich zeigen!

Einige Zeit später sitze ich im Nordosten Utahs auf einem Pferd, im Ashley National Forest, wo Schwarzbären und Pumas leben. Es war ein langer Tag, und wir haben noch mehrere Meilen vor uns, als die Nacht hereinbricht. Die Herbstfarben weichen der Dunkelheit. Ein paar Schneeflocken begleiten uns, und die Hufeisen der Pferde gleiten auf den glatten Felsen aus, sodass Funken durch die Nacht stieben. Mit taub gefrorenen Zehen kommen wir endlich auf einem Plateau in 3400 Metern Höhe an. Wir schlagen das Lager auf, ohne zu sehen, wo wir sind. Die Höhenkrankheit meldet sich, und ich leide unter heftigen, aber nur kurz andauernden Kopfschmerzen. In dieser Höhe ist jeder Schritt ermüdend, und wir brauchen fürs Aufbauen des Zelts doppelt so lang wie sonst.

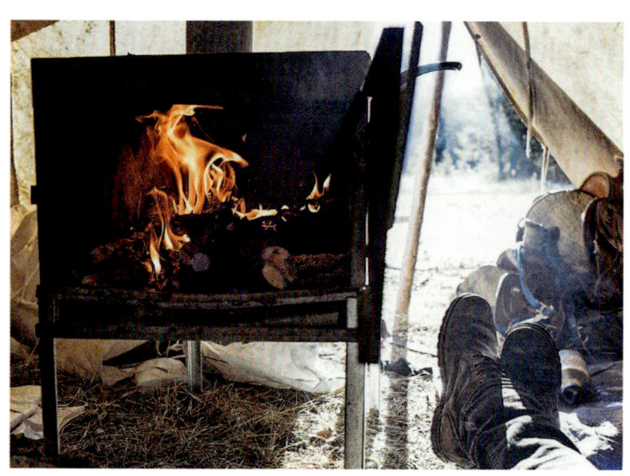

NORWAY

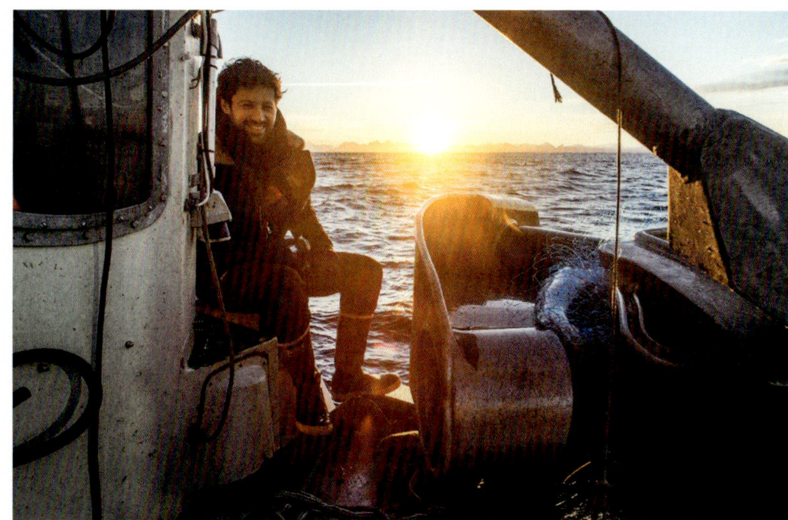

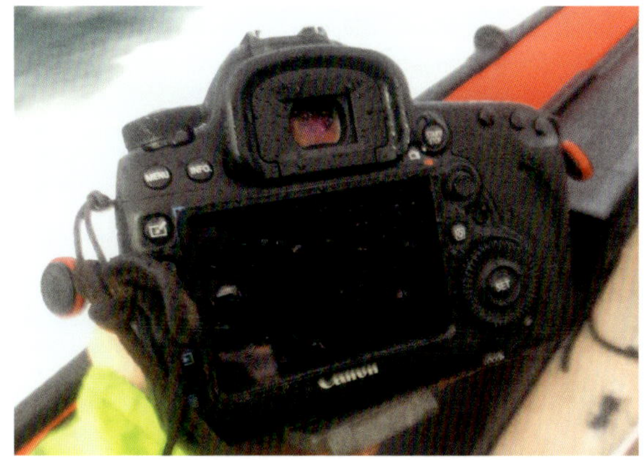

001 | I take advantage of being in Norway's Arctic territory to join some cod fishers on their fishing trip. From the Antilles to Nigeria, passing through Europe, the Norwegian fish is exported to countless countries across the world. Dried cod was also a staple of the Viking diet during their long journeys. At sea, ocean spray is inevitable and the seawater – following in the footsteps of the cold and the dust – once more tests the limits of my equipment.

001 | Ich nutze meinen Aufenthalt in der norwegischen Arktis, um mit Kabeljaufischern hinauszufahren. Von den Antillen über Europa bis nach Nigeria wird norwegischer Kabeljau weltweit in zahlreiche Länder exportiert. Einst war Stockfisch der Basisproviant der Wikinger auf ihren langen Reisen. Auf hoher See kann man der Gischt nicht ausweichen, und das Meerwasser ist – nach Frost und Staub – der nächste Test für mein Material.

002 | When I visit Elena in November, the sun disappears from the sky a little earlier every day. It's a strange feeling to be eating lunch at half past one in the afternoon with the sun setting in the background. Little by little, the sun leaves its spot in the sky and the Arctic night sets in with aplomb. Silent and seemingly never-ending, it will last for two days. A month of complete darkness set to the rhythm of crescent moons and northern lights dancing across the sky.

002 | Als ich Elena im November besuche, geht die Sonne jeden Tag ein wenig früher unter. Welch seltsames Gefühl, um 13.30 Uhr mit Blick auf den Sonnenunterganz zu Mittag zu essen! Nach und nach verdrängt die Polarnacht die Sonne von ihrem Platz. Diese stille, endlos lange Zeit dauert hier 32 Tage. Ein Monat totaler Finsternis, durchbrochen von Mondsicheln und Nordlichtern, die immer wieder den Himmel erhellen.

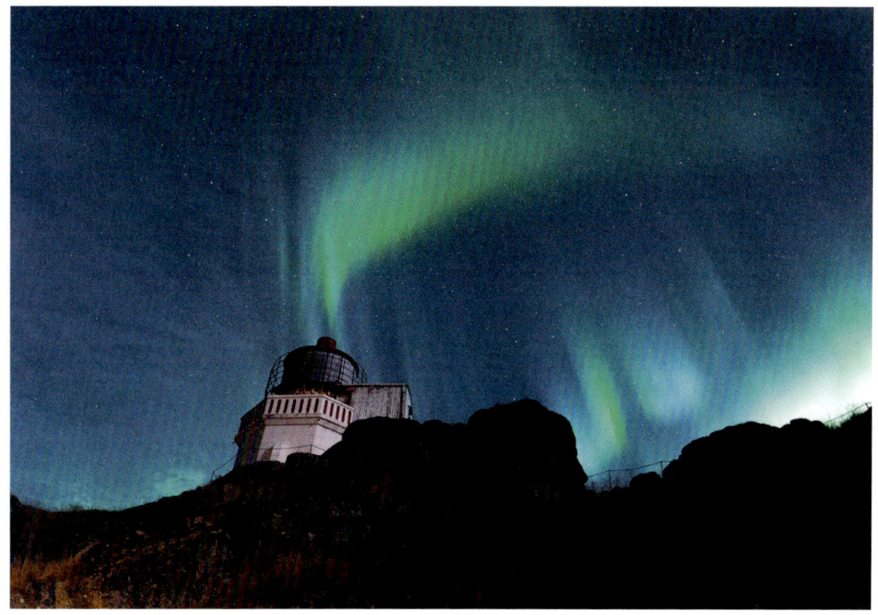

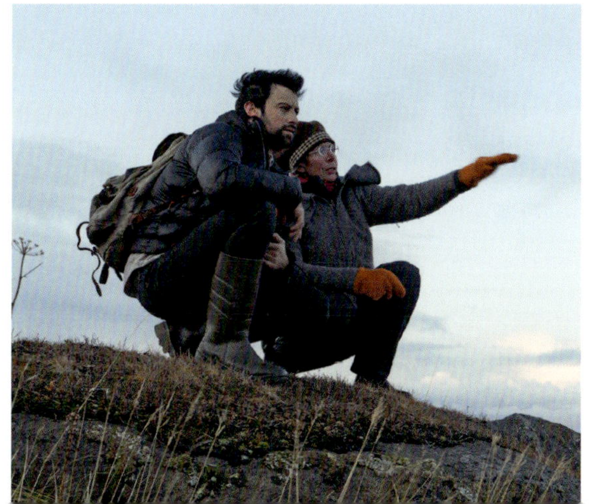

003 | At the island's summit, Elena shows me our surroundings. On one side you have the vastness of the Atlantic ocean, on the other the spectacular Lofoten Islands.

003 | Vom Gipfel ihrer Insel aus zeigt Elena mir die Umgebung: auf der einen Seite die Weite des Atlantiks, auf der anderen die spektakulären Lofoten-Inseln.

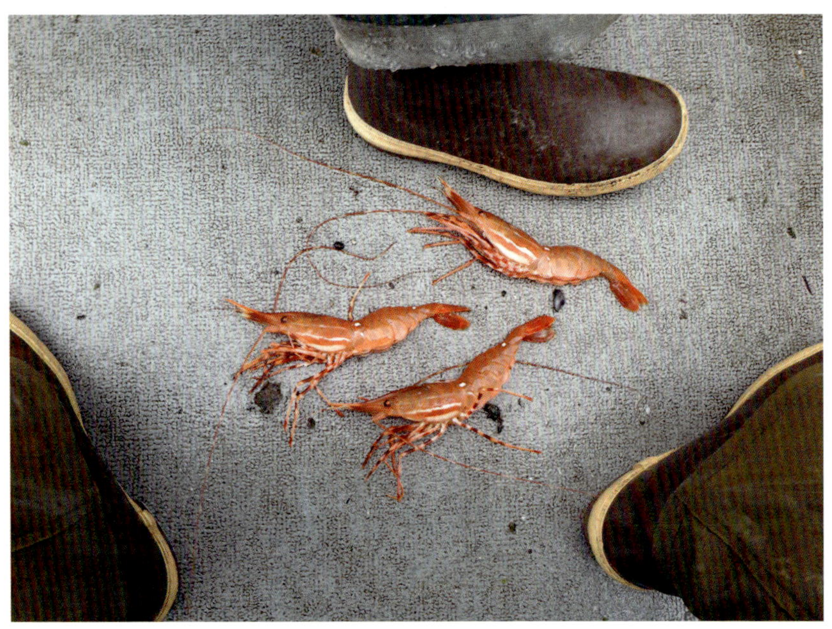

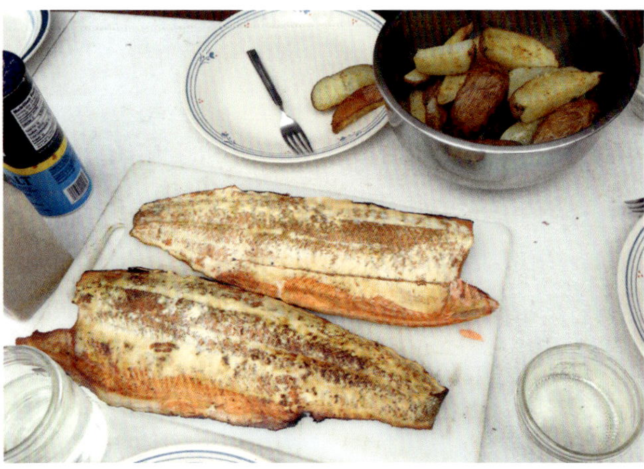

001 | Jerry catches numerous shellfish with the help of his traps. These spot prawns (Pandalus platyceros) will be used to flavour a spicy coconut milk soup. Crabs, clams and of course oysters, as well as lots of fresh fish such as salmon, halibut and rockfish, are served for lunch every day.

001 | In seinen Reusen fängt Jerry zahlreiche Meeresfrüchte. Heute werden Gefleckte Tiefwassergarnelen eine Suppe aus Kokosmilch und Gewürzen aromatisieren. Auf dem Mittagstisch finden sich täglich Krabben, Venusmuscheln und natürlich Austern, aber auch viel frischer Fisch wie Lachs, Heilbutt oder kleine Küstenfische.

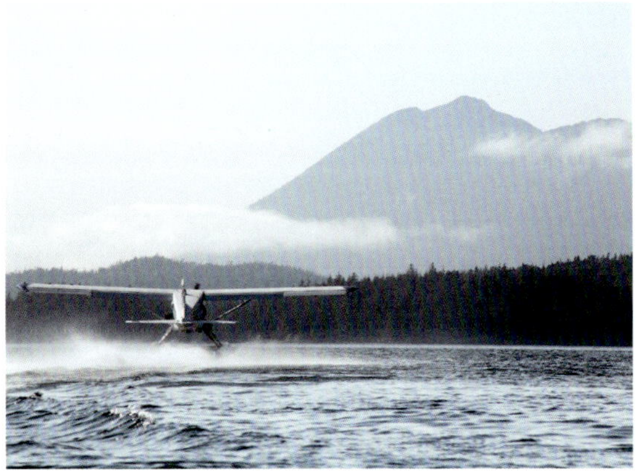

ALASKA

002 | After a few days in Ketchikan to pick up provisions, purchase a sturdy pair of boots and some oilskins, I head to the docks of the town one morning to arrange a seaplane flight. The plane has three rows: one for the pilot and co-pilot and two for the passengers. The rest of the space is free to fill up with all kinds of packages and parcels that nearly fall on top of us each time the plane lands on the water. For many of Alaska's inhabitants, the seaplane is the only link to civilisation.

002 | Nach ein paar Tagen in Ketchikan, wo ich Vorräte, ein ordentliches Paar Gummistiefel und ein Muschelzüchter-Ölzeug einkaufe, finde ich mich eines Tages am Hafen wieder, um über einen Flug im Wasserflugzeug zu verhandeln. Die Maschine hat drei Sitzreihen: eine für Pilot und Kopilot, zwei für die Passagiere. Der Rest ist bis zum Bersten mit Frachtstücken aller Art vollgestopft, die bei jeder Wasserung auf uns herabzustürzen drohen. Für viele Einwohner Alaskas stellt das Wasserflugzeug die einzige Verbindung zur Zivilisation dar.

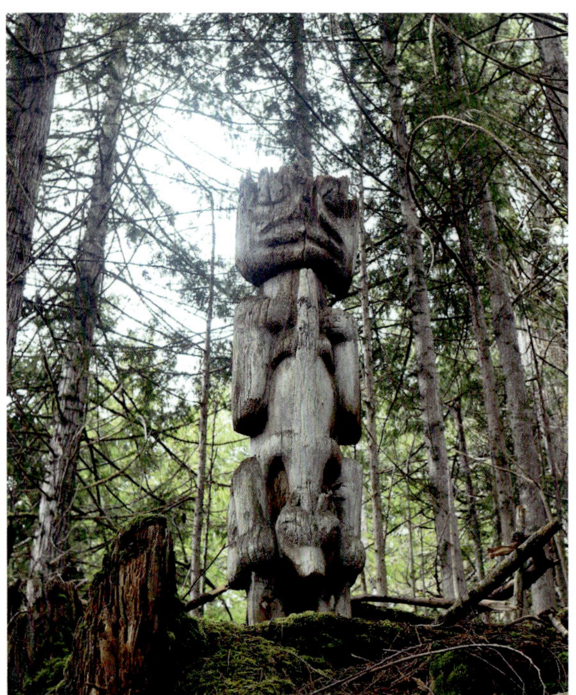

003 | Two mortuary poles from the Tlingit tribe are erected on an uninhabited island. According to local legend, anyone attempting to take hold of one runs the risk of dying an inexplicable death – one way of preserving them for some time to come before they are swallowed up naturally into the forest.

003 | Auf einer unbewohnten Insel stehen zwei Begräbnis-Totempfähle des Tlingit-Volkes. Nach einem lokalen Gerücht stirbt jeder, der sich ihrer zu bemächtigen versucht, eines unerklärlichen Todes. So werden sie noch einige Zeit erhalten bleiben, bevor sie ganz natürlich im Wald vermodern.

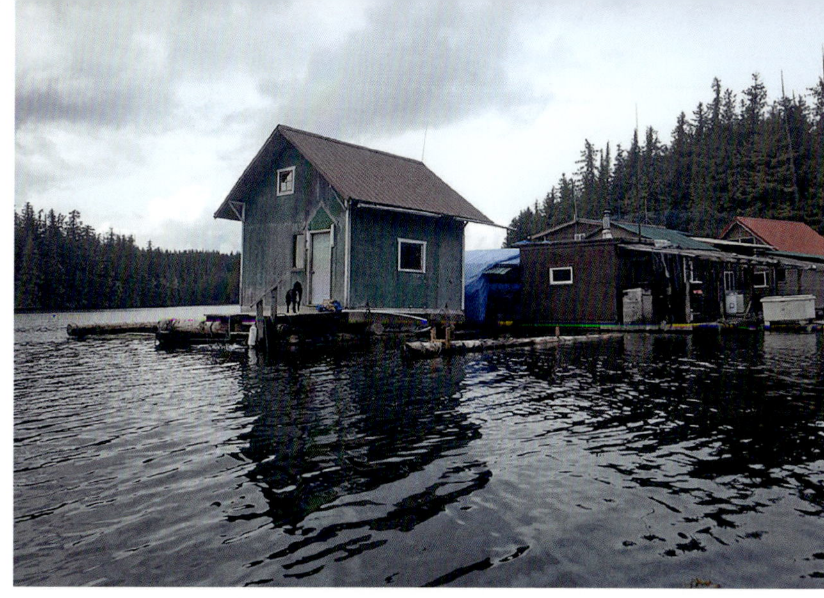

005 | Life in a floating house is fascinating. In spring, the weather changes up to twenty times a day, alternating between sun and complete calm to hail storms, snow, wind and heavy downpours. There are as many bald eagles as you would find pigeons in a French town. Despite the workload during these two months with Jerry, we enjoy a calm pace of life and the days are peaceful in this small hamlet. We draw our energy from the nature all around us and stress is non-existent. Now that I'm here in a place so rich in nature and open spaces, the noisiness of towns and cities suddenly seems absurd to me. Here, you're just a mere detail and nature is the norm – the complete opposite of urban life.

005 | Das Leben in einem schwimmenden Haus ist beglückend. Im Frühling wechselt das Wetter bis zu zwanzigmal am Tag, von Sonnenschein und Flaute zu Hagelschauern, Schnee, Wind oder Starkregen. Die Weißkopfseeadler sind so zahlreich wie Tauben in französischen Städten. Trotz der harten Arbeit in den zwei Monaten bei Jerry bleibt der Lebensrhythmus in dem kleinen Dorf ruhig und friedlich. Die allgegenwärtige Natur strotzt vor Energie, und Stress existiert nicht. An einem Ort, wo es so viel wildes Leben gibt, so viel Weite, kommt mir der Lärm der Städte plötzlich absurd vor. Hier ist der Mensch nur ein Detail, das Wilde die Norm – genau umgekehrt wie in der Stadt.

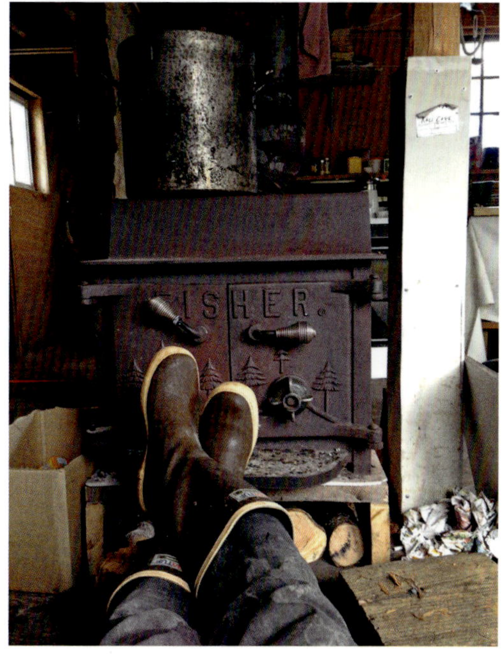

004 | The cabin I'm staying at while visiting Jerry has a wood-fired stove that can be used for cooking or heating up water for a bath. It takes a good hour to heat up 15 litres of water – just enough for a quick wash. By way of comparison, a conventional shower uses between 20 and 30 litres of water per minute.

004 | Die Hütte, in der ich bei Jerry wohne, hat einen Holzofen zum Kochen und zum Aufwärmen des Wassers, mit dem man sich in einem Becken wäscht. Es dauert etwa anderthalb Stunden, bis 15 Liter Wasser heiß sind, gerade genug für eine schnelle Toilette. Zum Vergleich: Eine klassische Dusche verbraucht 20 bis 30 Liter pro Minute.

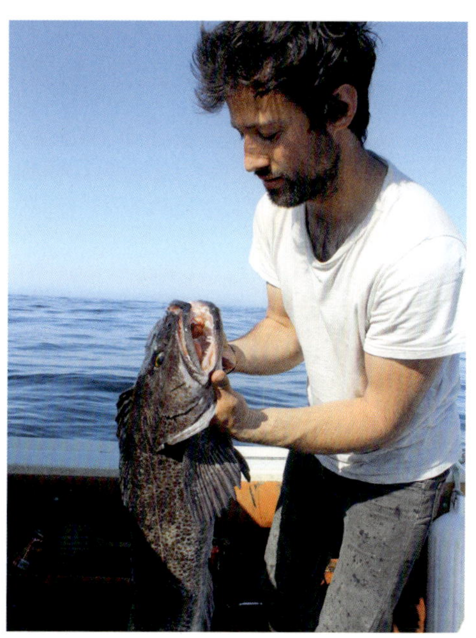

006 | Jerry uses long wooden logs to keep his home afloat, which is just as stable as a traditional house. Whenever a storm approaches, he goes around the buildings, just as you would a boat, to safely stow away anything that could be blown away, damaged or broken. In these conditions, the mooring system, made up of seven wire ropes, is placed under immense strain. During these two months with Jerry, I live far away from reality. We are cut off from the world, but connected to nature.

006 | Lange Holzstämme halten Jerrys Haus über Wasser; es ist ebenso stabil wie ein klassisches Haus. Wenn ein Sturm naht, umrundet er die Gebäude und bringt wie auf einem Boot alles in Sicherheit, was wegfliegen, zerreißen oder zerbrechen könnte. Bei solchen Bedingungen wird die Verankerung, die aus sieben Metallkabeln besteht, auf eine harte Probe gestellt. In den zwei Monaten bei Jerry lebe ich fern aller äußeren Verlockungen. Wir sind von der Welt abgeschnitten, aber in der Natur verankert.

Published by teNeues Publishing Group

teNeues Verlag GmbH
Ohmstraße 8a
86199 Augsburg, Germany

Düsseldorf Office
Waldenburger Str. 13
41564 Kaarst, Germany
Email: books@teneues.com

Augsburg/Munich Office
Ohmstraße 8a
86199 Augsburg, Germany
Email: books@teneues.com

Berlin Office
Lietzenburger Str. 53
10719 Berlin, Germany
Email: books@teneues.com

Press Department
Email: presse@teneues.com

teNeues Publishing Company
350 Seventh Avenue, Suite 301, New York,
NY 10001, USA

www.teneues.com

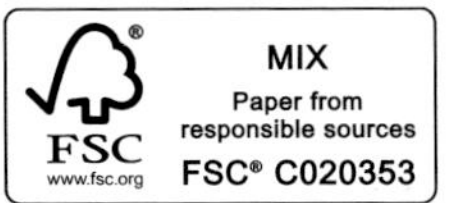

teNeues Publishing Group
Augsburg / München
Berlin
Düsseldorf
London
New York

teNeues